fXCk iT!
i'LL dATe
MYSeLF

101 SELF-LOVE DATE IDEAS

Listen Up!

For so long I thought I needed a friend or significant other to do the things I wanted to do, but I found out in my twenties that's not the case. You are free to do what you want when you want, and no one can stop you. But what do you want to do? Hopefully, this book can answer that question.

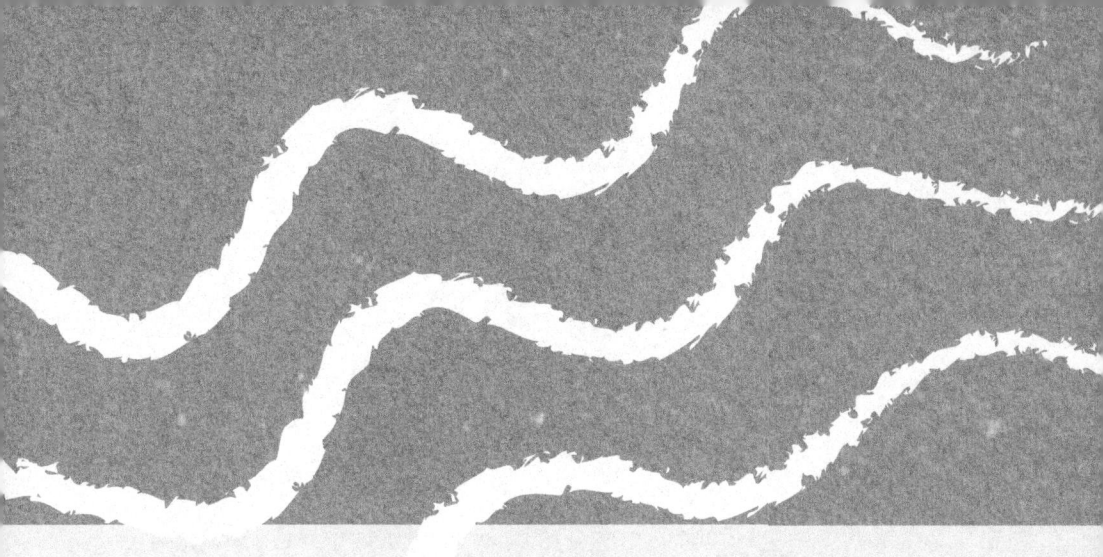

How to use this book

Flip to a page and pick an activity to do. If you don't like it pick another. Simple as that. If you come up with any of your own ideas write them down. There are pages at the end to use that for.

1. Movie & TV Marathon

This is a perfect way to spend time at home. All you have to do is find a movie or tv series you want to watch. They can be your tried and true favorites or something you've never seen before. You can even pick a theme such as romcoms, psychological thrillers (Gone Girl and the millions of spin-offs), or horror if you are brave! Get some snacks, and find a comfortable spot and enjoy the show! I enjoy watching series that uplift me such as the cult classic Pushing Daisies, Brittany Runs A Marathon and Wild. Inspirational movies and shows are the best because you come out on the other side of a binge feeling a whole lot less guilty about it.

2. Cook Something Fancy

I hate cooking but even I enjoy making a fancy meal for myself every once in a while. When you cook a fancy meal you are not only nourishing your body but there is a great sense of accomplishment that comes with making something impressive. I like looking at Alison Roman's recipes and picking one of the lists that speaks to me. Once you're done make sure to take pictures for yourself(or Instagram let's be honest).

3. Read

A good book can change your life in a serious way. Whenever I want to unwind I find a good book load it to my reader and get to reading. Try reading something inspirational if you're in a funk, or something fantasy-based if you want an escape.

4. Dance Party

It feels amazing to dance and let loose. Put on a great playlist, get in something comfy and dance like nobody is watching!
Also if you'd like search up digital raves. They popped up during the pandemic and are seemingly here to stay. They are loads of fun and you get to dress up and look silly and not worry about finding your way back home.

5. Online Shopping

this is self-explanatory but I enjoy a good online shop from time to time. I don't just shop for clothes, I love buying furniture, gifts for friends, organizational tools, and even trips to destinations. Be smart and don't go overboard. I set myself a budget that I don't go over and I make sure to not scroll endlessly otherwise it'll feel like a chore.

6. At Home Classes

ost peoples default at home classes are relegated to yoga, but the world is your oyster! I've done burlesque, Pilates, self-defense, language learning, and cooking classes from home. Think about a thing you love and search online for someone offering a class. I also found classes on Instagram and Facebook that have changed my life and I hope you find one that changes yours too.

7. Go Tubing

If you're looking for a fun and lazy activity to do go tubing! I personally like going in a lazy river at a spa but you can tube down a snowy hill in winter, or in a river in the summer. It's an adrenaline rush you can get for pretty cheap!

8. Rearrange Your Space

maybe you subscribe to the Marie Kondo method or believe in feng shui but a great way to spend a day at home is to change up your space. Reorganizing your space is said to spark creativity, ground you, and help you purge your space of old crap you definitely need. You also get the added benefit of deep cleaning and finding those stupid things you've been searching for.

9. Puzzles

Ok, hold on, I hope I didn't lose you but puzzles are some of my favorite activities to do at home when I don't want to stare at a screen. I buy the cheap crossword puzzles from the dollar store and it's a nice brain exercise. You can do regular puzzles, sudoku, brainteasers, and more. Just make sure it's difficult enough that you're not bored but not too difficult so that you're not...bored. It's a fine line y'know.

10. Make A Vision Board:

if you're anything like me you like visualizing the best life for yourself. The best way to do that is to make a vision board. It's like a collage but specifically for your goals. Get your sharpest scissors, collect some magazines or print some pictures and go to town. You can design it however you'd like but a word to the wise if you plan on hanging it up make sure it matches the vibe of your home.

11. Make Some Art

I love painting, am I any good at it? Hell no! That doesn't stop me and it shouldn't stop you either. If you want to learn how to do a specific style of art try it out. I started making paper art recently and it's surprisingly fun. Get over making it perfect and just make it. Keep your hands moving and create something you can be proud of. If it's too ugly though the trash can is always there to hide all the evidence.

12. Play Backyard Games

Grab a beer and head outside to play some games. You can play cornhole (obvs.), kan jam (frisbee horseshoe), and even giant Jenga. If you want to be fancy get croquet and swap the beer for sangria.

13. Bake

I love *Nailed It* and what I've discovered is you don't have to be an amazing baker to make something sweet and edible. Scroll through Pinterest for ideas, gather your goods, and get to work. Make something elaborate or keep it simple whatever you do just make sure you can enjoy it in one sitting. I've made the mistake of baking a three-tiered peanut butter cake, couple that with my lack and self-control and it was literally a recipe for disaster.

14. Meal Prep

Week after week you tell yourself "I'm going to meal prep" and you never do, so how about you keep that promise to yourself for once. Make a menu for the week, see what you need, and spend a day making it happen. I make theme weeks based on what cuisine I'm craving and purchase nice containers that make me feel like a boss. The goal is to make things you will eat so don't be too aspirational. otherwise, you end up with rotten asparagus in the back of your fridge.

15. Journal

Writing in a journal is something so many woo-woo wellness people recommend to better your life but they're right. I couldn't recommend journaling more especially during high-stress weeks. It is a great way to ease worry, and declutter your mind, and it's also a great tool for getting to know yourself better. If you aren't the stream of consciousness type there a so many great self-guided journals for whatever you need.

16. Clean Up Your Space

let go of that bronzer you've had since college please for the love of everything holy just throw it out now. Half of your stuff is expired, broken, ripped, or not necessary in your space. Once you do you'll find you'll be in need of a shopping spree.

17. Hangout With Your Pet

If you have a pet and work a regular job you might not be hanging out with them as much. Spend a day giving them the attention they deserve, make them some enrichment activities, find some recipes, and feed them something homemade or just cuddle them if you can.

18. Learn A Dance

 I love TikTok even though I'm way past the main demographic. Those dance trends are too fun not to try. Maybe you can learn that or even take virtual dance classes. I even love playing Just Dance on YouTube and memorizing the steps. Dance is great for memory and the body as a whole. Plus the feeling of finally nailing the dance is worth the amount of sweat. Post it online or keep it to yourself.

19. Scrapbook

maybe it's the 50-year-old mom in me but I love scrapbooking. It's an art form and a way to keep memories and nowadays it feels pretty cool and vintage to make one. You can print pictures at home and make a makeshift book with whatever you have on hand. On the other hand, you can go all out and buy a scrapbook to decorate. I personally like to make my own because I love being able to control the patterns. When it comes to memories you can scrapbook just about anything. I scrapbooked a trip to Cuba I took in 2019 and made a copy for my friend.

20. Learn an Online Skill

You can learn anything online nowadays so why not build skills and possibly earn money. A friend of mine learned excel and google suite skills and in 2 months was able to get a job where she makes twice her old income. She inspired me to learn to code so I can boss up my résumé. You don't need to learn just tech skills, anything goes when learning a skill so look up some tutorials on YouTube and surprise yourself.

21. Play An Instrument

Learning an instrument can be rewarding even if it's difficult at first. My sister is learning the guitar and 4 hours a day, in her free time, she is in her room strumming away. I've noticed a significant positive change in her mood and attitude since she's picked up a guitar so I can say this definitely is a great idea for spending time alone.

22. Herb Garden

If you like fresh herbs or you want a garden it has no space try growing an herb garden. It doesn't take too long to grow herbs from seed to sprout and when you put fresh herbs in your food it's amazing.

23. Fly A Kite

If you want to get outside but it's windy take advantage and go fly a kite. Surprisingly kite flying is great exercise, it's an awesome stress reliever, great for eye stimulation, and getting outside is always a plus. but don't be cheap on the kite, if you do you'll miss out on the stress-relieving benefits if you're unraveling string.

24. Do Nothing

That's it!
Just take a nap and do nothing. Sometimes rest and relaxation are productive even if you aren't making anything. Take a load off and learn to relax so you can be in tip-top shape.

25. Clean Your Feed

You probably have pictures or embarrassing social media accounts that you don't use anymore so why not clean up your social media? Delete old accounts, delete old pictures, and change your profile pics. Be sure that your profiles don't reveal too much private information so employers and creeps (same thing really) can't keep tabs on you

26. Make An Emergency Preparedness Bag

If you live in Tornado Alley like I do this is non-negotiable but anyone can do this for any occasion. A good starter pack includes water, food, flashlights, lighters, candles, blankets, change of clothes, first aid kits, utility knife, PPE, and a radio. You can add what you need depending on the area you live in so check online. This peace of mind is worth spending half a day making.

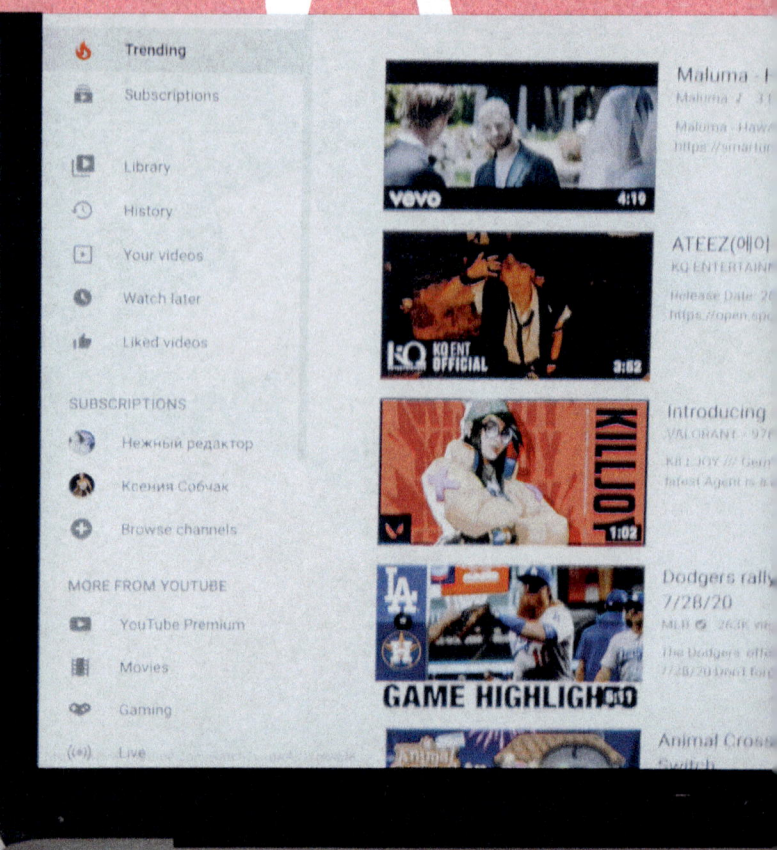

27. Make A Youtube Video

Have you ever made a YouTube video and felt a sense of pride making it. It's like creating a piece of art with no mess to clean up. You can make a video on anything you like but I think the best thing is to speak about what you know. You can teach people something or try making a product review you don't need to worry about going viral just make videos for fun.

28. Podcast

Podcasts are so much fun to listen to, so why not make one of your own. Pick a subject and record an episode of a podcast. Edit it down and post it somewhere. You can use Acast or Spotify to post podcasts. Or even post it to YouTube.

29. Do A Challenge

Is there anything you want to accomplish on your bucket list? Make it a challenge! Learn to meditate, work on your singing voice or learn to knit. Put a time limit on it and then it's a challenge that you can accomplish.

30. Spa Night

The quintessential night in for most women includes a spa and for good reason. The benefits for why you should do a spa night are endless but here's a few:
- Relieves stress
- Improves circulation.
- Helps slow down aging
- Maintains skin health
- Better sleep
- Improves mood

You can buy spa pampering treatments or DIY if you'd like. I love making the In To The Gloss' Green tea yogurt mask and running a warm bath. But you do you.

31. Connect With Your Inner Child

Yes you are an adult, but I firmly believe that nothing is better than stacking those little blocks and making something cool. So Get in touch with your inner child. Finger paint, make origami, or hula hoop, whatever it is make sure it makes you feel like a kids again.

32. Self Reiki:

  This one is a little different but reiki is a Japanese form of energy healing that's supposed to clear you of bad vibes and fill you with peace. From my experience it works but you usually have to go to a reiki practitioner. However, there is self reiki and you can find books and videos online and learn to do it yourself. It's relaxing and meditative so give it a try.

33. Self Message

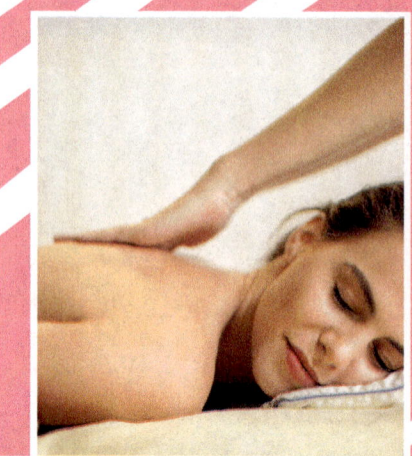

We all need to release some tension but did you know you could do it yourself? Get your mind out of the gutter! Self Massage is something you can do at home when you can't pay someone else to do it. You can use a foam roller or your hands to really dig deep.

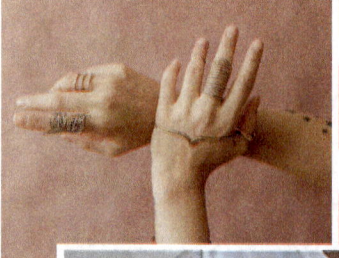

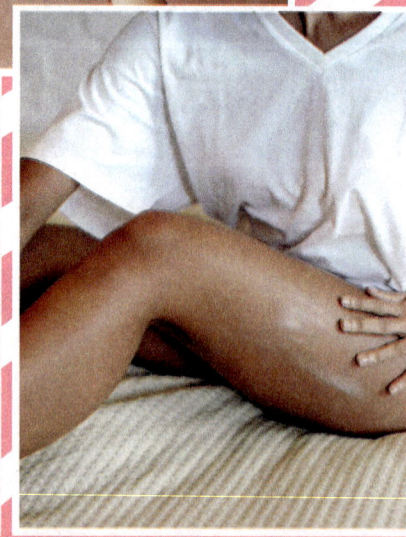

34. Thrifting

Spend a few hours searching a dedicated antiques mart, got to a tried and true flea market, or thrift store since you never know when you'll find your next one-of-a-kind furniture piece. There's a strong possibility you'll come across some unusual wardrobe alternatives as well. You might also get up early and go to the local garage sales. See what treasures you find along the way.

35. Go to a Pop Up Event

Some of the most interesting and experimental objects can be found in pop-ups. Whether the entrepreneur is just starting out or testing the market for a new type of food/drink/item, these "here now, gone tomorrow" mobile enterprises are typically economical. Seeing what's out there, in any case, is a fun experience.

Join local Facebook groups to learn about spontaneous activities in and around your city. With a simple Google search, you may find free and low-cost activities with like-minded people.

36. Hot Air Balloon Ride

Go on a hot air balloon ride – what's cooler than floating over beautiful landscapes with views for miles? This is a once-in-a-lifetime activity that everyone should try. If you are scared of heights, skip this but you'll be missing out on some awesome views.

37. Go To A Museum

Allow your creative side to drive you forward. When you connect with art, it can be therapeutic. Look it up because there are museums dedicated to just about anything nowadays. I've been to the Spy Museum in Washington, D.C., the Swedish History Museum in Stockholm, MOMA, and other museums. While some museums have high admission fees, many others provide free or discounted admission on certain days or hours of the week, allowing you to get cultured on the cheap.

38. Get in You Car

Make a decent playlist and go somewhere that will motivate you. Dopamine is released when you listen to music you enjoy. You'll undoubtedly spread positive energy. Alternatively, you may go to a drive-in movie. They're a lot of fun and ideal for those on a budget. You may even try your hand at stargazing. Take a blanket and search the sky for your favorite constellations. You can use apps like Star Tracker to get help if you need it.

39. Go To A Play

Take a break from reality and immerse yourself in pure fantasy. This is a fascinating method to get to know the characters and feel their emotions in real-time. You can observe the actors in action and, if you like, attend a musical performance. If you don't like musicals, I was in the same boat until I watched the reworking of Oklahoma! and it swayed my opinion. So give it a shot!

40. Volunteer

Giving back is thought to be one of the simplest methods to achieve true happiness. Being a part of your community is important because it gives you a different viewpoint. Clean up your neighborhood park or beach, then volunteer for the day at a local charity, such as a soup kitchen or a pet shelter. According to studies, acts of generosity improve pleasure and well-being, and couldn't we all use a little more of that?

41. Go Golfing

Golf ranges can be found almost anywhere, making this a simple night out. Most people consider golf to be a boring activity, but it is one of the most relaxing activities for a solo date around. TopGolf, for example, makes the experience enjoyable and all-inclusive. Work on your swing and, above all, enjoy hitting golf balls. Pretend to be a PGA champion and see how you do.

42. Learn Archery

Archery is so cool and connects you with something primal. It can Improve so many things like your focus, hand-eye coordination, and even your confidence. Book a day at an archery range near you and have a great time learning a skill that could come in handy. I mean you never know!

43. Food Tour

Most local brewery or winery tours are free, and you'll walk away with the knowledge to amaze your friends—and, of course, free sips of drink. Enjoy the magnificent outdoor facilities of vineyards and breweries if you're feeling fancy. But don't forget that some chocolate manufacturers provide tours, so if you've ever wondered how your favorite chocolates are made, now is your chance to learn and sample.

44. See A Psychic

A psychic can read your palms or tarot cards. You'll almost certainly uncover some predictions that will make you laugh. You don't have to be a believer of the mystical to go see a psychic, I am not but I did enjoy getting my fortune told. I treat psychics, tarot, and astrology as the same, it's interesting and a good reflection of whom we know we are. But as they say, take what resonates.

45. Go Skating

Take a couple of laps around a roller skating rink to relive your childhood (or a good '80s movie). Expect a few bruises and falls if you don't have the best coordination, but that won't make the skating any less enjoyable. Alternatively, you can bundle up and head to the ice rink. Then go get yourself a cup of hot cocoa or another hot beverage.

46. Go Camping

For the weekend, get away from it all and reconnect with yourself. Stay off your phone as much as possible to avoid distractions and to fully appreciate nature.

Construct a fire and create s'mores - you can do this in your own backyard, or go to a state park or the beach for a couple of hours and build a fire beneath the stars. Check out an indoor camping vacation if it's the dead of winter. If you don't want to rough it, Airbnb provides some beautiful glamping options.

47. Go Horseback riding

This is a unique and enjoyable alternative to a typical night out. With a guided horseback riding tour, you can view wildlife and learn about horses while having fun in the great outdoors. I adore horseback riding because it allows me to view some amazing sights while also spending time with some adorable animals.

48. Go Fruit Picking

Almost every season offers a fruit that can be harvested. In the summer, peaches, berries, and grapes; in the early fall, apples; and in the late fall, pears and pumpkins. Enjoy a pleasant day outside doing anything you like, and then prepare a delicious dinner with what you've picked!

49. Go Rock Climbing

Allow the adrenaline rush of a rock climbing wall to boost your endorphins. You can also hone your abilities and set goals for yourself to reach the top. It can be difficult to get into the swing of things if you've never climbed before, but once you do, you might find it entertaining and even addictive.

50. Go Swimming

Swimming is a terrific way to get some exercise and unwind. It's gentle on the body, and even if you can't swim very well, you should strive to learn. Swimming is a valuable life skill as well as a pleasurable exercise. If you're feeling daring, try skinny dipping. No, not at all. Stop blushing and go out and have some fun! Take a plunge in the moonlight at your neighborhood swimming hole. This is a great way to cool off and enjoy your own company this summer. Pack a picnic and spend the day resting in the sun.

51. Zipline

Check out your local adventure zone, or if you're lucky enough to live somewhere with forests, mountains, or a ski resort that offers zip lining when there's no snow on the ground, look into those possibilities as well! This is a unique (and entertaining) way to get your adrenaline going.

52. Explore a New Town

Put on your walking shoes and set out to discover a new city. Explore local communities and try out their restaurants, hiking paths, and stores. This is a fantastic day for a free weekend, so take advantage of it!

53. Go Foraging

Almost every season offers a fruit that can be harvested. In the summer, peaches, berries, and grapes; in the early fall, apples; and in the late fall, pears and pumpkins. Enjoy a pleasant day outside doing anything you like, and then prepare a delicious dinner with what you've picked!

54. Play Tourist At Home

Play tourist for a day and see what everyone says is the hottest area in town. You never know what's going on right in front of your eyes unless you take a moment to smell the roses. This is a fantastic way to explore while you're on the go. Grab a cup of coffee and go for a stroll around the block. If I go out later, I want to go to the hottest restaurants, local monuments, and even clubs. Put your own unique touch on this concept.

55. Get Out On The Water

If you don't get seasick, and if you live near water take a boat ride. It is a great solo date to be out on the water and romanticize your life. I went on a boat ride in Savannah and saw dolphins hopping out of the water and that is a sight you'll never forget. You could also rent a kayak, canoe, or paddleboat at a local lake or beach to test your sense of adventure. Rentals aren't too expensive, and you'll get some great shots on the water.

56. Go To A Comedy Club

Get tickets to a comedy club amateur night or an improv show when you just want some lighthearted amusement. It's guaranteed to make you laugh even if the jokes aren't on target, but at only $5, you're not taking a big risk.

57. RIde A Bike

Rent a bike or ride your own for a leisurely lap around a park or along a nature route. They are usually very inexpensive, especially if your city offers a bike-rental program. You may get a terrific workout while exploring your town.

58. Go To A Concert

Attend a concert or listen to music performed by a local musician. While singing your heart out in the car is enjoyable, nothing beats seeing your favorite band perform live. The music's vitality really comes to life. Or, better yet, attend an outdoor concert. You can sit on the grass and relax even if you don't make it to the front and center of the pit area. Bring a blanket and some water, and relax while listening to some great music.

59. Go Skydiving

Go skydiving to release your inner daredevil. It's a once-in-a-lifetime experience. Yes, it can be frightening, but the exhilaration far surpasses the danger. It's time to cross it off your bucket list, true adrenaline seekers. If you're not yet ready, try indoor skydiving.

60. Go Hiking

A morning trek on the nearby forest paths might provide a good exercise for the outdoorsy types. Is it autumn and you reside in a four-season area? Take a walk or hike through the magnificent fall leaves with your coat on. Being surrounded by pure silence and your own thoughts has a calming effect. This is a fantastic workout that can lead to some incredible adventures.

61. Snorkeling

Go snorkeling because it's a fun summer sport that allows you to take in the scenery. It's also a terrific thing to do on a budget because renting masks and fins is only a few dollars, and you can simply buy affordable gear at your local sports store or on Amazon.

62. Farmer's Market

This is a terrific outdoor activity. Visit your local farmers and sellers, get a bite to eat, and then return home to prepare a nice meal with your purchases. Or go to a flower vendor and get flowers for yourself. You don't have to wait for a man to buy you flowers.

63. Mani/Pedi

Get a Mani and Pedi, especially if it's been a while since you've had one. When I leave a manicure salon, I always feel like a boss! Choose an unusual color or pattern that you've never tried before and experiment with it. This is a wonderful way to pamper oneself.

64. Food Truck

Food trucks are a terrific way to get quality food at a low price. I enjoy going to the food truck lots, where there are so many possibilities and selecting an item from several locations. If I get a few things, I go exploring my city or taking a walk around a new neighborhood.

65. Paintball/Laser Tag

Paintball or laser tag is a wonderful adrenaline-inducing option for the competitive people out there. There are lots of lonely weekends at paintball fields if you don't want to do this with people you know. Laser tag is also a possibility if there are additional singles interested.

66. Go On a Picnic

Take your picnic basket and blanket to a nearby park and relax.

A picnic, whether it's an inside or outdoor affair, is a terrific way to mix things up on the cheap. Bring along your favorite appetizers, beverages, and desserts. You can unwind by watching a movie on your phone or reading your favorite book.

67. Art and Sip

Paint and Sip, pottery and sip, jewelry making and sip, whatever you want to make there is a and sip version that exists. I've made coasters, serving trays, and necklaces all while drinking mimosas so search it up online and pick your favorite.

68. Visit the Library

Although not every library has the same amenities, it is still a fantastic place to visit. Participate in a class, hear a local speaker, join a book discussion group or a book club, or borrow a book or a movie. At a library, there's always something going on, especially if you know the librarians.

69. Train Ride

Taking a slow form of transportation to nowhere, in particular, might be enjoyable especially after a busy week. Go sightseeing on the cheap, visit a new location, or simply sit and let your thoughts roam. For the holidays, there are also fantastic theme railroads such as the Polar Express in Chicago or the Royal Gorge in Colorado.

70. Go To A Resort

Despite the fact that resorts are often associated with families, this perception is changing. Resorts are increasingly catering to single tourists seeking an all-inclusive vacation. There are also a variety of resorts to choose from, ranging from wooded retreats to beach vacations. Check to see what resorts are available in your local state and make plans to visit.

71. Get Hot

When you enter a sauna, you will immediately feel the stress dissipate. If you're looking to decompress but don't have access to a pool or the weather isn't cooperating, try relaxing in a Jacuzzi. If it doesn't help you feel more alive, try hot yoga. Some people are fortunate enough to live near hot springs or lagoons, so take use of it. If done right, becoming hot is a well-known stress relief. Just be cautious.

72. Animal Cafe

This is a great experience even if the food is not the best. I enjoy going to cat cafes but nowadays there are cafes for all types of critters. There's even a raccoon cafe if you are interested in being around them I won't judge... too much.

73. Go To A Bakery

Take yourself to your favorite bakery for a treat. Don't skip out on that wonderful cake you've been longing to sample because life is all about balance. Being good to oneself includes allowing yourself to eat stuff you wouldn't normally eat.

74. Road Trip

A trip to a new location by car. There are numerous national parks and historical sites to visit throughout the weekend. You may even take a drive to a neighbouring town to see what they have to offer.
Try spending some time outside in nature; it might be precisely what you need. It's a good method to unplug from your hectic schedule and social media.

75. Dance Lessons

All you need is your positive vibes for this. You get to mingle with the other guests and meet new people who share your interests or hobbies. What's more, you're free to go at your own pace! It's not necessary to believe that you may become a wonderful dancer in one night; simply enjoy yourself.

76. Meditate

Get zen with this exercise and drop all your worries. There are many different types of meditation like candle gazing, body scanning, and transcendental so don't feel boxed in to just sitting down and letting your thoughts flow. No matter what you do you will feel better after you're done.

77. Go See Sports

I was raised in a baseball family (Go Braves!) so that's what I am partial to but any sport with high energy will do. Have you ever been to a Hockey game? It's like hunger games on ice! So Much fun and much better than watching it on TV.

78. Go To an Arcade

Take a trip to the arcade for a fun arcade night; all you'll need are some quarters and a good attitude. Play claw games, skee ball, video games, and more in the arcade.

79. Karaoke Night

Karaoke is a guaranteed good time, even if you can't hold a note to save your life. It's quite okay to go to a karaoke show by yourself. Many folks go alone and then meet up with their friends there. Others go by themselves and establish acquaintances with other karaoke fans.

80. Go To A Reading

By searching for nearby book readings, you can find poetry readings or performances of works by a specific writer. It's fascinating to hear the authors' motivations for penning their stories, and then you may meet them and discuss them further if you'd like.

81. Go To A Carnival

If you're in the mood for funnel cakes and cotton candy, go to a carnival. There is a lot to do. Visit a county or state fair throughout the summer. If you enjoy people watching, eating pie, or playing competitive games, this is a great solo date option.

82. Go Bowling

Bowling for a game that is normally performed with others, bowling is surprisingly enjoyable when played alone. You can play against other lone persons if you wish to have some friendly rivalry. The shoes are nasty, but you'll have a fantastic time nonetheless.

83. Try A New Workout

Try something new if you're trying to achieve your fitness objectives but are bored with your current regimen. A ropes course, weightlifting, or a rowing lesson are all good options. Something new is likely to motivate you more, especially if you become addicted to it.

84. Scavenger Hunt

Yes, you can do scavenger hunts solo with websites like scavengerhunt.com or you can make one by searching your cities name online and adding scavenger hunt after and seeing what comes up. Or try Geocaching it's one in the same but free and fun.

85. History Tour

Because every town and city has a history, take a historical walking tour. A short internet search might help you in compiling a list of sights to see. Alternatively, you can join a guided tour and meet new people along the route.

86. Go Out To A Bar

So Many different types of bars you should try them all. I prefer Dive Bars because the dart and drinks are fun. But if you want to be high class, the bars at fancy restaurants are the best for getting free drinks. I don't even try to get approached but the drinks keep coming and my friends have the same experiences.

87. Go to the Movies

If you usually watch one type of film try something different. Watch an acclaimed foreign film or a horror movie that is guaranteed to keep you. Pile on the popcorn and drinks and have fun at everyone's favorite pastime. No need to feel insecure it will be too dark and no one really cares if you are alone.

88. Go Paddle Boarding

Easier than surfing in my opinion but still nothing to sneeze at. Paddleboarding is as fun as it is challenging. Go out on your own at a leisurely pace and see the view. Or you can join paddle boarding groups and get taught the ins and outs of the activity.

89. Learn A Martial Art

Self defense, discipline and strength are all things you can pick up when you learn martial arts. From Judo, Krav Maga, Capoeira or even a self defense class you can learn so many different types that you can't really get bored.

90. Go To Dinner

Most people would shy away from a solo dinner date alone but not you! If you love good food why should you have to depend on someone else to enjoy it? Make a reservation to a restaurant you enjoy or somewhere new and eat to your heart's content and don't forget dessert!

91. Take A Trip

Solo trips are a great way for you to discover who you are as a person. Pick a place you've never been before and immerse yourself in the culture. You'll never know what you learn and see or who you'll be when it's over.

92. Take Up Photography

Photography is an excellent way to self-document. It shows how you see the world and how you want to remember it. Pick a place and start taking photos. If you want it memorialized get them printed professionally. No need for a fancy camera your phone will do just fine.

93. Go to a Rage Room

We all want to rage sometimes so why not go to a place designated for just that. Rage rooms also known as smash rooms or anger rooms are places where people can vent their frustrations by destroying items in a safer environment than home. You get to explore your emotions and be angry in a place where it's OK.

94. Improv

You can become a comedian, improve your self-confidence or public speaking skills, or improve your relationships with others by taking improv classes. Improv is harder to learn, but it is beneficial for students in many ways. You can connect with others and learn things about yourself while also having fun.

95. Learn a New Language

Not only will you learn about a new cultures and ideas learning a language is beneficial to your brain. It is evident that studying a second language has numerous cognitive benefits. Memory, problem-solving, and critical-thinking skills are all increased in those who speak more than one language. They also have higher concentration, the ability to multitask, and improved listening skills.

96. Pottery Classes

Making something with your hands is a fun and productive way to spend your spare time in the evenings. If you don't mind getting your hands a little dirty while working with modeling clay, this might be the ideal hobby for you. Before you invest in the materials and equipment, enroll in a ceramics class at a local art center in order to ensure that you will love the process.

97. Singing Lessons

There is an abundance of evidence that demonstrates the positive effects of singing on health and well-being throughout one's life. Vocal lessons assist you in developing a more refined understanding of a musical style and delivery. You will learn how to employ effective breath support, expand your vocal range, sing with ease and clarity, and project your voice.

98. Flower Arranging

According to research, flowers have an immediate positive impact on one's happiness and mental well-being.
So why not spend some time in the company of flowers while also creating a gorgeous arrangement at the same time? Flower arrangements make lovely gifts or can be used to beautify your own living space.

99. Jewelry Making

You can make beautiful jewelry while simultaneously building brain power. Jewelry making has many cognitive and physical benefits to your health and when you're done creating your pieces you have works of art to give to your friends.

100. Learn to DJ

You can find new music and have a blast while as a DJ. It is not just a great way to pass the time, but also an excellent way to meet people while traveling. DJs can even earn some money as well if they work hard.

101. Learn Calligraphy

Calligraphy is not only relaxing and meditative, but it also helps with fine motor skills and memory retention. We are most creative when we engage our hands. It helps us organize our thoughts and encourages us to think critically. It also helps us acquire confidence as we get better at the skill.

Make Your Own Self Dates

Write down a few self date ideas if you come up with any.

Make Your Own Self Dates

Write down a few self date ideas if you come up with any.

Make Your Own Self Dates

Write down a few self date ideas if you come up with any.

Make Your Own Self Dates

Write down a few self date ideas if you come up with any.

Printed in Great Britain
by Amazon

Become an
Influencer

ELMA SMIT

LAPA Publishers
www.lapa.co.za

© Text: Elma Smit 2020
© Publication: LAPA Publishers,
a division of Penguin Random House
South Africa (Pty.) Ltd.
380 Bosman Street, Pretoria
Tel: 012 401 0700
Email: lapa@lapa.co.za

Text editor: Glenda Younge
Cover design: Ian Dennewill
Cover photos: Letitia Lerm
Set in 9½ on 13 pt Stone Serif
by G.J. du Toit
Printed and bound by Novus Print,
a Novus Holdings company

First edition 2020

ISBN 978-0-7993-9985-1 (printed book)
ISBN 978-0-7993-9986-8 (ePub)

© All rights reserved. No part of this book may be reproduced in any way without the written permission of the copyright holders.

CONTENTS

1. **What is an influencer?** 1
   Actual queens, beauty queens and other royalty 1
   The chameleon effect 4
   What is engagement anyway? 5
   People follow people 7
   Who am I to write this book? 15
   The influencer industry is not a fad 17
   Beware the Fyre flop 18

2. **Where do you start?** 21
   Being "popular" is not the same as being an "influencer" 21
   Stay alert! Stay alive! 24
   Grab the chalk and draw your outline. 25
   But what if I have chosen the wrong thing – or I change? 28

3. **Find your tribe** 30
   The ghost in the machine 30
   Pumpkins are a niche too 37
   Hi, my name is … 39
   Should I be authentic or aspirational? 41

4. **Content, content, content**. 46
   What is your USP? 46
   Beware of pop culture blips and bubbles 50
   What to dish up and where 54
   Hashtags 58
   Killing babies. 60
   How often do you need to create content? 62

5. **Show me the money** 66
   What is my voice worth? 66
   Let's talk formulas 68
   How to build a media kit. 72

6. **And when I start making money?** 77
   Traditional media lessons apply 77
   Regulations: These are the rules 79

7. **What if I screw up?** 81
   Slacktivism and other ethical no-nos 81
   Where should you set your boundaries?. 85
   Risky business 89

Influencers worth following 93
   Mike Sharman's favourites 93
   Liesl Laurie's favourites. 93
   Rachel Kolisi's favourite 94
   Nadia Jaftha's favourites 94
   Bouwer Bosch's favourites 94
   Wian Magic's favourites on TikTok 95
   Katinka die Kat's favourites 95
   Maps Maponyane's favourites 95

Recommended reading 96

1

WHAT IS AN INFLUENCER?

Actual queens, beauty queens and other royalty

Influencers invented social media. Not the other way around.

Humans want to be accepted, to be part of a tribe, and to be a member of some community. We have always shared at least one thing, regardless of when or where we were born: the need to communicate, to engage.

Whether you do this by drawing stick-figures on cave walls for other Neanderthals to find or by sharing photos of your face with people you will never meet is simply determined by when you were born.

As any of the shareholders of Instagram, YouTube, TikTok, Pinterest, Twitter or Facebook will tell you, all these social media platforms would certainly become worthless relics overnight if all of humanity suddenly decided to stop posting content.

Being an influencer is nothing new. It is a skill, a hobby and sometimes an obsession. However, being good at one aspect does not mean that you automatically will be good at the others. Yes, it requires some talent and having this talent can be great for you, if you manage to turn it into a phenomenal career or a fulfilling pastime. But, as with any kind of (super) power, it can also be an all-consuming vice – one that can eat you up inside. It all depends on who you are, and why and how you are doing it.

Before I joined Facebook, Twitter or Instagram, I was a student at the University of Stellenbosch. Back in 2005, although you'd see people around campus or have their contact details, the only way you would know who they were dating was through the grapevine. Crazy, I know!

Sure, we took photos of ourselves at parties, on the beach and at graduation – even on digital cameras – but hardly anyone saw these unless we showed them the prints stuck on our bedroom walls or doors. And yet, freebies managed to find their way to me – or rather, I found my way to them.

I was a DJ at the campus radio station and, at the end of my first year, one of the other DJs told me that he had nominated me for the campus beauty pageant, Ms Matieland. His agenda was that he served on the student council committee, which leveraged the (relative) appeal of a beauty pageant to raise money and awareness for the Maties Community Service programme. He was looking for candidates on campus who could bring some legitimacy to the whole thing. I had spent some time in high school volunteering at a safehouse for abandoned babies in my hometown and later taught holiday programmes to primary school kids as part of this community programme at Stellenbosch University. Plenty of naturally gorgeous and far more glamorous young women roamed the campus, but I would be able to speak about community service with integrity.

However, let me be clear: I'm no Mother Teresa. I knew that I wanted to work in radio one day, even though I was determined to obtain a law degree first. I knew that competition for radio slots (both at our campus radio station and at radio stations where you were actually paid commercial rates) was fierce. This pageant would offer me the chance to gain a bit of influence on campus – not a lot, but perhaps enough to set me apart in the age before Instagram.

I decided that my pageant fundraising project would be a shavathon in aid of a leukaemia charity, the Sunflower Fund. With the help of another radio colleague, I convinced the branch manager of the bank in our student centre to pledge a cash amount for every head shaved or sprayed with colour. I then challenged the men's hostels to join the action. My line was, "If I shave my hair off, will you?" And yes, I did shave my hair off. All of it! I think we collected between R10 000 and R20 000 this way.

The prominence I was looking for came in the form of my photo on a billboard-sized banner in the student centre and front-page coverage of the shavathon in the town's newspaper.

As finalists, we were also given new jeans, a gym membership, a spa day and plenty of other smaller complimentary perks and freebies. Pageant sponsors could claim that they were supporting charity by getting involved and, at the same time, their clothes were worn and their businesses were frequented by the eight most-publicised faces on campus – for a month or two, anyway.

Soon after, and due largely to my short-lived stint as an almost-beauty-queen (who also worked in campus radio), I started landing more interesting work. I hosted hostel events, fundraisers, music gigs and award shows. I even presented a few of

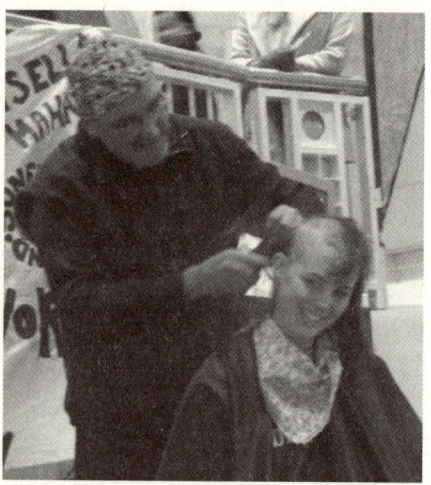

The CANSA shavathon in aid of the Sunflower Fund was a live event hosted in the Neelsie Student Centre at lunchtime on a weekday. I was obviously not thinking clearly when I set the date – it was done in the heart of winter, which should be avoided at all costs!

This was the actual billboard banner image. As you might be able to tell from the varying sizes of our heads, some major Photoshop work was done on this composite image to make us all appear the same height. From left to right: Elma Smit, Naomi Erasmus, Taryn Campbell, Irma Hurter, Caryn van de Coolwijk, Lize Visagie, Caren Dorrington and Keneilwe Kgasi.

those annoying shopping centre activations where they hand out branded pens, water bottles and lanyards, while an announcer (me) bellows promotional scripts over a loudspeaker. I said yes to anything that would bring me cash, some experience, exposure or a free pair of Sissy Boy jeans.

Before beauty queens, actual queens performed much the same role. In the 1500s, Queen Elizabeth I set beauty trends with her opulent dresses, fair skin, red lips, high hairline and strawberry-blonde hair. Many women at court plucked the hair from their foreheads in a bid to maintain a high hairline like the queen's, according to a fascinating section on the Royal Museums Greenwich website dedicated to the Virgin Queen. Women at court wore her old dresses or had copies made of them; they even blackened their teeth when the queen's rotted away and glazed their skins with raw egg white to achieve that marble-like look. You could say that she was the ultimate Renaissance beauty blogger. The website continues:

> An alabaster complexion symbolised wealth and nobility ... Concoctions used to bleach freckles and treat blemishes often included ingredients such as sulphur, turpentine and mercury ... As Elizabeth aged, her legendary sweet tooth caught up with her, causing her teeth to decay. Her influence by this time was so pervasive that some women went so far as to blacken their own teeth to mimic her appearance.

People wanted to emulate her, to gain acceptance and be associated with her power. In spite of reigning over an oppressively patriarchal society, she exercised great influence.

These days you don't need to be born into royalty. You don't need to tolerate marrying into a titled family. You don't even need to enter a beauty pageant or shave off your hair. Why? Because you have social media.

The chameleon effect

Is there anybody in close proximity to you right now? You don't even need to know them – just catch their eye. Now yawn. Yawn excessively. Don't hide it or be polite about it. Lean into that yawn, as Sheryl Sandberg would say. Make sure they can see you yawning; do it twice if you need to. Are they seeing you? Good! I bet they are also yawning by now. In fact, even if you are reading this all alone and you didn't just put on the most performative yawn on earth, are you feeling a great big yawn coming on? I'm yawning as I sit here writing this.

This is called unintentional mirroring – basically, influence in action.

Our brains do it all the time, in different and very interesting ways. Two scientists, Tanya Chartrand and John Bargh, ran experiments in the late 1990s and dubbed this the "chameleon effect".

They found that:

- When you work with people on a task, even if you do not consider them to be your friends, you naturally tend to start behaving like they do – often subconsciously. The more time you spend with them, the more you pick up their mannerisms, their postures and even their accents.
- When you mirror the behaviour that you see and hear around you, chances are people will automatically find it easier to like you.
- People who exhibit high levels of natural empathy are more likely to do this innately and they tend to be considered more likeable.

You don't need to read the whole study to know that this is true. Just think of your own school years or consider the social dynamics in any workplace. Whether you are trying to establish yourself in a new social environment or on a social platform, likeability is one of the key requirements for success.

So, where do you need to start if you plan to achieve this? Not by putting on some great show of strength. Not by living up to lofty materialistic ideals. Not by focusing on overcoming the crushing self-doubt you feel every time you look in the mirror.

You need to start by consciously studying your follower. The person you want to reach is not that different from the one who sits in the same office block or classroom as you do. Pay them attention – your most precious commodity.

This was one of the most useful things I did when I first started making inroads into establishing myself as a sports broadcaster in a male-dominated world. Long story short: I was the first woman chosen to report on a Rugby World Cup for the South African broadcaster SuperSport back in 2011. This was an incredibly daunting and intimidating task – and I still believe that it was my relative youthfulness (I was 25 years old) that made me foolish enough to take on the job.

One thing was even more crucial than keeping an eye on the actual ball during matches. More important, even, than getting to grips with the social shorthand of working with many very famous rugby pundits, some of whom were old enough to be my dad. I realised quickly that I needed to study the viewers, so I trawled the comments sections below rugby articles. I monitored Twitter, keeping tabs on popular hashtags and topics that dominated the conversations around water coolers and braais. This helped me gain a keen insight into the issues normal rugby fans were confused by and the broadly held opinions that could, perhaps, be unravelled, and even disproven, with the insight and analysis of my colleagues.

Sure, I needed a few years to get to grips with the job and I didn't enjoy uniform support – inside the company or on Twitter. But I found that when I started reading people's opinions and questions and attributing these directly to them on air, viewers flooded me with the one thing every content creator needs: engagement. Soon, people were tagging me in tweets, sending me detailed analyses in messages, and even making topic suggestions. They seemed to feel a much closer connection with me than with many of my more famous and experienced colleagues, not because I had suddenly convinced anyone that I held some mysterious rugby oracle capabilities, or that I had access to the reins of the @SuperSportTV account, but because I simply reached out first. That is what skyrocketed my direct engagement – on TV, but also online.

It was as simple and as uncomplicated as that. I went looking for what people were saying; I plucked them out of relative obscurity and attributed their ideas directly to them. That's what triggered the domino effect of engagement.

What is engagement anyway?

Engagement in social media is generally considered to occur when followers like, comment on, share or reply to your content. Engagement is the measure of how often they do this – how frequently they keep coming back for more – and how consistently this keeps happening, with new followers joining the ranks.

A rough sum looks like this:

$$\frac{\text{Likes + Comments}}{\text{Followers}} \times 100 = \text{Engagement (quantified in \%)}$$

On my profile on a recent post this works out to:

$$\frac{6177 \text{ Likes} + 71 \text{ Comments}}{97\,900 \text{ Followers}} \times 100 = 6\% \text{ Engagement rate}$$

Ideally, one would need to work this out over a month, or even three months, to get a fair estimate of an account's performance, but that is quite labour-intensive. Luckily, there are loads of engagement calculator websites, where you simply enter the account handle and they squeeze the metrics for you.

Below 1% is considered low, while 1% to 3% is considered a fairly good engagement rate. Between 3% and 6% is very high and over 6% is huge. Over the last 30 days, mine has been sitting at 3.99%, which is fairly healthy considering that I've had a book to write.

Comedians who really flex their comedic talent on social media tend to boast great engagement rates because comedians spend most of their time on stage telling us things we know about ourselves and each other. Yes, comedians often boast exceptional comedic timing, great charisma and some measure of stage presence. But what really sets great comedians apart is their ability to study people and distil our varied and unique experiences down to a few entertaining, universal notions.

Sharing in laughter makes us feel heard and recognised as we hear and recognise others. This is also why some sitcoms use what is called "canned applause" or "canned laughter". The script and performances are timed around a few seconds of applause after key punchlines. I'm sure you've wondered why you are able to hear the audience laughing, yet this mysterious audience is never shown? Yes, some sitcoms do actually record their shows in front of a live audience, which means that you are hearing the real reactions of that audience, but even then producers sometimes edit the laughter to make it continue for longer or start sooner – whatever is required to ensure maximum comedic effect.

This is a simple technique, but it works. Even when you know that the track is simply a recording of people laughing, you still laugh. Your brain is tricked into it. Producers rely on the chameleon effect to make sure you find their show funny enough to watch the next episode – and the following season as well.

Similarly, social media platforms make comment sections public. Haven't you wondered why these platforms don't just send the comments that people leave below your posts to you directly? After all, you are the person who created the post. Why show other consumers the comments made by your friends, the in-joke left by your colleague or if anyone liked your post at all? Even if you take the total number of likes away (as Instagram is doing), the mere suggestion that other people enjoy something or find it valuable enough to engage with it is often exactly why we take a second look. If you walk past a group of people crowded around something on a pavement (especially if you don't know what it is), chances are that you'll crane your neck to get a glimpse or ask a bystander about what is going on. This is no different to how social media works, and how hashtags and trending topics work.

But this is only half of the equation: it is a transactional relationship that needs to start with you. When you study and then cover the topics, ideas, concepts and trends your ideal followers care about, they will find your content easier to like (both virtual and actual likes).

What is it that they like? Pay attention: they'll tell you, one way or another.

People follow people

Influencer marketing exists because we have more faith in each other than we do in brands. This didn't happen overnight, though.

The earliest advertising can be traced back to Ancient Greece, Rome, Arabia and China. Of course, industrialisation really ramped up production and distribution, then television and radio changed the game during the twentieth century and, finally, the Internet came about.

What remained consistent throughout this time, however, was that brands traditionally created advertising featuring relatable-looking placeholder people. These placeholder people were using or consuming the products and services promoted. They all looked or sounded like you, your friends or your family. The scenarios were familiar and real; the products offered real solutions. But the people involved were clearly paid to do this.

Even when film stars, athletes and models first endorsed products under their own names, consumers accepted that this was an acting or a modelling job, much like their last movie, stadium billboard or advertising campaign; in other words, a commercial transaction.

Then, when social media kicked off, an exceptionally effective but rather limited kind of marketing exploded, almost overnight. The reach of our experiences with products and services became instantly shareable and searchable. We no longer had to take a company or advertising agency's word for anything. We didn't need to rely on celebrities in foreign countries or hand-picked, polished testimonials from one or two Satisfied Sallys to tell us that *"this* washing powder/moisturiser/car polish really works".

"Social proof" was easy to find and, before we knew it, it was all around us. Dr Robert Cialdini coined the nifty term "social proof" in his book *Influence*, where he went a step further than the "chameleon effect".

He found that we do not merely copy each other without realising it. He said that we copy each other *particularly* when:

- We are unsure of ourselves
  and
- The people we observe seem similar to us.

He wrote this in 1984, so the basic concept that underpins influencer marketing dates back to long before social media.

When I am not sure about what to do, I am probably going to default back to people who seem sure. Of all the people who seem sure, I'll probably copy the one who seems the most like me.

So, let's say that I am in the market for a new brand of mascara. I am unsure of which one to choose and I'm faced with four options:

- Product A is featured in a new TV advert.
- Product B is on a beautiful billboard I pass on my way to work.
- Product C was featured in a post by Kim Kardashian. She is gorgeous, but my lashes are naturally fair and quite sparse – not a problem I associate with her.
- Product D is used by a blogger who also does Pilates at my gym – a blogger with hair and lashes very similar to mine.

I am going to pick product D.

Brands soon realised that expensive television adverts create talkability; billboards give your brand clout; big celebrity endorsements deliver broad appeal; and a super testimonial from a gorgeous film star is certainly useful. However, sending lots of little advertising foot soldiers directly to a consumer's phone screen has become the ultimate shortcut to activate the ultimate marketing superpower: word of mouth.

People like me, solving problems like mine, with things I can access, where I am.

The more things change, the more they stay the same. Traditional marketing relies heavily on the infamous four Ps: product, price, place and promotion. We probably think of social media as 100% promotion and none of the other stuff. But social media can be hyper-local. It creates great opportunities to showcase a product in seamless and incidental ways with embedded links straight to an online store, which, in turn, delivers straight to your door or even your desk.

In an age in which we can rely on actual people over traditional forms of advertising, we tend to trust each other more than we trust the brands we buy. What do I base this on? The numbers. Of the 20 most followed

What is an influencer? | 9

accounts on Instagram, 17 belong to people and only three of them belong to brands.

See for yourself:

Instagram

Rank	Username	Owner	Followers (millions)	Profession	Brand account
1	@instagram	Instagram	332	Social media platform	✓
2	@cristiano	Cristiano Ronaldo	202	Footballer	–
3	@arianagrande	Ariana Grande	174	Musician and actress	–
4	@therock	Dwayne Johnson	171	Actor and professional wrestler	–
5	@selenagomez	Selena Gomez	168	Musician and actress	–
6	@kyliejenner	Kylie Jenner	161	Reality TV personality and businesswoman	–
7	@kimkardashian	Kim Kardashian	159	Reality TV personality and businesswoman	–
8	@leomessi	Lionel Messi	142	Footballer	–
9	@beyonce	Beyoncé	140	Musician	–
10	@neymarjr	Neymar	133	Footballer	–
11	@natgeo	National Geographic	131	Magazine	✓
12	@justinbieber	Justin Bieber	127	Musician	–
13	@taylorswift	Taylor Swift	126	Musician	–
14	@kendalljenner	Kendall Jenner	122	Reality TV personality and model	–
15	@jlo	Jennifer Lopez	113	Musician and actress	–
16	@nickiminaj	Nicki Minaj	110	Musician	–
17	@khloekardashian	Khloé Kardashian	104	Reality TV personality and businesswoman	–
18	@mileycyrus	Miley Cyrus	103	Musician and actress	–
19	@nike	Nike	100	Sportswear multinational	✓
20	@katyperry	Katy Perry	89	Musician	–

Figures accurate on 8 February 2020

But perhaps it's different on Twitter? Nope. Three accounts in the top 20 belong to organisations. The rest are all people.

Twitter

Rank	Change (monthly)	Account name	Owner	Followers (millions)	Activity
1	–	@BarackObama	Barack Obama	113	Former US president
2	⇧	@justinbieber	Justin Bieber	109	Musician
3	⇩	@katyperry	Katy Perry	108	Musician
4	–	@rihanna	Rihanna	96	Musician and businesswoman
5	–	@taylorswift13	Taylor Swift	86	Musician
6	–	@Cristiano	Cristiano Ronaldo	83	Footballer
7	–	@ladygaga	Lady Gaga	81	Musician and actress
8	–	@TheEllenShow	Ellen DeGeneres	79	Comedian
9	⇧	@realDonaldTrump	Donald Trump	72	Current US president
10	⇩	@YouTube	YouTube	72	Online video platform

Rank	Change (monthly)	Account name	Owner	Followers (millions)	Activity
11	–	@ArianaGrande	Ariana Grande	70	Musician and actress
12	–	@jtimberlake	Justin Timberlake	65	Musician and actor
13	–	@KimKardashian	Kim Kardashian	63	TV personality and businesswoman
14	–	@selenagomez	Selena Gomez	60	Musician and actress
15	–	@twitter	Twitter	57	Social media platform
16	⇧	@cnnbrk	CNN Breaking News	56	News channel
17	⇩	@britneyspears	Britney Spears	56	Musician
18	–	@narendramodi	Narendra Modi	53	Current prime minister of India
19	–	@shakira	Shakira	52	Musician
20	–	@jimmyfallon	Jimmy Fallon	52	Comedian

On Facebook, 10 brands clinch spots in the top 20; the other 10 go to individuals:

Facebook

Rank	Account name	Followers (millions)	Category
1	Facebook	214	Social media
2	Samsung	159	Products and services
3	Cristiano Ronaldo	122	Football player
4	Mark Elliot Zuckerberg	116	Internet entrepreneur
5	Real Madrid C.F.	110	Football club
6	Coca-Cola	107	Product and services
7	FC Barcelona	103	Football club
8	Shakira	100	Musician
9	Vin Diesel	97	Actor
10	Tasty	97	Internet media
11	CGTN	92	Television Network
12	Lionel Messi	90	Football player
13	Mr Bean	84	Public figure
14	Eminem	86	Musician
15	YouTube	84	Product and services
16	McDonald's	79	Product and services
17	Rihanna	79	Musician
18	Will Smith	77	Actor
19	Justin Bieber	76	Musician
20	China Daily	85	Newspaper

"People do not want to have a conversation with their chips" is a great quote from the Australian marketing guru Professor Mark Ritson. In an online lecture for the Australian Association of National Advertisers in May 2016 (still available on its YouTube channel), he explained that "social media is about people, not brands. 76% of people do not use social media to follow brands."

An updated, additional definition for the word "influencer" was included in the *Merriam-Webster Dictionary* in May 2019: "a person who is able to generate interest in something (such as a consumer product) by posting about it on social media". The editor of the dictionary remarked at the time that "all of us are consumers, even if all we are consuming is information".

Try to think of the last ten times you interacted with any brand on any social media platform. How many of those times did you simply reach out to complain or at least give critical feedback? We often use social media like a customer service careline, because we'd much rather drag the proverbial shopkeeper into the town square so we can shout at him (hopefully in front of a crowd!) for selling us rotten food than tell him quietly over the phone. When you love a product, chances are you'll be telling a friend before you reach out to the brand itself. You paid them for it, after all.

Whether launching your customer service tirades on social media is a good idea (or how to do it in a positive way) when you want to build a business out of partnering with brands is something I'll cover later in this book. But when it comes to brands marketing their products, social media soon showed marketers and advertising agencies that because people follow people, they would be more effective if they roped in the assistance of those people. Social media is exactly that – social!

Initially, brands and their agencies collaborated with large-scale influencers: athletes, celebrities, models, musicians, reality stars and actors. If you didn't command the attention of at least a few hundred thousand to a few million followers, you didn't mean much to brands. Your posts needed to be seen by as many people as possible. The entire digital advertising sales business is traditionally built on impressions: how many people saw the advert? Enough? Success.

But the problem is that even the US president @realDonaldTrump, with his verified account and more than 70 million followers on Twitter, could have as many as 15 million fake followers (according to twitteraudit.com).

What is a fake follower? A fake follower is an account that is not consistently active, has low fol-

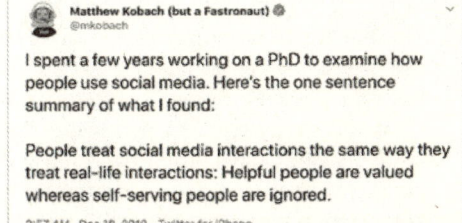

I could quote Matthew Kobach's impressive PhD to explain this, but I find that his Twitter feed serves as an excellent shortcut. He is head of Social at the New York Stock Exchange and is well worth following.

lower numbers, has been on Twitter for only a short while, does not stick around for long and could very well have been created by so-called bots (an abbreviation for Internet robots). Anyone can buy bot followers and you can also direct these bots to any nominated account you want to inflate. That's right: you don't need to be the owner of an account to be able to buy it some perceived support.

Yes, some of these accounts could belong to users who only passively consume content on Twitter from time to time. But most of them are created by programs written to create accounts under real or even imagined identities, because once there is a demand for a shortcut to becoming an influencer (being able to buy more followers, that is) someone will find a way to service that demand. Why some people have fake followers even when they didn't pay for this shortcut is unclear, but one widely held theory is that these bots follow a random number of accounts to raise the appearance of legitimacy.

Source: Twitteraudit.com

For the sake of transparency, my own account reflects a 7% fake-follower rating, according to the same website, and I have never bought followers. Musician, actor, producer and influencer Bouwer Bosch admitted in an interview for this book that he has been tempted to buy followers before.

> The thing about social media is, on the one hand, I feel like it is so filtered and fake. On the other hand, I feel like it's an amazing marketing platform. The more followers you have, the greater your pay cheque because the more people come to your shows.

The problem with fake followers, though, is that they can't go to shows.

> Yes, but it's the amount of ego involved that gets to you. In Afrikaans, at one point I was the leading Afrikaans alternative musician, in terms of followers. Maybe because my audience was so young, or maybe because I put a comedy spin on posts. But then suddenly guys like Jo Black and Francois van Coke started overtaking me. Then you start looking at other people, how they grow, and you start wondering about your own identity. You doubt whether people still like you. If it is perhaps your own fault that you're not keeping up?

Bouwer is sharing this important insight in the hopes that you realise that:

> Even people with 100 000 followers: "go through this identity crisis, but you should know that the algorithm is all about how frequently you post.

You need to keep up a very high frequency. And, of course, it also matters what you're posting. People loved it when Leandie [du Randt, his ex-wife and also a well-known actress and influencer] and I posted stuff together. Maybe because it held some sort of romantic aspiration? Those posts enjoyed so much engagement. That, and ones about feeling vulnerable and battling with depression. It shows you where we are as people, hey? We also want to know that other people are also scared, that they also battle.

The American digital and influencer marketing strategist Joe Scott manages global campaigns for Fortune 500 companies (the top 500 companies in the United States, as rated by *Fortune* magazine). I had the opportunity to work with him on a campaign during Rugby World Cup 2019 in Japan. Besides boasting a phenomenal karaoke voice and the ability to speak both Korean and German, Joe is an absolute student of the influencer industry. He concedes that brands cannot tell 100% if someone has bought followers, but that there are strong indicators they look for.

> With tools becoming more sophisticated, we can measure the activity of the followers, the rate at which the followers grew, and then the location of the accounts. For instance, let's take John Doe, an American influencer from Chicago, Illinois. This influencer grew from 50 000 to 500 000 followers in two months, without a particularly viral post. We also notice that Doe's average engagements haven't increased proportionately with the follower size. Finally, we see that over 25% of Doe's followers are randomly from the Middle East or another region outside the United States, without a clear connection between that region and the influencer. These could all be coincidence, but it raises many red flags.

I also asked another ad industry specialist – this time a leading voice here in South Africa – for advice on this topic. Mike Sharman (@mikesharman) founded Retroviral, an agency that has made more brands "go viral, globally" than any other agency in Africa. You will have seen his work on RocoMamas. Retroviral is the leading creative agency for the Smashburger brand, Russell Hobbs, Martin and Martin brands, and M-Net, to name a few. He has developed campaigns that have been classified as "truly viral" (like the "Last Dictator Standing" ad for Nando's). He was named one of the *Mail & Guardian*'s top 200 young South Africans in 2013 and is the co-founder of the influencer marketing platform webfluential.com, as well as retroactive.digital, a disruptive sports storytelling agency. Make sure your next read is his first book, *The Best Dick*.

Mike warns:

> There's an important distinction between buying bot-followers from click-farms in Asia versus paying to amplify your content, because all social channels now need a paid element. Organic is a very difficult thing to grow your base from.
>
> When you buy bot-followers you might get followers but no engagement and you'll soon be found out. There's a whole lot of fraud associated with

presenting yourself to a brand as something you're not. The brand won't get the sales though. And they're moving more towards a cost-per-click and cost-per-conversion sort of space. So, there's a lot of revenue sharing.

This is an interesting new innovation you'll see more of on webfluential.com and similar platforms. Basically, how this works is: "You drive the sales, you get the value ..." If you punt a company's sale, you earn commission on click-throughs or sales off the back of that. If you're a real, authentic influencer, you'll be able to make more money from conversions than off a paid post. Ultimately, it's a job, you need to make money. As an influencer your value is determined in your output.

As an influencer you will often deal with people like Mike and Joe, so I thought I'd take this moment to outline a few key terms and phrases that people bandy about in boardrooms and on e-mail in the influencer industry. Knowing this jargon will ease your progress through these conversations.

Ellen Ward-Collins – a planner with the UK-based branch of the advertising giant M&C Saatchi Performance – outlines the top three terms as follows:

- **Reach:** In order for your campaign to influence the largest number of people possible, the ideal influencer should be one who has an above-average audience size in a specific niche or market. However, as Donald Trump's millions of Twitter bots may demonstrate, the size of your audience is not actually the most important aspect. The way an influencer engages with their followers, and how lasting an impact they have on them, are much more valuable assets for a brand.
- **Resonance:** It is essential that the influencer selected for a campaign supplies content that resonates well with their audience, in a way that encourages further action. An influencer who creates content people crave and readily engage with will make a major wave with even a single tweet because the content resonates with their followers. Resonance can be measured via many engagement metrics, such as likes, comments, retweets or shares.
- **Relevance:** Although influencers are working with advertisers more and more, the vast majority of really successful influencers do this in a way that retains their authenticity: they will not "spam" followers to the detriment of their own brand. Influencers who always ensure that there is a strong overlap in what benefits the brand and what serves their followers maintain high levels of relevance.

Basically, when brands look to select influencers for their campaigns, they do not only look at the total number of followers an influencer has. Joe Scott explains that "every brand is different. Some are looking for the right influencer that matches their brand's values. Some are still looking for sheer numbers. When we build the profiles and personas for a brand campaign, we typically prioritise the following:

- **Engagement:** Median or average engagement rate.
- **Audience:** The influencer's audience demographic. Does their audience match the demographic target we are marketing toward?
- **Personal brand:** Their look and feel. Does the influencer's personal brand already communicate values similar to the brand's? Is there authenticity behind their storytelling and how they interact with the audience? Is the feed stylised and/or consistent?

Exactly how to ensure you generate high engagement isn't the only lifeblood of any influencer, though. You can certainly find inspiration, useful tips and constant learning opportunities in other places as well – radio presenters, TV producers, musicians and authors. They all spend their time creating content to inform, educate and entertain people.

Nobody does this with the expectation that their work will remain unwatched, unheard or unread. The whole point of the exercise is for it to be consumed. And you know what we really measure success by? Whether the consumer responds, in any way. Does the consumer change their behaviour? Do they tell a friend? Do they reply? Do they disagree and do they say so – on any platform? That is engagement and it is the name of the game, regardless of where or how you aim to inform, entertain or educate people.

Who am I to write this book?

You might have picked up this book not knowing much about me but rather because you're interested in this topic. In fact, even if you do know who I am, I'm hoping that you're here for the content, because this is why I wrote it.

In 2019 my career reached a turning point, but not the one most people would think of. I worked on two World Cup tournaments, across two different sports, for two massive global governing bodies as a digital presenter and producer: the International Cricket Council (on the 2019 ICC Men's Cricket World Cup in England and Wales) and World Rugby (on the 2019 Rugby World Cup in Japan).

From the outside it might have looked as if I had scaled up – I was working for truly global content platforms for the first time. This is true, at least in part. But what I really learnt from the experience was how these organisations leverage the appeal of their sport and, indeed, the appeal of live sport (the most real reality television on earth) on their digital platforms, and how they use a four-yearly event to take massive growth leaps in a matter of weeks.

In both cases, the teams I worked on saw their analytics return amazing results. We set well-documented records in our coverage of both events and I'm incredibly proud of our efforts. It was thrilling, inspiring and absolutely formative. Not only did I gain a much larger and certainly more global audience, but I also started looking very differently at what I was doing on my own platforms.

I described it to many people as going on a paid digital marketing and brand development course: a kind of boot camp where everyone in the team hustles under intense pressure to apply every bit of knowledge and skill they have garnered in their career, testing their knowledge with a live, global audience every day, with metrics and analytics immediately available – a massive departure from the way TV and radio traditionally work. This was a major leap for me, from my traditional broadcasting background, which often relies on quarterly viewer or listenership figures, paid research and a fair share of anecdotal feedback.

What surprised me was that if I had to measure my work in 2019, according to what produced the most lucrative result, it wouldn't be these massive events I got to work on – not directly, anyway. The value in both was certainly experiential: I built amazing networks, learnt many lessons and then, obviously, they also offered me great brand-building opportunities. But if one takes a closer look at the bottom line of Elma Smit, the business, what really paid in 2019 was social media. The sponsored content. Brands! My Instagram, Facebook and Twitter profiles generated a much greater return on investment than any of the radio, TV, event hosting or digital shows I delivered. You could argue that this was a direct result of the fact that it was the best year of my career, but it could also be argued that this was in spite of all my other activities.

The American thought leader and marketing guru Seth Godin is known for always emphasising that generosity is at the heart of content. At the end of 2019 I felt that this was truer than ever for me. When I returned to South Africa, I found myself telling people about the lessons I had learnt. Many who crossed my path showed an interest, even those whom I didn't think would be interested in influencer and content lessons. Too often, we keep a firm guard up and we don't share what we do and how, often enough.

On his blog, Godin writes:

> We choose to be selfish because we feel insufficiency ... Like a drowning person, we cling ever tighter to the life buoy ... The single best way to find sufficiency and confidence and trust and forward motion is to do precisely the opposite of what our instincts might tell us. In an economy based on connection, trust and attention, the posture of generosity is not only the highest-yielding strategy, it's also the right thing to do. Ideas shared go up in value. Doors opened turn into new opportunities for all.

So, I called up a few people in the influencer industry and asked them to open their books and share their knowledge with me and, ultimately, also with you. Instead of rejection and cynicism, I encountered the most amazing generosity. This shared passion ignited such a great spark of connection with people I've mostly admired from afar and we had awesome, compelling (and often very long) conversations – some of the most raw, inspiring and motivating conversations I've had in years. These lively conversations informed the writing of this book and they are available in full in an accompanying e-book, *Conversations with Influencers*.

Ideas shared really do go up in value. Please share yours with all the very generous people I have interviewed for this book. I can assure you that they are a remarkable collection of talented, committed and sharp-eyed experts in their fields. Thank you to each of them.

The influencer industry is not a fad

Some argue that the influencer market has peaked and that the downturn can already be spotted. However, the Internet certainly isn't a fad. Similarly, the inherent social nature of humanity also isn't, which is why I'd argue that social media (in one form or another) is here to stay. As long as the platforms attract users, there will be ways of turning influence on those platforms into income.

As Mike explains:

> Even brands also realise that if they're going to play in a social space, they have to actually be social. The brands who are doing well on social [media] are busy using banter, they are self-deprecating when they mess up. Brands now have very distinct personalities. Influencers are similar in that they are also brands, they are commercial properties, commercialised vehicles of audience.

This very interesting blurring of lines happens every day.

What brands and influencers have in common is that the foundation of everything they do when building a brand (as an influencer or as a marketer) is credibility. Anything that erodes credibility endangers the essence of what you're busy building when you're telling stories and trying to use your influence.

Joe Scott illustrates how this sets influencers apart from traditional media platforms in a very practical way.

> Traditional media tells me what I should think or how I should behave. Influencers should tell me what *they* think and how *they* behave. Their connection to a product should not be a glowing endorsement, but a recommendation based on their personal use. Not "you should use this because its good!" But rather "I use this because it helps me with ___. If you're like me, you may find value in it as well." A seemingly subtle difference, but a big one.

If you're actively positioning yourself as an independent voice you are also flexing your unique power to speak to a consumer in a way that brands cannot. This unique power, however, hinges on your trustworthiness. Trust is what turns your followers into a loyal community. When it goes missing, so does the work. This happened in Australia in 2019, when one small PR firm took the bold step to stop advising its clients to include social media as part of their PR strategies. The Atticism agency ditched spending on influencer campaigns altogether because it found that the same group of influencers in Australia would constantly be liking and commenting on each other's posts, which drives up engagement, but in a false manner. The agency claimed that it had bust a group of influencers for actively defrauding its clients, because the industry builds its rates on clicks (likes, comments, views and shares).

If you cook the books on your metrics, you are misrepresenting what you are delivering to the client. If you are actively skewing the reporting because you don't have confidence in your ability to deliver real value to your client, you had better know that they will eventually also notice it in their bottom line. They will change their approach sooner or later and the bottom of your influencer business will, ultimately, fall out.

Playing the long game – which is building a reputation that speaks of integrity and professionalism – is not only something that will stand you in good stead in the world of social media and making any kind of content, but it is also the hallmark of the influencers I interviewed for this book. These are the ones who have outlasted trends, who have earned their blue-ticked verified status, who have outperformed the norm and succeeded against the odds. They happen also to be the ones who under-promise and over-deliver, who treat their clients' businesses as they would treat their own business.

Beware the Fyre flop

The most high-profile reality check for influencers to date came with the unmasking of the famously failed music festival in the Bahamas, the Fyre Festival. The festival promoters, Fyre Media, captured the attention of thousands of fans through a series of sponsored posts shared by some of the most famous models on Instagram: Kendall Jenner, Bella Hadid, Hailey Baldwin and Emily Ratajkowski, to name a few.

It was a disaster, though. Bands cancelled at the last minute and guests found tents without beds in them. Nothing lived up to the hype and, ultimately, when the festival was supposed to be at its most fabulous and Instagrammable peak, chaos erupted. It turned out that the influencers involved had not disclosed that they had been paid to promote the event.

As Matt Higgins outlines in a paper in the *University of Cincinnati Law Review*:

> To the surprise of no one, lawsuits following the failed Fyre Festival piled up quickly. In a class action complaint ... plaintiffs named 1–100 "Doe Defendants" who deliberately and fraudulently marketed and sold tickets to a lavish, tropical destination music festival.

The class-action lawsuit against the influencers and the promoters was eventually withdrawn, but this wasn't the last the influencers would hear of it.

> Multiple influencers – including Jenner – were [also] subpoenaed by the Bankruptcy Trustee in the main Fyre Festival case against the organizers to uncover information regarding Fyre Media's financial affairs [i.e. where did all the money go?].

In the United States, the body tasked with policing sponsored content on social media, the Federal Trade Commission (FTC), has tried to stem the tide at the source.

> The FTC has pursued a claim against Warner Bros. for hiring influencers to promote one of its games without disclosing that they had been paid ... Of course, influencers should not be held as responsible for the actual perpetrators of the fraud, such as the organizers of the Fyre Festival. But, they should be held moderately responsible for their role in assisting and disseminating fraud.

What Fyre Festival exposed, outside of its inept promoters, is how the lack of regulation in the industry could ultimately cost influencers and consumers dearly. Maybe you're wondering why the influencers should be the ones asking any further questions of the brands they work with. The influencers were involved only in the promotion of it; they're not shareholders of the event, after all. They did their job, got paid and went on with their lives.

Not so. Whether you have to avoid a lawsuit or just plain old brand damage, being an influencer on social media is very different to being a model in a traditional advertising campaign. Honour, integrity and trust are essential qualities for being an influencer. Real people cut through the noise, mostly thanks to trust. You always run the risk of an unscrupulous influencer campaign coming back to bite you. Your integrity might survive it, but it also might not. Do you want to risk finding out the hard way?

Luckily, there is a simple way around this: Would you buy shares in this company with your own money? If so, work with them as an influencer on a campaign. Would you meddle with the metrics of a company you own shares in, if it meant you'd only be doing yourself in? No. So don't do it to your clients.

20 | Become an influencer

Instead of thinking of yourself as an "influencer", think of yourself as a shareholder.

Elma Smit ✔ @Elmakapelma · 2s

- Influencers have always existed; these days you just have a global platform.
- Pay your followers your most precious commodity: your attention.
- The key to engagement is knowing that you need to make the first move.
- Because people follow people, you can do stuff that brands and the media can't.
- I wrote this book because ideas that are shared go up in value.
- The influencer industry is here to stay.
- Influencers should think of themselves as shareholders.

2
WHERE DO YOU START?

Being "popular" is not the same as being an "influencer"
Joe Scott agrees:

> Anyone can be an influencer. Popular spaces like beauty, fitness and lifestyle are competitive and a bit saturated, but it's not impossible. Truthfully, one's influence is more about the quality of their content and consistency of output. A good example of this would be The Elegant Oxford. With over 100k subscribers [across platforms], this influencer built a following based on his dress-shoe restorations and shoe-shines. He was even invited to the Allen Edmonds factory with a select few influencers to witness how their shoes are made from end-to-end. That's about as niche as it gets.

"Begin with the end in mind." This is one of my favourite habits outlined by Dr Stephen R. Covey in his iconic self-help book, *The 7 Habits of Highly Effective People*.

This is a timeless bit of advice, particularly when you find yourself at the start of a new project. Covey elaborates on this idea by pointing out that "the physical creation follows the mental, just as a building follows a blueprint".

What is your blueprint? Mine is that an influencer is someone who creates content – content their audience enjoys so much that they interact with it. The engagement you gain from using your social media soapbox well can then be leveraged for money by partnering with brands.

Sometimes this relationship starts off as a barter: a brand gives you something that is naturally useful to you; you reciprocate by delivering content worth a similar amount in cash; you tag them in the content, allowing them to repost and engage with you. Progressing from this stage to actually generating cash from this content-producer adventure might feel like the point where you go pro. After all, in sport we consider athletes to be professionals when they start making money from their sporting pursuit.

However, in the influencer industry, true professional status arrives when you build repeat business – when you deliver such consistent value that the same agencies, brands and people you worked with before start coming back for more. That's when you've created a sustainable business.

Many influencers still squirm when you call them influencers, even the very successful ones. Others love it. My theory is that it depends on what you had in mind at the beginning of your journey on social media. Did you start off with "influencer" on your vision board? Was it the heading of your blueprint? Or is influence simply a by-product of a pursuit that stretches beyond your work on social media? Do you – deep down – prefer to consider yourself an entrepreneur or a storyteller? The latter is partly true for me. I am not uncomfortable with the title "influencer", but I do think that I exercise the same skill and obsession on my social media platforms that I continue honing and shaping in radio, TV, digital content and in writing. It's something I have always been doing in one way or another.

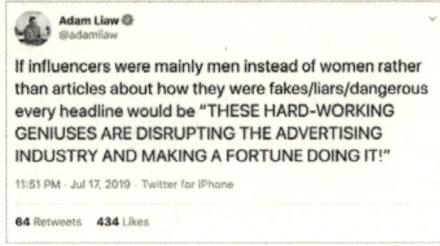

Adam Liaw is a Malaysian-Australian cook, television presenter and author. He was the winner of the second series of *MasterChef Australia* but tweets about parenting, race and the influencer industry nearly as much as he does about food.

When I was 11 years old, my class at school had to do oral presentations on the weather – I think it may have been for English. Pre-teen Elma then drew a poster of a very basic weather map and wrote a short weather-reporter script, closely modelled on what I had seen weather reporters do on television. My teacher was so delighted with the initiative I had shown that she took me around to other classrooms and had me perform my pretend weather report for kids and teachers in other grades.

I don't think she did this because it was a particularly useful weather report, since I had made it all up. But what she clearly picked up was the fact that I wasn't just watching the news and the weather reports every evening after dinner – I was actively studying how they were being delivered: the kind of inflection that was standard practice, the intonation, the correct posture and the arm movements. I mimicked what I had seen as closely as my little pre-teen brain could manage. Of course, it does help that I have no recollection of ever suffering stage fright in my entire life.

When reading, I have always studied the writing technique of the author, in the same way that I studied TV and listened to the radio. As well as loving stories and becoming fully absorbed in them, a part of my brain is always studying *how* people tell their stories. I don't consider it work; it's just the way I look at the world.

The point is that someone with an inherent gift for comedy might have used the same assignment to poke fun at the genre of weather reporting and the stereotypes in delivery. I think that a different approach would not have been wrong, but I instinctively knew that *my* take on "the weather" was to explore *how* we tell each other the weather story daily.

I don't think being an influencer is particularly special; it is just another strand of my business. I am using a skill I have honed by spending time on it; it is a skill that requires some innate talent but, as with everything, it is at least 80% perspiration and only about 20% inspiration. Beyond sport or music, TV or radio, I ultimately consider myself to be a storyteller and I don't do this for free. It's my business. I'm entrepreneurial in how I go about it.

Most photographers start taking photos as a hobby. Some manage to turn it into a business venture while others spend their free time doing it for fun. I tend to think of all of us who have social media accounts as hobbyists. The ones who manage to leverage this into a paying business with return clients are the professionals – the influencers.

I have no qualms about admitting that a lot of what I do, when I tell stories, is a commercial pursuit. I'm helping someone, somewhere, make money and I also get paid for it. You need to be mature about this and be careful not to underestimate your audience. They know that most of the content they enjoy is making someone, somewhere, some money or at least some equity. Earning some financial benefit from what you deliver to them is fair and justifiable. There is no need to be coy or embarrassed about it. It is also not particularly impressive because this is how commercial media has always worked. Influencers are not reinventing the wheel; they are just using it to explore new territories.

When I'm on radio in the mornings, we sell airtime (not only adverts, but also competitions and even entire events) to our clients, our advertisers – brands, as we call them in the influencer space. When the microphone goes on, it is our job as on-air staff to create value for those brands, because that is what our station requires to pay our salaries.

When radio listeners hear adverts and other commercial content that is well made, they often don't mind being sold something. It is only when the content does not create value for the listener (and in turn, the advertiser) that they tune out. The same goes for television, digital media and, of course, social media.

Having a logo on the shirt of your favourite athlete is not going to make you stop supporting them, is it? So why should sponsorships tank social media? If it is done well, is fully disclosed and creates value, it's a win-win relationship for all involved.

Choose to take up that space that Zozibini Tunzi, South Africa's Miss Universe 2019, spoke about. If she hadn't believed that a black woman with natural hair was inherently beautiful enough to win a global beauty title, no other opinion would have mattered. Yes, that belief alone didn't win her the title – it took many other things as well. But if you don't start with the belief that you have what it takes to create value for a group of followers out there, then no amount of effort will matter. Claim who you are – really own it. Own those things you innately do. Scale it up – that person you already are. Project that onto the screens of more people. Keep making the content. Don't wait for someone to come and pluck you from obscurity.

Stay alert! Stay alive!

Dr Covey also wisely points out that "if you don't make a conscious effort to visualize who you are and what you want in life, then you empower other people and circumstances to shape you and your life by default". Dig below the surface-level motivation – beyond wanting loads of followers, which is obviously what all influencers are looking for to prove their worth. Ensure that you can set yourself apart; take some time to figure out what you naturally do. Who are you when no one cares or is looking?

What are you always doing, even when you're on summer holiday with your family; when you're wasting time between work or studies? Bounce your ideas around with people who know you well and with whom you can't pretend to be anything you're not, because they'll tell you or call you out. Boil your essence down to as simple a practice as you can and remember that some fields of interest are fleeting.

Back in 2010, when I was busy planning my wedding, Pinterest hadn't taken off yet. The Internet tells me that it was created that year, but we certainly hadn't yet noticed it in South Africa. Either way, a wedding needed to be planned and, luckily, I found a variety of amazing wedding blogs, particularly American ones. I built Pinterest-like folders full of bits and pieces I loved, which I then used as references or briefs for flowers, hair, make-up and even the search for The Dress.

A lot of work also went into sourcing venue and entertainment options, and comparing photographers and the various packages they all offered. I was writing colour-coded running orders (like the ones we use on TV productions) for the weekend and the big day, to ensure everyone knew where they had to be and what had to happen at any given moment. Once I looked at all the work I had put in, I realised that I might as well start a wedding blog of my own. I had been studying the wedding industry so obsessively for my own purposes, that I had built up a treasure trove of useful information that I could share with the few followers I had found on Twitter, my Facebook audience and even the few souls who listened to me on 5FM. The American wedding bloggers I was following made it seem like such a cool field to specialise in and my TV work meant that I already had a bit of a following among people in their early to mid-20s – people who were also getting engaged and planning weddings. I decided that I'd review this urge to create a blog as soon as we got back from our honeymoon, to see if it was something I'd still enjoy once my own wedding was no longer on the agenda.

As it turned out, I never created that wedding blog, because once my own wedding was over, I never had the urge to open those wedding folders again. Instead of creating beautiful and practical tips and resources for brides – a noble enough pursuit – I realised that I always tend to gravitate towards a challenge and the chance to do something other than what is expected of me.

I needed the thrill of conquering a forbidden domain. It has always been this way for me. In primary school I spent my break times playing rugby and cricket with the boys. Later, I shaved my hair in the same year that I became a beauty pageant finalist. When I started working in radio, I was told again and again that an Afrikaans girl like me, with my accent, would never work on air at 5FM – but I proved them wrong.

I realised that I was relieved to be done with the business of being a bride and happy to move on to telling other kinds of stories. In fact, it was only a few months later that I leapt into the sports broadcasting industry and, by the end of that same year, I found myself in New Zealand covering the 2011 Rugby World Cup. I was breaking the rules and challenging convention again.

Grab the chalk and draw your outline

Something that might serve you in this process of defining who you essentially are is the awareness that no one expects you to come up with it all on your own. If you are stuck and none of the above has led you to an aha! moment of self-discovery yet, relax. A lot of people who have been on this influencer roundabout for years are still figuring it out. They're often the ones who are battling to grow or battling to create real engagement. An alternative and very useful approach is to start with defining what you are definitely not.

In crime movies they usually draw a chalk outline of a body to mark the exact position in which it was found, before the corpse is moved and the forensic processing of the crime scene can start. Now imagine your influencer identity – your brand – as a chalk outline. You might not know exactly what happens inside the lines just yet, but you can start by filling in the areas around it.

I had a really interesting chat with the YouTube vlogger and influencer Katinka Oosthuizen, also known as Katinka die Kat, about this very topic. She started building her audience when she was still a teenager, attending high school in the beachside town of Mossel Bay. Besides building an enviable audience on YouTube and Instagram before she left school, at the age of 19 she also became the youngest ever contestant on *Survivor South Africa*. These days she also works as a presenter, video producer, editor and entrepreneur.

> You just need to be yourself [Katinka says]. The niche will emerge without you even often noticing it. I never sat down and decided this for myself; I just knew what I was not. In the beginning I tried my hand at a variety of things, but I quickly realised what I didn't want to do more of and that it isn't necessary. Loads of things just didn't work on my channel, because it wasn't me. And then you often just don't have the inspiration required to really pull it off.
>
> Revlon once sent me [a pack of] 20 lipsticks and I just sat staring at it. I didn't know what to do with it because it didn't inspire me. And that's fine; they obviously found people that did feel inspired by it. Brands might think you're the same as a bunch of other people, but you need to know that you're not. Everyone is different, you are different. I think you can 100% choose who you want to be on social media, but ask yourself this: How long can you remain in a fake friendship? How long can you pretend to like something? I could probably choose to become a beauty influencer, but it will take so much energy to get into that mindset that I just won't ever get anything meaningful done. Never. That's why it just won't happen.

In my case, I knew very early on in my career – before Instagram even existed – that I didn't want to build my personal brand on pictures of myself in bikinis. I learnt this through dabbling in a bit of modelling while I earned my degree.

In the modelling industry, you build what they call a portfolio and a Z-card. Basically, these are photo albums featuring examples of your work and they are regularly updated so that you have something to show prospective clients. You want to give them an idea of how well you pull off a certain look or trend when you attend a casting. If you want to land toothpaste adverts, for example, you ensure that you have loads of photos showcasing your fantastic smile early on in your portfolio. If you're really into fitness and have very defined muscles, this would feature heavily in your portfolio.

Models, like influencers, can choose to actively position themselves in the market. Alternatively, you can leave it up to the industry to choose where they think you fit in, and then you will have to accept what you get. But I've never been a "take-what-you-get" girl.

For me, modelling was a shortcut to help me pay my university fees, but I quickly realised that I felt uncomfortable doing work that I would not still want to do in a decade or two. I wanted to build a business for myself that could be sustainable, and modelling was never the goal – it was a means to an end. I wanted to be able to look back at the work I had done when I was 20 years old and not cringe too much.

Then, when I graduated to working as a music TV presenter and radio DJ at 5FM in my early 20s, magazines like *Sports Illustrated* and *FHM* (*For Him Monthly*) featured the most prominent young actresses, models, musicians and TV presenters as cover girls. In a world before Instagram, I cannot overstate how important it used to be to feature in a magazine. Of course, these publications mostly featured cover girls clad in bikinis or lingerie. It was part of the deal. It was a case of "we give you a great big magazine cover to be on, and you show us what you've got".

While I didn't take any issue with my peers who successfully leveraged this platform to launch themselves into greater and more lucrative opportunities (and no, you don't get paid for appearing on a magazine cover), it simply wasn't something I was interested in doing. I was asked by both the music and the sports channels for whom I worked to consider doing features like this because they would yield good exposure for them. But I always replied that I wanted people to hear what I was saying and be less concerned with how I look. I've always been a total nerd in this way and I'm sure some might say that it was short-sighted. Either way, it's my body and the decisions I took then serve me well today. I wouldn't change a thing.

For Bouwer Bosch, his unique position has always been a focus on reconciliation through his work.

> My true passion is reconciliation ... I try to be the Afrikaner in the entertainment industry who also cares about things that don't only concern entertainment ... I need to be able to leave here and do business with everyone – not only Afrikaners. I cannot hide out in this Voortrekker laager. I was walking around Melville in one of my Steve Biko "Dis hoe dit is met Steve" T-shirts the other day. [*Dis Hoe Dit Is Met Steve* was a talk show hosted by Steve Hofmeyr, which ran for a decade from 2001 on the Afrikaans-language, pay-TV channel, kykNET.] Two black guys stopped me and started chatting to me about the message, the meaning of the Afrikaans words, the reference to Steve Biko, and it was great. I'm sure some Afrikaans people don't appreciate what I'm doing, I'll probably take a hit for it, but when I die one day this is the kind of work I want to be remembered for. For the fact that not many people had these difficult and important conversations.

The thing with being an influencer is that the Internet never forgets. Yes, people probably won't scroll back to what you posted five years ago – no one cares that much, and if they do, they're weirdos. (Block the weirdos!) However, your audience will notice if you try to sell them a version of yourself that doesn't echo your true values or that switches according to what is trendy. People will call you out on it or, even worse, they'll leave. You don't need to be everything to everybody. In fact, it's better not to be

– that's just bland. Make a list, draw that outline and list the stuff outside it. Check yourself against this and evaluate why you feel this way. The space that is left over might crystallise into a bit more brand awareness.

But what if I have chosen the wrong thing – or I change?

Take heart in the knowledge that nothing is set in stone. Pay real attention when selecting your niche, your topic, in determining who you want to be and who you want to reach. But take the same care in consistently re-evaluating that decision.

You are always going to grow and develop and so will your audience – this is actually the only thing we know for sure. Change is the only thing you can really bank on. Some of your tribe will migrate with you, others will not. If you're not completely immersed or inspired any longer, if you realise that you have been climbing that ladder with all you have, but it's actually leaning against the wrong wall, then stop. Be honest – with yourself and then with your audience.

If you're a wedding blogger who gets a divorce or a vegan influencer who goes back to eating meat (both of these have actually happened), as difficult as it might be, just be honest.

Prepare to watch the follower numbers tumble, but know that you might also be surprised by how many people also enjoy following the life not lived. Just because I don't have children of my own doesn't mean that I avoid all mommy bloggers. There are plenty of influencers in my feed who are into stuff that I don't really relate to: vegans, gamers, financial specialists, political reporters ...

Every now and again someone will comment on a sport-related post I create, to point out that they have been following me since I hosted a request show on campus radio, or that they used to watch me hosting music shows and they love how far I've come since then.

Have the courage to regularly (perhaps annually?) diarise and then prepare your own State of the Nation address: take stock, commit to new goals, talk about this to the people who follow you, and gather and even share their feedback. We tend to think that people only want to see content creators who have it all figured out, but what if your followers find even more value in seeing you adapt, seeing you grow?

Being real and transparent about your journey might just help you reach a level of trust with your followers that keeps them there, even if the content moves away from the topic that initially attracted them to you.

Elma Smit ✓ @Elmakapelma · 2s
- You don't need to be popular to be an influencer, but being an entrepreneur helps.
- Find your thing. Look deep inside. If that's difficult, start with what you're not.
- If you fear you've changed or might change, share that journey with your followers.

3

FIND YOUR TRIBE

The ghost in the machine

When engagement is low or when accounts don't grow the way people think they should, they often tend to lump one bogeyman with all the blame; the dark force that supposedly holds your account back from social media stardom is the algorithm.

Everyone who has battled to grow their account, from small bands to massive brands, up-and-coming influencers to world-famous athletes, has turned their attention to the algorithm and many have thrown their hands up in despair. But I have good news for you. The algorithm is not all that mysterious; it's not devious and it certainly doesn't want to prevent you from becoming a successful influencer.

What makes the algorithm tricky is that it's not a clearly codified set of rules. It is not like a set of commandments or laws. It is constantly shifting, improving and adapting, and it varies from platform to platform. This is also why we're constantly feeling our way through it, trying to understand it by playing with it. It's like a great big puzzle and often it can feel as though you are building it in the dark.

The other big issue to consider is that if you can't gain enough engagement organically, the chances are higher that you'll boost, promote or pay for posts to pop up in more feeds more regularly. You will advertise and this is part of how social networks make money. I think that while this is definitely true for brands, it is less so for influencers. When you're a digital creator, your content can certainly outperform a paid model, because you're not only posting and sharing commercially driven content: many of the stories you tell as an influencer are also perfectly human and relatable, which means you can build a much more impressive engagement rate than most brands are able to do. As explained earlier, regardless of a marketer's best efforts, people will always follow people.

You need to figure out ways of making sure you make the most of this advantage by developing content that builds a solid track record with your target follower. Ideally, you want your follower to "tell" (by way of their browsing habits) the algorithm to fast-forward the posts you send into the great big pool of content that is your social platform of choice straight to the top of their feed.

But let me start at the beginning so that we're on the same page about why algorithms exist.

Initially, as a social media user you saw every post from every account you followed. Posts were presented to you in chronological order. Imagine watching a bunch of social media posts standing in line like people, in a neat little queue. No post gets to jump the queue – first come, first browsed.

This makes a lot of sense, right? Yes, but then social media went pop! According to Instagram, we started missing out on as much as 70% of the content produced by the accounts we followed. We had so much happening on our feeds that we were stuck, looking at our distant cousin Helen's third child, drooling in high definition – while your crush had just posted a photo of himself at the beach … Of course, as luck would have it, this swimsuit post was uploaded immediately after you logged off. Sadly, your tolerance for baby spit ran out an instant too soon. Then, by the time you logged on again, just before bed, the swimsuit post had disappeared in the noisy, crowded mess that had become your home feed.

In came the algorithm, the solution to this chronological queue in which posts had to wait. The algorithm was created to ensure that you would see those swimsuit photos pop up the very next time you logged on, regardless of whether this was that night or two days later. This was not because the algorithm could read your mind, but because you had liked every single post your crush had put up for the past few weeks. You had spent ages thinking of witty comments to leave every time someone else tagged him in something and duly followed through. He liked your comment immediately. And, of course, you also spent an inordinate amount of time scrolling back on his timeline, studying his personality through the distorted prism that is social media. We've all been there – this is nothing to be embarrassed about.

On Twitter you used to be able to reset your feed, toggling back to that age before the big algorithm shift, but I don't see the function on my account anymore. On Facebook it is still there: you can shift your News Feed preference to "Most Recent" if you don't want the algorithm to automatically select the "Top Stories" for you, based on your browsing habits.

If you select "Most Recent" in your Facebook News Feed options, you'll basically switch back to the algorithm-free feed we first got to know in the mid-2000s.

The algorithm is designed to seamlessly improve your

browsing experience and it is constantly also learning from users, which is one of the reasons why it is not entirely predictable. The thing is that we're not predictable: our habits shift and change. In fact, the tech magnate Elon Musk says that it's a slippery slope from here to a full-blown, artificial intelligence, robot-run future. He told this to Joe Rogan on Rogan's immensely popular podcast series back in September 2018. Episode #1169 went viral for another reason – they smoked weed together – but the bit about search engines and algorithms, getting to know and predict our most intimate habits and preferences, was the most fascinating takeaway for me.

Simply put, the algorithm is deciding what features and what doesn't. And how does the algorithm decide on whether something makes the cut or doesn't? It takes its cue from you and from the network itself. You can't control the network, but you are teaching the algorithm what to show you without even realising that you are doing this.

The algorithm makes selections on your behalf, based on who you engage with and which keywords feature in the content that you read, view, share, like and comment on. Every time you fall down that rabbit hole of aimless browsing, you're leaving another series of breadcrumbs in a trail that you're constantly building for the ghost in the machine to follow, effectively telling the algorithm: this is what I like; I don't want to miss any of this or that kind of content; please give me more ...

Do you ever see the same person's Instagram Stories pop up first at the top of your Instagram home feed, over and over again? Perhaps your bestie, your significant other, your favourite celebrity or that influencer you discovered the other day. In fact, run your own experiment: make a point of finding and watching all the stories from any one account that you follow on Instagram. Search for them if the account doesn't come up and make sure you watch their stories every single day. Like every single one of their posts and drop a comment as well. Keep doing this for a few days and, before long, you'll see them popping up earlier and earlier in the carousel of Instagram Stories at the top of your home screen every day.

But where does that leave other platforms like TikTok? Wian "Magic" van den Berg is a 25-year-old magician and influencer from Frankfort in the Free State, who is one of the top influencers on the video-sharing platform. In fact, he is in the top 1% of the most followed creators, having built a following over roughly two years.

Wian explains the TikTok algorithm really creatively:

> When you upload a video, TikTok sends it to a sample of users. Let's say 100, but no one knows ... Then, if 10 of those people like the video, it'll just perform okay for you. But if 90 of those people like it, it'll be seen by another 1 000 and if 900 of them like it, it'll be seen by a million people. When I hit a million followers, my brother still remarked that he wonders

if it'll feel as if my growth slows down, because then you only see it tick over with every 100 000 followers, not in tens of thousands or even in thousands any more. And yet, it felt like it picked up speed after a million. I think that's simply because more people have a chance of seeing your video. It takes a few failures to realise what a great post requires; you just need to keep going and keep looking for a hit.

Cross-promotion is one simple way of ensuring you diversify the variety of platforms your audience follows you on. Share your Instagram feed posts on your stories and vice versa. Also, tease your TikTok/Twitter/Facebook followers about your Instagram content and vice versa.

In early 2020 Instagram released some information on what the Instagram algorithm looks at and this is useful across platforms, because it outlines some pretty universal truths about how platforms compile the feed you're presented with:

Interest: How much attention a post generates from those who see it. This is measured by how many likes, comments, shares and views your content attracts.

Timeliness: How quickly the post generates this interest. The quicker you start gaining reaction immediately after you've posted, the greater the chances that it will pop up in more feeds.

Relationship: Your friends and family tend to tag you in their posts and comment on yours. They direct message (DM) you and they search for you in the explore tab. If followers do this with an influencer's account, the account will start popping up in their feed as often as a friend's would. You need to build such close behavioural links with followers that the algorithm considers you friends. This means the reactions need to flow both ways, so you need to like and reply to comments.

Frequency: People who open the app often are less affected by algorithm ranking and see their feed in a more chronological fashion because they consume more content. Instagram wants to ensure that their regular users don't see the same post twice; the same with TikTok and Twitter. If your ideal follower browses any of these for only a few minutes every day, they will see a highlights-reel feed curated for them by the algorithm.

Following: If you follow more people, the algorithm will play a stronger role in selecting whose posts you see and which ones slip past you entirely. People who follow fewer accounts will see more of what those accounts post.

The following is more detailed Instagram-specific feedback:
- The platform also clarified that the algorithm does not prioritise videos over images universally, but if your follower responds to videos more than they do to images, they'll be presented with more videos than

photos. The practical impact of viewing video – the fact that you tend to pause on video content for longer than you do on an image – might also skew your feed to favour video.

- IGTV tiles are often presented four times larger than image tiles on the explore tab, so this means your chances to grow via the explore tab are increased if you present a really good IGTV tile. (IGTV is the Instagram long-form video format.) Instagram acknowledged that the machine-learning built into the algorithm is aimed at weeding out engagement pods and bots, in favour of truly authentic engagement. The widely shared myth that a comment doesn't get recognised as such by the algorithm unless it's longer than three words was also debunked. Verified or business accounts are not favoured by the algorithm – users see all the accounts in which they show interest and interact, equally.

Instagram clarified some points about its algorithm after users called for a chronological order feature.

- A simple way of boosting engagement is by using stickers that encourage engagement with your stories, like polls, questions and emoji sliders.

It is really important to keep an eye on any movement on this front. Obviously, loads of blogs, thought leaders and even news sites carry updates on algorithm trends. Another safe bet is to keep an eye on the platforms themselves.

Senior Facebook, Instagram and Twitter staff members shared some best-practice guidelines for creating digital content that performs well at a workshop I attended in May 2019. This was at the start of my two-month stint working for the International Cricket Council (ICC) as a digital reporter on the 2019 Cricket World Cup.

One of the key messages to come out of that session – and subsequent visits to Facebook's headquarters in London – was that video is a crucial component for driving engagement on both Facebook and Instagram. Regularly creating live videos longer than five minutes, preferably around the ten-minute mark – both for Facebook and Instagram – was a key part of the suggested best-practice strategies we used. Another thing I learnt from the experience was not to think of these live videos as tightly rehearsed, content-filled pieces like traditional TV (in performance or technical execution).

The aim is not to replace live TV, with professional lighting and high-end cameras. The point is to just be in the moment, to create a feeling of community with the viewers who join in, to break down as much of what creates distance between you and your followers as possible, and to create an authentic, immediate and interactive experience.

Nine weeks later, when the final of the 2019 Cricket World Cup played out to a thrilling super-over climax between the host nation England and New Zealand, we made our way from the media centre at Lord's Cricket Ground down to the side of the pitch and went live on the ICC's accounts. When I say we, I mean the digital reporters and the producers who worked with us.

We were not looking to replace or substitute what people were seeing on TV. We were not even showing the pitch – the camera was facing the stand, with us in the foreground. In fact, from where I was standing, I couldn't even see the pitch properly because of the advertising boards and the fact that the fans behind us kept asking us to crouch down so they could see!

We were waiting there because we were on standby to run onto the pitch and interview the winners as soon as it all wrapped up, but we hosted the live video feed in the final few minutes of the match to create a second-screen experience for fans who were already watching it on television. The point was to help our highly engaged digital fans feel closer to the action, as if they were there with us. We didn't provide them with expert commentary either, because an exceptionally talented bunch of commentators were already doing so on the TV broadcast.

What we were doing was simply opening up the experience of being pitch-side for five to ten minutes, so that more fans could hear the noise of the crowd and could identify with other fans (me, the people around me in the stands, my colleagues) because what unified us in that moment was the sheer exhilaration that only a great sporting event can deliver. We felt like we were all witnessing history and we loved being able to do it together.

Facebook, for example, has a wealth of information tailor-made for creators, available at facebook.com/creators. There you can find step-by-step instructions on how to link seamlessly and cross-post on your Instagram and Facebook accounts, for example. This way you do not need to create the same post twice – you can merely amend and tailor it slightly for the two different audiences and formats. Facebook provides step-by-step instructions on how to convert your personal profile into a fan page, with detailed information on monitoring how people view your content, so that you can learn more about what works and what doesn't. Mark Zuckerberg's own Facebook profile (which is public, by the way) is another great place to see which features the company would love to see you accessing and utilising.

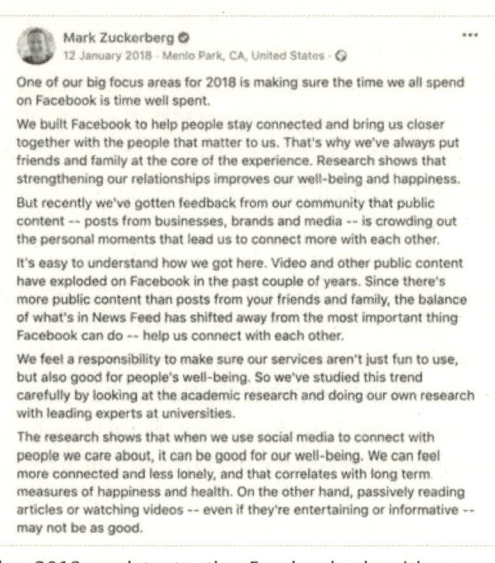

The 2018 update to the Facebook algorithm was designed to focus content on an individual's friends and family members, rather than prioritising spam from businesses.

At help.instagram.com you will find very useful and up-to-date outlines on how and why you should make the most of IGTV and convert your account status to content creator. It also outlines the interesting and important added features available to creator accounts: a two-tiered direct message inbox; the ability to monitor, as well as share, stories that mention you; and, of course, the all-important insights, also known as metrics or the numbers. This is where you can monitor the reach and engagement on your account.

Instagram's own Instagram account is always a reliable source of information on how to structure posts for their platform, how frequently to roll out new content and how to balance your content strategy (how much of it should be Instagram Stories over normal feed posts, how often to make carousel posts featuring multiple photos, and how to weigh up the benefits of making videos). The same applies to Twitter, TikTok and YouTube. They all roll out regular posts with useful instructions and advice.

Keep an eye on what your favourite social media platforms do on their own profiles. Useful features, important tools and best-practice advice gets updated regularly. Spend some time making the most of the resources that are freely available and also check back in for updates from time to time.

Pumpkins are a niche too

As you can see by our interest in the topic, influencer marketing only started coming into its own in 2016:

In the few short years since, a crucial shift has already taken place: industry experts are not only looking to partner with what we now call macro-influencers (people with a few hundred thousand followers or more). What we clearly saw in 2018 and 2019 was a push towards prioritising collaborations with micro-influencers (with roughly 10 000 to 100 000 followers) and even nano-influencers (with fewer than 10 000 followers).

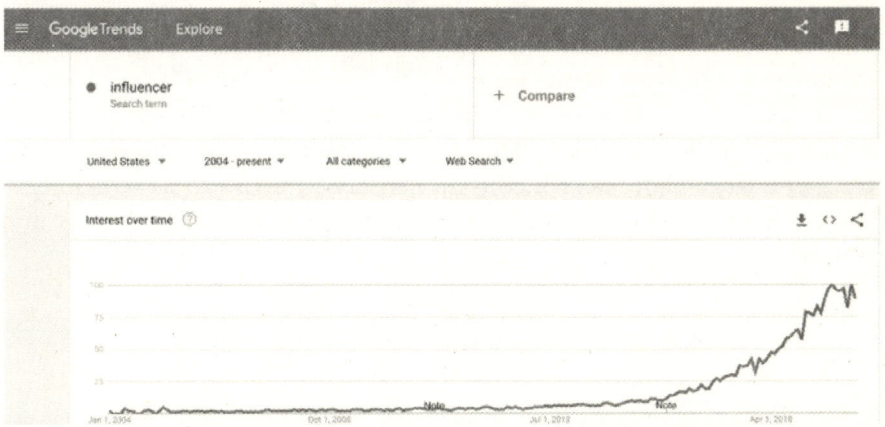

You can always do your own search on how often things are searched for. Google Trends is a phenomenal way to gauge interest in any niche area or topic.

There is a bit of disagreement about whether the latter is relevant in the South African market, but I'd say that in the nano-influencer space, you would often be looking at barter exchanges, small cash deals (if any) and invites to events (not paid appearances). In other words, you would ideally want to approach this as a phase. It is important to build relationships in this phase and to really make the most of the experiences afforded to you when you're in the nano-market, but if your aim is to generate revenue, then this is a phase you want to be able to scale out of – to grow through.

Micro-influencers offer an appealing opportunity to brands and if you fall into this category, it is important to be awake to the fact that the more niche your interest is, the greater the engagement rate tends to be. On what do I base this? The average Instagram follower of someone like the pumpkin-obsessed food influencer Maggie Michalczyk probably doesn't have many people in their social circle (in real life) who are also obsessed with eating pumpkin.

So, Maggie's followers find a sense of community with the other pumpkin lovers out there who are also commenting and interacting with this niche feed. This is why brands often opt to work with influencers on the scale of pumpkin-loving Maggie, even over a household name like Jamie Oliver with his 7.7 million followers. The Maggies of this world usually yield a low-cost-per-engagement rate, which is immensely attractive to some brands.

This is how you can calculate cost per engagement (CPE) quickly and simply:

$$\text{CPE} = \frac{\text{Total spend on sponsored post}}{\text{likes + comments + link click-throughs + shares}}$$

$$= \frac{\text{R2 000}}{176 + 22 + 2 + 0}$$

$$= \text{R10}$$

Compare this to a hypothetical macro-influencer: let's call them Person X. They boast 100 000 followers and this is why a deal could easily cost R15 000 per post (keep reading for more on how this fee is calculated).

Person X would then need to deliver 1 500 engagements to ensure the same CPE rate as someone with Maggie's following and engagement.

$$\text{CPE} = \frac{\text{R15 000 total spend}}{\text{1 500 engagements}}$$

$$= \text{R10}$$

For a brand manager, the option of spreading the same R15 000 budget between three micro-influencers (people like Maggie) and having them each create two or more posts could deliver more bang for the same bucks in CPE terms. If not more bang, at least they have lowered their risk by spreading their bets in the hopes that at least two out of the three influencers will deliver highly engaging content.

When you are trying to figure out exactly how best to position yourself, remember that bigger is not always better. Put yourself in the shoes of the marketer, solve their problem better and you are in business.

If you create content that your followers consistently find useful, interesting and entertaining, this will boost your chances of the algorithm rewarding your efforts by showing your content to more followers. Your engagement rate will increase and the value you create for eventual brand partners will start to look after itself.

Hi, my name is ...

In radio, it used to be the thing to have a very glamorous showbiz name. If your own was boring, you'd simply adapt or change it, or pick a new one.

I used to love listening to a radio DJ called Nicole Fox when I was in high school. She used to be on radio in the evenings while I was completing school projects or reading magazines, doodling in the margins of my schoolbooks or texting my boyfriend. She was so effortlessly cool that it actually intimidated the living daylights out of this aspiring radio presenter. I didn't inherit a fun, catchy surname, so I worried about never quite fitting the radio DJ mould. Imagine my indignation when I later found out that her real surname was Raubenheimer! If even her name wasn't real, I thought, what else about this person, whom I thought of as my ultimate study companion, was also contrived?

She wasn't alone, of course. Elton John was born Reginald Dwight. Lady Gaga is an act Stefani Germanotta created. However, I think the idea that a name will make or break your career, before it has even started, is fading along with the hierarchy that used to decide who had earned the right to entertain, inform and inspire (and who had not).

A crucial shift has taken place in popular culture over the last decade or two and I think it has much to do with the fact that the studio, the record label, the publisher, the radio station and the TV network have seen their powers eroded. There used to be quite a bit of distance between the entertainer or tastemaker and the consumer, which was created, controlled and sometimes abused by the owners of media platforms.

There have always been loads of talented people, natural content creators with amazing and powerful skills to share – ones we would have loved to listen to, to read, to watch and to learn from. But until social media took off, you didn't need only talent and skill to make it as a content creator; you also needed to be chosen. You had to land a record or book deal, an acting role, a job as a radio DJ or journalist, a residency as a comedian at a comedy club through a manager who would promote you and leverage their access to your chosen industry for a cut of your pay. You had to peddle your content from a soapbox that someone else owned. For about a century, key executives employed by large entertainment platforms mostly made the careers of content creators by choosing them – or not.

Cracks started to show around the turn of the century and, before long, the move away from this hierarchy gained such fierce momentum that it literally felt as though the earth was moving under our feet. Reality television shows such as *Idols*, *Big Brother* and *Survivor* elevated the Average Joe to Household Name nearly overnight. You still had to be *chosen*, but in this new century, the executive handed over the power to choose to the viewer, a tribe or a celebrity judge – in theory, anyway.

It was a very short journey from having Simon Cowell exercise that choice, to full on user-driven choice as we know it on social media now. Today, you are choosing who gets elevated to household-name status every time you like a post, save it, share it, download it, record it or comment on it – every time you spend more time scrutinising an influencer's feed than you do your best friend's.

As a creator you need to choose yourself, choose your audience and ensure that your content is chosen by them in turn. More risk, yes, but also loads more rewards. You don't need to share nearly as much of your power with an executive and their overlords anymore. However, you do need to remain directly attuned to your consumer, your follower.

Because traditional media executives don't have the final say about who we read, listen to, watch, laugh at and follow, I think we are increasingly picking our content creators based on more substantive things than their names. We have seen musicians launch new music albums with seemingly all-access documentaries accompanying their actual work, actively profiling and showcasing the real person behind the scenes.

To illustrate this: Lady Gaga makes music through the pain in *Five Foot Two*; Taylor Swift makes music despite sexual harassment and politics in *Miss Americana*; and, in 2017, Katy Perry lived in a *Big Brother* house of her own making (complete with live-streamed psychology sessions) during her YouTube live-streamed weekend called *Witness World Wide*. She did this to launch her album and generate interest in the themes of her new songs.

Strategists in the entertainment industry realised that we don't only want Lady Gaga to deliver the fantasy of a spectacular live show; we also want to be able to relate to Stefani Germanotta. We want to know what she looks like without the Gaga get-up, whether she experiences hardships of her own and has family members just like us, because it's about the followers. This is why the showbiz name, in effect, is over: your followers don't want to be fooled – not all the time, anyway. You don't need to choose a bogus name – just elevate the one you were given.

Should I be authentic or aspirational?

When I discussed this topic in quite some detail with Ridhima Pathak, one of my colleagues at the 2019 Cricket World Cup, she shared an interesting insight that underpins her approach to her work on social media.

Ridhima studied engineering but now works as a TV/digital presenter, popular event host and influencer, predominantly in India. During the tournament, she did quite a bit of influencer work, sharing a number of sponsored posts. In the evenings we'd go for a jog and I'd cheerfully share videos on Instagram Stories of my sweaty, red face on my run through the streets of Birmingham, while Ridhima took great care to carefully curate only the most manicured and polished images of herself and her environment for her own feed and stories.

Her theory was that because of the massive wealth gap in India, her broadest base of followers would probably never be able to travel to the United Kingdom themselves – certainly not for a Cricket World Cup tournament, but also probably not even as tourists. She saw it as her responsibility to ensure that her feed remained a form of escapism, of fantasy and aspiration for her followers, of ambition, yearning and desire. The basic idea was that even if I cannot go there and see this for myself, Ridhima is opening a portal into this wonderful world of glamour, wealth and adventure – how the other half lives.

Her approach was to give her followers a look behind the curtain only when it would inspire and delight them. She didn't bother to include the hard slog that is involved when you're scheduled to cover back-to-back game days, the late-night travel on jam-packed trains or the early-morning hours spent doing preparation and research. She could have shown the blisters you typically earn from the 30 000 steps we walked each day covering a cricket match, but instead she chose to focus on the excited fans she met.

Obviously, there is no empirically proven wrong or right approach here, but I realised then that I am very aware of the fact that my average follower (from their comments on posts and replies) tends to travel – or, at the very least, considers travelling to somewhere like the United Kingdom as reasonably possible at some point in their life. Travel is not entirely out of their reach or unimaginable, and they often leave me recommendations related to the destination or, at least, to the exercise of exploring new horizons.

I think my follower would see straight through me if I tried to maintain some sort of aspirational standard. I always assume that my follower knows that I don't have it all figured out and that no one's life is quite as amazing as it may seem. Of course, this isn't a universal approach, but I think the point here is that whether you lean towards aspirational or authentic (at all costs), it is worth your while to go through the exercise of defining it for yourself. If your ethos is crystal clear, you can ensure that a consistent approach is maintained throughout – one that speaks to the integrity you want to build to ensure longevity.

Mike Sharman believes that "a few experiences have shown that we don't want to be duped into following people who are selling us a lifestyle. I think aspiration has matured more into an authentic space."

Katinka Oosthuizen says her advice to her 16-year-old self (the age at which she started vlogging) would be:

> Post more content! I was so scared to post. I wanted to do a lot of stuff but I was always worried about what kids would say at school. I only realised after school that I never would've fitted in anyway, no matter how hard I tried. I think I held back a lot and did what I could with the confidence I had then. I wish I had taken more risks and had less stage fright then. I went through such an insecure period after someone once commented that I had gained weight, when I actually hadn't. I obviously realise now why people at school never understood me, but I wish I had known then that there was no point in being worried about what people would say at school.

TikTok star Wian van den Berg is by far the most productive influencer I spoke to and he believes that this approach applies universally.

> I think the mistake everyone, regardless of their platform, makes is to try to be too perfect. It's impossible. No one can be 100% perfect all the time. I think that's the mistake everyone makes, thinking that they'd rather not post something because it won't be perfect enough. They don't want to take the risk. They don't want to make a video in their room because they think it needs to be shot at the beach or at the mall. They don't want to do something when they've just come home from work.
>
> I know that something needs to be good to go viral, but it's just as important for it to actually exist. When people ask what matters more between quality and quantity, I always answer that they are both important. You can post six videos in the next ten minutes, easily. Anyone can. But these videos obviously then risk being not worth much, to anyone. However, you also can't allow perfectionism to paralyse you, to hold you back. Everyone is busy; we all have hectic schedules. But if you really look at your day, you'll find you have time. It's like any business, it requires time.

He says that some of the easiest clips he's made have yielded the best results.

> Sometimes the silly pranks I do with my mom, when I don't have the time to do my typical videos, do much better than my magic videos. Think of it as documenting, rather than creating. Try to work it into your life in a way that is easy. When you're watching TV, watch TV and make a post about it. When you walk into work, walk into work and turn it into a bit of content.

Nadia Jaftha's journey as an influencer took off after she started out as a fashion blogger and then began sharing the pranks she played on her mom, Nawal, which went viral. She concedes that this is still what her audience comes back for, even though she has gone on very glamorous trips and has shared loads of really gorgeous bikini shots in between.

> I think my brand is more about relatability than aspirational content. I never want to feel like I'm too far out of reach. I want people to look at me and say, "She did it, so why can't I do it?" You can be both aspirational and relatable, but it's all about balance – that's what I try to do. I definitely think I speak to the girl who is insecure and the girl who is confident. I never want anybody to feel excluded from my content, so I try to balance it out. I'll post funny videos with my mom, videos with my friends, outfit pictures, lifestyle pictures and business pictures.

Maps Maponyane started his career doing modelling in a gap year in 2009, but has earned his reputation in the entertainment and even advertising world in the decade since then, thanks to his fine understanding of branding and his insight into what people want. Maps is the kind of person other people talk about. People who run brands love bringing him in as an influencer or host on their events because he always delivers. Other influencers will tell you that they approach him for advice and sound counsel. Advertising industry professionals look to him as a great authentic voice in the market, a tastemaker and a curator. He speaks with great grace about the responsibility he feels as an influencer:

> It's super important to be real about what your life is really like; to be normal and authentic. There's too much of us sharing that "living my best life" idea, because each of those posts slowly adds to the mental anguish someone might experience from looking at your supposedly superior "best life" – until that follower starts asking, "Am I just not living life?" or "Why am I even here? My life isn"t worth living ...' It literally is that slow gradual spiral that comes with each and every post ... I never want to be part of that problem. I find half of social media so boring that I want to figure out how to have fun with it. I never want to feel like I *have* to do anything. When I work with brands, I want to be able to speak with my own voice, but have it so seamless that it is real.

Someone who is unashamedly creating gorgeous and aspirational content – at least in the main feed of her Instagram profile – is former Miss South Africa Liesl Laurie. "I think it's a personal thing, that's who I am as a person. I'm a little bit of both, don't forget I'm still 'hood'." Liesl grew up in Eldorado Park but didn't let her start in life determine the scope of it.

> I've always been *that girl*. My gran will tell you that. I like to position myself as that girl who can be a bit of both (aspirational and relatable) because it's easy for me; it's who I've always been.
>
> I think if you're just starting out, you could totally look towards someone like Nadia Jaftha, who was very authentic at one stage and then

she became very Instaglam at one point and now she's back at the relatable fun, family content. Sharing her grandfather and her mom alongside shots of her bringing the great fashion looks and full make-up …

But don't try and be Nadia – if you're not funny it won't work. If you're great at make-up like Mbali Nkosi, for example, and you only post make-up looks, then that's what your followers will be there for. She doesn't need to be Nadia, because it's not her thing.

So, how do you achieve this, practically? I read an interesting study on the "strategies that … influencers employ in performing an authentic persona", which was published by researchers at the University of Rotterdam in February 2020. In *Selling Brands while Staying "Authentic": The Professionalization of Instagram Influencers*, the first generally employed tactic Delia Dumitrica and Loes van Driel outline is that Instagram influencers often address the audience in the caption, usually in the form of some sort of question to generate an authentic tone.

"Another strategy, which serves to develop a connection with the audience, is the sharing of snippets from the influencer's backstage, everyday life to create a persona that the audience can relate to." A homesick travel blogger is often more relatable or feels more accessible than an uninterrupted stream of envy-inducing destinations, for example.

And, finally, they mention Instagram Stories as a supplementary platform where many influencers share more behind-the-scenes context than their main feed typically includes. This is a way to balance what influencers in the study perceive to be essential ingredients for any influencer: both aspiration and authenticity. Not aspiration *or* authenticity, as Ridhima and I defined ourselves over dinner one night in Birmingham.

"By adding details from their everyday lives, influencers give the audience the impression that they know the person behind the feed."

I would go further and add that if you're sharing honest and compelling insights with your followers, the followers' feeling that they are getting to know the influencer in the process will actually be true; it won't be an impression. If it's performative, the influencer – sooner or later – will risk slipping up and being found out. Building on integrity is far safer, more sustainable and more fun.

In fact, the same happens when we have strategy sessions in the radio and television industry. We have real and honest conversations around everyone's on-air persona, what our roles are in relation to the team, and which parts of our personal lives we'll share on air. Everything is not necessarily fair game, mainly because it is not necessarily useful to the listener or viewer. Focus on content, stories and conversations that are relatable enough for your follower to connect with. In radio, we strategically develop and position our stories, so that our content will transcend the distance (both literally and figuratively) between us and the listener, and the same is true for an influencer.

Elma Smit ✓ @Elmakapelma · 2s
- You can't control the algorithm, but the good news is that it responds to how your followers consume content. Serve the followers and the algorithm will serve you.
- Study the algorithm, the platform and the resources they provide.
- Cost per engagement can be your *x*-factor, even if you have a small audience.
- Carefully consider the level of balance your platform requires – sometimes it might be more effective to consistently document than to create or even curate.

4

CONTENT, CONTENT, CONTENT

What is your USP?

There is one simple departure point if you are trying to figure out how to stand out in an increasingly competitive and crowded influencer market. Your content needs to consistently reinforce your "unique selling point", also known as a "unique selling proposition" or simply your "USP". This is not something influencers came up with or even something we can credit traditional media with; it's basically a concept as old as commerce itself and it is equally useful across all entrepreneurial pursuits.

The *Cambridge Dictionary* defines USP as "a feature of a product that makes it different from and better than other similar products". Of course, you might not view being an influencer as a product, but when you are running a social media account to generate an income, I think this could be considered a production process and the product is your content.

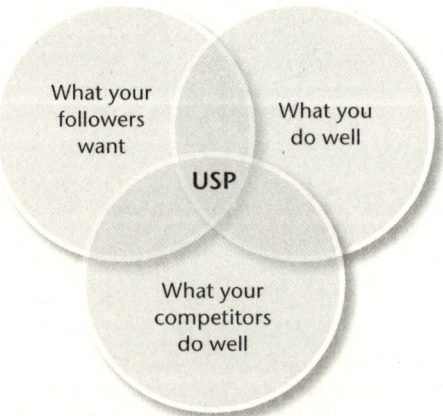

Your USP is the area of overlap.

Maybe it would help if I illustrate this USP idea with an example or two. Before Apple made market-leading cell phones, they broke open the music industry with their MP3 player, the iPod. iPods were not the cheapest mobile music devices available at the time, but they were so innovative that they set a new standard and reinvented the market to a certain extent. Suddenly you could carry thousands of songs around with you on a small mobile device, while a CD Walkman could play only as much as could fit on a CD.

The same could be said for Apple's subsequent foray into the cell phone market. Their major competitor in this market, Samsung, might not have been pipping Apple to the post in design terms from day one, but they are certainly perceived to be more affordable for similar technology (particularly of late). This is, essentially, Samsung's USP.

Charles Revson, founder of the make-up giant Revlon, always used to say that he sold hope, not make-up. He gave women a wide variety of beauty products at reasonable prices, distributed globally.

When you want to figure out what your USP might be, I would suggest looking for two or three things that you do, you offer, you are, you cover or you touch on. Look for things that no one else offers your followers in quite the same combination or way. Remember that the feeling you leave your followers with is also relevant. Do you inspire people? Do they feel like they have gained a friend, a source of laughter or, perhaps, self-deprecating fun?

Perhaps you review the latest technical gadgets, but you put your own dry, humorous spin on it and you are always looking for gear that you can actually afford while shopping with South African rands – as opposed to American voices in this niche segment, who might be able to buy a broader range of products because of their location and their strong currency. Your aim might be to leave your followers feeling like they're winning – that they enjoy a competitive advantage when they take your advice.

The 1990s hit movie *Speed* was famously pitched as *"Die Hard,* on a bus". Similarly, I developed and pitched a cooking show, *Buite Die Lyne*, to a TV channel in 2016 as *"Roer,* but with rugby players". *Roer* was a well-known kykNET cooking show where you got to know a different musician or actor in every episode by seeing them cook a meal for a loved one, in their own kitchen. Of course, the true value for the average viewer is seeing someone they admire interacting with their loved one – a mom or a sibling, a best friend, a partner or a mentor. I simply added a rugby spin to this format, offered it to a competing channel (Via) and *voila*! We made 26 episodes of *Buite Die Lyne*, fully commissioned.

It is important to note that the point of that show was never to create the impression that the rugby players who were featured were able to cook like Jamie Oliver. They were obviously very successful in a specific field, but they often made very simple (and, therefore, quite useful) recipes, while sharing very endearing and vulnerable moments with the viewer about their lives outside of rugby. We covered the loss of loved ones, the disappointments they had faced, the odds they had to overcome and how they all have people at home who worry about them (despite how invincible they may seem). Essentially, it was about how even very successful young superstars also battle to balance the demands of their personal lives and the professional pursuit of glory. The aim was always to leave the (predominantly female) viewer feeling as though she could somehow relate to a burly rugby player who takes massive hits every day. The USP was actually: "*Roer*, but with rugby players" PLUS empathy.

Another useful example of USP is Chrissy Teigen, a gorgeous model and the wife of John Legend. While these two aspects alone would probably have garnered her a large number of followers, what sets her apart from other models who are married to successful, famous men (and remember, there are many of these) is her feisty sense of humour, her love of cooking and the fact that she is the kind of mom who claps back at her haters. Many followers really relate and respond to the latter aspects: we actually root for her in spite of her exceptional, aspirational lifestyle.

My own USP could perhaps be outlined along the lines of "cat lady who pays for cat (and other) food by being a sports presenter". If a girl from a small town like myself, who didn't grow up speaking English or being considered a relevant voice in sport, could make it to the sidelines of two World Cup events in one year, then anyone can. That's what I want to leave my followers with,

Yes, my dear husband clearly won in the wife lottery!

after every single post. I want my audience to feel included, particularly if they don't fit into widely accepted stereotypes, because I also don't.

Based on my social media presence, you'll quickly be able to tell that I am (*a*) a woman, (*b*) often pitch-side at amazing sporting events, and (*c*) also a total nerd (who loves cats, gardening and sewing). Now there are plenty of other women who also work in sport, who lead lives that involve plenty of travel and speaking to household names – but are they also obsessed with their (four) rescue cats? And do they also take you along, behind the scenes, when they have a beer on the couch, to poke fun and marvel at the highs and lows of sport?

My deep love of having a beer, gardening and watching sport on the sofa is, traditionally speaking, seemingly incompatible with also regularly getting dressed up to host live broadcasts, award shows and events for big companies. Yet, I'm both the blonde woman in heels and the sports fan in sweatpants. I purposefully share the more real side of my life because I want my followers to feel as though they are always invited to hang out with me. I'm not on social media for your envy; I am there to open the door for you to also take a peek inside. Inside where? Wherever I am let in!

These are true interests that give me touch points with people who share my passions or who simply find the unusual combination entertaining enough to keep following – even if they are not actually a cat person or a sports fan. Perhaps some stick around because they relate to working in a male-dominated environment or find my access to big sporting events fascinating and insightful.

I recently stumbled upon a great example of how different feeds, all functioning within the same niche area, in the same geographic location, can present very different and beautifully unique characters without competing or crowding each other out. Robyn Donaldson's @almost_everything_off_ebay Instagram account has the following stories saved as part of her "Instabands" highlight.

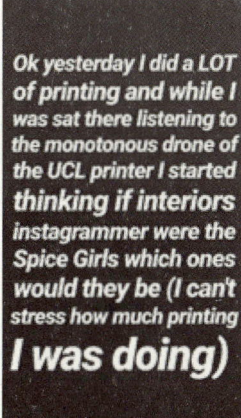

All of these are available on @almost_everything_off_ebay's Instagram Stories highlight titled "Instabands".

Not only does this show really good differences in the selling points of these influencers, but it's also a creative and practical way of networking on social media. This is just one example of how you can use your space and your voice in a way that showcases great lateral thinking. You gather content that stimulates your follower and interests you, and it can also effortlessly strengthen your relationships with other voices operating in the same space.

An often underrated way to really grow in a certain niche area is to actively collaborate and partner with other influencers in that field of interest. You can even put cash together and run a competition across your two or three profiles to give away a coveted voucher. If your audience is too small to secure a collaboration with a brand you might have on your vision board as a prospective partner, band together with allies who share the same conundrum. Attend events together and help each other gather content.

Generously share and repost their content, honestly ask for advice, share feedback and be the industry friend you wish you had. There is no guarantee that this will always work out the way you had planned, but the potential for growth and camaraderie – in what could be a very lonely pursuit – is a reward that is certainly worth the risk.

Being generous demonstrates to your followers that you don't feel threatened and that you are a positive force in a social media era that is often perceived as narcissistic. You are a great tastemaker or even an aggregator in your field of interest; you fully recognise that your own style isn't the be-all and end-all and you appreciate the creativity of others.

More truly is more!

Beware of pop culture blips and bubbles

Once you have figured out who you want to be, what your point of difference will be and what aspect of your story you want to put out there – what influence you want to have, basically – the next step is to figure out where best to do this.

Conventional wisdom points to the timeless value of creating your own blog or website platform – a central point that will collect all of your digital activities. We all know social media platforms tend to ebb and flow in popularity. Now add to this the fact that you (in spite of your best efforts at surfing these waves of platforms rising and falling) are ultimately also exposed to a powerful crosswind: the whims of algorithmic adjustments. As much as you can monitor, test and predict algorithmic behaviour, it does often leave influencers feeling as though they are only one adjustment away from invisibility. This is why some specialists in digital marketing still espouse the virtues of a corner of the web that you ultimately control: www.yournamegoeshere.com. A URL that you ultimately own.

This allows you to flex a bit of perceived power (even if it doesn't boast massive traffic) by always having an address that users can click through to – a shopfront on the web that is not bound by the limitations of any one social network: a digital patch of land where you can create a portfolio of your projects, and a showcase of your track record. A space that you can optimise for search engines to pick up on the useful projects to which you have contributed – particularly the ones where you collaborated with brands. A space where you can even host added-value opportunities to the brands you partner with, regardless of what the algorithm might make of it, and where you can even start building e-commerce opportunities that also turn you into a better influencer.

As Mike Sharman duly points out, you need to remember that:

> Every brand cent is accounted for, especially in tough economic environments. Modern influencers are learning a lot by experimenting with Shopify and those lessons are so valuable. Drop-shipping is another one: when you love a pair of sneakers, you can set up a store where people can buy them through you online; they're delivered straight to the client from the source in China. You become the face of the storefront, but the product doesn't ever actually pass through your hands. Ghost kitchens is another one: through Uber Eats you can now sell food that is available only through the delivery service; it's not a traditional restaurant with chairs and tables. Influencers and their virtual storefronts are becoming the middleman. If you understand commerce and you're commercially minded, there's a bigger chance you'd do well working with a brand.

Bouwer Bosch agrees wholeheartedly.

> Those things are all intertwined. I was 23 when [his Afrikaans band] Straatligkinders started doing well and back in the day we paid Loedi van Renen R20 000 for a music video. He was great, but then I realised he lives in Joburg and I lived in Potch, where we had a whole lot of bands. Loedi's camera cost R17 000, so I drove to the bank and asked them if I'd qualify for a R17 000 loan as a student. They said yes. I took that cash right there and bought the camera. I taught myself how to shoot and started making R5 000 music videos for people in Potch. Not all of the bands could afford R20 000 videos, but there was a demand for R5 000 ones. Then, suddenly Elvis Blue saw my videos and I shot three for him. Then Rocco de Villiers. Then Gangs of Ballet and, before you knew it, I shot two videos for Matthew Mole, one which got more than 2 million hits. All of this because I took the leap to buy a R17 000 camera. Now we're shooting R1 million ads!

Bouwer's story gets even more unbelievable from here.

> At one point I was even exchanging e-mails with Greyson Chance and his manager about making videos for him. This is the same guy who went viral with his Lady Gaga covers and was featured on *Ellen*. They found me on

> YouTube back then and I was honestly floored. No way, I thought! We were in Skype meetings trying to make the scheduling work, but I had to go for a back operation and he was in university and in the end it didn't work out. The point is, that was a clear gap that could have totally changed the course of my life. It only came up because I took a chance to make R5 000 videos, music videos no one else wanted to bother with. Nothing you do is ever in vain, not even R5 000 music videos.

I have always been fascinated by the amount of energy Bouwer ploughs into making a podcast. I actually featured in one of them, in exchange for one of his Liefde Wen hoodies. I asked him if he was worried about spending so much energy on a project that wouldn't generate an income. He was not bothered.

> The point of the podcast is to build a proven track record, so I can leverage that currency to land bigger interviews. Your clout isn't always measurable only in cash. I'm just building influence, for now. Playing the long game.

If this fires up your interest in setting up a site of your own, it doesn't have to cost much any longer. Thanks to services like Wix.com, designing a website is now even simpler than helping your grandparents set up a Facebook profile. Or you can build your website on Wordpress.com if you want to flex or strengthen your amateur-developer muscles. Regardless of which route you take, you can seamlessly and affordably set up hosting and e-mail integration on Google's G Suite in record time – complete with a fancy business-like e-mail address, such as info@yournamegoeshere.com.

In fact, while you're at it, take a short digital course on search engine optimisation (SEO) so that you can ensure your website pops up where it needs to. These skills are never wasted and even if you eventually abandon the idea of having the website up and running for whatever reason, at least you've parked your domain. Just in case.

I have a website of my own, I own a domain and although it is still visible and active for now, it has fallen entirely out of use, both by me and in terms of traffic on it. And for now, I'm totally okay with that. Any web platform remains relevant only for as long as someone updates it and there are users consuming what is on it. If those two things stop happening, it simply crumbles into irrelevance, like a sandcastle.

Proof of this can be found in the story of the biggest social media network on earth between 2005 and 2008: Myspace. At the peak of the Myspace era, it was synonymous with the words social and network – effectively it was Facebook before Facebook. Myspace boasted 100 million active users, which was incredible for the time. In fact, as a music portal it jump-started the careers of well-known musicians such as Calvin Harris, Sean Kingston, Lily Allen and the Arctic Monkeys. I even know a couple, who are now married, who met on Myspace.

So, if you've never heard of it, take it from me: it was a thing – a big one! And yet, it has since imploded so spectacularly that in 2019 all user data (images, music and videos) from before 2016 were accidentally deleted as a result of a faulty server migration. What makes it worse is that I didn't even know about the 2019 loss of data, even though I had a Myspace account, so I was one of those 100 million users.

This is not the only story of its kind. Google+ (sometimes written as Google Plus), a social network started by the mighty Google (of all companies), was another failed social network. It started in 2011 and closed down entirely in 2019.

I am not explaining all of this in such vivid detail because I enjoy a trip down memory lane – although it is fun to reflect and reminisce. I am trying to warn against the impression that all the data you have uploaded to social networks and the audience you have built on these platforms will exist forever. They might, but what if they don't?

Things change, they move on, and you need to ensure that your influencer business is nimble and substantive enough to outlive the platform itself, much like Calvin Harris's career outlived Myspace. It is important to remember that what feels like the career of your dreams at the moment (a massive audience on a particular social media platform) might turn out to be a pop culture blip in the long run. This also isn't unique to social media. I have hosted many TV shows that had faithful daily or weekly viewers for years on end, which have now disappeared. In fact, the entire TV channel that hosted the first TV show I ever presented no longer exists.

Your favourite platform might cease to exist, users might simply stop visiting it, or worse: you might lose interest entirely. If all three happen, for whatever reason, where would that leave you? If you can live with your answer, then proceed. If you can't, start building a digital bomb shelter of sorts.

This could mean building a website or perhaps simply diversifying enough that your content exists across a few different platforms so that you reach your audience through a variety of means. Perhaps what ultimately works for you is an approach that involves not only social media but also traditional media (which is probably the best way to describe my own business model) or one that isn't only content driven, but also has an entrepreneurial thread: making gorgeous wedding videos like Katinka does, or perhaps making adverts like Bouwer does. Perhaps it's starting a line of swimsuits, like Nadia Jaftha's, or a restaurant like Buns Out – *à la* Maps Maponyane?

What to dish up and where

On the topic of Buns Out, when I go to a burger restaurant, I walk through the door because I want food that is filling and prepared quickly. I am less concerned about how healthy it is or any frilly presentation. Instead, it needs to be affordable. In a fine dining establishment, however, a burger would have to be served on upscale crockery and with cutlery of a certain standard. I'd expect it to be made from only the highest-quality ingredients and for it to be pretty well balanced nutritionally. Also, I wouldn't stand for a paper napkin. Of course, this would come complete with a very different bill at the end of the experience, but that is what I went in for, after all.

The same applies when we consume social media, which can be divided broadly into four focus categories:

- Social networking (e.g. Facebook, LinkedIn)
- Microblogging (e.g. Twitter, Tumblr)
- Photo sharing (e.g. Instagram, Pinterest, Snapchat)
- Video sharing (e.g. YouTube, Vimeo, Facebook Live, IGTV, TikTok).

Let's take a look at how a brand adapts the same campaign and brand message across the four big platforms (Facebook, Twitter, Instagram and Pinterest). Even with Instagram and Pinterest both being classified as

Have you ever noticed how brand posts on Facebook always include an image?

Image quality on Twitter is less important. Note how this could very well have been a small photo report, lower down on a newspaper page.

photo-sharing platforms, the consumer patterns (and therefore content angles) are different.

For the purposes of this exercise, I gathered some screen grabs from Dove's Self-Esteem Project, which has enjoyed great acclaim worldwide. It is based on a study conducted in the United Kingdom, detailed on their website, which showed that while more than 1 million girls suffer from low body confidence, two-thirds admit that they feel prettier online than in real life.

> 1 in 2 girls say they are using social networks "all the time", across an average of 4 different networks and are increasingly considered as being "always on". The average UK girl takes 12 minutes to prepare for a single "selfie", thus spending 84 minutes a week getting ready for selfies.

Dove found that "the number of girls who say social networks make them feel worse about their appearance doubles between the ages of 13 years to 18 years" – from roughly a third to about two-thirds in only a few years.

They tell this story in striking ways, with the help of both images and great textual captions and hashtags, catering to the same group of consumers on different platforms but tailoring how they phrase it according to where it is posted. On Facebook, you will see that brands don't often post text-only status updates. They include highly polished images or videos with a great placeholder image. It almost looks like the kind of advert you'd see in a glossy magazine. Everyone looks polished: great lighting, beautiful styling, sometimes with text included in the image, but not too much.

Note how this image was clearly not taken with a phone. The image more closely resembles those family photo shoots you see on Facebook, where everyone magically appears to have dressed in white and denim that day. Where an entire family is arranged in some photographer's studio in an attempt to look as relaxed as possible, while obviously giving away that they're posing for a camera by looking straight at the lens.

On Twitter, the same campaign for the same brand presents more like a news post than a glossy magazine advert. It is clearly an image that was taken on the same day that it was posted – not nearly as much production involved. You can almost imagine it popping up in a newspaper, right? Perhaps it could even have been taken with a phone, but a phone is also obviously being used in one of the images. It is capturing a fleeting moment in time, reporting it for the sake of the information – it is not a portrait for the benefit of posterity. It is about the caption – a very information-heavy caption at that. While the Facebook post didn't feature hashtags, here you find more than one. These are crucial because they allow this post to align with global activities #ConfidentGirl or #DSEP2018 (Dove Self-Esteem Project 2018), which can be activated by Dove in different ways across the world. The hashtag allows all these worldwide activities involved in the same project to be searchable and accessible by users anywhere. It shows that the brand is truly committed and consistently involved, by creating a publicly accessible record of activities, but not only on the Dove website; they are also walking the talk on a platform where we love holding people accountable: Twitter.

On Instagram, the same campaign shows a post featuring two images as well, but here they are presented as a carousel – you have to page through – not as two separate but related posts on the same topic, but rather as a set-up-and-reveal tactic.

The first image in the carousel is of a young girl in school uniform and, as in the case of Twitter, this photo could very well have been taken with a phone. It is not nearly as polished as the Facebook post, yet some design work has been done to craft it into something that is much stronger, visually, than the Twitter post. It feels instant enough to fit into the aesthetic you've come to expect from an Instagram feed, but it is somewhere between Twitter and Facebook, from a style perspective. Once you page to the second image in the carousel, it reveals the campaign message. In this way, Dove echoes the message you would be able to read in one image on Facebook, but without crowding the image too heavily. This makes it appear similar to the kind of content that typical private users and influencers would produce and takes it further away from the usual branded content. In fact, neither of the images include Dove's logo or overt Dove branding. Even if you are scrolling so fast that you wouldn't normally take the time to read the whole caption, the message in the second image of the carousel will probably land well enough to entice you to read the caption. The caption here is also wordier than in either of the previous examples and features emojis and a whole raft of hashtags – 12 to be precise!

Content, content, content | 57

An Instagram caption lends itself to heavy emoji usage and loads of information.

On Pinterest, the typical user looks for and pins practical, useful, beautiful and inspirational content to digital versions of the cork board you used to have hanging somewhere within reach of your desk. In the days of actual magazines and print publications, you would cut or tear out bits of timeless and useful information for reference: recipes, instructions and style and decor tips. This is why Dove's "Beautiful Balance" board contains step-driven tips and useful information that don't explicitly sell deodorant but rather – you guessed it – promote ways to build self-esteem, particularly among teenage girls.

If you want to spread your influencer business across a variety of platforms, you need to be clear on the differences. Even when it is the very same user that follows you on all these different platforms, you need to understand that people open different apps for different reasons, so you must ensure that you are always packaging the kind of content they have come to look for.

As Wian says:

> No one opens TikTok to see Instagram-type stuff. They would've opened Instagram if they wanted to see their friends, family or celebs they love. But on TikTok, it doesn't matter who made the video, it just has to be good. On TikTok people can also scroll past within seconds, so you have to captivate them from the first second and because the sound is always up, right from the start your video also needs to be made differently.

I asked Wian to list the top three mistakes most people make on TikTok:

- People don't start strong enough. A video that did really well for me on TikTok fell flat on Instagram because there, many people watch the start of a video with the sound off and then only push up the sound a few seconds in. I think many people have good videos but because it doesn't start well, people scroll past it on TikTok. Videos need to be short, simple and you cannot waste a single second; on TikTok it needs to be interesting all the way through.
- People don't post often enough; they are too worried about quality and then not delivering enough quantity.
- Make content for TikTok specifically and if you don't know where to start, watch loads of TikTok videos. How did you learn what worked on Instagram or Facebook or Twitter? You spent a lot of time there.

No logo is visible on the Instagram images, yet on Pinterest it is a subtle footnote.

Hashtags

Fun fact: The father of the hashtag didn't work for Twitter.

Many people achieve exactly the opposite of what they intend with hashtags: you can tell by just looking at how they use them. Yes, the inclusion of hashtags will result in more people who don't already follow you seeing your posts. It could even deliver you some new followers. However, if you are just including irrelevant hashtags, thinking that this is a shortcut to gaining more followers, you will irritate the ones you already have and no new follower will gain value from what you're putting out there. As with anything on social media, if you are unsure, stay out of it or educate yourself quickly.

This was the first-ever use of the hashtag as we know it today. Chris Messina was a tech product designer in Silicon Valley in 2007. He was also part of the early wave of Twitter users who were trying to figure out how best to use the platform. Barcamp is a tech or web conference and Messina wanted to figure out how to organise the chatter about this event in a way that would be easy to access, both for him and the network of developers who were interested in it.

The use of hashtags really took off during a large-scale fire in San Diego County later that year, when Twitter users organically started using #sandiegofire to track updates. However, Twitter itself didn't want to adopt and promote the practice until two years later, in 2009. Hashtags have since been called "wormholes" or even the "veins" of the Internet. Eventually hashtags became commonplace on all social media platforms, to the extent that Instagram limits the number you may include in a caption to 30.

I absolutely cannot stand hashtags that shamelessly ask for likes and followers, such as #followme, #like4like, #follow4follow and #tagsforlikes. This is a pointless waste of characters that gives your followers the worst impression: that you are cool with spam, with bots and sneaky shortcuts. Real success on social media is about finding ways to create engaging content that elicits honest responses and trust.

As you can see in the Dove example, brands know better than to use a raft of hashtags at the start of a post and as a user you would do well to take your cue from them – after all, they have employed specialists to devise their strategy on this front.

Hashtags are not meant to be read, so think of them rather as little flags or signals you plant so that those who are interested in a particular topic can find relevant content. Use them for what they are worth by seamlessly integrating them in a simple caption (this is risky if not done well) or safely concentrate them at the end, spaced well clear of your precious, carefully crafted message.

I follow a few hashtags on Instagram; one example is #bonsai. This means that content from people I don't follow, but who are posting bonsai content, such as instruction videos on how to care for your bonsai or merely stills showing off beautiful bonsai trees, automatically pops up in my feed. If I see an account sharing really useful #bonsai content, I might choose to follow them, but mostly I am just keeping my eye on the bonsai scene in a much broader sense. When I work on a tournament, like the Rugby World Cup, I tend to follow the event hashtag #RWC2019 for that period as well, to get a feel for the content that users are generating: to see the event through the eyes of social media users who are out at matches, who are supporting their teams both in the host country but also around the world. It is great, free market research and provides me with useful insights I can incorporate in my work and, of course, provides an opportunity for me to pick up on the most interesting content creators in my field.

However, if I see a #bonsai or #RWC2019 post pop up in my feed that is clearly abusing the hashtag, because it doesn't actually feature content related to the interest area but cynically piggybacks on it to try to gain prominence, I can tell Instagram to stop showing this post under the hashtag by selecting the "Don't Show For This Hashtag" feedback option.

This is one way in which users can actively teach the Instagram algorithm what they want to be shown and what not. The other, simpler one is that they will simply swipe away. Regardless of the platform, hashtags allow your input to pop up in traceable global conversations on the topic you are passionate about, taking you into the feeds of people who might not have found you otherwise. If you are tweeting insightful, interesting, newsworthy or funny contributions with a relevant hashtag or two, chances are your posts will gain engagement quickly and rise to the top of the trending, explore, or for you pages – depending on the platforms of choice.

It is not about getting seen by many people, it is about getting seen by the *right* people. That's how hashtags lead to higher engagement and more followers. One useful, authentic and proven way of leveraging the power of the hashtag is to include an accurate one in the most important place of all: your profile biography. If you are a ketogenic diet enthusiast, #keto will allow your posts to link seamlessly with the searches and conversations around the topic.

Killing babies

When I think of the year I spent studying towards an honours degree in journalism at the University of the Witwatersrand, I feel as though we spent most of our time doing the exact opposite of writing: we were editing. This is something that would serve you well as a content creator.

It is effectively the practice of undoing, deleting, cutting, trimming, shaving or even destroying the writing you have already

Some more digital strategy advice from Matthew Kobach that works, whether you look after brand accounts or just your own influencer feed(s).

done. Editing is a euphemism for a very painful process our lecturer, Jo-Anne Richards, used to call "killing babies". We often think of writing as this creative, fun process where you are cheerfully stringing together a series of useful sentences with words, punctuation and a few key spaces. Easy peasy!

However, one of the key skills you learn in a journalism degree is that writing, in the traditional sense, is only the fun bit right at the start. Most of the real sweat and the true value of any piece is only revealed in the editing, where you refine the raw text into the most coherent, concise and, ultimately, the most useful version of itself. The news doesn't require frills and fuss; it needs to be understandable to everyone. Even if someone reads only the first sentence, they should already know the where, what, why, when and how before you use a full stop for the first time. This seems very simple, but you wouldn't believe how difficult it is in practice, especially if you get pretty attached to those words you so carefully selected and strung together. Just like a journalist, an influencer needs not only to edit their *words* ruthlessly, they also need to edit their *content* ruthlessly. Create it, save it, walk away from it, come back, review, critique and reconsider it.

Liesl Laurie explains her way of working:

> I draft a lot of my things in my notes app, complete with the correct tags and stuff, so I'm sure it's all there and then I send it out. I think you learn to be very mindful of what you say and how you say it when you're Miss SA, so I wouldn't even draft something in the app before I send it. I'll compose my thoughts somewhere I won't be able to press send or post by accident, ensure that it's right and ready and then copy it across. Sometimes I second-guess myself. If I'm uncertain about what I'm trying to say, I'll send it to my best friends or my cousins who know me well. They'll be straight up and honest with me. They'll tell me if it's coming across as pretentious. I am open about the fact that it's a work post; it needs to convey a certain message, but I want it to sound like me.

Some influencers and brands run private feeds called "test accounts", where they post all their content before they post it on their main feed. They check that it sits well with the rest of what is already on their feed. They make sure that the tags and details all show up correctly. They draft their captions, their tweets and their carousels with as much care and forethought as they would if they were the editor of *Vogue* or the *Washington Post*.

Someone who always generously shares her devotion to creating content and telling stories that are intentional and consistent is Rachel Kolisi.

> When I realised I had a following, I knew I had a responsibility. Everyone's an influencer in some way, because we all have a circle of influence

and are accountable for the message we send out to those watching. Yes, the capacity of my following may be larger than others – but I encourage everyone to be deliberate and intentional about their contribution to the world. So many eyes on me in a desperate world ... that is a responsibility I do not take lightly. I want to be relatable and have a positive influence on the lives of others. I never want someone to wish they had my life or that they were like me. My life changed for the better when I found content in my situation and in who I am. I wish that for every single person out there. As an influencer I have the same struggles, the same number of hours in a day, the same temptations and some bad days. I want my followers to know life is truly great with all its ups and downs and happy is a choice.

Every single element of your digital business, every aspect of every social network profile under your brand needs to carry that level of clear intent. All of it needs to communicate your message seamlessly and without contradiction or confusion. Your profile photo, the information in the biography at the top of your profile, your banner image, your pinned posts, your captions, your use of hashtags – these are all tools you have in your digital toolbox. Use them to colour in that space inside the chalk outline that encapsulates your influencer business.

Don't forget to audit the accounts you follow, as well. These are all the influences you take on board every time you open a platform. These are the sources you'll retweet, share and repost, and their impact on your voice cannot be overstated.

One of the sure ways to drive Instagram and TikTok engagement in ways that set the hearts of brands, agencies and marketers aflutter is to create posts that users will save or download. This is the platform's equivalent of pinning on Pinterest or likes on Twitter. Content that has timeless value, that is specific in its instruction or simply provides tips, will inspire your followers to mark and keep it for later use. Sharing content of this nature should always be pinned to your Instagram Story highlights as well – a great showcase area where you can briefly highlight what sets your account apart, for a prospective follower who has clicked through to your account biography in curiosity, by accident or because they saw or heard you on some other platform.

How often do you need to create content?

Nadia Jaftha, Katinka die Kat and Wian Magic are all convinced that they need to produce content every day in order to maintain engagement, but this is not a universally held opinion.

> I monitor the numbers every single day, [shares Nadia], because they keep changing. I have to post every single day. That keeps my engagement up; that keeps my numbers consistent. I need to do that so I can show brands that my metrics are consistent. My followers know that when they come

to my page there will be something new and something fresh. Whether it's funny, more lifestyle, there's always going to be something new. That's really important, to keep that relationship with your followers and make them feel like they can rely on you for new content.

It is about more than just engagements though; Nadia says the return on this investment is also brand loyalty and sentiment.

> It also makes them feel like they can support you with whatever you're doing. For example, I'm in my first movie now and it's very different for me: going from social media to cinema. When I shared that with my followers or my supporters, they responded really well to that and I was really surprised by how much love I got. I think that's really important: when your followers feel like they can grow with you; that when you succeed – they succeed. Essentially, that's what it is, at the end of the day.

In Katinka's case, she maintains a balance between video and photo content:

> I need to post a video at least every second or third day, while I need to post photos every day. People talk about what is trending, you know. You need to constantly pop up in their stories and you definitely get out what you put in.

Wian explains that instead of looking at what he's putting in, he measures his effort in terms of the results only.

> The motivational guru Gary Vaynerchuk changed my way of looking at this with his emphasis on the fact that we all have time, we just tend to use it wrong. You can only measure how you spend your time by looking at the actual results, not at your effort. Results are all that matters. Sometimes I plan videos, like a movie, for over two weeks and then they get the same engagement as something I came up with on the spot. I now try to keep my planning minimal, because every day that I spend planning and not posting costs me a day's growth. Most people treat their Instagram feed like a photo album, curated around a theme, and so perfect that not a single aspect of it is out of place. But how much growth do they miss out on, how much money and following do they lose because of this obsession with perfection? Quality is important, but not more than being productive.

Liesl is one example of an influencer who works on big campaigns regularly but doesn't prioritise social media every day.

> I often don't post over a weekend or for a day or two. I was recently on an influencer trip, hanging out with a few other influencers, and they explained to me how they work, but I've never bought into it. I do wonder if it takes away from being pure. I really only look at which day is best for me to post.
>
> I also know my personality and the A-type person I am can't afford to get too stuck into the metrics and insights. I think the big note here is that being Miss SA influenced a lot of how I think, to this day. It was a good thing for me. I realise how unrefined I was before the pageant and it wasn't

the pageant itself that refined me. I made conscious decisions about who I wanted to be in the world and it was the point in my life that got me to commit to that person I wanted to be.

Maps Maponyane talks about how he combats algorithm anxiety:

> I focus on my why and the things that make me happy. My journey, the work I've put in. I take stock a bit. A lot of the time I'd also just move away from social media. If I feel like it, I'll get back on. If I feel like it's changing me, I take a break.

Bouwer Bosch echoes this sentiment when he explains:

> I should probably post more consistently because then I'm sure it'll become more profitable, but I don't have the capacity to produce content daily, like Katinka die Kat does. Or even weekly. I'm just not in the mood to be funny every single day. I know from working with Nadia Jaftha on *Tropika Island of Treasure* that she's amazing and super disciplined at this. To me it often feels as if I'm bipolar because I often have to give myself a pep talk, that it's okay not to have something to post now. Because you tend to look at the profiles of others, their projects, the audiences they pull in and that's your downfall. When you start believing that your work doesn't have an impact. Then I usually go and look at what I'm actually busy with: Liefde Wen has more followers than Mr Price and Superbalist. Francois [van Coke] beats me on the follower front, but he primarily makes music. I get up in the morning and run Freckle, Liefde Wen and other projects. If you focus only on music, you'll probably eventually be able to also sell out the Sun Arena. But in my case, I make TV ads and I make movies too. It's important for me to sometimes tell myself "Hey dude, it's ok!" I love acting, I love TV and film and all those things. I recently did a live improv theatre show called *Intermissie*, which earned award nominations ...

I think the truth lies somewhere in the middle. You need to look at what your audience expects and what delivers real results, like Wian says, among that audience. I have experimented with a variety of approaches: long breaks between content, various posts per day, more video than stills, more trend-based stuff, and then the opposite of that in timeless "how-tos" as well. I have struck a balance that doesn't overlap with anyone else's approach here, which is why I think that, in the end, you just need to be consistent in whatever approach you choose.

Decide which expectations you can keep meeting while being generous, honest and productive at the same time. As Wian pointed out:

> The guy who has the second highest number of followers on TikTok right now, only posts every second day [he makes video editing tutorials]. His videos are amazing and generate loads of likes, so for him it works to post less frequently.

Elma Smit ✓ @Elmakapelma · 2s
- Figure out what your unique selling point is, what is at the crossroads of your offering, and how it makes people feel.
- Beware of spending years building a sandcastle that could wash away in the blink of an eye. Build a diversified business empire – not only an audience.
- In order to diversify successfully, take note of what works (and what doesn't) on each platform you tackle.
- The lightsaber of social media is the hashtag, but you need to wield it responsibly.
- Edit ruthlessly. Posting isn't free – every message you send out could cost you everything.
- Banish algorithm anxiety by setting a pace that you can sustain and serve wholeheartedly.

5

SHOW ME THE MONEY

What is my voice worth?

On YouTube it is relatively simple to start earning an income when you attract a solid following. They call it "monetisation", which is when the actual platform pays you cash for the adverts they run on your content – you only need to activate the monetisation setting on your channel and submit the information required.

The views you attract lead to eyeballs that also watch adverts and, eventually, YouTube shares a slice of the revenue you created with you. TikTok has a similar model, which allows viewers of live broadcasts to send creators monetary gifts.

As Wian explains:

> It works just like on Facebook, Twitter or Instagram Live, but viewers can send you emojis that are called gifts and they all have different cash values. Users can buy these emojis with actual money, so they're worth R100 or R200 or R400, and then when they send it to me while I'm live, I get half of the cash paid into my account and TikTok keeps the other half.

I am interested in what the viewer or follower gets out of sponsoring these emojis. Are we showing off how much cash we can splash or is it true organic appreciation from your fans?

Wian says it is more transactional than this.

> I'd suggest it to viewers along the lines of: "Send me gifts and I'll follow you back." The reason some of them want me to follow them is so I might like their videos and grow their engagement. Also, some just want me to mention their names in the video, to acknowledge them. To wish them happy birthday or whatever. Look, some nights it makes more sense for me to sit and answer my e-mails and set up event bookings or content deals, but on other nights R1 000 in gifts can totally make an hour's worth of a TikTok live worthwhile.

If your aim as an influencer is to build a solid enough following in order to earn an income, then this is the crux of the exercise. However, I know monetisation tends to be something influencers seldom discuss. There are a few people in the industry whom I know I can call to compare notes and we give each other a fair bit of advice, as well as support, because it is sometimes difficult to navigate on Instagram, Twitter and Facebook.

However, because of the inherently competitive nature of it all, I have also encountered plenty of people who don't want to share these trade secrets.

I like referring to webfluential.com or influencermarketinghub.com for guidance on this as well – these are like a kind of "Uber for influencers". The Webfluential platform was created in 2013 for influencers to sign up (you have to be vetted by a Webfluential employee) and be listed with a public profile. You even get access to guide prices on what other influencers with similar reach, relevance and resonance charge for sponsored content on a variety of different platforms (Instagram, YouTube, Facebook, Twitter, Snapchat, your blog, paid appearances, etc.).

You are welcome to set your rates at whatever you choose, but you give the platform a percentage of whatever you earn and, in return, you enjoy the support of a dedicated Webfluential staff member during any campaign. This person acts as the go-between for the brand's marketers and you the influencer. Essentially, they do what YouTube's monetisation function does for YouTube content creators, only now you can agree to what you charge before the advert features on your account. The downside is that you do not build a direct relationship with the brand, but the upside is that you get indirectly introduced to new clients outside your existing network.

They check that you received the information you need to incorporate and communicate in your sponsored post, that you load your post(s) in the agreed time frame, and that you provide the links to these posts as a report-back function for the client's benefit. Often, they will also give you instructions on how to change a few settings on your platforms, so that brands can promote or sponsor your content to pop up in more people's feeds as a paid-for advert. They also often help you to activate software that ensures that both you and the client get useful and important analytical data on how your followers engage with the sponsored content you created.

I have worked directly with marketers, brands and agencies as well, and these business relationships have their own pros and cons. They usually contact influencers via DMs or your e-mail address (if you have a public one), or you can seize the chance to set up personal relationships (these are probably the ones that yield the greatest return) by attending launches and events and networking with clients who are in attendance. Or you can just pitch yourself to them directly. I have googled the names and e-mail addresses of marketing managers at brands and e-mailed them pitches on how I wanted to add value for their brand.

An important aside, though: the guide price advice you can gather on websites like Webfluential does not consider supply and demand. At different stages you might have multiple offers coming your way and you will be able to push for higher rates, while at other times you might need to drop your expectations to stay busy. This is the nature of being a freelance content creator or, essentially, an entrepreneur.

Knowing when to push for more and when to take what you are offered is the stressful aspect inherent in any job that doesn't earn a straightforward salary. Sometimes you win, while other times you lose out.

When considering an offer and drawing up a quote, I always ask myself:

- What is the best that can happen?
- What is the worst that can happen?
- What is the most likely outcome?

If I am comfortable that I can face any of the answers, I proceed.

Let's talk formulas

There are two ways to approach rates. The one is to ask what the market is willing to pay and to adapt. Joe Scott also outlined the alternative, which is to figure out what you need to be able to make to do this work full-time.

> Value your time per hour accordingly [which can only be decided by you and your lifestyle needs based on the aforementioned question], and think about how long it typically takes you to film/edit/publish a typical video on YouTube, an image on Instagram, or whatever platforms make the most sense. For example, if I'm pursuing it full-time, and my goal is to make a working salary of around $20 [let's say R400] per hour and it usually takes me 20 hours to produce and publish a video, there's $400 [R8 000] right there. But then you have to account for your follower size [or average impressions] and its value, along with the cost of operation for your equipment, and the like.

Maps Maponyane says he initially worked on 50 cents per follower, which basically boils down to R5 000 per paid post if you have 10 000 followers.

> But then as your following increases, you need to drive that cent-value down. You have to be reasonable. It's not the US, where you're going to earn R500 000 for something. Even if you charge 10 cents per follower, I think you need to just be able to give a brand that breakdown, if they ask for it.
>
> In the branding industry they often talk about a forever mark, a brand that is beyond their current engagement rates; it is a brand with a story, that is established and has a track record. That's what I strive for. If every time you work with a brand, their sales shoot up, that's far more valuable to them than mere likes. You want to work to a point where your involvement drives their business.

There are plenty of very complex formulas out there. The South African digital marketing agency Nichemarket suggests working on an average of R70 CPM (cost per 1 000 impressions/followers) on its blog, but it also factors in a few other things: your engagement rate, a so-called brand-fit rating", a target group accuracy rating (what percentage of your followers actually form part of the target market), as well as "content value" (what it should roughly cost the influencer to produce the required content).

A lot of these are subjective or hard to quantify universally, but it does give you some insight into how agencies and marketers might get to the valuations they present to clients on what your voice is worth. On one of my own sponsored posts, I actually ran this sum:

R70 × 100 (roughly 100 000 followers) = R7 000 CPM

3 140 engagements: (3 140 ÷ 100 000) × 100 = 3.14% engagement rate (based on the actual post insights)

Target group accuracy = 50% (I'm guessing)

Brand-fit rating between 0.5 and 1.5 = 0.7 (I'm also totally guessing this!)

Content value = R2 000

R7 000 × 3.14 × 0.5 × 0.7 + R2 000 = R9 693

Incidentally, this basically boils down to 10 cents per follower or 10% of my follower total. The American social media analytics company Klear says that micro-influencers across a variety of territories charged about R2 500 per post on Instagram, R1 000 per story on Instagram, and R3 300 per sponsored Facebook post in 2019. This was according to a survey of more than 2 500 influencers across Instagram, YouTube and Facebook. YouTube content's cost of production and value in the international market is still comparatively high for the same bracket of influencers at R14 000 per video post, while an Instagram video, on average, earns only R3 300.

Influencer Rates
A survey of 2,500+ influencers rates, from Jan 2019 - Mar 2019

	Ⓘ Post	Ⓘ Video	Ⓘ Story	▶ Video	f Post
Nano 500-5K Followers	$100	$114	$43	$315	$31
Micro 5-30K Followers	$172	$219	$73	$908	$218
Power 30-500K Followers	$507	$775	$210	$782	$243
Celebrity 500K+ Followers	$2,085	$3,138	$721	$3,857	$2,400

klear | The Price of Influencer Marketing 2019

In its 2019 "Price of Influencer Marketing" study, American analytics provider Klear found that men make up only 23% of the influencer industry but they get paid much better: women earned 77 cents for every dollar a man earned in the influencer industry.

Influencer Rates: Instagram Stories

Introduced in 2016, instagram stories allows users to share an image or a video that will vanish after 24-hours.

Stories have been growing in popularity, surpassing Snapchat in daily usage. So, unsurprisingly, In 2018, 1-in-3 sponsored posts on instagram were stories

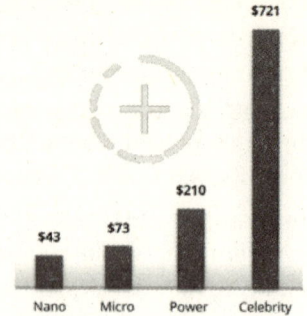

Nano $43 | Micro $73 | Power $210 | Celebrity $721

Fun Fact By early 2017 Instagram Stories had more daily views than Snapchat

klear | The Price of Influencer Marketing 2019

The study also pointed out how comparatively successful nano- and micro-influencers were, particularly on Instagram Stories. Nano-influencers with fewer than 5 000 followers, roughly 10% of the following of the average power-influencer, were earning roughly 20 to 25% of the fees that power-influencers earned on the same platform.

The digital publishing platform Hootsuite, which allows you to auto-schedule posts to go out at a certain time on a certain platform, suggested $100 (R2 000) per 10 000 followers as a pro rata rate in 2019. Rachel Kolisi and Nadia Jaftha, however, both mentioned a 10% approach when I asked them about their formulas.

Katinka die Kat elaborated on her recent experience in the influencer marketplace, which is that for a following similar to hers on Instagram:

> Someone the other day made R5 000 for a post and a story, as a package deal – I think it was to promote *The Bachelor*. Loads of people will also approach me with only R2 000 but then they want eight stories and six Instagram posts. [My audience] ... will hate me if I post six times about the same thing! I can't do that, so then I'll just explain what I'm able to provide and leave it up to them to make the call. I need to make sure people will still want to see my content, after all.

Liesl says she relies on influencermarketinghub.com to get an indication about going rates before she adapts them to the local market and the brand.

> Your comments, likes, followers, engagement rate, the rate at which you respond, all need to be taken into account. My recommended fee there is much higher than what I charge clients, but I use it as a guideline. You need to keep in mind what's happening in the market, our economy. With bigger brands I always point out that it's negotiable if we can build a relationship over a few months, instead of a one-off deal. I also often ask my friends in the industry what they charge.

When asked, Wian was very straightforward about his rates, explaining:

> Initially, when brands approached me to do this kind of thing, I was happy with just R2 000 for about three videos, but when a major beer brand approached me, someone suggested I speak to this guy who works in branding. He said the campaign should pay me at least R90 000 and they actually went for it! Another brand approached me and while we were negotiating, they told me that my valuation of my own account was too low, because I was willing to do a video for R25 000 for them. So, basically, I often ask other influencers for advice, or I wait until I can get a brand to make a price first.

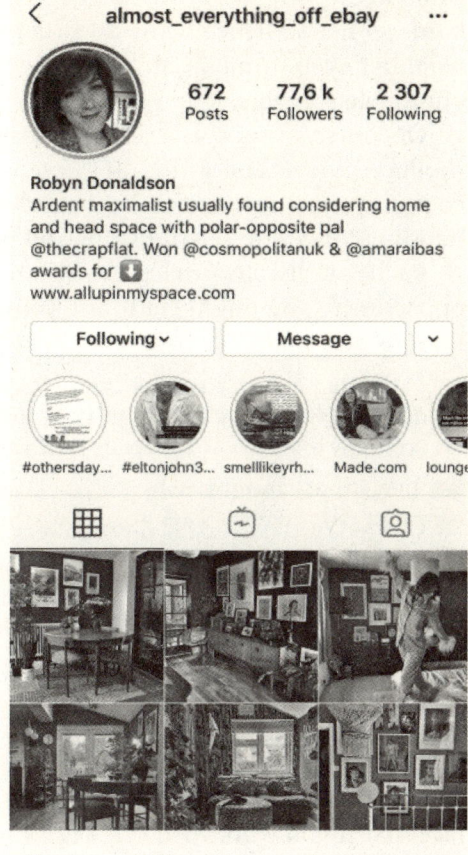

What you need to keep in mind, though, is that larger audiences or heavily branded content might yield lower-than-expected engagement rates, so even if your client is willing to pay that fee, your content might not generate the desired engagement or truly gain R25 000 worth of value. That's why overcharging might be a shortcut that leads you to a dead end: no return business. Always play the long game: under-promise and over-deliver.

Similarly, if you have fewer than 5 000 followers, you might not see offers of R750 per post. Brands might just offer a straight barter deal: R750 worth of product (you can, of course, negotiate this to be R750 cost price as opposed to R750 retail price – which would yield far more product) in return for a post and perhaps a few stories, as well as value-added tagging in a certain number of future posts.

Please note, though, that if you are a niche influencer with a smaller but highly engaged audience, you might be able to charge far more than the R1 500 guide price mentioned earlier. If the product or service has a likelihood of seeing massive value – a serious return on the investment – it could be well worth their money to spend R4 500 per post.

This brings me back to Robyn Donaldson @almost_everything_off_ebay: she shows that one can buy really interesting decor and beautiful interiors without breaking the bank. If eBay wanted to run an influencer campaign, particularly in the United Kingdom, they would be able to bank on her audience being all in on whatever she posted. Her followers wouldn't even mind because this is what they are there for: gorgeous but affordable interiors.

Of course, as soon as a series of posts – or a longer campaign involving produced video and a mix of content across more than one platform – comes up, you can certainly scale down the cost per post in favour of building long-term relationships and brand association.

Rachel Kolisi also makes an interesting point when it comes to the opportunity you might get to use your platform to help charitable organisations and small businesses.

> I allocate posts to charities and posts to small businesses where the rules don't apply. I really believe in the contribution of small businesses to the economy and I know the struggle of young entrepreneurs.

For her, it's all about trust:

> I have earned the trust of my followers and I can't keep it if I am promoting things I wouldn't actually recommend. I like to understand why they chose me to represent them and the intention behind the campaign. I turn down a lot of brands that I can't align myself with and I am very proud of the brands I have partnered with.

You don't want to be promoting one skin-care range at the top of your (digital) lungs for three weeks, only to have to switch to its competitor a month or two later, because your influencer business needs to maintain a certain number of sold posts to pay your rent. You need to allow for the fact that if you work with one brand in a particular market segment this month, you probably won't be able to legitimately pull off partnering with a competitor in the same space for the next few months. This is why negotiating a series of posts at a lower rate per post – but in the hope of setting up a relationship that leads to a consistent income over a number of weeks or months – is more sustainable.

How to build a media kit

We often think of influencers as people who do not have real jobs, so you might think that once your influencer ship comes in, you will never need a CV again. You would be dead wrong, though!

In the industry, we refer to an influencer's CV as a "media kit" and it is even more important than a CV, because you're constantly interviewing for new jobs. I always feel as though every bit of work I do is an audition, since as a freelance content creator, I invoice for every bit of effort. In this industry we have to maintain a level of performance, a certain kind of dedication to excellence that keeps us fit, disciplined and ultimately employed.

A media kit is a compilation of information that professionally presents your business and your strengths, and outlines your follower profile and the audience with whom you consistently engage. It can even outline your standard rates. If you are adept at using Photoshop, you can easily create a media kit, but even if you're not, you can find simple, free and user-friendly alternatives on the web.

Webfluential.com offers this as one of their free resources: you can simply let the platform do the hard work and build you a generic, digitally hosted media kit, which automatically updates your engagement rates based on recent posts and information on your audience demographic.

Mine looks like this:

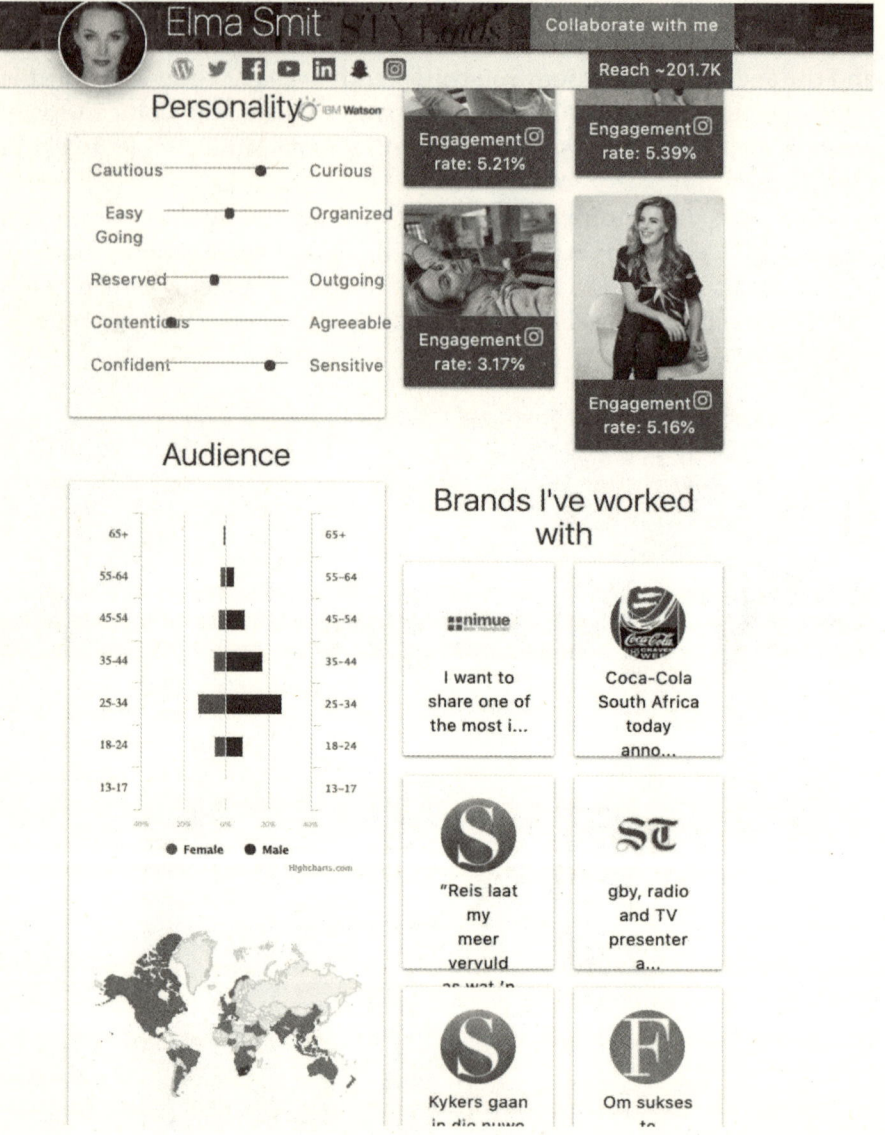

You can also build a fully downloadable one using a free media kit template available on canva.com. This gives you the opportunity to really fine-tune and customise:

Websites such as later.com also have free media kit templates you can download. One of the great – and I think essential – sections that they offer in their template is one where you can add testimonials from people you have recently worked with or for. Of course, you can simply build this into any other template you already have as well.

Facts, statistics and other quantifiable contributions are incredibly important. This is something I picked up from Maps Maponyane.

> I ask businesses to tell me about their key performance indicators, their agenda. I want to see the numbers after a campaign. I want to see what it did for their bottom line. We have analytics on the back end of everything we do now; it's good to see what that does. I want to see what the difference is that we get to make.
>
> I take it very personally when I get asked to do something – in them having hopes of a particular outcome. If it doesn't look like it's working, I'll just do the rest of the campaign at no cost. With a lot of brands, the value add will be: "Let's have a meeting; let's sit down; let's plan how we can do this." I don't think this is the right approach. This is where the market is at; this is the audience. I recommend these people to join this, so we can find more success.' I try to be as hands-on as possible. I'm probably more of a consultant than just an ambassador. I try to add real value.

Really flex the great value you have created for your partners; don't only focus on who you are and who your followers are. Let your previous clients tell your prospective collaborators all about you, in their own words. In fact, if you had to include a trackable link in sponsored content – to keep an eye on how many followers clicked through from your posts to a client's website – ask for the insights on that click-through rate and include these numbers in support of their opinions.

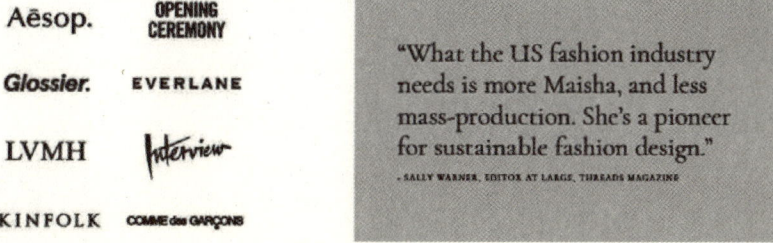

Elma Smit @Elmakapelma · 2s

- Setting and negotiating your rate is a complex decision you will have to review often; make peace with the fact that it is never straightforward.
- When you calculate your rate using a formula, ask around and keep the scope of the campaign in mind.
- If you build yourself a detailed, facts- and feedback-rich media kit, you increase your chances of landing great work.

6

AND WHEN I START MAKING MONEY?

Traditional media lessons apply

A close friend once asked me what my policy is when it comes to how much sponsored content I carry on my feed. It stopped me dead in my tracks. I still remember exactly where I was when we had this conversation. She was complaining about an influencer who seemed to feature sponsored content in eight out of every ten posts. She loved following this person for the other two posts but couldn't ride out the heavy commercial load any longer.

I have to admit that I hadn't thought of it as a hard number, or even a percentage, until she asked. It was just an intuitive balance I consistently kept an eye on and diligently maintained. I realised that I would probably pin my maximum number of sponsored posts at about three for every ten pieces of content – roughly 30% overall. But I must have got that idea from somewhere, right?

Someone else pointed out that in print media, they refer to the amount of sponsored real estate in a publication as the commercial "load". The balance in a newspaper used to hover around a load of 30% advertising to 70% content. When I worked as the music compiler at 5FM for about 18 months, shortly after I finished university, I used to build the playlist for the most lucrative commercial station owned by the state broadcaster, the SABC. This was a fun job, since you had access to the blueprint or the template of what made up every hour of every day of the week. Over the course of a week, that blueprint used to level out to a remarkably similar ratio: roughly one-third music, one-third content (features, news, traffic, sport, etc.) and one-third advertising.

For Liesl Laurie, this limit is about "three or four out of every ten posts" as well.

> I do plan around the fact that I don't want everything to be one paid or sponsored post after another. When I'm getting booked for things, I usually work out how often I generally post and how many sponsored posts the clients require, and then I space it out. Generally, I work with about four brands consistently and I keep them a few days apart, so it doesn't become spam. You don't want to post about the same thing over and over. I work about a month and a half in advance and I put it in my diary. I'll tell

clients that this week will be reserved for so-and-so and I don't know if you want your content to stand side-by-side with them ... Often, I have to plan a shoot with a photographer, a make-up artist; I often also create videos for clients and in all of this, we take on board the client's time constraints.

Nadia says that she tries to maintain a balance between sponsored content and the stuff she relies on for what she calls organic growth, because:

> I want to build an organic audience. You only do that by posting things where you're not selling a product. I do a lot of personal content and then sponsored content in between. I think you're building that organic audience when you share content that doesn't require something of your follower. People just want to sit down and not think or do anything. That's what I try and do for people.

One person who also instinctively came up with that 30% load as a guideline is Bouwer Bosch, but he cautions against the temptation to do more.

> I think if you're strapped for cash you might say yes to anything, but there's some benefit in guarding your brand and making it a bit more exclusive – both for you and the brands you partner with.

Mike Sharman says:

> I believe in an 80/20 model, which applies to a lot of things in life: 80% of the content is generated by 20% of the users. Everything in life tends to have an 80/20 model of sorts. That's a pretty fair description. I'd say two out of every ten posts is a good metric in your head. You also need to realise that you're an influencer because of your audience. You can't force-feed messages down their throats, because you'll lose them.

Ask any influencer and they'll be able to share a long list of products or service campaigns they have declined: weird beauty tools, weight-loss fads, accessories, clothing and even getaways all count among my own list of no-thank-yous. I have declined stuff or experiences I wouldn't normally spend my own money on, businesses I didn't think my followers would find useful, content I didn't think I'd be able to create with some semblance of integrity, and stories I didn't believe I'd be able to tell well. Often the deals simply don't offer enough reward to justify the effort. Every free gift or offer of a paid campaign you receive as an influencer has a *quid pro quo* attached to it and, as the English writer and influencer Bella Mackie (@mackie_bella) says, "the *quid* is often literally just not worth the *quo*".

I received a pair of vellies (veldskoene) recently – a pair I knew I'd never wear. I contacted the sender immediately and explained my position: that I was really flattered by their generosity; however, I didn't want their stock to go to waste since I knew the shoes were expensive, and out of respect for our relationship, they would be more than welcome to collect them if they felt they could extend the offer to a more receptive influencer. The pair was unopened and unworn, after all. They replied to thank me for the forthright feedback and insisted that they were happy for me to do whatever I wished with the shoes. Now it's not that I hate vellies or that these were not trendy enough (they were actually pretty cool), but I knew that I probably wouldn't wear them – a simple case of personal taste.

Follow a professional approach when it comes to your internal policy about the load you approve for your own feed. When you receive content offers, sponsorships or just a barter deal that you feel you cannot do justice to or if it is something your followers will not engage with, be mature enough to reach out and have that conversation with the marketer involved. You can offer an alternative solution or suggest another influencer you could pass it on to. Perhaps there is a product in their range with which you could interact more naturally or another story you'd be better placed to tell.

Cluttering your feed with sponsored content that your followers will resent you for is no way to build an authentic, relatable feed – or a business, for that matter. It is about your followers. Just because you need a new toothbrush and don't want to pay R150 for it doesn't mean that the followers on your "latest cars and bikes" themed feed care to see six posts on which model of electric toothbrush is currently parked next to your bathroom basin. Perhaps shelling out the R150 would be worth more to your influencer business in the long run?

Regulations: These are the rules

> Before that whole Fyre Festival incident I was a bit more ignorant than I am now [admits Liesl Laurie]. I would do what was asked of me, within reason. But since then I've read so many articles about what you should be doing as an influencer, how you should declare paid collaborations and why. I would often just call agents and brand managers I know in the industry to ask for advice. I don't have any pride when it comes to asking for guidance: when I don't know, I check things out. Having worked so hard, from where I've come from, I would never risk getting myself in trouble for a brand.

In 2019 the South African Advertising Regulatory Board (ARB) released a Social Media Code that serves to regulate the way influencers post, ensuring that consumers and influencers are all on the same page about transparency, accountability and best practice. The full code can be found on their website: http://arb.org.za/assets/appendix-k.pdf.

The code defines the three accepted hashtags you need to include if you share sponsored content "to ensure that consumers reasonably understand this to be a Paid Advertising as opposed to an Organic Social Media endorsement":

#AD
#Advertisement
#Sponsored

Even if you're not taking cash in return for sponsored content, but you have managed to strike up a barter deal where a brand gives you stock in exchange for posts, you need to disclose this as well:

> Influencers are required to disclose if they were provided (permanently or on loan) with goods or services in return for media coverage (whether this is expressly stated or not). This helps reinforce ... influencer integrity while clearly allowing the consumer to make an informed opinion of the applicable content, product or service.

The code also protects influencers by requiring brands to provide you with a written agreement.

> Marketers are required to have a written contract with any paid influencers that include the following information:
> 1. The details of the engagement/brief.
> 2. The remuneration (cash or cash equivalent), details and conditions of payment.
> 3. The obligation to publish only own content or to clearly disclose or credit the content creator, if and when the content is not self-created.
> 4. Mandatory disclosures and industry specific marketing regulations required by the marketer's industry.

Number 4 relates to gambling- or alcohol-related content, for example, which has an additional set of standard advertising requirements imposed on it.

Influencer content must also comply with the standards of the Code of Advertising Practice, which means that if you make a false claim about how good a product is, you can't protect yourself afterwards by saying, "It was just my own opinion". If your claim cannot be substantiated with facts, don't make the claim on your profile, no matter how truthful you may think it is.

If you want to check your draft post against the Code of Advertising Practice just to be sure, head over to the digital home of the Advertising Standards Authority of South Africa: asasa.org.za.

Elma Smit ✓ @Elmakapelma · 2s
- A commercial load of about 20 to 40% is best practice. Balance your clean content with the paid stuff so that you don't lose your audience along the way.
- The South African Advertising Regulatory Board has released a Social Media Code, which you can rely on for guidance and protection.

7

WHAT IF I SCREW UP?

Slacktivism and other ethical no-nos

Slacktivism is the practice of supporting a political or social cause through social media or an online petition, which on its own might seem harmless. It could even be very useful and potentially very effective, but the harm is typically done by the low levels of effort or commitment keyboard crusaders are known for. When you are considering taking up a paid-for collaboration with a brand that has some activist or other good-cause element attached to it, tread carefully. You run the risk of being accused of being a lazy slacktivist or of profiting from the distress of others.

In early 2019, the TV personality and rapper Nomuzi Mabena, professionally known as @Moozlie (on Instagram) and @Nomoozlie (Twitter), faced heavy backlash for a campaign she ran on her profiles, in partnership with motor manufacturer Volkswagen South Africa. She seemed to host a live video on Instagram one Thursday night in January, while driving. The live video was then cut off abruptly, in what seemed to be a car accident, judging by the noise and apparent breaking of glass visible before the video ended.

Her management refused to comment on reports that she had been in what appeared to be an accident for 14 hours after the incident, while her fans flooded social media with messages of concern and distress. Some on social media were already suggesting that it might have been a set-up, a stunt of sorts, within hours of the incident. She then took to Instagram with a carefully produced video, revealing that it was a stunt, but also a paid campaign:

"Take the pledge and make the change to #VWDriveDry in 2019. #Nomuzi"

What I found astounding is that she still only disclosed that she had "partnered" with VW but made no overt use of a hashtag such as #AD, #Sponsored or #Advertisement – of course, there is also Instagram's built-in disclosure function, which I often use. Four private individuals then duly took the case to the national Advertising Regulatory Board (ARB). The directorate ruled on the two main complaints: that the campaign was unduly graphic and that it didn't sufficiently disclose the fact that it was a paid campaign.

Even though it was found that this was advertising material that needed to be more clearly "labelled as such (by means of a hashtag or other appropriate identifier)", Mabena was ultimately excused because it was done in the name of a good cause. "The code is to be applied in the spirit as well as the letter … We do not consider that the purpose of clause 12 [of the regulation] can have been intended to undermine the strength of a message that is in the public interest and plays an important social responsibility role."

The regulatory challenge aside, the reaction in the court of public opinion was so vehement that she addressed the reaction with a follow-up video on Instagram three days after the event. In the update, she highlights how she had left a series of digital breadcrumbs in previous posts and in her Instagram Stories over weeks. She had apparently purposefully exhibited irresponsible behaviour relating to alcohol and driving for a while before the staged incident. The point she made in her follow-up video was that only four comments were reportedly made about "reckless driving" in the lead-up to the incident and the insights apparently showed that 300 000 people saw the campaign posts.

In other words, she felt the campaign was justified because almost no one had called out a celebrity for promoting drunken driving on social media.

Whether this campaign succeeded in promoting Volkswagen's and Moozlie's aims is beside the point now. What struck me was that the comments criticising the campaign were not aimed at the brand. Mabena's followers clearly wanted *her* – the content creator, the influencer – to exercise better judgement. Followers remarked that their trust in her was damaged, not their trust or faith in the brand.

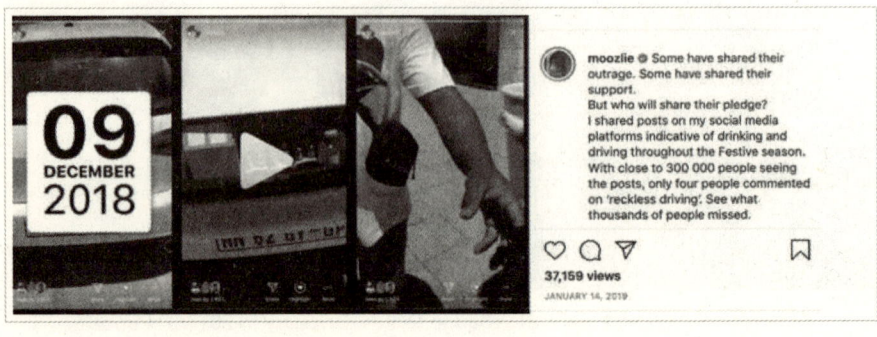

What if I screw up? | 83

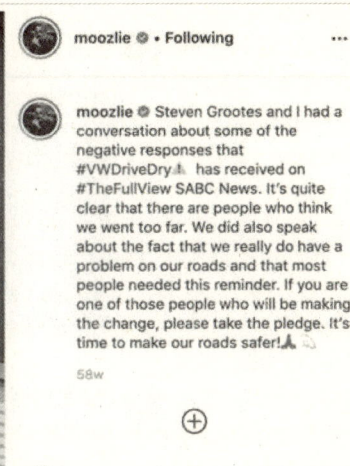
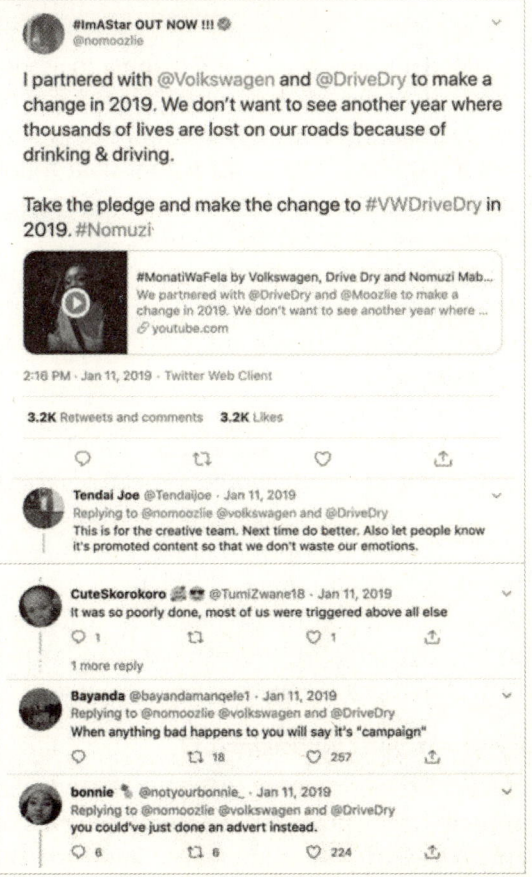

Perhaps the fact that this was a paid-for campaign is beside the point. I suspect that some of Mabena's fans would still have been angry if it had been done in partnership with a non-profit organisation as an advocacy stunt and not a paid one. The point is that your followers might not respond well if they feel that you are building better engagement statistics on content that causes them (or others) distress.

When you do start running paid-for (or even bartered) content on a profile, you cross a line into new territory: your entire profile and everything on it becomes a business and your followers will regard it as such, even if only subconsciously.

Whatever story you tell, any content you create on an influencer platform will be held accountable to a higher standard than your cousin's private citizen account. The average Joe can freely share their sentiments, opinions, thoughts, feelings and frustrations. They can prank and even outright deceive without facing many repercussions, but when you are building a brand, everything hinges on trust. Whatever you create under the banner of this brand is fair game for far more criticism and judgement and higher ethical standards than a private account that is run only as a hobby.

Where should you set your boundaries?

Let's say that you run a travel-themed influencer account and you happen to get engaged somewhere: a post sharing this detail will necessarily elicit more engagement. Win-win, you might think! But if you then also happen to go through a low moment in life, like a divorce, be prepared for a fair whack of scrutiny, judgement and even criticism around how that shows up (or doesn't) in your content.

This is not because there is an objectively right or wrong way of telling your story. You have created the perception that your followers are welcome in your personal life, so you should expect them to feel hurt when you shut that door in their face. Worse still, if you let people in, they might also criticise you for capitalising on something they find shameful. Hurt followers tend to express these sentiments in a variety of ways, many of which will not aid your healing or boost your influencer business.

Be very careful about which doors you open and the terms on which you open them. You determine the boundaries, the tone and the access you grant, but you will ultimately also bear the brunt and often this might not seem fair.

To keep your personal life personal when you're an influencer is easier said than done, because it is human to want to share your joy. Bouwer Bosch found this out the hard way when his high-profile marriage to Afrikaans actress and influencer Leandie du Randt ended in 2019.

> People have never become brands in quite this way before. We're all still figuring it out as we go, but in hindsight, I'd definitely have stronger boundaries. Going forward I'd be more careful, even though Leandie and I never purposefully tried to use our marriage on social media ... The thing with a break-up or a divorce is [that] it's shameful and when that shame is a public level of shame, it makes it much harder, but if you share the good times with your followers, you need to suffer through the bad times in full view as well. The weird thing with all of this is, of course, that people tend to announce things on social media that they could more meaningfully communicate with the person directly. Like, when people wish their kids happy birthday on social media or congratulate someone on a public platform. How many of those messages are really about the other person? I often wonder. And how much of it is actually about the person posting it?

For Liesl Laurie, the end of a high-profile relationship also changed her approach to sharing her personal life.

> I don't share the person I'm dating with social media anymore. I share my family, but I always ask them to approve every time before I share them, but I do tell that story. I love spending time with my family and I think it is part of who I am online. But my relationship isn't part of my social media presence because of the media in the past taking everything out of context when a relationship comes to an end. If media companies are going to make money off my posts and it's at the expense of my feelings, I'd rather be the one to make money off it first.

So, you don't want your unhappiness to make someone else money?

> Exactly. But it's easier said than done. Should I be comfortable and ready again – to share my relationship with the world – I will ensure that we benefit from it. I am tired of media companies using my name to sell copies of their publication, when things don't work out in my life.

Rachel Kolisi made the headlines for calling out women who sent her husband inappropriate messages on social media in 2018 and 2019.

> And I stand by every social media move or decision I have made. My Instagram profile is the truest reflection of me and if you follow me, you have a good idea of who I am. I was real at the beginning; there has never been a strategy, and I am proud of what I have put out there.

From a brand-strategist point of view, Mike Sharman advises two potential routes:

> You're either a "fuck that" personality or you're not. Rachel Kolisi is a good example of someone who stuck to her position. But you have to weather the storm. Yes, it'll be noisy but it will eventually be done.
>
> Or, you have to man up [sic] and say, "I fucked up, sorry guys". Someone screen-grabbed it already. Once it is out there, it's out there. Don't delete it – that makes it look like you're covering it up. If you wouldn't want to see a post on the front page of a newspaper, then why are you putting it out? Some people are controversial for controversy's sake. The true test is always, even on WhatsApp, are you willing for this to go on the most public platform you can imagine? If not, don't type it. Anywhere.

Katinka Oosthuizen can speak about experiencing deception and forgiving on a public platform like *Survivor*, which is known for high stakes, back-stabbing and tribe politics.

> Own it. Admit to it. Ask for forgiveness. Don't try to explain that it isn't how you meant it, though. I would almost forgive someone anything if they just own who they are and what they do. If you honestly don't feel like you did anything wrong, stand by that as well, but then prepare for the fact that you might lose people in the process. That's why you need to be yourself.

Nashville-based lifestyle blogger and influencer Tiffany Mitchell (@tifforelie) found this out the hard way when she shared photographs of her motorcycle accident on Instagram. Eventually she deleted the photos, but not before screenshots were posted to buzzfeed.com and she had become a cautionary tale. One photo featured a bottle of SmartWater positioned prominently in the foreground, and many critics questioned whether this accident was staged for the sake of undisclosed sponsorship.

Would this post have blown up in quite the same way if she had simply omitted the photo with the water bottle? Perhaps, but what if the bad taste was actually left by the fact that she seemed to hit the sympathy engagement button? Did she do this, at least in part, to boost the metrics of a professionally run influencer account? Cynical, yes. But, either way, she was so overwhelmed by the negative responses to the post that she deleted it and followed it up with a long and detailed explanation, denying the accusations of commercialisation and product placement:

> When I work with brands, they're ones I personally enjoy, and I disclose every single sponsorship. Accusing someone of faking or exploiting an accident is extremely serious – because what if you're wrong? It really happened to me, and I was scared … When I found out my professional photographer friend, who[m] I'd been shooting with earlier, took photos of everything, I was completely moved. I shared this on my feed with humans who have been on a journey with me for years because I knew they would understand what it meant to me and I understood what it would mean to them. I'm sad that something so true and personal has been treated this way, and disappointed in BuzzFeed for spinning it there. I would just ask that if you're here because of this, consider that the post I made was something real that happened in my life, that resonated deeply with me and those who have chosen to follow me. That's what it was intended for.

Mitchell also instructed an attorney to write to BuzzFeed to demand that the report with the screen grabs of the post be taken down, but the website stood by its reporting on the incident and it is still there. That's why there is no point in deleting a post that blew up for the wrong reasons, unless the content is defamatory or downright criminal (for example, if it injures the dignity of an individual or a group of people). Apologise, by all means, but nothing you create on the Internet truly ever goes away.

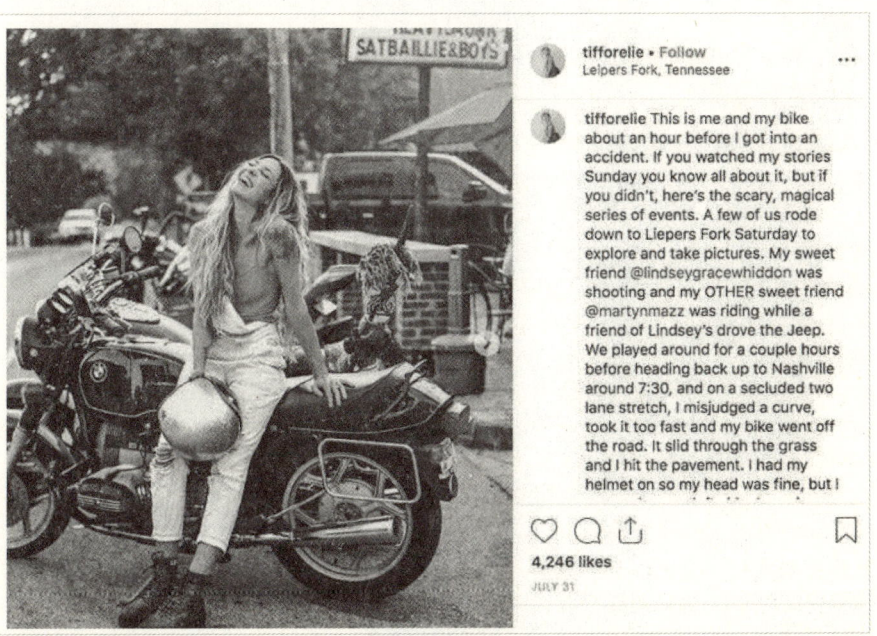

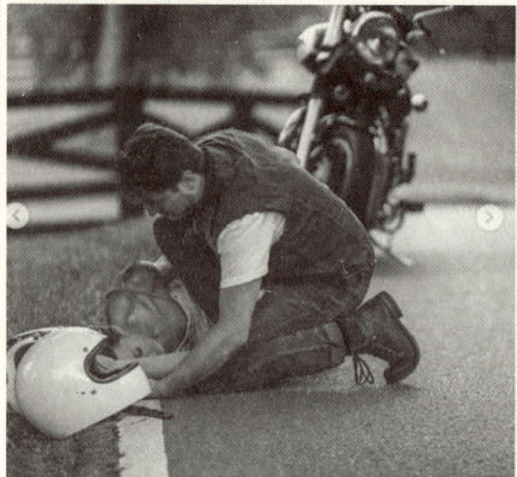

helmet on so my head was fine, but I scraped up my left side. I was in absolute shock laying on the side of the road. Scroll through the pics to see how much of it Lindsey captured! Unreal. I was scared, and relieved, and so thankful I could move all my joints and that I never lost consciousness. My friends were at my side immediately, an ambulance arrived within 10 minutes (CRAZY fast), and sweet strangers loaded my bike onto their trailer to haul it back to my house for me. I was in a haze the entire time. Losing someone in a moto accident makes something like this that much sharper. It brought back a lot of memories from 3 years ago when

4,246 likes
JULY 31

sharper. It brought back a lot of memories from 3 years ago when Kappel died and I in utter devastation had to decide how to move through it all, and whether it was worth it to ever get on a bike again.

We all drove back to my house with a green light from the angels that cleaned me up in the ambulance, sat with our new friends listening to music and laughing until I fell asleep. I felt so comforted. The next day I could barely move I was so sore, and I texted my mom (who raised me on the back of HER motorcycle) to tell

4,246 likes
JULY 31

Add a comment...   Post

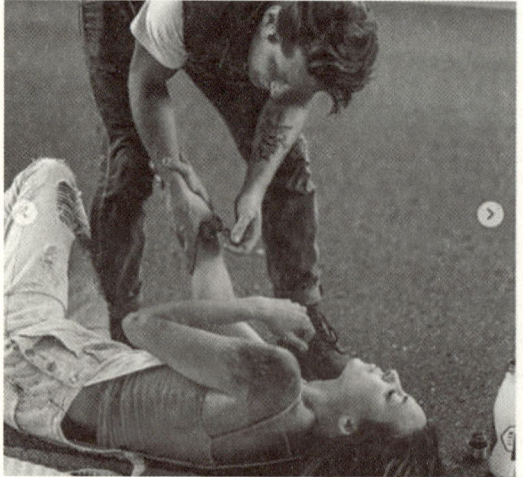

music and laughing until I fell asleep. I felt so comforted. The next day I could barely move I was so sore, and I texted my mom (who raised me on the back of HER motorcycle) to tell her what happened. I was so nervous but her response was magic. She asked if I would ever ride again, I said yes. She told me she was so glad I was ok, and that she's had her share of close calls too. Then she said it all, "Life is a gift and an adventure." YESSS. 😘❤️🥀

I'm resting and healing up my arm, and @ianwhitetattoos may need to touch up my wildflowers, but I am feeling so much better and guys, I am beyond grateful.

4,246 likes
JULY 31

You need to take a beat to decide if it is more important to you, in that moment, to be right or to win. In many instances you won't be right *and* win. Proving that you were right to post what you did will not necessarily result in a long-term win for your business – as much as you might feel vindicated.

Often, it requires great maturity and some patience to allow yourself to take the momentary hit that being "wrong" inflicts on your ego and dignity, in favour of winning the long game. When you have made a mistake, particularly when working with a brand, apologise if you were wrong and do what you can to rectify matters, if possible. Don't delete, don't pretend it didn't happen, don't deny that it did, and definitely do not fight with your haters – unless trolling haters is part of your brand position, as in the case of James Blunt's Twitter account.

Risky business

Brands are notoriously risk-averse. Holding extremely outspoken religious, political, moral or ethical opinions will certainly polarise not only your followers, but also the brands who are attracted and those who are repelled by your feed. This seems like a no-brainer, right? Yet, there is another side to this. To some followers, your strong opinions and tendency to court controversy could read as authentic – you are someone who stands up for what you believe and someone who displays integrity.

Bouwer is open about the fact that his reconciliation-above-all approach has cost him money; it is something he is refreshingly open about.

> When we were busy with preproduction on our movie *Thys & Trix* in 2017, one of our major sponsors pulled R100 000 in funding from the project because of my outspokenness on the topic of reconciliation. And that was fair game – people can do with their money as they please. But our country is bigger than what happens in the Afrikaans market and that small anxiety corner in our culture.
>
> The weird thing is that I then got a great gap with the Blue Bulls [rugby team] in 2019 – the same rugby union that used to be known for Steve Hofmeyr singing their theme song. I did a whole comedy-driven content

campaign for them during the Currie Cup. They said that their team consists of both black and white people: "We are not bothered by your political views at all." I actually think my divorce had a greater impact on my career and my opportunities than my political views, particularly over the last year. Liefde Wen [Bouwer's apparel line with a charitable element] definitely took shots, because people didn't seem to want to support the purpose of loving your neighbour if it is driven by someone whom they don't associate with romantic love any more. If my political opinions have some sort of impact on the work and opportunities I get, that's also okay, though. This country is bigger than one culture. I'm a South African, a *Suid-Afrikaner* as much as I'm an *Afrikaner*.

Joe Scott, the American influencer marketing strategist, says his experience in running global campaigns for Fortune 500 companies has shown that:

This is most definitely something that varies from client to client. Some brands are trying to boost positive sentiment on social media around their brand. So, it is important that the influencers they work with are not as critical, and more about keeping things light. However, influencers, especially in the tech space, have done remarkably well because of their unbiased, unpaid opinions regarding particular products, such as Marques Brownlee or Jonathan Morrison. Marques gets pretty much whatever he wants as a gift for review these days, but it is known by all of these companies that he will give a fair review with pros and cons.

Joe has a balanced guideline ready for influencers:

Feel free to be critical, but be fair. Don't go on a rant, completely dismantling a brand out of principle. Do your best to be objective with your critique, what you think would improve it, and [what] the redeeming qualities of a product are (if any). If you're an influencer that will review or critique a product (unless it's purely humour, in which case the brands you attract will be different anyway), play nice, be honest but fair, and refrain from letting personal vendettas shape the review. This leaves you open for partnerships with brands in the future, without alienating them or your audience should they make an offer you can't refuse.

You could even take the opportunity to turn this into future work by leveraging your unique voice. For example, if Reebok contacts you and says they will give you a year's worth of apparel for free, but you uploaded a four-minute video rant named "Why Reebok is Absolute Trash", your followers will think you're fake. However, if you posted a video called "Reebok: The Good, the Bad, the Ugly", a nine-minute video about what you love, what you dislike, and constructive feedback or solutions, then you now evolve from noise to someone that can influence a brand's decision-making moving forward.

This is not only valuable to the brand, but also helps your audience to understand you better.

As a listener, watcher, follower, I learn more about you and your unique style based on your feedback and solutions. From there, I can decide if your opinion is worth listening to. And if I can give one last bit of advice, it would be for influencers to always create content that presents the audience with takeaways about who they are as individuals, and a reason to keep listening. You can't do that if you're not expressing anything but criticism and complaints.

If you hold down a job alongside your influencer pursuits, always remember that what you post in your personal capacity – even on an influencer account you run in your spare time – can serve as grounds for your employer to dismiss you. Everything you do, whether in real life or on social media, reflects not only on you but also on your employer. Including a disclaimer, like the age-old "all views are my own (and not those of my employer)", in your profile is pointless. If you would not say it from a stage at an industry conference or in a job interview, do not say it online.

Even if you are reposting something that someone else posted on social media – whether you denounce them for it or not – spreading their offensive material also makes you guilty of spreading offensive material, regardless of whether you created it in the first place. Report them, do not retweet, share or screen grab the content – particularly if you think it might lead to criminal action.

In summary, things you should generally avoid or be careful about include:

- Profiting from someone's distress or a power imbalance, whether this be due to their poverty, their injury or their pain (emotional or physical). You might have the best intentions when showcasing a great cause on your feed, but consider the fact that this might not necessarily be construed as altruism, because your feed is essentially a business. Even when a post is not sponsored, you will be held to a very high ethical standard.
- Ask your friends and family members for their permission before you include them in posts on your influencer account. Allow people to opt out of your pursuit.
- Think twice about sharing photos of your children; they might not enjoy the attention a social media following affords them, if not now, then possibly later on in life. You can be a mummy blogger without having instantly recognisable kids.
- Think twice before you share images of anyone else's children, unless you have the parents' explicit consent. If someone is too young to hold down a part-time job, they are probably too young to consent to being featured on your social media stream without their parents' explicit permission.

- You can be taken to court for defamation or *crimen injuria* for what you post or share online. This is the unlawful and intentional undermining of someone's status, good name or reputation. You can generally only defend yourself against defamation if you can prove that the statement is true and in the public interest. Ensure that you can back up what you are posting or sharing and never provoke hate based on gender, ethnicity, religion, race or sexual preference.
- Constantly monitor the comments on your posts. As the host of those comments, you are as liable as those who leave them. If you know you are posting something that might attract controversial comments or if you know you will not be able to actively monitor the reaction to a post (for example, you're boarding a flight), close the comments section below the post.

The risk-and-reward balancing act that is the life of an opinionated influencer is a fine line to tread. Remember that a highly controversial approach is no worse than the other great sin: being boring!

Marketers will take great care to supply you with sample captions, set up actual photo shoots, and arrange completely produced videos and experiences that will delight and impress not only you but also your followers. However, marketers will not see the point in spending their budget on content that might as well have been created by a robot or any one of 15 other influencers in the same space. Have fun, be yourself and remember that what's true for your content is also true for the brands you partner with: you are all there to serve the followers.

Elma Smit @Elmakapelma · 2s

- Influencers are held to very high ethical standards: never risk being seen to profit (literally or simply by growing your audience) from the distress of others.
- When you are getting blowback, it's important to remember that hitting delete won't help. Rather choose whether you want to be right or whether you want to win.
- When you are being critical, be fair. When you are taking risks, be clear why. Be yourself, but always remember that the aim of creating content is to serve your followers.

INFLUENCERS WORTH FOLLOWING

Mike Sharman's favourites

Maps Maponyane (@mmaponyane) nails it. He really knows how to straddle the model lifestyle. He sells a triple threat: model, entrepreneur, success story. The quality of his content is always slick. It's consistently aspirational; he's not just posing in first class – he is flying first class. He doesn't dwell on negativity. He's always positive, consistently.

Trevor Noah (@trevornoah) is an incredible example because his product became part of this multiverse: the show, social, his book, he's a great face for ad campaigns. He's someone we can be very proud of. He stuck to his focus and it expanded into so many touch points.

Dale Steyn (@dalesteyn) has been great because he balances his personal life. We know he loves fishing and surfing. He's just himself, just a *gewone oke* from Phalaborwa. He built this massive Indian following from the IPL [Indian Premier League]. He's part of a special generation who cashed in on these massive, lucrative contracts. Dale is more human than AB de Villiers, for example. AB keeps his audience at arm's length. When you compare the two, Dale has always been more likeable than AB. That's why public opinion turned on AB when those rumours about the Cricket World Cup leaked in 2019 – whether they were true or not. We were much more understanding of taking Dale to the World Cup, even though he wasn't fully fit. Dale has always been about loving his dogs, loving his fishing, and he loves to surf. AB is only really loved for his performance on the pitch and then chastised for his musical exploits.

Bryan Habana (@bryanhabana_) understands brands and how to negotiate on a global level. He built a fan base across so many markets. He never allows himself to be embroiled in scandals and he conducts himself the same way on social media as he does in real life.

Liesl Laurie's favourites

Nadia Jaftha (@nadiajaftha) because I like that she seems to be herself. She's consistently that kind of girl, with a bit of glam, but she seems real and like a normal human being, which is what I like.

DJ Zinhle (@djzinhle) is a big brand and an influencer at the same time. Very real, very unapologetic about the choices she makes, which is what I like about her.

Mbali Nkosi (@theembalinkosi) is just exactly who she is. She isn't trying to be everything to everyone, and she really owns her field.

Rachel Kolisi's favourite

Emily Skye (@emilyskyefit) because she is always so real and I love that she's really busy changing lives too.

Nadia Jaftha's favourites

I try to be my own person as much as I can, to have my own unique style. That's very important. The people I look up to all do that.

Like Lasizwe (@lasizwe). He's turned his platform, his brand into a series; he has a lot of big deals; there's a lot of business that goes into it.

Internationally, I love **Emma Chamberlain** (@emmachamberlain). She's raw and real. She says it as it is. She has her own merchandise line.

David Dobrik (@daviddobrik) also has a few businesses and he is a great YouTuber.

Mostly people who have taken their social media influence to build some sort of business to sustain themselves in the long run. We're not going to be able to do this forever.

I've always loved **Liza Koshy** (@lizakoshy). She started off as a YouTuber and then acted in movies. She now has a talk show and a game show. She does red-carpet correspondent work … She's taken her brand to the next level and I really want to do that kind of thing.

Bouwer Bosch's favourites

Ryan Reynolds (@vancityreynolds) because I love how he markets brands. It's 100% him. Even when I know he doesn't drink Pepsi, I still enjoy his posts about it.

Schalk Bezuidenhout (@schalkiebez) is also good in that same way. Bennie [Fourie – Bouwer's business partner] and I often tease him about it, because his business sense is so honed. He even charged me R800 when I wanted to borrow his car for a shoot. Which is the right thing to do, but I just never would have thought of doing it, if the roles were reversed. He's so switched on.

Katinka die Kat (@katinkadiekat) hustles, man. She's constantly shooting. She's constantly sharing content that I love.

Coconut Kelz (@coconut_kelz) is cool because she makes fun of everyone. She takes white people out all the time and we love her for it; she gets away with stuff I never thought anyone would be able to do. She's so young and cool; she has a really great, unique voice. Companies are literally stealing her ideas – that's when you know you are hot property!

Wian Magic's favourites on TikTok

Loren Gray started on Musical.ly and still does really well.

Zach King makes six-second videos edited to look like he is doing magic tricks, which I love. He calls his videos "digital sleight of hand". He has been doing this stuff for years – on YouTube as well.

Charli D'Amelio is a super-interesting case because she had only one video on TikTok when she blew up and people started following her. She's like the Kim Kardashian of TikTok, where no one quite knows why she's famous, but she is. She's by far the most famous person on TikTok.

Katinka die Kat's favourites

Nadia Jaftha (@nadiajaftha). I enjoy following her. She's also very young and manages a great balance between glamour and relatability.

Chiara Ferragni (@chiaraferragni) shares a lot of her personal ups and downs.

Bouwer Bosch (@bouwerbosch). I love Bouwer's videos and the variety of stuff he's busy with: music, production work, his clothing business.

Maps Maponyane's favourites

People who have fun with it get it right. I'm sure most of the people you interview will mention **Nadia Jaftha** a few times, so I won't mention her as well.

Trevor Stuurman (@trevor_stuurman). He's always true. No matter how left-field it might be, it is consistently reflective of him as a person.

Lulama Wolf (@lulamawolf). If she speaks about stuff, it's pretty believable. She never veers away from being Lulama. She makes you want to be in her world. She's never overdoing anything.

Karabo Poppy (@karabo_poppy) because she leaves her mark on every brand she works with. You just know when it's Karabo, you know that it's real. You're always rooting for her. She just blows your mind with how she goes from strength to strength with her illustrative style. Her engagement is incredibly high in proportion to her following and her voice is consistent.

RECOMMENDED READING

Carnegie, Dale. (2010). *How to Win Friends and Influence People*. New York: Simon & Schuster.

Chartrand, Tanya L. & Bargh, John A. (1999). The chameleon effect: The perception-behavior link and social interaction. *Journal of Personality and Social Psychology* 76(6): 893–910.

Cialdini, Robert B. (1993) [1984]. *Influence: The Psychology of Persuasion*. New York: Quill.

Covey, Stephen R. (1989). *The 7 Habits of Highly Effective People: Powerful Lessons in Personal Change*. New York: Free Press.

Higgins, Matt. (2019). Fyre Festival aftermath: New rules for influencers? *University of Cincinnati Law Review*, March.

Sharman, Mike. (2017). *The Best Dick: A Candid Account of Building a $1m Business*. Johannesburg: Tracey McDonald Publishers.

FAMILY TRAITS

Sarah Jones

Cinderhill Publishing

Copyright © 2025 Sarah Jones

All rights reserved

This is a work of fiction. Names, characters, organizations, places, events and incidents are either products of the author's imagination or used fictitiously. Any resemblance to actual persons, living or dead, or actual events is purely coincidental.

No part of this book may be reproduced, or stored in a retrieval system, or transmitted in any form or by any means, electronic, mechanical, photocopying, recording, or otherwise, without express written permission of the publisher.

ISBN-13: 978-1-0682405-2-2
eISBN: 978-1-0682405-3-9

Cover design by: Get Covers

Photography by: Ian Jones

Proofread by: Mary Hoyle

For Ian

Thank you for the support, encouragement and patience!

CONTENTS

Title Page
Copyright
Dedication

1	1
2	4
3	11
4	19
5	26
6	33
7	36
8	47
9	52
10	55
11	61
12	65
13	68
14	73
15	78
16	82
17	87
18	94

19	99
20	110
21	115
22	121
23	123
24	126
25	130
26	137
27	140
28	145
29	151
30	157
31	164
32	169
33	172
34	177
35	179
36	183
37	190
38	193
39	197
40	206
41	214
42	221
43	227
44	229
45	235
46	240

47	244
48	248
49	255
50	259
51	266
52	270
53	277
54	280
55	282
56	286
57	290
58	296
59	300
60	302
61	304
62	309
63	313
64	315
65	318
66	323
67	327
68	332
69	334
70	338
71	339
72	343
73	346
74	350

75	352
76	354
77	356
Acknowledgement	363
About The Author	365
Books By This Author	367

1

Caro

Seventeen years earlier: Saturday, 25 August

Caroline Webster - Caro to her friends, or more accurately, Caro to everyone who knew the Webster family - had dreamed the afternoon away as she waited in the dunes. She had started off pretending she was dozing, fully expecting at any minute to be teased awake when he arrived. But the dunes remained steadfastly silent, no tell-tale shifting in the sand to signal that he was here at last. The only soft whisperings came from the marram grass, rather than soft lips murmuring against her ear. She had then shifted her position to lounge, in what she hoped looked a carefree pose, and attempted to read her book. But the words danced on the page and her mind was unable to get lost in this fictional world. Her thoughts only had space for him.

She decided she would head back to the Beach Hut. She wanted the loo, and didn't dare squat in the sand just in case he chose that moment to appear. Her face flushed at the thought of it. This new love seemed so precious but so fragile, and she was already understanding that the slightest wrong move would snatch this away from her.

She debated heading down to the harbour and nipping into the amusement arcade to use the toilets there, but dismissed that idea when she remembered she was avoiding Nat. Caro was cross with Nat, who had somehow switched her focus away from hanging off her friend's every word to embarrassing herself stalking the journalists - that strange pack who seemed to do nothing other than sit and wait for something to happen. She decided her best option was the Beach Hut. Kate had gone home now, thankfully, so she wouldn't be forced to make her a cup of tea or be badgered to go out and put up some more posters appealing for help to find her daughter. The girl everyone seemed to be obsessed with - the missing Samantha Chappell.

The Beach Hut was really the only place she could go, and she needed to have a quiet word with Jez anyway. He had been avoiding her since he had confronted them in the dunes, and she thought she could maybe explain and try and find out what he knew. At the same time, she could check that he wasn't planning to say anything to their mum and dad. She knew he couldn't have shared her secret yet, because if he had she had no doubt her mum would have been in hysterics, and she would have received the 'I'm very disappointed in both of you' from her dad. That's if he could spare the time to tear himself away from comforting the constantly sobbing Kate Chappell.

Caro found it incomprehensible that everyone was getting into such a state about a seventeen-year-old girl - or was she eighteen now? Caro had a feeling there had been one particular day when Kate had cried more than normal. It was something to do with Sam not being there to open the pile of lame presents that Kate had wrapped in the hope that Sam would be miraculously waiting for her at home. In the meantime, Sam was probably living it up in London, or somewhere else that was more exciting than her home town, and she was oblivious to the fuss she had caused. Caro couldn't wait to hear what her dad would have to say to Sam when she eventually turned up, tail between her legs and begging for forgiveness.

The need for the toilet had become more urgent and

Caro ran up the steps into the Beach Hut and sank onto the loo seat with a sigh of relief. Wandering back to the kitchen, she called out for her brother, hoping to tempt him from his room and put him in a good mood with the offer of ice cream. She called his name again, shrugging as she received no reply. No doubt he was still sulking or had his headphones clamped to his ears, lost in his own world. She wandered back to the fridge to cut off a chunk of cheese before feeling that the air in the house seemed just off. The hairs stood up on her arms and she suddenly felt afraid. At first, she wondered if there was someone in the house that shouldn't be. Had they been burgled? But then she realised it was the absolute silence of the house. The knowledge that she was completely alone. Alone when she shouldn't be, because Jez was in the house too.

Even with hindsight, she never believed she had an inkling of what she would see as she climbed the stairs to her parent's room, having first checked the bedrooms downstairs. She had opened the door and barely registered what she was seeing before she turned and fled. Her mind was still trying to make sense of what her eyes had seen, and Caro only remembers seeing his feet - noticing that he was wearing odd socks. On autopilot, she scooped up his friendship bracelet from the floor, before she turned and fled back through the dunes, screaming for her dad.

2

Caro

Present day: Friday, 21 June

Now that the funeral's done, it feels like no one really knows how life will start up again. Everyone is convinced they should be doing something, but as no one really knows what that something is, they are instead frozen at this point in time; everyone waiting for the next person to make the first move. Caro thinks in some way it is the same as when she's at work and addressing the room of students and she doesn't know what to do with her hands. She's OK once she gets in the swing of things - when her passion for her subject entices her mind away from the pettiness of the mundane, as she reels in those bright young minds to share her enthusiasm. But this is different to all that. There's no chance of forgetting the one huge thought that consumes every part of her brain, so much so that she's amazed she can remember to continue to breathe. It's a repetitive anthem in her mind, thumping to a dull beat that reminds her of the muffled music she hears escaping in a constant loop from her son's room.

'Dad's dead. Dad's dead.'

Caro feels she knows this bereavement process far too well. This time it's gentler, a little more standard, if there is such a thing as a standard death. It's the natural order of things that at some point you will lose your parents. At seventy-one, he wasn't a young man. But he wasn't an old man either. It shouldn't have been his time and Caro thinks it's the unfairness of it all that is causing so much of her distress. It was her mum who was supposed to go first. That death was the next chapter they should have reached, after living with the agony of losing her piece by piece; they had prepared for that change, almost welcomed it, in fact.

Just over a month since it happened and the shock is receding now. Thirty-four days when Caro found she could cope by dealing with all the death admin. The endless tasks that demand your attention when all you want to do is sink into a cocoon of silence and hope that maybe you will soon wake up to find it was all a horrible dream. A cliché, but somehow life after the death of a loved one seems to be full of clichés as if you no longer have the energy to be original. Thirty-four days since she had popped in to see Dad after work and found him sat outside in the garden, the local paper open before him, but his eyes no longer registering the stories that he would tell his shell of a wife when he made his daily visit. Thirty-four days of not stopping to think about it, instead dealing with things in her normal efficient way. Until suddenly it's all done, and Caro is left in the silence of the house. Nineteen days since the funeral and no more jobs left to do which will allow her to escape this new reality that she is forced to live in.

Caro registers the thump of the music has been replaced by a louder thump on the stairs as her son, Alex, makes his way towards her. She winces as she hears him skip the last three steps and knows he will have trailed his hand down the wall, adding to the grimy line that is embedded within the paintwork already. It doesn't matter how many times Caro mentions this - Alex doesn't see the issue with what he is doing, it doesn't matter to him, so he carries on, despite his mum's increasingly snappy reminders. Caro feels the familiar surge of irritation at his thoughtlessness but bites her tongue as she remembers this is his first experience of the death of a loved one. Still older than she had been when she felt the sucker punch of grief the first time, and the dawning realisation that this really was it.

'What's for tea, Mum? I'm starving!'

Caro reflects it would have been nice if he had given her a hug first or maybe asked her how she was. But then she tries to make allowances - he is only just sixteen, his recent birthday an afterthought to his grandfather's funeral. Still often a child, despite the fact he is living in a young man's body.

'I haven't even thought. Maybe we can nip out for a Chinese once Grace gets home.'

Grace, five years old and perfectly named. Calm, sweet, affectionate and the soothing oil poured over the troubled waters of Caro and Alex's current state of play.

'No time for that. I'm meeting Connor in half an hour. I'll probably stay over at his tonight.' He reaches into her bag and comfortably helps himself to a tenner from her purse. So comfortably that Caro absently wonders how many times he has done this when she isn't around.

'I'll pick up something in town.'

Caro knows she should stop him, so she makes a half-hearted effort with the reminder, 'Don't forget Dad's coming round in the morning.'

Alex pauses and Caro senses the neediness in him that craves parental approval. For a moment he looks eleven years old again, desperate for his dad to drag his eyes away from his new baby sister and see the painting he had drawn of them both playing football at the park. Then the little boy with the ready smile is gone, in his place the closed off sixteen-year-old with a body he isn't sure what to do with.

'He won't be bothered if I'm not here. He's only coming to see Grace anyway.'

Caro thinks about protesting that this isn't true, but that would make fools of them both. Swallowing the words, she beckons him over for a reluctant kiss and he is gone with a slam of the door, the whole house letting out a sigh of relief.

Caro watches him from the window, on his phone already, barely acknowledging his honorary aunt, Nat, pulling into the drive, ready to drop Grace off home. Caro waves at her friend and moves to the kitchen to put the kettle on. No need to open the door - Nat is as comfortable here as she is in her own home. The door slams closed after the new arrivals, but the noise holds a different quality to that which had rocked the silent house as Alex made his exit. Yet again Caro thinks she really needs to speak to him. It was her dad who would normally chat with Alex, the two of them close as they both tried to fill the empty space they felt in their lives. Alex sought the father figure his own dad was unable to provide, and Chris attempted to recapture the essence of the son he had lost. She will have to cut Alex some slack. He is feeling this loss deeply. Something else to think about, just not tonight. Maybe tomorrow, or next week.

Caro registers the sound of lighter footsteps thumping up the stairs and muffled giggles a fraction before she feels herself enveloped in warm arms. Arms that have been there for her since they were five years old. The same age as their own daughters are now. Sinking back into the familiar comfort, she allows herself to relax the tension from her shoulders for a few minutes as the two of them stand, breathing in sync, no need for words. Nat moves her hand to stroke Caro's hair, and it is this gesture that finally releases the tears, a gesture so reminiscent of the way she wishes her mother could care for her. Nat quietly reaches back for a tissue and allows Caro the space to simply feel.

Caro feels that she could have stayed like that forever, but the respite is ended abruptly when a second warm body flings herself between the two women, and Grace is there, assaulting her ears with requests.

'What's for tea? Can I have a bag of crisps to keep me going? Can I put on the TV and can you show me how to turn the Disney channel on? Can Annie stay the night?'

Nat gives Caro's shoulder a last squeeze and moves towards the fridge to pour them both a glass of wine.

'I missed you too, Grace!' Caro ruffles her daughter's hair and gives her a hug, removing any sting from the casual greeting.

'And in answer to your questions, no idea, no, yes, another time.'

Grace pulls a sad face but happily races back to join Annie.

'She's so easy-going. I wish Alex was a little more like her. I'm not enjoying these teenage years at all.'

'Ah, go easy on him, you know how much he adored your dad.' Nat passes her a cold glass whilst taking a large gulp from her own.

That desperate pull of the wine is something that tugs Caro out of her own world. Nat never has a drink when she is driving, and she is playing with the stacking ring she always wears on the middle finger of her right hand. They have always joked that this is Nat's equivalent of worry beads, her comfort, her solution of what to do with your hands when there is a difficult situation to be faced. Her mind races through the list of possibilities. Grace and Annie have fallen out, maybe? No, that can't be right as Grace had asked if her best friend could sleep over. Her eyes flicker to her friend's left hand, but she sees Nat's rings are firmly in place on her third finger. So clearly this isn't another bump in the road of her friend's rather rocky marriage. Nat is an expert at swinging wildly from madly in love to hating her husband, James, with a deep intensity that Caro marvels they ever recover from. Still, it seems these dramatic highs and lows are the living breath of their marriage, so who is she to judge? Clearly she's no expert given that Mark, her own husband, is no longer living in the family home.

Ah, that would be it. James had been meeting Mark last night for their weekly game of squash. Well, they meet at the sports centre but it always seemed the aim was to complete the game as quickly as possible so they could adjourn to the pub. Many a time, Mark had stumbled home after midnight, and she had been forced to take him to pick up his car the next morning. Looks like Mark has shared a secret with James and now Nat is the reluctant bearer of whatever news it is that Mark is too much of a coward to tell her to her face.

Caro takes a gulp of her own wine and moves to the fridge to collect the bottle, sliding a new bottle in the chiller in case it's a two-bottle conversation.

'Spit it out then, Nat. I've got the emergency supplies ready. Clearly you have something to tell me that I don't want to hear.'

Nat almost chokes on her last mouthful and smiles at her friend as she reaches forwards to top up her glass.

'We know each other so well, don't we? Might have known I couldn't keep up the pretence for long, but this must be a record!'

'It was the drinking when you have the car. I know how you feel about that.'

Nat's mouth moves to a smile that doesn't quite meet her eyes. 'I'm assuming I'm OK to abandon my car here tonight? James will collect me on his way home.'

Caro nods and decides to make it easy for her dear friend. 'Spit it out, then! What's the deal? Let me guess - Mark has met someone else and isn't sure how to tell me. Selfish prick! Just bloody great timing, as usual!'

Caro sits back with a satisfied smile, waiting for confirmation, but Nat simply looks confused.

'I've no idea what you're on about. Look, I've gone round and round in my head as to how I'm going to tell you this, so I think the best thing is if I just show you.'

Nat reaches for the phone that is never far from her hand and summons it to life before passing it over to her friend.

Caro isn't sure whether it's the wine that has blurred her vision, or the remains of the earlier tears, but it takes her a while to focus on what she is seeing. It takes a few seconds longer for her to understand what she is reading, but when she does, she feels her world spin wildly for the second time since she had discovered her father's body.

3

Caro

Present day: Friday, 21 June

Churcher's School – Old Pupils Group

Posted by: Anonymous. Thursday 20th June 11.53pm

Well, well, well! At last, the Wicked Witch – or should I say Wizard – is dead. Not sure many of us will be mourning the recent death of our old headmaster, the infamous Mr Christopher Webster. Died at seventy-one years old, which was about twenty years too late!

I wonder now if finally someone will have the guts to come out and tell the truth about what happened to Samantha Chappel. No doubt that dirty old paedo was something to do with it. If there's any justice, he will rot in hell.

25 likes

4 comments

JodieM: No idea he had died. It was never proven he had anything to do with Sam, so maybe a bit harsh.

Pam-Hopkins: Bit cowardly to post this after the old man died. But I reckon you're right. He was definitely involved in Sam's disappearance. I reckon he ran a cult!

David Hughes: He was a right 'cult' alright. Oooh, and then all that business with his son. No one ever got to the bottom of that.

Nat Morton: I am reporting this to admin and asking them to remove this vile post. Mr Webster was a fantastic headmaster, and his wife and daughter do not need to see shit like this. Shame on you.

Caro is roused from the screen by her friend pushing the cold glass of wine towards her, but at this stage she is desperate for her head to clear.

'What the hell is this?'

Nat shakes her head.

'I have been going round in circles over whether to tell you or not. It's been taken down now, but I took a screenshot and, in the end, I decided it was something you should know.'

Nat leans back, takes a long drink of her wine, and then blurts, 'Look, it's not the first time something has been posted on this page. I haven't said anything as I know you chose not to join the group, and I didn't see any reason to upset you with all this crap. But the posts are getting more frequent, and with your dad no longer here, this will only gain momentum.'

Caro can only blink at her friend, her brain struggling to follow the whole train of thought.

'I know it was always difficult for you as the daughter of the headmaster, but I think maybe you need to put a post on the page to let people know about your dad and show your full support for him. Just something to shut this thing down once and for all.'

Caro is aware that Nat is still speaking but is struggling to make sense of the words. She finds herself back in the mind of the girl she used to be, fighting to balance her friendships with family; the two inextricably linked given the dominating presence of her father in her school life. She had known that her fellow pupils didn't really like her – mistaking some of her insecurity for being standoffish - and she knew everyone had always thought she was a bit too pleased with herself. She had always felt like an outsider – ironic when her family were at the very centre of the school. How she had envied Nat and the way she was welcomed into most groups. Still, Nat had been a steadfast supporter of her friend - always there for her - and Caro knew she had relied heavily on Nat throughout her childhood, and now in adulthood too.

'Caro, are you OK?' She is brought back to the present by the glass of water shoved into her hand. Caro blindly obeys the instruction to, 'Drink this.'

Blinking rapidly until the room rights itself once more, Caro wipes away the sheen of moisture that has gathered on her forehead. Talking a swig from her glass, she splutters, and the sound breaks the tension in the room. She is able to raise a smile, probably more of a grimace, to reassure her friend.

Nat reaches to take her phone, but Caro shakes her head and snatches it back towards her.

'I need to read this again.'

On the second reading, Caro is able to understand what the words are saying, even if they don't make sense.

'Who would write such a truly horrible thing? And all these other people agreeing with them. It's vile, when he's not even here to defend himself.'

Nat nods in agreement, gently reaching to retrieve her phone.

'It's been taken down now. I think there were more

people than me that reported it, especially after the crack about your brother. I've fretted about telling you, wondered whether to leave it be.'

Caro shakes her head in bewilderment, wishing that her friend had taken that route. She really doesn't need this extra worry right now. She is aware Nat is still talking and focuses back on her friend's words.

'I'm concerned that they will post again, and I could miss it. I think, if you joined the group, maybe posted a tribute to your dad - it would make people thinking twice about sending such nasty stuff hidden behind the safe barrier of their keyboards.'

Caro nods, chewing her lip. 'I'll think about it.'

Nat laughs. 'That's a better result than I was expecting.'

Draining the last of her wine, Nat calls for Annie as again she moves behind her old friend and wraps her arms around her.

'Anything else I can get you before I head off?'

Caro shakes her head, allowing herself to relax back against the comfort of her friend's embrace. This is the thing she misses the most since Mark moved out. The comfort of being near someone. Of being looked after, rather than being the provider.

'We're all fine. Call you tomorrow?'

Nat nods then reluctantly moves away as they hear an impatient blare of a horn from outside. The friends exchange grins and then Nat and Annie have left the house, and Caro is alone once more. The trouble with being on your own, reflects Caro rather bitterly, is that you have plenty of time to dwell on your own shortcomings. In the months before Mark finally conceded defeat and left the house to move to the flat in town - for their temporary split that looks to becoming more permanent by the day - Caro has been able to focus on everything that he did wrong. The way he never put the used wet towels on the towel rail to dry - preferring to leave them in a heap on the floor. The endless scrolling of the YouTube videos - following people in places he would never visit and thinking she would be interested in an update of their latest antics. The snapping at Alex - his shaky tolerance of their son, highlighting still further his obvious adoration of Grace. Ah, yes! This is the big one. The root of it all. Caro is honest enough with herself to recognise that it's this disparity in his treatment of the two children that drove her to focus on his minor transgressions.

The last blazing row had started off with the normal bickering about who should have remembered it was blue bin day. Typically, they had both forgotten and the bin was overflowing, highlighting they were both breaking their rule of no alcohol during the week. Caro still isn't sure how they had moved on to Grace and Alex, but with a suddenness that should have given her whiplash, she was berating Mark for the way he was so different with the two children; picking open the scab that had been itching at her for months.

Normally Mark would let her continue to rant, choosing either a martyred silence, or more recently, leaving the room so she would be silently mouthing at the empty space before her. This time though he had worked through most of a bottle of wine and chose the words that he knew would hurt her the most.

'What do you expect? He's not my son. If I'm so useless, why don't you see if his dad would do a better job? Oh, I forgot, you can't because he fucked off and left you. Looks like he had the right idea.'

She knows he spat those words out at her in the heat of the moment. She knows he regretted them the minute they were out in the air between them. And if she's honest, she probably wishes more than him that she could snatch those words from the silence in which they had hung and press a magic button to pause and delete. But the words were out there, and Mark was out of the door a month later, Caro unable to ignore any longer the obvious truth that her husband still harboured deep resentment over her past.

Mark and Caro had met thirteen years ago when Caro was just twenty. She was working in the local coffee shop to help fund her way through art school. The two of them couldn't have been more different. Caro thought of herself as a free spirit, her hair colour changing with every month of the year, dreaming of escaping to a Greek island and painting on the beach as the sun set. The colours of her bright clothes clashed, as she should have clashed with the accountant, nearly ten years her senior, who ordered the same cappuccino every day and wore his different coloured ties on a strict rotation. Mark was sensible order and predictability. Caro thought she was chaos and a risk taker. But in Mark she found the ballast she needed to explore, knowing there was always a safe space to return home to.

They started chatting as she served him, until eventually she could stand the waiting no longer and asked him out for a drink. Mark was besotted. Caro represented his one shot at taking a risk. He hadn't realised how much he would need to bend until a couple of months into their relationship, when she explained there was someone very important that she wanted to introduce him to. That someone very important turned out to be her three-year-old son, Alex. Mark recognised immediately that if he wanted Caro, he would need to accept Alex.

They were married a month later and they were happy. Grace was born eight years after that, Caro having finished her degree and now lecturing modern art at the local Sixth Form college. Not quite painting sunsets on the beach, but a decent compromise. They seemed the perfect family. The couple that shouldn't really be together but had defied the odds and were flourishing. But Grace's arrival had coincided with Alex making the move to Churcher's. Caro's father had an account set aside to pay for his only grandson's school fees, and Grace would follow him, as was the 'family tradition'. Caro wonders if she should have been firm, said that they were going to sort their own thing. She had been so unhappy at that school and the fact that she and Jez had attended Churcher's, thanks to the discounted school fees courtesy of the fact her father was the headmaster, hardly made it a family tradition. Mark was adamant he didn't want Alex to go to that school, that he should be allowed to move on to the local high school with the rest of his friends. But her father was a forceful character, and she preferred to upset Mark rather than her father.

Alex loved the school. Unlike his mother, he adored the pomp and tradition of it all. He fell in with a group of confident boys from wealthy families. Caro felt they were forever chasing their tails to provide the funds for all the extras needed that weren't covered by the standard school fees. Alex developed what Mark called, 'a perpetual sneer', barely giving his parents the time of day. He had always known that Mark wasn't his biological father, and now to Mark's irritation, which Caro was aware masked a deep hurt, he started calling Mark by his Christian name. Caro felt he was hoping that his 'real' father was a more exciting man. In fact, she had once overheard him telling one of his friends that his father travelled the world managing the careers of Formula One racing drivers.

Caro tackled this in her normal way. In fact, in the way that her family had always tackled difficult situations. She ignored it and hoped that it would miraculously come right eventually. Mark seethed quietly, drank more wine and threw all his love, that he felt Alex had rejected, at Grace. Alex felt this deeply, even though he had been the one to start to withdraw from their father-son relationship. And so, the gulf between them deepened and Caro fell in the middle, unable to make things right, and making both unhappy with her refusal to accept there was a problem.

Alex began spending more time with his grandfather, who was happy to teach him to play golf and take him to the local shooting range. Whilst Caro was happy that Alex had a strong role model to turn to, she did worry that her father was using Alex as a replacement for his lost son. She couldn't help but feel uneasy, suspecting her father lavished all his hopes onto her son, using him to achieve all that he had hoped for Jez. And then her father had died. And Alex found himself adrift, unable to find consolation in his mother, and unwilling to accept the olive branch offered by Mark.

If Alex hears that someone has launched a campaign against his adored grandfather, he will be distraught. With a sigh, Caro recognises it's time to take her head out of the sand and tackle the present, and the past.

4

Nat

Present day: Friday, 21 June

Slamming the door behind them, Nat heads straight to the kitchen and pours two large glasses of wine. Taking a huge slurp off the top of them both, she refills the glasses before carrying them out to the garden, where James is pulling the chairs into the best spot to enjoy the evening sunshine.

They had been quiet on the car ride home, unwilling to talk in front of Annie, who has the knack that most five-year-olds have of being unable to sit quietly, unless she senses that something is being discussed that isn't for her ears. Instead, they had turned the music up and sat in companionable silence, as their daughter kept up a constant stream of chat about her and Grace's plans for the summer.

Now Nat feels she can at last take a breath as she sinks into the cushions, which still feel slightly damp from last night's downpour. They did mean to take them in each evening, but that intention normally fell by the wayside within the first few days of sunshine, and after the first relaxing glass of wine that inevitably led to just a couple more. No doubt they will neglect to bring the furniture in as the season changes and then will both grumble and swear to do better as they go to buy yet another set of cushions when the sun makes its reappearance next year. The two of them sit in the comfortable silence that comes when you have been with someone for a long time - and still like them.

'So, how did it go? Did she have a complete hissy fit at the suggestion that her beloved father may not be destined for sainthood?'

Nat can't help but giggle. James and Caro have never been the best of friends, but things have deteriorated since Mark left. James clearly feels he knows where his loyalties lie.

'Stop it, you know this is a difficult time.'

James knows better than to say anything, so he gives her hand a reassuring squeeze and limits himself to the comment, 'I bet you're glad you've told her, though. I know how it's been preying on your mind - all the hours you've spent glued to that bloody laptop trying to get it sorted out. You're a good friend Nat, too good really, considering the way she dropped you the minute you left school and moved away. Honestly, I think if she hadn't needed a friend at antenatal class, she would probably cut you dead in the street. It's lucky for her we came back here when we did. And that you are a much nicer person than she is.'

Nat knows there's no point arguing with James about this. He is fixed in his view of her friend and there is an element of truth behind his black and white assessment of their history.

'Hush now, you know how people drift apart when life takes them in different directions. I got to escape this town, see the bright lights of London, meet the man of my dreams.' At this Nat leans forwards and kisses James quickly on the lips - a promise of the night to come.

Pacified, James smiles at his wife and restricts himself to the mild, 'Well, you're just too nice, Nat. Not sure Caro deserves a friend like you.'

'Anyway, she took it much better than I expected. I hope I did the right thing telling her.'

'These things are always a flash in the pan. People will soon have something new to gossip and bitch about. Speaking of which, we have made great progress this week on the plans for the quarry.'

Nat is happy for James to change the subject. She knows that the redevelopment of the quarry is so important to him. Moving back here from London meant he didn't have the same opportunities in property development as he had when he worked on the redevelopment of the London docklands area. She had worried he would find the pace of life here too slow, would feel he was floundering in stagnant water. But he has embraced living in the small community, seeming happy taking on small projects. A bit of consultancy occasionally taking him back to London, allowing him to experience the best of both worlds. He is settled with the new pace of life. By contrast, Nat has struggled more. Moving from an aspiring journalistic career with one of the nationals, to covering weddings and fetes in the local newspaper has made her feel, at times, that she is suffocating.

She is envious that James has this opportunity to combine living here with his ambition. The development of the quarry, which has long been abandoned, to a site with luxury houses and a centre providing an area for various water sports, is a vision that he had shared with her one night after Annie had been born. They had laid on the grass in the back garden, enjoying the dark skies and the peace of their surroundings - congratulating themselves that things had worked out as well as they had. She hadn't been too bothered at the time, figuring it was the ramblings of a little too much wine. She had smiled, snuggled into him, and drifted half to sleep as he painted his castles in the sky. He had taken this as her agreement and before she knew it, James was photographed in the local paper beaming next to a giant hoarding which had been erected by the quarry entrance, proudly telling the world that the site had been acquired by

J.M. Developments.

Now, alongside the old signs, warning of the danger of steep drops and deep water, is a larger sign hunkered down to shelter from the sea breeze. It shows the artist's impression of the vision for the finished development. The picture shows it fitting tastefully in the landscape, with the stone of the houses mirroring the hue of the surrounding cliffs. The picture even includes seagulls proudly surveying the luxury residences, as if to proclaim that even nature's wildlife has welcomed this new addition to their habitat.

Unfortunately, you can't see the whole piece, as in front of it has been erected a sign from the 'RANDS' – the residents against new development. Their sign is not as eye-catching and there's too many words explaining a lot of reasons why the redevelopment should not go ahead. No one bothers to read this, and instead prefer to smirk that, predictably, someone has changed RANDS to RANDYS, with the appropriate symbols to make it clear what they mean.

Nat is dragged from her musings about the tension the plans for the quarry have caused in the town, aware that James is still talking about his dreams. His excitement is contagious, and she's happy to share in the anticipated glory.

'This will be the making of us, Nat. If it all goes to plan, I can see this site winning awards, which will really put my firm on the map. And the money will be just what we need. You can stop working for that boring rag if you want and be a lady of leisure. Spend your days doing downward dog with Caro and joining the club of ladies who lunch.'

Nat smiles, but he had lost her at giving up her job. Is she ready to stop chasing that dream? When she had started her career as an investigative journalist, she had imagined the story that was going to launch her onto the world stage. She had bided her time, put in the hours, smiled and congratulated others when they won the prize, all the time believing that it would be her turn one day. When they had decided to move back home, she had put the dream on hold, but it hasn't been snuffed out just yet. She still lives with the hope that there is still that story out there waiting to be added to her byline. Then she would be the one in demand, could write the pieces she chooses. Time to stop seeing writing about the failure of the council, yet again, to empty the dog poo bins as the culmination of her journalistic ambition.

The happy meandering of her thoughts is interrupted by a plaintive, 'Mum, I'm really, really hungry! What's for tea?'

'Pizza, though you'll end up looking like a pizza soon. James, will you do the honours?'

They had recently bought a pizza oven for the garden, envisaging turning their outside space into a replica of a Tuscan pizzeria. They had attempted homemade pizzas the first couple of times but recently had got lazy and normally ended up shoving in a frozen pizza from the supermarket. Nat reflects that she had more chance of making a name for herself reporting on a murder at the local WI, than ever mistaking their back garden for an Italian escape.

James groans. 'Tell you what, let's order a Domino's.' Annie greets this suggestion with enthusiastic appreciation and Nat has to admit it's preferable to sit drinking wine as they wait for the food to appear, than to struggle with the buyer's remorse over the outside oven.

Forty-five minutes later, James goes to answer the door, and Nat has some time to reflect on her visit to Caro. She has felt sick to her stomach ever since she had seen the words on the Facebook page; a harsh indictment of her best friend's father in black and white. Nat is aware of the adoration Caro feels for her father. Indeed, ever since the death of Jez, Caro has placed her father on a pedestal and devoted her life to making up for the fact that he had lost his favoured child. Before that, Caro had rebelled against the endless rules she was subjected to, her situation at home being merely an extension of the school day where there was no doubt that Mr Webster ruled the place with an iron grip.

Nat often wonders how different things would have been if they had not lost Jez the way they had. The two girls had always planned to take a year to travel the world. They had spent hours closeted in Nat's bedroom, planning and giggling with heady excitement all the adventures they had no doubt they would embrace. And then Jez died. Caro withdrew from everyone and despite Nat's efforts to keep close to her friend, she was cast adrift. In fact, Caro hadn't even shared with her best friend that she was pregnant. Nat had found that news out as she had stood waiting for the bus and spotted Caro across the street. She was walking with her mum, and Nat had shouted out a greeting. As Caro turned, Nat felt her own stomach turn a somersault as she noted the pregnant belly of her best friend. Nat never got the chance to ask Caro if she was OK. Mrs Webster had raised a hand in acknowledgment of the girl who had spent so many hours at their house, had been referred to as her third child, and then the two of them walked away.

Nat hadn't heard a word from her friend until she bumped into her at the doctor's eleven years later, and after a hesitation slightly too long to be comfortable, they had both smiled at their matching pregnant stomachs and the friendship was resumed. Nat never asked Caro anything about what had happened all those years ago. It was as if that period had ceased to exist, and their friendship resumed with an unspoken pact that they would only discuss the intervening years at a very superficial level.

This somehow made the effort of telling her friend about the post on the old school group even harder. It meant crossing a boundary that had been firmly established. An understanding that enables the two of them to proudly proclaim they are old school friends; simply omitting they stopped being friends during one of the most traumatic times of both of their lives.

5

Caro

Present day: Friday, 21 June

Caro and Grace are also eating pizza, but theirs is a frozen pizza which Caro had located at the back of the iced-up freezer compartment - found in a desperate rummage when she could no longer ignore Grace's request to be fed. As Caro slurps a freshly poured glass of wine (from a newly opened bottle) she reflects, not for the first time, at the differences between her children.

Alex had always been a demanding child, taking a long time to settle and never seeming to be content with anything for longer than five minutes. As a baby, if he was awake he was crying, and his sleep was fitful and confined to short bursts. It was exhausting and far removed from the bubble of baby bliss she had imagined. This didn't mean that Caro didn't adore him. She did without question, pouring all the love she had saved for the memory of her brother into this new person in her life who depended on her for his every need. Caro found that she liked this - being the centre of someone's world. The unquestioning adoration, even if sometimes she yearned for some time to herself. Some time to be free.

At first, Mark was content with the family unit of the three of them. When he first brought up the idea of them having a baby of their own, Caro had been reluctant. She didn't think she could face those early months again. The tiredness, the unrelenting schedule of the day and the isolation. But Mark had persuaded her it would be different this time because there would be two of them to share the load, until eventually Caro relented. She secretly hoped that maybe she would not fall pregnant so easily, but she could at least say she had tried, but sadly it was simply not meant to be.

As it happened, they got pregnant within a couple of months of trying, and from then on the months passed in a whirlwind. Every day Mark would come home with some new item that he had read was a 'must have' for every baby. In contrast to her pregnancy with Alex, this was a real time for celebration and Caro found that she enjoyed feeling so cherished and cared for. From the moment Grace was born, both her parents were besotted. She couldn't have been an easier baby, slotting seamlessly into the family life. It was such a welcome contrast to Alex, who continued to demand so much of his mother's attention.

Caro used to think about the difference between her children on the nights when she couldn't sleep. She would fret that Alex was too much like Jez, who her mother had always referred to as a sensitive soul. Her father was less gentle in his assessment that the boy 'just needed to toughen up.' Caro often wondered how often her father was tortured by those words once Jez had died. She would question whether Grace was so easy because she was the product of a loving union, whereas Alex came from a much murkier beginning. Grace was like her father. Mark was easy-going - happy to go with the flow whilst being fiercely loyal to those he loved. Alex's father – Caro didn't really know him well enough to see if his son had inherited any character traits from him.

Roused from her wanderings in the past by the beeping of the oven announcing the pizza was ready, Caro curses as she realises that once again, she has produced food that is a little too well done. Whilst she doesn't miss the arguments and the tension that had dominated their last year together, Caro does miss Mark's skill in the kitchen. And by the look on her daughter's face when Caro carries through the cremated pizza slices, Grace is wishing she was eating at her dad's. Still, she smiles at her mum and gamely tackles a crispy slice as she declares, 'Yum, I'm starving!'

'Good job, you'll need to be to eat this,' laughs Caro, deciding that maybe she will stick to a liquid dinner.

The two of them sit in comfortable silence, watching old episodes of 'Strictly', which Grace is obsessed with since starting ballet lessons and deciding she will be a professional dancer once she leaves school. Caro laughs as her daughter twirls in front of the television, but the easy camaraderie of the evening is shattered by the slamming of the door and the familiar heavy footsteps on the stairs as Alex returns home, not bothering to greet his mother or his sister.

Caro stands, tense and ready to confront her son, but Grace tugs at her hand.

'Don't be cross at him, Mum. He's ever so upset about Grandad. I could hear him crying in bed last night.'

Caro sinks back down on the sofa, drawing Grace in for a cuddle. Kissing her on the head, she once again reflects that Grace is wise beyond her years. In fact, she is probably the most grown up of all of them in the house. Caro heeds her five-year-old daughter's advice and gives Alex the space he seems to need.

Once Grace is in bed Caro makes her way downstairs and, pouring the final dregs of the wine into the glass, wanders down to the bench at the bottom of the garden, making a small detour to the shed to retrieve her emergency hidden stash of cigarettes. Tapping one out of the packet, she ruefully notices there are only five left of the pack of twenty. She feels a small frisson of panic that she may have to buy a new packet soon; she'd had this secret packet for so long, sneakily bought at a time you could still easily buy the menthol variety. Absently, she considers maybe swapping to a vape, then shakes herself and promises (not for the first time) that she will stop skulking round like a rebellious teenager and kick this habit once and for all. But not tonight. Definitely not tonight.

Settling herself on the bench, she takes a moment to enjoy the reassuring sounds around her. The garden is, to her mind, a place of peace. She can hear the rhythmic hum of traffic on the main road into town, and the occasional shout of laughter as people walk along the path on their way to wherever they have to be on a Friday night. Caro likes the companionship of this noise. Ever since they lost Jez, she can't bear to be sat in silence, needing the steady reassurance of background chatter to keep her safe.

Looking at her phone, she considers simply sending Mark a text. That would be the easy way to confirm tomorrow's arrangements; but sat alone on the bench where the two of them had spent many happy hours chattering nonsense, she feels the pull to hear his voice. Before she can change her mind, she presses the name that always used to be number one on her recent calls log. At first, she thinks he won't answer. *Well*, she thinks resentfully, *he does have the freedom now to do as he pleases on a Friday night.* So, she is already halfway ready for a fight when finally, the connection is made.

'Caro, everything OK?'

For a missed beat that lasts slightly too long, Caro is unable to speak, the sound of his voice taking her breath as she fights the longing to beg him to come home. To work with her to build the life they had promised themselves would be theirs for the taking. Instead, she hears her voice coming out sharp and cold.

'Oh, everything's just fine. You know, my father has died and our son, or should I say *my* son as you like to remind me, looks to be determined to make every bad choice available to him.'

There is a moment of silence and Caro can hear Mark sigh. She can imagine he is rolling his eyes, and this only adds fuel to the simmering rage she feels deep in the pit of her stomach.

'Are you drunk, Caro? Look, I don't want to fight anymore, and certainly not on the phone on a Friday night. I'll see you tomorrow when I collect Grace and Alex.'

'I doubt Alex will be coming. You've successfully made him feel worthless to you. I hope you're happy now!'

Caro knows she is being unreasonable - trying to provoke Mark to snap. But she wants the chance to scream at someone. Anyone.

'We'll discuss this tomorrow. For now, I'm busy. Goodnight, Caro.'

And she is left mouthing into silence. Her finger hovers over the redial button before sense prevails and she settles back on the bench, enjoying but hating the last few drags of the cigarette. As she feels the familiar buzz of the nicotine, her mind wanders to the screenshot Nat had shown her. Aware that trying to provoke the fight with Mark is her defence against thinking about this, she decides maybe it's time to face this particular demon.

Before she can change her mind, she opens the Facebook app and quickly navigates to the Churcher's page. It's easy to find, already in her search history: the siren of the past that beckons her whenever she has drunk too much. The desire to pick at the scabbed-over wounds of those school days some nights becomes overwhelming. But she has never taken the final step to 'request to join', preferring instead to consign herself to the sidelines - watching on and imagining what her fellow old pupils may be discussing. Rather like the reality of her schooldays where she had always had the sense of being at the edge of the friendship groups that were being established. Realising that whilst everyone knew who Caro Webster was, not many people really wanted to get to know Caro Webster.

Before she can change her mind, she clicks on the button to grant her access to the world of her past. Oh God, there are questions from the admin to answer. *Ridiculous!* It's a school reunion page - highly unlikely to be the target of a huge number of people who stumble upon it by accident.

Still, needs must, so she enters the requested information:

Name: Caroline Fraser (Webster)
Years attended: 2002 - 2009
Day or Boarder: Day
Headteacher: Christopher Webster

Hesitating, and hit by the sudden dread that pressing this button is going to send her spiralling wildly down a road she doesn't want to follow, Caro presses the 'submit' button and waits.

And nothing happens. A simple message:

Thank you. Admin is reviewing your application to join the group.

Caro isn't sure what she expected to happen. She supposes she anticipated that by now she would be scrolling through the posts of the group and recognising names. Maybe reading a few posts that fondly remembered her father's time steering the school. Whatever she had thought, she hadn't expected that after all these years loitering, flirting with the idea of opening this particular Pandora's box, that she would simply be left hanging - being judged if she was worthy to enter the hallowed portals of the Facebook group. This is all a bit too close to how she saw her time at school, always waiting to be accepted.

With a snort, she stumbles up the path towards the house, suddenly overcome with tiredness. Locking the door, she guzzles down a large glass of water, knowing that this is too little too late to stave off the inevitable hangover. Peeping in on Grace, she smiles as she sees her daughter spreadeagled across the bed, as relaxed in sleep as she is in life.

She hesitates outside Alex's door. If he is still awake, he will be furious that she is checking on him. But the fears of the past - and the last time a teenage boy hadn't been checked on - propel her forward. Alex is asleep, the paraphernalia of his gaming kit scattered around him, the covers scrunched in a ball as he makes small twitches in his sleep. Just like his sister's peaceful sleep reflects her contented day, his fretful rest mimics the nervous energy of his waking hours.

'Love you, Alex,' she whispers to the darkness, before making her way to her own lonely bed, where she prepares for the torture of her own restless night - counting the hours before she can feel the relief of the daylight.

6

Gus

Present day: Friday, 21 June

Gus pours himself another whisky, ruefully tipping the bottle only to confirm what his fuzzy brain is already telling him - that there is only a small glass left. This will be the last bottle he buys; he can't be trusted. That first glass is such a welcome relief from the inevitable shit storm of the day, but after that it becomes a mechanical treadmill of self-destruction. Inevitably he will wake cold and stiff in the early hours, realising he has fallen asleep on the sofa yet again and promising himself this will be the last time.

Glumly, he looks out across the land which stretches out until it hits the horizon, beyond which Gus knows is the churning sea, bashing against the rocks where he had spent so many days as a young boy, scrambling across the slippery seaweed in search of sea creatures to add to his plastic red bucket. Back then, as a seven-year-old boy, he loved this place. It was his home, the only place he wanted to be. He can't help but wonder why it has changed so much for him and how everything has gone so wrong that he is here again, stuck in the back end of nowhere, the days taking on the familiarity which he used to love, and which now serve to remind him that he is a failure.

He supposes the turning point was when he started at Churcher's. He had always been aware that he would be moving to the school once it was his turn to move to 'big' school. It was no secret, just as it shouldn't have been a shock that he was going to be there as a weekly boarder. Even though the family only lived five miles from the centre of town, it was the Redfearn tradition that the boys in the family boarded at Churcher's. That was the way it had always been, and things were going to be no different for Gus.

Gus had hated it. Eleven years of running wild along the coastline, an only child, he had learnt to love being by himself. And suddenly he was flung into being forced to live as part of a group. Whilst the boarding part of the school was small - the majority of the school being day pupils - for a boy used to the comforting silence of the sand dunes, the babble which surrounded him constantly (even the three other boys in the shared dorm either snored or spoke in their sleep) seemed to be utterly unbearable.

Every weekend home resulted in tears when it was time to return, clinging to his mother and begging her not to send him back, until his father threatened he wouldn't be able to come home at all during the term if he was going to create such a drama. It was Mr Webster and his wife who had saved him. Recognising that Gus was struggling to adapt, they singled him out for little tasks that gave him some time alone and room to start to adjust to his new life. He was responsible for running the grocery order, delivered to the school, over to the Headmaster's Cottage, where Mrs Webster would always take the time to ask him how he was and slip him a sweet treat to soothe him into the day. And gradually Gus adapted. He was funny and clever and soon found the best way to survive was to make friends. It was easier to cope with the long evenings confined to inside - instead of roaming the land by the pounding sea - if you could have a laugh with your fellow prisoners. And as he got to know his housemates, he saw that they didn't see it as a forced confinement. Instead, they seemed happy to be living at the school with the free time to roam the town.

By the time he was getting ready to move to Sixth Form, without even noticing the transition, Gus found he was starting to strain against the confines of small-town living. He felt that maybe there was something more for him away from this place. When Mr Webster had encouraged him to apply for Cambridge, he really did feel like he had the world at his feet; and once he had left to go to university, he rarely returned, other than the obligatory guilt-driven trip to visit his ageing parents. Instead of revelling in the wide-open space of the farm and the wildness of the sea, he found the breeze ripped through his cashmere jumpers, and the whole house always felt damp. He had never wanted to return. Never thought he would have to. When his parents died, he intended to sell the farm and then he would never have to see the place again, and that suited him just fine.

So how the hell had he found himself back here, rattling round this estate that ran itself, and stuck to remembering his school days as some of the best days of his life? The only excitement coming his way was getting his knickers in a twist railing against the redevelopment of the old quarry. Feeling very sorry for himself and very much alone, Gus drains the last of the bottle into his glass and hopes oblivion will come sooner rather than later.

7

Caro

Present day: Saturday 22 June

Inevitably, Caro wakes at three am before the welcome safety of the light, and, groaning, reaches for the glass of water beside her bed, cursing as she mistimes her reach and sends the water drenching the items on her bedside table. Muttering obscenities, she grabs a towel from the ensuite to mop up the worst of the damage, refills the cup and swallows down two paracetamols. She reflects bitterly that this is likely to be as useful as the sandcastle walls she would build as a child at the Beach Hut. Convinced each time this action would stave off the inevitable progress of the sea, it seems likely that, at best, the little white tablets will give her a couple more hours respite before the hangover returns in full force. When will she learn?

Sinking back into the pillows that feel hot and lumpy, she tosses and turns for a few more minutes, before giving in to the inevitable and reaching for her phone. Praying it has survived its brush with drowning, she is relieved to see it spring to life and, after a moment, reluctantly recognise her ravaged face and open to the Facebook app. Her heart is pounding in her ears, and she isn't sure if this is the effect of the wine or the nervous anticipation. Whatever the cause, it is a waste, as a quick check shows that her request to join the group is still pending. *What the hell!*

Caro furiously thumps the pillows, taking out her

frustration at the way everything is going, and decides there will be no more sleep for her. She debates getting up and making a start on trying to restore some order to the house. She frets she will be so tired all day now if she doesn't get a bit more sleep, and this worry sends her mind to a place where sleep will never claim her. She lays there for what seems like hours, throwing the covers off as her body boils in its attempt to remove the alcohol from her system, only for five minutes later to be huddling under the covers as she shivers in a damp sheen of sweat. *Never again*, she promises herself – which is not the first time she has made such a promise, and is unlikely to be the last.

Finally, as the birds start to sing to herald the start of a fresh new day, she drifts off to a restless sleep, and she would have slept the morning away were she not rudely woken by the slamming of the door, followed by the gentle voice of Grace asking what time her dad is coming to collect her. Opening eyes that feel gritty, she blinks, recognising that the room is out of focus, so at least she had remembered to remove her contact lenses. Rubbing her eyes, she beckons Grace towards her, pulling her in for a cuddle.

'Oh yuck!' Grace wriggles away. 'You're all sticky and smell funny.'

Caro feels the all too familiar flush of shame. Really, she needs to stop all this and get things back on an even keel. Today will be the day to do that.

'You're right. I'll jump in the shower and brush my teeth, and then how about a bacon sandwich for breakfast before Dad arrives? I bet even Alex will rouse himself once he smells that bacon cooking.'

'Alex has gone. He said he was going over to Connor's and they are spending the day in town. He said you knew all about this.'

'Did he?' Caro smiles reassuringly at her daughter. 'Ah

yes, silly me; would forget my own head if it wasn't screwed on.'

Grace laughs but concern still lingers in her eyes.

'You're not going all forgetful like Grandma, are you? Oh, please say you're not.'

Caro feels a surge of guilt. Whilst they had tried their best to shield both the children as her mother slid into the grip of early onset dementia, both Grace and Alex had picked up far more than she had considered possible. She thought they had explained it to them, had reassured them; but it appears that for Grace, at least, her grandma's illness is a real-life monster lurking under the bed.

'No! Of course not!' Caro bites back the admonishment to her daughter not to be silly. Too many times, when she was young, her parents had dismissed the concerns of both her and Jez as childhood silliness, and she swore never to diminish the concerns of her own children in the same way.

'I know what happened with Grandma is very frightening, but forgetting the odd thing is something that happens to everyone. Just like when you forget your plimsolls for P.E. It doesn't mean we are ill, just that we are normal!'

Reassured for the time being, Grace gives her mum a kiss and races back to her own room, calling back to her mum:

'That reminds me, Dad said to bring a swimsuit this weekend. If it's sunny, he's going to take me to the pool.'

Caro smiles. How she wishes her own fears could be soothed so easily.

They are finishing up breakfast when there is a tentative knock at the door.

'Dad!'

Pulling Grace in for a bear hug, Mark meets Caro's eyes over the top of her head. Caro notices he looks tired and unsure. Clearly, he is anticipating a repeat of their friction last night.

As Caro instructs her daughter, 'Go and get your bags, Grace,' Mark looks even more wary, and, sighing, raises a hand to his forehead to brush the now absent hair from his eyes. This familiar gesture tugs at Caro's heart, remembering happier times when he had the floppy fringe that her father used to complain needed a hairband, or preferably a decent cut.

'Look, I'm sorry about last night. It was a bit of a day and I'm afraid you bore the brunt of it.'

Mark relaxes slightly.

'No Alex?'

'No, sorry. He's meeting with friends.'

There was a missed beat that registers the hurt before the feigned nonchalant response.

'Can't say I blame him. I would have been the same at that age.'

Another beat of silence, then both start to speak at once. But neither get the chance to finish what they started to say as Grace reappears, itching to get started on the promised day at the pool. With a whirlwind of noise and hugs, they leave the house and Caro is once more left in the silence. *It's ironic,* she reflects, eighteen months ago she yearned for this time for herself. Now the silence is quite simply suffocating.

Putting the kettle on for yet another coffee, Caro is aware enough of her own coping strategies to accept that this is her way of delaying the visit to her mum. Jen Webster had always been a difficult figure in Caro's life. Up until Jez's death, Jen had been the life and soul of every social gathering, whether it was cheering from the sidelines at the school rugby match or glamorous in black tie for a school fundraiser. Jen was the centre of the household, pandered to by her husband and adored by her son. That closeness didn't extend to her relationship with Caro.

When Caro was small, Jen loved to dress them in matching outfits and parade her 'mini-me'. As Caro went through the awkward young teenager phase; Jen loved giving advice and glowed with the fact that all Caro's friends came to her for guidance on anything from the colour eyeshadow that would suit them to how to get the attention of the boy they had decided they liked. Being the wife of the headmaster of the school, where some of the pupils were boarders, Jen knew most of them by name. In fact, she prided herself on knowing the pupils, and of course everyone knew Mrs Webster.

When Caro turned fourteen, there was a rapid shift in their relationship. Obviously, she didn't wake up on her birthday transformed from an ugly duckling into a swan, though she thought maybe her mother would have found it easier to come to terms with things if that had been the case. Instead, she did fall head over heels in love - an unrequited love, and she doubted he was even aware of her existence. But she did start to want to look her best, and Jen was delighted that finally her daughter was looking for her help and guidance. Delighted that is, until Caro started to outshine Jen and the remarks of, 'There's no way you're old enough to have a daughter that age,' were gradually replaced by, 'Oh, your daughter is truly stunning,' and the very upsetting, 'She's just gorgeous - a much younger version of you.' This last comment was uttered by Chris Webster's secretary, who had always privately thought that Jen was a pampered diva and was delighted to seize the opportunity to take her down a peg or two.

Consequently, the relationship between mother and daughter was already showing small hairline fractures, and the death of Jez widened those tiny lines to a definite crack. Caro getting pregnant and the birth of Alex shattered the relationship into a million pieces. Whilst Chris seized onto the birth of Alex as a life raft to keep him from drowning following the death of his son, Jen would never forgive her daughter for making her a grandma.

From then on, Caro and her father's relationship had only strengthened - the two of them easily welcoming Mark into the mix. Jen would waspishly refer to them as: 'The Holy Trinity'. Whilst they focused their lives around moving forward, Jen was determined to stay forever thirty-nine. Frozen at the point where her son died; and when she was still young and the object of adoration.

Maybe it was this gulf between them that meant it took Caro and Chris some time to realise that anything was wrong with Jen. In fact, it was Mark that first tentatively suggested that Jen needed to have a chat with a doctor. Chris instantly dismissed this as nonsense; Jen had always been 'scatty' - the childlike helplessness been part of her charm. But when Jen had a couple of falls in the home and started talking to a boy in the room that only she could see, the family reluctantly conceded that maybe they needed a medical opinion. In all honesty, they expected to be told that it was a bit of anxiety and depression, maybe linked back to those terrible events years ago. Jen was complaining of feeling stiff and unsteady on her feet. Caro consulted Dr. Google and decided that her mother may have Parkinson's. After all the tests, she was ready to hear the diagnosis she already knew, so was blindsided when the consultant delivered his verdict. Lewy body dementia.

Caro would like to say she was devastated when she received the news, but the truth was, she was unable to comprehend what they were being told. They left clutching a handful of leaflets with follow up appointments and urges to join local support groups. That was three years ago and instead of bringing the family closer together, Jen's diagnosis threatened to tear them apart. Looking positively, Chris could be seen to have always been the staunch protector of his wife, taking the lead since the death of their son and striving to shield her from the world. If you were being uncharitable, you could say he was being controlling, needing to know her every move, monitoring where she went and the friends she made. This over-protectiveness only increased following Jen's diagnosis, and he was adamant that he would care for his wife at home, that he didn't need help, that this was what the vows in sickness and in health were designed for.

And now Caro blames her mum for her dad's death. The heart attack caused by the constant mental and physical strain he had been under. Chris had always joked that his wife would be the death of him, and it seems that this was finally no joking matter.

When Chris had died, alone in his garden, Jen had been in the first week of a two-week respite stay: organised by the local support team who had overridden Chris's protestations and insisted carers needed to look after themselves too. Caro was secretly hoping the arrangement would turn out to be more permanent and now tortures herself that it was this wish that had compelled a higher power to strike her father down. Because her wish has now come true, and Jen will be in full-time care until she finally joins her husband. Whilst Caro has resented her mother for many years, now she finds she hates her. And she hates herself for feeling that way.

Caro reflects on all this as she finally heads out in the car for her visit to Jen. The nursing home is a short twenty-minute drive and she finds she always arrives much quicker than she wants to. She knows the way the next few hours will go. The whole of the journey there will be dominated by a sickening dread of what is to come. Once duty is done, there will be relief for the first half of the journey home, with relief swiftly changing to guilt that she hasn't spent longer with her mother. The rest of the day will be dominated by sadness and regret that yet again she hasn't managed to be kinder - seeing instead this visit as a chore that needs to be ticked off the list.

Unconsciously, her foot eases off the accelerator as she makes the turn into the tree-lined driveway to her mother's new home: a rather grand façade that had brought a smile to Jen's face. Even as the illness robbed her of large parts of the woman she was - she remained at heart a bit of a snob, and so still appreciates living in this grand old house. Even if it had seen better days and the bells that rang were to summon harried care workers, rather than the Lady of the House instructing the butler they were ready for dinner to be served.

As is her usual habit, Caro takes a moment to sit in the car and take some deep breaths. She would like to join the small group of staff that she can see huddled by the bins - swapping stories and desperately dragging on a cigarette – but, proving she is her mother's daughter, she is too afraid of being judged. Not by the staff, but by the other visitors. Instead, she gives a vague wave in their direction, just so as not to appear unfriendly, and heads to the main door and rings the bell to be admitted.

In some ways, this is the worst part of the visit. Caro finds herself getting ever more impatient as the bell rings on and on throughout the building, as she hears sounds from the kitchen, the open window of which is close enough that many times she has wanted to scream at the faceless persons in there to 'open the fucking door!' At the same time, the delay is a welcome respite, even though it is temporary relief from the inevitable sound of the key code being punched in from the other side. This time there is a curse as the combination fails to open the door, and the whole process starts again. Still, Caro manages to have a fixed smile on her face as she is finally admitted and, almost on auto pilot, signs in to the visitors' book.

'Your mum's having a good day today. She's sat out in the garden making the most of the sunshine. Do you want to join her there?'

Caro nods, retaining the fixed smile which, spotting her reflection in the large hallway mirror, actually makes her look a bit deranged.

'That would be lovely.'

Of course, it is anything but lovely. Nothing about this is lovely. As the member of staff escorts Caro to the back garden (Caro isn't sure of her name and can't read the name badge as it is obscured by the plastic pinny), Caro can feel her pace slow. She knows it's a bad thing to wish, but if Covid could make a return, they will stop the visiting and then she will be off the hook. She can stay away, guilt-free.

'Jen, look who's come to see you, lovely. It's Caro, your daughter.'

Caro feels the fixed smile stretch even tighter as her mum looks straight at her, but through her at the same time. Each time she sees her mum here, she struggles to reconcile the figure before her with the idol, and later demon, of her formative years. Jen had never worn anything on her feet other than high heels. It didn't matter where they were going, she had to wear her heels. Here in the nursing home, she has on a sensible pair of flat Velcro-fastened sandals. The doctors suggested this might help her keep steady and lessen the ever-increasing number of falls. She had always been immaculately made up, black hair shining and Caro can see that her mum has had a recent haircut. For the first time she can remember, Caro sees the grey at the roots. She isn't sure why this causes such a pang - on some rational level she must have known that as her mother aged, her hair colour came out of a bottle. However, despite these small physical changes, her mum keeps the air that she knows she is a goddess sent to Earth to grace mortals with her presence. Caro thinks her mum has always believed that; and such was her conviction that the rest of them believe it too.

'Where's Chris? I want Chris. He promised he would go

and find Jez for me and now neither of them has come back.'

This is the other thing that strikes Caro - the sound of her mother's voice. Her mum had always had what you might class as a girly voice - breathy, with almost the hint of a little girl lisp. Now, her voice is weaker and quite simply whiny. Caro looks helplessly at the carer, knowing that there is no point telling her mum, yet again, that her husband and son are both dead. What is the point of inflicting this pain over and over - to see her mum's great distress as she struggles to process the news - only for her forget it all before the hour is up? Kinder to play along with her, even though Caro sometimes feels that she wants to scream the truth.

Taking a deep breath, Caro launches into the script that they play out on most of their visits. 'Dad and Jez are at the Beach Hut. I think they are getting it ready for the summer so it's all nice for when you have your friends round for drinks. They should be back tomorrow.'

Catching the nurse's eye, Caro nods to show that she is fine and, pointing to the buzzer which is there to summon help should she need it, Caro and her mum are suddenly alone in the garden. Rather ominously, the sun chooses that moment to disappear behind a cloud, and it seems that even the birdsong is paused as Caro desperately wracks her brains for something to talk about. She is about to launch into her normal patter of asking what was for lunch, chatting about the entertainment that she knows had been on the previous day, when Jen suddenly reaches forwards and grabs her daughter's hand. Caro gives a gasp, shocked at the strength in her mum's wasted fingers.

'I don't want them going to the Beach Hut. I told Chris to sell that place. It's too dangerous to keep.'

Caro is frozen, then decides to carry on talking about the piano player, dismissing the outburst as the hallucinations of her mum's embattled mind. She yelps as her mum squeezes her fingers harder. Looking straight at Caro, it seems that momentarily Jen's eyes clear.

'You need to go there and get rid of the stuff, Caro. Throw everything away, like your father promised he would. I need you to do this one thing for me.'

'Mum please, you're frightening me. What is it you need me to sort out?'

But Jen has disappeared again, her hands once more plucking at the hem of her blouse and looking blankly as she asks, 'Will Chris be here soon to pick me up?'

Caro presses the buzzer, and as soon as the nurse is in sight, she flees the garden, vowing to never visit again.

8

Nat

Present day: Monday, 24 June

Nat feels that she is constantly on a treadmill, where everyone else knows the trick to controlling the speed, or could even manage to get off, but somehow they haven't let her in on the secret. How can it be Monday morning again already? She feels like she spends the whole week longing to get to the temporary relief of Friday night, and then she time-hops straight to the start of the treadmill again, coming out of the weekend feeling more stressed and tired than before it started. Pushing the dark glasses up into her hair to act as what she hopes will look like a stylish hairband, she strides through the doors of the Roxcliffe Gazette and then curses as she realises that once again, she has forgotten her security lanyard.

She roots with hope more than expectation in the depths of her bag, and can feel the eyes of Tim, officiously manning the front desk, noting the discarded sweet wrappers and loose change that she tips out on the side. But still no lanyard. *Fuck*! She is going to have to ask him for a temporary sign in again.

'Hi Tim, good weekend?'

There is a dismissive grunt in response as Tim passes over the iPad for her to sign in as a guest, both of them familiar with this particular routine.

'Going for a full five days forgetting the pass, are we?'

Nat jumps at the hand on her shoulder and grins up at Ben, her boss. 'You know me. I can always be relied upon to be unreliable.' They both laugh, ignoring the disapproving glare of Tim, who is making it very clear that this is no laughing matter. Thankfully, the lift arrives and carries them away from the burn of his gaze.

'Bloody Monday already,' grumbles Ben, echoing her thoughts of minutes earlier. Nat smiles and takes a breath. This is a chance not often presented. Some time alone with her boss - her chance to sell her idea to him yet again.

'Look, I know I've pitched this to you before…' As she starts speaking, Ben is already sighing.

'Nat, we've gone over this, in fact so many times that I could do the pitch for you. The disappearance of Samantha Chappel, and…' he holds up a hand before Nat can interrupt, 'I'm well aware that her disappearance cut deep into the very being of this town. It affected everyone. You must remember, you were at school with her.'

Nat does remember - it was this event that had sparked her fascination with a career in journalism. Up until then, she had been a bit aimless. But seeing the national media descend upon their little town, reporting on the mystery of the girl who simply disappeared into thin air; she was drawn to watching them, was dazzled by the frenetic pace - by their relentless pursuit of anyone who could give them something to add to this story. The whole air around them seemed to fizz with an excitement that Nat had never experienced before. She spent hours just sat watching, hoping that by being near, she would absorb some of their energy. She knew then that this was what she wanted to do with her life.

Finally, after three weeks with no further developments, newer stories with more action grabbed the attention of this feral pack and they left the town as quickly as they had arrived. The majority of the locals had breathed a sigh of relief, although the landlord of the local pub was secretly gutted that his run of lock ins (when the drinks were all put on expenses) had come to an end. He supposed, looking on the bright side, at least it meant he might get to bed before midnight. His wife was complaining about the noise and the late nights, though she didn't complain when he explained this year they might be able to manage that two weeks break abroad - bring in a temporary manager like she had been nagging him to do for the last five years.

Nat made no secret of the fact that she was devastated. Suddenly the town seemed so much smaller - both in the area it covered and the small-mindedness of the people that lived there. The locals agreed Sam had likely stumbled off the cliff path, drunk on her way home from the school summer ball. It didn't matter that there were no witnesses to this or that a body was never located by the Coastguard. The town decided that was the most palatable explanation, and no one wanted to break ranks.

The school might have come under more scrutiny and criticism for allowing underage drinking to take place on school premises. Everyone expected that outrage to come. But then Jeremy Webster was found hanged in his parents' holiday home, and instead of criticism of the headmaster and the school, there was a steady outpouring of unquestioning support. This new development became a welcome distraction from the potentially sordid question surrounding what had happened to seventeen-year-old Sam.

Nat wasn't immune from this second event, Jez being the brother of her best friend. But Caro withdrew from Nat, seemingly still hurt by being abandoned for the journalists for all those weeks. Calls remained unanswered and visits to the house were politely rebuffed at the door, until Nat simply stopped trying and forgot all about the little town as she spread her wings at university and chased her journalistic dreams.

And now she is back where it all started.

'Just hear me out, Ben. Please!'

Ben rolls his eyes. 'You've got until I reach my office.'

Nat takes a deep breath. 'OK, so I've been doing some digging and we are coming up to the seventeen-year anniversary of her disappearance. I want to do a piece in the vein of 'where are they now': interview friends and family, see what they think happened all those years ago. I'll do it sensitively. I know this is a small place. In fact, I know this better than most people, given the opposition James has faced over the quarry redevelopment.'

At this Ben shifts uncomfortably, the paper being one of the cheerleaders for the opposition of the proposed changes. Nat decides to use his embarrassment to her advantage. 'Look, you know I'm professional enough not to let the paper's stance on the quarry affect my job in any way. But you said yourself the paper is facing challenging readership decline. A series of articles on the disappearance of Sam might be what we need to get people wanting to see what The Gazette has to say.'

'Hmm, and wouldn't hurt you if the nationals' interest were piqued?'

'Of course not, but that's not my main motivation. I think there's a story to be told here. And there was a bit of a development last week: a rather nasty insinuation on the school's old pupils Facebook group, hinting that maybe the headmaster was involved in more ways than simply turning a blind eye to the pupils' underage drinking. I think we could tell the story of that summer and show there were ripples affecting the whole community. I was thinking a series of interviews showing the range of the impact from those closest to her, to those who knew her as little more than a name in the papers. Please!'

Ben sighs. 'You're never going to give me any peace on this are you? Oh, bloody hell... OK.'

As Nat grins and moves to hug him, he takes a step back. 'But there are conditions.'

'Yes, I agree,' smiles Nat.

'You haven't even heard what I'm going to say! You can work on this for a month, but alongside all your other stuff. So no moaning about covering the town diary. And if Sam's family ask you to leave this alone, you allow them the peace they deserve. Deal?'

'Yes, boss!' As Nat throws her arms in the air, she feels the familiar pull round her neck and, reaching underneath her blouse, she triumphantly retrieves the missing lanyard.

'Looks like this week just got much better!'

9

Article from The Roxcliffe Gazette
Quarry Development To Finally Get Off The Starting Blocks

After three years of consultation and uncertainty, work is finally scheduled to begin on the redevelopment of the old Threlfell Rocks site on the cliffs above the town. J.M. Developments acquired the site, which covers around twenty acres, in 2019 for £1.2 million. The following year they submitted plans for an ambitious redevelopment project which includes the construction of ten luxury eco lodges around the base of the face of the quarry, together with twenty-four holiday pods scattered around the disused site.

The lodges will be built around two areas of water that are already in situ, with access to the public for swimming and diving. The plans show the leisure site will include three sauna pods on the shores of the water together with a number of swimming and diving jetties and a leisure centre for the hire of paddleboards and kayaks. The third area will be preserved for local wildlife that already populates the site.

The artist's impression of the new site also shows plans for an ambitious clifftop restaurant in Phase

Two of the development, together with a climbing centre, state-of-the-art gym and luxury spa.

Mr James Morton, Chief Executive of J.M. Developments, confirmed that the firm was looking to invest an initial £20 million in the Phase One development of the site adding, 'This is an exciting opportunity to create a stunning area which will attract visitors, as well as provide a beautiful location that can be enjoyed by visitors and residents alike. We are keen for the whole community to benefit from this project, so are not only using local contractors wherever we can, but envisage the operation will provide around one hundred jobs once the leisure facilities are fully operational. We appreciate there have been some concerns about the impact of this development on the area, but I can assure you we intend to treat the area with respect and preserve the eco system for the enjoyment of future generations.'

Mr Angus Redfearn, the spokesperson for Residents Against New Developments (RAND) greeted the announcement with some scepticism, telling the Roxcliffe Gazette, 'The quarry has been an integral part of the Roxcliffe coastline for many years, and has served as a haven for wildlife ever since it ceased to be operational over fifty years ago. Not only will this development destroy the habitat of many of the wonderful wildlife we are privileged to host in the area, but we also have grave concerns as to the feasibility of the existing infrastructure coping with the additional traffic and visitor numbers to the area. We are extremely disappointed that the council appear to have been swayed by false promises of the potential for increased wealth generation in the area, and will be monitoring developments very closely. We believe this is just the start of the destruction of everything that makes this area so very special.'

No one from the council was available to comment.

Do you have a story about the quarry or the company developing the quarry? If so, please email the news desk: news@roxcliffegazette.co.uk

10

Nat

Present day: Monday, 1 July

Monday morning again on the familiar treadmill of responsibilities. Nat had spent the previous week immersed in reading the archives from the time of Sam's disappearance. She remembered the hours when it first happened; the mid-morning phone call her mum received which prompted her to shout to ask Nat and Caro if they had seen Sam that night. Of course they probably had seen Sam, but she was two years above them and they had been confined mainly to the kitchen. They were honest when they answered they couldn't really remember. And they thought no more about it. No doubt Sam's mum carried on the ring round, and everyone assumed that Sam would eventually be located at a friend's house and that would be that. Of course, that wasn't the end of it.

The frisson of tension started in the town around mid-morning the next day, as the police organised a hasty press conference where Sam's distraught mum was paraded for the pack to get their first glimpse of this potential story. And still everyone thought she would turn up - no doubt a bit sheepish - but no one ever thought there wouldn't be a happy outcome to this little episode.

Nat is roused from her journey into the past by the buzzing of her phone. She is tempted to ignore it but then thinks she better answer - it might be Annie's school. She had been a bit under the weather this morning and Nat still feels that twinge of guilt that she had ushered her off to school, telling her she'd be fine once she was with all her friends. To her relief, it isn't the school's name flashing up; but she feels the familiar surge of irritation as she sees it's Caro.

'Hi love, sorry I can't really talk, working to a deadline.' Nat recognises that some of her irritation stems from guilt. At some point she is going to have to explore whether what had happened to her friend's family was linked to the disappearance of Sam. She tells herself that Caro will understand, will realise Nat is only doing her job, that it isn't anything personal. Still, it is this discomfort which means Nat finds herself agreeing to meet Caro for lunch.

As usual, Nat is late to arrive; having become engrossed in the archives and leaving far too late to have a chance of arriving on time. She grins in thanks and relief as she sees her friend has already ordered them both a panini and cappuccino. Kissing Caro on the cheek, Nat sinks down with a sigh and takes a gulp of coffee, spluttering as the burning liquid hits the back of her throat.

'Sorry I'm late.'

Caro looks at her friend and the easy smile doesn't quite disguise the irritation in her eyes as she comments, 'No, you're not. You're always late and if you were sorry, you would leave earlier! Anyway, I took a chance that we would do our normal trick of discussing everything on the menu and then order our usual, so I bypassed the whole palaver. I know you'll be in a rush, and I really need to talk to you.'

For a moment Nat feels a small spark of anger ignite in the pit of her stomach. This is so typical of her friend. Caro needs to talk to Nat, so she expects everyone to drop everything that is important to them and run to her aid. Tomorrow, she may be in a brighter place and Nat's calls will remain unanswered and her messages remain unread; until

Caro needs something again. Maybe James is right, and this friendship is very much a one-way street. Then she remembers Caro is really suffering. The separation from Mark, together with Jen's devastating diagnosis, had already pushed Caro to the brink. Nat needs to be there for her friend to help her deal with the blow of Chris's death and these horrible rumours swirling about her father and brother. Maybe when they are in calmer waters, she can make a move to set their friendship on more equal ground. For now, as is the norm, this is all about Caro.

Nat bites off a chunk of her panini and sips her coffee, giving herself time to put her head back in the right space and then smiles at Caro, reaching over to squeeze her hand.

'You're right, but I am sorry, honest!' Caro's mouth begins to soften into the start of a smile as her friend continues. 'What do you need?'

'OK, you're going to think this sounds bonkers, and I think it's a bit mad myself. But it's been going round and round in my head ever since Saturday and I can't stop thinking about it.'

Nat feels the lurch in her stomach as she recognises maybe she made the wrong decision to tell Caro about the post. Unconsciously, her fingers feel for her ring and begin the familiar twiddling of a calming ritual.

'Whoa, slow down. Are you talking about the thing I showed you on the Facebook page? Honest Caro, I'm sorry I ever told you. Best thing is to forget all about it. It's certainly not worth getting so upset.'

'No, not the bloody Facebook thing. Though thanks for reminding me that there's another piece of shit to add to my sandwich.'

Nat feels that ball of anger swell slightly. *Jesus*, she is only trying to help her friend, and now it seems she is being assigned the role of chief punch bag. Figuring the best thing is to say nothing, she takes another massive bite of the sandwich, filling her mouth to block the stream of bitter words that she would like to spew across to her friend. Picturing the look on Caro's face if she was forced to confront a few home truths helps to dampen down the fury. She is so lost in this happy little fantasy that she misses the start of Caro's story and has to hold up her hand to quieten her friend as she frantically chews and swallows her mouthful.

'Stop! Back up a minute. You've lost me here. Can you start again and take it slowly?'

Caro barely manages to stop the high-pitched tone of irritation from taking over her voice, but she matches the deep breaths taken by her friend and starts her story again. It is the familiar: moan about Jen, how difficult it is, and then she gets to the punchline.

'When I saw Mum last week, she started going on about the Beach Hut. She thought Dad and Jez were there and she started saying they needed to come back - that it was dangerous and that Dad should never have kept the stuff.'

'The Beach Hut? But I thought none of you had been back there to stay since, well, since poor Jez.'

Caro breathes out impatiently. 'That's what I'm saying to you. I've not been back there in seventeen years and, as far as I was aware, Dad just went back there to clean the place out. But now I can't stop thinking about it. What does Mum think is there that is causing her such distress? I mean, I know it's the place where they found Jez, but up until then it was really simply our happy place. You must remember, we had such good times there.'

And Nat does remember - it had been a very happy place, until it wasn't! The whole of the last summer they had spent there had been a time of discord, with friendships starting to fracture and the feeling that everything was coming to an end.

What happened with Jez - that only brought things to their inevitable conclusion a little quicker than if they had been allowed to limp on to their natural ending.

'Nat, are you still with me?'

Caro's voice drags her from the memories of the past.

'Sorry, yes, of course I remember. We all loved it there.'

For a moment Caro smiles. It had been the setting for some very good times, but also the setting for the worst of times.

'Once Mum started, it made me think. I'm assuming that Dad will have left me the Beach Hut in his will. It's this Webster family tradition thing. So, I was thinking…' At this Caro pauses and nibbles the stringy cheese at the side of her barely touched sandwich. 'Is there any chance you would come with me and help to clear it out?'

'Oh, erm, I'm not really sure. When were you thinking?' Nat's mind is grasping for an excuse. She only has the month to work on this story, so the last thing she wants to be doing is clearing out a building that has been left to rot for the last seventeen years.

Caro reaches for her friend's hand. 'I'm truly sorry to have to ask you this, Nat. It's just that I really have no one else to turn to.'

At this point her eyes fill with tears and Nat knows she will be unable to say no. Out of nowhere comes the thought, *this is exactly what Jen used to do when she thought she might not get her own way.*

Before she can change her mind, Nat finds she is returning the pressure of her friend's grip and nodding along.

'Of course, I understand. Are you thinking a couple of afternoons would do it? We can see what's involved in getting the place sorted and maybe stop off for fish and chips on the way home.'

Caro grins, happy now she has talked her friend round.

'That sounds like a plan, but I think we can make it better than that. I was thinking we should let our children have the summers that we used to have. As soon as school breaks up, we can recreate the good old days and decamp to live on the beach. The kids will adore it. Remember how we used to love the freedom of long days at the beach? I swear it was sunny every day.'

As Nat starts to mutter about the looming deadline, Caro brushes aside her protestations with a wave of her hand. 'I have a great plan. We can book the girls into the beach club there. They'll love it. That gives us until three every day where I can tackle the hut, and you can work on your article. You know you work at home anyway during the school holidays. Well, this way you get free childcare, and I get some moral support.'

Nat smiles. 'You seem to have it all worked out.'

'And in the evenings, we can order in takeaway and drink wine. How can you possibly refuse!'

As Nat walks back to the office, leaving Caro to sort the bill, insisting lunch is her treat, she reflects that the Websters somehow always get their own way.

11

Nat

Seventeen years earlier: Friday, 20 July

Nat was having an alright time - she supposed that was the fairest way to look at it. As usual, she was spending most of the summer holidays with the Webster family. The Webster family lived on the school premises in the modestly named Headmaster's Cottage. This always made Nat smile as, for her, 'cottage' conjured up a small building, pretty much like the fairytale house in the woods visited by Hansel and Gretel. The Headmaster's Cottage was nothing like that. With six bedrooms and three reception rooms, as well as Mr Webster's study, the accommodation was more like a small country house. She supposed the cottage label came from the fact it was a part of the much larger estate of the school. But every weekend from the start of the May half term, and for all the glorious seven weeks of the school summer break, the family would decamp to the much simpler Beach Hut.

Again, 'hut' been rather deceptive when describing the accommodation on offer. Set in the dunes, the romantically named beach huts were dotted amongst the landscape, as though thrown up there from the sea. They were the sought-after prize of the area, and most had been in the same family for generations. However, the owners from years ago wouldn't recognise their simple shelters. What were once places to sleep and get a cup of tea, were now reshaped beyond recognition to be luxury escapes, polished to a standard to be a lucrative holiday let when not in use by the owners. Fully booked every year, the huts never came for sale on the open market. You had to be in the know to be in with a chance, if the rare opportunity arose, to own this piece of paradise.

The Beach Hut - clearly the Webster family had run out of ideas when it came to naming their property - had been in the Webster family for generations. Nat always wondered why they had settled on that name when they were surrounded by the likes of 'Dune Cottage', 'Seashell Retreat', 'Seaside Escape' and so on. However, what they hadn't lacked was the imagination to turn the site into something very special. Gradually improved by each set of owners, what may have originally started as a simple hut was now a quite beautiful wooden coastal retreat. With five bedrooms, one of which was in the eaves, it was smaller than the Headmaster's Cottage. But the location meant that it was the preferred destination for the summer season. Chris and Jen had been gifted the property on their wedding day - a tradition in the family.

The hut had been Jen's project. She had spent months managing the whole operation: lovingly converting the bedroom and storage in the eaves into a large master with ensuite, and remodelling downstairs with the extravagant addition of a full wall of windows to make the most of the sea views. It was Nat's favourite view of the place; trailing up the sandy path as the sun went down and seeing Jen reading in the window of the hut. Nat was in total awe of Jen and always has been. Not only for her looks, as there was no doubt Jen was stunning. But her easy nature, the way she made everyone feel like they were the absolute centre of her world, whilst at the same time effortlessly dominating centre stage herself. And the way she was pretty much adored by everyone - but especially by her husband and son. There was no doubt that Jen was a man's woman.

Nat had always loved those long summers. Her and Caro

would spend hours down on the beach, paddling in the rock pools before returning to the Beach Hut, starving and grubby, sand sticking to their suntanned limbs. Little Jez had always tagged along, and they had enjoyed bossing him around, and he had been happy to be included in their exclusive gang of three.

But this summer was all different. Caro only wanted to loiter wherever Gus was likely to be, and Nat hated that trailing round, and the look that Gus would throw their way, far too aware of Caro's admiration, taking it for granted.

They had hardly seen Jez. He spent most of his time skulking around the house, not meeting with anyone and only emerging from his room to peer through his beloved telescope and grab food. Not that he seemed to be eating very much at all.

The summer seemed too overwhelming this year. The house had a constant stream of visitors and Jen was relentless in her need to have people around her all the time. Gus and Sam seemed to be practically living there, and Nat would catch poor Jez staring at his dad chatting and laughing with Gus. He must be suffering a real jealousy at their easy friendship. Nat wondered if he worried he was losing his dad, but it was impossible to ask him about it – he had simply withdrawn into himself, a shadow of the cheeky laughing boy of the summer before. Caro would be staring at them too, though her reason was very different to her brother's. Caro hadn't gone quiet that summer. If anything, she was more domineering than usual, demanding to be the focus of everything she and Nat talked about.

Maybe everything would go back to normal once Gus and Sam left to go to university. Still, Nat was starting to think that this would be her last summer at the Beach Hut - maybe she had outgrown this summer tradition, time for a change.

As it turned out, it was the last summer any of them

spent at the Beach Hut.

12

Alex

Present day: Monday, 1 July

Alex is killing time, as he does most evenings. Sitting in the doorway of the library, he scans the street to see if there are any of his friends from school around to help pass a few hours. He feels like the last few months of his life have been spent killing time. He knows his mum thinks he's depressed since they had lost Grandad, but the truth is he misses his dad. *Mark*, he corrects himself bitterly. He misses Mark and he really wishes he didn't.

He isn't sure when he first became aware that Mark treated him so differently to the easy affection he threw at Grace. It had probably taken him longer than it should have; in fact, it was Grandad's questions about whether everything was OK at home that had made him realise what a fool he had been. His parents - again he has to correct himself - *his mum and Mark,* have never made any secret of the fact that Mark isn't his 'real' dad. It had never mattered. He was secure in the family and had no desire to know any more about who his biological father might be. But then Grace had come along, and Mark was instantly besotted. And even then, Alex had been too naïve to recognise the way things were. If Mark had to say no to a couple of kick arounds in the park or couldn't always make it to watch him in the Saturday morning matches, well, that was the demands of having a baby arrive. All his friends seemed to have the same thing, and there was no doubt that Mark adored little Grace. I mean, how could you not?

And besides, Grandad, and especially Grandma, doted on him, constantly referring to him as their favourite. And he knew Grandad loved every second of the time they spent together, even if sometimes they focused on the things Grandad liked rather than the things Alex would have liked to do. It didn't matter because he quite simply felt safe and loved; even if it got on his nerves the way Grandma was constantly telling him he was 'her boy'. From quite young, Alex recognised that Grandma could be a bit over-the-top in her affection for him. It was sometimes a bit claustrophobic and overwhelming, but he didn't have the vocabulary to express how uncomfortable she could make him feel. By contrast, she barely threw a glance in Grace's direction. He wasn't the only one to notice, but it seemed to be accepted. In fact, his mum would laugh about it, brushing Grandma's behaviour away with the explanation that she had always preferred the company of men.

And then Grandma started saying odd things. He heard her tell Grandad that Mark was a saint for taking on a child that wasn't his, especially as none of them knew who his father was.

Grandad had hushed her but then had said, 'Let's hope he's still happy to have Alex in the house now he has his own child. Good job Grace wasn't a boy, else that really might have upset the apple cart.'

Alex had wanted to ask his mum and Mark about this, but the words somehow got stuck in his throat, and each time he tried to talk about it, the sounds came out wrong. Instead, he heard himself sounding like a toddler having a huge tantrum as he sulked over any attention Mark gave to Grace. So when Dad – again, he shakes his head as he corrects himself. When *Mark* moved out, he knew without a doubt it was all his fault. This was reinforced when Grandad was sent by Mum to have a 'man to man' chat with him.

Grandad hadn't really said much at all, preferring instead to take him for a brisk walk along the cliff tops, where the wind whipped their words away and there was no need to squirm through awkward silences. As they sat in the car afterwards, Grandad patted his knee and said, 'The thing is Alex, some men aren't man enough to take on other people's children. But you know you are part of my family, my flesh and blood, and will always be like a son to me. It's the old saying that blood is thicker than water, and you are part of my blood. Whatever the circumstances of how you came to be here, you are family and that is that.'

Alex hadn't said anything. He was trying too hard not to cry. Grandad didn't like anyone crying, but especially not men. He was certainly from the school of the stiff upper lip. That night, Alex had decided the best thing would be to avoid Mark as much as possible. He recognised any time Mark spent with him was done so out of guilt, and Alex wanted to make things easy for him.

It breaks his heart.

13

Nat

Present day: Wednesday, 3 July

Wednesday morning is the normal chaos for Nat and James. James is stressed as the investors are due to visit the quarry site and he is paranoid the visit will be blighted by a mob of placard-waving protesters. Despite him assuring Nat, and himself, that the general reception of the plans has been positive, Nat knows him well enough to understand he is not as confident as he would like to be. Nat is trying to be patient about it all, but really doesn't see why James is so bothered. The plans were approved months ago, the work is scheduled to start. Why waste time trying to soothe feathers that are determined to stay ruffled?

They end up arguing over who is going to drop Annie off at breakfast club, James conveniently forgetting that he had promised he could do the drop off, no problem. Suddenly, he has to be in the office for something that, supposedly, only he can deal with. Picking up that there was some dissension in the ranks, Annie had taken the opportunity to divide and conquer. Nat had lost the will to argue so now Annie is sat in the back of Nat's car, happily sporting a princess tiara and licking on an ice cream, which were her demands before she agreed to leave the house.

Nat is stony-faced as she drops her off, barely acknowledging Caro's wave at the reception gates. She needs to get in the right frame of mind for this morning's meeting. Samantha's mum, Kate, has agreed to meet her. The initial approach had been easier than Nat had expected. But when she had put the phone down, Nat worried at the hope she had heard in the other woman's voice. With that niggle of guilt chipping away at her, she had barely slept last night, fretting that Kate was expecting Nat to come up with the miracle that had eluded her for all these years.

Kate has obviously been looking out for Nat. The front door is flung open before Nat has time to compose herself and ring the bell.

'Come in, come in. You found me OK then? No, don't worry about your shoes. Tea or coffee? Come through, come through. Oh, I'm sorry I'm wittering on. I don't know if I'm nervous or excited to talk to you.'

Funnily enough, it is Kate's obvious discomfort that makes Nat feel more comfortable. She can do this. This is what she has always dreamed of doing. And a little voice is whispering, 'Wouldn't it be great if you solved this mystery? The story that started your career. You will have succeeded where all those other people have failed.'

And so what if she is driven by the idea of personal recognition? If Kate gets some answers too, then surely it doesn't matter that Nat's sole driver is to resurrect her flagging career.

'Hi Kate, don't worry, I'm nervous too.' Immediately Kate's shoulders drop a couple of inches and she breathes out as she leads Nat through to the back of the house.

'I thought we could sit in the conservatory if that's OK with you?'

'Wherever you feel most comfortable is absolutely fine with me. And a glass of water would be great - thank you.'

As Kate makes sure Nat is settled then leaves to get the

drinks, Nat is able to take a moment to have a good look around the room. Flooded with the morning sunlight, she can see immediately that Kate has green fingers. Maybe she finds some peace in the little oasis she has created. But the main thing that strikes Nat is that there are no photos that she has spotted anywhere in the house. Nat herself tends to be fairly minimalist and likes to keep her surfaces clutter free. However, whenever she has visited the homes of parents who have suffered some sort of loss of their children, the house tends to be full of photos of the child that is no longer there. The photos trying to live up to a forlorn hope that the static image could reflect some of the love and joy that had been present before tragedy visited.

She jumps as Kate leans over her to place a glass of water on the table.

'I love my garden. It's where I feel closest to my girl.'

'I can't even begin to pretend to understand how difficult these years must have been for you.'

Nat chooses to concentrate on opening her laptop, allowing Kate to quickly dash away the tears that have started to flow.

'People say I should have had a memorial for her. That I shouldn't have put away all the photos. But I refuse to turn my house into a shrine. And the photos I have aren't what Sam looks like now. And Sam could still be out there, waiting for the right moment to come home. She's no longer seventeen; she's a grown woman. She may have a family of her own. I never want her to think I gave up on her. Even if it sometimes feels like everyone else has.'

Nat nods, already feeling the heavy weight of this mother's expectations on her. Maybe Ben is right and this is a story that should be left in the past. But then Nat feels that familiar pull in her gut and knows that she is onto something here. And that, regardless of what Kate says to her over the next hour, she will be pressing on to write this story.

'Before we start Kate - am I OK to call you Kate?' Smiling at the other woman's nod, Nat presses on. 'Can I lay out to you where I am coming from on this?' Again, Kate registers the words with a nod and then leans forward to capture every word, as Nat begins to speak.

'OK, full disclosure: I was at the same school as Sam. A couple of years below, but I did know who Sam was and I was at the ball that night. I wanted you to know that before we start.'

Kate smiles. 'I appreciate you being honest about that, but I did already know who you were. You were best friends with the Webster girl. I used to see you at the Beach Hut. You used to like to come and chat. I don't know if you remember me, but I used to clean for Jen Webster.'

Nat frowns. 'Of course I remember. To be honest, I'm a bit embarrassed. I always meant to come and see you after Sam disappeared but... I got caught up in my own thing. Typical teenager - lost in my own world and oblivious of others around me.'

'Hah! Teenagers weren't the only ones to be oblivious of the hired help.' Kate smiles to soften the blow behind her words. 'I don't think Jen Webster said more than half a dozen words to me. Funny that we should both lose our children that summer.'

There is something else behind that statement of fact, and Nat knows it's an area she wants to explore. However, although she is tempted to barge in and ask so many questions, at this stage she just wants to set the scene and gain Kate's trust. She already knows she is going to tell Sam's story, whether Kate agrees or not. But it will be a much better piece if she can include quotes from the family. Rather cynically, Nat knows that for her piece to capture the readership she desires, she needs to serve up a ringside seat to the ongoing suffering of those who love Sam.

Jolted back to the present, Nat realises that Kate is looking at her expectantly, waiting for an answer to the question.

'I'm sorry Kate, I was lost there for a minute thinking of the Beach Hut. What were you saying?'

'I wondered if you still saw Caroline. I was ever so sorry to hear about her dad. Now, he couldn't have been more different than his wife. I had a lot of time for Chris, and he was so good with Sam - all the extra tutoring he gave her to make sure she would get the grades she needed to go to university.'

Again, Kate turns her head slightly to hide the tears which come at the realisation that the hopes and dreams from all those years ago were cut off without explanation on that warm summer night. Nat wants to reach out to touch the woman opposite, but instead she busies herself once again with her laptop, giving Kate the space she needs to regain her composure.

'Are you OK to start Kate? Please take your time. I think if you are able, it would be good for you to talk me through what happened when Sam disappeared. But I also want to know all about Sam, so I can present her as a real person - not just a victim.'

Nat flinches as she sees Kate recoil at her words. 'Sorry, victim is the wrong word. I mean I want our readers to understand who Sam was. To understand how much you loved her. Is that OK?'

Kate lets out a sigh and leans forward. 'Of course I'm ready. I've been waiting seventeen years for someone to ask me to tell my story.'

14

Nat

Present day: Wednesday, 3 July

Nat heads straight home after her time with Kate. She couldn't face the noise and bustle of the office and wanted to take some time to reflect on what she had heard. As soon as she closes the front door behind her she heads upstairs to the shower, discarding her clothes in a heap on the bedroom floor as she hurries to feel the warm water wash away the grief of the other woman; a sadness which she feels has started to sink into her very pores.

She stays in the shower, enjoying the feel of the warm water soothing some of the tension from her shoulders, grateful to have this time to herself. Her respite is short-lived as she is jolted from her near-stupor by the notification ping of her phone, followed by the strident ring tone. As she rinses the conditioner from her hair, she tries to ignore the persistent caller, but the phone keeps summoning her back to the real world. Grabbing the towel, she reaches for the phone, muttering a curse as she stubs her toe as she stumbles from the shower. When she sees the missed calls - all with Caro as the caller ID - she thinks, not for the first time, that she really should put her phone on 'do not disturb' for certain callers during the working day. However, she knows from experience that Caro will keep on calling until Nat picks up. It seems she is oblivious that Nat may be at work or may have other things going on in her life that means Caro may have to wait. Caro is not used to waiting for anyone.

Before Nat can press the call button the phone vibrates in her hand, and Caro's picture almost seems to yell to demand attention.

'Hi Caro, everything OK?'

'No, everything is fucking not OK!' Nat finds that, like a cartoon character, she is holding the phone away from her ear as she registers the near-hysterical screeching that is attempting to draw her in.

'Calm down, I can't tell a word you're saying.'

'Do not fucking tell me to calm down! I can't believe you didn't tell me about the latest post and just left me to find it! You need to sort this out like you did the last one.'

Sighing, Nat realises that she is going to have to get involved in this, regardless of the fact that she is so keen to get sat at her laptop and start work on her fledgling story. Adopting the tone that she reserves for Annie when she is overtired and on the verge of a tantrum, Nat sits on the edge of the bed, ignoring her dripping wet hair, and falls back into the role that she has fulfilled throughout their friendship.

'OK! I have absolutely no idea what you are talking about, so can we please go back to the beginning.' Nat lapses into a soothing sing-song voice as she attempts to bring her childhood friend back to the moment. For a second she thinks Caro is going to explode again, but then her friend gives a shuddering sigh. When she next speaks, Nat is relieved that it is with a more measured tone.

'I know I'm shouting but I've been going frantic trying to get hold of you, so I may have been a little overwrought when you finally decided you had time to answer.'

Nat grimaces. OK, maybe not really an apology, but as close to one as Caro is likely to give. Then she irritates herself as she hears her own reply.

'I'm sorry Caro, but I do have a job, you know.'

Why the hell is she apologising? This is the typical pattern of their friendship: Caro acts unreasonably, and Nat ends up apologising for some perceived transgression that has caused Caro to become overwrought. Maybe James is right. Maybe this is a friendship that should have ended when their time at Churcher's drew to a close.

There is a silence on the end of the line and then some indistinct words as Nat gathers Caro is taking her ire out on some pedestrian who has dared to use the pedestrian crossing in front of her.

'Look, why don't you call me back when you're not driving, and we can sort out whatever the issue is.'

'I'm on my way to yours – get the kettle on, I'll be with you in five minutes. You won't believe what's been posted on that stupid Facebook group now.'

The call abruptly ends with a flurry of expletives as Caro shouts some choice words at some bewildered fellow road user and Nat sits, stunned into silence. Sighing, she throws on jeans and an old t-shirt - her favourite comfy gear for getting lost in a story at her desk - and reluctantly turns away from her laptop, heading downstairs to wait for Caro's arrival. She supposes she should have a look on Facebook to see what has caused this latest outburst, and, not for the first, time wonders if she would have been better to leave Caro in blissful ignorance of the latest malicious post that popped up mentioning her father. A small voice whispers that she had told her to bring her friend down a peg or two. To knock Chris Webster a little off that pedestal that Caro worshipped at. But before she has time to explore this nasty little character flaw, the door is flung open and Caro makes her grand entrance, disturbing the air in Nat's home, the same way as her own son creates such a destructive energy in Caro's own space.

Sinking into a chair, Caro gives a theatrical shuddering breath, and Nat is disturbed to see her friend's eyes are filled with tears. When she finally speaks, it is between gulps of air that remind Nat of Annie stuttering out incomprehensible words in between sobs when she told her mum about the leg snapping off her favourite Barbie doll.

'Well? Have you looked at it? I don't know why someone would be that cruel.'

For a second Nat considers telling Caro that she has better things to do than look at Facebook in the middle of a working day. At the same time, a tiny voice whispers this is patently untrue. Spying on the picture-perfect lives and petty arguments on the community pages took up a great deal of time and was essential to relieve her of the boredom of reporting on the latest challenges facing the Hedgehog Conservation Society. But as these thoughts are flitting through her mind, she sees Caro is reaching over for her discarded iPad and pushing it across to her with an impatient wave of the hand.

'Go on, have a look! Then you will see exactly what I'm talking about.'

The iPad takes some time to spring to life, reminding Nat that she really needs to invest in a newer model. James was always hassling her to upgrade when the trade-in price was still worth having. But she grew comfortable with her items and would put up with the glitches and stutters until one day she was forced to consign them to the scrap. Then James would sigh and tut at the fact there was nothing worth trading in. He would then sigh even louder if he ever had to go in the cupboard in her home office - shaking his head as he was confronted with the crammed jumble of old phones, iPads and the boxes they had come in, together with the tangle of leads that one day might come in useful.

As the iPad lights into life - and after one false attempt

manages to recognise Nat's face, after she has slipped her glasses on - Caro snatches the tablet from her and quickly finds the Facebook group post she is looking for. She gives a rather dramatic little whimper, as if seeing it for the first time, so Nat feels she will be prepared for whatever vitriol has been typed by the anonymous keyboard warrior. Even so, the words swim before her eyes and she can't help her hand flying to her mouth as she gasps and looks at her friend. She suddenly feels bad for thinking that yet again Caro is making a fuss. This time the faceless poster really hasn't pulled any punches.

15
Nat

Present day: Wednesday, 3 July

Churcher's School – Old Pupils Group

Posted by: Anonymous. Wednesday 3rd July 10.17am

Well, well, well! So now with the death of the Wicked Wizard, his surviving Princess has decided to finally grace us with her presence. Caro Fraser, welcome to the group. So tell us, when did you realise your dad was a paedophile and a murderer?

Obviously, your brother couldn't live with it, but seems you are made of stronger stuff. I hope you don't abuse your pupils the same way – I would hate it to be a case of 'like father like daughter'.

Your poor, poor children, having a nonce for a grandfather. Hope you didn't leave them alone with him at any point. Did you learn nothing from what happened to your brother?

53 likes, 4 loves, 5 angry

42 comments

Admin: Comments have been closed on this post. Please can the group refrain from speculation on these tragic events.

'Fucking hell Caro, I mean, what the hell is this!' Nat twists the ring on her finger as she struggles to understand this latest post. There had been the odd snide remark on the group, and then the very unpleasant post that had prompted her to share the details with Caro, but this? This is a different level entirely.

Caro is nodding vigorously and the tears are streaming down her face, as if the acknowledgement by her friend has allowed the last bit of glue that has been holding her together to finally dissolve. Unable to speak through the sobs that are now shaking her body, Nat decides this is not the time to worry about whether somewhere in the world the sun is over the yard arm (or whatever that ridiculous saying is) and grabs a chilled botte of white from the fridge. Thankful that it is a screw top - as she doubts her trembling hands have the dexterity to manage the intricacies of a corkscrew - she sloshes a generous measure into the two nearest mugs that are draining on the side.

'Here, get this down you,' and, as Caro half-heartedly protests, 'Well, if you don't want yours, I can tell you I will drink that too.'

The two friends both gulp from the mugs and then for a few seconds stare at each other. Nat is aware that her mouth is opening and closing but that no sounds are coming out. She realises her brain doesn't have the capacity to be able to think of anything to say. Caro seems to be in the same predicament, though she sits completely still, as if the vile words on the page have robbed her of the ability to do anything. It can only have been seconds, but to Nat it seems like the longest moment of stillness she has ever had with her friend, and she almost gets the sense that she is holding her breath ready for what is about to be said next. It is like the moment she had marvelled at on the television when they showed that pause of deathly quiet as the waves roll back from the shore and the world held its breath, before the ocean unleashed the power of the tsunami on the poor souls who stood in its path.

When Caro finally speaks, it is with a steely calmness that reminds Nat of the school assemblies Mr Webster would preside over. The ones when he was clearly furious about a report of bad behaviour that had brought the school into disrepute. Nat remembered they all dreaded this quiet fury far more than the raging rants that would be the choice of some of the other staff members.

'I've contacted the admin on the page already. It's clearly not good enough to close this post to comments. It needs taking down immediately.'

Nat nods enthusiastically in agreement whilst making a mental note to screenshot the post. This might be very useful in the Sam story. At the same time, she sends up a silent prayer of thanks that Caro has acted and is not expecting her to take the lead on this one. Nat has no idea whether she has lost her ability to deal with the shocking since the move back home. Certainly, when working in the city she had almost become blasé about the terrible behaviours her fellow humans could inflict on each other. They were simply stories to be reported on - a welcome step to help her climb that ladder. Maybe she has become softer since having Annie, but she feels out of her depth on this one, and as she lifts her mug to her lips, she notes her hands are trembling. Now that Caro is taking control, she feels able to offer her own contribution.

'Yes, that's the starting point. Plus, whilst the post shows as an anonymous member, I know for a fact the admin on the site will be able to see the identity.'

Caro looks genuinely surprised at this and Nat continues. 'It came up on a story I reported on a few years back. I won't go into detail but in a nutshell, someone posted anonymously in a group asking for help with something quite sensitive. Anyway, the admin of the group basically told everyone she knew about it. Got her car windscreen smashed as a result. Can't say I had much sympathy for her, but it means we can ask them to tell us which account these posts have come from. Assuming it's the same person and they've used their actual account.'

Caro grins. 'I knew there was a reason you were my best friend! Genius! We've got them, and I might do something much worse than smash their car to pieces. Unless they're sat in it, of course.'

Nat gives a nervous laugh, knowing her friend isn't entirely joking, and feels obliged to dampen the celebrations. 'I can't see they will have used their real account. I mean, they might be vindictive and enjoying inflicting this hurt on you, but they're not going to be stupid enough to do it in a way that could be traced back to them. They're bound to expect that you will get the police involved - these accusations are so vile.'

Caro looks surprised at this. 'Oh God, you think I should go to the police?'

'It's a difficult one. I mean, they're basically accusing your dad of abusing his son and grandchildren and implying that maybe you could be doing the same. But then again, I do wonder if they want that reaction. That they will feed on your distress. It's just that it's a little bit more than unpleasant speculation about the disappearance of Sam and the accident with Jez.'

For a moment Caro stares at her friend, and then she gives a bark of laughter. 'You obviously listened far too much to Mum and Dad. They always liked to pretend that Jez's death was an accident. But come on Nat, how can you accidentally hook a rope over the top rafters in Mum's room and kick yourself out to oblivion? No, Jez killed himself. End of story. Maybe it's time I got the courage to find out why a fourteen-year-old boy would choose that.'

16

Caro

Present day: Wednesday, 3 July

Driving home, Caro is surprised at the icy calmness she feels. Pulling into the drive, she has already decided what she is going to do, and the first thing is to ignore Nat's advice to get the police involved. Caro doesn't want to think too deeply about why she is so reluctant to take this step. After all, the post was libellous or slanderous - she can never remember which way round it is supposed to be - and she smiles as she pictures her father shaking his head at her as he would remonstrate that you shouldn't use fancy words if you are going to use them incorrectly.

That was her dad - a stickler for the rules. She doesn't for a minute think there is a grain of truth in those horrid postings. And to be honest, it is laughable that anyone would even consider she has somehow abused her position of trust. She thinks, if anything, the poster has taken some of the power from their words by including that mention of her own moral behaviour. Clearly, it is someone with a grudge against the whole family.

Bearing all this in mind, why is she not marching into the local police station now and demanding something be done immediately? As she opens her laptop, the thought creeps into her head that she is reacting in exactly the way her parents did when Jez died. The fact that it was a suicide was quickly erased from history and instead, if it was mentioned at all, it was with the understanding that it was all an unfortunate accident. It was treated almost as if it was a bit of a misunderstanding; much like turning up to an appointment on the wrong day.

Whilst Caro knows both her parents had been devastated by the events of that summer, the family had reached an unspoken agreement that it was something that was better left in the past. Maybe they all realised that to speak about it may well inflict more pain on them than they could bear. They each withdrew to their private mourning and Jez was consigned to the laughing fourteen-year-old boy, captured in an oak frame, on display at the side of her dad's bed.

Caro had never found it odd that there were no other pictures of her brother in the rest of the house until Mark asked her about it. The one thing you could say about Mark was that he was a sensitive character. He quickly picked up that the Webster family had this huge wound at their core. A wound they had covered with strong sticky plasters which none of them had any desire to peel back to poke the scar. Seeing Caro's reaction to his question about the missing family photos, he knew this was a no-go area. And if he thought it was strange, he accepted that was the Websters' way of coping with the tragedy they had experienced that summer. They simply never spoke of it; because maybe if they didn't speak of it, maybe it hadn't happened.

Dragging her mind back to the present, Caro focuses on the Churcher's Facebook group. She isn't sure what to expect after that bombshell post had dropped. She supposes she expected a flurry of posts which would, best case scenario, be leaping to the defence of her father with pleas to remember the feelings of his family. She braces herself for pages of speculation, the past being dragged kicking and screaming from the locked room where it has been so safely hidden for all these years. It is with some disbelief, and then a sense of anticlimax, that she refreshes the page and sees the vindictive post is no longer showing, and the last post on the group is from a few days ago. She wonders idly if Nat has contacted the admin on the page to demand the offensive words be removed, then sets about composing her own message. Caro doesn't allow herself time to think too carefully about her words – no need as they have been running round in her head for the last seventeen years. As she types, she is instantly transported back to the girl she was, desperate to fit in and be liked, whilst at the same time battling to live up to the expectations of her parents. No wonder she hadn't managed to succeed in pleasing anyone, least of all herself.

> *I'm sorry that my first post here must be to address the recent accusations that have been made against my father, Mr Christopher Webster. As many of you know, my father recently passed away unexpectedly, and all our family are still struggling to come to terms with the great chasm this has left in our lives. As you can imagine, dealing with this loss and the natural grief we are all experiencing has brought back some very difficult memories of the time when we lost my much-loved brother, Jeremy.*

At this point Caro hesitates then slowly deletes the last sentence.

> *As you can imagine, dealing with this loss and the natural grief we are all experiencing has brought back some very difficult memories of the suicide of my dearest brother, Jeremy.*
>
> *So you can imagine how devastated I was to read the recent anonymous allegations posted on this page,*

and the disappointment I felt that those dreadful events of seventeen years ago are being discussed as if they are the latest soap on television. These are real life tragedies that impacted, and continue to impact deeply, the lives of both my family and the family of Samantha Chappell.

As I say, I'm sorry my first post couldn't be more frivolous, but I hope we can all agree to consign this to the past; and please give us the room to grieve and yet again try to rebuild our family and move forward with our lives.

Thank you for taking the time to read this. I hope to see you all at this summer's reunion, when I hope you will join me in raising a glass to remember my father, Jeremy and Sam.

Caro leans back and rubs her eyes. Is that last bit too much? Really, the last thing she wants to do is go to the school reunion - she has been using every excuse she could think of to make sure she couldn't attend since the first meet up was organised a little over five years ago. Before she can change her mind, she presses the 'post' button and sits back to wait for the reaction from her former school friends. Instead, she gets the rather officious notification that her message has been submitted for admin approval and will be posted in due course. Ah, that explains the inactivity on the site. Nothing to do other than wait.

Caro sighs, recognising that patience is not her greatest attribute. As she mindlessly scrolls down her timeline - which seems to be more suggested posts than news about people she actually knows - she sees she has a message. More accurately a message request, whatever that means. Navigating the messenger system, she feels for a moment the air has been sucked out of the room and that she will never be able to breathe properly again. Because laughing back at her, from the circular icon that bears his name, is a face from the past that she had never expected to see again. A face that she both longed to catch a glimpse of each time she walked down the high street, whilst at the same time praying he had left the area for good and would never return. Angus Redfearn, Alex's father.

17

Nat

Present day: Wednesday, 3 July

Once Caro has left the house, clearly seeing herself as a woman on a mission, Nat hesitates about what to do next. Normally she would ring round old school friends to rally a bit of support for the Webster family and would fire off a supportive post criticising the cowardice of the anonymous poster - clearly a troublemaker trying to dredge up scandals in the past where there really were none. Except she doesn't want to do this as - and Nat is ashamed to admit this, even only to herself - this latest development all plays rather well into the article she wants to write for the paper.

Of course, she is telling the story of something that happened a long time ago, but her aim was never to report a piece of historical narrative. No, she needs something new, a fresh angle, and Nat is ashamed to say that this latest drama on the school page has given her the perfect idea for her story. If only she dares to write it, knowing that it will potentially cost her Caro's friendship. But with this thought in mind, she decides to let things play out for a while. Instead of firing off a message to the admin on the Facebook group, pledging her support for Caro and expressing her disgust that the posts have been allowed, she heads to her study – more accurately, the small boxroom that has a desk crammed in alongside the boxes that they have still not unpacked from when they moved here over five years ago.

Nat has become skilled at ignoring these boxes, so sits at her desk and pulls out her phone and gets lost once again in her conversation with Kate.

Transcript of Interview with Kate Chappell – Wednesday 3rd July

KC: Sam and me, well, we were close. Probably unusually so for a mother and daughter. Sam was my best friend, and I think for a lot of her life I was Sam's best friend too. Up until the last few weeks, for sure. Sam never knew her dad. When I told him I was pregnant, he decided we had been a terrible mistake and that he didn't want anything to do with me or the baby. He went back to Ireland where I suspect he probably had a wife and children waiting for him. Of course, that's only something I've realised later. Back then I was a bit more naïve; and I loved him and was prepared to put up with pretty much anything. Anyway, you don't need to know this. Suffice to say, he showed his true colours and from then on it was just me and Sam. It's always been a weakness of mine, believing things people told me. Just like I believed the police when they told me it would be OK, that Sam was off partying, probably with a boyfriend. But I'm getting ahead of myself, babbling. I'm so nervous.

NM: Can you tell me a bit about Sam, how she was that summer?

KC: It had been a weird summer. Everything was changing around us and neither of us were good with change. You were at Churcher's too? So you'll know my Sam was there.

NM: Had she always been at school there? I can't remember, sorry.

KC: No, just for Sixth Form. Chris Webster had been involved in a programme for the students taking French and Spanish GCSE. Sam was very gifted at languages. No idea where she got that from, but it certainly wasn't my side of the family. Anyway, there were only two of them wanting to do GCSE Spanish, which meant the school couldn't really justify adding it to the timetable. But they worked with Mr Webster to arrange for the students to go to Churcher's and join the Spanish lessons there. I was a bit unsure at first. I mean, I know the two schools are practically next door to each other, but they are in different worlds.

NM: But it was a success? The collaboration between the two schools?

KC: Oh, yes. Sam flourished there. She got an A* in all her GCSEs and chose to do languages for A-Level. And out of the blue we had a letter from Churcher's offering her a scholarship. Again, I wasn't keen. I mean, all her friends were staying on at her old school and I worried that she would feel like a fish out of water - be seen as the charity case. But Sam didn't see it like that. She felt she deserved this chance, because of the talent she had. She really wanted to go to Oxford. Had her heart set on it. She said that Churcher's was her best chance of achieving that dream. In the end, I felt I had no other option than to say yes.

NM: So, Sam started at Sixth Form. And you'd had no concerns until she went missing?

KC: Sam was a good girl. You need to understand that. She'd never given me any bother. But that last year of Sixth Form, she did change.

NM: Change?

KC: I understood that she was feeling anxious. She was making her Oxbridge application and I know she felt such pressure to get an offer. I think she felt she would be letting Mr Webster down if she wasn't successful.

NM: Why would she feel she was letting the Head down?

KC: Well, not only had he given her the opportunity to study at Churcher's, but he also really helped her draft her personal statement for the application. Then did some private coaching, to let her know what to expect. She applied for his old college and I'm not really sure if he put a good word in for her, but she went for the interview and then we had to wait until after Christmas to see if she had been successful. That was a difficult time. I think Sam felt like she was floating in no man's land, and I think she missed the extra sessions with Mr Webster. I did worry that with Sam not having a dad, that she started to see Mr Webster as a father figure in her life. Maybe I should have talked to her about it, but at that time I got snapped at for even suggesting we watch something on TV. I tried to keep the peace and hoped things would be better once the letter from Oxford came.

NM: I remember well the stress of waiting for offers from universities. Not that I was ever bright enough to apply for Oxbridge. And Sam did get an offer, didn't she? I seem to remember there were a few pupils that year that we were all in awe of.

KC: Oh, yes. She got the offer. She needed two A*s

and an A. We were so excited, and then the self-doubt set in - that she wasn't going to achieve the grades. I tried to reassure her, kept telling her that she had a fantastic backup offer from Durham, but she snapped my head off. Said I didn't understand and that her life would be over if she didn't get the grades she needed. And she was right. I didn't understand. Just thought she was being a bit dramatic. Anyway, Mr Webster saved the day again. He offered to give her some extra tutoring after school at the Headmaster's Cottage. And in the holidays, she would come with me when I did my cleaning shift at the Beach Hut and worked with Mr Webster then. It really was very good of him, though Jen Webster always had a face like a slapped arse whenever I turned up with Sam in tow. Excuse my language. You won't put that in the article, will you?

NM: No, of course not. And was Sam the only pupil Mr Webster tutored?

KC: Oh, no. There was another pupil going to be doing the same course at Cambridge. Though, as Sam repeatedly corrected me, 'It's not taking the course, it's reading the course.' I'm not even sure I've got that right now. Sam used to despair of me. She had a real thing about me keeping getting that wrong. I mean, did it really matter? I had a tiny suspicion that Sam was a little bit ashamed of me. Her mum - the cleaner.

NM: It's funny the things that seem important to us when we are teenagers that we realise are of no consequence now.

KC: Yes, (muffled sounds) I'm sorry. It's just I'm thinking - Sam and I have never had the chance to look back and laugh at her teenager diva moments.

NM: Take as much time as you need. You were saying there was another pupil also being tutored by Mr Webster. Do you happen to know who that was?

KC: Of course. It was Angus Redfearn. I bet you knew him; I mean, everyone knew Gus.

NM: The Head Boy? Of course, we all knew Gus. I think every girl in the school fancied him too.

KC: And a few of the younger staff! Ha! He was a lovely boy, and I think was an added bonus to the tuition. It certainly used to put a smile on her face, though she would spend the rest of the time mooning after him.

NM: She wasn't on her own there. I was two years younger, and he was the real pin-up boy for all the girls, and some of the boys! And that is not very professional of me!

KC: (Muffled laughter) I wanted to tell Sam's story, but I've been scared as well. Not sure how it would make me feel talking about it. But with you it's just like chatting to a friend. It's easier, you already knowing the people involved. Thank you, Nat.

NM: I'm glad about that, but please don't pin your hopes too much on this. I'm just telling Sam's story; seeing if it stirs up any forgotten memories. I'm not promising it's going to give you any answers.

KC: Message received and understood. Now, I'm ready for a cuppa. All this talking is thirsty work. Can I get you anything? I have biscuits.

NM: Go on, then. Tea and two sugars please.

Break in interview.

18

Caro

Present day: Wednesday, 3 July

Caro leans back in her chair and isn't sure whether to laugh or cry. Angus Redfearn! How that name and face had haunted her on that last summer before she became pregnant. Everyone at the school knew Angus - Gus to his friends, which was the whole school really. Everyone liked Gus and he was always there with a ready smile to everyone he met. Head Boy, he was secure in his place in the world and was ready to fulfil his promise at A-Level and move on to Cambridge - no doubt followed by some glittering career in the city. Fifteen-year-old Caro had no idea what that career would be (other than glittering) but she did spend many hours fantasising about the two of them clinking fancy glasses in a toast as they looked over the Thames from the swanky penthouse apartment they shared.

This was the first secret she hadn't shared with Nat. It was her secret to hug close to her, though she was sure that Gus knew exactly how she felt. She could tell by the way he looked at her, the special smile he saved for her as she scurried past him in the corridor. But she was acutely aware that time was running out for them. Gus had finished his exams, so had left school whilst she was still confined to the sticky classroom, daydreaming as she stared out the window at the grass on the athletics field that was slowly turning brown and wearing down to dust as the sports of the summer took their toll. They had this final summer in the same small town and then he would be escaping to a new world; a world which she wasn't yet sure she would be a part of. She was pinning all her hopes on the end of term summer ball. Not that she was attending the ball as a guest, but her and Nat were working as 'staff' - probably taking coats or washing up in the kitchen. Still, it was better than being sat at home wondering who Gus was dancing with.

It had caused a bit of a row actually - her working at the ball. Jez had wanted to be involved but her mother had firmly stated that he was far too young. For once, her calm, easy-going brother had thrown a bit of a temper tantrum and stormed out of the house, muttering a few choice words that made Caro giggle. A summer that had started off so glorious though, if she thinks about it now, Jez had been weird for a lot of that summer. It is obviously something she has done her best not to think about; but sitting at her laptop now, it seems easier to think about that than think about whether or not to reply to Gus.

Moving upstairs to the bedroom, she opens the wardrobe door to remove the little tin that is secreted away behind the many shoe boxes. She has no idea why she has so many pairs of shoes, most remaining unworn as she chooses her favourite pair of trainers each time. Blowing the thin layer of dust off the top of the tin, she reflects that it really has been that long since she has opened this little collection of memories. Sinking to the floor by the side of the bed, she carefully opens the lid. She does so tentatively - as if the contents may explode and reduce the house to rubble. Which, in a way, she supposes they do. She always feels the events of the past have the capacity to wreak such havoc.

There is very little in the tin. A few pretty little shells from the beach. As Caro rolls them in her hand, she is whisked back to laughing with a nine-year-old Nat on the beach as they planned a cottage business of creating shell statues to sell to the tourists. These few shapes, whispering secrets from the sea, are all that remain of that disaster.

The ring pull off a can of Coke that she had watched Gus drink, tipping his head back to gain the last few drops, as he shielded his eyes from the sun and laughed at something her mother had said. That would have been that last summer at the Beach Hut, when Gus was doing some odd jobs for her father to supplement the money he was making from his job as a lifeguard on the beach. How ironic, all 'Diet Coke' breaks and 'Baywatch' that summer. Flipping the ring pull into her other hand, Caro reflects she really had been obsessed with the boy - remembering clearly snatching the discarded metal circle from the ground when no one was looking and secreting it in her precious tin. Sometimes at night, she would slip the ring pull onto her little finger and pretend it was a promise ring from Gus. A promise that he wouldn't forget her, which was a promise he would never make as he didn't at this point even know he was supposed to remember her.

Smiling at the memory of her naïve former self, the next item is the friendship bracelet she had found discarded on the floor of the bedroom in the eaves. She had picked it up without thinking on the day Jez had died, and wasn't sure why she had kept it, hidden away, other than because at that point she felt so alone, her parents closeted in their private world of grief. She was so desperate to have something, anything really, that let her keep a little bit of Jez. And finally at the bottom of the box, the photo of Jez, forever fourteen, a mop of curly brown hair framing the tanned face that she remembers was always laughing; eyes crinkled at some joke that he had found in the world.

'Oh, Jez,' she whispers to her brother. 'Why, just why?' But the photo is unable to give her the answer, and reluctantly she consigns these trinkets of the past back to the tin. She never likes putting the photo back and closing the lid. It reminds her too fiercely of Jez's funeral and her wails as the coffin was lowered into the ground. It was the last time she had seen her parents cling to each other. As time passed, and the grass grew over the earth mounded over the coffin, her parents found a new way of living. A way that almost erased Jez from their lives, other than the odd reference to the 'unfortunate' accident. And Caro had gone along with it, and not long after that had her own drama to deal with - finding she was pregnant at fifteen and facing the disappointment in her father's eyes and the total horror on her mother's face when she finally had to tell them they were to become grandparents.

Firmly shutting the past back in the wardrobe, Caro debates whether she should clean the bathroom - a job she detests - but which will put off going downstairs and opening the message from Gus. Remembering the fury that had driven her words to Nat earlier, she decides today is the day she will face the past without fear, and that includes seeing what Gus has to say. As with all these things, it is a bit of an anticlimax.

> *Hello stranger! Nice to 'see' you after all these years. I was so sorry to hear about your dad. He was a wonderful headmaster and inspired me to strive to apply to Cambridge. I will never forget the kindness of your parents encouraging me with my studying and employing me that summer as their odd-job man. I'm back home for a few months sorting some bits and pieces. Hopefully catch up with you at the reunion. Take care x*

Leaning back, Caro can't stop the giggle that bubbles up, and then finds she is laughing until the tears run down her face. The laughter turns out to be the outlet for the grief that has been threatening to overwhelm her for the last few days. Honestly! All that anticipation for this message of nothingness. Obviously, Gus had made it very clear all those years ago where he stood once she had told him about Alex. He had run for the hills without a backwards glance. Even so, she had expected something a bit more than this slap on the back meeting of old mates. Truly more than anything, this showed her that the great love story had only ever existed in her own head.

Wiping her eyes, she decides this is the wake up call she needs to focus on what is important. Clear the Beach Hut, finally lay the ghost of Jez to rest, and maybe try to rebuild her relationship with Mark. That is solid and real and for too long has been found lacking against a romantic fantasy that has no basis in reality. Feeling better that she has a plan, Caro is jolted to see the afternoon has run away with her and she needs to collect Grace from school. For the first time in quite a while, she leaves the house thinking that maybe there is some hope for a happy ending.

19

Nat

Present day: Wednesday, 3 July

James returns home well after Annie is in bed. Nat is catching up on typing a roundup of the town news for the week. Following an influx of letters berating dog owners allowing their pets to foul on the beach, Nat had managed to get a call with a lady who claimed her son had slipped and fallen in dog mess and had ended up in hospital with toxocariasis. Nat is googling exactly what that is and trying to decide if the story had any truth in it as she hears James climbing the stairs. Moving in behind Nat, James drops a kiss on her collarbone before he begins reading over her shoulder.

'Well, thank fuck for shitting dogs!' he laughs.

Nat can't help but grin back at him, whilst telling him off at the same time. 'It's not funny, James! It's a serious issue and that poor little boy could have died.'

She can't help but think of Kate Chappell and her sad calmness as she remembered the distraught sobs of the mother of the little boy who had just been discharged from the hospital.

'I'm not making light of what happened to them,' soothes James. 'It's just dog mess looks to be the perfect distraction to the last few objectors to the quarry redevelopment. With a bit of luck, the do-gooders can move with their placards down to the beach and do something to actually help the tourist business, rather than trying to stop the inevitable progress.'

Nat is familiar with this tune and has no desire to rehash the debate about whether progress always means improvement. She stands and stretches, her shoulders tense, and gives him a quick kiss. Leading him to the kitchen, she distracts him with the offer of leftovers before asking, 'So, how did today go?'

James nods through a mouthful of cold pasta, ignoring his wife's protestations to heat it up. 'It was good. Work starts at the end of the week - just the initial clearing - but we are ready to go. The investors are all delighted. I'm telling you Nat, this is going to be the making of us.'

Nat is surprised there is no hint of the niggle of the resentment she normally feels when James is caught up in the excitement of this career-making opportunity. She has her own star to chase now, even if it isn't going to give her the same monetary reward. The doors it will open will be incredible. She is so busy plotting ahead of how she will split the time working at home and the days when she will need to be in London, that she misses what James is saying until she is jolted back to an empty silence and realises that James is clearly waiting for her to make a response.

'Sorry, I was miles away. Say that again.'

Aware that James is looking at her rather strangely, Nat feels compelled to explain further. 'I had that interview with Sam Chappel's mum today.'

As James wrinkles up his nose in the classic giveaway that he is desperately searching his brain for who Sam Chappel is, Nat feels the familiar surge of irritation that things that are important to her are clearly of no consequence to her husband. And whilst she tries to show some interest and enthusiam for his projects - such as the quarry, which, to be quite frank, listening about the plans has bored the tits off of her – this interest is rarely reciprocated. After all, she thinks ruefully as James looks at her to give him another prompt, that's what you do for the people you love. Recognising that things are unlikely to change, Nat decides to let him off the hook and gives him a clue. 'You remember: the article I've been badgering Ben to let me write for the last six months. The girl who disappeared.'

James's brow clears with relief as he takes a welcome glug from the bottle of cold beer his wife now passes to him, seemingly unaware that she wants to shove the bottle somewhere quite different than his outstretched hand.

'Oh yes, the girl that you went to school with; the story that ignited your passion for being paid to be a nosey git.' He takes the sting out of the words with a hug and an offer of the bottle for his wife to take a sip. 'Come on then, tell all! How did it go? Is this the story you hope it will be? *The one!*'

Contrarily, now that James is showing an interest, Nat finds she wants to hug the story closer to her a little longer. She has always experienced this possessiveness each time she may be about to produce something significant. She enjoys the days or weeks when she nurses the embryo of a story to life. Her alone suffering its stumbles and falls, but enjoying the closeness she feels to it, before it is unleashed to the editorial scrutiny and the judgement of her peers. Once it is out there in print, the story no longer feels so special. Nat finds that now she doesn't want to talk about it, so brushes James away with, 'It went well I think, but if it's OK with you I'd like to finish off going through my notes. I was interrupted by Caro this afternoon, so I'm a bit behind.'

James fails to prevent his eye roll and Nat grins as the unspoken agreement that Caro can be a bit of a 'Drama Queen' flashes between them.

'Tell you what - let me get a shower, then I'll do bedtime and cook us a bit of fresh pasta and you can finish off whatever you need.' Nat gives him a grateful hug, and before he can start asking her where the pasta pan is or which book is the bedtime story of choice, she escapes back to her study, to settle down once again with Kate.

Transcript of Interview with Kate Chappell – Wednesday 3rd July

NM: Thanks for the tea. I was ready for that. So, can you tell me what happened the night of the ball? Pretend I don't know anything.

KC: OK. Gosh, this is harder than I thought. OK, so the exams were finally over and Sam was excited for the ball. We'd had a few fall-outs because she still wanted to come with me to the Websters' Beach Hut, even though the tuition was over. I let her a couple of times, but then Jen had a quiet word with me – actually, not that quiet - and asked me to leave her at home now the tuition was finished. I didn't see the harm in it but Jen was the boss, so what could I do?

She couldn't stop Sam coming to the beach though, even though she would like to pretend they owned the beach too! Sam would grab a lift with me and then sunbathe on the beach with her book whilst I worked. It seemed to keep her happy and to be honest, I was happy she was there. If you remember, that was the summer there were all the gatherings at the old quarry. I think they liked to pretend it was an illegal rave, though in reality I think it was cheap cider and menthol cigarettes. Anyway, I hated the idea of Sam going there. The place isn't safe. I'm pleased that something will be done about that once they get started on the development.

NM: It's nice to see someone who favours the development. I think you may be in a minority in this place.

KC: Of course - it's your husband who is leading the development, isn't it? And to be honest, I think most people are either in favour or pretty relaxed about what happens there - as long as something positive happens. Typically, there's a few with very loud voices who manage to create a fuss; and how ironic that Angus Redfearn is once again the one with the loudest voice. The leader with his little band of adoring followers! Well, it's like it was that summer. Now, what was I saying?

NM: You were talking about Sam spending time at the beach that summer.

KC: That's right. God, my mind - can't focus on anything at the moment. At one point I was scared I was going the same way as Jen Webster, and I thought that would be just my luck. My Sam would probably return when I had lost my marbles and couldn't remember who she was. But apparently it's the old brain fog that comes to women of a certain age. Or so the patronising young man at the doctors told me. Oh, see there I go again, getting sidetracked with stuff that's of no interest to you. I am sorry. Yes, so that summer Sam seemed happy to spend some time at the beach. I had a sneaking suspicion she spent all that time there hoping to see Gus, but whether they did meet up, I have no idea. I just know that the day before the ball, she came home in a foul mood and said she wasn't going. No tears, no explanation. Just shut herself in her room and didn't want to go to the beach the next day.

I couldn't believe it. I mean, she had spent weeks planning her outfit and was so excited. I wondered if her and Gus had had a row, but then they weren't going to the ball as partners, so it all seemed a bit dramatic. I was quite upset about it all and I ended up in tears at work. Thankfully it was Chris who found me crying, rather than his wife. I felt a bit of a fool, but he sat me down and made me a cup of tea and I told him about Sam. He told me not to worry, that he'd have a discreet word with her. Apparently he had some books to drop off for her – things he thought would help her at uni.

And when I got back, it was as if nothing had happened. Sam was all smiles and dashing out to get her hair done, and so excited for the ball. To be honest, I put it down to teenage hormones.

NM: Sorry to interrupt, but did you ask Chris what Sam had said?

KC: Not at the time and then with all the upset; I gave it no more thought. Afterwards when I had time to think – had nothing but time to think - I did call Chris and ask him. He could barely remember the conversation - so it was obviously something and nothing - but did say Sam was getting nervous about moving away to university. He said she was suffering from imposter syndrome, and I felt a fool because I had to look up what that meant after I had put the phone down.

NM: But she never said anything to you?

KC: No, but at that point, as I said, she really did see Chris as a father figure, and he understood so much more this new world she would be living in.

NM: OK, so Sam went to the ball as planned?

KC: Yes. We took the obligatory photos, and I dropped her off at school and arranged I would pick her up after the champagne breakfast. She teased me because the invite said, 'Carriages at midnight' and I was all excited as I thought there were going to be actual horse and carriages prancing along the school drive.

NM: (sound of laughter) I remember thinking the same when I first started at the school. So much more exciting than it just meaning 'home time'! I don't suppose I could have a copy of one of those photos? Would be nice to have a last picture of Sam. I'm sorry, that sounds terribly insensitive.

KC: I understand and yes, I can let you have a copy. Apparently, she's in quite a few photos that the official photographer took on the night. You know, the fly on the wall ones. To be honest, I couldn't bear to look at them. But her friends told me there were some good ones. I'll get them for you before you go.

NM: Thank you. And who were her main friends? I might try and see if I can talk to them. It would be good to get some detail of the night.

KC: Umm, there's Beth Huxby - she still lives locally. Works at Churcher's herself now, in the office. Then there was Lauren Green and Kirsten Hodgson. I'm sorry, I don't have contact details for them. They have both left the area, though Beth probably keeps in touch with them.

NM: That's really helpful. So, when did you first realise something was wrong?

KC: I was there to pick Sam up from about quarter

to. I didn't want to be late, and I was enjoying watching everyone leaving. Their excitement was contagious and sitting there I felt some of their enthusiasm for life rub off on me. Ironic really! I sat and sat until there was only the odd straggler and still no sign of Sam. To be honest, I was fuming. It seemed so inconsiderate. By this time, it was twenty past, and then I saw Chris coming back to school so I asked him if he could hurry Sam along. And - I'll never forget this - he looked all confused and told me Sam had left just before eleven. Said I had insisted on picking her up early. At first, I was furious that she had made me out to be the bad guy of the piece, when she was obviously sneaking off to be doing something she shouldn't. I drove home in a real temper, ready to give her a piece of my mind. And I waited and waited. Oh God, I feel sick thinking about it.

NM: It's OK, take your time.

KC: I rang round her friends, which was embarrassing as I woke people up and I could tell they were annoyed. I still thought she would waltz through the door at any moment. Then I drove round in the car, just looking, and eventually I found myself at the Beach Hut. I could see all the lights were on and Jen and Chris were both up. You know what that window was like. I never understood it, not having blinds or something. They were clearly having a blazing row, and I felt like I was watching something on the stage with them being all lit up like that.

NM: And what time was this?

KC: It was about four am. I hammered on the door and fell inside really. Chris was simply marvellous.

He took charge of everything from that point on. Looked after me, called the police. Jen just disappeared; like it was all a bit beneath her. I kept thinking this was all a dream. I didn't realise then that this wasn't a nightmare. That this was now my life.

NM: OK, so the police set up the search for Sam. What was that time like?

KC: At first it all seemed like it was happening to someone else. And whilst I was worried, of course I was, I also was panicking about all the fuss we were causing and how embarrassing it would be when Sam turned up. With the benefit of hindsight, I can see that maybe this denial was a form of self-preservation. I mean, if I had thought about it, I would probably have collapsed on the spot. Afterwards people have said silly things about how they wouldn't have been able to cope, that I am so strong. Of course that's all fucking nonsense! Sorry, am I allowed to swear?

NM: You are allowed to say whatever you want. This is your story to tell, and I want to give you the outlet to be heard.

KC: OK, well they were talking fucking nonsense! When stuff like this happens, you have no choice. You have to carry on, to show up to the press conference, to carry on with your life. Because my only other option is to curl up and die and what good is that? I mean, for all I know Sam could turn back up tomorrow. I have no choice in the matter whilst I continue to wake up in the morning. And even after all these years, I still have hope because again, what choice do I have?

Anyway, you were here so you know how the first

couple of weeks were. Press conferences, appeals for sightings. They enlisted the public for help and it was all on the news - footage of the search parties combing the cliffs and the dunes. And not a dicky bird. Nothing.

NM: I can't imagine what a terrible time that must have been.

KC: I hope you never have to experience it. I wouldn't wish it on my worst enemy. But funnily enough, that wasn't the worst of it. At least people were looking for my Sam. She was headline news and I knew whilst she was on the front of the papers, people would keep searching. But before I knew it, she had been missing for three weeks and there had been nothing. It was like she had disappeared into thin air. And gradually the journalists drifted away to cover new stories and my Sam was confined to the old news that was resurrected every now and then - normally in reference to another missing person's case. And that is how it has been for seventeen years.

NM: Kate, I am so sorry.

KC: The daft thing is I still walk the cliff path every day. The route they think she may have taken walking from the school home. As if, after all this time, I am going to find a clue. It's just I have to be doing something.

NM: I can understand that. Thank you for talking to me, Kate. I'm going to talk to some other people, and I may need to come back to you to clarify a couple of points if that's OK.

KC: Thank you, Nat. I don't want to die without finding out where my girl is.

End of interview with Kate Chappell.

20

Nat

Present day: Friday, 5 July

Beth Huxby is sat at the back of the café, casting anxious glances between the door, her phone and her watch. Her fingers are drumming a nervous anthem on the table; and she has kept her waterproof on. Every bit of her shouts out that this is a woman who doesn't want to be here; and will be looking to make her escape as soon as possible.

Watching her discreetly through the large glass windows, Nat struggles to see if she can place her, can dredge up a memory from their time at school together that she can maybe use to persuade Beth that they really are on the same side. But there is nothing there. With a deep breath, Nat pushes open the door of the café with a fixed smile on her face, hoping she looks friendly and approachable, rather than a predator showing her teeth. Judging by the way Beth shifts further towards the edge of her seat, ready to make a quick getaway, she has been assessed as a foe, rather than friend.

'Hi. You must be Beth, I'm…'

But before she can finish Beth blurts, 'I know who you are; and I want to say I wouldn't have agreed to meet with you, apart from the fact that Kate asked me if I would and, well, you know.'

Nat is concerned to see tears fill the other woman's eyes,

magnified behind the thick glasses that keep slipping down her nose.

'Look, I'm going to order a coffee. Can I get you another? Then we can have a bit of a chat. I don't want to cause you any upset, so let's see how we go. No pressure, I promise!'

Beth reluctantly agrees to another coffee and Nat orders a couple of slices of the chocolate cake too. She has found that cake rarely fails to break the ice when speaking to women, from the 'I shouldn't really,' to the ecstatic savouring of the first mouthful as the shoulders drop and her subject starts to relax. She is aware this assumption makes her a hypocrite of the worst kind. If James had dared to issue such a stereotypical comment about women and cake, he would have paid for it dearly. Sitting down opposite Beth, she tries a smile and gestures towards the cake, but is foiled by Beth's, 'I won't - I'm diabetic.'

As the two settle down, Beth studies Nat closely before remarking, 'Kate said you were at Churcher's at the same time as me, but I can't place you at all.'

I guess that makes two of us who aren't worth remembering, thinks Nat ruefully as Beth continues. 'She said you were friends with Caroline Webster. Now Caro I do remember. Always far too pleased with herself. I see her around town still and she doesn't seem to have changed much.'

Of course everyone remembers Caro. That is the thing with the Webster family - they were different characters, but all commanded centre stage.

Nat starts to explain to Beth about the article, aware she is using the same soothing tones that works on Annie when she is upset about the latest world-ending drama in her tiny life.

Beth ushers her to be quiet. 'Kate has explained all this to me, and I don't know what I can tell you. But I said I would talk to you, so ask away. I do work at Churcher's now though, so I would like my name kept out of it. The school has spent the last seventeen years trying to forget Sam ever existed, so I don't think they would look too kindly if I were a part of this story bringing the past back to life.'

Nat nods but pauses before she speaks. 'Obviously I can promise not to publish your name, but I can't promise that people won't speculate who contributed to the article. I don't want to give you any false promises that none of this will ever come back to you because that's simply not an offer I can make. What I can promise you is I'm trying to tell Sam's story, to find out what happened that night and hopefully bring Kate some sense of peace after all these years.'

Beth's tears threaten to spill over again and Nat passes over a napkin wishing, not for the first time, that she was the sort of organised mum who always has a ready supply of tissues in her bag. However, wiping her eyes with the scarlet tissue, Beth smiles for the first time and, leaning forwards, attacks the cake with the spare fork and takes a mouthful. Nat is happy to join her in giving the sweet treat the silent savouring it deserves; and then Beth is speaking, so softly that Nat is forced to lean forwards to hear her above the clatter of the plates and cutlery at the counter behind them.

'I don't like to think too much about that summer, because the last few times I saw Sam were not happy times. The four of us – myself, Sam, Lauren and Kirsten - were tight, always had been ever since we had started at Churcher's. We were all going off to different universities, so had promised ourselves to make the most of that summer, and then it all went wrong. Do you remember Gus?'

Nat nods as Beth continues. 'Silly question really - everyone remembers Gus. Sam was besotted. Like, truly obsessed. She always liked him, but once they started going to the extra tutoring with Mr Webster, she seemed to care about nothing apart from him. It was a bit embarrassing really as she made it so obvious, and he made it pretty clear that he simply wasn't interested in her that way.'

Nat nods. 'And it was definitely Gus she had a thing for; it wasn't, say, Mr Webster?'

Beth splutters on her mouthful of coffee. 'God no, I mean, Mr Webster was ancient.'

Nat thinks privately that fifty-three is hardly ancient, but understands it was to an eighteen-year-old girl. She waits for Beth to continue.

'That summer we had planned to meet up and spend time at the beach, maybe go camping - just make the most of the last few weeks we had together. Lauren and Kirsten both had jobs at Woolworths and I was working at the ice cream kiosk in the park so any time we could snatch together was precious, you know. But Sam never wanted to do anything. She always said she was too busy, or if she did turn up, she was talking about Gus and what he had been doing; and to be honest we all got a little impatient with her. She wasn't working or anything, so out of all of us you would think she would find it easiest to make time to see us. But she kept saying she had things to do and that she needed to spend time with her mum before she went away.'

Nat tries to marry this account with the narrative she had recorded from Kate. It did seem to be the case that Sam chose to spend time with her mum, though clearly the attraction was the Webster's beach house rather than precious mother-daughter time. As she considers this, she is aware that Beth is still talking, so drags herself back to the little café. She can check up on the details in Kate's story later.

'Anyway, it all came to a head the day before the leavers' ball. We had all arranged to go to Lauren's to get ready on the night of the ball, and her mum had bought some drinks in for us and had arranged for a lady to come and do our hair and makeup. It was so exciting. I was on my break from the ice cream van, and we had all agreed to meet by the little boating pond. Next thing, Gus turns up and asks to have a word with Sam. Oh, her face! She thought, well we all thought, that maybe he was going to ask her to go to the ball with him. After all, she never stopped going on about how close they had got when they had been doing the extra studying with Mr Webster. But next thing, Gus is going back to join his friends and Sam is running the opposite way. We tried to call her of course, but no reply, and then we get a text to say she's not coming to the ball. It was all so odd.'

'But she did go to the ball – I mean, that's where she was last seen. So, what happened to change her mind?'

'Honestly? I have no idea, and I can't really tell you any more than that. You see, that was the last time I saw Sam. Ironically, it was me who didn't make it to the leavers' ball. I'd been rather lax with my medication, and I ended up on a night out at the hospital instead whilst they tried to stabilise my blood sugars.' At the memory of this, Beth pushes the half-eaten cake away. 'So you see, I can't tell you much at all. But I have spoken to the others and they are happy for me to give you their email addresses.'

As Nat takes down the details, Beth stands ready to leave, clearly relieved to have done her bit. She hesitates. 'I do hope you can find something to bring Kate the closure she deserves. She was always such a kind lady and doted on Sam. I can't imagine how she has coped for all these years. But I'm sorry, I think maybe some things are meant to be left alone. Maybe it's best we don't know what happened. Maybe there are some secrets that should stay in the past.'

21

Nat

Present day: Monday, 8 July

The morning for work starting on the quarry redevelopment arrives in a blaze of sunshine - optimistically heralding that this may be the start of summer; that this year they may finally get the long summer days, meaning you start to take for granted that you can leave the house without a coat - maybe even risking not taking a jumper.

    Nat smiles as she feels the sun on her face and her brain registers that all she can hear is the faint hum of the traffic, rather than the rhythmic pattern of rain against the window. Opening her eyes, Nat sees that James's side of the bed is already empty, the indent of his head on the pillow already starting to fade. Which probably means he has been awake for hours. She lies for a moment, trying to calculate how long she will need to stay at the quarry to show herself to be a loving and supportive wife, as well as a committed unbiased reporter. This is never an easy line to walk - keeping James and her boss happy. And really, she doesn't want to be down at the quarry at all. She wants to be delving further into the past. She can see Sam on the edge of her vision, her hand reaching to her through the fog of people's memories. Not that things seem to be getting any clearer; but who knows, the next conversation could be the one to make sense of it all.

    Yawning, she has a quick look at the email to see if

there has been a reply from Lauren or Kirsten. She had emailed them as soon as she got home after speaking with Beth, but when she eventually dropped off to sleep last night, after hours of continuously refreshing the email, there had been no response. She had kept the message quite vague but was under no illusion that Beth and her friends would have already spoken. Who knows, maybe they had agreed on their version of the truth, and this would all be a dead end. There were new messages, but just the bill for the mobile and an invitation for the reunion ball at Churcher's. How funny to think they had come full circle.

As she comes downstairs James is scooping up his car keys and papers, gesturing to the coffee pot. 'I'll see you there, got to rush!' is spluttered through the piece of buttered toast he has grasped in his teeth. He attempts to blow a kiss that is all crumbs, and Nat theatrically pretends to wipe the debris from her face as she promises to see him very soon and wishes him good luck. Not that he will need it. All the hard work has been done. The local objections have been soothed with promises of extra tourism that will be attracted to the town, with the provision of much-needed leisure facilities for use by the community (there is even a whisper that it will be free for locals on the production of a valid postcode, though James swears he had nothing to do with starting this rumour). And there have been safety concerns raised for so long, with people pointing out that for many years it has been a spot that encourages teenagers to congregate to drink and smoke - Nat supposes they will be drinking and vaping now. It's the perfect place - if they scrabble down the path that has worn in the side of the scree they are safely hidden from view, so it is a popular place for clandestine meetings.

Nat remembers from her own teenage years that there would frequently be the charred remains of a fire - evidence of a gathering the night before, the embers still smoking. The favourite spot having been beside one of the three pools of water that filled the natural springs, now the quarry machinery no longer pumped the area dry. There were fears every hot summer that someone would drown in there as they laughed off the warning signs and decided it would be fun to go for a swim, deciding the murky depths were harmless; maybe lulled into a false sense of security by the life ring, carelessly attached to the odd fence post round the perimeter, the coating of green mould clinging to the orange rubber acting as a testimony to the fact it had never been used. So surely it was safe? The water was the town's version of 'something in the woodshed' and all the local children knew the rules. If the occasional holidaymaker was tempted to venture up there in the evening - bored teenagers looking for something to do - they were quickly put off by the nettles and thistles guarding the perimeter of the water, and so gladly turned their sights back to the twinkling lights that beckoned from the amusements and the welcome cafes down by the harbour. Soon the wildness will be tamed, and most of the town have come to terms with that adjustment.

That morning everything runs so smoothly, that afterwards Nat finds it quite ironic that there was no warning portent of the day to come. Somehow it would have been easier to accept the events of the day if there had been a series of mini disasters: Annie refusing breakfast, a spill of coffee down her cream shirt, stuck in traffic which meant she was late and couldn't get parked. Yes, if all those things had happened, she felt that the day, as it unfolded, would have made much more sense. But instead, Annie's mood is as sunny as the weather, her own reflection in the hallway mirror as they left the house (on time) shows a woman as pristine as she had been when she first got dressed, and every set of lights is on green, so they sail to school drop-off with time to spare. In fact, Nat finds she is one of the first cars to arrive at the quarry. Well, first after the small group of protesters stood haphazardly and looking a bit lost, holding banners proclaiming, 'Ducks not development' and 'Butterflies not building' which - whilst Nat appreciates what they are trying to do - thinks makes their cause sound a bit lame.

However, very aware that she is here representing the paper, which has been a focus for the local outcry against the plans, she approaches the group to get a statement. There is almost a party atmosphere amongst the little group, who seem to be enjoying the wait in the sunshine and are devouring bacon sandwiches that one of them is heroically rustling up from a camping stove at the back of his Land Rover. Clearly the desire to save wildlife doesn't apply to the inconvenience of having to give up his precious four-wheel drive. As she draws closer, she can see that there are a couple of familiar faces there - not surprising really, given the size of the town. And they clearly recognise her too, judging by the nudges, the wary glances and the silence that meets her as she raises her hand in a greeting. Of course, they will see her as the wife of James, the face of the development they are so upset about, rather than Nat the impartial journalist.

Good job I'm thick-skinned, she thinks to herself as she plasters a fixed smile onto her face. Which, judging by the step back the lady closest to her takes, maybe comes across as a little deranged, rather than the open and friendly greeting she is aiming for.

'Hi, Nat Morton from The Roxcliffe Gazette. I was wondering if you would be willing to share your thoughts today?'

There is a bit of shuffling and shared awkward glances, before a man Nat vaguely remembers from the school drop off steps forward. 'Hi Nat, I know Gus will be issuing a statement later, but I think I speak for all of us when I say we are very disappointed. It's not that we want to stop progress but, you know, this is such a big thing. However, a big day for your family.'

Nat judges the words, assessing whether they bear the obvious ill will that surely these people must hold against her; but instead, finds she is being offered a bacon sandwich and relaxes into the happy chatter of the group as they observe the activity in front of them. In fact, she recognises she dreads more the move down to join James and the rest of the rather serious-looking men in suits who are waiting to celebrate the first breaking of the soil (or whatever they call it).

However, with duty one being fulfilled, it is time to support James, who is rather badly attempting to disguise the obvious giddiness he feels. Nat feels a moment of tenderness for him pretty similar to the warm feeling that would wash over her when Annie would jump downstairs on Christmas morning, brimming with excitement for the promised treasures ahead. She moves to take his hand and gives it a reassuring squeeze.

'Just in time for the main event', whispers James, and Nat thinks again that really the morning couldn't have gone any smoother.

When the machinery finally roars into life, it is a bit of an anticlimax really. There is no jeering from the little group of protesters, who seem to be more interested in getting away to enjoy the beach on the first warm day they've had for some time. Nat thinks that reflects the general attitude of the town - a reluctant acceptance of change, too tired to put up too much of a fight. Snapping a couple of pictures of James grinning proudly, sporting an orange hard hat, arms flung out expansively to embrace the dream behind him, Nat judges ten more minutes should be enough; and she can make her escape back to the lost world of Sam Chappell. Planning to pick up a bottle of champagne for them to celebrate later, in her mind she is already back in her office, plotting the first line of the article, when she becomes aware that the steady thrum of the machine has grown silent and has been replaced by the shouting of the workmen. There is another moment of almost eerie quiet - then all hell breaks loose.

Afterwards she wishes she had been more aware, had thought to record the scene with her phone; after all, she was there at the start of the story. But instead, she stands confused, wondering if there has been an accident. Maybe one of the investors has fallen in, or a protestor chained themselves to a digger. She sees James shaking his head and dropping to his knees in the dust of his beloved quarry. She notices the last of the protesters stop and turn, as if invisibly summoned to witness the power of the quarry they have been so keen to protect; and she then notices the digger, half-tipped into the natural pool which is earmarked for the diving school. This is her favourite of the pools, with the ambitious plans to sink a plane and other underwater attractions which James had explained would draw members of the diving community from across the UK - even, he would speculate after a bottle of wine, from across the world. Unfortunately, he has not counted on the attraction that had been already hiding in the depths. Because proudly crowning the rocky, gloopy waste dislodged by the toppling digger, is a human skull.

22

Alex

Present day: Monday, 8 July

This is turning out to be an epic day - which Alex is learning is often the case when you really aren't looking forward to something. They had been studying the quarry for geography and Mr Harrison, the very boring relief teacher who had been brought in to cover sickness, had decided that it would be a good idea for them to visit the quarry to see the start of the development of the area. For once they were allowed to bring their phones - the idea being they would periodically take pictures as the development progresses, and they would write about the impact on the environment and the landscape. It had been an utterly boring project so far. They had spent weeks studying the impact of quarrying and the effect on the coastline, then had listened as Mr Harrison worked himself into a frenzy of excitement explaining how and why the quarry changed after the mining stopped. Alex never wants to grow up if stuff like this is the best thing you can get excited about.

To be honest, Alex and Connor have spent most of the morning ducking down behind the gorse for a sneaky vape and trying to chat up Liz and her friends, who are without doubt the fittest girls in their year. In fact, they are making some progress - tentatively agreeing to meet down at the amusements on Friday night - when Mr Harrison comes over with a forced grin on his face and urges them, 'Come on, can we concentrate on our work please?'

As the group disperses, clipboards in hand, Alex notices Nat near the diggers and thinks about shouting down to her. Instead, he focuses his phone camera on her and starts to film. It will be a laugh to show her and James next time they are round for a boozy BBQ. Especially as James looks such an idiot in his hard hat. He will caption it 'Bob the Builder'. He is about to finish filming when the digger tips off to the right and teeters precariously on the edge of the water. Alex zooms in, really trying to capture James's face getting redder and redder, as he waves his arms around frantically. He nearly turns away and if he had, he would have missed it. As he carries on filming and zooms in, he captures perfectly the expression change on everyone's faces. Trying to focus on what they are looking at, he curses again that his mum had refused to buy him the latest version of the iPhone that has just been released. The camera on that is so much better. However, as he stares at the screen, there is no disputing that he has filmed perfectly the moment they discover a body in the quarry. He can't wait to get this uploaded onto TikTok. It's bound to go viral.

23

Nat

Present day: Tuesday, 9 July

Nat can't believe that yesterday had happened at all really. Pulling in the driveway last night, Nat saw Annie waving to her from the window, and she had forced a smile on her face and waved back. Before she had left the car the front door had burst open and Caro called out a greeting, ushering her in the house and thrusting a glass of wine into her hand. Too tired to protest that she doesn't drink on a weeknight, Nat found she relished that first slurp to oblivion. Annie had clearly picked up that her mum might not be feeling the best and grumbled and grizzled about it being bedtime, but Caro was surprisingly efficient and was soon back downstairs, sitting down opposite Nat at the kitchen table. Both of them sat in easy silence, each lost in their own thoughts.

'Look, I'm sorry I've got to dash; Alex is watching Grace, but I doubt he will have thought to get her to bed. Is there anything you need me to do before I get off?'

Nat shook her head. She seemed to have been talking all day, and her brain had finally lost any ability to string a sentence together.

'It's so horrendous, splashed all over the internet. Honestly, I thought it was a joke when I first saw it. You know, like one of these Halloween decorations flung in for a bit of a laugh.'

'I can confirm it's certainly not that.' As Nat moved to the hallway to wave her friend off, eager to reclaim the silence of the house to herself, she caught sight of herself in the hallway mirror and was shocked by the recognition that she is looking at the spitting image of her mother. Was it really only twelve hours ago that all she had to worry about was whether Sam's old school friends would reply to her email?

Relieved that Caro hadn't hung around, she moved back into the welcome silence of the house and sat to wait for James. It was nearly midnight when she heard his car pull into the drive. When he walked in the room, he looked truly shattered.

'Any further news?' she asked, but he shook his head.

'If they know anything, they're not telling me. I can't believe this, fuck knows how long it will be before they will let us start work again; and in the meantime, I'll have to keep paying the standing costs. It's an absolute fucking disaster. Honestly Nat, if I'd been there on my own I'd have thrown the bloody thing back in the water. I'm hoping it's not going to mean the site is some ancient burial ground or some such shit.'

Nat made soothing noises but couldn't help feeling that James was overreacting. Yes it's an inconvenience for him, but for someone else it could mean that their world is about to be shattered.

By the time Nat gets to her desk the next morning, the small newsroom is buzzing with excitement. It reminds her of the hidden undercurrent of excitement that had surrounded the disappearance of Sam. Everyone agreed it was terrible, but at the same time couldn't help but feel a thrill at being on the periphery of a drama. They could enjoy all the twists and turns from a ringside seat and then go home at the end of the day, knowing that all is well in their world. She can see Ben frantically waving at her to join him in his office, and she has barely had chance to sit down before he is firing questions at her.

'What happened, did they know who it was? Did they know how it got there? Maybe it was sabotage from the RANDS?'

Realising that he isn't really expecting her to answer any of these questions, and is rather in a state of excitement at the possibilities this story offers their ailing little publication, Nat is content to sit quietly and gather her thoughts. God, it irritates her the way Ben slurps his coffee. Once she can stand it no more, she interrupts him and can see he is shocked into silence as she blurts out, 'Wouldn't it be great if it's Sam Chappel?'

Ben stares at her. 'Unlikely to say the least, and a bit heartless on your part. That's a rather big jump based on no evidence at all except your obsession with this girl and determination to make a story out of it.'

Nat doesn't bother to argue, knowing that she is indeed making a huge leap, and squirms inwardly with the knowledge how badly she wants this to be the missing Sam - despite knowing what this will do to Kate. But there is no denying this could be the rocket the story needs. And does it really matter if the body isn't Sam? Just some hint that it could be will be enough to spark the interest that Nat needs to get her story on the radar.

'Look, trust me on this. If I am right, we can get ahead on this. Think what this can do for the paper.'

And for me, her little voice whispers. *Oh, this could be so good for me.*

24

Caro

Present day: Monday, 22 July

By the time Caro has packed up ready to make the short trip to the Beach Hut, she is starting to wonder why she's bothering. When she was a child, the end of term and the packing up of the car for the six weeks stay at the beach was a time of giddy excitement. She wonders if that was because at that age she had no responsibility for the packing. Now her head is frazzled with managing the logistics of leaving one house and opening up another house that has been abandoned for seventeen years. She has felt a niggling ache behind her eyes for the last week or so, and she is hoping life in the sea air might release some of that tension.

Grace is looking forward to the adventure of it all, but Alex is taking every opportunity to point out it's the stupidest thing he has ever heard. His main gripe seems to be that they are literally packing up their lives to move ten minutes down the road to slum it in a place that is missing all the essentials. By which Caro understands he means his Xbox, which seems to be his main source of communication with all his friends. She had debated letting him pack it up and installing it in the Beach Hut, but the thought of enjoying evenings without hearing him alternate between screeching at his friends or laughing like a hyena kept her firm in saying no. She needs this time to be one of peace and as she pointed out, being down on the beach means it will be easy for him to meet up with his friends at the arcades and speak to them face to face like a normal person. As a result, Alex has been monosyllabic as they pack up the car and announces he will walk down and meet them at the house later. 'Oh, cheers for all your help Alex, not sure how we would have managed without you,' mutters Caro though gritted teeth as she watches her son slouch away down the road, looking at his phone rather than where he is going.

Caro isn't sure how she feels about all of this. She has spent the last seventeen years avoiding the place, doing her best to forget the house had ever existed. She thought her parents should sell it. Instead, it was kept as if frozen in a time capsule. Once a fortnight a local cleaning firm went in and checked there were no issues. But as far as Caro was aware, neither of her parents had stepped foot in the place since they had been ushered away with the blue flashing lights illuminating their way to the car.

She is pleased to have the distraction of Grace squealing with excitement. 'Oh, our very own house on the beach. This is going to be the best summer ever!'

Caro is aware that she feels a pang of sadness that she has lost the childhood knack of living in the moment. Of taking joy in the simplest of things. Pushing open the door, she braces herself to be catapulted back into the past and feel the loss of those no longer there. But in the seventeen years the house has been empty, the last of the whispering ghosts have left its corners, and instead the place feels almost like a prop on a film set. And in some ways, Caro finds that to be the saddest thing of all.

She is pleased that she has this time to herself before Nat arrives tomorrow. That is if she doesn't make yet another excuse to delay arriving. She is obsessed with this unfolding story. In contrast, Caro is doing her very best to pretend it isn't happening. Not easy when her son is on the verge of being an internet sensation.

From the moment she saw the footage he had recorded, she felt like she had been punched in the gut and had to rush to the bathroom to be sick. In truth the shaky film, accompanied by the hyena laughing of the teenagers who clearly thought it was some sort of joke, could have been something off the latest drama on the television. And Caro isn't able to stomach those either - any discovery of death sending her hurtling back seventeen years to finding the dancing puppet of her brother that still haunts her dreams. Wiping the tears from her eyes and swilling her mouth, she had stared at the haunted eyes looking back at her and felt a real sense of impending doom. How she wishes her dad was still alive. Sometimes it would be nice not to feel like the responsible adult.

Anyway, they are at the hut now and it is time to make some happier memories. Wandering from room to room, she can hear Grace clattering on the floors above, marvelling at the master bedroom in the eaves and claiming it as her own. Ah well, Caro can't blame her for taking a chance, but as it happens no one is having the master bedroom. It isn't even that the space is special. It is a space that needs to be changed completely before they can rid it of the ghost that clings to the wood of the eaves. They need to chase that spectre away with the happy memories they will create this summer.

Avoiding the room in the eaves for now, Caro takes the passage down the hallway to the four bedrooms that run along the back of the house. There is the original master bedroom, which she has nabbed for herself. Caro has very happy memories of sneaking into this room as a small child, to cuddle with her mum and dad and plan the endless sunny days that stretched before them. Then Jen Webster had decided that it was such a waste that all the bedrooms looked out over the dunes, instead of looking out to sea, and persuaded Chris it would be an investment to convert the attic to a master bedroom with a dressing room and ensuite. And of course, whilst the builders were in, it was sensible to put in the full height glass windows at the front so that they could feel like they were a part of the ocean. Caro can remember her childish dismay when she first visited after the renovations were complete. The cosy little hut was transformed, and Caro didn't like it one bit. On reflection, she still preferred the original character of the building. After all, they were happy then. And ironically, even with all that glass they had been blind to the storm clouds that were hurtling towards them, until they realised too late they had been engulfed.

Her old room is allocated for Grace and Annie to share. Superstition dictates that she doesn't want Alex to sleep in Jez's room, so Nat will be in there. And Alex can have the guest room. Whilst the house has been undisturbed for all these years, Caro is surprised to see that all the rooms have been stripped of any of the furniture she remembers and have all been kitted out with matching bedroom suites and plain white bedding. The walls are a bland sandy colour that Caro thinks is probably from a Farrow and Ball colour chart. All hints that this had once been a family home, with posters on the wall and belongings strewn messily on the floor, have been erased. It is instead a very impersonal holiday cottage, of which they are the first guests. And Caro is very grateful for that.

Lulled into a false sense of security, she is unprepared for the boxes bursting with memories that greet her as she climbs the stairs to confront the ghost of Jez and his dancing feet. Years after it had happened, she took herself off to see a therapist. It was when she had started catastrophising about the children and Mark - living in a permanent sense of fear that something dreadful was going to happen to them if she let them out of her sight. She was open about the trauma of finding Jez, but even with the gentle probing of a professional, she could remember only his feet – and the fact that he was wearing odd socks. She would give anything to stop seeing that macabre dance.

25

Nat

Present day: Monday, 22 July

The last two weeks have been a time of madness. Nat reflects that it really has been a case of that old adage, 'Be careful what you wish for.' She has been catapulted from dog poo wars into a different shit show and is discovering that maybe the life she had before - the safe little life that she had so railed against - is maybe a life that suits her better.

James is in pieces. He swings between manic, worthless bursts of activity and hours spent staring blindly at the computer screen, before dropping his head in his hands and reaching for the ever-present whisky bottle. Nat is trying to be patient but really finds it hard to be understanding - the behaviour seems a little melodramatic. Yes, finding a body wasn't the greatest start to his dream project - and she understands that he maybe felt his moment of triumph had been stolen from him - but at the end of the day it wasn't anyone he knew. In fact, she had tried to point out to him that all the newspaper coverage might be a good thing. After all, what is the saying, 'There's no such thing as bad publicity', or something like that.

And that's when James had told her. He was in debt up to his eyeballs. Or rather, *they* were in debt up to their eyeballs. Any delays on the project would start costing huge penalties; it was the only way he could secure the loan from the bank.

And he had been so confident that the project was going to be a runaway success and would be the making of them, that he had signed on the dotted line without a moment's hesitation. Seems he had figured there was no need for Nat to be involved in this huge decision - there wouldn't be a problem, so no need for her to worry about the little details. Except, thinks Nat, as she grumpily reverses the car from the drive, now that it seems it has all gone tits-up, he has decided the problem is a joint problem.

Added to that, Nat has had very little time to move forwards with the Sam Chappel piece and to her dismay, the opening article had been bumped in favour of the story of the body at the quarry. Nat is avoiding calls from Kate Chappel, who had been banking on Nat's piece bringing Sam back from the past, where she had been conveniently forgotten. Poor old Sam. It seems fate has conspired yet again to shove her from the centre stage.

With everything going on, the planned stay at the Beach Hut is the absolutely last thing that Nat wants to do. She has managed to wangle an extra day in the office, gently suggesting to Caro that she would give her some time there alone to make some peace with her memories. Nat knows she isn't being a very good friend but, as she suspects, she is failing at motherhood, work and marriage - what is one more area of shortcoming to add to the list?

For once she has remembered her pass, but even this small victory doesn't lighten the mood, and she is not impressed to see Ben beckoning for her frantically as she heads to her desk. All Nat wants to do is retreat to Sam's world of seventeen years ago - never mind what rubbish Ben is about to pile on her. Ben is fizzing with excitement. He has been this way for the last couple of weeks. *Seems like I'm not the only one hoping there's a story that will whisk me back to the nationals*, thinks Nat, as Ben ushers her into his office and closes the door.

'Any news on the body in the quarry, Nat?' is his opening gambit. Nat tries not to sigh, as this is the question he asks her every day. He seems to think that because James is leading on the contentious redevelopment, that he will have some fast-track to the police database, allowing the local paper to be breaking news. Nat knows she should try and show some interest, but she is still pissed off that her piece on Sam had been bumped. It's not like this is the first time a body had been found in the quarry.

When Nat was around eight years old, every few months the town would see the arrival of Stan. No one knew if that was really his name, but that was what everyone called him - one of the politer things they called him! Stan was what her parents called a tramp. Nat remembered she was very frightened of him, though he had never done anything to her to justify the terror she would feel if she was playing out and glimpsed him in the distance. The minute she spotted him, trudging along the road, wearing his tatty long overcoat whatever the weather and muttering a tale to himself that no one else was interested in hearing, she would flee inside.

Once when it was bitterly cold, her mother had made him a cup of tea as he sat on a bench at the side of the road. After that, Nat and her father refused to drink from the mug she had used for Stan, even though her mother protested she had washed it and used boiling water. It was a dark blue mug, the inside a shiny white. In the end, her mother had thrown it away because she obviously didn't want to drink out of it either! Funny the things you remember. And then after a few years, Stan stopped appearing and no one really remarked on it. The next summer, a group of boys were playing at the quarry and discovered his body. It seemed he had sat down to rest there and simply never woke up. No one had reported him missing because no one missed him. Even now, Nat feels a twinge of guilt as she recalls how she would run away from him as he would wave a hand in a cheerful wave. He had been so grateful for that cup of tea, but never complained that he was never offered another.

Dragging herself back to the present, Nat takes a deep breath. 'You'll be the first to know if we hear anything, but I don't think we get preferential treatment! But I'm pleased I caught you.'

'Oh dear, looks like I made a mistake asking you in here. Let me guess: Sam Chappel.'

Nat manages a smile. 'Come on Ben, I kept my side of the bargain and I got you a good story on the drama at the opening ceremony. The least you can do now is run my first piece of the Sam series. I've got lots more to come, but I'm hoping this first article may tug at someone's hidden memory. Someone out there may know something that they didn't realise was important at the time. They may have forgotten all about it and I need them to come to me!'

'Well, you'll be pleased to know it's going online tonight. Providing nothing else happens at the quarry.'

'Ben! I could kiss you. But I won't.'

Ben grins and pulls a relieved face before dismissing her with a wave of his hand as he turns back to his computer, frowning. He is obviously looking at the updated weekly circulation figures. Nat would have liked to make a coffee and take five minutes, but she is aware the day is running away with her, so she opens her laptop and feels the familiar jolt in her stomach as she realises that she finally has a reply from Sam's friend Kirsten. About time. It has been days since she had fired off her initial email, and she has followed it up twice. She wanted to make it clear that she wasn't going to go away.

The email is brief and to the point:

Hi Nat

I'm sorry it has taken a while to get back to you, but I wanted to speak to Lauren and Beth first. I did then check in with Sam's mum. I'm sure you can appreciate that I was reluctant to accept that you had Kate's blessing on your word alone. As I'm sure you are aware, this was a very upsetting time for us. Whilst I always hope for news on Sam, I'm afraid after all this time, we have all come to accept that Sam isn't coming home.

I'm back in Roxcliffe visiting my parents this weekend and would prefer to meet with you face to face. Lauren is abroad and has no plans to return in the near-future. We have spoken, so I can pass on everything the two of us remember from that time. Could we say ten at the Beach Café on Saturday? I don't think there is much I can tell you, but I feel I owe it to Kate to help in any way I can. Please let me know if this is convenient for you.

Regards

Kirsten

Nat grins and fires off a quick response agreeing to the proposed meeting. As she sits back on her chair, she considers her next move. She had planned for the second piece in the series to be driven by the recollections of Sam's friends and their feelings today, seventeen years after the trauma of their teenage years. However, she had been forced to jiggle things around a bit when she hadn't heard from Kirsten and Lauren. She plans now to follow Kate's story with details of the police investigation. On reflection, this may have turned out for the best as she is hoping that as the piece attracts attention, there may be others willing to speak to her and she can work her charm offensive at the school reunion. All in all, Nat is feeling really pleased with herself when her phone rings. She is sharply reminded that real people are involved in her story when she sees Kate's name flash up on the screen. She hates that her first instinct is to dismiss the call and feels a familiar impatience that Kate is bothering her now when she has so much to do. After all, she has already told Kate's side of the story. But the nicer side of her - the part of her that pretends to like hot chocolate because Annie loves the family ritual of making the stuff on a rainy Sunday afternoon - that side of her presses the 'accept' button.

'Hi Kate – listen, I know you'll be eager to know when the article is coming out, but I've had it confirmed it's this week. Kate, can you hear me?'

At first Nat thinks they have a bad connection, but then she realises Kate is there but is unable to speak through the tears.

'Don't move, I'm on my way.'

As Nat runs from the office to Kate's bungalow, she curses that she isn't the hard-nosed journalist she so aspires to be. She bets when she gets there, it will be something daft. Maybe Kate has had second thoughts as the anniversary approaches. But when Kate opens the door, Nat can see she is in pieces.

'I'm sorry, I didn't have anyone else to call,' is her opening greeting; and then she stumbles against Nat, who instinctively hugs her close. As she strokes her back as Kate sobs on her shoulder, Nat finds herself cooing the soothing noises she had used when Annie was a fractious baby, struggling with colic. Eventually, Kate's sobs die down to a hiccup and Nat leads her to the kitchen and puts the kettle on. Kate seems to be in a trance as Nat finds the cups and makes the judgement to add two sugars to Kate's tea. Isn't sugar supposed to be good for shock? Not for the first time in her adult life, Nat wishes her mum was here. She would know so much better what to do.

Placing the steaming cup in front of Kate, Nat settles down opposite her and sips at her own drink, giving Kate the chance to talk when she is ready. Eventually the older woman clears her throat and, retrieving a hanky from the sleeve of her top, blows her nose and then uses the sleeve to wipe her eyes.

'I'm sorry Nat, it's so good of you to come. I feel a bit silly now.'

Nat has learnt that often the best way to encourage people to talk is to say nothing. She has lost count of the times she has sat opposite a person in silence, knowing that it's human nature to want to fill the void. Nat has her own technique of running through her grocery shopping list in her head and totting up how much it will cost. It distracts her from breaking the silence with her own rush of words. She has only got to the end of the vegetable aisle when Kate speaks.

'It's all been such a shock, I suppose. I mean, all this time I knew it wasn't going to be good news. But there's always hope, isn't there?'

Nat simply nods, struggling to see where Kate is going with the conversation. For a moment Kate stares into a spot in the distance, lost in a different world; maybe a world where Sam had come home after the leavers' ball, and she is now sat in the kitchen watching her grandchildren play in the garden.

Dragging her gaze back to Nat, Kate swallows deeply and then, clearing her throat, whispers. 'It's the body in the quarry. They think it might be Sam.'

26

Nat

Present day: Monday, 22 July

When Kate drops those words into the silence of the kitchen Nat has, for once, not had to resort to her technique to stop her breaking the silence. She feels like the words have been snatched from her and her voice lost until Kate shares the details. It's almost as if now the initial outburst of grief has subsided, Kate is numb. That she is now just a shell of her former self, and Nat wonders now if that will be Sam's legacy to her mother: Kate condemned to going through the motions, waiting for the time when she can escape the land of the living and finally be reunited with her daughter - if she even believes that such a place is waiting for her.

Kate speaks in a quiet voice - flat, defeated. 'I thought I wanted to know, but it seems I was fooling myself. I hated living with the uncertainty - thought it would be easier if I knew Sam was dead. That she was never coming back to me. But it turns out I was wrong. The prospect of living without that little glimmer of hope, I'm not sure that's something I can bear.'

'But what's made you think the body is Sam? I mean, there's no way her body could have been there for all these years. Look at Stan, the tramp. He had no one looking for him and he was found after a few months.'

'I don't understand any of it, but they were pretty clear

in what they were telling me. I was sat in the garden, thinking about the anniversary, and there was a knock on the door. I thought it was Pat dropping my Avon order round; that spray that is supposed to stop you getting bitten.'

Nat manages to hide her frustration and bites back the snapping, 'Just get to the point, will you,' recognising that for Kate, sharing the details is one step closer to making the unthinkable real. So they sit there in the peace of the kitchen, the birds singing in the sunshine, proving that life really does go on. Even though for Kate, her world has been shattered.

'Anyway, it was a man and a woman in suits. I thought it might be the Jehovah's Witnesses and so I was already saying I wasn't interested when they introduced themselves. I can't even remember their names now, though they left me a card.' Kate gestures over to the kitchen counter, where Nat can see what looks like a business card. Her inner voice makes a note to take a photo of it before she leaves the house, then she drags her attention back to Kate's words.

'I knew as soon as they asked if they could come in that it wasn't going to be good news. The woman even asked the chap to make me a cup of tea, and I've watched enough stuff on TV to know what this sort of thing means. Anyway, to be honest it was all a bit of a blur, but they explained they had reason to believe the body in the quarry could be my Sam. They asked for details of her dentist - said they would ask for dental records - and then asked if Sam had ever broken any bones, had to have surgery to repair the joint. I explained she had broken her wrist falling off a bloody donkey when she was fourteen. I mean, who pays for a donkey ride at that age? I told her it served her right. Poor donkey probably couldn't wait to get her off its back. And the minute I mentioned it, I saw the look they gave each other.'

Nat reaches over to cover Kate's hand with her own. 'Maybe they are contacting the families of everyone missing within a certain area,' is the best she can offer. Though even to her own ears, it sounds weak.

For the first time, Kate is dragged back fully to the present, and her eyes flash with something approaching contempt as she snaps back. 'Don't be bloody stupid! You're a journalist - you know better than most what it means if there are reports of a missing person followed by the discovery of a body. They say they are keeping the family of so and so informed with the latest developments, but you know what we all think. It's only a formality before they make the announcement.'

Nat is unable, or unwilling, to meet Kate's eyes, knowing the other woman is right. And knowing the reassurances she has tried to give are not to comfort the older woman, but to allow her to escape to her computer. Her heart is racing; she has a head start on this one. She needs to tell Ben to get her first piece on the front page. Then they can update it with the breaking news once the identity of the body in the quarry is confirmed. Maybe she should get in touch with a few of her old contacts, give them the heads-up and offer them the first chance to take her story.

She is itching to escape, dreaming of being fought over by the nationals. But she forces herself to sit with Kate until there is another knock on the door. And this time it is Pat and Nat is able to slip away, with promises to check back later.

'Thanks for coming Nat, I really do appreciate it.'

'We will find out what happened to your Sam. I promise.' Nat flinches as she says the words, aware she is making a promise she has no idea if she can keep.

Kate seems comforted by the empty assurance, whispering, 'I hope so. My poor baby, she hated the water - couldn't swim. I can't bear to think of her being there all that time. She must have been so afraid.'

27

Gus

Present day: Monday, 22 July

Glancing at his watch, Gus judges it is still too early to have the pint he has been thinking about all day. Obviously, it isn't just the one pint he is craving. What he craves is the peace he is striving for that too much alcohol will give him. He knows he is fooling himself.

It was last night and that bloody Tik-Tok video that had done it. Once he had reached the halfway point on the whisky bottle, he had gone down the rabbit hole of social media, firing off emails to the RANDS committee with suggestions as to the next step. Becoming increasingly frustrated at what he perceived to be the tardy responses from the rest of the group, he had been furious at one message suggesting that maybe they should focus instead on the rumoured new housing that was to be situated on the site of the old Middle School playing fields. Easily distracted, the rest of the group had seized on this new challenge with glee and were back and forth with suggestions of how the site could instead be utilised for the community. Idiots! Recognising that now was not the time to spill forth his thoughts on how useful they all were, he instead found himself tumbling down the black hole of social media.

It was all the usual stuff: a few bits of speculation on local forums about the discovery of the body. But the general consensus was that it was likely a repeat of what had happened before - someone with no family or friends to miss them had fallen ill whilst sleeping rough at the quarry and had remained undiscovered until the developers had disturbed the site years later. There was a bit of chatter that maybe there would be some archaeological significance to the site, but this was swiftly shot down by some know-it-all explaining that the site was a working quarry up until fifty years ago. So, it was unlikely there had been any ancient civilisation living inside the rocks that were blasted away to form the quarry as it exists today.

And then it had suddenly appeared in front of him: the moment the digger revealed the gruesome parting gift of the quarry. Uploaded on Tik-Tok and playing in a macabre reel, over and over. The image was grainy, but there was no mistaking what it was. The camera had quickly switched from its focus on James - zooming in to his smug grinning face framed by the ridiculous orange safety helmet. This had obviously been the objective of the video as the person behind the camera was clearly humming the theme of 'Bob the Builder' in between sniggers, and the comment of 'Here we have the lesser-spotted James looking like a right knob!'

And then as the digger lurched towards the water and the shouting began as the footage switched from the living to the dead, the only noise from behind the camera was deep breathing and a sworn obscenity. The filming was interrupted in response to some indecipherable command off-camera and the view swung around, before filming the unwelcoming landscape of jagged rocks to which the prickly clumps of yellow gorse clung, before finally finishing.

Gus had caught his breath as he watched the footage again. He wasn't interested in the discovery of the bones. He had scrambled for his reading glasses so he could see clearer, and his stomach had churned as he realised there was no doubt about it. The little shit had unintentionally managed to capture Gus as he had stood, thinking he was hidden from the view of both the workers in the quarry and the protesters who were enjoying their picnic in the sunshine. It was a deeply private moment as he mourned the desecration of the quarry he had fought to protect.

He was furious last night. Still is now. He has no desire for his obvious misery to be broadcast for strangers to laugh at. He looks like some sort of pervert lurking in the bushes. He knows it's unlikely he will even be noticed by the majority of viewers - they will only be interested in the emergence of the body - but that isn't the point. Gus is absolutely beside himself.

At three in the morning, when he had woken with his heart pounding and his mind racing with the thoughts he had tried to drown out the night before, he had sworn it was time to get his act together. He had wallowed in the misery over the way things had turned out for him for far too long. After tossing and turning for a couple of hours, he had given up and stood under the dribble of a shower, the power shower from his flat in London being one more thing to miss so bitterly. Ironic that he can't feel the power of clean water to wash away the grubbiness that seems to cling to him now that he is back in this place. He has spent the rest of the day feeling like he is drowning in the salty water that he can see from each high point on the estate. Brushing his teeth repeatedly hasn't stopped his mouth feeling like he has slept face-down in the sand of the beach, and he has spent most of the day rubbing his eyes to try and clear them from the scratchy grit that is all in his mind.

By mid-afternoon, when he finally makes it to the farm office to look at the accounts, (which he has been promising himself he would do for the last two weeks) he flinches as he catches a glimpse of himself in the computer screen before he switches his camera off. Resolving that today he will start to sort things out, instead he decides to have a quick scan of the email, telling himself this is work as there might be something there that he needs to pull that quarter's figures together.

Scanning through the unread messages, he lets out a relieved breath when he realises there is nothing new there about the development at the quarry. It has been a strange time since the grand opening, which had turned out to be rather more the opening of a can of worms. He isn't sure what he has been expecting, but is relieved to see there isn't a flurry of messages saying that he had been spotted on that bloody video which has apparently now gone viral, whatever that means.

He should learn a lesson from this: best to keep his head down and get on with the jobs that have to be done. He hadn't meant to get involved in the campaign to be honest - the quarry was far enough away from his family estate that really, he could pretend it wasn't happening. Some suggested he should be concerned as it may impact the popularity of the holiday cottages dotted around the estate. But Gus was confident they were appealing to different price points. Really, if the quarry was opening new attractions such as the diving and swimming lakes, he just saw that it was enhancing the appeal of the area, which really could only be good for him. But sat one evening in the pub, he couldn't help but eavesdrop on the noisy group who had set up headquarters around the large table in the corner, and listening to their arguing and disjointed plans of action drove him demented. And then he thought maybe this was what he needed. He had thrived on high pressure bids in the city, excelled at leading and motivating a team; it had been that way since school, and he really thought that if he had to face many more weeks with nothing but the easy predictability of the estate (which in reality ran itself), he might end up drinking himself into an early grave. On the spur of the moment he'd wandered over, introduced himself, and as he knew he would, had taken over and turned the campaign into something with half a chance of success.

He would have been amazed if they had managed to stop the development. But they had made enough of a nuisance of themselves to get some local news coverage and to cause a bit of a headache for the investors. And as he got more involved in the campaign, he became more convinced that the quarry should be left to the nature that had embraced it once it had been abandoned the first time around. How ironic that they had been so concerned about disturbing the living wildlife, when it would be the dead that succeeded in stopping the work. Though Gus has no doubt it is simply a short-term reprieve.

He has never liked the quarry. Avoiding it at all costs, turning his head away if the school planned a cross country run along that part of the coastal path. He can't explain why it still makes him so uncomfortable. He had tried to tell Mr Webster once - how he felt drawn to the edge, and even though he didn't want to, feared something would compel him to step off the path into oblivion and be enveloped by the cool depths below. Mr Webster had looked at him a little odd, so Gus decided not to mention it again, just as he never mentioned the calling of the sea, persuading him to walk into its soothing arms and keep walking until he belonged to the salty waves.

Dragging himself back to the business of the accounts, Gus instead finds himself pushing back his chair and with a 'Fuck it!' he heads out to make his way down to the harbour to sink into the safe comforting arms of a pint.

28

Caro

Present day: Monday, 22 July

'Mum, Mum I'm hungry!' The feel of a warm body wrapping around her legs and the plea for food drags Caro away from the screams of the past.

'I can make us a mini picnic?'

Grace's mouth turns downwards in an expression rarely seen on her face, but which instantly reflects the young Alex. 'I was thinking chips and an ice cream before the amusements.'

The difference between her two children, Caro reflects as she packs up a sandwich, is Grace is easily pleased. With the promise of a trip for fish and chips for tea, Grace is happy to set up with her colouring on the decking of the hut, allowing Caro to make a start on the desk in the room her father used as an office. Walking into the room, Caro is struck again how different this space is from her father's office back at Churcher's. At the school it was all heavy dark furniture, the walls groaning under the weight of wooden panelling, the darkness broken by an occasional painting that had been gifted to the school. The paintings were all the same in Caro's opinion: dull! The perfect backdrop for her father, always formally dressed wearing a tie, even on the most sweltering summer's day. The school prided itself on its long traditions. Its critics would say it struggled to move with the times.

By contrast, the office here makes the most of the natural light. Her mother had painted the walls a shade of blue that seem to absorb the colour of the sea. A young Caro had always marvelled that the room seemed to reflect the weather outside until she realised, as she got older, that the paint reflected the light that streamed through the window that ran the length of the wall. There was no need for pictures on the walls of this room. The window framed the most beautiful landscape imaginable - a perfect living picture. The furniture was light wood, her mother declaring it should look like driftwood from the beach. Whilst this had always been her dad's space at the Beach Hut, Caro had spent hours in the room; always choosing to sit and read with her dad when the rain was clamouring against the window. It was in this room where her dad tutored his favourite pupils. Not always the brightest. Just the ones in which he saw a spark of something. Caro often wonders if he had ever seen that same spark in her.

Standing in the door of the room, she expects to get a sense of her father - the hint of a scent of his aftershave, allowing her to believe that he is still with her. But the room smells a little musty and the colour of the walls is grubby and flat - no longer a reflection of the light, but simply a faded blue. The room looks old and in need of some care and attention. Caro just can't understand why her parents never sold the place. It was made very clear they didn't intend to pass it on to Caro to use when her family was small, and they never even walked down to the beach since Jez had died, so they would never enjoy the hut again. It seems a form of torture that they had kept it on. It must have been a constant reminder every time a bill needed to be paid, or the cleaners alerted them to work that needed to be done. It was so out of character for her father and the way he had dealt with everything else surrounding Jez's death.

Sitting at the desk, with the main doors flung open to try and let some air into the place, Caro finds the afternoon slipping gently away from her. She keeps breaking off to admire Grace's latest masterpiece and is able to tell when it's late afternoon as the sound of the sea intensifies, signalling high tide, and the light changes to a kinder sunlight that dances on the cobwebs in the high corners of the room. Caro is lost in a world that had been so safe and familiar seventeen years ago. She feels underneath the desk drawer to reach for the key that her father used to Blu-Tak there, him laughing as he told her to close her eyes as he was doing top secret business. Her father knew Caro could be trusted, and she feels an irrational surge of guilt as she uses the key for the first time to access the little wooden cupboard which sits alongside the desk.

Caro finds treasure, worthless to anyone else; but she greedily sifts through the mementoes her father had safely entrusted to the four boxes stored away. Who knew if her father remembered he had kept these things? She wonders if he ever walked to the hut and quietly spent some time revisiting his memories. It seems they both kept their boxes of special things and she regrets bitterly that she hadn't shared her own keepsakes with her dad when he was still alive. Instead, she visits the past alone, her dad now gone and her mum simply disappearing.

Lots of photos of the family at the beach, playing cards out on the decking, her mum raising a champagne glass in a toast as she presides over a steaming bowl of mussels displayed triumphantly on the kitchen table. The photos tell the story of endless carefree summers, and Caro finds she is both smiling and crying as the past clamours to be remembered. They had been so lucky in the life they had. It seems inconceivable that it could have gone so wrong. Vowing to get these photos safely back to her own house and maybe choose some favourites to put on display, Caro imagines the happy hours she can spend with Grace and Alex, showing them that she was young once too. It will be nice for them to see their grandparents looking so fit and carefree. Caro had forgotten how mesmerising her mother was. She shouted for attention in every photo she was captured in and, even if she was caught on the sidelines, your eyes drew her to centre stage. And she had been the centre stage at the Beach Hut. Their door was always open and there was a constant stream of visitors all happy to give Jen the attention she demanded.

It's funny to see herself and Jez growing up in the photos. As was typical of her dad - the boxes had been organised into strict date order - and as she opens the last box, Caro is reluctant to discover the contents. These must be the last photos they had at the Beach Hut. The last summer as a family of four. The last summer of Jez. But the photos continue the happy theme. Her mother seems to glow more than the previous year, if anything looking younger. Her father has developed a furrow between his eyes, but she remembers it had been a tough year at school and he had been spending hours tutoring his chosen waifs and strays. Speaking of which, there they were at the first BBQ of the summer break.

Her breath catches as she strokes Gus's image and smiles at the look of adoration on her fifteen-year-old face. He must have known exactly how she felt about him. Looking at the photo, she can see that she wasn't the only one. Her expression is matched by Sam's. Mousy Sam, hidden away at the back, close to Chris - as if being near him would make him the father she was missing from her life. Gus is brandishing the BBQ tongs and laughing at the camera. Jez is scowling at the camera and Caro frowns as she flicks through some of the other photos, noticing that Jez looks sulky on most of them.

She also notices that even on the brightest day, when others in the photos are sporting swimming things or shorts and t-shirts, Jez was never out of a long sleeve top and tracksuit bottoms, normally in black. What a change from the summer before when he was a young boy, happy to wear the colourful outfits his mother bought. Funny how she can't remember him changing to a sulky teenager. She supposes she was too caught up in her own worries. Maybe they all had been. Certainly, they all missed the signs that would have helped to save him.

The last photo is the night of the leavers' ball. Jez must have taken this photo as it was Caro in the middle of her mum and dad, Chris looking like an old-fashioned Hollywood movie star in his pristine tuxedo. Next to him was Caro. She remembers her mum arguing her black skirt was too short and that she needed to do up the top few buttons on her white blouse. In contrast, Jen commanded all the attention in the photo. She literally sizzled in a dress of silver sequins, which should have looked tacky but instead made her look like a beautiful mermaid. Her long dark hair fell gently round her shoulders, and she wore no jewellery aside from her gold wedding band and a simple pair of diamond studs. Caro remembers the dress looking so demure at the front, which was unusual for Jen, who was never shy about showing off her figure. Caro had been puzzled by her mother's choice, until she turned away and showed the back of the dress, cut so low that it skimmed the top of her mother's perfectly pert bum. Caro giggles to herself as she remembers her dad trying to persuade his wife to cover her bare back with a throw, complaining it was highly unsuitable for a school ball. Jen had refused, eyes glittering in evidence of the two glasses of champagne already consumed.

Declaring it was important to show at least one cleavage - and wiggling her bum to make it clear what she was flaunting - she had crackled with a dangerous energy that night. Caro thinks that was maybe the last photo of her mother looking like a young model, rather than the headmaster's wife and mother of two. The tragedy of that summer stole Jez from them but also stole something integral to the character of her mother. It sounds corny, but Caro can see that the light inside her mother had simply been stubbed out that summer. Caro thinks this photo is maybe the saddest she has seen. She scours their faces to see if they showed any hint of recognition that tragedy was ahead. But it is clear that none of them had any idea that in a few short days they would be set on a path that would change their lives.

29

Nat

Seventeen years earlier: Saturday, 4 August

Caro and Nat had fallen out on the night of the leavers' ball. They were both working that night. Caro had been torn between wanting to be at the ball so she could keep an eye on Gus and the rather less glamorous fact that she would be there serving canapes to the people who actually had a ticket. Nat was glad of the money. They had to be there for six-thirty and were running late as Chris had made Caro go back and change once he saw the length of the black skirt she had thought she could get away with. Nat had thought he would tell Caro to wash her face at the same time, but as usual Caro managed to get away with pushing to the limit what her father deemed to be acceptable.

They had spent all afternoon doing their makeup. More accurately, Caro had spent all afternoon doing her makeup and Nat had spent that time offering the admiring words that were required at frequent intervals. Caro had finished off with a triumphant swipe of the expensive rich red lipstick that Nat could see immediately was Jen's. Nat caught her looking and winked at her. 'No, she doesn't know I took it, but she won't miss it. She's always losing things and already has a new one to put in her bag this evening. Besides it looks better on me. I think Mum's getting too old to get away with red lipstick.'

Nat thought that nothing could have been further from

the truth. Jen wore her lipstick like it was a part of her. It drew attention to the full slightly parted mouth that could seductively tempt every male in the room, whilst spitting venom at those who had displeased her. The splash of red seemed to emphasise that if you were on the receiving end of either of these, you were in trouble. It was just that one sort of trouble was a lot more pleasurable than the other. In contrast, Caro looked like she been rooting in her mum's dressing up box. The richness of Jen's lipstick had transformed to a garish slash of colour that made her look trashy, rather than the siren she wanted to be. Wisely, Nat kept this observation to herself.

Because they were the last to arrive, it meant they got allocated the shittiest of jobs, so weren't even out serving - but instead were refilling trays and piling up pots for the washing up. Stuck in the back, Caro was sulking and bitching that she would never get Gus to notice her at this rate. Somehow that got turned around to all of this was Nat's fault.

'If I didn't have you and Jez trailing round after me like a couple of losers, then I reckon he would have asked me out by now.'

And Nat was tired of all this. For one thing, Jez hadn't trailed round after them for the last eighteen months. Caro hadn't even noticed but her little brother only had eyes for Sam and followed her round like a little lost puppy, blending easily into the background so no one, least of all Sam, ever really noticed that he was there. And it wasn't Nat that was stopping Gus noticing Caro. Normally Nat would have let it go, but she snapped back, knowing that she was reacting to the summer of managing Caro and her moods, and that she would end up feeling like she had been unreasonable.

'Gus probably doesn't look at you because you're such a bitch, Caro.'

For a moment Caro had stood there with her mouth open, her reaction as shocked as if Nat had slapped her round the face. Then she burst into tears and went off somewhere round the back, clearly expecting Nat to follow her and apologise. Instead, Nat carried on with the stacking of the dirty dishes - thinking this was typical that Caro had got out of doing any of the work but would still end up getting paid exactly the same as Nat.

It was a long night, and by the time Nat could hear the disco starting the last slow dances her feet were killing her. She thought she better go and search for Caro, seeing as she was supposed to be staying with her that night. She could see that a few of the waiting staff had obviously been hanging round by the bins and had left the evidence of an empty half litre bottle of vodka and a couple of smoked cigarette butts, one of which was stained with the distinctive lipstick that Caro had nicked from her mum. This irritated Nat even more, knowing her friend had been happily drinking and smoking whilst she slogged away doing the work that should have been split between the two of them.

Wandering back towards the entrance lobby of the school, Nat saw Chris Webster ahead of her and recognised she felt a pang of relief. With the mood Caro was in, she wouldn't have put it past her to have left her at the school to make her own way home. Chris was in full benign headmaster mode. He was having a word with every pupil who would soon be leaving the school, no doubt aware that one day he would be writing to these former pupils to ask them to donate to the school's latest fundraiser. Most of the pupils were heading towards the steady stream of cars, driven by whichever parent had drawn the short straw that night. Nat could see Kate waiting at the end of the drive and looked round for Sam. It was likely that Sam and Gus would be the last to leave. They both adored Chris Webster and if he was still there, then they would be found not too far away. But as the crowd leaving the school thinned out to the last few stragglers there was no sign of Gus, Sam or Caro.

Nat felt a bit awkward then. Chris looked to be getting

ready to leave and she wasn't sure whether he knew she was staying back at theirs. Vowing that this was the last time she would arrange to stay with Caro, she couldn't help the smile that spread over her face as her friend hugged her from behind and gave her a kiss on the cheek.

'I'm sorry Nattykins. I've been a real bitch, haven't I?'

Nat was aware that Caro didn't expect her friend to agree with her on this. So instead, she hugged her back and whispered, 'I've missed you!'

Caro's eyes were slightly glazed, but other than that she was steady enough and waved over to her dad, who smiled as he saw the pair of them approaching.

'That's good timing. Mum's gone already. She had a really bad headache. I think that might have been a bit too much Mr Brigham though. Still, she charmed the old bugger, and he left us a very nice cheque. So sorry girls, it's just the three of us walking home.'

Caro grimaced. 'Can't we get a taxi? My feet ache. We've been slaving away all night.'

Nat had to stifle a giggle. This was why she loved Caro. She really did have absolutely no shame and, in a typical fashion, she got away with it. Chris hesitated and Nat could see that once again her friend was going to get her own way. But before he could reach for his phone, they were interrupted by Kate Chappell. Caro rolled her eyes, but Nat smiled a welcome to her, as did Chris.

'Hello, Chris. Looks like it's been a brilliant evening, though there may be a few sore heads in the morning.'

At this Nat couldn't help but glance at Caro, who steadily met her gaze. If she ever took up poker, she would be unbeatable!

Chris laughed. 'I'm pleased it's all done for another year, and we managed to raise a decent amount too.'

'Any chance you could call in and ask Sam to get a move on? You know what she's like. If Gus is in there, no doubt Sam will be too!'

Caro stiffened and Nat thought it odd that her friend really was oblivious to those she thought to be on the periphery of her world. As Jez had mooned after Sam, poor mousy Sam had trailed round after Gus, and, like Jez, she remained unnoticed - of no more importance than the other bits of background scenery in the drama of his life.

'Sorry, Kate. Sam left nearly an hour ago now. Said you were picking her up early.'

Seeing the flush appear on Kate's face, Chris laid a hand on her arm. 'Is everything OK?'

Kate laughed nervously. 'Yes, no problem. What am I like? I've got muddled up on the times. Sam will be cursing me if she's had to walk all the way home. I better get off and try and catch her up.'

With that, Kate hurried back to her car.

'That's odd, Dad. It won't have taken Sam an hour to walk home, even if she didn't take the shortcut on the coast path.'

Chris nodded. 'Come on, we can keep an eye out on the way home.'

Caro looked at her father and smiled rather slyly. 'Oooh, do you think Miss Goody Two Shoes has gone off drinking and smoking when she should be tucked up at home in bed?'

Chris didn't bother to reply, even as Caro continued. 'Remember last year - that group went skinny dipping. That will be Saucy Sam tonight!'

'Shut up, Caro! You really can be very childish. Come on, we can walk home along the cliff path; and if we see Sam about, then I can make sure she gets home to her mum.'

The three of them trudged off, Caro grumbling about her poor feet, unaware that this was the last night in a while that they would have the energy to bicker about nothing.

30

Nat

Present day: Monday, 22 July

Nat takes her time walking back to the office, choosing instead to wander down to the harbour. She always likes coming here - the harbour is solid and busy with boats. Whilst the fishing boats have declined over the years, these have been steadily replaced by the boats for the tourists, offering daily sailings throughout the year. The booths that once were the focus for the sale of the fish hauled ashore, now shelter a couple of bored-looking women, usually with a book or some knitting to pass the time, as they tempt the passing tourists to experience the best boat trip on offer. The place is bustling and singing in the summer, and a little lost as the colder weather sets in, with only a few hardy souls braving a trip on the winter seas.

Almost on autopilot, she soothes her racing thoughts with an ice cream, barely registering the taste as she tries to make sense of everything she has just heard. She definitely feels out of practice on all this. More raw. Ten years ago, she would have covered this story with no thought or care for the emotions of those involved. Is it having Annie, becoming a mum, that has made her soft? As her breathing slows and she is lulled into relaxation by the familiar noise of the seagulls who are circling ahead, tempted by the ice cream treat, she formulates a plan of action for the rest of the day.

She is working with a very small window of opportunity

now. If the body turns out to be Sam, the town will once more be inundated by the national press. But as well as the professionals, she has no doubt they will see the arrival of the amateur sleuths. She has marvelled at this so many times in the last few years. How the TikTokers circle the scene of a tragedy, pretty much the same as the seagulls are circling her ice cream, both greedy for a bite. She needs to make the most of the small amount of time she has.

Nat debates what to do with the information she has from Kate. She knows that Ben will tell her to contact the police officer in charge of the case; to hassle them for a statement. But Nat is reluctant to do this. If there is a hint that the press are sniffing round, linking recent events to the disappearance of Sam, they may decide to issue a press release and tip off the rest of the pack. For now, Nat decides to keep the information to herself and press on with the plan she has in place for the day.

Checking her watch, she curses and discards the remainder of the ice cream in the bin, where the bravest seagull risks swooping down and carrying away its prize for its daring, hotly pursued by those trying to steal it away. Nat thinks that is pretty much how things will work out for her with this story, so she needs to make sure she twists and turns and moves swiftly so others don't steal her opportunity. By the time she has climbed the cobbled street up to the bustling streets near the newspaper offices, she is sweating and feeling slightly sick. When will she learn that ice cream really isn't her friend? Flashing her pass at an unsmiling Tim, she reaches her desk in record time and, grabbing her laptop, gets settled into the empty meeting room she has booked with minutes to spare. Logging onto Zoom, she can see that retired DI Stephens hasn't yet joined the call, so she takes the time to smooth her hair and make sure she is ready to make the most of the time she has.

When the retired detective appears on her screen, Nat

feels a jolt of recognition, coupled with shock, with how he has aged. She doesn't know why she feels so surprised; it is seventeen years since she had tried to catch a glimpse of the man as he had strode purposefully into the police station, looking wearier as the weeks passed with no positive news to impart. Nat has read somewhere that all police have the one case, unsolved, that they can never get out of their minds. She is hoping that the disappearance of Sam Chappel is that case for DI Stephens.

DI Stephens had seemed old to sixteen-year-old Nat, but he would have been in his late forties, at a guess. So now he will be approaching seventy, and the lines on his face show every one of those years. Nat remembers he had been brought in from regional headquarters, so she guesses his job had exposed him to some gruelling cases. But he smiles at her as they make their introductions and his voice is strong and authoritative - just as she remembers when she had watched him on the local news, giving updates on a case where there was nothing to say.

'Thanks for your time, Detective Inspector,' starts Nat, but is interrupted.

'Retired Detective Inspector. I think it's important to make sure that is clear. So why not call me Mike?'

Nat smiles. 'Mike it is. I really do appreciate you talking to me about Sam Chappell. I grew up in this town and went to school with Sam, though I'm a couple of years younger. I remember her disappearing so clearly, and the huge effort that went into trying to find her. As you're aware, I now work for the local paper and I'm writing a series of articles - with the blessing of Kate Chappel - to see if we can find out anything new.'

'I did take the liberty of speaking to Kate. Not that I don't trust journalists or anything.' Mike flashes a grin at Nat which quickly fades as he continues. 'I always felt bad for Kate. I mean, we did everything we could at the time, but I always felt that we had let her down somehow.'

'Let her down? Can you tell me more about that?'

'Oh, it was nothing that was wrong with the investigation. We followed best practice to the letter. But it was like Sam disappeared into thin air. I've kept an eye on it over the years. Up until my retirement seven years ago, every six months or so I would run a standard check. You know, any claim for benefits, any application for a passport. All the usual stuff; and there was never anything. Not that I expected there to be.'

Nat tips her head, inviting the older man to elaborate.

'Look, we never said at the time, but within a couple of days, the feeling of most of the team was that there had been foul play involved. I mean, there were no credible reports of Sam being seen after she left the school. No one came forward to say they had seen her walking out of town or had given her a lift. We trawled the CCTV of the town bus station and then widened that review to cover a larger area. And nothing. If Sam had left town, it must have been by car. And if someone gave her a lift, they weren't coming forward to tell us about it. That's not a good sign that their motives were innocent.'

Nat nods. 'That makes sense. So, you didn't think Sam had maybe run away?'

Mike thinks about this for a moment. 'The local police initially thought Sam had likely stayed out with a boyfriend. She was seventeen - a week or so short of eighteen - getting ready to go off to university. So there wasn't a particular urgency when they first received the report. Even though her mum was going frantic, insisting this was all very out of character. But without sounding too jaded, that's what they all say.'

Remembering Kate's account of the night Sam disappeared, Nat thinks you couldn't judge the police too harshly for this assumption. Kate too had been annoyed at what she thought was Sam's lack of consideration in sneaking off - definitely irritated before the fear started to take hold.

'And when did all that change?'

'We got another call the following lunchtime. To be honest, I think the local police would have left it longer, were it not for the involvement of Sam's headmaster. He was a very forceful character, to say the least.'

'That would be Chris Webster?'

'That's right. He was brilliant with Kate. She was on her own, no other family really, and didn't appear to have many friends; and Chris, he went above and beyond. At one point we did query whether there was something more to his relationship with the family.'

'Sorry, what do you mean by that?'

'Well, he was involved as much as any family member would have been. He rang the station every day, even after the case had gone cold. We did wonder if maybe he and Kate were in a relationship. But there was never a scrap of evidence to suggest that was the case. Seems he was a decent man who was doing his best. Poor bugger had his own tragedy to deal with after that, and understandably his calls to the station stopped around then.'

'Ah yes, the death of his son.' Nat is surprised how there is no emotion in her voice. How can she speak of Jez like that? The little brother of her best friend. The little boy who had trailed round after them for years, until he reached an age where it wasn't cool to hang around your sister and her friends.

'Yes, completely tragic. By this time, we had taken statements from everyone who had been at the leavers' ball. We had even spoken to staff and pupils who hadn't been there. We had scoured hours of CCTV of the high street, the bus station, the railway station. My team had spoken to all the local taxi drivers and had kept widening the search area just a little bit more, but no joy.

'As a last resort, we did a reconstruction of Sam leaving the ball and heading towards the clifftop path. Just to see if it jogged anyone's memory. The trouble was, we didn't know where Sam had gone once she reached the path. Had she followed the path towards the harbour or turned towards the quarry? And we had some luck. Two different calls both confirmed she had been seen heading towards the harbour, and this supported the idea that she had been making her way home. We focused quite some man hours to that area, even sending out the divers to search the coastal waters after the Coastguard had tracked the currents, and we were able to pinpoint where we should concentrate our efforts. And we came up with nothing. Like, zilch.'

'So the case was closed?'

'Oh no, it was never closed - the team was scaled down, until eventually it remained an open case that no one was working on. About eight months later, we had an anonymous call to say Sam had been spotted in London, near Kings Cross Station. We obviously flagged her description with the force there, as well as alerting the homeless shelters. But nothing came of it. I know Kate was holding on to the idea that Sam was making a new life for herself and would one day return. But it never rang true. I mean, it takes some planning to intentionally disappear off the face of the Earth. Skills and resources that I don't think Sam would have had. She was really still a child. As I say, I periodically ran checks to see if Sam had surfaced but I never expected to find anything. My gut told me after a few days that we were looking for a body rather than a runaway. But there was never any evidence to support that, so Sam remained a missing person.'

After Nat ends the Zoom call, she reflects grimly that

Mike's gut instinct may sadly have proved to be far too accurate. It looks like the missing Sam Chappell has finally been found.

31

Caro

Present day: Monday, 22 July

Ironically, Grace has drawn a picture of their own family. Still a family of four, with the stick figures depicting Caro and Mark sporting smiles half the sizes of their faces, hands touching, a bright sun shining. Promising that they will set off very soon, Caro moves back to the office and tips out the assortment of trinkets in the bottom of the final box.

It's a strange collection, but Caro understands the significance of most of the items. A half full bottle of Chanel Allure perfume. That one is easy - it was the perfume her mother had always worn, a scent that hung in the air after she had left the room and which clung to you long after she had released you from her embrace. Her mum had stopped wearing the perfume after Jez had died. Just as she had stopped wearing the clothes that Caro had thought were too young for her and laughing too loud as the centre of attention. In fact, her mother had stopped laughing at all.

There is a faded polaroid photograph taken from the night of the leavers' ball. She remembers Jez had been given the polaroid camera for his birthday. He had been a complete pain that summer, snapping pictures of them, until he had spent all his birthday money on film and had to save up his pocket money. Caro remembers they had all been relieved by that. She is looking at a stiff posed photo of Chris and Jen flanked by

Sam and Gus. As usual, Caro feels a jolt in her stomach as she catches sight of eighteen-year-old Gus. Studying his youthful face, she can see parts of his features in Alex and wonders if they ever meet, if they will feel a recognition. She boxes that thought away, as she has done for the last sixteen years, as it is too hard to deal with. She will deal with that when Alex turns eighteen.

Sam looks faded. Not just the age of the photo, but she is stood next to Jen, who seems to have absorbed all the light from the young girl who stood there looking so awkward in her strapless dress. She is looking away from the camera towards Chris, who has the same frozen expression on his face that she had noticed in the earlier photo. Maybe they *had* felt the storm approaching.

Next is a small diamond earring. Caro remembers this was an anniversary gift from her father to Jen: the exact ones Jen was wearing on the night of the ball. Her mother had worn them all the time, and Caro can't actually remember when, or if, her mother had stopped wearing them. Odd for her dad to keep just the one. It would have been nice to have the pair, and she could have saved them for Grace, who will never really know her grandma.

Next is a crumpled piece of paper - the ink smudged, the paper thin. It is a love letter from Jen and Caro smiles. Her mother had always been difficult to read, whereas her father never hid the fact that his wife was the absolute centre of his world. In fact, at times Caro had felt that her and Jez were an unwanted intrusion. The letter is so personal and filled with desire that Caro feels a bit sullied - that she is looking in on something not meant for anyone else's eyes.

My darling

Yesterday was simply amazing. I have been unable to stop thinking about you and the way you make me feel. I honestly feel sometimes that I could come without you even touching me, just by the way you undress me with your eyes.

You know I love you and I dream of the day it will be only the two of us. Spending long days in bed, with no one needing anything from us. I will tire you out!

I know I could have said this to you, but I wanted you to have something you could read at any time. Especially when you are stuck in the middle of your dreary books.

I love you, eternally, and would do anything for you

Your Jen xxx

Caro can feel herself blushing; even as an adult, you don't want to think about your parents having sex. But she can see why her dad had kept it, especially as he lost the essence of his wife and became her carer rather than her lover.

And then a diary from the year Jez died. Her dad had always kept an A5 diary, where he marked down all his important appointments. They were carefully filed away in year order in his filing cabinet at the school, so Caro is surprised this was left abandoned at the hut.

Flicking through the pages, she sees that the entries stopped after the 25th August 2007. The date of Jez's death. It was the usual mundane stuff of organising a life.

7th May :   Boiler service at the Beach Hut – ring to remind them to check the carbon monoxide detector at the same time

9th June: Pete and Anne – Marcos 7.30.

22nd June: Caro exams finish

8th July: Jez cricket match

4th August: School Leavers' Summer Ball

They were the passing glimpses into a life that Caro knew had been so busy and rich. They had mocked Dad, trying to persuade him to get an electronic organiser, to move with the times. But he had liked his paper diary and had kept one going right to the end, insisting his phone was to make calls only. Now she is pleased she gets to keep this mundane narrative of their past.

As the days neared the end of term there were odd little notes, as if her dad was trying to figure a pattern out.

He looks glum, sad, I hope this isn't going to all go wrong.

Bit of a chat but not sure he got what I was trying to say.

Sam not her usual self, do I need to chat with her?

Things seem calmer. Just need to get through summer and then all should be well!

Caro sits back and contemplates these funny little snippets of a commentary on life. Had her dad noticed that things weren't quite right with Jez? If so, she can barely imagine the guilt he would have had to live with - to know that he'd suspected something was wrong, but was still unable to prevent the tragic events running their course. How ironic that they never got to the end of summer: the magical time of new beginnings that her father was pinning all his hopes on.

Caro doesn't want to look at any more entries. It's all too sad, and she has become skilled at shutting this period away in a little box in her mind. She matches that with repacking the items back in the tin, but the lid won't close properly. Clearly there is a knack to packing this thing up. Typical of her dad, he liked to make the best use of the space. Emptying the items from the box, she finds the culprit nestled in the bottom of the tin. But it doesn't make any sense. Because her dad had kept Jez's friendship bracelet. The leather plait that never left his wrist. But if this is Jez's bracelet, what had Caro picked up off the floor all those years ago?

32

Alex

Present day: Monday, 22 July

Alex is on his own down by the harbour. His mates have all ditched him to head back to their homes, claiming they are starving. Alex knows he should do the same; he only has to walk across the dunes to the Beach Hut, but he doesn't want to see his mum. She makes him feel uncomfortable - all the time looking at him with that sad little expression on her face. Alex can't decide if she is trying to figure out just what he is, or if she is trying to understand just how he has managed to wreck all their lives, simply by being born.

Two more years and he will be eighteen. He can escape from here and they will forget all about him. He sometimes feels sad about this but mainly, he tells himself, because he knows Grace will miss him. He is her adored big brother, and it doesn't matter how grumpy he is with her, she loves him and takes every chance to let him know it. When Mum and Dad – *bugger, he keeps doing this*. When Mum and Mark sat him down to tell him he was going to have a baby brother or sister, he hadn't been excited in the least. In fact, it was the last thing he wanted. He had taken some time to adjust to Mark coming into their lives, to him not having his mum to himself anymore. The last thing he wanted was for his mum's attention to be spread still thinner. He had been all set to hate the baby as soon as it arrived.

When Mark took him to the hospital to meet Grace, he had refused to wear the 'I'm the big brother' T shirt and had shuffled along the corridor into the room, his face set as he tried his best not to cry. He had peered into the funny little glass thing in which the baby lay and was confused at the bald wrinkled-faced alien that stared back at him. Grace had had no choice and was sporting a pink babygrow declaring 'I'm the little sister'. She was making a terrible noise, and Alex marvelled that something so small could make that much racket. Unlike when he was shouting at the television, his parents hadn't told her to stop. But stop she did when he peered in at her. She fixed her wide blue eyes on him, and in that instant Alex was lost. He loved her with a fierceness that took him by surprise, and that love has never wavered. He can't even resent her for taking all the love Mark has. But he is jealous, maybe not of the relationship she has with Mark, but that he doesn't have a relationship with his real dad. His mum refuses to talk about it, his grandad had told him his dad was worthless and not worth any of his energy. In desperation, he had once tried to ask his grandma, but it was when her mind was slowly taking her from them, and she seemed to have confused him with Jez, and simply told him how much she had loved his father.

One of his friends at school is adopted and talks endlessly about the day he turns eighteen and will be free to try and find his real family. But that same avenue isn't open to Alex. He has seen his birth certificate, and the name of the father shouts out as a blank space. He will need his mum to share the secret, and he wonders if his mum knows the answer. What he does know though is that the need to have that relationship is becoming overwhelming, all-consuming, and he doesn't see how his mum can't see how much the not knowing is hurting him.

And then there is the stupid pressure of the ghost of his uncle. An uncle who died when he was younger than Alex is now. Alex had learnt early on that the trouble with trying to compete with a dead person is that there is no chance that you are ever going to win. It is as if the moment they die, all their faults are wiped clean from the slate, and all people remember are the good things - the happy memories. And that seems to highlight even further that Alex is a poor substitute. Alex feels that whatever he does is wrong. If he is quiet, he's being moody. If he's laughing with his friends online, he is making too much noise and disrupting the whole house. If he stays in his room, he's wasting the day when he should be outside. But if he goes to see his mates, he's accused of never being home. There are times when Alex secretly thinks that if Grandad had ragged on Jez as much as the family complains about his behaviour, there was no wonder he hung himself from the rafters. Thinking of this, he groans as he remembers he is being forced to endure a summer at the Beach Hut. It's alright his mum pointing out that they are close to the harbour here so it will be easy for him to hang out with his mates every day. What she doesn't get is a lot of the time his social life is online, and the Wi-Fi at the hut is shit. Bloody hell, after six weeks he might be ready to swing from those beams too.

33

Caro

Present day: Monday, 22 July

Caro isn't sure how long she sits staring at that tattered circle of leather in her hand. She jumps as a hand touches her shoulder and she is roused back to the present by Grace, looking unusually solemn, quietly declaring she is getting a bit hungry now. How different to Alex at that age, who would have been yelling loud enough to rival the seagulls, demanding to be fed. Glancing through the window, she can see that the afternoon has passed and the sun has lost some of the fierceness of earlier in the day. A look at her watch confirms that it is coming up to seven o'clock.

'Oh God, I'm sorry Grace. You must be starving! Come on, this calls for fish and chips and ice cream. Let's get this holiday started properly!'

Locking the door to the hut, Caro drops a text to Alex, letting him know they are heading out to the harbour. She doubts he will come and find them. She realises, with a jolt of self-hatred, that a part of her is hoping that he will sort himself out. The day has already been emotionally challenging and she would like to enjoy the simple companionship of Grace, who makes no demands and who looks at her with adoration, rather than the dislike she has started to search for and find in her son's eyes. Still, she has given him the option - more to absolve her own guilt and out of a sense of obligation than because she wants him to join them.

'When I was your age Grace, we never locked the door of the Beach Hut. In fact, lots of times the door was left open, and we came and went as we pleased.'

Grace smiles at her mum. She always enjoys the stories about Caro as a little girl. 'Weren't you scared someone might steal your things?'

'I never even thought about it, and I'm sure Grandma and Grandad didn't either. Then Grandma started on her grand renovation, and she started to panic that things might get spoilt. The final straw was one night we had been on the beach, paddling as the sun went down. That was Grandma's favourite time on the beach as she liked to climb back to the hut and see the lights shining from the window. She said it made her think she was returning to her own castle, following the lights to a magical place.'

Grace is listening closely, mouth open. 'What happened then?'

Caro laughs at the memory. 'Me and Jez had run ahead and when we got to the hut, there was a pile of rags on the porch and a trail of sand leading to the lounge. We were both scared and ran back to Grandad. We thought maybe it was some sea creature that had made its way up from the beach.'

Grace laughs too. 'A sea creature? But Mummy, you know that mermaids can't survive too long out the water and would never have managed to slither all that way across the dunes.'

Caro looks at her daughter, relishing the jolt of love that hits her in the pit of her stomach. This is typical Grace. Caro and Jez had both feared sea monsters - something dark and ugly bringing malevolence into their world. Grace can only think of the fairytale mermaids with their pretty faces and beautiful voices. She has yet to realise that even their beauty can be the disguise for an ugly terror.

'Grandad told us not to be so ridiculous and stomped into the house. And next thing a man ran out, completely in the nude. Grandma screamed, we all screamed, the man screamed! He picked up the pile of rags and ran off in the dunes, his bottom bobbing like a big moon.'

Grace is giggling, as she does at any story that involves bottoms. 'Who was the man?'

'It was a man who used to travel around, sleeping beneath the stars. I don't even remember his name. Grandad thinks he saw the lights and got confused, thinking it was maybe public toilets. Anyway, he was having a wash in the kitchen sink. And after that the door was always kept locked. Although the spare key was hidden under the rock by the back door, in case of emergencies.'

Caro remembers the fury on her mother's face when her husband had come up with this explanation. That her beloved Beach Hut - that she had spent hours transforming to something that could grace the pages of Ideal Home magazine - could be mistaken for public conveniences sent her into a fury; that was the only time her mother would seem ugly. Her father had sorted out new locks and shiny sets of keys first thing the following morning.

Grace stands still and tugs at her mum's hand. 'The man won't come back when we are there, will he Mum?'

Caro understands she sometimes forgets Grace is a little girl, who still occasionally gets her mum to check for any monsters who could be lurking beneath the bed or inside the wardrobe.

'No, he won't come back. He lives under different stars now, like Grandad.'

Grace considers for a moment then attempts a wink at her mum and laughs. 'Maybe Grandad is telling him off for getting him into bother with Grandma.'

Caro laughs, and the two link hands as they move from the soft sands of the dunes to the cobbled streets that lead to the harbour. Already, they can see the flashing lights of the arcades and hear the constant music and mechanical voices that fight for airspace for the hours the arcade is open. It is still quiet, with just a couple of little ones pushing two pence coins into the machine that houses the trembling rock of coins, which seem to promise will fall at any time. Just one more coin. They are clearly in the care of their indulgent grandparents, who patiently stand waiting for the pile of coins to be finished and bracing themselves to deny the plea for a few more goes.

The queue for the fish and chip shop snakes lazily along the street. They have hit the end of the teatime rush, entering the lull before the dash to line stomachs ready for a Friday night drinking. Grace chatters away to Caro as they stand, but Grace abruptly breaks off her story and squeals out 'Alex!' then jumps up and down waving frantically. Caro remains amazed that such a sweet, small girl has a voice that could rival the foghorn that used to call into the night from the lighthouse. Alex tries to look like this little child is nothing to do with him, but Grace pulls free of Caro and runs to him, before flinging herself in his arms and covering him with kisses. Alex tries and fails to look cool, and laughs, swinging her around in his arms.

Caro catches the infectiousness of their affection and is laughing, half blinded by the glare of the evening sun, wishing she had a camera to snap this moment of innocent adoration. As the two of them move towards Caro, she feels the overwhelming sensation of being watched. As she turns round, it takes her eyes a few seconds to adjust from squinting against the light; and in that time Grace and Alex have reached her and Alex greets her with a, 'Hi, Mum.'

And in that moment, Caro's eyes focus on the man walking towards them who seems to have frozen, his own greeting stolen from his mouth, his smile fixed. This is really not the way Caro wanted father and son to meet for the first time.

34

Gus

Present day: Monday, 22 July

Maybe it is the last of the summer sun that distorted his vision, or the four pints which were drunk quickly but failed to quench the thirst deep inside him; but Gus is shocked to a sudden halt when he sees Jen Webster stood in line waiting for fish and chips. It takes a while for his brain to make sense of the scene before him - seventeen years have passed but Jen, if anything, looks even younger than the last time he saw her. He had read that Chris Webster had died recently, and although Jen was younger than Chris, she certainly hadn't been frozen in time. He is roused from his trance by the squeal of a young girl who had been clutching the hand of the woman who was not Jen, and his eyes track the girl as she runs across the harbour to meet a teenage boy. A boy who is trying to look like he isn't delighted to see her.

For the second time Gus thinks he is losing his mind, for he feels like he is looking at a film of himself as a teenage boy. He is catapulted back to the summer days of years ago when Jen would be buying bags of chips for them all to enjoy as they let the sun dry their sea salted bodies. Maybe he has drunk more than he thought, and his mind is playing tricks on him, taking him back to the time when he had been welcomed into the home of Jen and Chris, and for the first time had felt truly loved and wanted.

And then as the woman turns and looks at him, and the boy greets her, Gus is dragged back to the present and is suddenly stone cold sober. He sees the truth of his realisation reflected in her face. And for the second time in his life, he turns and walks away from Caro.

35

Caro

Present day: Monday, 22 July

In that split second, Caro sees the knowledge wash over Gus's face, and she knows that everything is now going to be changed forever. She isn't aware that her feet had blindly shuffled along to the front of the queue until Alex elbows her. 'Mum, what do we want?'

On autopilot, she trudges back to the Beach Hut and they sit out on the decking in a companionable silence, Grace darting in and out as she brings her masterpieces from the afternoon for Alex to admire. Caro is overwhelmed with relief when Alex slinks off to his room as soon as it's time for Grace to go to bed. For once, she doesn't wish he would sit with her. She needs to be alone to try and work out what she is going to do now. It has been seventeen years since the last time she saw Gus. It had been a magical summer, like a fairytale. But like all good fairytales, there had been some unpleasantness looming; and in this particular story, there had been no happy ending.

Caro had wanted Gus from the first time she saw him, head bowed over some book, in her father's office at the school. Of course, she knew who he was. Everyone knew who Gus was even before he had been made Head Boy. He had that presence about him, and Caro could tell if he was in the room even if she couldn't see him. She would tell herself that it was the force of their attraction that made it this way. But she had a strong suspicion that everyone in the school felt the same.

She knew that he would be leaving to go to university; how could she not know this when it was all her dad had gone on about for the last year? His two prized pupils aiming for Oxford and Cambridge. There had been the stress of the applications, the relief when they both got interviews, followed by a tense Christmas as they waited to see if they would get an offer. As other pupils started to get offers for their first choice of places, it seemed their delight only fuelled the weight of expectation resting on Gus. And Sam. Though no one seemed to consider Sam - she was just there, loitering in the shadows, unnoticed. It's funny, Caro reflects, although the pair of them had spent hours with the Webster family, she could barely remember Sam. Whereas she is haunted by every inch of Gus's face, the inflection of his voice, the way he would tilt his head when considering anything, and the slow smile that would bring a sparkle to his dark eyes and make you long to do anything to make him happy.

She is dragged back from the past by the vibration of her phone, showing a new message. Nat's photo fills the screen and for a moment Caro, still half locked in the past, is shocked to see how her friend has aged.

> *Hey, how's it going there? I'm looking forward to joining you but wondered if you could do me a quick favour? I've got the chance to do an interview I need in the morning, but James can't watch Annie. He's still making a drama out of the crisis at the quarry. Any chance I could drop Annie off with you a bit early and I'll join you as soon as I'm done?*

Caro really wants to refuse - to reply that she needs Nat to come and watch her! But she already appreciates the friendship is being pushed to the limits by her asking Nat to stay at the Beach Hut with her - this place with its raw memories of happy times, before everything changed between them.

Of course, no worries at all. I'm looking forward to seeing you.

The phone pings immediately, and Caro can feel the relief in her friend's reply:

Thanks, you are a star. I'll tell you all about it when I get there. I think you'll be interested. I'll say two words - Sam Chappell. Hint hint hint.

How funny, thinks Caro, *it seems today is the day for ghosts deciding to push their way back into the present.* The coldness in the pit of her stomach starts to rise into her throat, and for a few seconds Caro feels she can't breathe. Her own reply certainly doesn't reflect the panic that is threatening to overwhelm her:

Can't wait to hear all about it. I'll get a bottle of wine in the fridge ready for you. Sleep well x

Never mind the bottle of wine tomorrow, Caro realises she needs something now. Splashing warm white wine in a glass, she grimaces as the liquid coats her mouth, the taste not altogether pleasant, but providing some measure of relief as it hits her stomach. As she drains the remainder of the glass, she feels she can start to breathe normally again.

The phone shouts the arrival of another message out to her, and she clicks expecting to see Nat's goodnight message; but the sender is a simple grey circle. Unknown contact.

I think we need to talk. Tomorrow at 2. Usual spot.

36

Caro

Seventeen years earlier: Wednesday, 22 August

Caro was starting to hate this year. The day the letter had arrived for Gus, with the exciting news he had been accepted to Cambridge, should have been a day of happiness and celebration. And for her dad and Gus it was - Caro had been quietly devastated. It was real now; she was going to lose Gus before she had even won him. He would go away and meet lots of new people and she would never see him again - her life would be over. Her mum had been in a mood about something - likely a dress that had gone out of stock or someone booking the last spot at the Pilates class she wanted. Caro couldn't remember, she just knew that day was the beginning of the end.

Sam got her offer for Oxford a day later. And once again, the celebration felt like a bit of an afterthought for poor forgotten Sam. Caro had bitchily remarked to Nat that it was debateable whether Sam was heartbroken more at the thought of leaving Gus or Chris Webster, who she clearly idolised.

And now Sam was missing.

Caro was sat at the beach on her own. Up until the leavers' ball, her and Nat had been inseparable as always - Nat happy to tag along with the plans Caro had made for the two of them. Sometimes, she would pull a face and have a moan. 'You're so like your mum Caro, always used to getting your own way!'

But that had changed almost overnight.

To be honest, Caro hadn't really noticed at first that Sam being missing was serious. Of course, she knew that the police had been to the house, and that Kate Chappell seemed to have taken up residence in the Beach Hut kitchen, with everyone fussing round her like she was ill or something. Even Jen Webster was rallying round not seeming to mind that, for once, she was not the centre of attention. But two weeks later the fuss was continuing, and it was all rather boring.

Today she needed to find Gus so she could carry on with 'Operation get Gus to notice me'. The summer days, whilst still hot, were starting to shorten in length, as if to draw attention to the fact that Caro was running out of time. She'd expected that Nat would come with her to hang about by the beach or the little boating lake in the park, but Nat was completely obsessed with Sam and where she could be. She didn't want to talk about how good Gus looked in the blue shirt that emphasised his dark eyes and clung his body, instead snapping that there were more important things to worry about and flouncing off to God knows where. Caro was left on her own, which made it so much more obvious that she was Gus's new stalker. Trust bloody Sam Chappell to ruin everything, just to try and get a little bit more attention.

Caro did consider seeing if Jez wanted to come and hang out down by the beach, but he had shut himself away in his room and had turned the music playing through his headphones up so loud that Caro could hear the heavy beat vibrating thinly in the room. When she flung the door open, she was surprised to see he looked to have been crying, before he turned his face to the wall and screamed at her to get out of his room. *Fuck him!* thought Caro; he was so bloody moody at the minute. She would be better on her own rather than dragging that lanky, spotty child round with her anyway.

Bloody idiot looking like he was dressed up to scare the children at Halloween, rather than enjoying the heat of the summer.

Caro had stomped from the Beach Hut without shouting goodbye, afraid that if she did her parents would try and rope her into sticking some of the 'Help Find Sam' posters up that they had wasted hours getting ready. *Honestly*, Caro thought, as she hesitated at the fork in the path, *how embarrassing for Sam when she did turn up to see her face splashed across every lamp post in town. Just typical of people round here to overreact.*

Caro decided to head to the beach first. She could hear the waves, and even though the crisp crash was muffled by the dunes, she guessed there was some decent surf, which meant there would be a good chance Gus would be out with his board, showing his friends how it should be done. Lovely! She could arrange herself on the sand and watch him from behind her dark glasses. If she set up her blanket close to where his group had left their stuff, there was a good chance he might come and chat to her once they had finished in the water. She cursed the fact she hadn't thought to bring a book so that she could pretend to be engrossed in reading and that she hadn't even noticed them out mastering the waves. Too late now, no chance she could risk going back for it.

But as Caro broke through the dunes, she could see that whilst the beach had the usual smattering of holidaymakers - children building sandcastles whilst their parents wrestled with the windbreaks - the sea remained an empty expanse. There were no figures dancing along the line of the waves. Caro was disappointed, but decided to head to the harbour. Maybe they were meeting there and would come down to the beach later.

Again, she drew a blank. The harbour was unusually quiet. The lifeboat was getting ready to be launched and this usually drew quite a crowd, but this time there were few spectators and a sombre air, rather than the electric excitement that usually filled the harbour as they watched the boat slip down the ramp. Caro idly thought it was unusual for there to be a practice session during the day. Most of the crew had other full-time jobs so they tended to carry out their drills in the evening, especially with the good weather and the longer summer days.

She spotted Nat in the crowd and waved over to her, but Nat was engrossed in watching, not the lifeboat, but the people watching the vessel. Caro walked over and hugged her friend from behind.

'Christ, you made me jump!'

'Sorry.' Though Caro didn't feel sorry at all. 'What's happening here, then?'

'They haven't said, but clearly something to do with Sam.'

Caro huffed; she was getting a bit sick of hearing about Sam. Funny that someone who blended into the background when she was around, trying to take up the least amount of space possible, almost looking guilty for using up air, could now be causing such a fuss. Maybe this was the whole idea behind her pulling the disappearing act.

'Shall we go to the park and maybe get an ice cream?' Caro started to walk away, expecting her friend to dutifully follow. She was shocked when she turned to see Nat hadn't moved and was shaking her head.

'I want to stay here, it's really interesting. Most of these here are local press, but there's a whisper a television crew will arriving shortly. It's all looking serious, Caro. They think she might have drowned.'

Caro shook her head in wonder and curled her lip in a sneer as she snapped. 'Honestly, I expect she got cold feet over this Oxford thing. There's no way she will ever cope with being somewhere like that. She'll be home before you know it and will look a right twit. And you'll look like a fool too for wasting your time on all this nonsense!'

Caro registered the look of hurt on Nat's face before her friend turned away, but not before she muttered, 'And you don't look foolish mooning round after Gus. I suppose that's OK because it's you.'

Caro paused and considered a smart retort, but struggled to think of anything when faced with something that held more than a grain of truth. Instead, she stomped away towards the park, hoping that her silence said all that needed to be said. No doubt Nat would be round with a grovelling apology later. Minutes later, Caro had made the first circuit of the park and could see that there was no sign of Gus or his mates. She debated getting an ice cream, but the little kiosk remained shuttered and in darkness with a handwritten note hastily taped to the glass informing disappointed customers that the kiosk would not be open due to staff illness. *Bloody hell,* thought Caro. No wonder the town was seeing such a decline in holidaymaker numbers. In her opinion, there wasn't that much to appeal about this shit tip of a place to start with, and now you couldn't even get an ice cream.

She debated heading back to the harbour to see if Nat was still there but then remembered they had fallen out, so decided to head home and see if she could sneak in to get her book and maybe steal a couple of cold beers from the fridge. Caro didn't really like the taste of beer, but it was something to pass away the boring hours that stretched out in front of her.

Rather than head back across the beach, she decided to cut through the dunes. The path was overgrown, and the marram grass scratched at her bare legs as she fought her way across the soft sand. She was sweating and regretting her choice, realising it would have been quicker to go the longer way round. It had never seemed this hard work when her and

Jez had spent hours playing in these sandy mountains. They had a red plastic sledge they would haul up the steep banking and then launch from the top, screeching as their mouths filled with sand and they fell in a heap at the bottom - just to do it all again. Her mum would grumble that the sledge was for use in the snow and that one day they would send some poor walker flying, but her dad had sensibly pointed out that they hadn't had snow deep enough to sledge in for at least five years and that no one in their right mind would choose to trudge through the dunes when they could enjoy the firm sand and stunning views that were a few hundred metres away.

Glancing round, Caro could see that the dunes were deserted. It felt like a different world here and completely isolated from the laughter and shrieks that occasionally wafted on the breeze from the direction of the beach. Stood at the top of the dune that had been their favourite spot, Caro launched herself from the top at a run, remembering how her and Jez would race to the bottom, arms flailing and feet sinking into the soft sand until they were in danger of toppling forward. Breathless, she reached the bottom and collapsed in a heap in the soft, warm sand. It had been more fun and not as hard work when she was younger.

'You looked like some mad woman heading towards me then. I was in fear for my life.'

The voice made Caro jump and then blush a dark red as she saw Gus lounging in the hollow at the bottom. He had set himself up with a blanket and cool box, which looked to contain bottles of wine. By his side a radio was playing Radio Two, which seemed an odd choice for the boy Caro thought she knew. Wiping her eyes clear from the grit, Caro hoped he would think she was red from running across the dunes, rather than recognising the heat of desire that had flushed her features. Gus smiled again and Caro had the disconcerting thought that he knew exactly the effect he had on her.

'Take a seat, I could do with some company.'

Caro hesitated, but then Gus passed her the bottle of wine, inviting her to, 'Take a swig,' and Caro sunk down beside him, before her trembling legs let her down. Afterwards, Caro would like to think they sat for a while in companionable silence. But in reality, she had felt incredibly self-conscious and the silence seemed fraught and so she was forced to blurt out, 'Do you often come here, then?'

Gus laughed. 'Is that your version of the traditional chat up line?'

Caro felt her face heat further still, until Gus took pity on her and nudged her arm. 'I'm only kidding you. I like to come here, it's private and I never see anyone - until you ran towards me like some sort of sand monster!'

Caro looked at him uncertainly, but seeing he was grinning, managed to match his smile with her own.

'Truth is, I was meant to be meeting a friend here but looks like they can't make it. But… it seems like this is my lucky day, as you are a much prettier companion to share the wine with.'

They had sat that afternoon, taking turns to sip from the bottle, until Gus said he needed to head back home. Caro thought she might cry. This had been her one chance, and she had blown it. As he set off back towards the harbour he turned back to Caro, who was struggling to keep the tears at bay. 'Say hi to your mum and dad for me will you; and say I hope to see them soon.'

Caro couldn't speak, so instead simply nodded. Then Gus continued. 'It's been really nice, Caro. See you again tomorrow – same time, same place?'

And Caro nodded, unable to stop the grin that spread across her face. It was finally happening.

37

Nat

Seventeen years earlier: Wednesday, 22 August

Nat had hung around the harbour for another hour or so; but then the little crowd had started to drift away towards the pub, clearly deciding that the boat was unlikely to bring in anything newsworthy. The place had been buzzing with different stories, but they did all agree that Sam had last been seen heading along the cliff path to the harbour. The fact the lifeboat was being launched - the crew unusually quiet, faces grim - you didn't need to be a seasoned reporter to guess how this story was looking to play out.

It had been nearly three weeks now since the leavers' ball, eighteen days since she had last seen Sam. She would bet any money that Sam's mum could tell you how much time had passed in hours, maybe even minutes. Nat had always liked Kate Chappell. Sometimes when the noise and competitiveness of the Webster family became overwhelming, Nat would sneak into the Beach Hut and chat to Kate as she quietly and efficiently restored the living space to the pristine condition Jen Webster demanded be shown to the outside world.

Last night Nat had bought a card to send to Kate. She hadn't known what to say, so in the end had said nothing and the card remained on her desk. She hoped that Kate would know how much people cared, even if she couldn't quite find the right words to say to her. Nat had walked past Kate's house a few times. She had planned to call in and say how sorry she was, but to her relief the house was in darkness and Nat assumed Kate was still staying with the Websters. She could imagine how pissed off Jen was about that, and wondered if she was persuading Kate that doing jobs for the Websters would help take her mind off things. Nat allowed herself a smile at this thought. Jen Webster knew how to look after Jen Webster, even when appearing to look after others.

Since Nat and Caro had become best friends when they were five, that friendship had never wavered. The Webster family had embraced Nat into their gang, and the long summer holidays had been spent mainly at the Beach Hut which helped Nat's parents, both of whom worked full-time. But for the first time, Nat and Caro were drifting apart.

Nat couldn't say for sure the first time she realised with a jolt that there were some members of the Webster family that she didn't like at all. It was probably when she was about thirteen that she started to be wary around Jen, seeing the older woman somehow always got exactly what she wanted. The mood of the day would be dictated by how Jen was. If Jen wasn't enjoying herself, then you could be sure that no one would be allowed to have a good time. Chris Webster was easier to deal with. At first, Nat had found it weird spending so much time with her headmaster. But Chris was funny and welcoming and made it easy to relax into her summer family. But as she got older, she noticed that Chris prioritised his wife above everything. Jen was the obvious favourite, the centre of his world, and she sometimes thought that his adoration of Caro and Jez was a simple extension of his overwhelming love for Jen. They were a bonus, but not the necessity, for his world to keep turning. Sometimes, she saw Jez longing for the full attention of his dad but failing to steal even a half day of the limelight from his mum. Jen simply wouldn't allow it, and Chris was too enthralled by his wife to see that maybe his children needed to feel like they mattered too.

And then there was Caro. For the last six months, Nat would get a bit of a horrible feeling in her stomach when she thought about her best friend. She didn't want to feel like she did. But the truth was as Caro got older, she was becoming more like Jen in more than just the way she looked. Caro had always been the leader in their friendship and Nat had been happy to follow, secure in the knowledge that Caro would always be there for her when it mattered. But recently Nat had started to feel that Caro was only friends as long as Nat would give Caro what she wanted. Nat didn't want to admit it even to herself, but she was starting to dislike her best friend.

38

Caro

Seventeen years earlier: Thursday, 23 August

Nineteen days since Sam had gone missing. One day since Caro had sat in the dunes with Gus. Both huge events, but Caro really only cared about one of them. And that wasn't the missing Sam.

Caro had found it easy to escape the house. Kate decided it was better for her to be at home - in case Sam turned up there - so Chris and Jen had accompanied her. Why the woman couldn't be on her own was beyond Caro's understanding. She had managed on her own for all these years, so surely she didn't need Chris and Jen to make her a cup of tea. Still, at least it made it easy to sneak a bottle of wine into her bag and head off into the dunes.

Seeing that Jez's door was firmly closed, Caro did hesitate as she thought she heard a funny noise coming from the room. It almost sounded like her brother was crying. He was maybe taking Sam's absence badly. He had liked Sam, and she had always had plenty of time for him, always greeting him with a smile even when she was with all her friends. Now she thought of it, Caro could see that Jez had almost hero-worshipped Sam - almost the same as she had moped around after Gus. Remembering that Gus would hopefully be waiting for her, she decided she would persuade Jez to go down to the arcades with her later. Her conscience temporarily cleared she headed off, her head full of love and a fantasy of her future.

When she reached the little dip in the dunes, she saw she was the first to arrive and sank down on the soft sand, realising she was pretty much hidden from view. She glanced at her watch nervously. Maybe he wouldn't come.

She sensed his arrival before she saw him. Alerted by the trickle of sand as his steps disturbed the fragile surface. Then he was flinging himself down next to her, greeting her with a hug. And they spent another afternoon sipping from the bottle of wine and sharing their hopes and dreams. Or rather, Gus shared his hopes and dreams. Caro was content to listen as he described how he would make his escape; leave this little town without a backward glance, free to discover a new world.

By then, Caro had thought that if Gus didn't make a move soon, then she would kiss him herself - the pain of rejection couldn't be worse than the endless torture of being so close to him and yet so far away from what she wanted. As it was, she didn't need to make a move. There was a different energy about Gus and his blue eyes were cold as he stared at her as she drank from the bottle. As she passed it to him, he set it down in the cooler and pulled her towards him. Caro had been hoping for this for so long, but she had to admit this wasn't quite the tender first kiss she had imagined. Instead, he kissed her as if he didn't like her very much. Still, after so much anticipation, Caro was determined to see it through to the end.

Afterwards Gus cried and kept saying sorry. Caro held him in her arms and comforted him, knowing that he was now hers forever. She enjoyed holding him, stroking his hair as he relaxed against her. Both dozing in the sunshine.

Which was where Jez found them.

'Caro, what are you doing?' was the high-pitched voice that roused her from sleep. Blinking as her eyes became accustomed to the bright sunlight, Caro could see Jez staring at them with a look of horror on his face.

'Oh God, of God, oh God, Caro. I was watching through the telescope, but I didn't think it was you.'

At that Jez launched himself at Gus, attempting to punch him in the face. He was no match for the older boy, who easily pinned his arms to his side.

'What the fuck are you doing, Jez?'

'You're a fucking monster, Gus. I know exactly who you are. I'm going to tell Dad, then you'll be in real trouble!'

At this point Jez was hysterical, and Caro looked nervously around, expecting that at any minute his shouts of distress would rouse more people from the beach. Her brother carried on trying to swing at Gus, who looked helplessly at Caro. 'Fucking hell Caro, do something! I really do not need this! Pretty disgusting really - not ashamed to admit he's a nasty little perverted peeping Tom. What is it with this drama queen?'

Caro grabbed her brother's arm, surprised at how skinny he felt. When had he lost so much weight? As he felt her hand on his shoulder, he turned towards her and collapsed against her. Although he was taller than her, he was so slight that it felt like holding onto a fragile child. He simply buried his face in her shoulder and cried. He was mumbling to himself but was so distressed that Caro was unable to hear the words properly - and what she could decipher certainly didn't make any sense.

'Oh Caro, what have you done? What have you done?'

Gus took a step back and met Caro's eyes over the top of her brother's head. She tried to smile at him, but the blankness of his features snatched the smile from her lips.

'I think it's best if I go.'

Caro could only node mutely, knowing if she tried to speak, she would start to cry too.

'I'll see you around, Caro,' was flung carelessly over his

shoulder. That was the first time Gus walked away from Caro, and for seventeen years that was the last Caro saw of him.

39

Nat

Present day: Tuesday, 23 July

'I really could do without this trip to the Beach Hut,' is Nat's opening line as she pours herself a coffee from the pot James has set going.

'Yes! You may have mentioned that! In fact, you never stop mentioning it. Well, I could do without a body in the quarry. I suppose we all have our crosses to bear.'

Nat turns to look at James and feels a pang of guilt that she has been so caught up in her own dramas that she has failed to even greet him with a 'good morning' or ask him how he slept. Jesus, maybe spending all this time with Caro means she is catching some of her friends less attractive traits.

'Let's start again. Good morning,' and a kiss on the cheek helps to ease some of the tension in the air. Nat doesn't bother to ask James how his night has been. It isn't that she doesn't care. Rather the dark circles rimming his eyes, the pronounced furrow on his forehead and the hair sticking in all directions, bear testament that James had not seen much rest during the hours of darkness.

Still, he does manage a smile. 'Good morning. And I'm going to be really up against it for the next couple of weeks, so at least I don't have to worry about trying to get home to spend time with you and Annie if I know you're having some fun at the beach.' Noticing his wife grimace, James kisses her hard on the lips to stop the protest escaping from her mouth. 'You know you always have fun with Caro in the end. She's like a drug you just can't give up. Every time she behaves badly you swear never again, but then forgive her. You're a Caroholic!'

Nat laughs, unable to deny the truth of what he is saying, and they part on good terms with promises to speak later in the day. Annie is beside herself with excitement. The prospect of a couple of weeks living with her best friend means that the noise level has ramped up a notch and the twenty-minute drive tests the last bit of Nat's already short fuse.

As Caro opens the door to them, Nat can see that her friend has obviously had a similar night to James. Wrestling between feeling she should ask her how she is and needing to get away to get her own head in the right space for her upcoming coffee date, Nat settles on a rather unsatisfying mixture of both. 'Morning lovely. No offence, but you look shocking! I can't stop - got this thing, you know - but as soon as I get back, I need to know everything!'

Driving away in the car, seeing Caro still standing in the doorway, Nat is struck again how her friend is looking more like the Jen she remembers from her teenage years. Ironic really that Caro is more like the woman she claims to despise, both in character and looks, than the dad she had always professed to adore. And that's a weird one too. Because when it came down to it, Chris Webster really didn't seem to care for anyone apart from his wife. Making sure Jen was happy seemed to be the purpose of the whole Webster family.

Bloody hell! Even now that family has wormed its way into her thoughts when she needs to be thinking how to tackle this conversation with Kirsten. Turning up the music in the car, her ears are assaulted yet again by the irritating lyrics of 'wheels on the bus'. Turning it off, she opts for silence instead, and by the time she parks up in town she is 'Nat the journalist'.

There is a small line of people waiting at the takeout window, obviously planning to make the most of the sunshine. Skirting round them, apologising in case anyone thinks she is pushing in, Nat opens the door and triggers an old-fashioned tinkling bell which sounds uncomfortably loud as it echoes round the nearly empty cafe. It's easy to spot Kirsten. She has tucked herself away in a corner and looks as though she is hoping that she will somehow blend in with the furnishings of the café so Nat will be unable to spot her. Then she can go on with her life with a clear conscience, telling herself, 'Well, I did try.'

Kirsten has obviously shared the same sleep experience of James and Caro and struggles to raise a smile in reply to Nat's greeting and introduction. She does however thankfully accept the offer of another drink. Clearly, she is running on caffeine. Picking up a selection of croissants and jams, Nat settles herself at the table and spends some time preparing her breakfast, doing her best to put Kirsten at ease. After a couple of minutes of passing over butter and jam, the two of them sit eating the flaky comforts until Nat takes a gulp of her drink and decides it's best to dive straight in.

'I really appreciate you seeing me Kirsten, and I know you have your misgivings about resurrecting that time. But I think now, more than ever, is the time to try and tell Sam's story.'

For a beat of silence that holds on a fraction too long to be comfortable, Kirsten looks at Nat before setting aside her plate. 'So, is this anything to do with the body at the quarry?'

Nat is unable to keep the surprise from her face. As far as she was aware, Kate hadn't spoken to anyone else and there has been no hint that local gossip has even considered this a possibility. For most people in the town, Sam is ancient history.

Before she has chance to consider her answer, Kirsten

continues. 'Come on, don't look so surprised. Like you've not thought that might be the case. Sam was one of my very best friends. I know you've spoken to Beth, and you are aware that the last summer was a weird time for our little group. We were getting ready to move on to the next stage of our lives and we were all nervous and excited about that. It felt like we were on the brink of a precipice at times. About to jump and no idea whether we would hit warm or cold water. But despite all that, there is no way that Sam would have disappeared like that without a word to anyone. I guess we always knew that something bad had happened to her. It was just that none of us wanted to say it out loud.'

Nat nods. She supposes this is no surprise really. It's just that Kirsten is brave enough to say out loud what probably many people thought at the time. Remembering watching the lifeboat launch to search the coves along the cliff edge, there had been speculation that there had been a repeat of the skinny-dipping incident. Only this time with a tragic outcome - the cold water shock, mixed with alcohol, leading to Sam's disappearance. The sea hadn't ever given up its victim though - if that is what had happened.

'And can you tell me a little bit about the last night you saw Sam? I'm trying to put together a picture, but no one really seems to remember anything very clearly.'

'You were there that night, weren't you?'

Nat nods, surprised that Kirsten has remembered her.

'Oh, don't worry. I would never have recognised you. But Beth mentioned you were best friends with Caro Webster, and she was there that night. I figured if she was there, you wouldn't be anywhere else.'

Nat smiles but doesn't like the feeling in the pit of her stomach. It isn't nice that people continue to see her as Caro's little hanger-on.

'I was there. Working, unfortunately! But I was stuck in the back, refilling plates and washing dishes. It was a bit grim, actually. So, I didn't really see any of the ball.'

'It had been a good night. At least at the beginning.' Kirsten smiled and her face transformed to show her younger self, before the worry lines made a mark on her face and she learnt too young the vulnerability of life as you expect it to be. 'We were all really disappointed that Beth couldn't come. She'd had a diabetic episode - she'll have told you all about that. But Sam did turn up and was in good spirits. She was more back to her old self. I know loads of people thought Sam was quiet and shy and that she faded into the background, but once you got to know her, she was really funny. She was witty and sharp and had us in stitches all night with her comments on other people. I suppose were being quite bitchy, but you know what it's like at that age.'

Nat smiles in agreement, unwilling to break Kirsten's train of thought.

'We had been drinking, I won't deny that. I mean come on - it was the ridiculous the fuss that was made about this. We were all eighteen - or going to be withing a few weeks - and the majority of us were hoping to head away to uni, when no one would have a clue how much we drank, or whose bed we slept in for that matter. So I did think all the nasty tittle-tattle aimed at Mr Webster was desperately unfair. As if he didn't feel bad enough about it all; and then that dreadful thing with his son.'

Nat smiles understandingly and swallows back her frustration. She wants to tell Kirsten to get on with it, but guesses this is maybe a difficult story for the other woman to tell. 'Dreadful. Jez was a really nice lad. I'd known him years, just never would have thought he was so sad. I can't believe, young as I was, that I didn't see how desperate for help he was.'

'He was the best of the whole family, that's for sure. Still, for all their faults, his parents didn't deserve that.'

Nat wants to probe this further but recognises she is here to find the material she needs for her article on Sam, not to indulge in gossip about her former best friend - probably not former now, which again is something Nat recognises she needs to revisit in a quiet moment – to figure out exactly how she feels about Caro's presence in her life.

She limits herself to a grunt of agreement. 'Was Sam very drunk then? I'm not sure that has been reported before.'

'She'd had a drink. Fair to say that she wouldn't have been able to drive a car. Not that she could drive a car anyway as she'd never bothered to learn to drive. No idea why. Most of us couldn't wait to get some independence.'

Nat bites down on her frustration and takes a large bite of croissant to stifle the groan of annoyance and the snappy, 'For fuck's sake, get to the point, will you!' that she can feel itching to be set free.

'So yes, she was tiddly I suppose. But she was a happy tiddly. She had kicked off her shoes and was dancing to every record. She even managed to get Mr Webster up on the floor for a dance. Jen Webster was furious - sat there with a face like a slapped arse and left shortly after that. Mr Webster said she'd got a bad headache, but I think she couldn't bear the fact her husband was getting more attention than she was.'

'When did Sam leave then?'

'As I say, all was OK. We were all dancing and sneaking slugs of vodka into our soft drinks, and then Sam saw Gus head outside with his friends for a cigarette. She'd been dancing with Mr Webster again, and she clearly was feeling irresistible. You know how Mr Webster always boosted her confidence, well…'

'Sorry to interrupt - but what do you mean, boosted her confidence?'

For a moment Kirsten looks like she wishes she could

snatch the words back. Still, Nat isn't going to let her off the hook on this one.

'Did Mr Webster treat Sam different to the rest of you?'

Kirsten takes a sip of the drink that by now is no doubt going cold. Nat recognises when someone is playing for time and feels a pull of excitement. Her fingers reach for the comfort of the stacking ring, attempting to stop the tremors of excitement she can feel running through her body. Is this going to be the answer? Is there actually some shred of truth in those anonymous posts?

'Look, I know what you're thinking. And I do want to say that I saw those Facebook posts on the Churcher's school page, and I was absolutely disgusted by them. Maybe Mr Webster did treat Sam a little bit differently. But not in some pervy way. He simply recognised that Sam had real potential, if she could have a bit more self-belief, so he used to really work to improve her confidence. And she spent hours at the family home being tutored for the entrance exam, and then to make sure she got the grades. You know Sam didn't know her dad. So yes, Sam saw Mr Webster as something more than her teacher. But she saw him as the father figure she was missing in her life. I think sometimes Mr Webster worried about this, and he was always careful to act professionally. I know for a fact he never tutored Sam on her own. And I know this because Sam was ecstatic that Gus was always there. Sam saw Mr Webster as a safe parental figure. In the romance department, she had her sights firmly fixed on Gus.'

Nat stores this away - not quite ready to fully let go of those rather vicious allegations - but smiles at Kirsten to encourage her to continue.

'Anyway, off Sam went, saying she was going to ask Gus if she could cadge a cigarette. She told us not to worry if she was gone some time. I'll always remember that. She winked as she said it and then laughed. She was high on life, and we were all giggling with her.'

'And was that the last time you saw her?'

'Oh no, it all turned to shit after that. Sam reappeared fifteen minutes later, and she was manically happy. Like, completely over the top, but looked like she had been crying a bit as well. She grabbed her bag from the table and said she was going home - that her mum was coming to collect her. Mr Webster obviously noticed she was upset and followed her out the hall. We saw them talking. Sam was talking at Mr Webster, who looked furious and tried to persuade her to come back, but she shook him off and ran towards the exit. Mr Webster came back in and sat down and by then things were slowing down, and we all figured she'd had too much to drink and that Gus had likely led her on a bit and then knocked her back.'

'And when did you first realise that there might be a problem?'

'The house phone rang in the middle of the night. I didn't hear it. I'd had my fair share of the vodka and wasn't really used to drinking alcohol, so I'd practically passed out. I know Mum spoke to Kate, who asked if Sam had come back to ours. Apparently, Mum came in and checked I was still in bed and that we hadn't sneaked Sam in; but I was oblivious to all of it. Then the next morning Mum woke me up early. I remember I was really snappy with her as I had a banging headache. In fact, I've not touched vodka since that night. She told me Sam hadn't come home and asked me if I knew anything. Well, of course I didn't. Nothing more than what I've told you. It was the same as I told the police. Sam said she was going home early and that her mum was picking her up. That's all I know, really.'

As Nat smiles her thanks Kirsten's eyes fill with tears. 'I hope you find out what happened to Sam. It's awful, but with me moving away it was easy to forget about her. And now, I hope Kate gets the answers she needs. The thing is - is it easier to live with not knowing but always having hope, or to have confirmation that he worst happened, and that Sam is gone forever?'

'Honestly, I don't know. I would have said it's better to know. But since having my own daughter, I think sometimes a little bit of hope can help you to survive what is the unthinkable.'

Nat stays at the table after Kirsten leaves. She types up her notes, but something the other woman had said tugs at her memory and she checks through to Kate's account. Yes, there it is. Kate had said Chris Webster told her Sam had left as her mum was picking her up early, but from what Kirsten had said, it sounded the two of them had a much more fraught encounter. She doesn't suppose it matters; Sam seemed to have told the same story to all her friends. Still, the one thing she has learnt is that it is often the small inconsistencies that can be the thing that allow you to see things clearer. Why did Chris not mention to Kate that Sam was so distressed when she left the ball? That may have prompted a call to the police much earlier. Very odd. Nat files that away to slip into the puzzle when she has a few more of the pieces.

40

Caro

Present day: Tuesday, 23 July

Caro thinks that Nat is never going to get back to the Beach Hut. It is already nearly one. She has spent the morning looking at her watch. At first the minutes seemed to have come to a standstill, time moving slowly. Alex still hasn't emerged from his room, and Caro knows better than to try and rouse him from his bed. Thinking of her younger days, she remembers her parents had no such qualms. The door would burst open, the curtains drawn wide to allow the light to glare in as she was told it was far too nice a day to spend in bed. With a grin, she fantasises trying that with Alex.

She has spent the morning on the beach with the girls, sat on a blanket whilst they paddled at the edge of the sea. Squealing at the sight of the odd jellyfish, they happily built their sandcastles and chattered away until Grace declared she was hungry, and it was finally nearly midday. Time to head up for some lunch. As they reached the hut, the girls grumbling quietly that it was so much further on the way back, Caro is disappointed to see there is still no sign of Nat. If her friend had been there, they could have shared a bottle of wine.

She feels in desperate need of a bit of Dutch courage, but it's twenty-to-two by the time she hears Nat's car pull up on the track. The girls have been nagging her to go to the beach again. Alex has emerged with a grunt and has left the house with barely a goodbye. She wants to shout after him to ask if he has cleaned his teeth, but then reminds herself, he is sixteen. No longer a child. Maybe she should pick which battles are worth fighting. *God, why does this have to be so hard?*

As Nat shouts out a cheery hello, Caro grabs her bag and, not giving her friend a chance to say anything more, rushes out the door.

'I'm sorry Nat, I've got an appointment I can't miss. Help yourself to anything. You know where everything is. I'll grab some more wine on my way home.'

Nat doesn't get chance to reply as she is accosted by two excited five-year-olds, dressed in their swimsuits (though Annie appears to have put both legs through one leg hole) and brandishing fishing nets. The little group of three are laughing as Caro turns round to blow a last kiss. She wishes she was going down with them to explore the hidden treasures of the rockpools left by the receding sea. It will be much more fun than whatever monster she is about to unleash on her family by lifting the heavy rock of the past.

The trek through the soft sands of the dunes is much harder work than she remembered. Clearly, she had been a lot fitter as a teenager. When they had met here before, she had been the first to arrive - excited to see Gus. This time she is red-faced and sweating and right on time. Typically, Gus - who in the past had been late, making her fear that he might not show at all - is already there. This time there is no brightly coloured picnic blanket spread for the two of them to sink down into each other's arms, no tinny music blaring from the cheap radio and certainly no cold bottle of wine waiting for them to share as they whisper their secret dreams to each other.

This time there is no rush to touch each other. Rather an awkward silence as they stare at each other, trying to reconcile the adult stood before them with the memory from seventeen years ago.

It is Gus that speaks first. 'Thanks for coming.'

Caro has a speech all prepared but before she can start, she feels the tears start to roll down her cheeks and all she can manage is, 'I'm sorry,' before the pain of the last few months rips the voice from her throat. And she finds herself with Gus once more holding her. She can feel the tension leaving her body as the tears fall. She knows she's crying for lots of things: the loss of her dad, her guilt over Jez, the pain that Gus has never wanted to know their son, the struggles with Alex, the pain of losing Mark. All these things that have been carefully boxed away, too painful to look at too closely, are now all clamouring to be heard and Caro doesn't know if she is strong enough to face it all. Even though it has been seventeen years, being with Gus feels so familiar, so safe. Sheltered in the dunes from the sea breeze, the distant sounds of the beach seem to be in a different world.

Caro isn't sure how long they stay like that. Neither of them seems to want to let go, to break the spell and let the real world and its problems into their bubble. That had always been their problem, she reflects bitterly as she wipes her eyes with a tissue Gus has passed to her - they have never spent any time together in the real world. When Alex was first born, she would have given anything to be meeting with Gus. To be sharing the news that they had a son. Now she doesn't really know what to say and there is a moment of silence as they both consider saying the words that will turn their worlds, and the lives of many other people, not least of all Alex, completely upside down.

'I was sorry to hear about your dad, Caro. He was very good to me.'

Caro nods. 'He was so proud of you, Gus.' It seems unnecessary to mention that Gus's name has never been mentioned since the day he left to go to university.

There was another moment of silence which Caro wants

to not end. She knows they have to have the next conversation, but she wishes she could avoid it.

'Gus, I...'

'So, your son...'

Typically, they both speak at the same time before Gus gestures Caro to go first. And what can she say? How can she explain all those years of hurt, the grief she had felt when she realised he wasn't going to respond to her letter and had just left them?

'Obviously, this is awkward. It's been so long. But I'm guessing that having seen Alex, we need to establish some ground rules for going forward.'

Gus looks at Caro, mouth agape until he shakes his head in disbelief.

'Fucking hell Caro, you certainly are a Webster through and through. I find out - completely by chance - that I have a son. In fact, I didn't really know for sure - it was just he looked so like me. Then I saw the look on your face. And you stand there, all matter-of-fact in front of me, calmly informing me we need to figure out a way to all live in the same place. Unbelievable!'

This time it's Caro's turn to look at Gus in disbelief.

'So, you're now rewriting history, conveniently forgetting that you walked out on me. Even after I wrote to you and told you, I never heard another word. And me and Alex - that's your son's name, in case you're interested - have done fine, so don't worry that we will be asking for anything at all from you. At this point, all I care about is that Alex doesn't get damaged by the mess we have managed to make.'

'Alex... My son.'

Caro looks at Gus and is shocked to see tears streaming down his face. There is a flicker of doubt somewhere. Would

Gus really have left it all these years? And there was no denying the look on his face that evening by the harbour. Maybe it wasn't horror that he had bumped into them, when he had done his best to forget they had ever existed. Maybe it was because he really didn't know. But how could that be?

'Yes, the son that you didn't want anything to do with. Gus, I don't want to sound like I'm being unreasonable here but Alex and I, we had to learn to make a life without you in it. And you can't decide now that you want things to be different. It's not that simple. Alex has a man he calls his dad.' At this, Caro feels that familiar pull in her stomach as she silently acknowledges that at the moment that relationship is looking pretty ropey. Still, that's nothing Gus needs to know. 'Alex is at a very vulnerable age, and whilst I'm not denying he has every right to know his biological father, I think you need to respect that the choice is his and not yours. You gave up that right to be involved when you walked away all those years ago.'

Caro is pleased with her speech. It came out exactly as she had rehearsed it last night. And when she had rehearsed it, she imagined that Gus would smile at her in agreement that all that was reasonable and then walk away. Crisis averted. Instead, the man stands before her looked completely shell shocked.

'But I didn't. I would have never. I… What can I say? I had no idea you were pregnant. God, I would never have walked away from that and missed out on all those years of having a son.'

And Caro finds she believes him.

Still, she reasons with him, 'I sent you a letter. I was desperate to get in touch with you and I wrote to you, care of the college at Cambridge. When I didn't hear, I thought your silence gave me all the answers I needed. It was a truly terrible time, what with Jez dying and Mum falling to pieces. I didn't have the energy to chase you anymore. It took everything I had just to survive.'

Gus looks completely defeated. 'I swear Caro, I never received any letter. I hadn't wanted to leave you without saying goodbye, but your dad had made it very clear that me going was non-negotiable.'

'My dad? Are you saying he spoke to you?'

Gus shifts awkwardly. I never saw your dad, but he sent me a letter which said all that needed to be said. I was certainly left in no doubt about where I stood with you.'

Caro stares at Gus and struggles to keep the scepticism from her face. Seeing this, Gus reaches in his pocket and passes over an envelope.

'Here, read this; I received this from your dad a few days after Jez had died.'

Caro is reluctant to see what her father had chosen to share with Gus, but knows this is something she can't avoid. Funny to think that after seventeen years of successfully running from the past, it has caught up with her with a vengeance. Clearly it is true that you can't outrun your past deeds forever.

Gus

I wanted to come and see you but didn't trust myself to keep control. You have destroyed my family and have left me to pick up the pieces. As promised, I have enclosed a reference letter. Should you need anything further, please contact school admin. I will not respond to any further communication and nor will any of my family.

I still don't think you have any comprehension of the impact of your actions. I have agreed to keep quiet, but do not think I am doing so out of any regard for

> you in anyway. I will regret for every day of my life that I allowed you into our family. That I spent all that time with you, thinking I was encouraging you to make a good life for yourself.
>
> I treated you like a son - to my shame, I probably treated you with more kindness than the way I treated my own son. I will have to live with the consequences of my poor judgement for the rest of my life. I hope you feel shame at your actions and find it difficult to live with yourself, but I am starting to understand that you will breeze on past this and will give no further thought to those you have hurt so badly.

The first page of the letter is ragged and torn, the ink smudged in places where the page had been folded and unfolded. Clearly it has been read and held many times, and she appreciates it clearly hurt Gus deeply. Why else would he have kept it all this time? The letter continues on the second page in a similar vein, and Caro finds it hard to reconcile the coldness in the words with her memory of the easy friendship that had developed between the two men that last summer.

> I blame myself for not seeing your true character, so how can I blame her for being deceived in the same way? She does not want to see you ever again. Do not try to contact her in any way, or make no mistake I will go to the police.
>
> C. Webster

Caro reads the letter through then glances up to see Gus watching her intently. She reads the letter through a second time, reeling at the punch of betrayal deep in her gut. All those times her dad must have heard her crying in her room, and all the time he knew that Gus would never come back because he had told him she didn't want to see him ever again. Had threatened reporting Gus because Caro hadn't been sixteen. All those years wasted because of her dad. The life she and Alex had could have been so different. After all, part of the problem with Mark was due to the simple fact that he wasn't Gus. Yes, he is kind and safe but that made her yearn for the excitement that was Gus. Alex could have had a father that he adored and looked up to. And now her dad is dead so she can't even ask him why he did it.

'Oh God, Gus! I had no idea. All those years wasted!' And then they are both crying and clinging to each other as Caro processes the depth of the betrayal by her father. Afterwards, they sit in the warm sand and share the details of their lives since they have been apart. Looking at her watch, Caro is surprised to see it's nearly five.

'I've got to go, but we will sort something out. I'll try and make this right for you and Alex.'

'Between us, we can sort this. All that matters now is that Alex doesn't get screwed up because of our actions. He needs to come first in this. Obviously, I hope he chooses to have a relationship with me, but I will understand and respect his decision if he decides he doesn't have room for me in his life right now.'

Caro nods, not trusting herself to speak, finding herself feeling just as she had seventeen years ago when she had wanted Gus to never leave her again. As she wanders back over the dunes, she feels dazed but can't help but think that maybe this will be a new start for all of them. Maybe it's not too late to be the family they always should have been.

41

Nat

Present day: Tuesday, 23 July

The afternoon has flown by, and Nat realises they need to head back to the Beach Hut – Caro will be wondering where they are. Nat and the girls had spent most of the afternoon at the beach, wandering from rock pool to rock pool hoping to find some little creature to capture in their buckets. Nat's job had been to carefully lift the bigger rocks to see if anything would dart out from the shadow. To say they had limited success would be being kind to the girl's efforts. There was lots of splashing and squealing but not a lot of catching. Still, they all had fun and are tired as they troop back to the hut.

    Nat has always loved this part of the return to the hut. Climbing the small incline from the beach up the wooden steps, you are suddenly faced with the hut. Her favourite is when the light is fading and the inside lights illuminate anyone in the lounge, like they are actors performing on a stage. Today, there is no sign that anyone is at home. Nat had expected Caro to join them down on the beach, and for a few seconds she feels the familiar resentment that Caro has expected her to be around that afternoon to provide the childcare. She then realises that this time she is being rather unreasonable - given that she had dropped her daughter off that morning without a second thought, because it suited her to do so. Nat swallows down her irritation together with her first small glass of wine.

By the time Caro appears, the girls had showered the beach away from their bodies and are eating pizza, and Nat is on her second, much larger, glass of wine. Seeing Caro's face, Nat bites back the sarcastic greeting that is itching to escape her lips. Her friend looks truly terrible. She has obviously been crying, and Nat is almost surprised to see that Caro can look quite unattractive. It isn't a trait that you usually associate with the Webster women. Nodding towards the girls with a shake of her head, Nat understands that their conversation needs to be delayed until they are safe from prying ears.

Grace and Annie are delighted at the offer of two films of their choice, as long as they promise to go straight to bed after. The deal is sealed with the bribe of ice cream, and the pair of them are soon safely settled in front of the TV whilst the two women close themselves away in the kitchen. The patio doors at the back of the hut are open and the evening breeze brings with it the smell of the nighttime ocean. Nat remembers the hours her and Caro had sat here years ago, sharing their dreams and planning a future that was a world away from where they have ended up.

Caro stands at the worktop setting out cheese and crackers. Nat recognises a delaying tactic when she sees one and, pouring them each a glass of wine, moves towards her friend and lays a hand on her shoulder. She is shocked that Caro is shaking.

'Come and sit down, tell me what's happened.'

Nat can honestly say that Caro's tearful confession is the last thing she had expected. Her head is so full of Sam's last evening at the ball and her weirdly close relationship with her headteacher, that she half expected Caro to share that she had found something at the Beach Hut that made her question her father's role in Sam's life all those years ago. That maybe she had seen something that had made her think those unpleasant allegations on the Facebook page had a grain of truth behind them. But Angus Redfearn being Alex's father. Now that Nat really hadn't seen coming.

When the rumours first started that Caro was pregnant, there had been very little speculation about who the father might be. The town was still reeling from Sam's disappearance and then the suicide of Jez. So as far as Nat could remember, it was assumed that Caro had hooked up with one of the many holidaymakers visiting that summer; and it was usual for the local teenagers to enjoy a string of holiday romances through the summer season.

Years later, when Nat had returned to the town with James and rekindled her friendship with Caro, they would sometimes speculate about who Alex's father might be. But again, idle gossip, assuming that Caro didn't know who the father was either - she had made no secret of the fact that she had left that box blank on the birth certificate. Caro had always made such a big thing about the fact that Mark was the only father Alex would ever need.

When Caro finishes talking, Nat takes a long drink of her wine and moves to the fridge to top both their glasses up.

'Bloody hell Caro, I don't know what to say.'

Caro sniffs. 'To be honest, there isn't really anything you can say. It's all such a mess and whatever I decide to do, someone is going to get badly hurt. I don't want that somebody to be Alex. But funnily enough, I do feel better for telling you.'

Nat understands that. She has seen it throughout her career - the relief of unburdening your secrets. It's the thing that makes people decide to share their story - when often it might be better, all round, for them to continue in silence.

'But your dad writing to Gus like that. You had no idea?'

'Absolutely none.' Caro gives a bitter laugh. 'And the weird thing is, I never told Mum and Dad who Alex's father was. I assumed they went along with the belief that it was a casual fling with someone who had left the area. How could Dad have known all these years and not said anything? And to threaten Gus with the police. I mean, I know technically Gus had broken the law with me being fifteen, but let's face it, we were both just kids. Gus must have been terrified.'

Nat nods in agreement, but her brain is struggling to make sense of it. It's all so odd. Yes, the Websters would have been deeply disappointed in Gus, and maybe they weren't thinking straight - dealing with the shock and grief of losing Jez. But Chris had always liked Gus, treated him like a son really. Surely there were worse things that could happen? But to threaten him, meaning Caro was left alone and Alex never got the opportunity to have a relationship with his father, it doesn't add up.

Caro obviously reads the confusion on Nat's face. 'What?'

Nat curses the fact that she has always been a bit of an open book as far as her friend is concerned.

'Don't you think it's a bit strange? I mean, a bit of an overreaction from your dad. To be honest, I would have been less surprised if he'd forced a shotgun wedding - he liked Gus, and you know what he was like about keeping up appearances.'

Caro nods slowly, her face creased as she tries to make sense of it all. 'I agree, but it was a funny time, Nat. Honestly, it was like we had all lost our minds when we lost Jez. And maybe, once he'd sent that letter, he thought it was best to not tell me what he'd done - it probably wouldn't have changed anything.'

Nat nods but bites back her retort. Chris Webster had ridden roughshod over everyone's lives, doing what he thought was the right thing, without giving those that it affected much choice in the matter. To her, those weren't the actions of a loving father. Gus was a nice lad – his family was decent. She would have thought Chris might have been secretly pleased with the way things turned out.

'Anyway, I can't think about it anymore tonight. I need to sleep on it and decide what to do. So come on, tell me how you got on with your hunt for the ever-elusive Sam. Do you reckon you're going to find her hiding out somewhere and get the scoop on her emotional reunion with her mum?'

Nat knows that Caro is being flippant to disguise the hurt and confusion she's feeling, but even so, she feels a flash of irritation at the complete lack of empathy shown by her friend.

'Mmm, I'm not so sure there is going to be a happy ending.'

Not wanting to break Kate's confidence that Sam might have been found a little closer to home than they'd ever expected, Nat looks to distract Caro. 'Oh, you'll never guess what. I've got a pack of photos from the leavers' ball. Kate Chappell gave them to me, and I haven't looked at them yet. Let's see if we can spot anyone we know. There's bound to be some of your mum and dad, and we might even be there in the background, slaving away!'

The two of them spread the photos out and spend some time giggling over hairstyles and unflattering frocks. Nat is looking for that snap of Sam, the one that might give her a clue. She doesn't know what the picture will look like, but she is convinced that it must be there somewhere. She is lost in that world, transported back seventeen years, and is barely aware that Caro has left the room. Looking at the handful of photos that include Sam, she is struck by the fact that Sam is always on the periphery of the shot. That she always seems to be looking in, rather than being a part of the picture. It's also striking that whenever Gus is in the picture, Sam would be somewhere at the edge of the photo - looking. Not at the camera, but fixing her gaze on Gus. Well, that fitted with everything Beth and Kirsten had said about her obsession with the boy. How funny that her and Caro were both going through that same painful unrequited attraction.

'Come on Sam, where did you go?' But the pictures keep their secrets of that night.

'Talking to yourself is the first sign of madness.'

Nat laughs, pleased that Caro seems to have regained some of her composure.

'See if these photos help at all.'

Opening the box she had been carrying, Caro takes out the photos she had been looking at earlier of her parents, Gus and Sam.

Adding them to the collection, Nat continues to study the images, thinking that maybe if she stares at them for long enough something will jump out at her. She is brought back to the present by Caro giving a little gasp beside her.

'Oh my God!'

Nat has to fight back a snap of irritation. Why does Caro have to be so dramatic about everything? Her friend is picking up each picture with a shaking hand, looking at the image closely, before throwing it down and snatching up the next one. Moving to the box, she roots in the bottom before retrieving a leather friendship bracelet.

'Look! At Sam's wrist. She's wearing this bracelet.'

Nat looks at the photo and then manages to gently prise the circle of leather from Caro's trembling grip. Looking from the photo to the bracelet, she can see the similarity, but they aren't the same item.

'Look Caro, the beads are different, this one has them grouped in twos whereas the one Sam is wearing just has a single bead. And there's some sort of charm on Sam's bracelet. But you're right, they are very similar.'

Instead of calming down, Caro seems to shake more violently. 'Nat, this bracelet was in this tin. Dad had kept it. It was Jez's.'

Nat nods, not really seeing where this is going.

'But the thing is, for all these years I've kept what I thought was Jez's bracelet. I picked it up off the floor after I walked into the room and found him. I'd slipped it in my pocket and ended up keeping it just for me. It made me feel close to him. But that wasn't Jez's bracelet, so who did it belong to? And why does it look so like the one Sam was wearing on the night she disappeared?'

42

Nat

Present day: Saturday, 27 July

Nat isn't sure what she expected the next few days to bring. But after the tears of Tuesday night, the storm seems to have blown over and Caro is acting as if nothing of any importance has happened. True, Nat notices her friend looking at Alex a moment longer than maybe she normally would. Nat wonders what she is seeing, what she is thinking? Does she find herself lost in a world of what might have been? Nat feels unable to ask her friend, and she remembers this has always been the way of the Webster family. If they decide to share anything, it will always be on their own terms.

The weather for the first week is perfect. The sun shines and there is a soothing sea breeze that keeps the temperature comfortable, but isn't fierce enough to blow the sand into your eyes and try to wrestle the rug from your hands. They have fallen into an easy routine with Nat hiding herself away in Chris Webster's old office until mid-afternoon, when she takes over the role of chief entertainer to the demanding five-year-olds. At that point, Caro either opens the wine - and the two sit gossiping about nothing - or takes herself off for a walk. She returns with her cheeks flushed and bringing with her an atmosphere of manic excitement. Nat thinks she is likely meeting up with Gus - but again doesn't feel she is able to ask her friend about it. Still, her second piece about Sam has been published. It included a photo of Sam taken by Kate on the night of the ball, as well as the photo Caro had allowed her to use of Sam stood with Jen, Chris and Gus. As with the previous piece, the end of the article was an appeal for anyone to come forward if they remembered anything, however small. So far there has been a resounding silence.

Nat hasn't been able to stop thinking about the bracelet. On the Wednesday, Caro had nipped home and brought back the bracelet she had kept for all those years, thinking she was holding a piece of Jez close by. The two women took turns holding the bracelet and the photo of Sam. Nat had the genius idea of taking a photo of the picture with her phone so they could zoom in on the bracelet, but this made the image grainy and harder to see. There was no doubt that, after their scrutiny, they were as sure as they could be that the bracelet Caro had picked up from the floor of the bedroom all those years ago was the same as the one Sam had been wearing on the night she disappeared.

On Friday night, with the girls once more settled in front of the TV, Caro finally decides to speak again about what she had found.

'Do you think I should go to the police, Nat? I mean, I don't even know if they would be interested after all this time.'

Nat pretends to consider this for a while, then shakes her head. 'It could be a coincidence, Caro. You know what it's like around here in the summer. You can pick bracelets like that up from nearly every little gift shop, as well as the open stalls that set up near the beach car park. The bracelet might be the same as Sam's - but let's face it, there were probably hundreds of bracelets like that sold over the summer. And in the picture, Sam's bracelet definitely had a charm attached to it, and there's nothing like that on the bracelet you have.'

Caro considers this but isn't quite ready to let it go. 'I just thought if I took it to the police, they might be able to run a fancy test or something. I don't know...'

Her voice trails off and she takes another gulp of wine. Nat feels sorry for her friend, she really does, but selfishly she doesn't want this nugget of information out in the open. What she really wants is to drop it as a bit of a bombshell in her next piece. Maybe even go so far as to question whether there is a link between Sam's disappearance and Jez deciding he couldn't face living any longer. But she is torn, recognising that Caro will never forgive her if she puts this speculation out there for everyone to make their own assumptions. Nat really doesn't think she can do that to her friend who, for all her faults, doesn't deserve the shit storm that will rain down on her and her memories if the internet sleuths pick up on this link, however tenuous.

Saturday morning dawns with dull skies and the hint of a storm in the air. Nat has a cracking headache - likely due to the fact she has tossed and turned all night wrestling with her conscience. Maybe this is the killer instinct that she has always worried she lacked. Maybe this is why she will be stuck writing about local grumbles for the rest of her life.

As it happens, the decision is taken out of her hands. She mumbles a good morning to Caro - who looks like she has suffered all night the same as Nat - and they both sit in their own little worlds held in a phone. Nat is having trouble focusing through bleary eyes, and is already on her second cup of coffee in a futile attempt to jump-start the day. Her mindless scrolling is interrupted by the notification there has been a new post on the Churcher's group. Expecting an admin update on the reunion dinner, she realises Caro is reading the same post when she hears the whimper that escapes from her friend.

Churcher's School – Old Pupils Group

Posted by: Anonymous Saturday 27th July 08.17am

Well, well, well! Has the penny finally dropped? At last, someone is telling the real story about what happened to Sam Chappell. Interesting to read the latest article in the paper by our esteemed old girl Natalie Morton. For those that don't remember, Natalie was best friends with Caroline Webster. So, I suppose you could say she was part of that inner circle.

Does Nat know something that the rest of us don't?

Interesting that the photo chosen to accompany the article included the late, not lamented Mr Webster and his beautiful wife Jen, who - rumour has it - is away with the fairies. Maybe she finds it easier to live in cloud cuckoo land than face up to the knowledge that her son couldn't live with what had happened to Sam Chappell. Because, let's be honest here, we all know that Sam's not living a happily ever after anywhere. Quite nice to see the local rag is actually leading the way for once. Justice for Sam!

27 likes, 15 sad, 2 angry

4 comments

JohnB: Whilst I feel it's unfair to drag the Webster family through the mud like this, I do think it's about time Sam's case was investigated again. There's no way she left of her own accord, and you can't help but think it's no coincidence that the school should experience two tragedies in the same month and that they aren't linked.

PinkyPen: Good point – it's not like we have ever had anything like this happen since. Not in the school. Not in the town.

CarlaBarnes(nee Simpson): Got to ask when the police are going to update us on the mysterious case of the body in the quarry!

JohnB: The quarry which just happens to be developed by Natalie's husband! She definitely knows more than she's ever let on.

Nat quickly takes a screenshot, guessing it's only a matter of time before admin takes the post down. Caro is quiet. In contrast to her rage at the previous posts, this seems to have destroyed her. She doesn't flinch when Nat moves over and wraps her arms round her.

'It's going to be OK, Caro. We can get through this, I promise.' Nat flinches as she whispers the words. Mindful that yet again she has made a promise it is very unlikely she will be able to keep.

Caro almost jolts back to her old self, and for a moment Nat thinks she is going to tell her to stop being so ridiculous. Instead, she holds Nat's hand as she nods. 'You can't make this right, Nat. It's no use pretending all this is fine. When Jez died, we had the funeral and then Mum and Dad almost acted like he had never existed. We never spoke about it. Never asked why. I mean, they never even attended the inquest. So, will you help me?'

Nat looks at Caro, unsure what her friend is asking her to do.

'You're a journalist. You can tell Jez's story. Because the one thing I do know, is my brother would never have harmed

Sam. At least, not intentionally. But something happened that meant he couldn't bear to live any longer, and I think it's about time we faced the truth - whatever that is.'

And as Nat tries to appear that she is being talked around, is reluctantly agreeing to help her friend, all she can think is that she really hadn't needed to worry last night. Things have a way of turning out just the way you want them to.

43

Caro

Present day: Monday, 29 July

Caro is parked up outside the police headquarters. She had rung the local station earlier that day and had been on hold for so long, she nearly took it as a sign that she should really let the past stay in the past. After all, this whole thing is completely ridiculous. But then she had thought of those vile anonymous postings and realised that until the truth about Sam was finally discovered, there would be no peace for either the Chappell or the Webster family. Eventually a rather flustered voice on the phone told her that the case was being dealt with by Detective Inspector Gillingham who was based at the regional headquarters, and Caro got the impression they couldn't wait to get her off the phone. No doubt they had been inundated with callers since Nat's article triggered a new appeal for witnesses, and she hates the idea that she may have been bunched in with the so-called crank callers.

Part of her had hoped she wouldn't be able to find a parking space, and she could take that as a sign that she wasn't meant to be here. But sods law she sailed into a spot, right by the pay and display meter and conveniently located by the pedestrian exit that leads to the building she needed to get to. Looks like fate has a different idea for her.

Announcing her name at the front desk, she is ushered to a seat in the waiting area and Caro can't help but feel a bit detached from it all; like she is making a guest appearance on a TV show.

When someone eventually comes to collect her, Caro is surprised that they aren't wearing a uniform. She had expected to be accompanied down some dingy corridor to a room which would hold a very functional table which would be fixed to the floor. Of course, one wall would be dominated by a large mirror, which everyone knew was really a viewing point from the room on the other side, where the clever detectives were peering in on you, scrutinising your every word. Instead, she is shown to a small room with a couple of comfortable chairs where the young man introduces himself as Detective Constable Coles. Strangely, the realisation that the detective in charge is not wasting any time to come and see her and has, instead ,sent a junior member of the team, immediately reassures Caro - the police obviously don't think she has information of any importance. Just as she thought - she really did have nothing to tell.

She did think about apologising for wasting their time and making a swift exit. But then she thinks about those horrible posts that are getting more vicious every time, so takes a deep breath and tells the detective all about finding the bracelet and her suspicions. She points out the photograph of Samantha, taken on the night of her disappearance, and the detective asks if he can keep the items. Caro finds herself signing a load of paperwork and is then outside, blinking in the sunshine, unable to comprehend what has just happened. Did they take her seriously, or will she be filed away in the box labelled 'nutters'?

Either way, it's done now and was the first step in shutting down the murmuring gossip once and for all.

44

Nat

Present day: Monday, 29 July

Nat is pleased to escape the Beach Hut to get a couple of hours in the office. Caro had volunteered to drop the girls off at holiday club and had said she should be OK to collect them at the end of the day. She had been vague about what she was intending to do with the day, but Nat didn't press her too hard. She didn't want to get roped into keeping her company when she is keen to get on with the next part of her article.

She'd been working on it most of Sunday night, and her eyes feel gritty from lack of sleep and staring at the screen. Ben had been reluctant when she had first messaged him, but sat now in his office reading her piece, she can see that he is seeing the potential in this twist on the old story.

'And you say the Webster family have spoken to you about this?'

Nat nods. Caro really was the Webster family now. Jen didn't really count, seeing as most of the time she didn't even remember she had a son who had died.

'It was Caroline Fraser, Jez's older sister, who asked me to look into this. She has been very upset by the anonymous posts on the Facebook group and wants the allegations investigated. And that's what I do, investigative journalism. Or at least, it's what I should be doing. It's why you pay me and the boost this paper needs.'

Ben acknowledges this but still looks doubtful. 'And is she prepared for the fact that people might jump to the conclusion that her brother did have something to do with what happened to Sam?'

Nat pretends to give this some thought, when in reality it is all she has thought about whilst writing the article. She can't escape she has a personal connection to Jez, and she truly can't believe that the quiet, sweet, awkward teenager she remembers could have been involved in any way in harming Sam. She was probably his first love. And as it turned out, his last.

'She has thought about this Ben, and I have to say I see where she's coming from. You know this town. It's a small place and there's no way that post, practically naming her brother as the villain of the piece, is confined to the old pupils of Churcher's. It will have been screenshot and made its way throughout the town by now. And the fact it names the paper as fearlessly tackling the issue…' At this she steals a sideways glance at Ben, knowing she is shamelessly appealing to his vanity. 'That gives us the perfect excuse to run with the story.'

Nat nervously fiddles with her ring but then relaxes. She knows she has got him as he smiles. 'Go on, then. It can go up on the website.'

'You're the best boss in the world. I could kiss you! But I will remember we are professionals and content myself to making you a coffee.'

Ben grins. 'I hope you remember I am the best boss in the world next time I assign covering the town council meeting to you.'

Laughing as she pretends to hang herself, Nat finds her smile slipping, reflecting that the gesture may be in rather poor taste, bearing in mind poor Jez. Returning to her desk, she scans through the piece one last time, making a last few minute tweaks. Admittedly, the headline of 'Death and Disappearance' is designed as clickbait, but after that she thinks the piece has enough behind it that it could get picked up by one of the nationals. She is allowing herself to dream of the approach from Netflix, to front a documentary on the mystery that is gripping the nation, when she is brought back to the reality of the cramped offices and her desk by the toilets, by her phone ringing.

Seeing it's Kate, she presses the 'accept' button, feeling a pang of guilt that she hasn't made the time to see how Kate is since the last time she had answered the other woman's distressed call. This time, there are no tears. In fact, there is no emotion at all as Kate speaks. Putting down the phone, Nat realises she will need to change the headline and play around with a few of the details, but what a bloody great story she has! This time, she really has fallen on her feet.

Murder and Suicide - a deadly coincidence?

By Natalie Morton

The peace of the town was shattered three weeks ago when the development of the quarry was brought to a standstill by the discovery of a body. Whilst the discovery caused a sensation on platforms such as TikTok, most of the town carried on as normal. The general consensus being it was unlikely to be anyone local, and it appeared the gruesome find may be decades old - nothing to disrupt the comfortable rhythm of life in a seaside town.

And life has followed a comfortable rhythm here for seventeen years. Many residents either didn't live here, or are too young to remember, the last time tragedy hit our little tourist honeypot. Sadly, today police issued a statement that the body recovered from the quarry was that of the missing teenager Samantha Chappel, who disappeared in 2007.

In the first coincidence, the Roxcliffe Gazette has been running a series of articles documenting the disappearance of Samantha, fondly known as Sam by those close to her. The search at the time drew a blank and, whilst the case was never closed, it was shelved away waiting for new evidence to bring it back to life. Sadly, that new evidence is in the form that has brought Sam's mother, Kate Chappel, closure but more pain. When Kate heard the news, she told me how she had expected to feel relief, but instead was overwhelmed by the torrent of grief that struck her once the small light of hope had at last been extinguished.

Finally, Sam has a new chance to find justice, but her story doesn't stand alone. At Churcher's School, the building on the hill that looks out over the town, there have been some unpleasant rumblings that started with the death of the retired headmaster, Christopher Webster. Mr Webster was well-known for championing pupils to achieve the very best they could and, seventeen years ago, Sam was one such pupil who was lucky enough to receive his support. Mr Webster was devastated by Sam's disappearance, and Kate Chappell is a staunch supporter, stating publicly that she would never have survived those first few weeks without the help of Christopher.

Little did they know that shortly after Sam's disappearance, the Webster family would experience their own tragedy when their fourteen-year-old son, Jeremy, took his own life.

For seventeen years, the two families have had to learn to live without their children. But today, another more difficult question is raised. Is the link between them something more than has been looked at up till now? During the course of my investigation, I have spoken to Sam's mother and her best friends. I have my own memories of Sam, as I was at the same school as her. And I have my own memories of Jeremy, as his family embraced me into their home. Jeremy was a quiet, kind boy. He had an easy smile and was, at fourteen, just in that awkward part of growing up, when you start to make the transition to adulthood, with all the turmoil that can bring. But there was never anything that indicated to his family that Jeremy was thinking of taking his own life.

As you would expect for a boy of that age, Jeremy was starting to be interested in girls. It would appear that he had a crush on Sam, who was a regular visitor at the house for tutoring sessions. The feeling was unreciprocated, and no one really noticed that Jeremy may have become obsessed with Sam. What was noticed, was that in the last few weeks before his death, Jeremy did change. The people I spoke to remarked that he became sullen, shut himself away in his room and seemed angry most of the time.

In the last few days, there has been a new development which may suggest there is a link between Jeremy and Sam. The evidence has been passed to the police, and so as not to hinder their investigation, we won't reveal the exact details until we have their permission to do so. I was made aware of this by Caroline Webster, who remains my friend. I spoke to Caroline about recent events, and she told me this:

'I have been very distressed at the anonymous postings that have appeared on the Churcher's school site, accusing my father of some vile things. I find it particularly sickening that this person waited until he was dead to start these rumours, giving my father no chance to defend himself. When they started to drag Jez into their sordid accusations, I knew I couldn't ignore it.

'I was at school with Sam and remember her disappearance very clearly. I never had a hint that any of my family could have been involved, and I continue to stand by that belief to this day. However, I am keen to assist the police in any way so they can concentrate their efforts in finding the truth of the matter. I believe that truth will totally exonerate my family, and we can move forward remembering with love my father and brother, who we miss so deeply.'

In the meantime, the town waits for the day when they can finally allow Samantha and Jeremy to rest in peace.

45

Alex

Present day: Monday, 29 July

Alex knows something is up with his mum. I mean, there's always something up with his mum. Mark always said she was a bit of a drama queen. It was something they had always laughed about together. Before it all went wrong. But she is being weirder than normal. She thinks he doesn't notice, but he can feel her eyes lingering on him. Watching him even when he is just making himself a drink. It's like she is trying to see something else in him, and he isn't sure what it is. He just knows it makes him feel uncomfortable. He wishes he could talk to Mark about it, ask him to have a word with Mum. Mark always knows what to do - could always make everything right. Until he stopped caring.

It has been a bit of a crap summer so far. OK, they have only been off for just over a week and the Beach Hut is actually pretty good. But all his mates seemed to be jetting off on holidays that sound to be much more fun that being stuck here for the whole summer. He'd enjoyed the flurry of activity that had followed his upload of the body in the quarry, but nothing else had happened since and so he, and everyone else, had lost interest a bit. And he is skint. He really ought to look at getting a summer job, but he has probably left it too late - hoping one of his mates might invite him to join them on a trip abroad. So now he is stuck here with no money to do anything

- even if there was something to do. Which there isn't, because there never is. He can't wait to get away from here, move to a university in one of the big cities. He's far too lazy to work hard for Oxbridge, but he figures if he can get to London, or even Manchester or Leeds, he will be much happier.

He had been glad when Monday had rolled around. It meant Grace and Annie were heading off to holiday club, so he wouldn't be badgered to go with them to the beach or be forced to have family fun time. Really, did his mum think anybody really enjoyed these artificially jolly gatherings? Today he can please himself, and that means hanging around with his mates, hoping that some of the older ones will go and get some booze and vapes for them. He's already helped himself to twenty quid from his mum's purse, so that's his share of the kitty sorted.

Opening a can of Coke out of the fridge, he sees there are the dregs left in the bottom of the bottle of wine, and he takes the bottle with him as he sits at the table. Crisps and a chocolate bar for breakfast satisfy more than his growling stomach. He knows his choices will piss his mum off and he can hear her nagging him to eat a proper breakfast. I mean, who decides what a proper breakfast is? Raising the bottle in a silent toast to Caro, he takes a large gulp and tries to hide the grimace as the sour liquid hits the back of his throat. He has no idea why his mum and Nat seem to enjoy sitting drinking this stuff. Still, he does like the warm glow that follows - after his stomach stops churning in revolt. Soon the bottle is empty, and he stashes it with the growing pile of empties stacked by the back door, waiting to be taken down to the recycling.

It's nice to have the house to himself. Sometimes he feels that everyone else is sucking all the air out of the room, leaving him nothing left to breathe so that he slowly suffocates whilst no one notices. He idly flips open his mums iPad and waits while it updates to the Cloud. He sometimes has a sneaky look - to see if he is ever mentioned in the messages between his mum and Mark. He never knows what he's hoping to see. But he does know that it doesn't feel good when his name is conspicuous by its absence. Even though he knows where he stands, it isn't a great feeling to have that knowledge confirmed.

There have been a couple of messages since the last time he'd sneaked a look, but just general life admin. Details of bills that need to be sorted and the pick-up and drop off arrangements for the favoured Grace. He is about to swipe the iPad closed when a new message thread catches his eye. Unusually for his mum, she hasn't saved the contact as a name, so it is a simple number with no accompanying picture. He feels a bit weird opening this thread up. Different to reading anything Mark has to say - he justifies that as he needs to know things that will have a direct impact on his life. He tends to respect his mum's privacy in terms of the other messages – besides, he has no interest in the frivolous gossip he imagines she exchanges with her friends.

Unknown: I think we need to talk. Tomorrow at 2. Usual spot.

Caro: Despite everything, it was so good to see you.

Unknown: It was good to see you too.

Alex cringes a bit reading this. Did his mum have a new boyfriend? The thought makes him feel a bit sick. Anyway, surely, she is far too old to be bothering with that sort of stuff - though he knows Cameron's dad has recently moved in with a new girlfriend, which is just gross! Maybe he shouldn't read any more. But then his own name jumps out at him from the screen.

Unknown: So, Alex. I can't stop thinking about him. I'm starting to get my head round it, but what the fuck! I have a son. I appreciate this won't be easy, but I do want to get to know him. I know I can never get back all those years I've missed, but I would like to try and make up for that now.

Caro: Let's talk about this in person. It's not going to be easy, and Alex is at a very vulnerable age. I think the main thing to remember in all this is Alex. Regardless of how we both feel and what we would like to happen, it comes down to what he wants.

Unknown: I agree, but I would like to at least be given a chance. After all, it's not my fault I wasn't involved in his life. I would never have left if I had known you were pregnant.

Caro: That does make me happy to know that. But please, we do need to take this slowly. This is all going to be a huge shock for Alex. And the rest of the family. Mark is the only father he has ever known, and we do need to be considerate of everyone.

Unknown: OK, but please understand I won't just walk away.

Caro: I understand. And I don't want you to walk away. I want you to be a part of Alex's life.

Caro: And mine x

Alex doesn't really know what to feel at this point. He has dreamt of meeting his real father so much over the last couple of years. Yearning to create the same bond that he saw between Grace and Mark, and now it's within his grasp. His dad is somewhere nearby. Close enough for his mum to have met up with him - and still, she has denied him that chance. How he hates her, and Mark and this town. Without giving himself time to be nervous, he grabs his own phone and dials the number of the unknown contact. It rings for ages, and he is about to give up when the call connects and a man's voice speaks a little warily. 'Yes?'

At this point Alex realises he doesn't know what to say. He wants to put the phone down, but before he can disconnect the call the voice speaks again. This time, the hint of impatience is gone.

'Hello. This is Angus Redfearn, who is this?'

'Hello Dad, this is Alex, your son.'

46

Nat

Present day: Monday, 29 July

Nat is sat in her car just down the road from Kate's house. She supposes she could just march up to the front door and knock - try and feign the confidence that she will be granted admittance to that inner sanctum of grief. She has seen numerous others try that tactic as she watches the street descend into the press rabble that will become the norm - until there is a new development, or a more interesting story breaks elsewhere. On top of the traditional press, there is a new phenomenon. The social media detectives. In fact, it seems this group has rather snatched the attention away from the murder investigation, with more time of the police appeals dedicated for them to please leave the area, to stop trespassing, to please leave the families alone to grieve. Nat fears it's only a matter of time before one of them stumbles upon the Churcher's Facebook page, and then Caro will be faced with trial by online jury.

    She is roused from the paralysis of indecision by the vibration of her phone:

> *Are you going to sit out there all day? Come round the back, I can meet you at the gate to the garden.*

Leaving the car, Nat casts an anxious glance towards the press pack, but they are focused on the little bungalow that houses their prey. Stood in groups, appearing to be swapping idle chit chat, but each constantly checking if their opponents have something that will make their story the breaking news. Joking as they debate whose turn it is to try another knock at the door that they have no expectation will be opened to them. Still, at this point they have nothing better to do.

Ducking around the corner, she counts the backs of the houses until she sees the little gate to her left cracked open and a white-faced Kate ushers her through, before firmly locking it behind them. It feels natural for the two women to embrace, and Nat struggles to hide her shock at the years that have been added to Kate's face. Grief and loss are etched into the lines around her eyes and mouth with skin drawn tight over her cheekbones.

Entering the bungalow, Nat can see that it's not just Kate's appearance that has changed since she was last here. Framed pictures of Sam are on every surface, telling her life story from the studio portraits of the baby days, through to toddlerhood, junior school, teenage years and that final summer. Pride of place is given to Sam stood arm in arm with her mum, dressed ready for the leavers' ball. Nat struggles to understand why Kate would want that reminder of the last night she would be with Sam - but then she sees the photo depicts the two women looking at each other, rather than at the camera. It captures the obvious deep affection between them so perfectly, that Nat understands there is no way this photo could be consigned to a drawer - despite everything that followed.

'No point not having the photos out now.' Kate notices where Nat's eyes have been drawn. 'I know that my little girl will be forever seventeen. Those eighteenth birthday gifts that

I saved for her coming back - they'll never be opened.'

There is an awkward silence when Nat knows she ought to be offering Kate some words of comfort - she just doesn't have anything to say that will make any of this better. Thinking of her own daughter, Annie, Nat can't stop the tears that roll down her face, and so Kate ends up comforting her. 'There, there, have a tissue. I know, I know.'

Afterwards, the two women sit at the kitchen table, hands cupping mugs of tea, as Kate speaks about Sam. Nat doesn't want to break the spell by getting her notebook from her bag, but she does manage to flip her phone into record mode, feeling a moment of guilt that she is somehow intruding on a private conversation that journalist Nat has no business with.

'I wanted to thank you, Nat, for everything you've done so far.'

Nat feels the heat rise in her face, Kate's words of thanks adding to the conflict she is battling.

'I know the case would have been reopened anyway, what with them finding my little girl and all. But you'd already forced people to remember. Reminded them that my daughter did exist and was still out there, needing to be rescued. Now I can let her rest easy.'

'Have you made any plans yet?' Again, Nat is torn, knowing that she will probably publish these details in the paper.

'The police haven't really been able to give me a timeline of when I can have a funeral. Not that there's any hurry - it's been seventeen years - so I guess a few more weeks won't matter. But I have spoken to the school chaplain and I'm having a memorial service for my girl next Saturday.'

'At the school?' Nat knows from the quick glance that Kate shoots her way that the other woman has picked up on the note of shock in her voice.

'Well yes, I mean, it was where Sam had spent the most time over the last years of her life. Despite everything, the school years were happy years for Sam, and they gave her the most marvellous opportunities. If only things had turned out differently.'

Nat nods, her fingers seeking comfort from the circles of metal on her right hand, trying to reconcile this with the information she has about Jez Webster.

Seeing the doubt in her eyes, Kate continues. 'I know what you're thinking. I'm not daft. I know about the rumours flying back and forth about Chris and Jez, and I read the piece you wrote. I can tell you one thing: that dear sweet boy, there's no way he was involved in this. He adored my Sam. Probably a bit too much, but he would have grown out of it, and he would never have harmed her. If anything, I'm scared he killed himself because he couldn't bear to live without her. You know how things feel when you're a teenager. And if that's true, whoever hurt my Sam - they murdered two people that night.'

Sneaking back out of the garden, Nat hopes that Kate's version is correct. That would be such a story - a real pull on the heartstrings. Hurrying back to her car, she barely glances at the small crowd who remain peering at the bungalow. She has the next instalment of her piece to write. Something good is going to come out of this for her. She can just tell.

47

Caro

Present day: Monday, 29 July

Pulling up by the Beach Hut, Caro hopes that Nat is back. She wants to share how the visit to the police had gone - to dissect every moment and every word. She wants to find something in there that indicates they took her seriously, but at the same time reassures her that she really is fretting about nothing. Instead, she is greeted with that empty silence that tells you, even before you shout out a questioning hello, that there is no one else home.

  Flicking the kettle on, her brain carelessly turns over the fact that it is unusual for Alex to emerge from his bed before lunchtime. At the same time, she taps her iPad and sees it is open at the string of messages she has exchanged with Gus. Her mind fights against the rationale of what this means - desperately shuffling through the possibilities that are more palatable than the one that is screaming in her face.

  Maybe she left it open on those messages - but she knows she's grasping at straws. After all, she has been so careful not to save Gus's name and even looked at how she could lock the chat - until she got distracted by something and thought no more about it. Her heart is threatening to burst from her chest and her stomach is recreating the reaction to a ride on a rollercoaster. There is only one explanation: Alex has somehow seen the chat and knows about Gus. She is unable to imagine the confusion her little boy must be experiencing right now, and she wants to wrap him in her arms and make everything alright for him - even though she knows that is beyond her capabilities.

She isn't sure how long it takes for her mind to process all this, but then she is reaching for her phone and frantically checking for the missed calls she expects to see. Nothing from Alex; a few months ago she would have expected him to go to his grandad, but that is obviously no longer a possibility. Maybe Mark - would he have reached out to the only father he had known? But Mark would have called her surely, to reassure her that Alex is safe. Oh God, Mark! He will be so hurt by all of this.

Pressing on his name from the recent call list, she wonders when he had dropped so far down the screen. Not that long ago he had always been at the top. It seems to take forever for him to pick up, and it crosses her mind that maybe he is looking at his call notification and debating whether he can stomach talking to her. How have things changed so much?

'Hello, I can't really talk now - I'm at work.'

Caro knows at this point that Alex isn't safe with Mark and is about to make her excuses and put the phone down when Mark speaks again. 'Caro, are you OK? Is everything alright?'

That's all she needs to lose the little control she has, and she is unable to answer from the tears that are choking her voice to silence.

'Stay at the Beach Hut. I'm on my way.'

Mark has obviously not stuck to the speed limit as he arrives in record time. Looking flustered, he bursts through the door and is nearly knocked sideways by Caro flinging herself into the safety of the man who had rescued her once before.

It's a few minutes before Caro can get the words out. At first, Mark can't really make sense of what she's saying, but then the realisation slowly dawns and he holds her away at arm's length, looking at her in disbelief.

'Christ, you really are taking the biscuit this time, Caro. All these years, you've never spoken about Alex's father. Your parents pretended they didn't know who he was. And all this time, the bastard has been living in the same town.'

Caro shakes her head helplessly. 'It's not like that Mark, he wasn't here. He left before Alex was born and has only just come back.'

The words tumble from her mouth as she shares the events of the last few days. 'We'd agreed to take it slowly. I mean, this is mind-blowing for Alex and I know it's a huge thing for you to come to terms with.'

'Well, that's nice of you to consider my feelings in all of this.' Mark spits the words out, leaving Caro in no doubt of the contempt he feels towards her. 'But leaving that aside, the main thing now is to find Alex and give him the help and support he needs. But this isn't over, Caro. Not by any means. Anything I do to help you, know I am doing for Alex. As far as I'm concerned, you can rot in hell alongside your dear father.'

Yet again, words spoken in the heat of the moment hang between them, unable to be snatched back or unheard. The stalemate is broken by the sound of a car door slamming outside and, looking out the window, Caro only feels relief as she sees Alex; then a sickening dread as she sees he's accompanied by Gus. As the two walk up the path, Caro hears Mark's sharp intake of breath. He can't have failed to notice the similarity between the boy he has brought up as his son, and the man following him towards the house. Time seems to go in slow motion and Caro thinks the pair of them are never going to reach the door, to enter the house, and that her and Mark will be stood there for eternity. Simply waiting for the next moment - which is likely to destroy everything they have spent so long trying to build.

As the two enter the Beach Hut, Caro is suddenly aware of how Gus, as usual, takes the spotlight and the rest of them are there simply to help him shine brighter. Alex is calm, but he looks so much older than the boy she had left sleeping in bed that morning - his sleep-softened features reminding her of the little boy who liked to fall asleep in her arms, twiddling her hair in his hands as comfort. Next to the energy of Gus, Mark seems to shrink, and he clearly feels it too as he clears his throat, preparing to speak to Alex. But whatever it is that he plans to say never gets the chance to escape from his mouth, as Alex ushers him towards the door.

'Mark, good of you to come, but we've got it now. It's a family thing, you see. Something for me to discuss with my mum...' Here Alex hesitates as if debating whether to deal the killer blow. 'And my dad.'

48

Nat

Present day: Monday, 29 July

Returning to the Beach Hut, Nat's head is still full of poor Kate Chappell and the lonely world of grief she is trapped in. She's submitted her piece and it will appear online later - the exclusive interview with Sam's mother has caused a flurry of interest in the local paper, and Ben has texted her to say that several of the nationals have been in touch to get her contact details. For the first time, Nat is feeling uncomfortable that the worst outcome for Kate is having such a beneficial impact on Nat's own career. She knows she can't afford to go soft now, but seeing the car parked outside that she doesn't recognise, and realising Caro has company, she considers driving away, not sure she is up to making polite conversation with a stranger.

Maybe she should go and pay a supportive visit to James, who also isn't faring as well as Nat is from the discovery of a body in the quarry. As she sits debating where she can go, she sees another car pull up behind her and recognises the two occupants from the police press briefings she has attended. That's made the decision for her. No way she is missing out on a visit to Caro from the police, and she hurries from the car and into the Beach Hut before the next lot of visitors have gathered themselves together - Caro needs her at this time. It is the right thing to do for her friend. No other agenda!

'Caro, you've got visitors!' Nat bursts in, breathless, and

is aware her voice has more of a hint of excitement than concern, but she skids to a halt as she drinks in the tableau of three people that appear to be frozen before her. Caro is pale-faced and has obviously been crying. Alex is pale and stands stiffly, as if shielding himself from any contact, and the third person, well, that is Angus Redfearn. He's aged but there is no mistaking Gus, who still fills every inch of space in a room as he always had when they were at school. So that all makes sense. But what doesn't make sense is how Nat has never noticed that Alex is the spitting image of Gus. Even though Caro had shared her secret, Nat wasn't sure she had really believed it; but there is no disputing the evidence before her now. The likeness is unmistakeable. Bloody hell, everything had been going on that summer - and she had missed it with her obsession with what had happened to Sam.

The awkward silence is broken by the knock at the door, which makes Nat jump even though she should have been expecting it. After all, it was the arrival of these visitors that had prompted her own decision to dash into the house. She needs to get the inside scoop on whatever involvement the police have decided the Webster family may have with the investigation into the death of Sam. For a second, Caro looks as if she will ignore the door - in fact, she seems incapable of moving - but then Nat hisses. 'Caro, it's the police!' and her friend manages to shake herself into action.

Gus and Alex both dither by the back door before Caro ushers them outside.

'I need to deal with this, and it's not something you two should be involved in. Gus, I'll come up to the farm as soon as I can. Is that OK?'

Alex hesitates. For all his bravado, at this point he looks like he just wants his mum. But then the knock comes again on the front door, this time a little louder and with a hint of impatience, and as Caro moves to answer it, Gus ushers Alex away. Nat runs through her options and decides the best bet is to establish herself in place before anyone gives a thought to ask her to leave. Putting the kettle on to boil, she is already reaching for the mugs when Caro returns to the kitchen, followed by the two detectives Nat had spotted earlier.

'Hi there, tea, coffee?'

Caro looks a little flustered. 'This is my friend - Nat. She knows all about the bracelet and stuff.'

The older of the two detectives gives a forced smile. She looks tired and her trousers and T shirt both look like they are on the second or third day of wearing. Trainers that are coated in a thin layer of dried mud complete the less than glamorous outfit. 'Yes, we know who Nat is.'

Nat can't help but wince. The words convey that not only do they know exactly who she is, they don't think much of her. Or the story she is writing.

'Hi Mrs Morton, I'm Detective Inspector Gillingham. If Caro would like you to sit in on our conversation, then at this stage we have no objections. But I must stress, the conversation needs to stay in this room. I will take action if anything said today finds its way onto the pages of the Gazette.'

Nat smiles and does her best to look confused at the accusation that she would even think of such a thing. 'Of course, that goes without saying.'

The younger of the two detectives gives a disbelieving 'humph' which is converted quickly to a cough following a sharp look from his boss.

'I'm Detective Constable Bryce. And thank you, tea would be great. White, no sugar.'

Nat busies herself with the various drinks orders, keeping one ear on the conversation around the kitchen table. It's just the normal stuff, explaining Caro isn't under arrest - but they do need to caution her - and they are speaking to her to gain further clarification relating to the report she had made earlier that day. Nat puts a reassuring hand on her friend's shoulder as she places the mug of coffee in front of her. Caro is probably scared witless. At the same time, Nat is surprised that her friend had acted so quickly. Caro normally prefers to see how things go, hoping difficult things will resolve themselves, so this has been quite a step for her.

DI Gillingham takes a sip of her own coffee and, shooting a final warning glance at Nat, flicks through her notebook before giving a reassuring smile at Caro.

'Mrs Fraser, thank you for coming into the station this morning. I'm sorry I wasn't available but as you can imagine, we are dealing with a number of issues at the moment.'

Caro relaxes slightly and nods. 'I understand of course, and please call me Caro. To be honest, the more I think about it, the more I'm afraid I may have wasted your time. I'm thinking maybe I am allowing everything that's happened to lead me down a road that simply doesn't exist and so I'm sorry for adding to your list.'

Once again, DI Gillingham flashes that reassuring smile, but Nat can't help but notice that the smile never quite meets her eyes. She will need to tread very carefully here as there is no way she wants to get on the wrong side of this woman.

'I always think it's best in these circumstances to tell us everything. It doesn't matter how small the detail, or how unimportant it may seem. Let us judge if what you have to say fits into the bigger picture we are building. I can assure you that if we decide your information is not relevant to Sam's death, there will be no judgement from us that you've wasted our time. We appreciate anything people can tell us to help us find out just what happened to Sam.'

Nat wishes she had the nerve to switch her phone to recording mode. She would love to be able to report these words, to stress the passion of the woman leading the investigation to ensure that justice was done, but she is aware that DC Bryce has never taken his eyes off her, so she decides she had better behave. Better to get them on side, then they may remember her kindly when they are ready to drop a few crumbs to the press.

Caro starts her story, beginning with the anonymous post before the body had been found. Even though Nat knows the story, hearing it told from the beginning makes the excitement start to fizz in her stomach. DI Gillingham listens intently, asking the odd question, whilst DC Bryce makes careful notes. When Caro talks about finding the bracelet which her father had saved, DI Gillingham interrupts. 'So, the bracelet you brought into the station, your father had kept that for all these years, and you had no idea?'

'No, no, well yes, he had kept a bracelet for all that time and I was unaware of that fact until I came to clear out the house. Like I said, since Jez died here - as far as I was aware, the house was simply shut up and left as a museum to the days we had here before we lost Jez. No, the bracelet I brought in was the one I had kept all these years.'

'And you thought that belonged to Jez?'

'Yes.' Caro nods, tears rolling down her cheeks as she continues. 'I picked it up from the doorway before I realised what I was seeing. Before I could make sense of why his feet were suspended in the air. I ran to get my dad, and I must have slipped the bracelet in my pocket. Afterwards, it was a way for me to keep Jez close. It was only when I found the other bracelet that I realised that I didn't have Jez's bracelet. And then Nat here,' Caro gestures towards her friend, 'was showing me the pictures she had pulled together as part of the article she was writing on Sam's disappearance, and that's when I saw the bracelet Sam was wearing on the night of the ball. And I hope I'm wrong. But I can't get the thought out of my head that, for some reason, Jez had Sam's bracelet. And he must have taken it the last night Sam was seen.'

There is a moment of silence round the table and Nat breaks the fundamental rule she learnt when she had first started out as a journalist - the instruction to never be the one to fill a silence. But at this point she isn't a journalist, but is Caro's friend and is fifteen again and ruffling Jez's hair, her friend's goofy little brother. She blurts out. 'I mean, there must have been hundreds of those bracelets sold, so it's not going to be Sam's, is it. But we thought it best to let you know. More for our own peace of mind than anything. You know how these things can haunt you and let you come up with irrational stories if you let them fester.'

DI Gillingham stares at Nat and Nat feels the heat rise in her face and knows her chest will have that tell-tale blotchiness for the next few hours. The Detective quite deliberately angles her body away from Nat, so that Nat feels an invisible door has been slammed in her face. 'Caro, I want you to try not to worry about this until we can give you some answers. We will be running some tests and will update you as soon as we are able.'

Caro smiles in gratitude and Nat feels the familiar annoyance that somehow, the Webster family always ended up being treated with sympathy. She forces herself to focus on DI Gillingham's next words. 'In the meantime, would you like to file a report about these malicious posts that have been appearing on Facebook?'

This is absolutely not what Nat wants. These are her potential lead into anything new and the last thing she wants is for press attention focusing on these posts. However, thankfully Caro is shaking her head. 'Thank you, but to be honest it's just an upgrade on schoolgirl graffiti on the toilet wall. Truly not worth my time, and certainly not worth yours. Besides, at this point I really don't want to draw any more attention to my family than I have to.'

The detective nods. 'Understood, but please let me know if you change your mind.'

Nat jumps to her feet to usher the pair out the door and does her best to look suitably hurt as DI Gillingham fires the parting shot. 'Remember, I better not see anything resembling this conversation in print, Mrs Morton.'

'Message received very clearly and understood,' smiles Nat as she closes the door. However, there's nothing to stop an interview with Caro Webster, is there? She just needs to persuade her friend that the best thing to do is to tell her side of the story before the gossip starts. Where is the harm be in that?

49

Alex

Present day: Wednesday, 7 August

Alex can't really believe how his life has spun full circle, upside down, back to front, thrown him in the air and then somehow set him the right way up and continued. That day sat frozen at the kitchen table seemed a lifetime ago - and in many ways, he supposes it was. He knew who Angus Redfearn was. Of course he did. Everyone did around here. The so-called city slicker who had returned home to run his parent's estate and had taken on the mantle of leading the opposition to the quarry. When he heard the voice on the other end of the phone, he knew exactly where to find his father and he didn't want to waste another minute.

From the minute Alex had taken a chance on his greeting with the words 'Hello, Dad,' he had known that whilst Gus might be shocked that his son had called him, he already had the knowledge that he had a son. What Alex wanted to know was how long this man had been aware of his existence. Had he chosen to ignore him for sixteen years, or had he been manipulated by Caro into having no part in his life? By the time he reluctantly returned to the Beach Hut with Gus, he had no doubt who he blamed in the whole matter.

He wanted to scream at his mum, and even though Gus had explained that really everyone was a victim of misunderstandings, his words did little to dampen the fury that was burning in Alex's chest. Seeing Mark at the Beach Hut actually knocked the breath out of him. Mark looked so sad, so unsure, and Alex didn't think he would ever forget the look in Mark's eyes as he closed the door on him, shutting him out of the building and shutting him out of his life. Yes, that's one relationship he is glad to see the back of. At least, that is what he tells himself at night when he is struggling to sleep and he misses the calm solidity of Mark. Mark, who has the most ridiculous rules which Alex struggled against as he got older. But whose rules somehow always make him feel safe.

By contrast, the days are now a whirlwind. It's like Gus and his mum are trying to fit sixteen years of missed life into a few days. Alex spends hours up at the farm where there are really no rules. Gus has told him this is his heritage, his inheritance, so it is important he learns how it all works. Alex would have preferred to spend that time alone with Gus, really getting to know him, but his dad seems to prefer to have his mum there too, fussing round after her and making sure she isn't left alone too much.

He is avoiding the Beach Hut, other than to sleep, as he doesn't want to get cornered by Nat again. He had clocked the look on her face that day and it was obvious Caro had hugged her secret tightly to herself, not even sharing with her best friend. Nat has obviously told James, who no doubt will have been in touch with Mark, and Alex feels Nat is trying to find out information to report back to his adoptive father. And he doesn't want Mark to know anything. He wants him to suffer - to feel a little bit of the pain of rejection Alex had felt when he had seen how Grace was favoured.

The days have fallen into an easy pattern and even though it has been little more than a week, Alex likes the new rhythm of life. After breakfast at the Beach Hut, during which he smiles and laughs with Grace and Annie, he sits in the passenger seat of his mum's car as she drops the two girls off at holiday club. This is the danger point, the time when

Caro might suggest he stay at the house as she will be driving back that way. Nat always looks hopeful, and he has a sneaky suspicion the two women have decided they may lure him in this way. But he stubbornly sticks to his guns, unwittingly assisted by Grace who loves the fact she gets to spend an extra fifteen minutes in the car when she can talk at Alex.

Then they go on to meet with Gus and the days stretch out - walking the fields and Gus teaching him how to shoot rabbits. Alex doesn't really like this. He would have preferred to shoot at cans or some other non-breathing target, but he is eager to please his dad so closes his eyes and hopes that sometimes he will hear the exclamation, 'Oh, unlucky!' and know that he doesn't have to go over and inspect a body, or even worse, 'Best put it out of its misery.'

Caro joins them at lunch, and they sit in the sun and talk. Some idle chat, but mainly Caro sharing stories of Alex growing up and Gus sharing similar stories from his own childhood. Alex squirms a little when they talk about how they had met and is sad when he hears about the letter his grandad had written to scare Gus away. Not only does he grieve for what might have been, but he also mourns the loss of a memory of a man. A man it seems he had never known. The grandad that could be so cruel to his own daughter and the father of her unborn baby.

Then it's time to collect Grace and Annie, head back to the Beach Hut and break the concentration of Nat, who is often sat where they had left her, tapping away at her laptop in the kitchen. After a couple of days, his mum had begged her to go and work in the snug, which Grandad had always used as his office. Alex thinks it isn't so much the mess that bothered his mum, but the photos scattered around her. A constant reminder of a time that seems to cause his mum such unease. Alex longs to sit and leaf through those memories, to see his mum and newly discovered dad as they were then and to daydream about how life would have been so different for all of them.

The only difficult bit he struggles to reconcile with this fantasy is Grace. Because if life had worked out differently, there would be no Grace, and Alex can't imagine life without his annoyingly loving little sister. Still, Mark can be scrubbed from the picture and, going forward, there will be a new family of four. Alex just can't wait to see how that life will unfold.

50

Nat

Present day: Wednesday, 7 August

Nat feels like she is drowning in a sea of information and is struggling to get her head above the waves to figure out what is true and what might be a false memory. A slight misdirection - whether intentional or not. Most days, Caro leaves the house with Alex to play happy families with Gus, and Nat pretends to be writing at her laptop, or engrossed on the phone, just so she doesn't have to talk with her friend.

Nat is struggling to understand Caro - which she recognises is the general pattern of their relationship for as long as they have been friends. Caro has always been skilled at shutting off things that don't suit the narrative of her life. She has made her report to the police, and now she is ready to close that door and move on with this new chapter. Whatever this new chapter is. Her relationship with Mark needed a bit more work, so Caro decided better to throw that one away and start with a brand new one. Nat can almost see the cogs turning in Caro's mind as she works out how she will rewrite history - present herself as the victim in all of this, if the police decide that Jez had some link to Sam's death.

For her own part, Nat simply can't see a way how this could be a reality. Whilst she is struggling to get any words on the page to move the story forward, her mind probes everything she could remember about that night, everything people had told her, and she just can't see how Jez was involved in any way. Banished to the old study, Nat fears she will end up being swallowed whole by the memories of the past and, shaking her head at the fact she is losing her professional grip on this story, she wanders to the window and stretches like a cat, back arched, as she feels the sun warm her stiff shoulders.

Pride of place in the window is a telescope. Nat pushes up her reading glasses and squints through the lens. She has always been rubbish at seeing anything through this. She remembers when they were young Jez had been obsessed with scanning the dunes, looking for the various species of birds that he would tick off in some notebook that was never far from his side. Nat smiles as she remembers her and Caro used to tease him for being a 'Peeping Tom', accusing him of trying to spy on couples kissing in the dunes. Jez would vehemently protest his innocence, flushing red, until the two of them would take pity on him and laugh to show they were only teasing. Now Nat wonders if maybe Jez took all these words to heart much more than any of them had ever realised.

Moving the telescope round, Nat marvels at the detail you can pick out in the sand and understood for the first time Jez's obsession with the quiet watching - waiting to spot some rare sighting that would be unaware they were in your vision. Turning away, Nat absently walks to the desk and opens the drawers. This is a dreadful habit of hers she acknowledges - the overwhelming urge to have a little snoop through other people's belongings. To have a little look at the tiny pieces of their life that they shove away in a drawer, hidden from view. James teases her, not always without a note of true annoyance, whenever she excuses herself to use the loo when visiting friends. 'You been rooting through the bathroom cabinet again Nat?' would be the comment, with eyes narrowed and a grin tugging at the corner of his mouth. For all his disapproval, he would be keen to hear of any juicy titbits she had discovered. And where's the harm? She never shared her secrets further than James, and she would leave the room as she had found it. No hint to anyone that someone had been snooping in their hidden lives.

Today, she really needs to crack on to get some stuff over to the paper. Last night, she had been at the town council meeting, and she must get the summary typed up and over to Ben for them to print in the weekly roundup. Instead, she lets her fingers dip into the drawer of the desk, feeling for just one thing to take out and examine. *Just one thing*, she promises herself, before she dedicates herself to what she should be doing. Her fingers feel the shape of a box and, sitting down in the chair, she pulls it out and recognises this must be the box Caro had found the bracelet in. Opening it, she rifles through the contents, with a little less care than her friend had done the week before.

When she gets to the letter, she has time to pause. Why would Chris have kept this letter? It seems so obvious that this is a letter written from a woman to a new lover. A lover that isn't her husband. So why would Chris choose to keep proof that Jen was having an affair and how did he come to have it? Puzzled, Nat shuts up the box and reluctantly returns to her Town Hall Report. It seems the bracelet isn't the only thing odd that Chris had chosen to squirrel away in his box of secrets.

As the hours drag by, Nat finally emails her report off to Ben and, standing to stretch the stiffness from her shoulders, she crosses to the window and debates if she has enough time for a quick walk on the beach before everyone once more returns, bringing noise and chaos and different demands on her attention. She allows her mind to puzzle over the letter she had found and tries to reconcile that with the memories she had of growing up with the Webster family. Chris, aloof and, to the children, a little dull. Nat had always been a little scared of Chris, not helped by the fact that for a vast portion of her life, he was also her headteacher. But as far as she could remember, of the little interaction she had had with him, he had been nothing but kind.

Jen was the very opposite of her older husband. Stunningly attractive, most of the boys in school had a little bit of a crush on Mrs Webster. In fact, Nat reflects with a wry smile, quite a few of the girls felt the same way too. She remembers hearing her parents discussing the Websters after one school fete. Nat's mum had made some sharp remark about the fathers following Jen round with their tongues hanging out, whilst her dad had laughed and teased her for being jealous. Her mum had tutted and turned away to make tea, simply muttering that she felt sorry for Mr Webster and she didn't know how the man put up with all the craziness. At the time Nat had only been half listening, and assumed her mum meant the craziness of living at the school with the responsibility for all the staff and children. Now it seems maybe her mum was more astute than Nat had ever given her credit for.

Nat idly looks through the telescope and smiles at the sight of a couple entwined in the dunes. Thinking themselves alone, they are unaware of the watcher far away in the Beach Hut, and if they glance her way, they will be none the wiser. Nat suddenly feels uncomfortable and quickly moves out to the back decking where she has the best chance of getting decent mobile signal.

'Hey Mum, just a quick call to check you're all OK.'

Nat patiently listens to her mum's story about the latest drama at her walking group. Something to do with the car share arrangement. Recognising her mum is settling in for one of her legendary rants, she manages to interrupt.

'Mum, sorry I haven't got long as the girls will be home soon, but I just wanted to quickly ask you something.'

Nat's mum falls silent.

'We're seeing you on Sunday, so tell me all about it then.

Karen sounds like she is being... well... a right Karen.'

Nat's mum laughs and, feathers successfully soothed, Nat presses on with the reason for her phone call.

'Look Mum, I know this will sound weird, and I will explain at the weekend, but Chris and Jen Webster. Before Jez died, what were they like?'

There is a moment of silence on the phone and for a minute Nat thinks her mum is going to come out with some platitudes, some breezy generalisation, but the silence stretches a little longer until her mum carefully speaks.

'What makes you ask that Nat, after all these years?'

And that, thinks Nat, is the nub of it all - why is she interested after all these years?

'I don't know, Mum. Maybe it's being back here at the Beach Hut and seeing my memories through adult eyes now, and things don't seem quite so straightforward as they did back then.'

There is a sigh from the other end of the phone and Nat can picture her mum closing her eyes for a second and rubbing her left ear, the way she always does if she thinks the conversation may become difficult.

'Oh gosh, Nat you do pick your moments. It's all so long ago, so what does it matter?' There was another beat of silent before her mum asks, only half joking, 'You're not going to quote me in some bloody article in the paper, are you?'

Nat laughs. 'No Mum, you can be sure of that. It's just, I'm starting to remember some odd things and I'm not sure if I'm making it all up. You know, with the benefit of hindsight.'

There's another beat of silence, then a loud sigh. 'I don't want to say anything nasty - Chris isn't here to defend himself and Jen is in no fit state either. You adored spending time with the family. Me and your dad we weren't quite so keen.

Oh, it was nothing bad, it was just the whole family, with the exception of little Jez, they were all a bit, how can I put this politely? All a bit up themselves.'

Despite herself, Nat can't stop the snort of laughter that escapes. 'Oh Mum, never change! If that's you being polite, I would hate to get on your wrong side!'

There's a giggle from the other end of the phone and Nat reflects how we sometimes forget that our parents are human too. That they have the same emotions running through them and are capable of bad and good behaviours like the rest of us. Funny how she had always seen Mum as a mum, and she wonders if Annie will be the same with her.

'Look, there was nothing wrong with Chris. Your dad used to say it was me getting worked up because he was the headmaster at school, so I was always on edge, always felt like I had to be on my best behaviour. He was just a bit stern I thought, and I never really understood how him and Jen had ended up together. Now Jen. That was a different matter altogether. Not that I ever had much to do with her, I was the wrong sex entirely to hold any appeal to the gorgeous Mrs Webster. I used to think one day she would up and leave. Especially as Caro was growing up and was proving to be some competition. And then poor Jez. That sealed the deal really. I suppose they were forced together as they understood the pain each of them was going through. Chris carried on until retirement. But we saw very little of Jen. She literally went from being the life and soul to a hermit overnight. I know you are judging me now Nat, so don't roll your eyes.'

Nat smiles again. How does her mother know her so well?

'I mean, the woman lost her son, and in truly awful circumstances. I always think you must be haunted as to what you could have done to make things different. But she did have Caro to think of. But it was as if her life ended on the day Jez's did. Chris battled on, in many ways seeming unchanged. But that was Chris. As long as he had Jen, nothing else mattered. I used to say to your dad, and I feel awful repeating this now, but I thought at the time that Chris was relieved that it was Jez rather than Jen who had died that day.'

There is a moment of silence again on the phone and Nat understands her mum is speaking the truth. Putting into words what everyone had always recognised. Jolting back to the present, she realises her mum is still speaking.

'And Caro, I know she could be a madam, but you had to feel sorry for her. I mean, Jen was happy to parade her round like a little dog when she was younger, but the minute that girl needed a bra, Jen saw her as a threat. What woman sees her daughter as the competition? I used to say to your dad, "God help Jez's friends when they get a bit older. Never mind Mrs Webster, it will be a case of Mrs Robinson!" And your dad used to pretend to be shocked, but he saw it too!'

'Mum!' Nat doesn't know whether to laugh or be horrified. No one wants to think of their parents having sex, and she is once again struck how we strip our parents of the normal human urges, forgetting that they are just like us.

'Well, it's true Nat. Poor Chris, for all his faults, I think he lived his life in constant fear that one day he would lose Jen. Either to illness, or even worse, to someone else. Anyway, what time do you think you will be here Sunday? Your dad's keen to try out the new BBQ. Again! Honestly, I'm going to look like a sausage at this rate.'

Nat recognises the conversation about the past is done. Her mum has said all she wants to on the matter, so they chat briefly before Nat hears the door slam and says her goodbyes. She is thankful for the chatter of the girls, meaning she doesn't have to think too much about what she thinks might have happened. She will unravel that tomorrow.

51

Caro

Present day: Wednesday, 7 August

Although Caro feels she is living in a special bubble where all her old fantasies are coming true, real life has a habit of intruding rather rudely. Whilst Grace is a sunny, easy-going little girl, she is starting to ask when her daddy will be coming to the Beach Hut. Clearly Grace envisages that this is a temporary state of being - that by the end of the summer everything will return to her safe normal, and Caro isn't sure what their new future is going to look like. She only knows that she hopes it will include Gus, and that means speaking to Mark. To start to navigate a way forward for all of them.

They agree to meet at a small pub on the outskirts of town. One of the chain-type stopovers attached to a hotel which specialises in mid-week packages for those working away from home. It's impersonal and bland and not somewhere they had spent time at before, meaning there is no need to battle memories of happier times.

Mark is already sat at a table in the corner nursing a pint. She notices he hasn't bothered to order a drink for her, and feels a pang of longing to return to how they used to be. To the days when she was the centre of his world and felt safe and steady. Maybe that had been their problem - the mundaneness of it all that hadn't stood a chance against that passionate flame she had experienced. A flame that had been deadened but never been stubbed out and had flared back into life, as strong as ever, once it was given the air to breathe again.

Giving a wave to Mark, Caro gestures she is heading to the bar and pointing at his glass questions if he wants a refill. Mark shakes his head. Clearly, this isn't going to be an easy meeting - probably best if they both have reasonably clear heads. Though Caro feels her head is about to burst with the events of the past few weeks. How could life have changed so much?

Taking a gulp of her wine and wincing at the not-quite-cold-enough sharpness, Caro sits down opposite Mark and decides to open with small talk. 'How are you?'

Mark grunts in reply. 'Let's get straight to it, Caro. I've reached out to Alex a couple of times, but he has now blocked me from his phone. I'm not going to go in there all guns blazing, but I could really do with your support on this.'

Caro hasn't expected this as an opener, and her feelings are clearly written all over her face as Mark continues. 'What, you think I'm just ready to accept that you have decided to trade me in for a new model? Rewrite history and pretend I was never a part of Alex's life? Look, I know I said some stuff - hurtful stuff - but that doesn't change the fact that Alex is my son. I am the only father he has ever known, and I won't be pushed out now your fling has decided maybe he wants a ready-made family.'

'I'm not sure that's fair, Mark. Gus wasn't aware of Alex's existence and now that he is, he is keen to be a part of his son's life.'

Mark gives a snort. 'Didn't know he had a son. Oh, come on Caro, you're telling me in this small town, in your even smaller precious school alumni, he never once heard the gossip about the headmaster's daughter getting herself knocked up and keeping the baby. That he never looked at the timings and thought that maybe it was something to do with him.'

Caro bristles, not liking the fact that Mark is putting in the open the doubts that have swirled in her mind ever since Gus had come back into their lives.

'Why is it such a surprise, Mark? As you said yourself, maybe I was such a tart that the father could have been any one from a number of candidates. If that's the case, there should have been a steady stream of people lining up to take responsibility.'

Mark rubs his eyes, and Caro sees he looks tired. He has aged this summer. Suddenly changing from the young man she had first known to the greyer man sat opposite her now. A man who looks like he has the weight of the world on his shoulders.

'I know I shouldn't have said that, Caro. I'm sorry, you know I don't think that of you. I was just lashing out because I felt so hurt. I hope you can understand that I am concerned for you and Alex now. And for how this will impact Grace, of course. You can't just erase me out of your life, pretend these last thirteen years haven't happened and resume your happily ever after. There's a lot more to sort out.'

Caro thinks she prefers it when Mark's angry, when he's shouting at her, rather than this quiet man who looks so defeated.

'I mean, you don't know anything about him Caro, why he's come back now after all this time? I asked James what he reckoned about it all, and he told me what he knew. None of which was complementary. James thought it was all very shady. One minute the guy's supposedly a hot shot in the city and the next he's back here, playing Lord of the Manor with his main focus seemingly lobbying against the redevelopment of the quarry. All very odd.'

Caro sighs. 'James isn't going to say anything nice about Gus, is he? That protest group made his life a misery - as we heard every time they invited us round for dinner. And there were plenty of locals opposed to James's grand scheme. Not everyone is happy with the change that is bound to affect the town.'

Mark's mouth sets in that grim straight line that reminds her of the way her father would look once he had made up his mind, but he sighs and when he speaks his voice is soft and calm.

'Look Caro, we can agree to disagree on why Gus is here. Surely, the most important thing now is for us to make sure Alex is safe and not going to get hurt. He is still just a child. Our child. You, Alex and Grace, you're my family, and you know I would do anything for you. Please, let's talk this through, see if we can start to make things right again.'

Caro can't help herself, knowing that she is reacting as she always does when she feels backed in a corner. She lashes out in an effort to wound others before they have the chance to really hurt her. 'I'm not sure Alex would agree with you that he is a child Mark, and the fact you refer to him as such just reinforces my belief that you stopped seeing Alex for who he is once you got your own precious Grace. Alex has had to adjust to the fact you decided he wasn't good enough to be your son, and now he's lucky enough to have a second chance with his real father. In fact, we both have a second chance with his real father. We can formalise the arrangements for Grace - and you know I'll be more than reasonable - but we are done here. There really is nothing else left to say.'

And leaving Mark staring at her, mouth open and the colour drained from his face, Caro pushes back her chair and storms from the pub. In the car, she can't help but feel that maybe she has been a bit unfair. Was she running away as usual, taking the easy option? Oh, if only her dad had not interfered, life would be so much more straightforward.

52

Nat

Present day: Thursday, 8 August

Nat couldn't sleep that night. She had tossed and turned until the early hours when she had given up and, switching on the light, reaches for her iPad and begins reading through the various notes she has made over the last few weeks.

She starts to jot down a timeline of the night Sam disappeared, just to get it straight in her head where everyone was. There were some gaps, but by the time the rest of the house starts to stir she thinks she has a good understanding of the events of that evening. Reading through her notes once more, she is satisfied she has done as much as she can. The one person she doesn't know where they had been, is Jez. She has always assumed that Jez had remained at the Beach Hut - his parents deciding he was old enough to be left alone for the evening. But that simply doesn't make sense if he had ended up with Sam's bracelet.

Had Sam made her way to the Beach Hut before Chris arrived there, and Jez had somehow got hold of her bracelet then? But that doesn't make sense either, because Jen Webster had returned home earlier than that, so would surely have seen Sam. Likewise, if Jez had sneaked out and met Sam somewhere near the quarry, Jen would have seen that her son was not where he should have been. Nat knows that Jen could be self-absorbed and had said that night she had a migraine, but surely she would have noticed if her fourteen-year-old son was missing from the house.

And if Jez had seen Sam, he had clearly not shared this with anyone, which didn't look good at all. Whichever way Nat tries to spin it, she is starting to think that the only explanation is that Jez knew something about Sam's disappearance, and whatever that knowledge was had driven him to think he couldn't live with himself any longer. A part of Nat wishes that Sam had stayed where she was in her watery grave because the way things were looking, more lives are about to be destroyed. Kate has lost the shred of hope that had sustained her though the years, and Caro may be about to have the memories of her much-loved younger brother smashed to pieces.

She supposes the only consolation is that Chris and Jen will never learn the truth about their son. The thought crosses her mind that maybe they had always known on some level and that was why he had been effectively erased from the family home. Photos packed away and his name rarely mentioned. No loving tribute on anniversaries or birthday, just a focused determination that life should continue, as if Jez had never been a part of it. Nat has always thought that was odd, but had decided maybe that was the only way the family could cope with the gaping hole that had been blasted through their lives. But as she sits at the table, bleary-eyed and squinting into the sun that is already promising them another beautiful day, she starts to think that maybe she has never really understood at all.

After dropping the girls off at holiday club, Nat finds herself driving over to the quarry, telling herself it is because she needs to see James. This is easier than admitting she feels a draw to the place where they found Sam's body, as if willing her ghost to whisper the secrets of the past so they can all move on. There is a small cluster of white vans parked up. Nothing like the volume of traffic that should have been there if the development was in full swing. There are no protesters at the site today - they are either back at work or have decided to enjoy the sunshine down on the beach. Besides, they have done all they could do. It looks like Sam Chappell might do the rest. At the site entrance, there are a small cluster of flowers, dead in their plastic covering, the words on the cards blurred by exposure to the rain and sun.

As she stands looking at them James walks from the quarry to join her, and they stand together in silence looking at the sorry little tribute.

'I don't know what to do with them, Nat. I mean do I just throw them away? Try and keep the cards for her family? I just don't know.'

Nat is surprised to hear a catch in his voice and turns to look at him properly. She is instantly overwhelmed with guilt that she has been lost in the world of seventeen years ago, whilst failing to notice that her husband is struggling in the present. She really does need to bring this Sam Chappell story to a conclusion and move on with her life. Move on with all their lives. It had been rather arrogant of her to think she could present a neat solution to something that had baffled so many professionals. She squeezes James's hand. 'I'll sort it for you now, then you can make me a cup of that disgusting coffee and let's make a plan.'

When she has finished clearing away the tributes Nat feels a little dirty, not just from the bits of slimy stem that have stuck to her fingers as she scoops the dead flowers into the black bag, but she feels tainted by the feeling that somehow this is all her fault. She had started the digging in the past just as her husband had started the physical digging in the quarry.

'Thanks Nat, I really appreciate that.' James handed her a chipped mug and grinned. 'Sorry, this was the best I could find in the portacabin.'

'Ah well, beggars can't be choosers and all that. It's so

quiet here.'

James grimaces. 'Yes, not at all how I had thought it would be but,' his mouth shifts slightly from the hard-set line into something approaching a smile, 'we finally get to work on Monday. Not sure that I'll use the fact the site has been a temporary graveyard for the past seventeen years on the sales literature though.'

Nat can't help but smile. Journalists are used to the gallows humour; it is sometimes the only way to get through the day.

'Well, time to move on now, for all of us.'

They sit in a companionable silence, enjoying the feeling of the sun on their faces, both of them lost in their different dreams of what the future will look like. James is the first to break the silence. 'Talking of moving on, what the fuck does Caro think she's playing at? I had Mark round last night. He's absolutely broken, just can't believe what's happening. Did you know?'

Nat shakes her head. 'If you're asking if I knew that Angus Redfearn was Alex's father, then no - I didn't have a clue. I mean, I knew Caro had an almighty crush on him that last summer, but so did most of the girls in the school.' As she spoke, Nat remembers ruefully that Sam had been one of those girls to be a member of the Gus Redfearn fan club. 'But honestly, I didn't have a clue that it had come to anything. For the little I knew, Caro's pregnancy might as well have been the second immaculate conception.'

James smiles. 'From the way Alex was doted on by his grandparents, you would have thought he was some mini deity.'

Nat giggles, remembering how they had laughed after attending the nursey nativity where they had been practically knocked off their feet by Jen taking photographs of her darling grandson.

'But seriously Nat, you need to have a word with Caro. I'm not sure she knows what she's dealing with.'

Nat raises an eye and knows she is looking at James in disbelief.

He reacts defensively, as expected. 'Why are you looking at me like that, as if I'm an idiot?'

Nat sighs. She really doesn't want to disturb the happy rapport they have established. 'It's just you might not be the most rational where Gus is concerned, given all the bother he caused you with his protest group. And let's face it, Mark is never going to be a fan of the bloke. I'm just thinking you both might be a bit biased, that's all.'

'I wish that's all it was, Nat. I'll even admit there's been times where I wondered if he somehow staged that blasted skeleton in the quarry. Just so he could destroy me.'

As Nat rolls her eyes, James smiles a genuine smile for the first time that day. 'I know, I know, all this is driving me a little bit crazy. But there's something about the bloke. Look, you're going to be pissed off with me, but when that group started to make some noise objecting to the development, I paid a bloke to have a poke around in their background. Nothing seedy. I just wanted to know who I was dealing with.'

Nat looks at James in disbelief. 'And you never thought it might be worth mentioning this to me? After all, that can't have been cheap. So, whilst you have me stressed out about whether we will be able to pay the mortgage, you're off squandering money on some dodgy bloke poking around in people's private business. Just so unnecessary!'

'I knew you'd be like this, that's why I didn't say anything. You're on your typical double standard. Like it's OK for you to go poking around in peoples' business, but it's a different rule for me.'

Nat stays silent, unable to think of a cutting reply to what James is saying. His remarks are far too close to the disquiet she has been feeling for most of the week.

James, recognising he has somehow scored a winning point, carries on speaking. 'Anyway, whether what I did was right or wrong, it's done now, and I found out some interesting stuff on your Mr Redfearn that I'm sure you aren't too morally upstanding to hear?'

Nat laughs and the tension is broken. 'Come on then, spill. It's a fair cop - I'm all ears.'

James takes a furtive glance round, even though the site is deserted, and leans in closer to Nat. 'Well... the so-called city hot shot turned out to be more of a damp squib. He did finish university but with a very mediocre degree, and it seems family connections secured him the job with the investment firm. Some distant cousin of his father's was a senior director there and that seems to have done the trick. There were rumours of some unpleasantness at university - some nasty rumours spread by an ex-girlfriend - but again, these conveniently disappeared.'

'So, he got a leg up through family connections. Nothing new there. If either of us had been able to get a little help along with our careers, I'm sure we would have been happy to take it.'

'Yes, yes, you're right. But he started at a junior level, and he just stayed there at that junior level. Year after year, people got promoted above him, and he was just there. Until last year - he left. No huge fuss, no grand move to another job, no restructure in the firm that might have affected him. It was all done very quietly and my guy couldn't really find out why, other than the vague comment by a junior secretary over a lunchtime wine that he had been encouraged to move on. Likewise, he couldn't find anyone that knew he had moved back here. I mean, he had worked there for thirteen years, and no one bothered to keep in touch with him? Just odd.'

As Nat drives away from the quarry, she thinks that odd isn't really the word for it. Resolving to make sure she corners Gus at the upcoming reunion, she pauses as she reaches the junction. Before she has time to change her mind, she turns right towards the outskirts of the town. She is sure Jen Webster would be grateful to have an afternoon visitor, and a chance to reminisce about the past.

53

Caro

Present day: Thursday, 8 August

Returning to the Beach Hut that afternoon, the girls giggling in the back of the car, high on the promise of fish fingers and ice cream for tea followed by yet more screen time, Caro reflects that she isn't in line for any mother of the year awards. She frowns as she pulls up and sees that Nat's car isn't parked up in its usual place. Seems like she isn't the only one who is being a bit lax with her motherly responsibilities. There is, however, another car parked near the house and as Caro pulls in, the doors to that car open and she feels a flicker of unease as she recognises DI Gillingham and DC Bryce, clearly waiting to speak to her.

    The two detectives give her half smiles as she waves a hand in greeting, and they follow her up to the door of the house. Clearly, they expect an invitation to come inside; probably expect a cup of tea as well, Caro thinks grumpily. They all troop into the house, the girls unusually subdued as they sense their promised treat may be delayed. Caro grabs a couple of ice creams from the freezer and despatches them off to the lounge with the instruction to watch some TV quietly. This gives her time to compose herself, to brace herself for whatever storm is about to be unleashed on her now.

    Returning to the kitchen, she sees the two are still stood awkwardly where she had left them. 'Oh God I'm sorry, where are my manners? Do have a seat. Tea?'

Relieved that they both shake their heads as they sit down, Caro takes a deep breath and sits opposite them, hands clasped as she focuses on breathing steadily.

'We wanted to update you on the bracelet, Mrs Fraser. Mrs Chappell confirmed that, to the best of her knowledge, the bracelet did belong to Sam, and from us studying the photos we have of that night, that would certainly seem to be the case.'

Caro nods. It isn't unexpected news, but she had so hoped they would tell her that she was wrong, that she was a hysterical woman who had wasted valuable time and resources.

'However,' DI Gillingham gives a theatrical pause, and Caro struggles to hold back the snort of impatience. The woman isn't on a bloody made-for-TV drama; clearly, she's watched too many detective shows. She realises the others are looking at her oddly and the DI has stopped talking.

'Sorry, thought I was going to sneeze there - allergies you know. Anyway, you were saying?'

'Yes, we wanted to inform you that we will be making a statement shortly. We have already updated Mrs Chappell, but we will be ruling Sam's death accidental. Obviously, I'm not in a position to share all the details, but we believe Ms Chappell left the ball, probably intoxicated, and became disorientated in the dark and likely tripped and fell. It would appear to be a tragic accident. Obviously, Jez can't confirm our story, but we are told he spent a lot of time birdwatching, both in the dunes and up on the cliff path, which means he likely spent time at the quarry. We think he probably found the bracelet up on the path and slipped it in his pocket, not realising the significance of what he had found. Unfortunately, at the time there was no evidence to suggest that Sam had taken that path and there was no hint that she may have fallen. Again, after all these years it is difficult to confirm exactly, but it is our belief she would have become unconscious very quickly once in the water - if not before she hit the water, if she had hit the rocks at all - and so there would have been no different outcome if Jez had identified what he had found.'

Caro finds she is struggling to process the words and is aware she is staring at the woman sat opposite her, who again is regarding her with some concern.

'Are you OK Mrs Fraser, can we make you a drink?'

Caro just wants to be left alone, so she makes an effort to smile at them. 'Thank you for coming to me so promptly with this news. Obviously, I thought there would be some straightforward explanation, but I didn't want anyone to think I was hiding anything.'

As she stands in the door watching the car drive away, Caro knows she should feel relieved. She has done the right thing going to the police, rather than living as her parents had and trying to hide the truth away - to refuse to accept any unpleasantness by simply pretending it had never happened. Instead, she feels on edge, her stomach a fizzing churning of giddiness, similar to the feeling she used to have as a child as she rode the spinning waltzers. Glancing at her watch, she is relieved it is an acceptable time to open the bottle of wine which she had put in to chill that morning. Setting out a second glass in preparation, she wishes Nat would hurry back. Maybe talking to her will make things feel better; or maybe, she reflects grimly, her parents hadn't got it so wrong after all.

54

Press statement issued by North Yorkshire Police: Thursday 8th August

Following confirmation that the body recovered from the quarry on the 8th July was that of Samantha Chappell, investigations have been ongoing in respect of the circumstances of the death of the missing teenager.

Samantha, aged seventeen, was reported missing from home by her mother, Kate Chappell, when she failed to return home after a social function at Churcher's School on 4th August 2007. Following that report, an extensive search was carried out of the area. This was a large multi-agency incident, and the search teams included Mountain Rescue and the Coastguard. The investigation continued for around 18 months before a decision was made to scale down the search. The case continued to be reviewed on a periodic basis by experienced officers, and the case has remained open.

On 8th July, we received reports that a human skull had been found during excavation work as the quarry was being redeveloped. Work at the quarry ceased and a search commenced, with forensic scientists on site to assist officers.

Due to the passing of time, it is impossible to

determine the medical cause of death and also the exact circumstances of how Samantha came to be in the quarry. However, the discovery is not being treated a suspicious and a file is being prepared for the coroner.

Specialist officers are supporting the family of Samantha, and we would like to extend our condolences to all who are affected by this sad outcome.

55

Nat

Present day: Thursday, 8 August

Nat arrives at the nursing home to be met with the familiar smell of boiled vegetables, even though it is hours since lunchtime. It makes her wonder if these places all place a bulk order for some peculiar-smelling air freshener, maybe labelled 'institutional aroma'. Impatiently ringing the buzzer for a second time, at one point she decides this is her sign to escape, to leave Jen to her own secrets; but then the door is flung open by an out of breath staff member who smiles a greeting, and the chance to escape is lost.

'Oh, Mrs Webster will be pleased to see you, she doesn't get many visitors since Mr Webster died. We do miss him. Such a lovely man, and devoted to his wife.'

Nat finishes signing in the book, seeing that entries are scarce for the last couple of weeks, when the glorious weather has made it too much of a chore to endure an hour out of the sunshine - visiting a relative you no longer know and who you persuade yourself doesn't even know whether you're there or not.

'It's just a flying visit this time, I'm afraid.'

'She will enjoy seeing you, I'm sure. The only time she seems to smile is when she gets a visit from her lovely son. He's always so nice, just so charming, and always spoiling the staff with little treats.'

Nat thinks about correcting the nurse, pointing out that Alex is her grandson, but is distracted as the other woman continues. 'I'll show you to her room. Maybe you can persuade Mrs Webster to sit out in the garden with some of the other residents. It's beautiful out there and we are all having ice creams. But Mrs Webster refuses to join us.'

Nat realises this is exactly how she would expect Jen to behave. Ice creams in the garden with a bunch of old ladies would be sneered at, but cocktails on the terrace with a few dapper gentlemen may hold more appeal.

'I'll do my best but to be honest, I don't fancy my chances!'

After a rap on the door and a cheerful, 'Mrs Webster, I have a nice surprise for you: a visitor,' Nat finds herself sat in an upright chair in the window, politely declining a cup of tea as the other woman declares, 'I'll leave you to it - just press the buzzer if you need anything.'

Now that she is here, Nat can't think what to say to this woman sitting opposite her. A woman she recognises from her outward appearance, though the Jen Nat remembers would be horrified that her hair has been allowed to go grey. However, she remains impeccably dressed in black trousers and a cream silk shirt. Her mouth still highlighted in the familiar slash of red lipstick that, on closer inspection, has seeped into the deep lines that now frame her mouth. The heat in the room is stifling but Jen seems unaffected by it, the curtains half closed, adding to the oppressiveness of the room.

'Hello Mrs Webster, it's me - Nat. I'm a friend of your daughter's, Caro.'

Jen's face remains blank, staring at the space where Nat sits with unseeing eyes. Nat pauses and carries on chatting, recalling the summers at the Beach Hut, even mentioning happier times with Jez, desperately searching for something to rouse the woman from her private world. She starts to have some sympathy for Caro and her reluctance to visit her mother. Privately, Nat and James have always been very judgmental of how Caro would make any excuse to avoid a visit to the home. But sat in the visitor's seat now, Nat can understand the agony of only seeing the faint shadow of someone you had once loved. Suddenly, she isn't so sure she would behave any differently if it were her mother still alive, but lost.

Her mouth dry and for once at a loss of anything more to say, Nat is about to reach for the buzzer when Jen looks her straight in the eye and whispers, 'How's our boy?'

This is Nat's worst nightmare. Jen asking about her dead son, unaware of the heartache that is waiting to be revealed once more. But then she remembers reading that the best thing is to go along with the fantasy - what's the point of distressing Jen with the truth when she will only forget it again, stuck in a cycle of forever living the moment of hearing that devastating blow.

'Oh, you know, doing just fine. Enjoying the sunshine, I'm sure.'

Jen smiles, the first time she has looked happy since Nat arrived. 'Oh, is it the summer holidays? How lovely that it's nice weather for the children to be off school.'

Nat plays along, struck that Jen is stuck back in the past where her boy would forever remain fourteen years old. Not facing the reality that he is buried in the ground - the same as Sam Chappell who had been interred in the watery depths of the quarry.

'He's our boy you know - mine and his father's. So like his father. At least I got to keep him once I'd lost everything.'

Nat is struggling to keep up with this train of thought

now, so just nods, playing along.

'I do miss him. Tell him to pop in and see me soon.'

'Of course I will. And on that note, I really need to get off. I'll come again next week.'

Nat is happy making false promises, safe in the knowledge that Jen will be unlikely to remember she even had a visitor. She presses the buzzer and after a minute or so that passes in an awkward silence, as Jen resumes her study into nothingness, Nat finally hears footsteps approaching. Honestly, what had she been thinking? Expecting the shell of a woman sat before her to reveal the secrets of her past which really were no one's business but her own.

Following the nurse out of the room, desperate for the fresh air and sunlight that wait for her, Jen calls after her. 'Don't forget to tell my boy, tell Alex to come and see me soon.'

And that, reflects Nat as she pulls up at the Beach Hut, is all she has achieved. Time wasted discussing a boy, long dead, whose mother can't even remember his name.

56

Nat

Present day: Saturday, 10 August

Nat is torn over attending the memorial for Sam. She is still reeling from the issued police statement judging Sam's death to be an unfortunate accident. Ben had quickly pulled her latest article, and she knows it's only a matter of time before he instructs her to concentrate on the job he employs her to do.

Caro had already declared that she wouldn't be there, making the excuse that she needed to be around for Alex and Grace. Nat had assumed that Gus would attend, seeing as he had spent so much time with Sam over that last year, as they had both crammed for a future that hadn't turned out the way either of them had planned. But scanning the crowd, there is no sign of him. Clearly, he has decided the events of the past are not important enough to distract him from the new life he seems hell bent on creating with his new family.

James has insisted on accompanying her - stating he needs to show his face to prove that Sam was a human to him and not just an inconvenience to be overcome for the development to move forward. Privately, Nat thinks she recognises a PR stunt when she sees one and is irritated that James couldn't be honest with her. However, she can't argue that the events of the last few weeks have knocked James, and they make a sombre couple as they shuffle into the school chapel. Maybe she is judging him too harshly here - just because he hadn't known Sam, didn't mean his life hadn't been impacted by her death. Resolving to be more tolerant, she gives his hand a squeeze as they take their seats towards the back.

Nat finds it weird to be sat in the chapel after all these years, remembering a girl who had been forgotten for as many years as she had lived. The atmosphere is oppressive and very different to the gatherings she remembers from when they were at school. Normal assembly was held in the hall, with the chapel reserved for the Christmas carol concerts, prize giving and leavers' ceremony. The school chaplain is clearly talking about a girl he hadn't known, and Nat feels James start to fidget beside her as the service drags on.

Nat feels her attention drifting as she surveys the room and sees Kate flanked by Kirsten, Beth and a third woman who Nat has not seen before but who she assumes to be Lauren. Bloody hell! She could do with speaking with her, but maybe now isn't the right time. It must be strange for the girls to be here remembering a friend who had been a part of their lives for such a short time, but had made such an impact. She isn't sure, if she was in their shoes, if she would know just how she should be feeling. Although it sounds callous, life moves on and these women have different lives now – children, jobs, the stress of starting to be responsible for their own parents. It must be strange to be here mourning a friend who hasn't been a part of their lives beyond childhood. If life had panned out the way it should have done, they may not even have been friends still - maybe an invite to the evening reception of each other's wedding where they would swear they would keep in touch, whilst wondering how soon was too soon to make an escape. No doubt the disappearance of Sam has strengthened the bond they have now - an invisible tie that will always keep them together.

She is brought back to the present by James clasping her hand tightly and she hears a few coughs and shuffling of feet as the chaplain brings his monochrome eulogy to an end and announces the last hymn. And finally, they are out in the sunshine. Seeing Kate is surrounded by a crowd of people keen to offer their condolences, Nat decides she will pop in and see her in a few days. Kate will need the company then, when people have forgotten she is on her own whilst they move on with the life she had expected to share with her daughter. She links arms with James, and they start to make their way to the cliff path when she hears her name being called. Turning, she sees that the woman she had assumed to be Lauren is making her way over.

'Hi, it is Nat, isn't it? I'm Lauren.'

'I guessed as much. I was so sorry to hear about Sam.'

Lauren smiles in acknowledgement. 'I feel a bit of a fraud here, to be honest. Don't get me wrong, Sam was my friend, but it was so long ago and so much has changed since then. I know you were keen to talk to us all, but I don't think I can add anything extra to what Kirsten and Beth have already told you. As you can imagine, it was all we talked about when it happened, and to be honest it's all we've talked about since Kate asked us to talk to you.'

Nat nods in acknowledgement. 'Yes, Kirsten did say the two of you had spoken.'

Lauren reaches into her bag. 'I just wanted to give you these. I know you have some photos of that night, but these are the pictures from this disposable camera that had been put on the tables. I'd forgotten I'd taken the camera in to be developed to be honest, but I looked for it once I knew this memorial was going ahead. I don't think there's anything much on there - most of the pictures are from the end of the night and they are blurry. But they make Sam seem real, if you know what I mean. If you could pass them on to Kate once you've finished with them, I would appreciate it.'

Nat nods her thanks and slips the envelope in her bag. 'That's all I ever wanted from this story, really. To make sure

Sam was remembered.'

Liar, a little voice whispers. *Don't pretend you didn't have purely selfish reasons for resurrecting the memory of Sam.*

'I'll look through these and see if there's any I can add to the final article.' Nat is tempted to cross her fingers that there would be a final article.

'Mmm... well, as I say, we were all a bit tipsy at the end. There's nothing awful in there, but I think there are better photos of Sam that night. Anyway, Kate asked me to pass them on, so I think it's the least I can do.'

Promising that Kate would have the final sign off on any photos used, Nat rejoins James who is loosening off his black tie and looking keen to escape.

'Come on, lets sneak off for ice cream before we collect the girls from Mark.'

'If you change ice cream for gin, then we have a date!'

And just like that, Nat reflects wryly, she can move into the sunshine - whereas Kate will forever live her life in the shadow of what should have been. This story really is more than just her career, and she swears she will tell it to the best of her ability.

57

Caro

Present day: Saturday, 10 August

Caro feels uncomfortable that she has not been to the memorial service. Part of her thinks that she, and by default her father, will be judged by their non-show. If everything had been normal, there is no doubt that Chris Webster would have been there. Sam's mentor, caring headteacher, no doubt addressing the congregation to deliver the eulogy remembering Sam's short time on Earth and speculating over just what she could have achieved if she had not got drunk and fell in the quarry. Of course, he wouldn't have put it like that. Tragic circumstances beyond anyone's control. Yes! Those would have been the likely words he would use.

Afterwards, he would have solemnly shaken the hands of those who attended. A word for each of his former pupils. Caro always marvelled how he could remember all those little details about the pupils who had passed through the old wooden doors of Churcher's. Chris Webster always made them feel like they were special - that he would always remember them. No doubt that was part of why he was so successful in securing cheques from the old school network.

Caro should have attended. She should have represented her father and the Webster family and been there to support Kate, who had worked for the family all those years ago. But she simply couldn't face it and as Gus had told her, she didn't owe these people anything. As he said, it was likely they would all be whispering behind her back anyway, so sod the lot of them. Caro hadn't needed telling twice!

Instead, she decides to pay penance by visiting Jen. She can take Grace with her, who will act as a distraction - it will give her something to talk about, and Grace chattering away will ease the awkward silences that fill so many of her visits. She doesn't know how her dad had coped with visiting every day. He was always content to simply sit in silence with his wife, happy to just be in her presence and requiring nothing further from her than that.

Signing in the book, Caro is distracted from Grace's constant commentary by the sight of a familiar name on the page. How odd that Nat had been to see her mum, and odder yet she hadn't mentioned it. She must be out of her mind. Caro is only there because she feels she has to be, so there is no way she would visit if she felt she had a choice in the matter. She must remember to ask Nat why she had popped in.

Grace is running ahead down the corridor, and they find Jen in her usual spot. For a moment her eyes light up when she sees the door opening, but her face soon takes on the familiar dullness of disinterest and she flinches as Grace moves towards her to give her a kiss. Caro sighs. Maybe this hasn't been such a good idea. Whilst Grace is used to being the centre of most people's world, for Jen, Alex is the one who sparks the most intense emotions. Caro has always assumed it was because he gave his grandma the chance to imagine how her own son would be growing. Now it seems she often thought Alex was Jez, and so showers him with a love that she had never shown her son when he was alive.

The visit, as expected, isn't a success and Caro is glad to escape home to the Beach Hut - her duty done; now she can maybe not think about Jen for another couple of weeks. Her mum didn't seem to know she was even there, so what did it matter if her visits were infrequent?

She's pleased to see Nat's car is back, and even more pleased when she sees her friend has opened a bottle of wine and has hot dogs and ice cream waiting for Grace. Loading her plate, Grace runs to the lounge to find Annie and catch up on whatever film has been selected for the evening.

Pouring herself a glass of wine, Caro downs half of it in one long drink and refills her glass, before taking the rest of the bottle and joining her friend out on the decking. The two sit in silence for a while; and then Caro asks the question that has been burning in her mind all day.

'How did it go?'

Nat turns towards Caro, shielding her eyes from the late afternoon sun, and considers her answer as she reaches for the bottle to top up her own glass.

'The memorial? It was fine. A bit surreal really. It's so long ago and I'm sure half the people there had forgotten all about Sam, other than an interesting anecdote to tell at a dinner party about the school friend who disappeared off the face of the earth. I suppose they have an exciting end to the story now.'

Caro nods, aware that her friend seems on edge - almost spoiling for a fight.

'I just couldn't face it myself. Just everyone looking at me and whispering about my dad. Did anyone ask where I was?'

Nat hesitates for a while and looks at her friend as if she is seeing her for the first time.

'Funnily enough Caro, and you may find this hard to believe, but you were not the centre of attention today. Jesus, can't you even let Sam take centre stage at her own memorial service?'

'Wow! Want to tell me how you really feel, Nat?'

Nat opens her mouth and for a moment Caro thinks she is going to take her up on her offer. Then she sighs and takes another gulp of wine.

'I'm sorry Caro, and I do know how difficult all this has been for you. It's just today was so bloody sad. It dawned on me how few people there were who really cared about Sam. I'm not sure it gave Kate what she wanted either. I think she thought she could turn back the clock, have the memorial she would have had seventeen years ago if Sam's body had been found straight away. It would have been standing room only then. People lining the streets, a huge pile of tributes left at the quarry. Instead, for most people it was a bit of a day out. Nothing that impacted them and they were only there because they either felt they should be, or they were hoping to find out a bit of gossip.'

'That's so sad. I suppose people just move on.'

'They do, but Kate hasn't been able to move on. Maybe she can now. Now she knows there's no hope left, and she has to make a different life.'

The two women sit in silence and Caro reaches for Nat's hand. A squeeze of her fingers from her friend tell her all is well between them once more.

'Talking of finding a different way to live the life you have left, I popped in to see Mum today. Why didn't you tell me you had been to see her?'

Caro sees the colour appear on Nat's neck and chest and her hand takes up the familiar twisting of her ring. She takes sympathy on her friend. She had figured it out in the car. She knew that Nat and James sometimes thought she was uncaring when she moaned about her mum, and she guessed Nat had felt sorry for Jen, and thought she could ease some of the pressure on Caro.

'It was very kind of you Nat, and I really appreciate it. I

find it so hard, and it's nice to know there are other people who will step in to help now Dad's no longer around.'

Nat nods vigorously. 'No problem. That reminds me, talking of your dad. There's a couple of pictures of him here. Lauren gave me these photos from the leavers' ball and there's some of your dad in his element.'

Nat reaches in her bag and passes the envelope to Caro. The pictures are grainy and many out of focus - the images hazy, just as blurred as her memory of that time. She laughs as she looks at Chris, still immaculate in his tuxedo, surrounded by spent party poppers and empty glasses.

'He looks like he would rather be anywhere than there right now! I bet he wishes he'd thought to have a headache so he could have escaped like Mum.'

Nat laughs in agreement and the two continue to leaf through the pictures. The last photo in the pack is Sam smiling to her friends as she waves goodbye. Caro and Nat both take a long drink at the same time, struck that this is the last image captured of a girl who thought she had her whole life ahead of her. It would have only taken a friend persuading her to stay at the party, and everything could have been so different.

Caro looks at the photo and then holds it closer. Standing up, she takes it to the light, not really understanding what she is seeing.

'Caro. Are you OK? You've gone white as a sheet.'

'Look, Nat. Look at the picture of Sam.'

Nat looks at the picture and then at Caro. 'I'm not seeing anything, Caro. Care to enlighten me?'

Instead Caro disappears, and Nat can hear her rummaging in the desk drawer that she had been guilty of snooping through days before. When she returns, she is holding a faded polaroid photo and the diamond stud.

'See this earring? That was Mum's. She wore them all the time and was wearing them on the night of the leavers' ball.'

To prove her point, she shoves the old polaroid photo towards her friend and jabs her finger at Jen's image.

'Look, there. Mum was wearing the earrings on the night of the ball.'

'OK. But what has this got to do with Sam?'

'Look at the photo, Nat – the one of Sam as she is leaving – and tell me what's different about her from that photo and the photo at the start of the night?'

'Apart from the fact she's smiling at the end of the night, which is more than can be said of the first photo?'

At Caro's grumble of exasperation, Nat manages to remove the smirk from her face and focuses on the picture. Gosh, she is more drunk than she had thought. Gin in the afternoon was never a good thing. Glancing from one photo to the other, like a photographic spot the difference, Nat suddenly freezes as she sees exactly what Caro is looking at.

'How odd. When Sam left the party, she looks to be wearing your mum's earrings.'

Caro nods. 'Exactly! And if Sam was wearing the earrings when she left the party, how come Dad had one of those earrings hidden in his desk drawer?'

58

Nat

Present day: Friday, 16 August

Nat is pleased it's Friday at last. All she wants to do is go back to her own bed. Not the bed at the Beach Hut, but the bed in her modern home that only holds the memories she, James and Annie have made there. Instead, she has this blasted reunion to go to. But after that, she promises herself, time to look to the future. No more living in a past that can't be changed and dreaming of a future that might just jeopardise the person she is. She has risked enough on this story, and she doesn't ever want James, or Annie, to know just how low she has sunk.

Was it only a week ago that her and Caro had poured over those two photographs and the solitary earring that Chris had kept for all these years? The earrings in the photograph worn by Jen certainly looked to be the same as the ones in Sam's ears at the end of the night. But it just doesn't make any sense. At least, it doesn't make any sense to Caro – Nat has started to have a nasty feeling that she knows exactly what had happened, and that put her in a bit of a difficult position.

Ben had been reluctant to go ahead with the piece she had submitted that Monday. Started muttering about needing to get the lawyers involved if Nat was going to make an allegation like that. There was no way the family would accept the publication of what they would see as malicious speculation, involving two people who were in no position to defend themselves.

Nat had been passionate in her argument. 'I'm telling you, Ben. If we can write this the right way, I'm sure it's something we can get away with.'

Ben had looked unconvinced. 'You're telling me this has nothing to do with the fact that the story about poor Sam turned out to be rather less dramatic than you had first hoped for and failed to give you the exposure you were banking on? I'm guessing this is your second bite at the apple.'

'Cherry, Ben. I think you'll find the saying is second bite of the cherry.'

Ben had banged on his desk in an uncharacteristic show of short temperedness and Nat saw how tired he looked.

'Nat, you have to understand the seriousness of this. The paper's circulation is dropping by the day. People aren't clicking on the subscribe button to read the online articles and our advertising revenue – we can't give the space away. The shareholders just need a tiny excuse, and they will shut us down without a second thought. What you're proposing, that could be just what they've been waiting for.'

'Look Ben, I just know there's something there. Just give me this week to work on it. I'll smooch Caro and Kate too. Get the families on side. If I can get that, will you at least give it some thought for next week?'

Ben had given in as Nat knew he would, though she did feel a twinge of guilt as she left him slumped at his desk; but if she got this right, he would be happy to share in the glory, so a bit of stress now seemed like a small price to pay.

Nat has a theory. And it isn't a very nice theory. She had mulled it over all night after Caro had finally gone to bed; and really, it seems to be the only thing that makes any sense. Chris and Sam were obviously lovers – everyone said how close they had been. He had told Sam that night it had to end – after all, if it ever came out, he would be destroyed. No doubt, to soften the blow he had given his teenage mistress a parting gift. Probably the same earrings he had given Jen as an anniversary gift. Nat cynically thought he had maybe got them on a 'buy one get one free' offer. Sam, distraught at losing him, had run into the night, probably throwing the earrings back at him, before jumping to her death. No doubt if she goes to the nursing home again, she will find Jen still has her own pair of earrings. So not a tale of murder, but one of a man in a position of authority preying on a young girl in his care – and those stories sell well too.

Now, at the end of an exhausting week, where Nat has done her best to avoid Caro, she calls Kate and manages to get a number for Lauren. Kate had wanted to chat about the memorial, but Nat manages to fob her off, pretending that she is doing a write up for the paper – a celebration of the life of Sam. Not giving herself time to feel guilty and promising herself she will write a glowing piece about Sam once all this is done, Nat ignores the voice in her head that says no one will care what is written afterwards. And she probably won't care either, if she can just get this final explosive piece into print.

Lauren answers on the second ring and pauses for a moment as Nat gives her name.

'Oh, I didn't expect to hear from you. How did you get this number? I can't really talk right now – I'm on a train on the way to the airport.'

'I'm sorry to bother you, Kate gave me your number. Can I just ask you a very quick question?'

Nat carries on without giving Lauren the chance to make the excuse she can't talk now.

'The night of the ball, Kirsty mentioned Sam left early and that before she left, she had been speaking to Mr Webster. Can you remember if that was before or after she came and collected her things from the table?'

'Umm, oh God, it was so long ago. But funnily enough, I do remember. It was after. Sam was on her way out of the door and made a point of going to give Mr Webster a kiss on the cheek. It's no secret she was a bit tipsy. She would never have done it otherwise. And he sat there looking horrified. Next minute, he stands up and follows her and catches her by the door. He was gesturing towards her face and looked really annoyed, but Sam shrugged him off and away she went. Funny, I'd forgotten all about that. I mean, if she hadn't disappeared it would have been the talk of the ball – her going for it with Mr Webster like that.'

Putting down the phone, Nat thinks all this ties in with her theory. She just needs to figure out how to prove it. And maybe make sure the story doesn't hit the internet before she has moved out of the Beach Hut!

Getting home later that night, Nat finds her friend in a joyous mood.

'I feel so much better, Nat. I've realised what happened. Mum was dreadful when she had a headache. I remember she would take her earrings out and massage her ear lobes. I bet she left her earrings on the side and Sam, the little bugger, decided to try them on. Probably lost one, and Dad picked it up thinking Mum had the other on at home.

Nat smiles at her friend. It seems pointless not agreeing with her. 'Of course, it's so obvious now you've said it. Come on, let's forget about it and plan what we're going to wear for the reunion ball.'

59

Churcher's School – Old Pupils Group

Posted by: Anonymous. Saturday 17th August 2024 03.00am

Are we in for a treat tonight! Roll up, roll up for the long awaited Churcher's Old Gits Reunion!

I hope you are all ready to shed false tears about how sad it is about poor Sam and remember not to speak ill of the dearly departed Mr Webster, who I hear is to have the new library named after him. Quite apt for all hours he spent lurking in the dark corners tutoring all those gorgeous young things. At least, he called it tutoring!

Funny how none of his protegees were ever unattractive – male or female. Maybe he wasn't bothered either way!

Sadly, we won't be joined by the recently widowed Mrs Webster, who apparently can't remember her own name, never mind the names of all the young things she was happy to invite into her house for her husband's 'good deeds'.

Still, it will be sad to miss her glamour – always the life and soul until that last ball, when she had to leave early due to a headache. I reckon she was sickened with the realisation of just what her husband was up to. Must be pretty gutting to realise that even though you started as a child bride, you're no longer child enough for your husband. That thought gives me a headache too!

Anyway, food for thought, and I shall be raising a glass to those no longer with us – whether they are missed or we are celebrating seeing the back of them. Looking forward to hearing you talk all about this post later at the party.

3 likes, 6 angry, 50 care

Comments: The author has turned off comments on this post

10.30am: The post is deleted by an admin followed by a post reminding members of the group rules.

60

Gus

Present day: Saturday, 17 August

Gus looks at himself in the mirror, enjoying seeing himself in the tuxedo which emphasises his broad shoulders and brings out the icy blue of his eyes. He is pleased with how he looks and knows he will attract those same admiring glances that had sustained him the last time he had been at the school.

He remembers the last time he had attended a ball at Churcher's and Jen helping him with the bow tie, while Chris looked proudly on. Chris, the man who had been like a father to him, but who had never forgiven him for his betrayal. Gus doesn't like to think of how his behaviour had affected Chris, so he simply doesn't. Gus has always been good at not thinking about things that make him feel uncomfortable.

Which is why tonight he is not going to think too much about Alex. When he had found out about his son he had soon got lost in a fantasy of just how life would be, but it had not turned out like that. Alex had deeper ties to his old family than he had thought possible, and he can sense it will be a difficult transition for the boy. He had wanted to snap his fingers and have everything just fall into place; but instead it was a long waiting game, with the promise of 'soon' dangled in front of him, egging him forward.

But tonight he is going to enjoy taking his place at the centre of attention, for he knows they will all slot back into the roles that were allocated to them at school. And at school, there was no doubt he was the star of the show.

He hadn't expected to be able to come back here at all. Chris had made it so clear that he needed to stay away or face the consequences. Instead, he spent his life playing a very minor role in a show where other people were the stars. And then he had heard that Jen was ill, and his heart had broken a little bit, afraid that as she forgot that last summer, that time would maybe cease to exist for all of them and then who would he be? He had been consumed with an overwhelming feeling that time was running out and he wasn't sure if he was sad for the Websters, or for that version of himself who had failed to live up to his early promise. And then the second body blow: Chris Webster had died, and suddenly he had no excuse not to return home. He could pick up where he had left off. But of course it wasn't like that, and he had been regretting his choice, until he had seen his son down by the harbour and it was suddenly clear what he needed to do.

Maybe tonight would be the start of things falling into place. He supposes it was the last leavers' ball that was the start of this path he has chosen to tread. She had come out with the smuggled bottle of alcohol, an air of giddy wildness about her, and he had seen her. From then on, there was an inevitability about everything that had happened. They had come full circle, and he couldn't wait for them to be together. Just the three of them, the way it should have always been.

With a last glance in the mirror, Gus turns and leaves the house, looking forward to once more being the king of the Churcher's castle.

61

Caro

Present day: Saturday, 17 August

Looking in the mirror, Caro is momentarily shocked to see the shadow of her mother reflected in her face. Leaning in, she can see where her foundation has clung to the fine lines around her mouth and her eye shadow has creased into her lids, and she tuts and corrects the damage, the same way she remembers her mother doing.

She has a churning in the pit of her stomach. As Grace likes to say, her tummy is whizzing like the washing machine on spin. She smiles at the thought of her dear sweet Grace, then feels the threat of tears as she struggles with the hurt Grace will experience at the break down of her safe space - her family.

It's funny - a few weeks ago, she wouldn't have even thought of attending the reunion. Why would she want to be dragged back to remember things she had spent a fair bit of money on therapy to try and forget? Then she heard from Gus, and suddenly she has been looking forward to going back. It's as if she's been catapulted to the past and given the chance to pick up where she left off - to live the life she has always dreamed of with Gus and their son. And then she had woken up to that vile message on the chat board, and the reunion is now the last place she wants to go.

Caro hadn't cried or lashed out in anger when she had read the message. She just thought she had lost the ability to feel anything. Nat had found her white-faced at the kitchen table, shivering even though the heatwave was looking set to continue. Her friend had known immediately what the problem was, holding her own phone open on the same message that had greeted Caro that morning. Nat felt the anger on Caro's behalf, and was straight on with tracking down the admin to have the post removed. A task that was easier said than done on a sunny Saturday morning when most people were out enjoying the glorious weather.

'I'm not going tonight, Nat. I just can't face it. Everyone there will have read that poisonous post and will be looking at me with gleeful false sympathy - pleased to see the Webster family put in their place at last.'

Nat hadn't tried to persuade Caro otherwise and had wordlessly put the kettle on. The two friends had sat in the company of their own thoughts, both struggling with the emotions dragged to the surface by the anonymous message - Nat's fingers flying across the screen, her frustration evident in the tapping of her fingers, as if she could reach through the glass and drag out the writer and give them a piece of her mind. Caro simply sat in silence, lost in memories of the past and wondering if her father had always been despised. Could she trust her memory at all?

Despite everything, Caro had enjoyed that morning with Nat, both content to enjoy the quiet. It had always been that way. Sometimes they talked non-stop, completing each other's sentences and switching back and forth so fast that their friends would smile in confusion and admit defeat in understanding whatever the two of them were jabbering on about. And then at other times, they would sit for hours in a silence of contentment. Enough to brush the other's hand as Nat scribbled away on her latest piece of writing and Caro dreamed of love to a background of Coldplay. They had probably sat doing exactly that seventeen years ago, waiting to head to the ball where they would be onlookers to an event at which they will now take centre stage.

Eventually, Nat reached for her friend's fingers. 'Caro? You should really have a look on the Facebook group. There's been some lovely posts.'

Caro had shaken her head, staring at her friend, who squeezed her hand and smiled at her.

'I know that you want to stick your fingers in your ears and sing *la, la, la I'm not listening*.' With this, Nat did a perfect demonstration of her words. 'But you have to listen, Caro. It's one person. One vindictive, cowardly person, and if you don't turn up tonight you will have let them win. Plus, I went to all the effort of buying a new dress, and Mum is looking after the girls. I've even persuaded James to be our taxi driver for the night. Come on, it will be a laugh.'

'Nat, I just don't know if I can do it.'

'I know exactly how you feel. I know it's not the same, but I used to hate it when I could see the RANDs people collecting signatures for their petition around the town. I felt like everyone was looking at me and whispering about me. But I forced myself to show my face. I'd done nothing wrong, and whatever happened that night, you've done nothing wrong either.'

Caro had snatched her hand away from her friend. 'And what's that supposed to mean? I've done nothing wrong. Are you implying that there's some truth in these nasty posts? That my dad did do something he shouldn't have done? God Nat, I thought you were my friend.'

'I am your friend, and that's why I need to say this to you now. As a friend. I think we need to be open to the possibility that maybe something was going on that we were oblivious to. Maybe your dad did get closer to Sam than was wise.'

Seeing the fury on Caro's face, Nat recoiled before continuing. 'Maybe Sam read more into the situation than she should have. She didn't have a strong male presence in her life and maybe the attention your father showed her, whilst all above board, made her think there was something else between them. Your dad could have found himself in a very difficult, well, nearly impossible, position.'

Mollified, Caro nodded. That was a truth that although unwelcome, could be made acceptable.

'Look Caro, now's not the right time to discuss this in depth, but after this weekend, let's have a chat. Maybe it's time for you to tell you story and put a stop to these rumours once and for all. For now, let's show them just how we've got so much better with age!'

And that's how Caro came to be now looking in the mirror, not seeing herself, but the image of her mother reflected back at her. She hadn't consciously chosen a dress reminiscent of the dress her mother had been wearing at that last leavers' ball, but here she is. There is no mistaking she is Jen Webster's daughter.

Nat looks taken aback when she first walks in the room and gives a little shiver. 'God, I just had the almightiest sense of déjà vu. I never realised how alike you and your mum are.' She quickly covers her confusion with a smile as she thrusts a glass of ice-cold wine into her hand. 'Get that down you! For tonight, Caro, you will dazzle!'

James lets out a theatrical wolf whistle as he arrives to drop them off at the school, although Caro worries he is rather cold with her. She feels judged and uncomfortable, recognising that she has always had a need to be liked by people. Even people she doesn't like herself. Nat picks up on her discomfort and gives her hand another reassuring squeeze. Caro gazes out of the window, focusing on the pretty fairy lights that dance down the drive, distracting herself from the tears that just recently never feel too far away.

James drives away with a kiss for his wife and a rather

dismissive wave to Caro. The two friends stand in the sweeping driveway in front of the grand entrance to the school. It brings back memories of all the years this entrance had been out of bounds, and Caro can't help but feel a shiver of excitement - feeling as if the night is starting on a daring note. She gives a small laugh. Is this what her life has come to - when she gets a thrill of excitement from breaking long forgotten school rules? The sound of excited chatter drifts out on the warm summer evening breeze and, taking a deep breath, Caro takes the plunge back into her past.

Thankfully, it is rather like that first dive into cold water. The anticipation is far worse than the initial shock of submersion and, once you get in, you find it to be exhilarating. Caro and Nat find themselves engulfed by faces from the past. People clearly making an effort to show that they may have read the piece online, but as far as they are concerned, it's nonsense. Caro is assailed with condolences about her father and kind enquiries after her mother. She loses count of the number of times she hears, 'Your dad was such a brilliant headmaster, such a positive influence on my life, so sad to hear of his death.' Nat is smiling over at her friend and mouths 'Told you so,' and blows a kiss to remove any trace of cattiness from the comment.

Caro can tell when Gus arrives. It's the same as it had always been. The energy in the room seems to ramp up a level and she feels her eyes drawn to him as he makes his way towards her - a smile and a word for everyone he passes until he reaches her and kisses her on the cheek. 'God, you look stunning. It's like being catapulted back in a time machine.'

Caro smiles and decides to accept the compliment as it stands, rather than arguing that she bears little resemblance to the girl he knew all those years ago. With Gus at her side, Caro feels she could take on the world.

62

Nat

Present day: Saturday, 17 August

The evening is flying by, and Nat is surprised that, other than the initial flurry of conversation about Mr Webster, there has been no chatter about the anonymous posts. More shocking is the fact that the ghost of Sam Chappell isn't acknowledged at all. It seems to suit everyone better to pretend that any unpleasantness simply hasn't happened - the memorial service has closed that chapter.

The drink is flowing and now Nat is sat in a small group which includes Caro and Gus. Nat notices that Gus has retained the same magnetism he had as Head Boy and she doesn't think he's had to buy himself a drink yet, with plenty of admirers happy to do the honours.

Leaning in towards Caro, Nat whispers. 'Bit different to the last ball we attended when we were waiting on, eh?'

Caro laughs. 'Yes! And now it's full circle with my son being a very handsome waiter.'

Nat follows Caro's gaze and sees Alex, who might be a very handsome waiter but certainly doesn't have a smile on his face.

'He looks about as happy to be waiting on as you were all those years ago, Caro. The only difference being that he does actually look to be doing the job he's supposed to. As I remember you sneaked off and abandoned me!'

'Ah yes, menial work was never my forte!'

Nat can't help but laugh. 'Yes! You were a lady born to live a life of luxury.' She leans in closer and lowers her voice, making sure not to be overheard. 'And looks like Mr Redfearn will be able to make that Lady of the Manor a reality.'

Caro laughs and blushes, but Nat notices she doesn't deny that this is in her future plan. Nat doesn't doubt that Caro had been drawn to Gus all those years ago by his looks and his charm. But the fact his family were very wealthy had certainly helped. Poor Mark never really had a chance. Gus is just in a different league.

'So, tell all! Was it when you were supposed to be helping me that you got together with Gus the first time? I always wondered where you sneaked off to.'

Caro laughs. 'I wish! I did go off to find Gus. I was determined to make my move that night. In that waitress get-up, what man could resist?'

Nat is aware that Gus has finished his conversation and is listening to Caro talk. He moves in closer and puts his arm round her in a clear signal that they are together, and Nat is sure it's in her imagination, but the whole room seems to hold their breath as they realise the two of them are a couple.

'I'm sure you looked stunning as a waitress Caro, but I have to say I prefer the version of you tonight. It's like being sat with Jen all those years ago.'

Nat feels the prickle of unease in her stomach. What an odd thing to say.

Beth looks thoughtfully over at Caro. 'You may look like your mum, but you're not really like her in any other way, are you? I mean, you're a one-man woman. Just a pity that recently that one man seems to have changed.'

There is a moment of awkward silence and Nat notices Caro pull away slightly from Gus, but then she laughs. 'Good things come to those who wait.' Moving in closer to Gus, she continues. 'And seeing as you weren't captivated by my waitress outfit all those years ago, it's just as well I didn't manage to find you then. I saw you slipping from the room and followed you with the bottle of vodka I'd somehow ended up with. But all in vain! I ended up drinking it myself, crying about lost chances. Probably the reason why I can't stomach vodka now.'

The group of people they are with all laugh as Caro continues. 'I was rumbled by my mum, who was leaving early because she had a bad headache. I got such a shock when she appeared in the back yard. Surprisingly, I got off lightly. In fact, I think she had some sympathy for me as she looked like she'd had a bad night too, and who can blame her? Stuck on a table with all the old farts when she would have been much happier on the dance floor.'

The laughter continues as they all acknowledge the difference between Caro's mum and dad. Mr Webster, the headmaster, a stickler for the rules and a reputation for being a bit dull. It was a well-worn conversation as to how he had managed to ever hook Jen Webster, who was just so stunning and full of life.

In the corner Beth continues to laugh a bit too loudly, and a fraction longer than everyone else, so that she is suddenly the focus of attention. Through her laughter she splutters, 'Oh, Lauren told me they thought she was sneaking off to meet some young lover. Poor Sam was horrified by it. Terrified your dad would find out, and you know how she adored your dad, Caro.'

This time the laughter that greets the remark is a little more hesitant, until Caro joins in and Nat feels the tension ease once more. But looking across at Gus, she sees his lips are white and he looks totally furious. Just what's eating him? And if he hadn't been with Caro that night, then just where had he been?

63

Alex

Present day: Saturday, 17 August

Alex is a little bit pissed off. It's bad enough he's been made to dress up like a penguin and hand round silly little plates of fish and chips on a stick and mini burgers, but hearing everyone whispering about his mum and dad makes him feel a bit odd. He hates to admit it, but the gloss of finding his real dad is starting to wear off, and he realises there are a few things about Gus that he doesn't really like.

It had started a couple of days ago when his dad had messaged to see if he wanted to go out for a drink. At first, Alex had liked the fact that Gus didn't treat him like a child. Mark would never have invited him to the pub - unless it was a family meal where he would be confined to a pint of coke. He had once let him have a bottle of beer at a BBQ, but other than that Mark would bang on about how he was still too young to drink and now was the time to enjoy life without getting drunk. And although Alex would bitch about these stupid rules to his friends, his grandad and anyone who would listen, he is starting to realise that these rules somehow make him feel safe. And although he feels many things when he's with Gus, safe is not one of them.

And when they were at the pub, Gus just started to go on at him about that stupid TikTok video and insist he delete it. Alex had done so, with Gus peering over his shoulder the whole time to make sure it was done. Alex genuinely couldn't see what Gus was getting so stressed about. I mean, he was barely in the shot - just stood there glowering over at James. The way he was kicking up a fuss, you'd swear he'd been caught with his pants down or something.

And then there is Grace. Alex loves Grace with all his heart. He is her big brother and will do anything to make sure she is never sad. But his dad is starting to talk about them moving away to make a new start, and Grace is firmly excluded from these future plans. Gus makes it quite clear that it will just the three of them going forward - and Alex doesn't like that at all. He realises he doesn't want to move away from here just yet. Yes, he can't wait to break free from the shackles when he goes to university, but he realises that freedom will only be enjoyed as long as he knows he has home as a safe haven to come back to. And that home is with people he loves, and Grace is very firmly included in that picture. It seems to him that Gus is trying to rewrite the past, and in doing so, erase Grace from existence. And that worries Alex. He wants to talk to his mum about it, but she is too loved-up to listen to anything that might be difficult. And then he realises he wants to talk to Mark, to hear his quiet reassurance - but how can he, after everything he has said?

Hearing another burst of laughter, he sees his mum leaning into Gus, clearly smitten. God, this is just so embarrassing. But something about the way Gus is looking at his mum makes him feel uncomfortable. He is studying her with a look of... well, a look of disgust. Before he has time to change his mind, he takes out his phone and calls the name he still has saved as Dad.

64

Nat

Present day: Saturday, 17 August

Nat volunteers to go and retrieve their coats, although they won't be needed as the night is still warm. As she walks alone towards the cloakroom, she is unable to shake the feeling of unease. Ahead of her she sees Alex, who is clearly in a world of his own, and to her horror she sees he looks to have been crying. At that moment Alex spots her approaching, and looks equally horrified to have been caught out in this moment of vulnerability.

'Alex, are you OK? Do you want me to get your mum?'

'No!'

Nat recoils slightly from the violence of that one word.

'Oh Nat, everything's gone wrong. I need to speak to Dad, well Mark, but he won't pick the phone up to me and I can't say I blame him. After all, I'm not his son and I said some truly dreadful things to him. I bet he hates me.'

Nat curses her timing. Providing reassurance to teenage boys is not her thing at all, and she has a brief flashback of all the times Jen Webster would soothe troubled youngsters in the Headmaster's Cottage. Maybe that's why Alex visits his grandma so regularly, seeking some comfort that she can still provide.

'Come and sit down.' Patting the seat beside her, Nat

persuades Alex to join her on the row of chairs by reception. 'Now I don't know much Alex, but the one thing I do know is that Mark loves you. He considers you his son, and so whilst he may have been hurt at things you've said, the thing about parents is, we love you unconditionally and are quick to forgive.'

Alex seems to relax slightly. 'But Grandma always said Mark never really wanted me and that the only person who would truly be there for me was my real dad. She always promised that one day he would come for me.'

Nat shakes her head. 'You have to remember your grandma's very poorly - and she was poorly for a long time before anyone realised. There were times when she might have seemed OK, but, really, she was very confused.'

Alex looks doubtful and Nat once again remembers how at that age you trust adults are telling you the truth. God knows what bitter seeds have been sown by Jen's unintentional rambling.

'Is that why you visit your grandma so often, Alex? To talk through everything that's going on with Mark and now Gus?'

Alex looks confused. 'Visit Grandma? No way! I know its horrid of me, but I don't go near the place unless Mum says I have to go with her. And she hates going too, so thankfully it's not a regular thing. Grandma either stares into space or rants on about nonsense and cries. And...' Alex leans forward with the first smile he has managed in the last few minutes, 'The place stinks of piss!'

Nat lets out a splutter of shocked laughter, though can't deny the accuracy of what he is saying.

'Alex!'

The pair of them sit giggling, Nat feeling like she is sixteen again and is flung back to the last ball she had attended at the school. She had expected to be sat giggling with Caro that night, but her friend had disappeared. As had Jen and Gus. A little niggle of a thought is starting in her brain, but it's so unpleasant she doesn't want to think about it.

Alex jumps to his feet. 'I'm going to head over to Mark's. Maybe you're right and I need to have a conversation with him, and that's better-done face to face.'

Nat gives him a hug and is surprised that he doesn't pull away from her as he has done ever since he reached that awkward teenage phase.

'Wait on and James will give you a lift when he picks us up.'

Alex straightens and narrows his eyes. 'I'm not sure that's the best thing with Mum and Gus there, and they have both been drinking. Mum's bound to get all emotional and Gus can be a bit full on - if you know what I mean.'

Nat nods. She does know what he means. Even at school, Gus was well known for his obsessions. When he took something on, he certainly took it on with a passion. Maybe that was why so many of the girls strove to be his latest obsession.

'I'll cut over the cliff path. It's still light and I'll text you as soon as I get to Mark's. Thanks, Nat.'

Afterwards, Nat never forgave herself for not stopping him, but she is so pleased that he has taken her into his confidence, has shown that affection that had been so freely given when he was a young child, that she didn't wanted to spoil the moment. And there is no doubt she is distracted by the worm of an idea that's burrowing in her mind and shouting louder to be heard. So, she stands and watches Alex head down the path towards the cliff tops. Following the steps Sam Chappell took all those years before.

65

Caro

Present day: Saturday, 17 August

By the time James arrives to collect them, they are amongst the last to leave. As Gus flags down the car, he greets James with a jovial, 'Ah, here at last, my good man. Straight back to the Manor and don't spare the horses.'

Caro laughs but she sees the glance that passes between James and Nat, and she realises they think Gus is a bit of a dick. This increases the swirling in her stomach, because, as the days pass, she realises there are lots of things about Gus she doesn't like very much. It turns out that her fantasy becoming a reality isn't going to be the sweet smooth sailing she had hoped for. But having come this far, she can't see a way to steer the ship in a different direction.

As James follows the winding road that leads to Gus's family home, Caro sits up straighter in the car, attempting to stop her head from spinning. She isn't sure how much she's had to drink - just vaguely aware that her glass kept getting refilled - but it has clearly been too much.

'Better drop me back at the Beach Hut please, James. I need to make sure Alex gets home OK.'

She can see Nat's shoulders tense in the front seat; then her friend speaks, feigning a casualness she obviously doesn't feel.

'I saw Alex. He was heading over to Mark's. Think he wanted to sort things out between the two of them, which is a good thing, isn't it?'

Beside her, she feels Gus stiffen as he barks back to Nat, 'And you've only thought to mention this now?'

'He's going to message when he's safely there, so I'm expecting his text any minute.'

Caro knows when her friend isn't been entirely truthful, and she sees Nat's fingers seek out the stacking ring on her hand and picks up on the slight tremor in her voice.

She tries to sound relaxed as she asks, 'When did you see him, Nat?'

Nat glances at her watch. 'An hour or so ago now. Honestly, I'm sure he'll message soon.'

At this point, James decides he should take charge. 'An hour ago? He should easily be there by now. Look, I'm going to give Mark a call, just make sure he made it there OK.'

By this point, Caro can see that they are pulling up at Manor Farm. Gus jumps out. 'No need for you to call Mark, James. I think your wife has done quite enough for one night. We will take it from here. Come on Caro, we need to get this mess sorted.'

Caro is torn. She wants James to ring Mark, then she wants to go home. Not to the Beach Hut, but to her proper home. The home she had built with Mark. But she can't say that to Gus, who is looking furiously into the car. With a helpless shrug at Nat, she climbs out.

James hesitates, clearly unsure what to do. But as Gus slams the car door, it seems he makes up his mind. As Nat calls, 'Let us know if you hear from Alex,' he pulls away up the drive. Caro has a suspicion he will be straight on the phone to Mark the minute they turn the corner, and for that she is glad.

'Right Caro, you go and wait in the house in case he turns up here. I'll follow the path along the cliffs. Bound to catch up with him at some point. There's no way Alex would be heading to see Mark. He doesn't want that man to be any part of his life. He'll have made up a tale to throw Nat off the scent. No, I bet he's meeting mates for some sneaky drinking up at the quarry. Just the same as we used to do, back in the day.'

Caro wants to say that she had never gone drinking up at the quarry, but now doesn't seem the time to make a fuss about the details. Gus thrusts the house key in her hands and, with a barked instruction to stay close to her phone, strides off into the night.

Caro shivers as she enters the farmhouse. Whilst the house is grand, it somehow kept a chill about it, even on the warmest of days. She misses her modern house and flinging all the windows open to gain some relief from the relentless summer heat. What she would give to be tucked up in her own bed, moaning that it was far too hot to sleep.

For something to do, she walks through to the kitchen and puts the kettle on but is distracted by the 'no signal' sign on her phone. Desperate not to miss a call, she wanders around the house, phone aloft, desperately seeking the elusive bars. Remembering Gus works from home, she figures his office will be the best place to try; he must be reliant on phone signal, or maybe she can hook up to the Wi-Fi there.

Opening the door, she feels on edge. This room is strictly 'out of bounds' each time she visits - Gus emerging from the door and firmly closing it behind him, making it clear that it is an area not open to visitors. She guesses he keeps confidential stuff in there relating to the farm and the investments he is managing for his clients. For a moment, she forgets her worry about Alex as she looks around the room. There doesn't seem to be any signs that Gus has been working here, but she figures maybe everything he does is kept on the laptop.

Moving towards the window to see if she can pick up any signal, she growls in frustration that the phone stubbornly remains closed for business. She will have to connect to the Wi-Fi so she can use her phone that way. Checking her settings, she sees the Manor Farm network there but when she clicks to connect, is quickly prompted to enter a password. Bloody hell, this is just typical. She needs to call Gus to ask him for the password, but she can't call Gus without getting on the internet.

'For fuck's sake!' Caro whispers over and over as she has visions of Alex desperately trying to reach her, or Mark calling to say there is news, or Gus telling her they are on their way home. He will be furious with her. The last thing he had said was to make sure she was by her phone.

Knowing Gus would hate her prying, but deciding this was a real emergency, Caro tentatively opens the top drawer of the desk, hoping he has written down the password - the same as she always does. Mark always said if they were ever burgled, the thieves would be able to clear all her accounts within minutes. But she still writes everything down just the same. Otherwise, her whole life would be spent requesting password resets.

It appears that Gus has a better memory. As she makes her way through the drawers, she is becoming more frantic as she is greeted with yet more pristine pads of Post-it notes and neatly lined up pens, all with the lids intact and filed in colour order. It really doesn't look like there is much productive work done in this office.

The third drawer down is messier but is mainly stuff to do with the protests against the quarry. Odd notes scrawled on paper - seeming to be Gus's thoughts as to the best plan of action. She recognises some of the phrases as the building bones he had used to draft his impassioned speeches, but nothing that looked like a password.

Caro holds her breath as she opens the last drawer.

'Please be there, please be there, please be there.'

It looks more hopeful - a jumble of papers with what looks to be bank account numbers. If he has written the password down anywhere, Caro thinks, this is where she will find it. Her frustration grows as she frantically rummages through the pile of papers, before she manages to calm herself and decides to take everything out the drawer and put it back methodically. That way she will be doing Gus a favour, as how he ever finds anything he needs in all this clutter is beyond Caro.

She is about halfway through, tempted to give up and just sit in silence with no phone, when she spots the printed combination of letters and numbers

ANGJEN140607

As she types the details into her phone she smiles as she sees she finally has connection, then smiles again as she recognises Alex's birthday as part of the password. Gus must have changed it recently, as soon as he had found out about his son. Honestly, she needs to persuade him to let her sort some of his stuff out, rather than jotting things down on old scraps of paper. Checking her phone, she sees the Wi-Fi has dropped off and remains steadfastly unobtainable. Yet again, she is cut off from everyone and is desperate to be out there doing something.

66

Nat

Present Day: Saturday, 17 August

'For God's sake, Nat - will you just sit down and stop pacing the floor!'

Nat spins round to glare at James. 'I'm not sure you realise how serious this is, James.'

James makes a dismissive snort and for a moment Nat thinks he is going to confine his feelings to that, but it seems he is determined to say his piece.

'Serious! Are *you* serious, you mean. The two of you, and counting Gus makes it three, are behaving like a bunch of hysterical mother hens. And all because a sixteen-year-old boy has decided to walk over to see the man who has been a dad to him for most of his life. Ooh, let's call the police right this minute!'

Having said his piece, James turns to pour a glass of wine, then thinks better of it and switches the kettle on.

'I'm sorry Nat, I don't mean to sound dismissive. It just all seems a bit dramatic. A typical Caro drama. But look, I'll do my bit and make tea.'

He grins at his wife who, after a moment's hesitation, smiles back at him.

'You're right, I know you're right. It has just been such a

weird time.'

'You're telling me! Want to tell me what's bothering you?'

The two of them settle down in the snug, nursing their tea as they look out over the blackness of the dunes.

'It's a stunning spot this, Nat. Imagine what you could do with this place.'

Nat splutters. 'Don't even think about it! It's bad enough you found poor Sam Chappell. Let's not go disturbing the ghosts that may rest here. Though I have a nasty suspicion that Jez isn't resting in peace.'

James shifts closer and touches her hand. 'You're shaking, Nat. Come on. Tell me all. Is this something to do with Sam?'

'Sort of. Well, that how it started - and I think it's linked - but God, I just don't know anymore. It's Jez, you see. Caro's brother. I think his death is somehow linked to Sam.'

James interrupts. 'Now, hang on. That's a hell of an accusation to make against a fourteen-year-old boy.'

Nat holds up a hand. 'No, let me finish. That's not what I'm suggesting at all. Jez was a really sweet kid. He was gentle and kind and quiet.'

'Not like the rest of the family, then.'

'No, but the main thing is he was unassuming. We all just forgot he was there. All he was interested in was logging the birds he spotted in the dunes. And I think he found something out. And it was that something that made him feel he couldn't live anymore.'

'OK,' James lets out the word on a sigh. 'And what makes you think this?'

'Right, you're going to love this bit. I reckon Jen Webster was having an affair with Gus.'

James looks at his wife. 'I think you're losing the plot a bit on this, Nat. I have no idea what would have made you think that.'

Nat blushes. 'OK, I'll admit I'm not a very nice person, but the truth is I went to visit Jen at the nursing home.'

'Bloody hell Nat, you know how ill she is. I mean, she's lost her mind. She could tell you absolutely anything.'

'I know, I know. I realised that as soon as I got there. But she kept going on about their son, and she kept calling him Alex. I thought she was likely just confused, but then the nurse was talking about how her son visited all the time. I assumed that was Alex, but then tonight Alex told me how he feels guilty because he avoids visiting his grandma. So just who has been visiting Jen, because it sure as hell isn't her long-dead son!'

James laughs. 'So now Jen Webster has a thing for young boys. Never mind the fact that Gus was having a fling with Caro. Nothing like keeping it in the family!'

'But that's the thing. Gus was eighteen, so not a child. And I know you don't like him, but nearly everyone in the school was a little bit in love with him. And this thing with Caro - no matter what story he likes to tell now, it was no great love affair; and I'm starting to think maybe it was Gus lashing out at the family once things had ended with Jen.'

'That sounds like Gus that's for sure; and Nat, you know I despise the man, so I'm happy to think the worst of him, but you said that it was like a Romeo and Juliet love affair. Torn apart by her dad threatening to go to the police.'

'I know, so I can't figure that out at all. Caro showed me the letter her dad had written. It was very plain what he thought of Gus, and it set out in no uncertain terms that he wasn't to see Caro again. Look, it's here somewhere - have a read for yourself.

Nat fetches the letter from the drawer, ignoring James's tut of disapproval at the casual ease in which she locates the item, and hands it to James, who reads it quickly. Then he turns back to the first page and frowns.

'But this doesn't make sense at all, Nat. It's all wrong. Look at the date.'

Nat does, and at that moment everything seems to fall into place.

'Fuck, the letter's dated before Caro could have possibly known she was pregnant. This letter isn't warning him to stay away from his daughter. It's warning him to stay away from his wife.'

James sits quietly, then gets to his feet. 'Fuck it, I'm having a whisky.'

'Get me one too please, will you? Honestly James, I have a really bad feeling about all of this. And I can't get hold of Caro, so God knows what's happening.'

67

Caro

Present day: Saturday, 17 August

Caro can't face putting everything back neatly, so decides to just dump the rest of the papers in the drawer. Gus will be none the wiser. As she scoops up the first pile, she hesitates as she spots yet more familiar writing, and the rest of the papers flutter to the floor as she reads the words her father had written. The beginning of the letter is missing and, as Caro reads, she struggles to make sense of the words that now shine a light on the past in a way she doesn't want to see.

> *I don't know if you set out to make her fall in love with you or if you did have some element of genuine feeling. The more I begin to try and understand you, the more I fear this was just a game to you - just another way to prove that you really can have just anything you want. What I do know is my wife thinks she fell in love with you and was prepared to throw away our family for this supposed connection she feels the two of you have.*
>
> *And I do believe she may have gone with you. Where no doubt I would have been left to come running to the rescue once you tired of her as you tire of everything once you know they are yours. But you have frightened Jen with your actions on the night of the ball.*

I doubt I will ever find out the truth of what happened that night, and I'm not sure that Jen even knows the full story. All I do know is that a girl is missing - a girl who had the misfortune to stumble upon your sordid little secret. A girl so infatuated with you, who allowed you to walk her home to explain that things were not what they appear. That much I have gleaned from Jen. She chooses to believe Sam then fled, heartbroken, deciding to start a new life where she didn't have to live with the pain of seeing you so in love with my wife. One of Jen's many faults are she chooses to paint a story to erase any hint of any unpleasantness, but I think deep down she knows this is not the truth.

I pray every night that is what happened. So maybe I am as bad as Jen for keeping that glimmer of hope alive. Maybe I can only live with myself, and my wife, if I choose to believe that everyone is living happily ever after. No real harm done.

But make no mistake. It ends here. If you attempt to continue this sordid relationship with my wife, the mother of my children, I will not hesitate to inform the authorities about everything I know. Make sure you leave and don't ever think about coming back.

I will have to live with this decision. I hope you are haunted by the memories of what you have done for every second of whatever miserable life you have left to you.

Caro feels her breathing quicken and become shallower until she feels she can't breathe at all. Her body is telling her to run, that she needs to get away from this house, to be with her children. She needs to tell someone, but her phone steadfastly refuses to find any signal. Instead, she sinks to the floor and sobs whilst her mind races to find a different explanation to the truth her father's words are telling her.

She can't say how long she has sat there when she is roused by a banging at the door. Frantically, she looks around for somewhere to run. She can't face Gus right now, not with all these questions swirling round her head. Then logical Caro takes over. Why would Gus be banging on his own front door? Stumbling to her feet, she risks a look out the window and feels her body relax as she recognises Mark's car.

'I can see you up there, Caro! Come on, stop playing silly buggers and let me in. I promise you; tonight is not the time to play drama queen.'

Mark is still speaking but Caro can't make out what he is saying as she hurls herself down the stairs, two at a time, and wrenches the door open, ready to envelop Alex in a hug and have Mark drive them away from this place. But there is only Mark stood outside, running his hands through his hair so that it is messed in all directions.

'I came as soon as I got Alex's message. He sounded upset. Where is he?'

Hearing Mark's words, Caro collapses again to the ground, finding that now the tears have broken through that dam of control, there is just no stopping them. She tries to speak to Mark but can only gulp out sobs as she struggles to catch her breath.

'Caro, come on Caro, sit over here.' Mark stops shouting and is leading Caro to the bench by the front door. 'Just breathe, just concentrate on breathing. Come on. A deep breath in for three, that's right. Now a breath out for three.'

As Mark counts in a steady rhythm, Caro finds the beats of her heart slow to match the soft rumble of his voice, and she leans into him, knowing that somehow Mark will make sense of all this.

'OK, you're safe now, Caro. Now what on earth is going on?'

Cara wishes she could rewind the clock, but in light of the letter she has just read, would she need to rewind back seventeen years? To wish that Alex had never existed? She can't do that. She loves her boy and, looking at Mark, she realises he loves their boy too.

'Alex wanted to come and see you.'

Mark makes an impatient noise. 'Yes, I know that. I had a voice message from him saying he was on his way to the house. I was just sat by the harbour, thinking things through. I headed straight home as soon as I got the message, but there was no sign of him. I've tried his mobile but it's straight to voicemail and he just sounded off on the phone, so I thought I better come and check. I've been to the Beach Hut but no sign there - I guessed maybe the three of you were here.'

Caro recoils at the way her husband spits out the reference to the three of them, but realises her horror isn't because of fear of his anger, but because, for the first time, she is understanding the deep hurt her actions have caused. She is ashamed to admit, even to herself, that she has followed this exciting path with no thought for Mark. And to be truly honest, even if she has given his feelings a passing thought, she has been too caught up in what she believed was the romantic story of her youth now coming to a happy ending; she has blocked out anything that might tarnish that fantasy. Instead, she has simply chosen not to think of Mark at all. Going so far in some fantasies of the future to imagine his death in a tragic accident. That way, she hasn't had to try and figure out where he will fit in this picture of the future.

'Oh Mark, I don't know where Alex is. Gus was furious when he heard he was coming to see you, so he headed out to try and catch him up on the cliff path.'

Mark looks puzzled. 'Why on earth would he take the

cliff path?'

'He was working at the school - waiting on - so that would have been the quickest way to you.'

'OK, so hopefully Gus will have found him. Can't you give him a ring? Check that all's OK?'

Again, Mark looks confused at Caro's inability to use her phone. 'Look Caro, I know I've been angry. I'm not going to try and excuse things that have been said. Let's try and make a fresh start. You know I didn't want the family broken up, but now you seem to have made your choice, can't we at least work together to find a way forward? For the sake of Alex and Grace, if nothing else.'

'Oh, Mark. We have to get to Alex. Something's dreadfully wrong.'

Mark looks like he wants to roll his eyes. He is used to the dramatics frequently displayed by the Webster family, but something in Caro's voice seems to alert him that this time she is serious.

'What do you want to do? We can wait here for Gus to bring Alex back and then I can take the two of you wherever you feel safe. Or we can head out to look for them.'

Caro is already running towards his car. 'Let's go and please, we need to hurry. I'll explain everything on the way.'

68

Caro

Present day: Saturday, 17 August

Mark parks the car at the end of the green lane, having got as far as he can. As he had driven down the narrow strip, Caro prayed no one was coming the other way as they wouldn't have a chance of stopping. As he drove Caro told him about the letter, and how Gus had shown her a part of the letter to explain his sudden disappearance all those years ago. But now, seeing the missing pages, it was a completely different story.

'I think Gus always knew about Alex and either didn't care or was too afraid to risk seeing Dad. But as soon as Dad was dead, he was free to come back and pick up where he left off. The thing is, I don't think I was intended to be in that future picture. I think I was a very poor substitute, in his eyes, for my mum.'

Mark doesn't reply, but she sees the clench of his jaw and his hands tighten on the steering wheel, making his knuckles turn white, and the car goes a little bit faster.

Caro is first out of the car - not waiting for Mark – and, using the torch on her phone, she stumbles along the path. The route is overgrown with the blackberry brambles that will soon feed the birds, and the people organised enough to forage for free food. The dancing midges are picked up in the light and she can see tiny creatures scuttling away to avoid her feet. The nettles sting her legs as she makes her way down the narrow path, and she wonders how long it has been since she has been up here. The path has always been fairly quiet, but in recent years it seems to have been left to nature, and she can see no sign that anyone has made their way along here before her tonight.

Behind her, she hears Mark curse as he stumbles; but he quickly catches her up and the two of them move at a steady pace, breathing in the night air that gives no hint there is anyone else sharing this space.

'Are you sure they would have come this way, Caro?'

'Why are you whispering?' Caro whispers back, and the two giggle, dispersing some of the tension that surrounds them.

'Nat saw Alex head down the school drive and he had said he was coming to see you. This is really the only way he could have gone. And he used to like it up here, said it was his thinking place. I think that was what we hoped when Gus went after him - that he would have chance to catch him up and speak to him.'

In the darkness Caro senses Mark's anger at this, and she understands he feels Gus was trying to prevent Alex from reaching him. Caro is starting to wonder if maybe that was the case. Still, none of that matters now, she just needs to get to Alex - and get him far away from the man who isn't fit to be called his father.

69

Sam

Seventeen years earlier: Saturday, 4 August

Sam wished she had stuck to her original gut feeling and not come to this stupid ball. She had been so excited by it, spending hours daydreaming about how she would look in her new dress. Picturing the look on Gus's face when he saw her and realised that, after all this time, he loved her. She only wished he looked at her the way little Jez did. At least she knew what it was like to be adored, even if her admirer was a skinny fourteen-year-old boy.

And then all those dreams had been brought to a sudden halt. Sam had been hanging around at the boating lake and Gus came to find her. She thought he had come to ask her to the ball. In fact, to her shame, she thinks she blurted out an excited 'Yes, please!' before he had a chance to ask his question. Gus had looked quite taken aback but then had smiled that slow, wide grin of his and explained that he would like to get Mr Webster a bottle of whisky to say thank you for everything, and did Sam want to add her name to the card? She felt a right idiot and had mumbled some nonsense and fled the park, avoiding the pitying glances thrown her way by her friends.

Later, Sam had gone with her mum to the Beach Hut, happy to hang around there on the off chance that Gus might turn up. Maybe she could brazen it out and he hadn't noticed what a fool she had made of herself. Bored, she had wandered through the dunes, knowing without looking that Jez's eyes would be watching her through the telescope that he spent hours peering through. She had sunk down into the dry sand, enjoying the feel of the grains shifting, almost tickling against her legs, and had started to doze off in the sun.

Only half awake, she was jolted back from the fantasy of being stood with Gus, receiving their doctorates at the same time and being called the bright young things of the future. Mr Webster and her mum would be there smiling proudly, all of them together as a new family. For a moment, she thought that Gus's voice was in her dream, but then she heard him speaking clearly.

'You know I love you. I'll not go to uni. You leave here. We can be together. Happy.'

There was a moment's silence as whoever was on the phone responded.

'I'd do anything to have you. I can't live if you are not there to help me breathe. Please let's meet later - we can sneak away from the ball. I just have to see you. I just can't stop thinking about you.'

Gus was still murmuring into the phone, but Sam was unable to hear what he said as he moved further away towards the harbour. She wasn't aware of the tears that had started to stream down her face. All she could think was, *I've lost him. He's in love with someone else. Someone he can't live without. He can't live without her, and I can't live without him.* Wiping her tears, determined to let no one see how she was hurting, she made her way back to the Beach Hut, where she told her mum she wasn't going to the ball. What was the point? She just didn't think she could bear to see Gus with whoever this girl was.

But everyone nagged at her on and on to go and, in the end, Mr Webster was despatched to have a word. Sam could never bear to disappoint Mr Webster - he had been the closest thing to a father figure she had experienced in her life, so she had reluctantly agreed to attend. It hadn't been as bad as she thought. Gus was showing no particular attention to anyone in the room, although every so often his eyes flicked to the door, as if checking out an escape route. Maybe she had misunderstood the conversation she had overheard - after all, she had barely been awake.

It was later in the evening when she saw Gus casually swipe the bottle of prosecco from behind the grandly named 'Cocktail Station'. As he headed to the back door, she saw that bloody Caro Webster watching and, right on cue, she grabbed her own bottle of contraband spirits and followed him. Bloody hell! She might have guessed it would be that little bitch getting her claws into Gus. She was far too young for him, but everyone knew if Caro wanted something, then Caro usually got it. Well, not this time. Not if Sam had anything to do with it.

As she slipped through the back door, she was struck once more by the ugliness of the rear of the school building. Clearly Churcher's showed its best face to the world and secured its less attractive bits out of sight. *A bit like some of the people round here*, she thought, wiping away the tears that were threatening to overwhelm her again. She could still hear the low beat of the music as she moved away from the building, and every so often the still of the night was pierced by a shriek of laughter from those inside. Sam wished she was one of them - that she had never fallen so hard for Gus, that she didn't feel she could enjoy anything unless he was close.

Rounding the corner, she nearly tripped over someone sat on the floor. The girl had no reaction to Sam's appearance, simply sitting with her head in her hands, swigging directly from the bottle of vodka beside her. Sam's first feeling was one of overwhelming relief. It was Caro Webster, which meant she wasn't with Gus after all. To her shame, the surge of happiness this brought her was further increased by the knowledge that Mr Webster was going to be severely pissed off that his daughter was in this state, letting the school and him down. *Oh, yes!* Caro's status as golden girl was going to be severely tarnished by this event. Quickly turning away, Sam began to head back to the school, delighted to be the one to be the bearer of such distressing news. She must remember to wipe the grin from her face when she told him.

The back door opened again, spilling out the light and allowing the inside party noise to escape on the night air, and Sam slipped into the shadows as she saw Nat, Caro's friend, move outside. In a theatrical whisper, she called for her friend a couple of times, and then with a shrug she went back inside, slamming the door. *Oh, what a night this was turning out to be!* Looked like Caro had finally managed to piss off her adoring friend too. This was nearly as good as things working out with Gus. Sam still harboured a secret hope that things may come right in that department too.

As she stayed in the shadows, she heard a murmur of voices and her stomach plummeted - just like the time she had ridden a rollercoaster at Alton Towers. She hadn't liked the sensation then, and she suddenly knew she wasn't going to like what she saw if she followed the sound to see who was hiding in the dark. Afterwards, she did wonder how different things might have been if she had gone back to the light of the party that beckoned her to safety. But by that point it was too late, and she was falling to the darkness that would end things.

70

Caro

Present day: Saturday, 17 August

Caro stops suddenly and is jolted forward as Mark runs into the back of her, grabbing her arm to stop her falling to the ground.

'What? Why have you stopped?'

'Sshh, I can hear voices.'

The two of them stand, straining to listen above the sound of the night, and Caro feels Mark tense beside her as they both catch the rumble of men's voices floating towards them on the breeze. Though she can't make out the words, there is no mistaking the harshness of the tone - the sound jarring against the gentle chirruping of the insects who seem to be chattering in protest at the disturbance of their nighttime peace.

'Come on, they're this way.'

Mark is off and Caro knows she must follow, but her legs don't want to work. She knows where they are. They are at the quarry.

Afterwards, she wonders what would have happened if they hadn't heard those voices - if they had carried on following the path towards the town. But in the moment, she has no choice but to follow the path, and she is engulfed by the darkness.

71

Sam

Seventeen years earlier: Saturday, 4 August

At first, Sam's brain couldn't make sense of what her eyes were seeing. Gus was stood in the corner of the yard, hidden rather unromantically by the huge kitchen bins, the night air tainted by the slightly sweet smell of rotting food. His head was bent in low towards the woman smoking a cigarette by his side - the woman who was old enough to be his mother. Jen Webster.

Sam ran through every possible scenario. Maybe Gus was confiding in the woman he had come to see as a surrogate parent, sharing his fears and disappointments. But then he leaned in closer and the two of them shared a kiss that left the hidden watcher in no doubt of the feelings that sizzled between them. She turned to flee to the sanctuary of the party - devastated for herself, but also for dear Mr Webster, who she knew would be destroyed by this betrayal. Maybe she should just keep quiet - pretend she hadn't seen anything then leave for university and try to forget all about it. But then how could she keep seeing Mr Webster, share her future successes that he had set her up to achieve, all the time knowing he was the victim of such a nasty little secret? There was only one thing for it - she would have to tell him and just hope he didn't hate her as the messenger. This time, there was no danger of her revelling in passing on this news.

'Hold on Sam, where are you off to in such a hurry?'

She jumped as she felt a warm hand grasp her arm and spun round to see Gus standing there, a lazy grin on his face as he reached forward and brushed her hair away from her face. She couldn't help her heart pounding, and for a moment wanted to believe that she had misinterpreted the scene that had been played out before her eyes. But there was a tic going in the corner of his left eye and she got the impression that the lazy indifference was just an act. The air was charged with something and, despite her misgivings, she started to relax against him as she smelt the familiar tang of his deodorant, the smell of beer on his breath and the hint of tobacco where he had sneaked a forbidden cigarette. Sam felt drunk on it, but was unable to ignore the unmistakeable scent of a woman's perfume. It was Jen Webster's. She would recognise that scent anywhere. Like everything about Jen Webster, her perfume was rich and unmistakeable.

Gus seemed to sense the change in her and, for a fraction of a second, his eyes narrowed. The change in his face was so brief that she would have missed it, had she not been on high alert.

'I really need to get back, my friends will be looking for me.'

Gus smiled again, but this time rather than feeling that familiar warmth of basking in his approval, Sam felt herself shiver. She had been praying for weeks to get some time alone with Gus at the ball, and now she found she really didn't like it at all.

'They won't have missed you yet, Sam. Everyone's a little drunk and enjoying the party. I doubt they've even spared you a thought.'

Gus delivered the words with a smile that failed to take the sting out of them, and it struck Sam that she had always known that Gus could be cold and cruel. She had just been willing to overlook this because she had believed she was in love. Any traits about him she didn't like, she forced herself to ignore - preferring the fantasy of the man to the real-life version with all his flaws.

'Come on, walk with me, I think you may have misunderstood what you just saw. Besides, I have a little going away gift for you. I've been waiting for the right time.'

Sam hesitated, chewing on her lip as she wondered what to do.

'My mum is coming to pick me up. Perhaps I had better call her and let her know.'

'No need. We will easily be back before the party has finished, so she will be none the wiser. I won't take up much of your time, I promise. This might be the last time you and I get to spend any time alone together before we head out to the brave new world we have been gifted, courtesy of Mr Webster.'

Sam hesitated again but part of her still longed to be noticed by Gus, and she had drunk more than normal. It wasn't impossible that she had misunderstood what she had seen. If she saw Jez as being far too young for her, why on earth would Jen Webster see Gus as anything more than a surrogate son?

'You do look beautiful tonight, Sam.'

Oh, how she had longed to hear those words. Gus cupped her face with his hands and then, reaching in his jacket pocket, drew out the most beautiful diamond studs Sam had ever seen.

'I saw these and just knew I had to get them for you. They should be a reminder that you will always shine bright and that I will always be with you. Put them in now and promise me you will wear them forever.'

Sam was dazzled, not just by the earrings Gus had produced like a magician from his jacket pocket, but by his words which seemed to hypnotise her. This was so much better than she had even imagined it would be.

The decision was quickly made, although she didn't understand the decision wasn't really hers to make - the idea that she had a choice was simply an illusion.

'I'll need to nip in and get my things. I'll tell everyone Mum is insisting on coming to pick me up early.'

'Don't be long, I want to make the most of every minute of this magical night.'

Sam dashed in and said breathless goodbyes, smiling as Lauren snapped a photo of her. She made sure to sweep her hair behind her eyes so that the earrings were on full display and as she laughed, she saw Mr Webster giving her the strangest of looks. She ran over to him, giving him a quick kiss on the cheek - after all, none of this would be happening if it wasn't for him. She felt giddiness overwhelm her as she noted the shocked look on his face replicated on the faces around the room. That would give them all something to talk about; but just as she was making her escape, Mr Webster appeared behind her and grabbed her arm.

'Sam, those earrings - just where did you get them from?'

Feeling bold with the consumption of alcohol and the promise of Gus waiting for her in the night, Sam laughed. 'Not that it's any of your business Sir, but they were a gift.'

Sam went to leave, but gave a small cry of shock as Mr Webster grabbed her tighter by the arm.

'Was it Gus? Was it?'

Sam pulled away as Mr Webster continued. 'You should know that those earrings were not his to give.'

Pulling away, Sam looked at Mr Webster and shook her head before running through the door to join Gus. Why did everyone always try and spoil things for her? Without a backwards glance, she joined Gus and enjoyed the feel of his arm around her shoulder, the warmth of his body next to hers, as he led her towards the cliff path.

72

Alex

Present day: Saturday, 17 August

Alex wants to be anywhere but here. Gus had caught him up on the cliff path. It was his own fault as he had dawdled, sitting smoking a sneaky cigarette and draining the dregs of the vodka he had swiped, whilst he waited to see if Mark would reply to his message. Normally he would have been happy to turn up unannounced. It wasn't anything he had ever had to think about, secure in the knowledge that he was always welcome at home. But now he was uncertain of everything - not even sure where his home was.

When he had heard a man's voice shouting his name, he had felt a rush of relief and happiness, thinking for a moment that Mark had come to find him - to tell him everything was going to be alright. But then he recognised the figure of Gus, his new father, and had a sickening realisation all over again that with Gus, he didn't feel safe at all.

At first, he had been so carried away on the fantasy come true of finding his real dad, that he had been blind to anything else. But as the days went on, he had started to have a funny feeling, and realised the truth was he didn't like this stranger at all. He didn't like the way Gus sometimes studied his mum when he thought no one was looking. Not a look full of love, but a look which Alex struggled to interpret. At first, he thought it was puzzlement, which figured because he certainly had never understood his mum. But in the middle of the night, as his brain refused to switch off to allow him a rest from the feeling that he was living on the edge of a drop from which he could fall at any moment, he suddenly realised what it was. Gus looked at his mum the same way that Grace looked at the solitary sprout on her plate at Christmas dinner. Like she didn't want it to be there. That she knew she had to because it was a necessary part of the Christmas tradition, but she still felt slightly sickened at the fact that it was there. Which just didn't make any sense at all, seeing as it was supposed to be Caro and Gus - the great love story.

With all that swirling in his head, Gus is the last person he wants to see striding towards him, calling his name and looking cross, rather than relieved to have found him.

'What are you up to then, Alex? Your mum is fretting about you. Come on, let's head back to the farmhouse.'

Alex wanted to stand his ground. He wanted to calmly tell Gus that he is on his way to see Mark - that there is no need for his mum to worry. She hadn't been that worried about him when she had been obsessed with reconnecting with Gus. But Alex found that the words are caught in his throat. He doesn't want to antagonise Gus any further and he senses that the man next to him seems to be quivering with tension, as if he is just itching for a fight. He decides the best thing to do is to follow Gus back to the house, and he can reach out to Mark in the morning. Things might not seem so dark and scary then.

The path is narrow so the two walk silently in single file, with Alex becoming more anxious as he finds he is completely disorientated. He is sure they should have turned off a while back. They don't seem to be heading inland, where the thought of a comfortable bed and his mum fussing round him seems so appealing, but instead are heading towards the quarry. And that is so far from where he wants to be, with this sullen man striding grimly ahead, that Alex just wants to cry and for his mum and Mark to come and tell him everything is going to be just fine.

73

Caro

Present day: Saturday, 17 August

Caro wants to shout to Mark to wait for her, but she can't catch her breath to allow the plea to leave her lips. Instead, she concentrates on moving as fast as she can seeing that, despite her best-efforts, Mark is getting further away from her. Suddenly, she nearly runs into the back of him and is about to ask him what the hell he is playing at, when she sees he is transfixed by the sight of Alex and Gus stood facing them.

For a moment she is filled with relief that they have found them, and that Alex is safe; but then she sees they are stood at the edge of the quarry - far too close to the edge of the quarry. Gus is holding Alex's arm in a grip that doesn't look to be friendly, and Alex is trembling. Something about all of this is dreadfully wrong.

Mark is clearly thinking the same, as he holds out a hand and calmly speaks.

'Pleased we have found the pair of you. Alex come over here, away from the edge. I think we will all be pleased to get home tonight, and I for one could do with a drink. I've got a nice bottle of whisky at home Gus, if I can tempt you to join me for a glass.'

Caro marvels at the steadiness of Mark's voice - at the fact he sounds as if he would like nothing better for this man, who he despises, to come and sit in his house and drink his whisky. For a moment Gus seems to relax, and Alex makes a move towards Mark. But Gus pulls him back with a yank that sends his feet skidding and small pebbles tumbling over the edge. It seems that time slows down for them to count the endless seconds it takes for the stones to make the fatal fall to the bottom.

'Careful!' Caro can't stop the cry of alarm, and she feels Mark's hand close around hers in an attempt to calm her.

'No need to worry Caro, they are being careful. Gus knows this area and wouldn't do anything to put his son in danger.'

Caro bites her lip and nods, but she thinks Gus looks like he is capable of anything at this point.

'Your darling soon to be ex-wife doesn't look convinced, Mark. I'm not sure she thinks I am a nice man. I saw you'd managed to get on the Wi-Fi, so I'm guessing you had a good root around in my office, dear. That is unfortunate because I'm guessing you may have read a bit more of what your father had to say to me, and I'm not sure I can rely on you to keep that to yourself.'

Caro can't help the swift glance towards Mark. Gus notices and gives a harsh bark of laughter. 'As I thought; no doubt you've already tattled to good old Mr Reliable here, so now it's only a matter of time until you tell Nat - who will be the first to tell you to call the police. After you've promised her an exclusive, of course!'

When Mark speaks next his voice is calm, but Caro can see his hands are shaking.

'Look, it's been a long night. Let's get back home and we can sort all of this out in the morning. In fact, we don't need to sort anything out. We can all just forget tonight ever happened and life can continue - no need to get anyone else involved. Isn't that right, Caro?'

Caro nods frantically in agreement but understands Gus is unlikely to be fooled by this sentiment. He must know that there is no way she will keep quiet about his involvement in the disappearance of Sam.

As if reading her mind, Gus gives another unpleasant laugh that seems to echo around the stillness of the night air, taking up all the space. 'That's a jolly nice sentiment Mark, but we all know it's a load of bollocks. The first thing you'll do when you leave here is call the police, and they will then try to destroy my family. I let Chris tear us apart seventeen years ago, but I'm not going to repeat that mistake.'

Caro moves towards Mark and touches his arm, trying to signal that there's no point talking to Gus. He has lost his mind – it's the only explanation. She can see the tears on Alex's face, and she knows she will do anything to stop anyone hurting her son. Gus is inching back towards the edge and Caro can't stop the cry that escapes her lips. Alex seems to come to life at the sound and starts to fight against the man who seems intent on taking him over the edge.

'Keep still, Alex! It will be over in a second and it won't be too long before Jen joins us, and we can be a family at last.'

For a second Gus is distracted by his attempts to restrain Alex. Whilst Gus is considerably stronger, fear has given Alex the extra edge as he struggles to be free of the man and for a moment it looks like he will slip away from danger. Gus concentrates all his efforts on keeping his son in his grasp, determined to take him with him to whatever fantasy he has designed over all these years. Caro darts forward, willing to sacrifice herself to save her boy. But she is too late. Mark leaps forward with a roar. 'He already has a family, you sick bastard!'

Gus loosens his grip just enough for Alex to break free and shove past the man, before running to the safety of Caro's hug. They watch in horror as Gus and Mark struggle on the edge, before both disappear from sight, crashing down to the rocks below.

74

Alex

Present day: Tuesday, 3 September

Alex is sat by his father's bed, chatting to him about all the things they will do when he is out of the hospital. Caro worries that he doesn't understand that Mark has a long road ahead. Ironically, his fall had been cushioned by landing on Gus - which had likely saved his life - though it had been touch and go for a few days.

Alex doesn't remember much about that night. He does remember feeling safe for the first time in quite a while, despite the horror that was unfolding around them. His mum had looked pale but determined as she had calmly taken out her phone and dialled 999. Alex had wanted to look over the edge, but his mum had held him back. Not knowing what else to do, he had sat on the floor shivering, counting silently in his head until he heard the distant sound of the sirens and the night became alive with the flashing blue lights and the urgent clamour of strange voices.

James had arrived shortly after and had ushered Alex and his mum back to the Beach Hut, where Nat made them hot chocolate and treated him like he was five years old again. Alex found that he liked this, being looked after. It was only an hour or so, but seemed much longer, before there was a knock on the door and a grim-faced DI Gillingham came in. She had explained there was one fatality but one survivor, and all Alex could think was, '*Please let my dad be alive, please let my dad be alive. I can't lose him, not now we've just found each other again.*'

He heard his mum's gasp of relief as the police confirmed Gus was dead, and he thought his own heart would burst as he realised his desperate plea bargaining had been heard. Mark, the man who had shown himself to be his father, was alive and Alex had a chance to make things right between the two of them. He hated to think of all the time he had wasted searching for his 'real' dad, when it turned out the father he needed to love and protect him was there all along.

Now he sits by his dad every day, sometimes alone, sometimes with Grace and his mum, and he doesn't resent that when Grace visits, all eyes are on her. He knows he is loved, and he is secure in this family – Mark proved his love out there at the quarry - and promises himself he will spend his life trying to be everything Mark would like him to be. Like father, like son.

75

Caro

Present day: Tuesday, 3 September

Caro hopes that the memories of that night will fade as time goes on. For now, whilst the events are still a muddled blur, she continues to be haunted by the moment when she realised just who Gus was, and knew without a doubt that she was about to lose her son forever. She will never be able to tell Mark just how grateful she is for what he did. She only hopes that in time he can forgive her, and they can be a family again. For now, it is enough that those she loves most in the world are safe.

She had spent hours talking to the police, piecing together the events of that night and the events of seventeen years ago. It seems there was no doubt Gus had pushed Sam Chappell to her death after she had stumbled on the truth of the relationship between him and Jen Webster. The police were taking the view that Gus had acted alone, and Caro knew she had spun the story to imply it was almost a schoolboy crush, unreciprocated, that had spiralled into an obsession verging on madness. The police seemed to accept this version, though she could see DI Gillingham watching her, a query in her eyes that indicated the woman knew there was more to this story than would ever be shared beyond the surviving circle of three that were there that night.

Caro is relieved that her dad is not alive to have to hear the whispers that follow her around the town. She doesn't know if he would have been able to live with the knowledge of the woman his wife was. Now it is time to concentrate on the living and to build on the strong foundations that had been forged that night on the rocks of the quarry. Because, when it comes down to it, family is everything.

76

Nat

Present day: Tuesday, 3 September

Nat sits in her car at the entrance of the nursing home, debating whether she can risk a final visit to Jen Webster. She had filed the last piece on the disappearance of Sam Chappell: the mystery finally solved. A rather bland piece in the end that chose to let the main characters of the story maintain the lie. Nat really didn't feel she could do anything different. She had wanted to talk to Kate, but the bungalow was shuttered up and a neighbour told her Kate had decided to go away for a while. Nat had wanted to ask if there was any way to contact her, but the look in the woman's eyes made her swallow back the words and her face flamed red as she tried to reach the safety of her car before the tears came.

There is no danger of bumping into Caro visiting her mum. After the horrific events of that night two weeks ago, Caro has vowed her mum is dead to her. Nat had caught Caro burning the missing pages of the letter her father had written to Gus. She guessed that Chris Webster had been aware of the truth all those years ago but had chosen to protect his family and keep quiet. His death had allowed the monster to return to their lives.

Deciding she has nothing to say to Jen - because what is there to say? - Nat instead makes her way to the office. Logging on her computer to write a feature on a planned litter pick at the beach, she realises she will always have her own share of guilt to carry. It was her visit to Jen Webster that had started her own obsession with the Sam Chappell mystery. She had only been at the nursing home to drop some toiletries off for Jen. Caro had been snowed under with the funeral arrangements, and it seemed such a small task that would help. How Nat wishes she had never stepped foot in the place.

She could have just dropped the bits off at the office, but she had felt sorry for Jen, living in her own little world where she wasn't even aware that the husband who adored her wouldn't be coming to visit anymore. Feeling rather virtuous, she had decided to stick her head round the door and say hello.

Jen hadn't known who she was, and Nat wasn't even sure she was aware there was someone in the room with her. She was just whispering the same thing over and over. 'He did it for me, you know. He knew it would destroy him. Living with the horror of what he'd done. But he did it anyway. That's how much he loved me. Silly little child, but he did it for me, you know…'

Nat had stood horrified, because she assumed Jen was talking about Sam Chappell. And she thought she knew that Jen was talking about her husband. After all, she had eavesdropped on her parents whispering that it was a hell of a coincidence - Jez killing himself just after Sam disappeared without trace. She thought lots of people probably said the same thing at the time, just not out loud!

She had created that anonymous account and started the nasty little posts on the Facebook group. Just to try and get people talking again. To get to the truth. She hadn't meant any harm, but she had got it all wrong and almost destroyed the memory of a man who had acted foolishly but had acted out of love. Poor Chris Webster. What a burden to have carried for all these years. And now Nat will live the rest of her life carrying her own little secret. It doesn't feel very good at all.

77

Chris

Seventeen years earlier: Saturday, 25 August

Chris Webster was a man in turmoil. There was no doubt in his mind that Gus had something to do with the disappearance of Sam, and he feared the absolute worst. In some ways, he hoped she was dead; that way she couldn't tell the secret that wasn't hers to tell.

Chris had always been aware that his wife had some major character faults. Whilst he loved her unconditionally, it seemed she was always looking for something. Something that her life with Chris and the children couldn't give her. And for some time, he feared that she thought she had found what she was looking for in Gus.

Night after night he lay awake, fretting that things were getting out of hand, but in the cold morning light he would tell himself he was being ridiculous - Gus was barely more than a child. But then Jez had come to see him in tears, clearly not knowing what to do but wanting his father to reassure him about what he had seen his mother and Gus doing in the dunes. That damn telescope!

Chris had spoken to him, laughed and told him it was all fine - nothing to worry about. But he had seen the way Jez had started looking at his mother and caught the sideways glances his son threw his way. The glance that was no longer filled with admiration, but which held a tinge of doubt - judgement even - with the knowledge that his father was not the man he thought he was.

Things had come to a head on the night of the leavers' ball. Chris was amazed that no one else seemed to notice, or maybe they were just too polite to say anything. He hated the fact that people may have been sniggering at him behind his back. Jen looked gorgeous that night, but instead of feeling proud that she was his wife, that she had chosen him, Chris was gripped by the fear that all this was about to be snatched away from him. At one point he had grabbed her as she made her way to the ladies and had hissed a warning in her ear. She was drunk, and for a moment he feared he had pushed her too far, but then the light seemed to leave her eyes, and she nodded in agreement. Twenty minutes later she had whispered she was going home, that she had a bad headache and that she was sorry. Chris had offered to call her a cab, but she said the fresh air would help her. Chris wished he had not accepted her words at face value, but he was so overwhelmed that for tonight at least she was still safely his, that he had watched her go with relief. A relief that was short-lived once he saw Sam Chappell wearing earrings that undoubtedly were his anniversary gift to Jen. He knew then that Gus had given those earrings to Sam - just as he knew Jen had given those earrings, the symbol of their love, to the man she now saw as her new future. He had felt sick to the stomach, and vowed tomorrow he would sort this all out - put a stop to it and try and rebuild his family.

The night had passed by smoothly after that, and he hadn't had chance to think about his wife and Gus because Kate Chappell had arrived and the whole nightmare had started. At first, he thought it was all a bit of unnecessary drama, but then she had hammered on the Beach Hut door in the early hours, and the flashing blue lights brought more fear and chaos than Chris had ever known. Jen was actually quite helpful, making tea and quietly preparing food. Chris knew something wasn't right - his wife had never missed the opportunity to make a drama out of a crisis, the chance to make it all about her, but he chose to believe they were heading for calmer waters. Maybe Jen had realised she had pushed things too far this time and was quietly making amends. At least, that was what he thought he could believe, until he saw that she had a single diamond stud in her jewellery case - almost like a trophy - and he was sick to the stomach with the realisation that Gus had given it to her. Proof of what he would do for the woman he loved.

As the days passed, life fell into a new routine - which really consisted of just waiting. Chris wasn't used to this. He was a man used to being in charge, of getting things done. Instead he was forced to simply sit, dependent on the crumbs of information the family liaison threw their way. Chris knew he was being unfair when he snapped at the man to give them something useful. There was simply nothing to say.

Then the hours had turned to days and then a week. Kate had gone home; the tabloid press had moved on to stories that had a bit more going on, and slowly life in Roxcliffe was returning to normal. Chris supposed this was now his new normal and thought he should start to prepare for the new term. Instead, he took to wandering aimlessly in the dunes, enjoying the escape, breathing in the sounds and smell of the sea he loved so much. He told himself this chosen solitude was to clear his muddled brain so he could be more use to those who so clearly needed him. Afterwards, he wondered if the truth was that part of him knew he was somehow responsible for what was happening to the Chappel family. Not directly of course, but his silence made him complicit and so, even early on, he was struggling to look Kate Chappel in the eye as he repeated the worthless platitude that everything would turn out just fine. The truth he couldn't acknowledge was that he couldn't bear to be near his wife, knowing what she was.

When he saw his son running towards him across the

dunes, he thought for a glorious moment that Sam had turned up. For a second he vowed they would move away from this place, make a fresh start and he would tell Jen to either commit to the family or they would part and go their own ways. He couldn't continue living like this. Then he saw the tears streaking down his son's face and knew his world was about to change yet again.

Afterwards, he thought how he had wished Jez had been so distraught as he was bearing the news that Sam had been found dead. Chris knew this was deeply selfish, but he would have given anything for the discovery of Sam's body to be the cause of his son's deep distress. Jez had thrown himself into his dad's arms and clung to him in a way he hadn't done for a few years now. Chris held him tight, realising with a shock how skinny his son felt, and recognising that Jez needed his dad. When the words eventually came, Chris didn't want to make sense of them.

The two of them sat on the warm sand and Chris felt his heart split in two and his stomach fill with an ice cold dread, as his son told him Jen was wearing Sam's bracelet. That he had seen Gus give it to her earlier that day. That it was definitely Sam's, because she had hung a little charm pendant dolphin from the leather to make it her own. Chris had whispered some meaningless platitudes to his son how everything would be OK, that there was bound to be some sensible explanation, that he would sort it out. Then, with the instructions to not say anything about this to anyone else, Chris sent his son on his way.

Resolute, he knew what needed to be done. Chris would not allow his family to be ripped apart. He had headed straight back to the Beach Hut and confronted Jen. At first she had taunted him, until he had pointed out what people would say about her - a desperate old woman forcing Gus to kill for her. That her life going forward would be people whispering behind her back as she waited for visiting times to see her young lover, who would spend the rest of his life in prison. This was of course after she had served her own sentence for whatever part she had played in the whole sordid affair. Then she cried, begged him for his silence, told him she would never betray him again. She had handed over the bracelet and earring and he had thrown the dolphin charm into the ocean. The bracelet was then just like any other trinket that had been sold that summer from the pop-up stalls by the harbour. A bit of cheap tat that he consigned to the kitchen bin. But the earring, he couldn't bear to part with. A memory of the best and worst of times. This he hid in his little box of shame.

He had gone to see Gus and given him the letter. Told Jez that the matter was sorted - just a misunderstanding. The bracelet wasn't Sam's, and it was terribly sad she was missing but they needed to try and move on with their lives. He tried to pretend that his son believed him. He would feel sick every time he saw Kate Chappel and asked her if there was any news, knowing but not knowing the truth of the matter.

On that last day of his life as the father to two living children, he had been working at the school - half-heartedly reviewing the new timetable and signing off on a pile of invoices for the building maintenance carried out over the summer. He had sat in with the bursar as they discussed the proposed fee increases and the effect on pupil numbers, and for a while had felt that maybe life could continue as before.

When he had let himself into the house, he had thought he was the only one there and was about to settle down with a well-deserved whisky, when he heard a noise from the bedroom above. At first, he was filled with a rage that Jen had let him down again, had sneaked Gus into their bed whilst he was working to give her every material thing she wanted; but then he recognised the sound was one of distress, rather than passion. The sound suddenly stopped, and for a moment Chris wondered if he'd imagined it. After all, he imagined Jen and Gus together most of the time; it was like a reel in his head that refused to stop playing over and over.

He was roused from his private hell by a crash upstairs, and he reluctantly got to his feet to investigate. The sight that met him would haunt him for the rest of his life. His son had tied a rope round his neck and kicked away the chair that was keeping him in this world. In his hand was that bloody bracelet, retrieved from the rotten discards of their life. His feet were dancing in a crazy dance that Chris would think afterwards was a grotesque mimicry of the Irish dancing they had so admired one year on the TV.

For a second Chris froze. This was the moment he should have rushed in - supported his boy, taken him to the hospital and told everyone what had led his boy to this terrible act. That's what Chris should have done, but he wanted Jen, and maybe the loss of his son was the price he had to pay to the gods to let him keep this woman who consumed him. Chris didn't even need to think about it; he simply turned and walked away.

ACKNOWLEDGEMENT

Thank you to every one who has taken a chance on reading this book. It always feels strange that the words I have hugged close to me for so long, are finally out there in the world.

I'm lucky that my family are my greatest cheerleaders, so thank you Ian, Charlotte and Ben.

ABOUT THE AUTHOR

Sarah Jones

Following a degree in Theology from Durham University and a successful career in the world of finance, Sarah saw the opportunity to take early retirement and fulfil her lifelong ambition to write a book.

Fascinated by people watching and amateur detective work via social media, these pastimes form the basis of the unsettling stories Sarah writes.

Sarah lives with her family and dogs in rural North Yorkshire and completed her debut psychological thriller, A False Reflection, in 2024. Family Traits is her second novel and she is now working on the first instalment of an exciting new series.

Instagram: @sarahjoneswrites
Facebook: Sarah Jones Writes
Website: www.sarahjoneswrites.co.uk

BOOKS BY THIS AUTHOR

A False Reflection

Family Traits

Printed in Dunstable, United Kingdom

THE WEREWOLF DELUSION

THE WEREWOLF DELUSION

Ian Woodward

Paddington Press Ltd
New York and London

Library of Congress Cataloging in Publication Data
Woodward, Ian, 1941-
    The werewolf delusion.

    Bibliography: p. 244
    Includes index.
    1. Werewolves. I. Title.
GR830.W4W66   001.9'44   78-21699
ISBN 0-448-23170-0 (U.S. and Canada only)
ISBN 0 7092 0873 1

Copyright © 1979 Ian Woodward
All rights reserved
Filmset in England by SX Composing Ltd., Rayleigh, Essex
Printed and bound in the United States
Designed by Sandra Shafee

IN THE UNITED STATES
PADDINGTON PRESS
Distributed by
GROSSET & DUNLAP

IN THE UNITED KINGDOM
PADDINGTON PRESS

IN CANADA
Distributed by
RANDOM HOUSE OF CANADA LTD.

IN SOUTHERN AFRICA
Distributed by
ERNEST STANTON (PUBLISHERS) (PTY.) LTD.

IN AUSTRALIA AND NEW ZEALAND
Distributed by
A. H. & A. W. REED

Contents

INTRODUCTION *11*

1   A Dreadful Superstition   *14*

2   Wolf Nature:
Its Ancestry and Superstitions   *30*

3   The Werewolf Symptom:
How to Recognize a Werewolf   *42*

4   Delusions, Dreams and Hallucinations   *58*

5   The Werewolf in Antiquity   *69*

6   Servant of Witchcraft and The Devil   *80*

7   Torture, Trial and Execution   *96*

8 Man into Wolf – Wolf into Man   *113*

9 "The Devil is Exceedingly Chastised":
   Cure and Exorcism   *136*

10 The Vampire Connection   *147*

11 Bloodlust   *156*

12 Rabies and the Werewolf:
    A Case of Mistaken Identity?   *162*

13 A Bizarre Contradiction of Terms   *169*

14 "An Unsettling Display of Bare-Chested Lycanthropy":
    The Werewolf in Literature   *174*

15 A Mere Twist of Fact:
    Wolfman and The Cinema   *191*

16 The Commercial Werewolf *205*

17 Were-Animals *208*

18 A Chamber of Global Horrors *221*

19 Fact or Fancy? *236*

APPENDIX:

What's in a Name? *238*

FURTHER READING *244*

PICTURE CREDITS *247*

ACKNOWLEDGMENTS *249*

INDEX *251*

Oh! ye immortal Gods! What is Theogony?
    Oh! thou, too, mortal man! what is Philosophy?
Oh! World, which was and is, what is Cosmogony?
    Some people have accused me of Misanthropy;
And yet I know no more than the mahogany
    That forms this desk, of what they mean; – Lycanthropy
I comprehend, for without transformation
Men become wolves on any slight occasion.

                    BYRON: *Don Juan*

Introduction

"Werewolf!"

HOW THE WORD STRIKES DEEP into the imagination of the Western peoples. How it impresses itself upon our common speech and, like the word "vampire," sends fearful chills down our spines at its very mention. The werewolf, inescapably, is synonymous with something grim and awful, a specter terrible to behold and dangerous to mind and body. Of this, as the story which is about to unfold will demonstrate, there is no shadow of doubt.

The fear of werewolves is universal; although werewolfery reached its peak of horror during the Middle Ages, it has never quite lost its ancient power to shock the senses and make the blood run cold. In secluded areas of France, Germany, Scandinavia, Eastern Europe and elsewhere, the superstition and heart-sinking terror which surround the werewolf legend can still shock people to the marrow. Yet today, with society generally being both more skeptical and enlightened, people are more inclined to *question* the tales they hear. That is good.

Stories of men capable and willing to transform themselves into animals, and most frequently into wolves, have been told for thousands of years. The first known traces of them are to be found mingled with the pagan sorceries which abound in the writings of the old poets of Greece and Rome, and there have since been, right up to the present, accounts of the werewolf's foul deeds. Once transformed, the only instinct of these monsters is to ravage and devour human victims. They thirst in particular for youthful blood, and carry off children and women with reckless audacity.

The means by which their transformations take place are as involved as they are bizarre. An association with black magic and the Devil, and the use of all manner of occultist ceremonies, incantations, potions, unguents, garments, lycanthropous water and spells form a vital part of the werewolf's foul life-style. To comprehend the werewolf mystery spiritualism, theosophy, the church, cannibalism, rabies, satanism, psychiatric medicine, and an understanding of the ancient mind must all be investigated. Many people today believe that the archetypal werewolf of the past was a creature which existed on what the theosophists refer to as "an astral level." This means that if an utterly depraved person was to use the technique of astral projection his body could be seized upon by astral entities and materialized, or made solid, not into human form but into that of an animal, usually the wolf. Astral projection is a very real technique about which there has been much research; but for those unfamiliar with it in the past, it could have disastrous effects.

The hunt of the werewolves, the obligatory torturing sessions, the trials and inevitable executions at the stake – they were burned to prevent them becoming vampires after death – constitute one of the most gruesome and fascinating aspects of the werewolf saga. Many of those who stood trial were genuinely deluded into believing that, at certain periods, they could transform themselves into wolves (whereas in fact their *physical shape* never changed); these poor souls were in reality victims of the terrible mental ailment known as lycanthropia, or lycanthropy. Most of those who were hauled before the courts not only swore that, with the help of the Devil and special potions and animal girdles, they could metamorphose into the shape of wolves, but witnesses also testified to that effect. A peculiarity of these trials, it needs to be said immediately, was the vast number of prisoners who confessed so readily to crimes of werewolfery that were more than likely never committed. Torture accounts for many such "confessions." And as for "witnesses" – well, how easy it was to make false accusations, to fabricate "evidence" and by so doing conspire to have the accused convicted and executed. In one period of little over a hundred years a staggering 30,000 cases of werewolfery were recorded in France alone, and the mind literally quails at the thought of how many innocent people went to their deaths for no other reason than the fact that a vindictive neighbor had trumped up some wild allegation of werewolfery against them.

Yet, as many experts today agree, there can be little doubt that the werewolf as a psychic phenomenon could, did, and perhaps still does exist. What superstition, one that is a thousand years or so older than Christianity, could survive to the present day if there were not a germ of truth somewhere? For there are as many reasons why the werewolf could have existed as there are reasons why it could not. All authors who write of the supernatural are in effect voicing their curiosity about its existence, no matter how vociferously they declare their skepticism along the way.

Being curious as well as skeptical of the werewolf legend, and greatly aware that thousands of years of ignorance have clouded even our most basic understanding of the subject, I decided to try, once and for all, to expose the myth and disentangle fact from fancy. My researches have taken me all over the world, and the project has proved to be one of the most engrossing courses of investigation I have ever undertaken. The supernatural sphere of the werewolf is known throughout the world, and so I wanted to know what it was about the phenomenon that still enabled it to exert such a powerful and chilling influence over people. I was fired by a deep compulsion to find out and then to write *The Werewolf Delusion*.

So why should men wish to practice the vile art of werewolfery? A vexed question, the answer to which may possibly be found in the narrative which lies before you. It can in any case be said with conviction that no other branch of the occult, save the main artery of witchcraft itself, has so dramatically asserted its damnable influence on man. But as to the *whys?* and *wherefores?* – who knows, who rightly knows? Perhaps, as the Belgian poet-dramatist Maurice Maeterlinck observes of the supernatural, we should not search for rhyme or reason, but simply acknowledge that it *is*.

1 A Dreadful Superstition

OR SEVERAL DAYS during the bleak winter of 1521, the oak-timbered courtroom in the old French city of Besançon was packed to the rafters. Locals, and others from all around the diocese, flocked to witness what was to become one of the most notorious trials of werewolfery ever put before the public. Even for a period in history when hundreds were sent to trial for practicing black arts and consorting with the Devil, and punished in most instances by being burned alive or broken on the wheel, the trial of Pierre Bourgot and Michel Verdung remains unsurpassed in blood-curdling repulsiveness.

The Inquisitor-General of Besançon, Maître Jean Boin, heard how Bourgot and Verdung, after transforming themselves into werewolves, set out to wage a series of unspeakable atrocities on the community. Under cross-examination, Bourgot, a shepherd, confessed that nineteen years earlier a terrible storm scattered his sheep over a wide area. As he went to look for them he was approached by three black horsemen. One of them asked, "Where are you going, my friend? You appear to be in trouble." Bourgot explained that he was looking for his sheep. "Take courage," said the horseman. "If you show faith, my Master will protect the straying sheep and see that no harm comes to them."

They agreed to meet again in four or five days, and soon after he found all his sheep safely in one place. He then learned that the black horseman was a servant of the Devil. If Pierre served him likewise, said the stranger, his flock would be given his Master's complete protection, and Pierre would be provided with money.

Pierre Bourgot then told the court:

> I foreswore God and our Lady and all saints and dwellers in Paradise. I renounced Christianity, kissed his left hand, which was black and ice-cold as that of a corpse. Then I fell on my knees and gave in my allegiance to Satan. I remained in the service of the Devil for two years, and never entered a church before the end of Mass, or at all events till the holy water had been

sprinkled, according to the desire of my master, whose name I afterwards learned was Moyset.

All anxiety about my flock was removed, for the Devil had undertaken to protect it and keep off the wolves. This freedom from care, however, made me begin to tire of the Devil's service, and I recommenced my attendance at church, till I was brought back into obedience to the evil one by Michel Verdung, when I renewed my compact on the understanding that I should be supplied with money.

In a wood near Chastel Charnon we met with many others whom I recognized; we danced, and each had in his or her hand a green candle with a blue flame. Still under the delusion that I should obtain money, Michel persuaded me to move with the greatest celerity, and in order to do this, after I had stripped myself, he smeared me with a salve, and I believed myself then to be transformed into a wolf.

I was at first somewhat horrified at my four wolf's feet and the fur with which I was suddenly covered, but I found that I could now travel with the speed of the wind. This could not have taken place without the help of our powerful master, who was present during our excursion, though I did not perceive him till I had recovered my human form. Michel did the same as myself.

When we had been one or two hours in this condition of metamorphosis, Michel smeared us again, and quick as thought we resumed our human forms. The

A man looks on, terror-struck, while his friend is attacked by a werewolf, in this sixteenth-century woodcut from Johann Geiler von Kaisersberg's *Die Emeis* (1516).

In search of human blood and flesh, this werewolf – and it could easily be Bourgot or Verdung – pounces on an unsuspecting traveler. A nineteenth-century illustration by Maurice Sand.

salve was given us by our masters; to me it was given by Moyset, to Michel by his own master, Guillemin.

The judge and the crammed courtroom then heard that after this first attempt Bourgot and Verdung frequently transformed themselves into werewolves. On one occasion, said Bourgot, they attacked and tore to pieces a boy of seven, but because the child screamed so loudly they were forced to beat a hasty retreat. Shortly afterwards, in a nearby field, they attacked and savagely mutilated a woman who was collecting peas; and when a M. de Chusnée came to her rescue, he was similarly attacked and killed. Their lust for blood and palpitating flesh became more and more intense and, consequently, more gruesome.

One day, as werewolves, they came across a little girl of four years old, and pitilessly consumed every ounce of her warm body, with the exception of one arm. "Michel thought the girl's flesh particularly delicious," Bourgot told the court, "although it gave him indigestion."

Later they pounced on another little girl, strangled her mercilessly, and lapped up her blood. They repeated this type of foul crime a great many times, said Bourgot, because they were particularly fond of consuming warm flowing blood. Sometimes they appeared to commit their disgusting deeds as "a form of play" and on these occasions they would either leave the body un-eaten or else eat only a portion of the stomach.

Bourgot's confessed crimes were apparently boundless. He recounted how, one evening at dusk, he leaped over a garden wall to prey upon a girl of eight or nine who was weeding the flower beds. He told how she went down on her knees and begged him not to harm her and how he ignored her pleas. Instead he cracked the girl's neck between his keen white teeth, tore out her throat, and left her corpse quivering among her flowers.

Neither were their odious crimes restricted to the human population of the area. Bourgot described how they killed a goat near to the farm of one Pierre Lerugen, by setting on it with their teeth and eating the raw flesh. There were many confessions like this. They also delighted, said Bourgot, in having intercourse with she-wolves, deriving more pleasure from this coupling than in the natural entering of women.

An interesting point which came to light during the trial – at which, incidentally, Pierre Bourgot's confessions were fully corroborated by Michel Verdung – was that Verdung could apparently transform himself at will with his clothes on, whereas Bourgot had to strip (the classic course) and rub in ointment to achieve the same result. The whole heinous business only came to light by accident. In his werewolf form, Verdung attacked a traveler who, in turn, wounded the animal, which fled into the undergrowth. The traveler followed the blood, which took him to a hut where Verdung – who by now had resumed his human form – was having his wound bathed by his wife.

With a third werewolf named Philibert Montot, Bourgot and Verdung were duly executed for the trail of bloodshed they inflicted on a fear-struck community. Pictures of the three werewolves were subsequently hung in the Jacobin Church at nearby Poligny. France, once more, had rid herself of the dreaded werewolf . . . but not for long.

Bourgot and Verdung were but two examples of a dreadful condition which plagued not only France but all of Europe and elsewhere, and even today the werewolf still strikes terror in the hearts of people in many countries. The irrefutable fact is that half the world believes, or believed, in a curious psychic phenomenon, the werewolf – a wretched person who has been cursed with the power of transforming himself into a wolf and who possesses, while in the lupine state, the intelligence of a man, the ferocity of a wolf, and the irresistible strength of a demon. In this condition he feels obliged to go in search of blood and flesh, usually human. Like the werewolf's first cousin, the vampire, he might become a werewolf as a curse from God, or be an innocent victim, or suffer from an atavistic tendency, such as a cannibalistic craving for blood. Like the vampire, too, the werewolf is under a curse that impels him to prey upon those dearest to him. He is controlled by a demonic spirit. The human being who, in his normal personality, is kindly and gentle, becomes a jungle beast with ravening instincts.

The wild and howling night winds may have given the first notion of demon wolves to the trembling listener as they passed shrieking by his solitary tent or hut. Our fear of the "wolf creature" is almost certainly instinctive and deep-rooted in the subconscious, while the old, primitive belief in the werewolf itself spans the globe. There are few cultures where stories of the transformation of a living human being into an animal do not exist. Usually it will be transformation into a wolf in regions where the wolf is or was common; into a lion, hyena or leopard in Africa, where these animals are common; into a tiger or serpent in India; and, in other localities, into those animals characteristic of the region. Most universal, though, is the transformation of man into wolf.

In his great narrative work *Metamorphoses*, written two thousand years ago, the Roman poet Ovid recounted many legends involving the miraculous transformation of man into beast, from the Creation to the age of Julius Caesar. He vividly describes stories of men who roamed the woods around Arcadia in the form of wolves. Much later,

The Roman poet Ovid was one of the most prolific and enthusiastic chroniclers of the ancient werewolf stories. Even so, he was merely *retelling* the legends he had learned from earlier authors.

between 1520 and 1630, there were 30,000 recorded cases of werewolves in France alone. And as recently as 1975, newspapers in Britain were reporting the macabre case of the seventeen-year-old boy who believed himself to be a werewolf.

Certainly the werewolf tradition is long and curious and littered with much that smacks of the fanciful and preposterous. The "werewolf delusion" – my own term for a terrible hypochondriacal condition in which the patient believes irrationally and falsely that he is transformed into a ravening beast – is doubtless purely mythical in its origin; although in its developed state it is composed of a curious and overpowering mixture of mythical, historical and psychological elements. On the other hand, the belief *is* supported by a vast amount of evidence which can neither be argued nor laughed out of court.

A definition, now, of what is generally meant when people refer to a *werewolf* and a *lycanthrope*.

"Lycanthropy" is a Greek word formed from "wolf" and "humanity" which initially became used in connection with the dreadful folklore of men converted into werewolves. Most psychiatrists today regard lycanthropia as a fundamental delusion. So a lycanthrope is a human being who, on account of some peculiar twist of insanity, believes himself to be a wolf and acts accordingly. He refuses to eat anything but raw, bloody meat, he lets out hair-raising bestial howls and indulges in unrestrained sexual attacks on any victim he can overpower. Physically, he retains his human form, but mentally he is suffering from wolf-madness. Many lycanthropes experience dreams where transformation, bloodshed and diabolical murder are principal themes. Again, the person remains in his human shape while asleep, although in his dream a psychic "transformation" takes place. The grim horror of it all is subsequently retained in the patient's psyche during his non-sleeping hours. The seventeen-year-old youth described later in this chapter was, in essence, a lycanthrope.

The origins of the term "werewolf" are explained fully in the Appendix to this book, but as it is commonly understood a werewolf is a human being who either voluntarily or involuntarily is transformed into the apparent shape of a wolf. In this form he displays the characteristic ferocity, appetite, strength, cunning and swiftness of that animal. He remains in this shape usually for the duration of an evening, but sometimes longer or shorter – and occasionally permanently. The ability to metamorphose into animal form is customarily effected in the first place by the initiate calling on the help of the Devil and black magic and by the liberal use of special potions, unguents,

Illuminated capital "L" from Henry Boguet's *Discours des Sorciers* (1590), which, as part of the decoration, depicts a sufferer of lycanthropy.

An early werewolf illustration, taken from Comestor's thirteenth-century bestiary manuscript, *Historica Scholastica*.

animal skins and incantations. In the Middle Ages it was held that while the werewolf was in his human form the hair grew inwards; transformation was achieved – or so it was supposed – by turning himself inside out.

Both the werewolf and the lycanthrope undoubtedly exist, or existed, although our present knowledge of psychiatric medicine would lead us to suspect that many of the reported cases of werewolfery in the Middle Ages were in fact sufferers of lycanthropia. Simply by *behaving* like wolves, even if physically they were clearly human beings, was often sufficient justification in a less-enlightened age for the gullible in a community to cry out in mortal terror, "Werewolf!"

It is interesting to note how the seventeenth-century English dramatist, John Webster, viewed the phenomenon in his tragedy of suffering, *The Duchess of Malfi*. Here one of the murderous brothers goes mad and imagines himself to be a wolf:

> ... Two nights since
> One met the duke 'bout midnight in a lane
> Behind Saint Mark's Church, with the leg of a man
> Upon his shoulder; and he howled fearfully;
> Said he was a wolf, only the difference
> Was, a wolf's skin was hairy on the outside,
> His on the inside.

Webster wrote *The Duchess of Malfi* in 1613, at a time when werewolfery was rampant and at its loathsome peak. He did not need to do his academic homework. The curse was manifesting itself all around him.

Physicians of the Renaissance, among them Johannes Schenck von Grafenberg, tried to look at mental aberrations from a unified *medical* point of view. In Schenck's *Observations* (1665), for instance, he refers to lycanthropy as a "natural" disease. The English scholar, Robert Burton, also discusses the delusion as a very definite "disease" in his *Anatomy of Melancholy* (1621), explaining that "men run howling about graves and fields in the night, and will not be persuaded but that they are wolves or some such beast." Twenty-four years earlier, in his *Daemonologie*, James I of England had noted with some perception that werewolves were victims of a delusion

Werewolf devouring a man, from a medieval bestiary.

With the help of modern illustrations like this, together with the influence of books, films and stage productions, the werewolf superstition has survived well into the twentieth century. The picture accompanied J. A. Rio-Neuhof's short story "Die Weerwolf" in the South African magazine *Die Brandwag* (November 29, 1974).

induced by a state of melancholia. The conflict raged, however, as to whether the condition of lycanthropia was a physical or a mental disease, as, often, it still does.

Sabine Baring-Gould, the English parson and prolific author and writer of the famous hymn, *Onward Christian Soldiers*, published his now classic *Book of Were-Wolves* in 1865. Many of his conclusions, in the light of science and hard evidence, have long since been questioned. But as far as his conception of lycanthropy is concerned, he remains dead right. "Truly it consists in a form of madness," he tells us, "such as may be found in most asylums."

Today the werewolf legend has understandably retreated into the realms of a more subjective reality, but has done so without losing any of its grim horror. As a recent history of demonology explains, "The werewolf is a monster of the unconscious, one to which folklore and superstition formerly gave fleshly reality and occasionally still does, in modern times." We may live in a period when people are reputedly more rational, more educated, more

Suicide youth feared he was a werewolf

By JAMES GOLDEN

APPRENTICE joiner Andrew Prinold plunged a knife into his heart because he feared he was turning into a werewolf.

He told of his fears in a desperate phone call to a friend minutes before he killed himself.

Shaking

His death came after he had started attending seances in a bid to contact his dead father, an inquest at Eccleshall, Staffordshire, was told yesterday.

His weird flirtation with spiritualism started after he saw the film The Exorcist, it was said.

The first seances were described by 18-year-old workmate Stephen Williams, who told the jury: 'Five lads took part. They put a glass on the table with numbers and names round it and started talking to it.

'Within five to ten minutes Andrew started shaking. He was sweating, moaning and groaning.

'Five or ten minutes later they held another seance. Andrew didn't take part but within minutes he started shaking again.

'Andrew said the devil was inside him. I had to punch his jaw to bring him round and he remembered nothing. Then we went off on our motorcycles and Andrew said he could not see, but later he was all right.

'The Monday before he died he said he saw his father in the mirror.'

Stephen then told of the telephone call. He said: 'Andrew said his face and hands were changing colour and he was turning into a werewolf.

'He would go quiet and then start growling. I told him to see his brother. He said he had a knife and was going to kill himself.'

Andrew's girlfriend Celeste Martin said he had mentioned suicide.

Pathologist Dr Frank Pick said Andrew's wound appeared from its angle to be self-inflicted.

Verdict: Andrew killed himself.

Legacy

Later Andrew's mother, Mrs Edith Prinold, who did not attend the inquest, said: 'I know nothing about seances. I just know he was killed. He was due for a £400 legacy in October. I can't believe he killed himself.'

Andrew's half-brother, David Cartwright, 26, said: 'I must accept the verdict but I am not really satisfied. It was just not like Andrew. I knew nothing of any seances until today.'

How the British *Daily Mail*, in its issue of April 29, 1975, covered the tragic story of the youth from Staffordshire in England who believed he was a werewolf. The entire British press gave the werewolf affair massive coverage.

sophisticated and therefore less easily "taken in" by the idea of the supernatural. The wolf as a universally dreaded species may also be on the decline. But the werewolf superstition – if only the *knowledge* of the superstition, from films, books, magazines, etc. – persists, and as long as it does, there will always be people, if only deluded people, who will read into werewolfery a certain bizarre reality.

In relatively recent times – over the last one hundred years, say – there have been periodic reports in the press concerning so-called werewolves. Many of these reports are of dubious origin and authenticity, but in some cases the patients displayed symptoms of sufficient conviction to warrant our attention. In April, 1975, for instance, a seventeen-year-old youth from the village of Eccleshall in Staffordshire, England, was so horrified by the personal belief that he was turning into a werewolf that one night he plunged a switch-blade into his heart. A few months before his death this apprentice carpenter developed a fascination for spiritualism and the occult and attended several seances, during which he tried to establish contact with his father who had died five years previously. At one of these seances, he told a friend, he became possessed by the Devil; at another he was taken over by the spirit of a black cat, and he began scratching the table at which he was seated with several other people. He was never the same again. At the inquest the coroner was forced to admit: "There has been considerable publicity recently about this sort of thing and I do not feel I am qualified to comment."

On the evening before his death, the young man made a frantic midnight telephone call to one of his teenage workmates, who later informed the inquest jury: "He told me his face and hands were changing color – and that he was changing into a werewolf. He would go quiet and then start growling. I told him to see his brother. He said he had a knife and was going to kill himself."

His body was found by a passing postman near the village crossroads at six o'clock next morning. He had stabbed himself through the chest with a knife. Who knows what mental tortures, what horrible lycanthropic delusions he endured before taking his life? Yet one thing is certain. By his behavior-pattern alone in these moments of anxiety, and by his subsequent eleventh-hour "confession," he would assuredly have been accused of werewolfery in the Middle Ages. If he had not taken his own life first, the judiciary would certainly have obliged him later. Thus the irony and the injustice of the werewolf delusion.

Sixty miles west of Eccleshall, only ninety years ago, an Oxford professor and his wife were confronted by a phantom werewolf. During the summer of 1888, in company with a friend, they had gone for a fishing holiday at a remote lake in Wales, in a mountainous region of Merionethshire. Here, on the edge of a pine forest, they rented a cottage. One day while wading in the lake the professor stumbled across what he took to be the skull of an unusually large dog. He took it back to the cottage and placed it on a kitchen shelf with the intention of examining it more closely another time. That evening, while the professor and his friend were out, his wife was startled by the sound of soft pawings outside the cottage, followed by snuffling and scratching at the kitchen door. She gathered her wits together, since she feared a savage dog was on the prowl, and ran quickly but nervously into the kitchen to check that the door was locked. As she turned, her eye caught sight of something at the window – there staring at her was the hideous head of an enormous beast, part human, part animal. Montague Summers, in his book

The Werewolf (1933), explains what happened that night:

> The cruel panting jaws were gaping wide and showed keen white teeth; the great furry paws clasped the sill like hands; the red eyes gleamed hideously . . . half-fainting with fear she ran through to the front door and shot the bolt. A moment after she heard heavy breathing outside and the latch rattled menacingly. The minutes that followed were full of acutest suspense, and now and again a low snarl would be heard at the door or window, and a sound as though the creature were endeavouring to force its entrance. At last the voices of her husband and his friend, come back from their ramble, sounded in the little garden; and as they knocked, finding the door fast, she was but able to open ere she fell in a swoon at their feet. When her senses returned, to find herself laid on the sofa and her husband anxiously bending over her, she told in halting accents what had happened. That night, having made all secure and extinguished the lamps, the two men sat up quietly, armed with stout sticks and a gun. The hours passed slowly until, when all was darkest and most lonely, the soft thud of cushioned paws was heard on the gravel outside, and nails scratched at the kitchen window. To their horror in a stale phosphorescent light they saw the hideous mask of a wolf with the eyes of a man glaring through the glass, eyes that were red with hellish rage. Snatching the gun they rushed to the door, but it had seen their movement and was away in a moment. As they issued from the house a shadowy undefined shape slipped through the open gate, and in the stars they could just see a huge animal making towards the lake into which it disappeared silently, nor did a ruffle cross the surface of the water. Early the next morning the professor took the skull, and rowing a little way out from the shore flung it as far as possible into the deeper part of the tarn. The werewolf was never seen again.

"... there staring at her was the hideous head of an enormous beast, part human, part animal. . . ." This imaginative werewolf illustration by John Giunta first appeared in the November 1942 issue of the American pulp magazine *Weird Tales*.

Was the presence of the beast's skull in the kitchen sufficient to energize into physical materialization a former werewolf? Could the combination of the skull and the old cottage have recalled a grim association from the past? There are a number of accounts on record of phantom werewolves, and this would appear to be a notable example. A few years ago the incident formed the basis for a spine-chilling play on British television; it was accused by the critics of being far-fetched. Another phantom werewolf was said to haunt the Valley of the Doones in Exmoor, England, at the turn of the century. Such sub-human

Seven hundred horror-film fans attended the 1976 London preview of *The Squirm* dressed in horror gear. Here four of them, including a blue-jeaned "werewolf," pass through Piccadilly Circus en route to the theater.

apparitions are, by all accounts, the spirit of those werewolves whose depraved cruelty has compelled them, after death, to remain earthbound. They are the most unusual, and the most dreaded, of all phantasms of the night.

What emerges from this account, and from several other reports of werewolves in fairly recent times, is that the incidents almost invariably occur in remote country districts – districts, I suspect, where rustic folklore and local superstition still inspire an atavistic fear. How much these tales are twisted and embroidered in the telling, it is impossible to know; yet every story, I believe, possesses at least a kernel of truth; the authenticity of others, because they stem from reliable authority, I have small reason to doubt. Just before the First World War, three werewolves were said to haunt the forested Ardennes area of Belgium, a country where belief in the werewolf still pervades the minds of some country people. At about this time, or rather just after the First World War, a shepherd who lived alone in a desolate part of Inverness-shire in Scotland, was said by people in the area to be a werewolf. His eyes were "unusually piercing" and he had "heavy brows which met so as almost to form an arched bar across the forehead." His behavior was "odd," and "the evidence seemed conclusive" that he was a werewolf. But what *was* that "evidence?" I cannot say.

In the case of the werewolf boy of Alsace, in northeast France, evidence was rather more forthcoming, for in November 1925 the whole village testified that the boy possessed the devilish power of animal metamorphosis. The episode came to a head when the village policeman of Uttenheim, near Strasbourg, became convinced that the lad was a sorcerer who was responsible for his terrible visions of human-faced animals and shot the boy dead in a fit of haunted desperation. Everyone agreed that the boy had made a pact with the Devil and practiced the diabolical act of werewolfery, and that the policeman was the chief target of his mischievous abuse. That a whole village in the twentieth century should testify to the effect that a boy was a werewolf may sound incredible; but this was a remote part of France, remember, close to the German border. Here, such beliefs die hard.

Just five years later and two hundred or so miles southwest of the area, at Bourg-la-Reine, another French werewolf incident reached public notice. Pierre van Paassen recorded it in his book, *Days of Our Years*, published in 1939:

> We had a werewolf scare in the winter of 1930 through the disappearance of a farmer named Richard who had a bad reputation as a sorcerer, blighting the corn through his evil eye. He prepared love-philtres. Upon his death there were found in his cabin bottles, various herbs, magic stones, amulets with "druidic" inscriptions, the head of a calf, assorted powders, waxen

Arguably the most horrific wedding of 1975 took place in Hollywood. A "werewolf" acted as chief witness while two horror-film fans, twenty-year-old Keith Reber (dressed as Frankenstein's Monster) and his nineteen-year-old ghoul-friend Katherine Engel (as the Monster's Bride), joined in unholy matrimony. Werewolf and Co., who later drank blood-red cocktails, were specially made-up by experts at Universal Studios in Los Angeles.

27

manikins labelled with the names of various persons in the neighbourhood long deceased, dried salamanders, a pair of leather gloves. The man was believed to walk by night in the shape of a wolf.

Did anyone see him do so? We are not told. Yet the community feared him just as surely as if he were a savage werewolf of antiquity, and fear has always been the werewolf's – or the supposed werewolf's – foremost ally.

A few years after the last war, during a humid summer's evening in 1949, a police patrol was called to a house in the center of Rome, where howls could be heard coming from some bushes in the owner's garden. A werewolf was believed to be in the area. Cautious investigation soon revealed the creature responsible for the wolf-like behavior – a young man, covered in mud, was howling and furiously digging the ground with his sharp fingernails. There was a full moon. When he was taken to a hospital, the young man said that for three years he had regularly lost consciousness at periods of the full moon and had found himself wandering the streets at night, driven by uncontrollable instincts. The man was clearly suffering from lycanthropic delusions. Perhaps he should have been thankful that the time was an enlightened 1949: had he suffered the same delusions in 1549, and "confessed" his "crimes," he would certainly have ended up in court on charges of werewolfery. His fate would have been a foregone conclusion.

Police were also called in to help hunt down a suspected werewolf in Singapore in 1957. A particular nurses' hostel on the main island had a long history of what the authorities believed were werewolf attacks; and then the hostel was demolished and a new complex built in its place. Soon after, in 1957, the supposed werewolf attacks were resumed, and a hundred nurses slept fearfully behind locked doors and barred windows. Yet, despite all precautions, a young student nurse fell prey to the beast. "I woke," she said, "to find a horrible face, with hair reaching to the bridge of the nose, glaring down at me. The creature had two long protruding red fangs. I saw him clearly because the room was bathed in moonlight. I tried to scream but could not. I staggered into the corridor and collapsed." The mystery, as far as I know, was never solved. Because of the nature of the attacks, including the infliction of teeth-like punctures on the girl's wrist, student tom-foolery could be ruled out. Supernatural groups are rife on the island, and it would not have been beyond the realms of possibility for the nocturnal intruder to have been a soul initiated into the horrors of werewolfery.

'Werewolf' attacks nurse in haunted house

Sunday Express Correspondent
SINGAPORE, Saturday.
POLICE with Army tracker dogs tonight patrolled the grounds of a nurses' hostel, waiting for the return of a "werewolf" who attacked a student nurse at dawn today.

The werewolf of Singapore, as reported in Britain's *Sunday Express* (December 29, 1957).

We have Werewolf killer, say police

From ANDREW McEWEN in Paris

A MAN was charged last night with the 'werewolf' murders of seven women in seven years.

The grimy, rain-soaked railway sidings of suburban Paris yielded the vital clue to the identity of the killer.

Police believe the link between the deaths was the suburban railway line.

Detectives alleged that father-of-two Marcel Barbot, 35, was the man who terrorised women along the railway between the suburbs of Creil, Nogent-sur-Oise, Villers-St Paul and Laigneville to the Gare du Nord in Paris.

'Jacques the Ripper's' trademark was to kill with a ·22 long-barrelled rifle and strip his victims of their underclothes, but not rape them.

All the girls were brunette and very ordinary. Only women who blended into the suburban g r e y n e s s were chosen.

Police were convinced that the killer spent weeks selecting and trailing each of his victims before striking. Each murder was carried out with precision, leaving not a fingerprint or other clue.

An eighth victim was a man, who died because he was with a girl selected to die.

Yesterday police said they found a ·22 rifle, bludgeon and dagger at Barbot's home.

The werewolf of Paris, as reported in Britain's *Daily Mail* (December 17, 1976).

Occasionally werewolves replace the traditional role of pink elephants, blue snakes, mauve lizards and giant green spiders. In 1964 a man from West Kensington, London, told a court of law that he had been drinking whiskey, barley wine and beer just before he saw a werewolf. "It had terrible, long fangs and glaring eyes," said the man with vivid recall of memory. "I could feel its presence even when it was out of sight. It was chasing me round a privet hedge. I ripped at the hedge to keep my balance." After being fined for disturbing the peace, the man added: "This has finished me with drink. I hate to think what may happen next time."

French police in 1976 charged a man with the murder of seven women in the suburbs of Creil, Nogent-sur-Oise, Villers-St. Paul, Laigneville, and the Gare du Nord in Paris. He was dubbed the "werewolf murderer" – though exactly why is not clear. The thirty-five-year-old family man killed his victims with a .22 long-barreled rifle, and then stripped them naked. Rape was never committed. The police chose to describe the man in terms of the most horrible creature in French folk mythology. He had to be a werewolf, a term used by the tyrannical judges of the Middle Ages. Today such deluded souls languish in comfort in state institutions, whereas their predecessors of past centuries could once expect, with grim certainty, to forego care, comfort and understanding for a rigorous regime of torture, trial and execution . . . as will soon be apparent.

2 Wolf Nature: Its Ancestry and Superstitions

ROBERT EISLER, the British anthropologist, puts forward an intriguing theory in his book *Man into Wolf* (1951), about the peculiarly savage psyche of the werewolf. He draws our attention to the fact that a great many ancient Indo-European tribal names, like Luvians, Lucanians, Dacians and Hyrcanians, mean "wolf-men," and that numerous personal surnames in Germany, Italy and Greece mean "wolf" and "she-wolf." This clearly proves, he says, that the transition from the fruit-gathering herd of "finders" to the lupine pack of carnivorous hunters was a conscious process accompanied by a deep emotional upheaval still remembered by man's subconscious, superindividual, ancestral memory (an idea reminiscent of Jung's "concept of archetypes"). In turn, this became reflected in the "superstitions," or rather the surviving atavistic beliefs, surrounding lycanthropy.

Clearly, there must be more substance to the traditional concept that werewolfery invariably struck those who were least able to rationalize clearly. There are two interrelated possibilities: first, that suspected werewolves came mainly from lowly, peasant stock, where logic and intellectualizing was replaced by a willingness to believe in the absurd; and second, that their malady, in mind as well as deed, is a genetic throwback to the black savageness of the primeval beast. Along with the cave-bear and the cave-hyena, the ferocious wolf was among the fiercest enemies of prehistoric man. This is why our fear of the "wolf creature" is deep-rooted, even among the vast majority of us who have never made his acquaintance (and probably never will) in his natural environment.

Our knowledge, and perhaps even our instinct, tells us that the wolf, because of its unbridled cruelty, bestial ferocity and ravening hunger, must be viewed with the utmost suspicion. As Montague Summers points out in *The Werewolf*, "His strength, his cunning, his speed were regarded as abnormal, almost eerie qualities; he had something of the demon, of hell. He is the symbol of Night and Winter, of Stress and Storm, the dark and mysterious harbinger of Death." And so, whether as a devourer of lambs in the New Testament, or as a monstrous sun-devouring wolf of Nordic mythology, the creature comes down to us today mainly as an emblem of the principle of evil, within a pattern of ideas which is unquestionably related to the Gnostic theory of the creation of the universe. It is no coincidence, either, that the Nordic wolf-myth is also associated with all other concepts relating to the final annihilation of the world, whether by water or by fire. The werewolf's inheritance, therefore, is one of maniacal savagery: to destroy and, the ultimate fate, to be destroyed.

From time to time, although now less frequently, reports reach us from different parts of the world of wild children reared by wolves or other savage animals. These stories go right back to the time of Romulus and Remus, the legendary founders of Rome who were rescued and suckled by a wolf, and may have strengthened the belief in half-human animals. In 1852, Dr Hubsch, physician to the hospitals of Istanbul (then Constantinople), saw a wild-child in one of the Central African tribes, which he describes as having a tail and feeding constantly on human flesh. Sabine Baring-Gould, in his *Curious Myths of the Middle Ages*, chronicles the history of John Struys, a Dutch traveler who visited Formosa in 1677. One of his companions, it seems, captured a wild man who earlier had murdered one of their party. "He had a tail more than a foot long, covered with red hair, and very like that of a cow," Struys wrote in his journal. More well-known, and nearer our own time, were the two wild girls found in Midnapur, India, in the 1920s, who were said to have been reared by wolves and later cared for by the Rev. J. A. Singh.

All these accounts from tropical countries have much in common with tales of wild individuals who roamed naked and speechless in European forests, such as the Bear Boys of Lithuania (1657), Wild Peter (1724), the girl of Châlons-sur-Marne (1731), and the Wild Boy of Aveyron (1798). They certainly generated a great deal of interest among early students of man, and, because their behavior had more in common with animals than with humans, the eighteenth-century Swedish botanical scientist, Linnaeus, classified them as a separate species, *Homo ferus*, or feral man.

Yet as intriguing as these stories of feral children may be to the anthropologist, or even to the man in the street with an interest in the bizarre, to try and correlate the

Wild children, like the two shown in this sixteenth-century woodcut, led many early historians down a false trail regarding the possible explanation for some werewolf stories.

The wolf-reared Romulus and Remus, seen here in a painting by Zender, fired the imaginations of those who wished to believe in the existence of half-human animals.

behavior of wolf-children with werewolves would not only be spuriously contrived and misleading, but downright dishonest. But, for the record at least, they should be mentioned.

The gray, common or timber wolf (*Canis lupus*), which is a wild species of the dog family, is the best known and most widely distributed of all types of wolf. It is also the largest and most dreaded of the wild Canidae; a fine Northern male wolf may measure something like seven feet in length, including the bushy two-foot tail, and weigh ten stone. Because of its fearlessness and savage

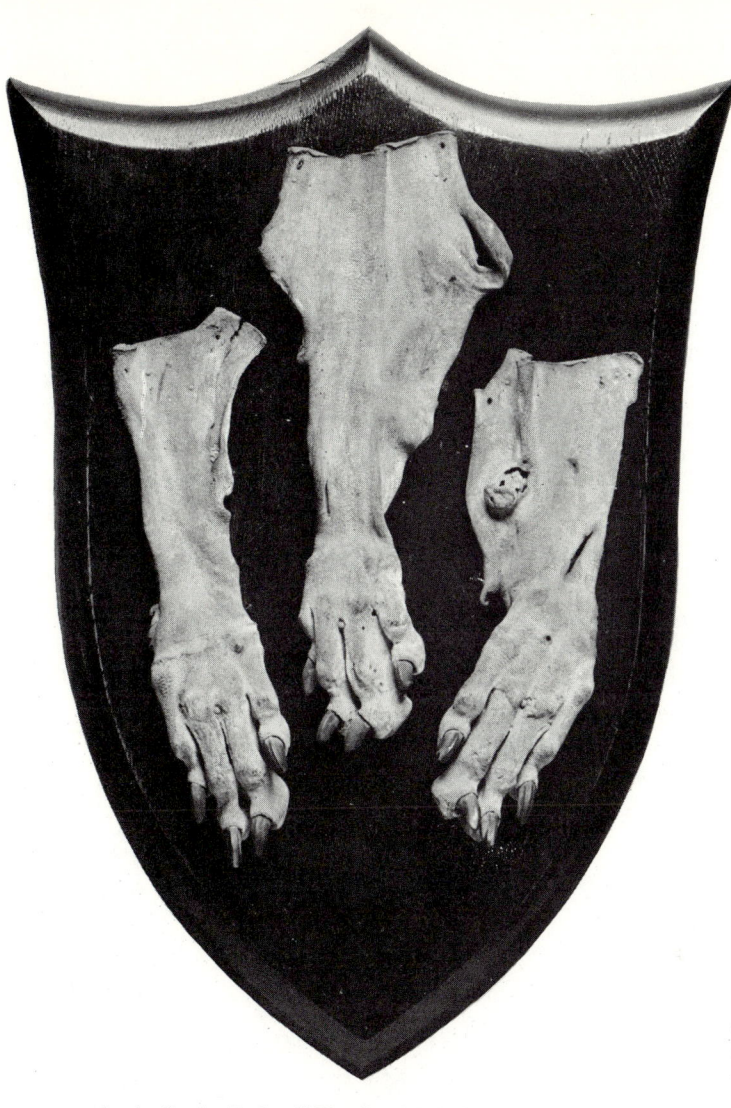

These Welsh wolf pads were presented to the National Museum of Wales in 1977. Until the 1920s, though, they hung in the great hall of Island House, Laugharne, in the old administrative county of Carmarthenshire. They stem from about 1560, when werewolfery was raging through Wales. Who knows what terrible crimes inspired the slaughter of this particular wolf?

strength, it finds little difficulty in bringing down an elk, bison or horse; a man, bereft of a defensive weapon like an ax or gun, is easier still.

The latest geographical survey of the wolf, to quote the *Encyclopaedia Britannica,* indicates that "although once widely distributed over North America and Eurasia, they are now found from Alaska through northern Canada to the northern plains states, making rare appearances in the Rockies, and are extinct in the British Isles and only occasionally seen in the winter in west-central Europe. They may occur as far south as India." Nonetheless, their blood-curdling howls can still put the fear of God into those peoples living in the wilder and more mountainous regions of France, Belgium, Austria and Hungary, and their abundance throughout the Soviet Union produces annual wolf scares.

It was this same fear which, after the First World War, was seized on by a German para-military underground group known as "the Werewolf Organization" – a gang of terrorists who "organized" themselves into wolf-packs and hunted down their victims in the dead of night. In the closing days of the Second World War, the Nazis relied heavily on these "Werewolves" for heinous acts of terror. The organization, said Himmler, should harass "like werewolves"; and Hitler was thinking of werewolves when he said he wanted "to see once more in the eyes of a pitiless youth the gleam of pride and independence of the beast of prey." Just after the war, in 1945, Goebbels re-organized the Werewolves as an underground resistance movement, complete with its own "secret" broadcasting station. Its task, like that of the Werewolves generally, was to create unbridgeable hatred between the occupation authorities and the German people. A typical radio message was: "The members of the Werewolf Organization use any means good enough to harm the enemy. Woe to the enemies of the country, but thrice woe to the traitors of our own people who put themselves at their disposal!" It was not the first time, either, that an organization had adopted the legendary name of werewolf. During the Thirty Years' War of 1618–48, German peasants rallied together and called themselves the Werewolves, their function being to form a defense against foreign soldiers who were then ravaging Germany.

To return to wolves proper – in southeast Poland, an

How Britain's Communist newspaper, the *Daily Worker* (now *Morning Star*), viewed the Nazi underground terrorist "army," the Werewolf Organization, in its issue dated April 9, 1945.

> **WEREWOLF MAN TAKEN TO SECRET PRISON**
>
> 20 APR 1946   Express Staff Reporter
>
> THE man who is believed to have led the German Werewolves, the last-gasp guerrilla organisation, is in Allied hands. He is 57-year-old Captain Horst Gustav Friedrich von Pflugk-Hartung.
>
> Von Hartung was brought to England from Washington on...

End of the road for the pack-leader of the Werewolf Organization. News report in the British *Daily Express* (April 20, 1946).

area once heavily populated by the species, they had dwindled to no more than two hundred in 1975, while in the remainder of the country they are now almost extinct. A survey conducted in Sweden recently revealed even sadder figures: there were only ten wolves left in that country. In the mainland United States, where wolves were hunted for bounty until 1959, there is estimated to be fewer than a thousand timber wolves, and these are all in Michigan, Wisconsin, Minnesota and Montana, although there are greater numbers in Alaska and Canada.

But in those countries where the wolf has managed to hold its own, the werewolf superstition is still keenly believed. This belief is stoked by the frequent wolf scares which plague certain areas. A few examples:

In January, 1967, two huge and hungry timber wolves attacked the mayor of the snowbound little Italian village of Montefredane. They hurled themselves at his car and then killed two dogs.

In February, 1967, starving wolves, driven into the summer resort of Zabadani by Syria's worst snowstorm for years, savagely mauled five people, including a mother and her two children. Police armed with rifles and civilians with picks and axes drove the wolves off after a desperate one-hour battle.

In January, 1968, wolves forced down from the mountains by snowstorms attacked and ate eighteen people around Hamadan in Persia.

In August, 1968, wolves carried off three children from the town of Sherkot, eighty miles from New Delhi, India.

In September, 1968, a man-eating wolf was haunting the village of Gestosa in northern Spain. On one occasion the wolf snatched an eighteen-month-old boy in

35

The werewolf superstition remains at its most feared today in those countries where wolf scares are still common.

full view of his parents. Eventually, after being pelted with stones, the startled wolf dropped the child.

In September, 1969, a four-year-old girl was attacked by a wolf and seriously injured while playing a few feet from her home in the small village of Gomesende, again in northern Spain.

In December, 1972, shepherds in Yugoslavia's Bjelasica Mountains discovered the body of a man next to the corpse of a wolf. It was thought the man strangled the wolf before dying from injuries received in the fight.

In February, 1973, a telephone repair man in Sabzavar, Persia, was trapped at the top of a telephone post by four wolves waiting for him at the bottom. He sent a call for help via the wires and was rescued.

In March, 1974, in Gornia Teslic, Bosnia, a nineteen-year-old man was attacked by three wolves while he was sleeping in a small cellar under a tumbledown shack on a farm. He killed one wolf with his bare hands, the other two with a threshing flail.

In July, 1974, wolves killed two young boys within a week in the San Cyprian district of Orense province, north-west Spain.

In November and December, 1975, fifty-strong wolf packs were scaring inhabitants of villages in the isolated mountains of central Italy.

In October, 1976, marauding wolves in eastern Finland forced parents to organize transport to get their children safely to school. Farmers pleaded with the authorities to have the wolf removed from the list of protected species.

Small wonder then that all over the world the wolf has become an omen of death; small wonder, too, that wherever the wolf is still looked upon with fear, the werewolf belief remains at its strongest.

Although loyal and obedient to the pack leader, the bravery of wolves in the pursuit of prey seems to exist only during those occasions when they are particularly ravenous; as a general rule, though, wolves appear to be somewhat cowardly and easily scared. In the days when wolves were regularly trapped, they would be so terror-stricken as to offer very little resistance to their captors.

Discretion and caution are also strongly developed features of their character. They display a marked aversion to any combination of ropes and poles, and will avoid any enclosure marked off in this way. Wire fences they view with the gravest suspicion, and in Norway it has been found that even the erection of telegraph posts and wires effectively keeps wolves from a neighborhood for many years. In the United States, hunters frequently cash-in on this wolf-caution. By tying a fluttering strip of cloth to a stick, and planting it beside the carcase of their prey, the prowling wolves are often forced to remain at a respectful distance until the sportsman returns and carries off his trophy.

A rather curious example of the wolf's cowardice once occurred near Leningrad. Here, while driving his sled, a Russian peasant found himself pursued by eleven ravenous wolves. As soon as he caught sight of them he urged his horse to gallop as swiftly as possible, so successfully that he was still happily ahead of the pursuers when he arrived home. The entrance to his courtyard was a swing-gate, which was closed, but the speed with which the horse dashed against it threw it open and the sled entered safely – but so closely followed by the wolves that nine managed to gain entrance while the door was swung back on its hinges. They were effectively trapped. The moment the wolves noticed that all means of escape had been denied them, their courage utterly failed. Instead of showing the bravery they are widely thought to possess, they shrank back cowering into corners and were easily killed by the peasant.

But for all his negative attributes there are many instances of the wolf being used to cure diseases, develop strength and courage or ward off evil. *Medicina de Quadrupedibus,* a medical treatise of the seventeenth century, informs us that wearing the skin of a wolf provides a cure for rabies and prevents epilepsy, while the skin of the head is an infallible precaution against male-

American animator Walt Disney saw the wolf's famed ferocity not in terms of the werewolf but as a straightforward rogue. Yet his Big Bad Wolf can also be seen as pure symbolism, for it reflects the same evil bloodlust as his lycanthropic aberration, the werewolf, with the Three Little Pigs – one of which is depicted here – taking the role of the victims of his loathsome raids.

volent demons, just as a supper of well-seasoned wolf's flesh cannot be bettered as a safeguard against satanic apparitions. The same volume assures us that the finest cure for insomnia is to place a wolf's head under your pillow. A wolf's skull, thoroughly burnt and finely pounded, was guaranteed to heal excruciating pains in the joints, and an ointment prepared from the right eye of a wolf was the most valuable prescription known to the Saxon oculist. Another seventeenth-century work, *De Virtutibus Herbarum*, recommends that if you hope never to be angrily spoken to you should wrap a wolf's tooth in a bay leaf and wear it as a charm, while in an Aesop fable the skin of the wolf is recommended by the fox as a cure for the sick lion. At one time it was believed that if the penis of a wolf is roasted and eaten it weakens that person's sexual desire, though whether that is a cure or a cause of a malady is a matter of point of view.

One of the strangest superstitions regarding wolves is to be found in China to this present day. Here it is considered lucky, if a child has died of any infectious disease, that a wolf should carry away the corpse, because by doing so he removes the cause of the disease and prevents it from spreading to other children. In Mongolia, until very recently, it was the custom to throw out the dead on to the plains for this same purpose.

Strength and courage, at least while he is on the attack, have always been accepted as attributes of the wolf, however much he may be feared and loathed. The Sicilians still believe that a wolf's head will increase the courage of whoever puts it on, and in Agrigento, near the south coast of Sicily, the belief remains that children's shoes should be made of wolf's skin if their parents wish them to grow up strong and pugnacious.

The wolf has even so far drifted on to the side of good that he has been seen as a custodian of religious truth and the friend of the saint. In the year 617, according to the sixteenth-century Italian ecclesiastical historian, Caesar Baronius, a number of wolves broke into a monastery and tore to pieces several friars who were known to hold heretical opinions. Another wolf guarded and defended from wild beasts the head of St. Edmund the Martyr, King of East Anglia in England during the ninth century. In another story, stemming from the twelfth century, St. Norbert first forced a wolf to let go of a sheep it had clutched in its jaws, and then persuaded it to guard the rest of the flock all day without touching them.

But, as might be expected, the wolf is generally seen as the ultimate in the depraved, ferocious savage. In The Bible he is not only bloodthirsty and treacherous, but is also a heretic: "Beware of false prophets, who come to you in the clothing of sheep, but inwardly they are ravening wolves" (Matthew, VII, 15). When Christ told his disciples to cast out unclean spirits, he said: "Behold I send you as sheep in the midst of wolves" (Matthew, x, 16). Again, the Good Shepherd, speaking of the tragedies which were about to crash down on his church, exclaimed: "But the hireling, and he that is not the shepherd, whose own sheep are not, seeth the wolf coming, and leaveth the sheep, and fleeth: and the wolf catcheth and scattereth the sheep" (John, x, 12). And in offering his last farewell, Christ is quoted by St. Paul as saying: "I know that, after my departure, ravening wolves will enter in among you, not sparing the flock" (Acts, XX, 29).

Olaus Magnus, in his great history of Sweden, *Historia de Gentibus Septentrionalibus* (1555), writes that wolves, attracted by the smell, will attack pregnant women, and it is probably in this belief that we find the origin of the old custom which says that no pregnant woman should go outside unless accompanied by an armed man. Wolves tore to pieces and devoured Milo, the Greek athletic hero of the sixth-century B.C. Olympics. Wolves, according to Servius, the Latin scholar of the fourth and fifth centuries, carried off the entrails of a victim sacrificed by the Hirpini tribe in southern Italy to Pluto, and thus brought a plague down upon the land. It seems that mid-winter was the time when wolves in medieval Britain were at their most savage, and perhaps because of it the Anglo-Saxons bestowed on January the name "Wolf-month."

No wonder the wolf is known to us today as a beast much to be feared, when historically and in reality as well as mythology, it has been invested with so many gloomy superstitions and beliefs that are all too often horribly real and true. It should be feared on account of its teeth alone, which are sharp-cutting blades of great strength. When biting it gives a rapid succession of vicious snaps, compared to the firm, retaining hold which characterizes the bite of a healthy dog. Frequently, too, they indulge in wanton killing, and their mass slaughter of sheep and cattle appears to result from nothing more than sheer physical exuberance, which is one reason why man has tried to exterminate them by shooting, trapping, snaring, driving, lassoing, pitting and poisoning.

The character of the wolf's voice is mainly directed in producing long-drawn, dismal howls of a peculiarly eerie nature. They do this mainly when they are hungry or lonely. They sit on their haunches, noses pointing skywards, and let out a series of long, full-throated wails – the sort directors of horror movies are so fond of

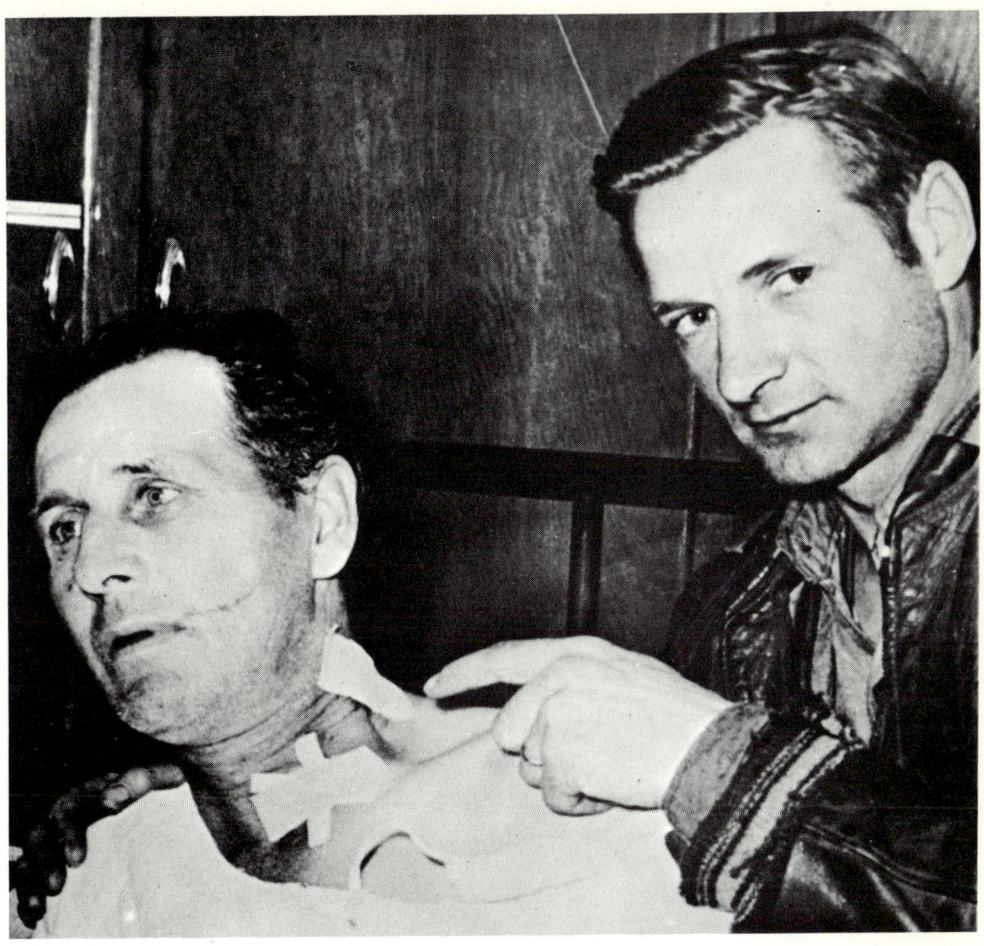

inserting into their Gothic extravaganzas to make our hair stand on end.

The cruel, treacherous expression of the wolf's obliquely set eyes betrays just how different is the wolf-spirit from that which looks out through the kind true eyes of the faithful dog. Though they are of the same family, there is a natural hatred which exists between wolves and dogs. This is not surprising when one considers that wolves actually devour dogs, a gruesome trait which smacks of cannibalism.

It is this willingness on the part of the wolf to attack and consume the flesh of its own kind which leads us naturally to the parallel of the human lycanthrope or werewolf who perpetrates similar crimes on his fellow men. The close association between the savage wolf and man's atavistic bestiality is one reason why belief in the werewolf has endured to the present day. With each there is the ferocity of attack, followed by an inordinately evil appetite, and with each the desire for blood and flesh drives them on to commit even more diabolical crimes.

One man who lived to tell the tale. Isadore Carre was attacked by a wolf on his northern Ontario farm, near River Valley in Canada. The wolf leaped for the farmer's throat as he left his stable to investigate why his dogs were barking. The wolf's fangs just missed the artery. His wife killed the wolf with an ax and he and his son-in-law (in the picture) forced the wolf's head away from his throat.

41

3 The Werewolf Symptom: How To Recognize a Werewolf

ONE DAY IN 1821, Count von Breber, the chief-of-police of the German city of Magdeburg, was looking into the ominous disappearance of a number of children when, in pursuit of a particular line of investigation, he found himself outside a large building on the perimeter of the city. Here, after a few moments, he could hear the most appalling sounds coming from the other side of the door: a frantic to-ing and fro-ing, peculiar soft patterings, agonized human screams coupled with the growls and snappings of an animal. His curiosity grew more intense by the minute, even though the noises coming from the building made his blood run cold and his hair stand on end.

Summoning courage, he beat down the locked door, and the sight which greeted his eyes made his stomach turn over a dozen times. Everything, the floor, walls and furniture, were splattered with blood; in front of him lay the body of a woman, her face mutilated, her breast and stomach ripped open. Everywhere else, over every square inch, were mangled human remains – possibly, he feared, those of the city's missing children.

But what he next saw, skulking in one corner, completely took his breath away, for in the yellow glow of a lantern his eyes picked out the beast responsible for the carnage all round him. The specter was a monstrosity: a thing with a woman's breast, a woman's hair, golden and curly, but the face and feet of a wolf; the hands, white and slender, ended in long, glittering nails, cruelly sharp and dripping with blood. He was face to face with the werewolf of Magdeburg; its gruesome days were now almost over.

One evening not long after, near Vienne in southeast France, an English writer tried in vain to hire a horse-and-trap to take him to a nearby hamlet. The problem was that the driver would be compelled to return alone, which no one would agree to as they all felt that it would put their lives in peril. The area, it seems, was plagued at night by werewolves.

"Picou tells me that he saw the werewolf only last night," said a peasant. "He was down by the hedge of his buckwheat field, and the sun had set, and he was thinking of coming home, when he heard a rustle on the far side of the hedge. He looked over, and there stood the wolf as big as a calf against the horizon, its tongue out, and its eyes glaring like marsh-fires."

Here, then, are two quite different eye-witness accounts of a werewolf, its deeds and its physical form. Most people would probably regard the first description as the one nearest to their own conception of the werewolf: a creature with a human body but the face and feet of a wolf. Yet out of all the great mass of evidence I have acquired on the subject, the beast from Magdeburg is the only instance which describes the werewolf along these

The tremendous strength attributed to many werewolves is dramatically represented in this eighteenth-century engraving. A giant werewolf carries off a young woman, although her rosary, which might ward off a vampire, is obviously powerless where this werewolf is concerned.

lines. The werewolf of Vienne is nearer the mark.

How would we recognize a werewolf if we saw one? The answer to that might seem simple enough to anyone who has seen a movie like *The Wolf Man* or *Curse of the Werewolf* or *Legend of the Werewolf*, because here the creature resembles an over-hirsute man with large lupine teeth, growling voice and foaming mouth, and it viciously attacks (but never actually consumes) its victim. But the sort of beast which was portrayed by Lon Chaney, Jr, Oliver Reed and David Rintoul on the cinema screen is merely the result of one of the biggest con-tricks ever perpetrated by the film industry. For, historically, a werewolf in its animal shape resembles a large wolf. Hollywood, perhaps in the belief that it is difficult to make a wolf *act*, stuck yak's hair onto an actor and passed this off as the real thing; and by so doing gave birth to the popular myth of the twentieth-century werewolf. It is pure fancy. If it is your misfortune to bump into a werewolf, and you are not sure whether it is a human being or a real wolf, there is, according to tradition, one infallible test. You should throw steel or iron at the animal under suspicion, whereupon, if it is a genuine werewolf, the skin will split crosswise on the forehead and the man will come out naked through the opening. This "werewolf test" obviously stems from the medieval belief that suspected werewolves have their fur growing on the inside of their skin and that they become werewolves by simply turning themselves inside out.

Countless fully documented trials tell of prisoners who were closely interrogated as to how this inversion was accomplished. As far as I know, none of them gave a convincing answer. At the moment of change, their memories seem to have become temporarily befogged. Now and then a poor devil had his arms and legs cut off, or was partially flayed, in an attempt to detect the in-growing hair. But I cannot find a scrap of evidence to suggest that the torturers ever found the ingrowing hair they so desperately needed in order to "prove" their case against the convicted werewolves. When one considers that a werewolf in his animal form looks like any other wolf – except that he might be larger and more savage and voracious than ordinary wolves – the problem of how to recognize one is difficult.

In his animal form the head, claws and hairy skin are like those of a real wolf, but he retains his human voice. The surest test of the werewolf's identity, however, lies in his complete absence of a tail. A tendency to transform is believed to wax and wane with the seasons and to be subject to the influence of the moon. His clothes, too, are sure to be found not far from the scene of slaughter.

A strange impediment, which is found in many historical accounts, is that the werewolf falls down quite a lot. This may have something to do with physical exhaustion, because the werewolf also seems to be constantly thirsty. Many of the werewolves in Hungary and the Balkan countries, for instance, were said to be witches who became wolves in order to suck the blood of men who were born during the night of a full moon; by so doing they preserved their health. In their human form they apparently had "pale, sunken faces, hollow eyes, swollen lips, and flabby, weak arms," and after their blood-baths they experienced an acute thirst.

According to some accounts, the werewolf is sometimes frozen with the cold, and on such occasions he is invulnerable to ordinary weapons. The traditional way to wound him is to shoot at him with balls of eider pith or, since we have advanced somewhat from the days of the powder-and-ball flintlock, with bullets of inherited silver.

A valuable eye-witness account of a suspected werewolf attack in the Jura Mountains in 1598 is given by the infamous judge Henry Boguet in his famous *Discours des Sorciers* (1608). He describes how a fifteen-year-old boy named Benedict climbed a tree one day to pick some fruit when he saw a wolf attacking his younger sister, who was playing at the foot of the tree. He instantly descended the tree to try and protect her with a knife he was carrying, but the wolf quickly turned on him and, with a fierce blow of its paw, tore the knife out of his hand and drove it into his throat. Before he died from the mortal wound, however, Benedict was able to offer a description of the wolf which attacked him. Its forepaws were shaped like human hands, covered on top with thick, bushy hair, while its hind feet were completely covered with fur. A young and demented girl, Perrenette Gandillon, later confessed to the crime and admitted that she was a werewolf, after which she was torn limb from limb by the community. The Gandillons were a particularly loathsome family, and several of them were arrested on charges of sorcery and werewolfery. In prison they behaved as though they were possessed, walking on all fours and howling like wild beasts.

The first symptoms exhibited by someone undergoing transformation into a werewolf are extreme restlessness and anxiety. After much inner turmoil, when the man seems to be wrestling with the savage atavistic beast within him, as if trying to make an eleventh-hour effort to curtail his terrible impending fate, he develops the instincts and characteristics of a wolf. More often than not he acquires enormous strength. As he has now developed the nature of a carnivore, he has a lust to kill and devour flesh.

Although his body has taken on the shape of a wolf, his eyes remain unchanged, and out of these windows of the soul a human being looks out. His intelligence, darkened by the shadow of malignity or passion more characteristic of the lower orders, will be minimal. His eyes will be sunken and glazed, as a consequence of which he cannot see very well; his tongue will be burning with a parched dryness and, because the saliva is dried up, he will have an unquenchable thirst.

As the transformation is taking place, he falls to the ground and is seized with fearful writhings and pangs, after which his limbs quiver and contract violently. He then lets out a long, mournful howl and rushes off on all fours to the nearest forest, or to any place where he can shun the light which seems to cause him such agonies. Here he prowls about through the night searching out his victims, which he kills in the normal manner of a wild beast, tearing off their limbs and feasting on their flesh. In this state he literally quivers with a demoniacal ferocity and will bite anyone who may cross his deadly path; but his hair-raising howls, which echo all around the stricken district, are usually enough to warn local people to keep well away from his tracks.

The sixteenth-century physician, Gaspar Peucer, offers a slightly different picture of the symptoms endured by the demon werewolf. According to his *Commentarius de Praecipius Diuinationum Generibus* (1572):

> Those who are changed suddenly fall to the ground as if seized with epilepsy and there they lie without life or motion. Their actual bodies do not move from the spot where they have fallen, nor do their limbs turn to the hairy limbs of a wolf but the soul or spirit by some fascination quits the inert body and enters the *spectrum* of a wolf, and when they have glutted their lupine lusts and cravings, by the Devil's power, the soul re-enters the former human body, whose members are then energized by the return of life.

Human transformations, and the projections of astral bodies, will be examined more closely later on, but Peucer's theory is an intriguing one: that it is the *ego* of the individual which becomes enclosed within a wolf's form, with all its accompanying bestial motions and ferocity. It differs in essence from a very striking case of lycanthropy described in 1852 by another physician, Dr Morel, but since the actual *symptoms* he chronicles in

Many sufferers of lycanthropia experience an acute passion for raw meat. The lycanthrope in this nineteenth-century French print by Léonce Petit apparently hoped to appease his diabolical appetite by consuming one of the local farmyard beasts.

his *Études Cliniques* agree so remarkably with the descriptions of werewolves in the Middle Ages, his reports are well worth our serious consideration. It is important to remember, though, that the sufferer who came under the doctor's care was a classic example of a lycanthrope, a man utterly convinced that he had taken on the shape of a wolf, even though witnesses around him could testify to the contrary.

"See this mouth," cried the victim, touching his lips with his fingers, "it is the mouth of a wolf; these are the teeth of a wolf. I have cloven feet; see the long hairs which cover my body and my paws. Let me run away into the woods so that you may shoot me there!" During the moments when the patient was in a calmer state of mind, Dr Morel would sometimes allow him to see children, sometimes members of his own family, whom he loved dearly and would tenderly embrace. But when they had left he would cry out, "The unfortunates, they have been hugging a wolf!"

"Give me raw meat," he would yell on other occasions, "I am a wolf, a wolf!" Coincidental to his attacks of lycanthropia, he was an unfortunate victim of the morbid wolfish hunger known medically as lycorexia. Raw meat, he said, was the only food he could touch; but when offered this food, he would first attack it ferociously and devour a portion of the meal, and then he would push the remainder away, complaining that it was not decomposed enough.

Of all the cases of lycanthropy I have studied during my research, this is by far the saddest, for during his delusions he undoubtedly suffered the most terrible mental agonies; he accused himself of, and thereby tortured himself by, the guilt of monumentally gruesome offenses which he had certainly never committed. When he died of mental exhaustion and physical consumption at the asylum of Maréville, he was diagnosed by Dr Morel as being in an advanced state of spiritual dereliction. We can but hope that this was the climax of his trial, for what stands out clearly from the medical reports of the case is that the victim was suffering from diabolical possession. It is doubly unfortunate that a qualified exorcist was not called in to rid the patient of his imitative madness.

But the atrocities which Dr Morel's patient imagined he had committed on mankind seem insignificant compared to the very real acts of werewolfery perpetrated by Jean Grenier in the early seventeenth century. Grenier was partially idiotic and of strongly marked canine physiognomy: his jaws were large and projected forward, and his canine teeth were unnaturally long, to the extent that they protruded beyond the lower lip. He was thirteen when he was brought to trial for the murder of several children, and for devouring their flesh and drinking their blood; the court, taking into consideration the tender age of the boy, sentenced him to life imprisonment within the walls of the Monastery of the Cordeliers in Bordeaux.

Grenier had been at the Franciscan monastery for seven years when he was visited by Pierre de Lancre, who relates that the prisoner was of diminutive stature, with black eyes which were deep-set and haggard, and he refused to look anyone straight in the face. His nails were black and, in places, worn away, and his teeth long and protruding and a dirty brown color. His mind, completely blank, seemed unable to understand the simplest things put to him.

He boasted to de Lancre of his former exploits as a werewolf and told how, when he first arrived at the monastery, he preferred to run around on all fours. He also said that he still felt a craving for raw flesh – "especially for that of little girls, which is delicious; if it wasn't for my confinement it would not be long before I tasted it again." He added that he had been visited twice by the Lord of the Forest, as he called the mysterious person who had given him the wolf-skin which originally converted him to werewolfery, but on both occasions he had driven him off with the sign of the cross.

Grenier may well have found it impossible to comprehend the smallest things, but his power of recall was amazing. His account of the murders of several years earlier, his story of the compact he had made with the Devil, the methods by which he had effected his transformations – all this was identical in every detail to that which came out in his trial and in former statements.

Grenier died, aged twenty, soon after de Lancre's visit. It seems he did not die in vain, for his trial and imprisonment heralded a new era in the conviction and punishment of werewolves. Throughout the trial, the court consistently referred to the whole matter of lycanthropy as an aberration of the brain and not as a loathsome branch of black magic. Medical men also began to look upon lycanthropy as a form of mental malady which required their serious attention and skilled treatment and not, as previously, a crime warranting the severest punishment by law. Even so, prejudice against the werewolf was deep-grained and stubborn, and not all courts of law by any means showed the wisdom and courage as the one which sat in judgement on Jean Grenier.

Although de Lancre's physical description of Grenier is a supremely graphic one, it came seven or eight years after the youthful werewolf's bestial attacks on young children; far more useful would have been a description of the boy's features at the time of his arrest, because it is at this time that a werewolf is thought to be distinguished by some peculiarity in its appearance. The meeting of the eyebrows on the bridge of the nose, for instance, and curved, almond-shaped, reddish fingernails, are particular features of the werewolf in his human form. Sometimes a werewolf may be identified by an exceptionally long third finger on each of his broad hands; sometimes by an overall hairiness, especially on the hands and feet; sometimes by the ears, which are set rather low, and far back on their heads; and sometimes by a noticeably long, swinging stride, which is strongly suggestive of some animal. These features, or a good many of them, are always to be found in hereditary werewolves, and they are sometimes developed in those people who voluntarily become werewolves. Among the Russian peasantry it is still believed that while all witches have tails, and all wizards have horns, so a werewolf may be detected (if examined) by the bristles which grow under his tongue.

The year 1598 heralded an epidemic of werewolfery throughout France, and produced one of the most notorious of all werewolf trials. Jacques Rollet, the man-wolf of Caude, was accused of devouring a little boy, and in court confessed to having killed and eaten several women, lawyers, attorneys and bailiffs, the last of which he found tough and tasteless. When caught in a forest he was half-naked, with long hair and a beard, and his hands

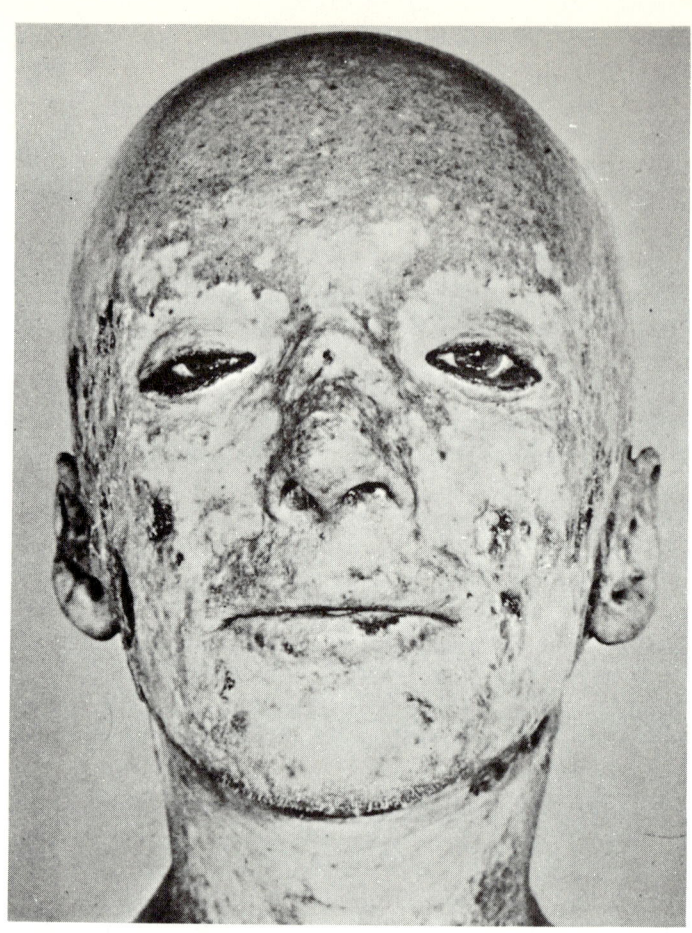

A victim of the rare recessive-gene disease, congenital porphyria. Patients suffering from this complaint in the past, suggests one member of the British medical profession, may have been mistaken for werewolves.

were covered in blood; on his claw-like nails were found shreds of human flesh. He was condemned to two years' sentence in a madhouse.

In recent years an attempt has been made by at least one member of the medical profession to connect the behavior and physical characteristics of early werewolf reports, particularly those in the Middle Ages, with the pitiful victims of a rare disease, porphyria. I am thinking specifically of a paper which was presented on October 2, 1963 at the Royal Society of Medicine by Dr Lee Illis of Guy's Hospital, London. The paper, "On Porphyria and the Aetiology of Werewolves", was subsequently published in the *Proceedings of the Royal Society of Medicine* (Vol. 57, January, 1964), and I am grateful to the Society for placing these findings at my disposal.

I only wish I could be enthusiastic about Dr Illis's argument. He states his case right at the beginning: "I believe," he says, "that the so-called werewolves of the past may, at least in the majority of instances, have been suffering from congenital porphyria. The evidence for this lies in the remarkable relation between the symptoms of this rare disease and the many accounts of werewolves that have come down to us."

He later defines the disease (technically, I am afraid) in this way: "Congenital porphyria is a rare disease, due to a recessive gene, in which there is an inability to convert porphobilinogen to porphyrin in the bone marrow." Among the most convincing symptoms, when trying to relate porphyria to documented werewolf cases, are severe photosensitivity, red or reddish-brown teeth ("due to the deposition of porphyrins") and nervous manifestations ("ranging from mild hysteria to manic-depressive psychoses and delirium"). But most of the other symptoms seem to be less relevant to the argument.

Admittedly, some of the mental symptoms of porphyria described by Dr Illis, as well as one or two physical deformities, could easily be applied to those of both the werewolf and the lycanthrope – but then I have no doubt that they could also be correlated with the symptoms of other medical and psychological ailments. I believe Dr Illis does not give enough thought to the fact that a true werewolf resembles a large wolf and that a lycanthrope only *imagines* himself to be a wolf, since visually he is to all intents and purposes like his fellow men. The horrific skin lesions on the face and hands of the porphyria victim could hardly be mistaken, even in less-enlightened medieval times, for the physical characteristics of the werewolf and certainly not for those of the lycanthrope.

Remember, ancient eye-witness accounts either describe a horrible wolf (when the werewolf is in its animal form) or (when he is in his human shape) some physical characteristics connected with the positioning of the nose, the shape of the eyebrows, the color of the fingernails, the degree of hair on the hands and feet, the kind of stride, and so on – but practically never the nature of the skin-type. I say "practically never" advisedly. It may well be that there is evidence among the vast stockpile of ancient and not-so-ancient literature to corroborate Dr Illis's thesis, but I have seen precious little of it. In fact, my own extensive researches reveal only one very brief description which could be used to support the case for porphyria. The ancient scholar Altomarus concludes his remarks on werewolves (that is, those in their human shape) by explaining that "they have usually hollow eyes, scabbed legs, very dry and pale". But, as strikingly similar as the description may be to that of the victim of porphyria, I would be much happier if there were several other descriptions through the ages to support it. But it seems there are not. And just as one swallow does not make a summer, so I am not prepared to acknowledge that a solitary description from the ancient past justifies acceptance of Dr Illis's porphyria theory.

A far better case could be made, if we wished to find a medical explanation for the belief in werewolves, by equating it with the unfortunate victims of a disease called hypertrichosis – or, scientifically, hypertrichosia universalis congenita. This is an hereditary genetic malfunction which can affect a family through three generations. It is first noticed in the baby, when long hair will be seen to be growing from the ears; gradually, as the child develops, the hair increases to anything up to ten inches in length over most parts of the body, except on the lips, the fingertips, the ends of the toes, the palms of the hands and the soles of the feet. It affects both sexes, and is extremely rare: about one child in every billion born. Documented cases of the disease go back many centuries, although one of the most famous was Théodore Petrof, who appeared for many years in P. T. Barnum's circus during the second half of the nineteenth century; one of his sons was also born with the disease.

It is easy to see how people afflicted by hypertrichosis, at a time when the disorder was not understood, could be mistaken for werewolves – although the rarity of the disease rules out this happening on a large scale. Similarly, it is also possible that some victims of porphyria may on some occasions in the distant past have been viewed as werewolves; but neither the porphyric nor the hypertrichosiac could have flourished on the same grand scale as the archetypal werewolf, which goes back many thousands of years, and it is precisely this fact which invalidates both these medical disorders in the attempt to rationally explain the werewolf superstition.

Porphyria certainly cannot explain some of the werewolf's more depraved physical characteristics, such as his insatiable lust or equally intense craving for blood. Nor the blackness and thickness of his blood, which wells in great clotted gouts. And while in many countries the werewolf is looked upon as wholly physical, in others it is regarded as partly, if not entirely, supernatural. In some parts of the world, for instance, the werewolf exerts certain occult powers to numb his victim's faculties and, cutting up the body, extracts the liver, which he eats. He then joins the parts of the body together again so that the friends of the dead man will not discover how he came to lose his life.

Also, there is no known physical ailment that could account for the one characteristic upon which Boguet, de Lancre and other eye-witnesses emphatically agree, and

OPPOSITE Could at least some reports of werewolves have been attributable to people seeing the unfortunate victims of an hereditary genetic malfunction called hypertrichosis? Here, in a photograph taken around 1888, is Théodore Petrof – the dog-man of Barnum's Circus – who was born with the disease.

that is the horrible "werewolf eyes," the windows of the bestial soul, or for the uniquely animal behavior and movement which the werewolf displays even in his human form. Jean Grenier certainly walked more easily on all fours than upright as a human being, and his agility in clambering and leaping was almost supernatural.

Another thing. Grenier was scarred on the buttocks with the mark of the Devil. When he was first captured, this spot was hard and insensitive, although very conspicuous; but later, after he renounced his sorceries, it

The Devil marking an initiate werewolf. Witches and warlocks are participating in the ceremony. An Italian woodcut from Francesco Maria Guazzo's *Compendium Maleficarum* (1608).

grew tender and soft, and eventually could hardly be seen. Montague Summers tells us, interestingly enough, that "all werewolves – I do not speak for the involuntary ensorcelled transformation – are witches, and therefore all werewolves will be found to be branded with the Devil's mark." I doubt this. Certainly there is little evidence to support the theory, but it is a colorful one all the same. Yet of all the Devil's servants, the werewolf is undeniably the most depraved.

On werewolves in general, de Lancre also gives serious thought to the "Command of the Demon." This "Command" was that a werewolf must not cut the nail of his left thumb, which grows to a considerable length and becomes horny and as hard as the talon of a wild beast. De Lancre considers this to be merely a piece of foul superstition, which in itself is harmless, but which does highlight a certain mindless obedience to the Devil, even in small details. Consequently, an excessively long left thumb nail is an obvious characteristic to look for in a suspected werewolf.

In Sicily, an island with a rich abundance of werewolf folklore, a child who is conceived during a full moon will become a werewolf; it is a belief which subsequently spread northwards into Italy, France, Germany and a few other countries. It is also said in these countries that any man who, on a certain Wednesday or Friday, sleeps outside on a summer's night with the moon shining directly on his face will become a werewolf; his eyes will sink deep into their sockets and take on a glazed expression, and he will fall to the earth in a wallowing heap, whereupon he will gradually take on all (or certainly some) of the classic werewolf symptoms. Avicenna, writing in *The Canon* (a system of medicine) in the eleventh century, asserts that "this malady troubles men mostly in February; they lie hidden for most of the day, and go abroad in the night, barking, howling, at graves and in the desert" (Avicenna was an Arab).

Many a werewolf who, through no desire of his own, finds himself stricken with the dreadful curse, must suffer an additional agony: how to protect those around him, whom he loves, from his own bestial cravings, over which he has no control. If he is lucky and his dreadful desires come over him slowly, he can sometimes give his family or friends advance warning, telling them to leave him in a room which has been securely bolted and barred and from which there is no means of escape; no matter how persistently he demands to be released during his ravings, they should not under any circumstances obey him, and certainly not for a good twelve hours after peace has fallen upon the room.

A particularly depraved attribute of the lycanthrope is his insatiable appetite for consuming recently buried corpses. There is considerable documentation about this trait, such as that to be found in the *Annales Medico-psychologiques* during the last century, but it is far too revolting and gruesome to detail. It would be wrong, however, to overlook the malady completely and so I will document one extraordinary case which was brought before a court-martial in Paris on July 10, 1849. Baring-Gould's description of the case is so good – particularly as it was written only fourteen years after the event – that I have chosen to cite his version of it in full:

> In the autumn of 1848, several of the cemeteries in the neighbourhood of Paris were found to have been entered during the night, and graves to have been rifled. The deeds were not those of medical students, for the bodies had not been carried off, but were found lying about the tombs in fragments. It was at first supposed that the perpetrator of these outrages must have been a wild beast, but footprints in the soft earth left no doubt that it was a man. Close watch was kept at Père la Chaise; but after a few corpses had been mangled there,

the outrages ceased.

In the winter, another cemetery was ravaged, and it was not till March in 1849, that a spring gun which had been set in the cemetery of S. Parnasse, went off during the night, and warned the guardians of the place that the mysterious visitor had fallen into their trap. They rushed to the spot, only to see a dark figure in a military mantle leap the wall, and disappear in the gloom. Marks of blood, however, gave evidence that he had been hit by the gun when it had discharged. At the same time, a fragment of blue cloth, torn from the mantle, was obtained, and afforded a clue towards the identification of the ravisher of the tombs.

On the following day, the police went from barrack to barrack, inquiring whether officer or man were suffering from a gun-shot wound. By this means they discovered the person. He was a junior officer in the 1st Infantry regiment, of the name of Bertrand.

He was taken to the hospital to be cured of his wound, and on his recovery he was tried by court-martial.

His history was this.

He had been educated in the theological seminary of Langres, till, at the age of twenty, he entered the army. He was a young man of retiring habits, frank and cheerful to his comrades, so as to be greatly beloved by them, of feminine delicacy and refinement, and subject to fits of depression and melancholy. In February 1847, as he was walking with a friend in the country, he came to a churchyard, the gate of which stood open. The day before a woman had been buried, but the sexton had not completed filling in the grave, and he had been engaged upon it on the present occasion, when a storm of rain had driven him to shelter. Bertrand noticed the spade and pick lying beside the grave. He managed by some excuse to get rid of his companion and then, returning to the churchyard, he caught up a spade and began to dig into the grave. "Soon I dragged the corpse out of the earth, and I began to hash it with the spade, without well knowing what I was about. A labourer saw me, and I laid myself flat on the ground till he was out of sight, and then I cast the body back into the grave. I then went away, bathed in a cold sweat, to a little grove, where I reposed for several hours, notwithstanding the cold rain which fell, in a condition of complete exhaustion. When I rose, my limbs were as if broken, and my head weak. The same prostration and sensation followed each attack.

"Two days after, I returned to the cemetery, and opened the grave with my hands. My hands bled, but I did not feel the pain; I tore the corpse to shreds and flung it back into the pit."

He had no further attack for four months, till his regiment came to Paris. As he was one day walking in the gloomy, shadowy, alleys of Père la Chaise, the same feeling came over him like a flood. In the night he climbed the wall and dug up a little girl of seven years old. He tore her in half. A few days later, he opened the grave of a woman who had died in childbirth, and had lain in the grave for thirteen days. On the 16th November he dug up an old woman of fifty, and, ripping her to pieces, rolled among the fragments. He did the same to another corpse on the 12th December. These are only a few of the numerous cases of violation of tombs to which he owned. It was on the night of the 15th March that the spring-gun shot him.

Bertrand declared at his trial that while he was in the hospital he had not felt any desire to renew his attempts, and that he considered himself cured of his horrible propensities.

The fits of exhaustion which followed his accesses are very remarkable, as they precisely resemble those which followed the berserk rages of the Northmen, and the expeditions of the lycanthropists. At first the accesses chiefly followed upon his drinking wine, but after a while they came upon him without exciting cause.

The manner in which he mutilated the dead was different. Some he chopped with the spade, others he tore and ripped with his teeth and nails. Sometimes he tore the mouth open and rent the face back to the ears, he opened the stomachs, and pulled off the limbs. Although he dug up the bodies of several men he felt no inclination to mutilate them, whereas he delighted in rending female corpses.

He was sentenced to a year's imprisonment.

Bertrand, who was afflicted with the foulest of the foul of all varieties of lycanthropia, endured the classic symptoms of physical exhaustion once his demented attacks were at an end. The lycanthrope and the werewolf both suffer in this way. He is left weak and debilitated, with dry throat and tongue, poor vision, hollow and discolored cheeks and, in those places where he has been hurt by his victim struggling for life, extreme soreness.

The werewolf, too, once he has shaken off his madness and resumed human shape, undergoes the most painful nervous depression. He suffers tenfold for his catalog of horrors the night before. He is not simply the most depraved of Satan's servants, but the most remorseful.

4 Delusions, Dreams and Hallucinations

Delusion: *a false, irrational belief which is held with great conviction by the individual, cannot be corrected by logic, reason or suggestion and is not held by others of similar class or culture.*
Myre Sim and E.B. Gordon, BASIC PSYCHIATRY, 1972

Dreams and hallucinations: *The experience of some mentally sick patients, who misconstrue their hallucinations as real events, may be classified as dreams despite the fact that the patients are by no means asleep. Their hallucinations are often responsible for the abnormality of their speech and conduct.*
ENCYCLOPAEDIA BRITANNICA, 1969

Lycanthropia, *or wolf-madness, when men run howling about graves and fields in the night, and will not be persuaded but that they are wolves ... Aetius and Paulus call it a kind of* melancholy; *but I should rather refer it to* madness, *as most do.*
Robert Burton, ANATOMY OF MELANCHOLY, 1621

N OCEAN OF THOUGHT, and three and a half centuries, divides *Anatomy of Melancholy* from *Basic Psychiatry*. In Burton's time, the body was still being entrusted to the physician, while the mind and the soul remained the property of the Church; today the mind and soul have moved within the domain of medicine. Also, Burton's era was one of flagellantism (self-injury), tarantism (dancing mania), mass madness, hypochondriacal delusion, projection or hallucination, and (of course) lycanthropy. Elton B. McNeil explains in *The Psychoses* (1970):

Attitudes reflected a psychology influenced by the belief that "whom the Gods will destroy, they first make mad." Madness, as an expression of the will of God, became epidemic. Its cure became a religious ritual designed to use the psychotic as a target for religious persecution and as a means of reaffirming the worth of the blessed, innocent, and pure. Blessed were those who exposed persons who had sold their souls to the Devil. The classic "hunt of the witches" was a side product of the search for salvation.

The "hunt of the werewolves" was also a major factor in man's search for salvation. The witch trials and the werewolf trials were not just interrelated: they were aberrations of the same occultist blood-group. Lycanthropia was, still is, all things to all men. To Robert Burton, in his celebrated medical treatise, it is wolf-madness; to Richard Madden, the nineteenth-century surgeon, it is "werewolf superstitious insanity"; to Johann Wier, Johannes Schenck and other Renaissance thinkers, it is a "natural" disease; to anthropologists like Robert Eisler it is imitative madness; to Alfonso Ponce De Santa Cruz, the seventeenth-century physician to Philip II, it is a symptom of melancholic humor (a product of the bile which attacks the brain); to most psychiatrists today, however, it is little more (or less) than a fundamental delusion, the outcome of restitutional processes. Somewhere here there may be the answer to a terrible mental-spiritual condition, affecting equally men, women and children, which I have termed "the werewolf delusion."

Later we will look at the proposition that man perhaps can, under certain conditions, be metamorphosed into the form of a wolf, but here we are dealing with a far more complex creature, the man who believes he is (but in fact has never been) a wolf – the lycanthrope. Grenier and, a few years earlier, Jacques Rollet, were not only treated by the courts as lycanthropes, but – much more enlightening – were referred to by the judges as the deluded victims of an ailment of the brain. In the tenth century lycanthropes were known by the scientific name of *melancholia canina*, in the fourteenth century by that of *daemonium lupinum*; Dr N. Parker, writing in the *Journal of Mental Science* in 1854, discusses "these sufferers of wolf-madness" as victims of "a variety of isania zoanthropica"; while Dr Daniel Hack Tuke, in his *Dictionary of Psychological Medicine* (1892), terms their ailment quite simply "endemic insanity." People *have* tried, often without success, to *understand* the lycanthrope.

An aged lycanthrope, flanked by two fallen angels, from Jean de Nynauld's *De la Lycanthropie* (1615). All shape-shifting, Nynauld insists, is mere hallucination.

Nearer our own time the British anthropologist, Dr Robert Eisler, makes the fascinating observation in *Man into Wolf* that Adolf Hitler, no less, may have been a lycanthrope. He talks of the famous eye-witness account of the Führer "biting the carpet" in his fits of rage, and then explains, "If the stories about Hitler's rages are true, they would appear to have been manic lycanthropic states and not melancholic bouts of repentance as were the depressions of Nebuchadnezzar." This assumes added dimensions when we view it in conjunction with a particular incident concerning Hitler's arch-enemies, the Russians. In the 1920s the Soviets were putting out stories to the effect that Lenin began life as a bear! "The bear Lenin," they told their more backward regions, "lived for a long time in the virgin forest. There came a Russian general in the forest and tried to trap the bear. He placed a barrel of vodka in the forest, and Lenin, having drunk it, became intoxicated. Thus he fell into the hands of the Russian general, who compelled him to wander about all over the world and to dance for him. Finally he escaped, became a man, and now he is revenging himself on all generals."

In 1935, the British College of Psychic Science, in its quarterly journal, *Psychic Science*, published an amazing account by Dr Gerald Kirkland, formerly Government Medical Officer in Southern Rhodesia, of two natives actually transforming themselves into jackals. If a distinguished, rational and indeed skeptical man of medicine, a respected surgeon, can be deluded into thinking he has seen metamorphosis taking place, then what mental trickeries can a more susceptible mind be expected to experience? This is his story:

> One of the most secret rites of savage Africa today is the ritual of the animal dance. I am one of the odd dozen Europeans who have ever seen one of these. And one moonlight night in a clearing of what at home people call "the jungle," I saw the "Nyan na lo Laklass" – the dance of the jackal. I saw men and women stealthily collecting, forming a circle, drinking furiously – drinking, drinking, drinking. The tom-toms are beating that maddening rhythm so impossible to reproduce, so ventriloquial that it seems to come from inside one's head. The beaters glisten with sweat as their bare hands beat with incredible rapidity upon the stretched skin.
>
> In the circle drunken men and women are dancing, each in their place faster and faster as the drums' fierce rhythm seeps into their blood, and the beer inflames them. Then there is a hush as the witch-doctor, in his

beads and teeth and jackal tails, begins his amazing dance. No human unpossessed could sustain the terrific strain of that dance. I am certain that from that moment he becomes supernormal. Mediumistic if you prefer. Blood and saliva foam from his lips and nostrils. At last he falls in a deep trance. The scream of a hunted jackal echoes through the trees. The drums cease. A shiver runs through the squatting bodies, a little movement as of wind in standing corn. A woman whimpers – like a jackal bitch. A man growls – like a jackal dog. And then it begins. The details are horrible. I can only say that those men and women imitate the actions of jackals with such uncanny accuracy, that one is compelled to believe that they take on the nature, if not the form, of the beast.

Now the climax. Exhausted, the jackal men and women crawl back to their circle to growl and lick their wounds. The witch-doctor comes out of his trance and dances again, and again falls, this time apparently in the deepest coma. And now a boy and girl leap into the circle to dance. If the imitations of the crowd are uncanny, those of the pair are miraculous. More and more nearly do they resemble the animals they portray until suddenly, before my eyes, two jackals are standing in that ring. One noses the entranced witch-doctor with canine curiosity. Then they leap off and away while I blame my fatigue for a trick of the sight. But was it? I do not know. Perhaps it was a coincidence that I treated a native girl in the district for severe jackal scratches (an unheard of thing). Perhaps! I am not sure.

In a paper published in *The Journal of American Folklore* in 1945, the American psychoanalyst Dr Nandor Fodor

Lycanthropic dreams, explains American psychoanalyst Dr Nandor Fodor, are used symbolically by the patient as self-denunciation for secret fantasies or desires.

Hallucinatory werewolf figures as seen by James Callot, a noted seventeenth-century engraver from Nancy who was inspired by a multitude of sins.

interprets the phenomenon described by Dr Kirkland as "an evolutionary regression, an escape from the human onto the animal level." The medical officer's account exposes "the psychological motive behind the lycanthropic ceremonial he witnessed. . . . eating ill-smelling meat and heavy drinking was apparently part of the self-persuasion necessary for the lycanthropic climax."

Dr Fodor goes on to talk about lycanthropy as "a psychic mechanism," and he records a number of dreams which were reported to him by his patients, in which the werewolf figure is a prominent subject. Transformation, bloodshed and cruel murder form an integral part of these "werewolf dreams," the crucial transformation being used symbolically as self-denunciation for secret deeds, fantasies or desires. A few examples from Dr Fodor's notebook will serve to illustrate just how strongly the symbolic wolf/werewolf association can sometimes haunt the mind of the mentally deluded:

A London woman awakes in the morning to find two gleaming eyes in the head of a wolf-shaped animal glaring at her from near the fireplace. In terror, she switches on the light, whereupon the animal vanishes. She believes it was a werewolf.

On being asked for associations, wolf becomes the name of a man through whom she had lost a lot of money and who had climbed into her bedroom in France at night and threatened to strangle her if she would not leave her husband and be his. By his brown, large and baleful eyes, he qualified for the werewolf. Only – the werewolf vision took place before the man invaded the lady's bedroom. Nevertheless, the association gives us a clue to the understanding of her hypnopompic hallucination. It represents her sexual sadistic expectations. The glare in the eye of the wolf was the glow of her own desire for assault and the fireplace was a fitting topographical symbol for the passion from which she burned.

A New York girl dreams of trees the trunks of which are cut off in the shape of a "Y". Each of the trees had a huge cat or panther in the crutch, eating bloody meat, head down, except one whose head was up eating entrails. She suggested that the Y shape stood for the human body with extended legs and that the dream must have a sexual significance. It had. A year before she had an abortion. The entrails referred to the fetus and the cat or panther was herself. The motive behind her lycanthropic dream is self-castigation. She changes into a leopard because her conscience wants to represent her as a beast feeding on the flesh and blood of her own body.

Another woman comes in a state of intense excitement to her thirty-third analytic session. She discovered that she was a werewolf because of her destructive fantasies against her younger sister, Piroska (the Hungarian equivalent to Little Red Riding Hood). Symptoms of cannibalistic guilt appeared from the fact that she could not eat bread because Piroska was often called "piritós" (toast) and "cipó" (loaf of bread); nor could she eat red meat or suffer anything that reminded her of blood. Gisella, her other sister, was also engulfed by these fantasies because she happened to have married a man called Lamb (Bárány) and thus lent herself well for symbolizing the victim of the wolf. Previous to her own lycanthropic discovery, the patient had arrived at a session with a book called *Lady into Fox*, and insisted that I should read it. It was a tale of lycanthropy, the transformation of a woman into a fox – a sign that the lycanthropic fantasy was breaking from her unconscious into her conscious mind. Suddenly, she recalled a neurotic symptom which until then she had failed to describe. She used to feel that there was a long pipe in her body, elastic and dark, which sometimes closed up and then she could not relax. The pipe began high up in her chest and went down to the back of her waistline curling around. Now she knew what it was: the tail of the wolf, anchored in her coccyx. The Hungarian word for wolf is "farkas" and "fark" means tail. With a slight linguistic license, "farkas" can be translated as "the taily one." Thus, psychologically, the lycanthropic element is excellently represented by the tail fantasy and the motive is criminality as in the previous dream.

One final werewolf dream recorded by Dr Fodor comes from a Russian woman; it is part of a longer recurrent nightmare about wolves. She relates it like this:

> I come into a circular room with Roman columns. There were greyish brown hangings all around the room, a long table on my right with benches on each side. On the farther side lies a man with his hands clasped on his breast and his eyes closed. On the nearer side a woman, burying her face in her arm. On my left in the corner stands a female figure clad in a long Roman toga and holding over her shoulder the head of a putrefied woman.
>
> When I come in, the three of them say: "It is time you should have come, we have been waiting for you so long." The woman on the left said: "You saw this head before, it was here" – and she lifted it up toward her face; "now it is here" – and she placed it between her shoulder and head; "it will disappear but you must come and lie with me in the coffin."
>
> Then suddenly there was a new woman sitting there and I was that woman. The dead man was moaning: "Dying, dying ... Bertha, why are you afraid of dying? Dying is being born, there isn't anything to fear about dying."
>
> Then I saw that the hangings were not hangings but the flatulent movements of the womb. They were slimy. I knew then that I was in my own womb.

Dr Fodor interprets the dream in this way:

> Slavering with freshly spilt blood and with human entrails hanging from her mouth, the dreamer presents the traditional picture of a ravenous wolf that has made a kill. Her body retains the human shape, she only changes sex, but the psychic transformation is complete. The link between this dream and that of the two wolves on the hillock reveal the shape-shifting purpose of her fantasy, the grim horror of which may well compete with medieval chronicles on lycanthropy. In her

In this gruesome woodcut by the sixteenth-century German painter, Lucas Cranach, a shaggy-haired lycanthrope has adopted the aggressive stance and predatory behavior of the wolf he imagines himself to be. He is making off with a baby, long the favorite prey of these demented human monsters. All around lie the horribly dismembered remains of the lycanthrope's earlier expeditions.

childhood, Russia was still rife with werewolf superstition. Many people believed that by certain practices men could change their bodies into the shape of beasts. She vividly remembered a story about a certain prince and his servant which she herself had been told. The servant threw himself three times on the ground and became a wolf; whereupon the prince sprang on his back and rode away on some nefarious business. The story sent cold shivers down her spine. When her growing intelligence rejected it, it receded into the hotbed of her unconscious fantasy life from where it flowered into nightmares.

In the sixteenth and seventeenth centuries, these werewolf dreams would almost certainly have been interpreted by the judiciary as self-condemnatory. Since they came within the forbidden religio-legal domain of "dreams and visions," the obligatory confessions in court would no doubt have constituted adequate testimony of the dreamers' guilt as werewolves, though, as was noted earlier, James I of England was perceptive enough to regard lycanthropes as "victims of delusion, induced by a natural superabundance of melancholy." The English, American, Hungarian and Russian women cited by Dr Fodor, in a less favorable age, a world without benefit of psychoanalytical therapy, would undoubtedly have perished at the stake. Psychiatry tries to explain today what the torturer could never explain: the motivation behind, and the ancestry of, a patient's delusions, dreams and hallucinations.

Through all ages there have been men who could *imagine* themselves as beasts, and make not only other people believe them, but the beasts also. MacGregor Mathers, the leading light of the late-nineteenth-century magical society known as the Hermetic Order of the Golden Dawn, was one day walking with a friend through a field of sheep when he said, "I am going to imagine myself a ram," and instantly all the sheep came bounding after him. What would have happened if he had imagined

The werewolf in contemporary fantasyland, as seen by artist Nick Neocleous for the British comic-book fanzine, *Comics Unlimited* (March 1978).

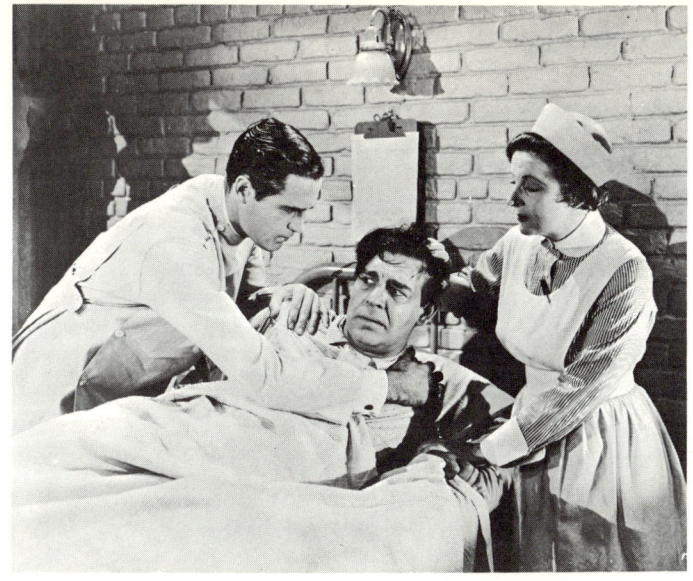

Larry Talbot, played as poignantly as ever by Lon Chaney, Jr, suffers from more than just delusional qualities in the 1943 film *Frankenstein Meets the Wolf Man*. He *is* the wolfman. Doctor and nurse should take heed before it is too late.

himself a wolf? Would people have bounded away from him in morbid fear?

Later on it will be seen how, in the case of a seventeen-year-old youth, a powerful projection of hate against an enemy can assume visible form in an hallucination. Richard Cavendish, in *The Powers of Evil* (1975), refers briefly to a similar instance of "hate projection," and he tells us that:

> Dion Fortune said that she once unintentionally created a werewolf in this way. She was in bed, half asleep and brooding over her resentment against someone who had injured her. The thought of casting off all restraint and going berserk came into her mind, and then the thought of Fenris, the monstrous evil wolf of Norse mythology. "Immediately I felt a curious drawing-out sensation from my solar plexus, and there materialized beside me on the bed a large wolf." When she moved, it snarled at her and she had to muster all her courage to speak sharply to it and push it off the bed. It went meekly enough, turned from a wolf into a dog and vanished through the wall in the northern corner of the room; but next morning someone else in the house reported dreaming of wolves and waking in the night to see the eyes of a wild animal glowing in the dark.

"... the gleaming eyes of the classic werewolf dream...." Illustration by Peter Coccagna for the 1930s American magazine, *Fantasy Fiction*.

Here we have the gleaming eyes of the classic werewolf dream as recorded by Dr Fodor, except in this particular case the apparition of a wild animal was not self-motivated but was the overtly mental repercussion of someone else's projection of hate. Psychic transformation was the grim outcome.

There have been many cases, too, where the homicidal or cannibal craving has been accompanied by genuine hallucination and by certain forms of insanity in which the afflicted persons imagine themselves to be brute animals. John Fiske, writing in *The Atlantic Monthly* in 1871, says, "I once knew a poor demented old man who believed himself to be a horse, and would stand by the hour together before a manger, nibbling hay, or deluding himself with the pretence of so doing." Such hallucinations are far more common than most people perhaps realize; they stem principally from melancholy, and specifically from melancholic humor, which, as was established earlier, is a product of the bile which attacks the brain. The *World History of Psychiatry* (1975) confirms that if this humor attacks hypochondriacs and is "accompanied by obstructions," then it produces hypochondriacal delusion; the book gives such instances as "the thirty-year-old patient who first fell into a melancholy, then developed a monomania which made him believe that he was transformed into a wolf (lycanthropy); he fled from men and sought refuge in the mountains, where he spent the nights howling, visiting the graveyard and invoking the dead."

Dr Thomas Freeman, of Holywell Hospital, Antrim, Northern Ireland, mentions in his book *Psychopathology of the Psychoses* (1969) several cases where his psychiatric patients saw in him, and other doctors, certain delusional qualities. One patient, for instance, asked the author if he was a man or woman. "Later," says Dr Freeman, "he told a nurse that he was surrounded by 'paranoidals' who were half man and half woman and who preyed on humans. He believed a woman doctor was a vampire. This idea was stimulated when he saw her take a blood-sample from a patient." He could just as easily have associated the woman doctor, of course, with a werewolf or some other savage beast. It would certainly have been a reasonable enough hypochondriacal delusion – a classic example, in fact, of "the werewolf delusion." It is also reasonable to suppose that many so-called "eye-witnesses" in the distant past who claimed they saw werewolves, and perhaps even testified to this effect in court, were simple people who were themselves victims of melancholia.

So, if a myth or superstition is a piece of unscientific philosophizing, it must sometimes be applied to the explanation of obscure psychological as well as psychic and physical phenomena. Where the modern man calmly taps his forehead and says, "Arrested development, hallucinations, delusions," the terrified wretch in the Middle Ages made the sign of the cross and cried, "Werewolf!"

5 The Werewolf in Antiquity

ON THE NIGHT OF A FULL MOON in June, 1954, a Montreal doctor of philosophy, Dr Joseph de Nobilis, took sixteen of his students up the mountain of Loup Garou in Quebec – a reputed haunt of the werewolf of French-Canadian folklore. His mission was to disprove the validity of such a legend. He believed, naively, that if neither he nor any of his party were attacked by a werewolf, then the legend must be false. Not unsurprisingly, none of them were attacked . . . but then the werewolf has seldom, if ever, appeared to order.

All the same, Dr de Nobilis's "werewolf expedition" does illustrate just how forcibly the belief in animal metamorphosis has permeated into the second half of the twentieth century, thousands of years after ancient man first shuddered at the grotesque specter of the werewolf. The idea of a being, half-wolf, half-man, who is the possessor of terrible demoniacal qualities, is certainly a very curious piece of old-world superstition, but it is a belief which still exerts a magical power all over the globe, and no doubt strengthened, if misguidedly, by the occasional discovery of children who have been carried off and cared for by wolves who preferred the role of foster-mother to that of devourer.

But as the superstition is so widespread – France, Germany, Eastern Europe, Africa, Asia, North America – it could be assumed that it arose at a very early time in Man's history, when all the world's peoples were in communication with each other. Another possibility, much favored by modern science, is that the superstition arose independently in various continents during the course of the natural psychic development of the human race.

My own view is that the werewolf legend in Europe was born while the Greeks, Romans, Celts and Germanic peoples were still in friendly contact with each other. When one race began to partition off its particular identity from the other, the superstition became slightly modified – in some cases intensifying its grip on the ancient imagination – according to local needs and cultures. With the growth of culture, too, came the growth of

The Greek philosopher Plato, author of the earliest werewolf story. He asks us if we *know* the story.

supernaturalism, from the roots of which grew werewolfery.

Around 370 B.C., the Greek philosopher Plato wrote the following dialogue:

"And what are the first steps in the transformation of the champion into a tyrant? Can we doubt that the change dates from the time when the champion has begun to act like the man in that legend which is current in reference to the temple of Lycaean Zeus in Arcadia?"

"*What legend?*"

"According to it, the worshipper who tasted the one human entrail, which was minced up with the other entrails of other victims, was inevitably metamorphosed into a wolf. Have you never heard the story?"

"*Yes, I have.*"

Of course he had. Romans and Greeks alike were familiar with it. It is the oldest werewolf story on record, and is mixed up with another legend relating to the practice of sacrificing human victims. Anyway, the story tells of Lycaon, King of Arcadia, who was turned into a wolf as a punishment for offering human flesh to the gods.

Pausanias, the Greek traveler and geographer, writing in the year A.D. 166, discusses at some length the magical

rites of werewolfery which were still being practiced in Arcadia. He observes:

> Lycaon brought a human babe to the altar of Lycaean Zeus and sacrificed it and poured out the blood on the altar; and they say that immediately after the sacrifice he was turned into a wolf. For my own part I believe the tale: it has been handed down among the Arcadians from antiquity, and probability is in its favor. They

Lycaon, ax in hand in readiness for the sacrifice of a human victim, at the altar of Lycaean Zeus. A copperplate engraving by the sixteenth-century Italian artist Agostino de' Musi.

say that from the time of Lycaon downward a man has always been turned into a wolf at the sacrifice of Lycaean Zeus but that the transformation is not for life; for if while he is a wolf, he abstains from human flesh, in the ninth year afterward he changes back into a man, but if he has tasted human flesh he remains a beast for ever.

There are several Arcadian tales along these lines. One legend speaks of the family of Anthos who, selected by lot, made for the shores of a lake in Arcadia. Here, after hanging his clothes on the branches of an oak, Anthos dived in and swam across and changed into a wolf for a period of nine years. Then there is the story of Demaentus who, during a sacrifice of human victims, tasted the entrails of a boy who had been slaughtered and was immediately transformed into a wolf; ten years later he was victorious in the pugilistic contests at the Olympic games.

Herodotus, the most probing travel-reporter of all time, tells us that the Neurians became wolves for a few days once a year, and then returned to the form of men. Virgil and Propertius confirm the story. The werewolf was commonly called a "skin-changer" or "turncoat" (*versipellis*) by the ancient Romans, and similar epithets were applied to him in the Middle Ages. The medieval theory was that, while the werewolf kept his human form, his hair grew inwards; when he wished to become a wolf, he simply turned himself inside out. In ancient Denmark it was believed that if a woman were to creep through a colt's placental membrane stretched between four sticks, she would for the rest of her life give birth to children without pain or illness – but all the boys in such cases would be werewolves, and all the girls Maras, or nightmares.

Marcellus Sidetes, writing in the second century A.D., talks of men who at the beginning of every year were afflicted with a form of madness, during which they believed themselves to be wolves or dogs, and spent the night prowling about burial grounds. In many European countries this prevailing belief may have acted on some weak minds who were perhaps naturally inclined to lunacy, and some madmen may have really believed themselves to be possessed by a wolf spirit: they may have acted the part well enough as to strengthen the popular superstition associated with werewolves – that they were the undoubted servants of the Devil. Norwegian and Icelandic sagas are full of references to this belief.

It is easy to see how such tales were developed by the medieval imagination into a popular belief in werewolves. Beginning as a figurative explanation of meteoric facts, it

Arcadia, an ancient Greek Shangri La and the mountainous center of the Greek Peloponnese, was also the seat of the first European werewolves.

next became a hieratic mystery, and then descended from the domain of religion to that of magic and popular myth. But not everyone was a believer. Pliny, the great Roman scholar, certainly refused to give credence to the possibility of Arcadian werewolves. "That men may be transformed into wolves, and restored again to their former shape," he writes, "we must confidently believe to be a great lie, or else give credit to all those tales which we have for so many ages found to be mere fabulous untruths."

Of course, there may possibly be a simpler explanation for the apparent transformations into wolves of some of those present at the sacrifices to Lycaean Zeus. Just as the medicine-men of modern totem clans often wear costumes resembling their totem animal, so the priest who officiated at the Lycaean rite may have clothed himself in a wolfskin. Whatever the answer, the Arcadian belief in werewolves clearly illustrates the complicated manner in which a number of mythical conceptions and misunderstood natural occurrences all combined to generate a long-enduring superstition.

We should also remember that the story of Lycaon takes us back not just into antiquity as we usually regard it, but back to a period which the historians call pre-history. These were the days before a flood covered the world, the age of the Giants and the Titans, for Lycaon was the son of Pelasgos, who in turn was the son of Mother Earth. Furthermore, it was when Nyktimos, the son of Lycaon, ruled his father's home that the deluge of Deucalion swamped the continents. We are literally in deep waters when we touch upon the origins of the werewolf legend.

One of the best-known of the ancient werewolf stories comes from Petronius Arbiter, a contemporary and fellow countryman of Pliny. It is told by one Niceros, at a banquet given by Trimalchio, in the *Satyricon*:

Petronius Arbiter, director of entertainment at Nero's court, tells a fine werewolf yarn in his satirical picaresque romance, the *Satyricon*.

> It happened that my master had gone off to Capua to take care of some business. I took the opportunity and persuaded a young soldier who was staying in the house to accompany me on a journey. We set off at about sunset, and before long the moon was shining bright as midday. We were on the main road, with the gravestones on either side of it, when my companion went off to one side (I assumed) to relieve himself among the tombstones. After a while I looked around to see what the fellow was up to, and by the gods! my heart leaped into my mouth. He had taken off all his clothes and piled them in a heap at the edge of the road; and then I saw him piss in a circle all around his clothes, and just like that – pop! he turned into a wolf.
>
> He then began to howl horribly, and with that ran off full tilt into the woods. I was half dead with fear. So I drew my sword, and as I made my way along the road I kept thrusting at the haunted shadows until I finally reached my pretty mistress's house. "If you had only been here a little earlier," Melissa said, "your help would have come in mighty handy. A huge wolf had just broken into the place and made sad havoc among the cattle and sheep. But Master Wolf didn't get off scot-free, though, because our servant gave him a good jab in the neck with a pike."
>
> When I heard all this I couldn't so much as close an eye; but as soon as it was daylight I made hurried tracks back to the house of my master, Gaius. When I got to the place where the fellow's clothes had been turned to stone, I could see nothing but a ghastly pool of blood! Finally I reached home, and there I found the soldier in bed, bleeding like an ox in the slaughterhouse, while a physician was busy dressing a deep gash in his neck. It was then that I knew he was a werewolf.

From ancient times up to a period nearer our own, there is this recurring theme which binds together the whole damnable werewolf superstition: the peculiarity of a wound being dealt to the werewolf being reproduced in the human being.

Little Red Riding Hood being attacked by the wolf. A nineteenth-century illustration.

One of the germs of the European werewolf myth seems to be the Aryan conception of the howling wind as a wolf. The Maruts, the young men of mythology who rode the clouds and made rain, sometimes changed themselves into wolves on the occasion of sudden storms. Throughout all Aryan mythology the souls of the dead are supposed to ride on the night wind, with their howling dogs, gathering in their company the souls of those just dying as they pass by their houses. Sometimes (as is explained more fully in Chapter 2) the whole complex conception is wrapped up in the notion of a great ravening wolf who comes to devour its victim and extinguish the sunlight of life, just as that old wolf of the tribe of Fenris gobbled up Little Red Riding Hood with her cloak of scarlet twilight. The storm-wind or Howling Râkshasas of Hindu folklore is, to quote Baring-Gould, "a great misshapen giant with red beard and red hair, with pointed protruding teeth, ready to lacerate and devour human flesh. His body is covered with coarse bristling hair, his huge mouth is open, he looks from side to side as he walks, lusting after the flesh and blood of men, to satisfy his raging hunger and quench his consuming thirst. Toward nightfall his strength increases manifold. He can change his shape at will. He haunts the woods, and roams howling through the jungle." He is, in short, to the Hindu what the werewolf is to the European or American.

It was also a primeval viewpoint that dogs and wolves

Nebuchadnezzar, the King of Babylon, having incurred the wrath of God, "was driven from men, and did eat grass as oxen, and his body was wet with the dew of Heaven, till his hairs were grown like eagles' feathers, and his nails like birds' claws" (Daniel, iv, 33).

were to be found among the inhabitants of Hell. Actually, this belief was taken very seriously by the early Hindus. And there are some mythologists who would like us to believe that these infernal animals were real werewolves: men upon whom such a transformation had been inflicted as a punishment. We are, therefore, never far away from the Arcadian concept of Lycaon being turned into a wolf in retribution for offering human sacrifices to Jupiter.

The great Babylonian warrior-king, Nebuchadnezzar, who died in 562 B.C. after restoring his country to its former prosperity and importance, has become the center of many legends. One of these concerns a strange lycanthropic malady which he suffered for several years during his reign. The British anthropologist, Dr Robert Eisler, in his study of sadism, masochism and lycanthropy, *Man into Wolf*, explains that "it is perfectly conceivable that he suffered from a cyclothymic manic-depressive psychosis, the elation of a 'Caesarian' megalomania of the divinized world-ruler being succeeded by a depression in which he developed a sense of guilt and responsibility for all the blood shed at his behest and wanted to return from the accursed state of a blood-stained predatory werewolf or lion-man to the innocence of the grazing cattle." Complex indeed are the ways of lycanthropy.

Bypassing Lucian, Apuleius and other ancient writers, we find the werewolf superstition in vogue among the Scandinavians as late as King Gustavus I of Sweden, who died in 1560. In his great history of Sweden, *Historia de Gentibus Septentrionalibus*, published in 1555, Olaus Magnus devotes three long chapters to werewolfery, discussing transformations both in ancient times and as he found them in his own day.

> Between Lithuania, Samogitia, and Curonia, there is a certain wall left, of a castle that was thrown down; to this, at a set time, some thousands of werewolves come together, that each of them may try his nimbleness in leaping. He that cannot leap over this wall, as commonly

Transformation of men into wolves at the sabbath. Woodcut from Olaus Magnus's *Historia de Gentibus Septentrionalibus* (1555).

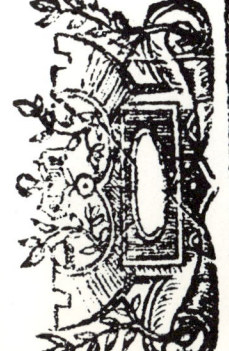

George Sand's illustration (from his *Légendes Rustiques*, 1858), showing "a certain wall" where "some thousands of werewolves come together, that each may try his nimbleness in leaping."

the fat ones cannot, are beaten with whips by their captains. And it is constantly affirmed that among the multitude are the great men and chiefest nobility of the land.

We come across such a wall, and such a contest among werewolves, in a number of West European stories, although it is rare to encounter it in the ancient sagas of the North. Throughout Scandinavia in general, and Finland in particular, werewolves in ancient times were credited with demoniacal power, and even well into this present century Finnish peasants cowered in fear at the merest mention of the word werewolf; superstition dictated that they could not even mention its name. In the ancient sagas, old women who possessed the power of metamorphosing into wolves were said to be able to paralyze cattle and children with their eyes and to have deathly poison in their nails.

Generally speaking, while Gaul has been the favorite haunt of the werewolf, Scandinavia has been preferred by the were-bear and India by the were-tiger. But bulls, too, as well as bears, figure in Northern werewolf mythology. Ari Hin Frode, the Learned, wrote that Dufthac was "a mighty skin-changer," and so was Storwolf o' Whale. It seems they got into a quarrel about some rights of pasture, so the one turned himself into a bear, and the other (rather weakly it seems) into a bull. They fought it out and, as might be supposed, the bear won. The valley where they fought looked as if there had been an earthquake; both were so bruised when they resumed human shape that they had to go to bed.

King Harold I, known more popularly by the Norwegians as Haarfager (the Fair-haired), who ruled between the years 860 and 930, had a body of men called Ûlfhednar (wolf-coated) to distinguish them from the Berserker (bear-skin shirted). These men were supposed to acquire the strength and fierceness of the animal whose skin they wore. The myth of the giant wolf Fenris, the offspring of the evil Loki and the giantess Angurboda, who created such a disturbance among the gods in Asgard, gave a semi-religious authority to the man-wolf idea in Scandinavia. The werewolf itself was commonly known as *vargr*; as for the berserker, who in earlier times were also men who had acquired superhuman strength by transformation into either bears or wolves, they will be returning later in the story.

Another ancient legend, this time stemming from sixth-century Ireland, tells how St Natalis inflicted a curse on an Irish family of high degree. Each member, male and female, was subject to the horrible doom where, at some period of life, he or she (and sometimes both) had to assume the form and behavior of a wolf, and for seven years had to roam the countryside before once again taking his or her place among fellow human beings.

Throughout the fifteenth and sixteenth centuries in Europe, the belief in these transformations equaled the belief in witches and wizards, and those suspected of being werewolves were burnt, decapitated or hanged in the most cruel manner. And yet it is easy to understand the wrath of the governing authorities when we remember that most of those accused of werewolfery during this period had committed the most atrocious butcheries.

Consider the case of Peter Stump, who died a penitent near Cologne in 1589, prior to which he had pleaded guilty to the crime of magical self-transformation. Today we might be inclined to regard him as being as fanatical as his judges were credulous. Yet he freely confessed to having killed thirteen children, two women and a man, usually in the most savage fashion; and so the violent death of sixteen people in one neighborhood is a notorious fact we can neither ignore nor question. The madness of Peter Stump, we must now assume, was precipitated by an advanced state of lycanthropia.

Time may prove that there is probably less in lycanthropy than the superstition of the sixteenth century supposed, and more in it than we, with all our apparent sophisticated reasoning and infinite wisdom, can clearly comprehend. That proposition will be explored later on.

6 Servant of Witchcraft and the Devil

ATAN, the supreme embodiment of evil – vengeful, intensely malicious, ruthless and subtle – is the constant companion of the werewolf. There are many satanists, in fact, who insist that all werewolves are witches and therefore branded with the Devil's mark. But this has never been proved, although there are a number of isolated instances on record. What is more certain is that in the Middle Ages witches often avenged themselves on those they or others hated by inflicting on them the evil curse of the werewolf. Numerous knights and ladies were victimized in this way, although it seems to have been more commonly directed toward people of a less exalted class.

During the sixteenth and seventeenth centuries, when werewolfery was rampant, the learned men of the day reasoned that if the Devil could enter swine, he could just as easily enter wolves; and his influence on witches was never held in doubt. This is well illustrated by a woman who was apprehended at Lyon, in 1601, on suspicion of being a werewolf. She was asked by the magistrate if, in return for his sparing her life, she could show him how she went about practicing the art for which she was then standing trial. She agreed that she could, but, as a necessary preliminary, she would require a particular pot of ointment. When a clerk of the court had obtained this potion from her house, she smeared various parts of her body with it, and then fell into a deep sleep lasting some three hours. After awakening she told the court, in answer to their numerous questions, that during her sleep she had taken the form of a wolf and made for a neighboring town where she had mangled a sheep and a cow. The magistrate immediately sent an official to the place in question to inquire whether such an attack had been committed on these two animals, and was told that it had indeed. The court was suitably impressed, although the records do not state precisely whether or not the magistrate kept his word and spared the life of the witch-cum-werewolf.

Some interpreters of this case think that the Devil was the real author of the killing and slaying, and that he influenced the woman to dream that the credit was due to herself. Certainly Satan has been at the center of many werewolf cases. Jean Grenier, for one, often told people that he had sold himself to the Devil and that he had acquired the power of ranging the country at dusk in the form of a wolf.

In the South of France, as recently as a hundred years ago, it was believed that the Devil had destined certain men to be lycanthropes, especially in the old district of Périgord, where the werewolf was (and perhaps still is) called *louléerou*. Baring-Gould explains:

It is always at night that the fit comes on. The lycanthropist dashes out of a window, springs into a well and, after having struggled in the water for a few moments, rises from it, dripping, and invested with a goatskin which the Devil has given him. In this condition, the *louléerous* run upon four legs, pass the night in ranging over the country and in biting and devouring all the dogs they

The Devil . . . the chief instigator of many a lycanthropic and werewolfic crime?

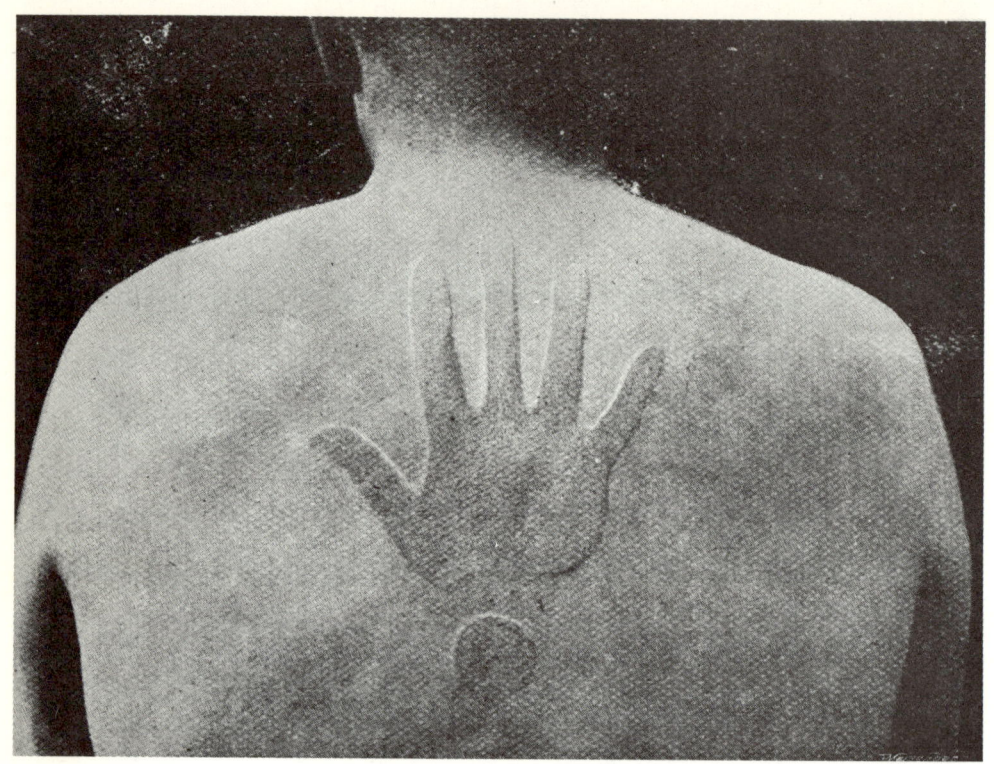

Mark of the Devil. A late-nineteenth-century photograph by F. Meheux of Paris.

meet. At break of day they lay aside their goatskin and return home. Often they are ill in consequence of having eaten tough old hounds, and they vomit up their undigested paws. One great nuisance to them is the fact that they may be wounded or killed in their *louléerou* state. With the first effusion of blood their diabolic covering vanishes, and they are recognized, to the disgrace of their families.

Baring-Gould also points out that men in Normandy who are afflicted with the curse of the werewolf clothe themselves every evening with a skin – their *hère* or *hure* – which the Devil has generously loaned them. "When they run in their transformed state," he says, "the evil one accompanies them and scourges them at the foot of every Cross they pass. The only way in which such a werewolf can be liberated from this cruel bondage is by stabbing him three times in the forehead with a knife."

A fascinating example of a late-medieval sermon was delivered at the cathedral of Strasbourg in 1508 by Dr Johann Geiler von Kaisersberg, "the German Savonarola," whose bold, incisive, denunciatory sermons won for him a wide fame. These were taken down by a barefooted friar, Johann Pauli, and published in Strasbourg in 1516 under the title *Die Emeis*. This is a valuable document for the student of lycanthropy, both for its graphic descriptions of

Johann Geiler von Kaisersberg: "What shall we say about werewolves?"

contemporary werewolf belief and for the Church's attitude to a type of man who supposedly consorted with the Devil.

Dr Geiler begins by asking his congregation, "What shall we say about werewolves? For there are werewolves which run about the villages devouring men and children. As men say about them, they run about full gallop, injuring men, and are called *ber-wölff*, or *wer-wölff*. Do you ask me if I know anything about them? I answer, Yes. They are apparently wolves which eat men and children." He lists seven reasons for this:

1	Esuriem	Hunger
2	Rabiem	Savageness
3	Senectutem	Old age
4	Experientiam	Experience
5	Insaniem	Madness
6	Diabolum	The Devil
7	Deum	God

But it is principally the last two factors which most interest us here. Geiler says:

Many demonologists argue that with the command of God the Devil can be given the power to transform a human being corporeally into a wolf.

Under the sixth heading, the injury comes of the Devil, who transforms himself and takes on him the form of a wolf. So writes Vincentius in his *Speculum Historiale*. And he has taken it from Valerius Maximus in the Punic Wars. When the Romans fought against the men of Africa, when the captain lay asleep, there came a wolf and drew his sword and carried it off. That was the Devil in a wolf's form. The like writes William of Paris – that a wolf will kill and devour children, and do the greatest mischief. There was a man who had the fantasy that he himself was a wolf. And afterwards he was found lying in the wood, and he was dead out of sheer hunger.

Under the seventh heading, the injury comes of God's ordinance. For God will sometimes punish certain lands and villages with wolves. So we read of Elisha – that when Elisha wanted to go up a mountain out of Jericho, some naughty boys made a mock of him and said, "O bald head, step up! O glossy pate, step up!" What happened? He cursed them. Then came two bears out of the desert and tore about forty-two of the children. That was God's ordinance. The like we read of the prophet who would set at nothing the commands he had received of God, for he was persuaded to eat bread at the house of another. As he went home he rode upon his ass. Then came a lion which slew him and left the ass alone. That was God's ordinance. Therefore must man turn to God when he brings wild beasts to do him a mischief: which same brutes may He not bring now or evermore. Amen.

The assertion that God sometimes imposes a curse on certain people so that they will be ravaged by wild beasts, wolves included, is strange but enlightening. Reading the werewolf literature, and reflecting on the numerous instances where saints, men of the Church, and even God himself, have placed lycanthropic curses on men who have incurred their respective wrath, one can only conclude that the Devil is not the only perpetrator of the sad affliction of the damned.

But it is the Devil who is most often behind it all. The accused of one werewolf crime in the seventeenth century confessed to the court that a *female* Devil had given him a magical belt, and whenever he buckled it around him he was instantaneously changed into a wolf. When he was back in his human shape, he was always telling people that he had not the faintest idea where the bristles went which, in his wolfish form, had covered him from head to toe.

Because Satan's subordinate demons can take possession of men's bodies, afflicting them (II Corinthians, XII, 7) or making them diseased (Matthew, XII, 26; Luke, XI, 18), it is commonly believed among respected demonologists that Satan can hold lycanthropes and werewolves in his power by any one of three ways:

Firstly, that the afflicted men commit certain depredations, such as mangling cattle, while they are in their human shapes; but they do this in such a state of hallucination that they are firmly convinced that they *are* wolves, and others who see them execute these crimes are similarly convinced of the wrongdoers' wolfish form. Although they are not true werewolves, but lycanthropes, they nonetheless hunt in packs like the animals they believe themselves to be.

Secondly, that they leave their bodies lying fast asleep and "send out" their imagination in a dream in which they believe they have injured, for instance, several cows; but it is the Devil who does what is suggested to them by their thoughts.

And, thirdly, that the Devil induces real wolves to do the terrible crimes, but impresses the scene so vividly on the mind of the sleeper that he considers himself to be guilty of the act; this certainly seems to have been the case concerning the witch-werewolf of Lyon who had

Satan, with whom so many medieval werewolves swore they had entered into compact. Illustration from a fifteenth-century French manuscript.

demonstrated the process to the court.

In her scholarly book, *Human Animals* (1915), Frank Hamel discusses an intriguing case which underlines much of the above, and it has double the fascination for us today because it clearly illustrates a form of hallucinatory predicament in which both the attacker *and* the attacked believed that the latter was a wolf. Hamel explains that a man was starting on a journey in Latvia when he saw a wolf attacking one of his sheep:

> He fired and it fled wounded into the thicket. On his return he was told that he had fired at one of his tenants, called Mickel. Mickel's wife, when questioned, said that her husband had been sowing rye and had asked her how he could get some meat for a feast. She said on no account was he to steal from the master's flock as it was well guarded by dogs. Mickel ignored her advice and had attacked the sheep. He came home limping badly and, in a passion, had fallen upon his own horse and had torn its throat. It seemed as though he were bewitched or in a trance.

The werewolf, being invariably a practitioner in witchcraft and sorcery, has made a pact with the Devil and, as Francesco Guazzo explains in his *Compendium Maleficarum* (1608), these pacts "are not only vain and useless; they are also dangerous and immeasurably pernicious." Nicolas Remy also observes in his *Daemonolatria* (1595) that any werewolf, or wizard of black magic, who has surrendered himself to the power of the Demon, has in effect become weary of his tyranny. A great number of werewolves suffer from melancholia and manic-depression because of this: they are bitterly conscious of the loathsome nature of their crimes and are continually trying to throw off their blind obedience to evil. But so harsh and unjust a taskmaster is Satan that, at their every attempt to steer towards good, at each inspiration of spiritual grace, they are scolded and severely punished by the evil one; and so, just as the Devil aids the cat-witch – that contemptible creature who stealthily finds her way into bedrooms, who leaps walls and runs with great nimbleness and speed – so he will energize the werewolf, who will from that point on be possessed of all the savagery and fiercest instincts of a ravening wolf.

It is pertinent to mention briefly here the views of the great Jean Bodin who, in the second volume of his *Démonomanie des Sorciers* (1580), puts forward the always controversial notion that Satan can materially metamorphose the body of a man into a wolf or some other animal by means of black magic, via the diabolical sorcery of his

OPPOSITE By means of a magical rite, sorcerers and witches are being transformed into werewolves. The painting, *The Witches' Kitchen,* was one of six produced by the Spanish master, Francisco de Goya, in 1798.

Having made a pact with the Devil, werewolves and witches embark on an orgy of terror. The illustration appears in a German broadsheet, published in Augsburg in 1591.

disciples. As Montague Summers points out in *The Werewolf*, there are other equally learned writers who have maintained that, under God, the Devil has the power actually to change a human being corporeally into a wolf, but it was Bodin who was universally regarded and so violently attacked as the chief exponent of this argument. Summers writes:

> From whatever cause this shape-shifting may arise, it is very certain by the common consent of all antiquity and all history, by the testimony of learned men, by experience and first-hand witness, that werewolfism which involves some change of form from man to animal is a very real and a very terrible thing. But it cannot, of course, take place without the exercise of black magic.

Bodin's faith in the powers of Satan, as they apply to werewolfery, is all the more remarkable because for more than a thousand years, from the time of Saint Augustine to the publication of Bodin's treatise, scholars (certainly church scholars) had condemned out of hand all such unearthly powers. There is no stronger critic, in fact, than Saint Augustine himself who, in his *De Spiritu et Anima*, tells us:

> It is very generally believed that by certain witches' spells and the power of the Devil men may be changed into wolves and beasts of burden, and when their work

is done they return to their original shapes, but they do not lose their human reason and understanding, nor are their minds made the intelligence of a mere beast. Now this must be understood in this way: namely, that the Devil creates no new nature, but that he is able to make something appear to be which in reality is not. For by no spell nor evil power can the mind, nay, not even the body corporeally, be changed into the material limbs and features of any animal . . . but a man is fantastically and by illusion metamorphosed into an animal, albeit he to himself seems to be a quadruped; and as for the burdens which the beast carries, if they be real they

Surrounded by assorted demons and watched over by a guardian angel, Saint Augustine works on the manuscript of his *De Spiritu et Anima*. Illustration from a fifteenth-century French manuscript.

are supported and borne by familiars so that all who see the seeming animal may be mocked and deluded by diabolical glamor.

Jean de Nynauld, in his *Lycanthropie* (1615), generally supports Augustine and categorically rejects Bodin's belief in the material transformations of men into wolves. The title of his first chapter is adamant: *That the Devil cannot in any way transform men into beasts. Moreover, the Devil cannot separate the soul of a sorcerer from the body, in such fashion that after a while the soul returns to the body and the sorcerer is alive.*

But this is clearly heretical, as is the following statement from the last chapter: "Regarding the reality of this

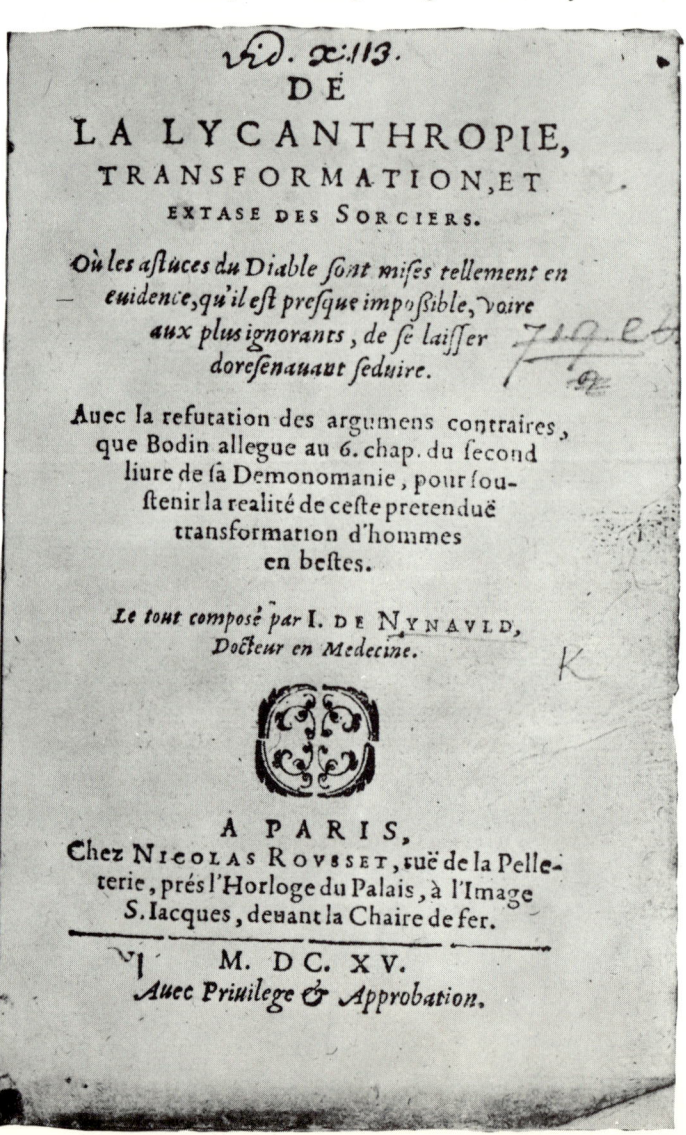

Title page of Jean de Nynauld's *Lycanthropie* (1615). "Metamorphosis of men into beasts," says the author, "cannot be achieved by any natural means."

metamorphosis of men into beasts, I have already proved that it cannot be achieved by any natural means, nor even by the Devil even if he strains to the utmost of his power, for he cannot even make a fly. God alone is the Creator and Preserver of all things." This is just not so. Countless examples could be quoted as to exactly why it is not so, but one should be enough. "Aaron stretched forth his hand upon the waters of Egypt," we are told in the eighth chapter of Exodus, "and the frogs came up and covered the Land of Egypt. And the enchanters also by the enchantments did in like manner, and they brought forth frogs upon the Land of Egypt." In other words, it was by God's permission that the power of Satan produced these frogs, and Nynauld obviously makes nonsense of the very Scriptures he is trying so desperately to defend.

The celebrated professor of Leipzig, Joannes Fridericus Wolfeshusius, is just as keen as Nynauld to come to the defense of "the omnipotence of Almighty God" in any argument which couples the Devil with the werewolf. "Is it possible," he asks in his *Lycanthropis* (1591), "that a man may by magic spells or the power and craft of the Devil verily and indeed assume, and transform himself into the shape of a wolf or some other animal, or are all those histories and accounts which we read of lycanthropy, in particular as detailed in authors who have written of the peoples of far Northern climes" – he is obviously referring here to Olaus Magnus – "merely fantastical, and if we accept them do we in any way seem to impugn the omnipotence of Almighty God?"

Another canonized scholar, Albertus Magnus – or Saint Albert the Great, the German philosopher, theologian and scientist of the thirteenth century – is, however, prepared to compromise in his attitude toward God's omnipotence. He maintains in his book, *On Animals,* that "the Devil can, with God's permission, make imperfect animals." Since it is universally agreed that the werewolf has no tail, and is therefore an imperfect animal, it follows (at least according to Magnus's argument) that the Devil can make a werewolf. This certainly seems to be the view of Jacob Sprenger in the *Malleus Maleficarum* (the "witches' hammer"), published in about 1486, which formed the handbook of anti-Satanism in Europe between 1486 and 1600, and which was used by the Inquisition in its many trials of alleged witches, satanists and werewolves. Here, Sprenger reviews the Canon Episcopi (attributed to a collection of ecclesiastical decrees issued by Abbot Regino in A.D. 906), and it appears that "when it says that no creature can be made by the power of the Devil, this is manifestly true if 'made' is understood to mean 'created'.

Albertus Magnus, who died at the age of eighty in Cologne, in 1280, was canonized and proclaimed a doctor of the church in 1931. He was a champion of the view that, with God's permission, "the Devil can make a werewolf."

These evocative engravings come from Theophilus Laube's *Dialogi und Gespräch von der Lycanthropia*, published in Frankfurt in 1686.

RIGHT The Devil contemplates the havoc being caused by his werewolf disciples.

RIGHT A suspected werewolf is hanged in the town square, while a portrait of the accused sorcerer is prepared for public display; this was common practice in Germany until the beginning of the eighteenth century.

FAR RIGHT A werewolf harasses a shepherd's flock.

FAR LEFT The same werewolf is later tracked down and shot.

LEFT Another werewolf carries off a lamb.

FAR LEFT This werewolf is also subsequently caught and clubbed to death.

LEFT It is dawn and the werewolves change back into their human-sorcerer shapes.

But if the word 'made' is taken to refer to natural production, then it is certain that devils can make some imperfect animals."

So, assuming a man of an utterly depraved character wishes to indulge in werewolfery out of pure choice – as opposed to the vast majority who have the curse inflicted on them involuntarily – how should he proceed? "In the first place," explains Montague Summers, "an essential circumstance and condition is a pact, formal or tacit, with the demon. Such metamorphosis can only be wrought by black magic. This is in itself a mortal sin, for, as Saint Bonaventura instructs us (in Book 2 of *Sentences*, 1477), it is sinful to seek either counsel or aid from the demon. Again, the werewolf is a sorcerer well versed and of long continuance in the Devil's service, no mere journeyman of evil." And, as Guazzo tells us in his *Compendium Maleficarum*, "this seems particularly worth noting: that just as Emperors reserve certain rewards for their veteran soldiers only, so the demon grants this power of changing themselves into different shapes, as the witches believe, only to those who have proved their loyalty by many years of faithful service in witchcraft; and this is, as it were, a reward for their long service and loyalty."

The "evidence" which is commonly offered to support the belief that werewolves are transformed witches is that the beasts have no tails. According to this theory, any animal minus a tail is a witch in disguise – so beware the Manx cat! One of the prime reasons why bewitched animals were formerly burnt alive was a belief that the human being is in the animal and that by burning you compel him to assume another shape. Conversely, many witches who were condemned to the stake in the Middle Ages confessed to having taken the shapes of cats, hares, dogs, horses and wolves, adding that they were prompted into such transformations by the Devil, with whom they were in league.

The accounts given by R. R. Madden in Volume 1 of his *Phantasmata* (1857) of the confessions of several medieval werewolves, who were apprehended in what is now Latvia, throw much light on werewolfic sorcery. All the confessions had a kind of consistency to them which made them all the more believable, even though they were all elicited by means of torture. All the same, they generally agreed – separately – that they had entered into compact with Satan; that they were in the habit of assembling twelve days after Christmas, being led by a young man with a lame foot; and that they were urged on by another person of large stature, armed with a whip of wire and chains twisted together, who inflicted severe wounds on

A sorcerer, having changed into a werewolf the night before, returns home in the early hours. A sixteenth-century woodcut.

every person who had been driven to the chosen rendezvous. They were all left with horrible weals and scars. When finally they reached the appointed meeting place, after numerous rites and ceremonies, they were all transformed into wolves. They then went their separate ways among the fields and forests, attacking and devouring sheep and other animals, although they were bereft of any power to harm human beings. For twelve days they behaved like ravenous wild beasts, after which they resumed their human form.

It is, of course, of great significance that at a time in history when witch trials were the order of the day, there was a proportionate number of werewolf trials. It was a black period indeed, and as Summers concludes in *The Werewolf*:

> not without reason did the werewolf in past centuries appear as one of the most terrible and depraved of all bond-slaves of Satan . . . Hateful to God and loathed of man, what other end, what other reward could he look for than the stake, where they burned him quick and scattered his ashes to the wind, to be swept away to nothingness and oblivion on the keen wings of the nightly storm.

7 Torture, Trial and Execution

RANCE IN 1573: one of the most notorious of all werewolf trials, at the Supreme Court of the Parliament of Dôle, drew to a close. The courtroom was alive with expectation as the judge, Henry Camus, doctor of law and councillor of the king, returned to deliver his verdict. At the end of a detailed summing-up, he pronounced the following sentence:

> Seeing that Gilles Garnier has, by the testimony of credible witnesses and by his own spontaneous confession, been proved guilty of the abominable crimes of lycanthropy and witchcraft, this Court condemns him, the said Gilles, to be this day taken in a cart from this spot to the place of execution, accompanied by the executioner, where he, by the said executioner, shall be tied to a stake and burned alive, and that his ashes be scattered to the winds. The Court further condemns him, the said Gilles, to the costs of the prosecution. Given at Dôle, this 18th day of January, 1573.

The case of Gilles Garnier is one of the most distressing examples of pure ignorance, superstition and cruelty in the history of jurisprudence. Garnier was sentenced to death upon his own confession, wrung from him while he was suffering from the tortures of the rack. It is not possible to consider the crimes of such werewolves in anything like a proper perspective without first taking into account the no less serious crimes committed by those who administered the law of the land. There are few names more closely associated with werewolfery, or more stained with the blood of the damned, than that of Henry Boguet, Supreme Judge of the St. Claude district in Burgundy and author of that black treatise on witchcraft, *Discours des Sorciers* (1608), in which he details many of the sixteenth century's principal werewolf trials. As we now know, a vast number of condemned werewolves and lycanthropes were burned to prevent them from becoming vampires after death. Boguet claims the principal portion of these judicial murders. Wherever this inhuman monster presided, a campaign of torture and terror produced admissions of guilt and culminated in the inevitable burnings at the stake.

Boguet, lamentably, was not alone in encouraging ruthless barbarity in the name of the law: torture was the sixteenth century's principal weapon in eliciting "confessions," even though it was sometimes held that the Devil could counteract its effects by anesthetizing his servants. Henry Camus, presiding judge at the trial of Gilles Garnier, was just as guilty as Boguet. For that particular trial he drummed together fifty people "to bear witness," and he subjected the accused to the rack, which, as might be expected, produced an unreserved "confession." Among the evidence produced at the trial was a letter from Daniel d'Ange to the learned Matthieu de Challemaison, Dean of the Church of Sens. In this letter, which was read to the court, d'Ange testified:

> Gilles Garnier, lycophile, as I may call him, lived the life of a hermit, but has since taken a wife, and having

Pages 332 and 333 of *Discours des Sorciers* (1608) by Henry Boguet, Supreme Judge of the St. Claude district in Burgundy and the most fearless enemy of Satanists. The first edition was published in 1590, and there were more than twelve reprints between that year and 1611. The judge died in 1619. "I maintain," he says in the book "that for the most part it is the witch himself who runs about slaying: not that he is metamorphosed into a wolf, but that it appears to him that he is so."

no means of support for his family fell into the way, as is natural to defiant and desperate people of rude habits, of wandering into the woods and wild places. In this state he was met by a phantom in the shape of a man, who told him that he could perform miracles, among other things declaring that he would teach him how to change at will into a wolf, lion or leopard, and because the wolf is more familiar in this country than the other kinds of wild beasts he chose to disguise himself in that shape, which he did, using a salve with which he rubbed himself for this purpose.

The Hermit of Dôle, by which name Garnier became known, lived miles from nowhere in a small hut of the crudest sort, with a roof constructed from turf and walls covered with lichen. He was a somber-looking man, with a pale face, leaden complexion, as if discolored by bruising, deep-set eyes hidden beneath a pair of coarse and bushy brows, which met across the forehead. He seldom spoke and he walked in a stooping gait which, combined with a long grey beard, made him a very odd sight indeed.

The indictment read out in court by Henry Camus stated that the accused had killed a girl of twelve, after tearing her to pieces, partly with his teeth and partly with his wolf's paw; after dragging the body into the forest, he then ate the larger portion, reserving the remainder for his wife, Apolline; it also said that by reason of injuries inflicted in a similar way upon another young girl he was likewise responsible for her death; also that he had devoured a boy of ten, tearing him limb by limb; and that he had killed another boy of twelve or thirteen, and it was only the approach of men which hindered him from eating the victim; and that he displayed the same unnatural inclinations even in his proper (human) shape.

Was Garnier a werewolf or a lycanthrope? In every instance, it would seem, he was fully convinced that actual transformation into a wolf had taken place. His mind was apparently clear and he knew exactly the extreme nature of his crimes. He was accordingly burned at the stake.

Scattering Garnier's ashes to the winds did not put an end to the matter. The fear of werewolves, both real and imagined, had reached such epidemic proportions by the autumn of 1573 that the very same Court of the Parliament of Dôle, in Franche-Comté, had to draw on the help of the local population to suppress the nuisance. So the following authorization (unique, I believe, in such cases) was issued:

According to the advertisement made to the sovereign Court of Parliament at Dôle, that, in the territories of

Various methods of torture were employed by Boguet and other judges to extract confessions from suspected werewolves. Use of the wheel was one method. Boguet would question each prisoner while a scribe took down the confession. Another judge, as a witness to the confessions, would invariably "sit in."

Espagny, Salvange, Courchapon, and the neighboring villages, has often been seen and met, for some time past, a werewolf, who, it is said, has already seized and carried off several little children, so that they have not been seen since, and since he has attacked and done injury in the country to some horsemen, who kept him off only with great difficulty and danger to their persons: the said Court, desiring to prevent any greater danger, has permitted, and does permit, those who are abiding or dwelling in the said places and others, notwithstanding all edicts concerning the chase, to assemble with pikes, javelins, clubs, and sticks, to chase and to pursue the said werewolf in every place where they may find or seize him; to tie and to kill, without incurring any pains or penalties. Given at the meeting of the said Court, on the thirteenth day of the month September, 1573.

It is too horrible to imagine what appalling atrocities were inflicted on completely innocent victims. I have no doubt that the *carte blanche* invitation to commit murder would have been quickly taken up by a certain portion of the population with black minds and malicious scores to settle. A *loup-garou* (French for werewolf) was eventually caught; whether he was in fact guilty – and by that I mean guilty in *fact* – is quite another matter.

Boguet devotes a complete chapter in his book to an account of six individuals at whose trials, in 1597, he sat in judgment. They were charged with practicing sorcery and lycanthropy, with frequenting the Devil's sabbaths and using diabolical ointments and potions, and with transforming themselves into wolves, killing children for their loathsome orgies, and causing many people, as well as cattle, to die a horrible death. With Boguet presiding over the legal affairs, we can be sure that no prisoner was spared the damnable use of terror and torture.

In another chapter he refers to some of the extraordinary theories of Jean Bodin, whose controversial *Démonomanie des Sorciers* has already been referred to. Here, for instance, Bodin relates the confession of a woman, the substance of which is that sorcerers – and therefore werewolves – could only shed three tears with the right eye. Boguet derives much mileage out of Bodin's "tear theory" as a means against which to judge the six werewolves brought before him. He informs us enthusiastically:

> The doctors esteem it one of the strongest presumptions that exist as a test in crimes of sorcery. I wish to report what has come to my knowledge. All the sorcerers whom I have examined *in quality of Judge*, have never shed tears in my presence: or, indeed, if they have shed them, it has been so parsimoniously that no notice was taken of them.
>
> I say this with regard to those who seemed to weep, but I doubt if their tears were not feigned. I am at least well assured that those tears were wrung from them with the greatest efforts. This was shown by the efforts which the accused made to weep, *and by the small number of tears which they shed*. But if I spoke to them in private, they shed tears and wept with all possible vehemence. The same happened when they confessed. They then showed themselves more lively and joyous than they had previously been, as if they had been delivered from a great burden. Besides, it is probable that sorcerers do not shed tears, since tears serve principally to penitents to wash away and cleanse their sins.
>
> Nevertheless, if you demand of sorcerers why they do not shed tears, they answer you that it is impossible for them to weep, because they have the heart too much oppressed at seeing themselves disgraced by the imputation of a crime so detestable as that of sorcery.

How many poor wretches suffering from psychiatric delusions and diabolical possession were sent to the stake by Boguet for no other reason than the fact that they failed to shed a tear is too hideous to contemplate. The figure certainly runs into many hundreds, possibly thousands. But the matter does not rest there, because Boguet –

described by some people as a "man-devil in judicial authority" – was impertinent enough, in the same treatise, to explain in a high tone of dignity how other judges should act in cases of lycanthropy. This is the man, remember, who could wring tears from human misery, and could do so with all the coldness and calm composure that he thought becoming his high office; who could measure the meager drops that came from tear-ducts dried up with fear and horror and the anguish of judicial terror; who could use a prisoner's absence of tears not simply as a legal yardstick but as evidence of guilt against all accused werewolves and lycanthropes who failed the test – this was the model judge who was to teach his junior brothers of the Bench how to deal with cases of sorcery and lycanthropy.

One of Boguet's victims was Clauda Gaillard. At her trial one Jeanne Perrin gave evidence before Boguet that she was walking through a wood one day with Clauda when Clauda suddenly disappeared behind a bush. An instant later a tailless wolf appeared from the same bush, and she was sure the beast's hind feet were like those of a human being. It frightened her so much that she made the sign of the cross and ran away in terror. From this scanty testimony, and from the fact that Clauda later told Jeanne that she should not have been afraid of the wolf because it would not have harmed her, it was assumed by Boguet that Clauda had taken the shape of the wild beast and was therefore a werewolf.

In fact, Boguet regards the werewolf trial of Clauda Gaillard as such a perfect model of its kind that he devotes a whole chapter to it. "Common report was against her," he writes, adding: "No one ever saw her shed a single tear, *whatever effort might be made to cause her to shed tears*" (Boguet's italics, not mine; it is difficult even to imagine what tortures she had to endure to pass the judge's "tear test"). She was convicted because she went to the Devil's sabbath, because "she varied often in her answers," because she committed "several acts of sorcery," and because she "caused the deaths of six goats of Peter Perrier, and caused a mare of his to fall sick, and afterwards to have cured that mare, and to have moreover transformed herself into a wolf. It is however quite true that the witnesses who deposed to these acts were for the most part single witness, but as they were of accord as to the crime of sorcery, they so far confirmed it, although they were all either relations or connections of Clauda Gaillard."

Clauda perished at the stake.

Elsewhere, in Germany in 1589, the trial, torture and execution of Peter Stump, along with his daughter and mistress, were sufficiently barbaric to have impressed even St Claude's Supreme Judge. The Marquis de Sade himself, had he been there, would likewise have been amply satisfied by the physical atrocities inflicted on Stump (or Stumpf, Stube, Stubbe, Stub – the spellings vary). Not that Stump was a deluded innocent: his crimes, over a period of twenty-five years, were tenfold those of his legal torturers. He very quickly became a bizarre folk-legend throughout Europe.

A pamphlet detailing Stump's life, deeds, torture and execution was published a few months after his death, and it is this publication (in the English translation of 1590) that I have used as my principal source. Like so many werewolves, Peter Stump was indoctrinated into the art of metamorphosis by the Devil, who presented him with a wolf's skin for this sole purpose. As soon as he had tasted, while in wolf form, the flesh of his first victim, "he took such pleasure and delight in shedding of blood that he would night and day walk the fields, and perform extreme cruelties."

While transformed into a wolf, he would go in search of young women working in the fields, pursue them and, changing back into his human shape, rape them. When his lust had been satisfied, he would proceed to violate them and eventually murder them by the most obscene means imaginable. During the first five years of his pact with the Devil he had murdered thirteen women and young children, and two pregnant women, tearing the unborn babies from their mothers' wombs and devouring their hearts "panting hot and raw." On top of this he killed countless lambs, kids and other young beasts.

Stump lived with his daughter, Beell, with whom he committed nightly incest, and eventually she gave birth to his child. He later took a mistress by the name of Katherine Trompin, "a woman of tall and comely stature," and all three slept in the same bed. His lust for blood was so intense that he could not even resist consuming his own son, finding the boy's brains "a most savory and dainty delicious means to staunch his greedy appetite."

For twenty-five years Peter Stump continued this vile way of life, sometimes in the form of a wolf, sometimes in his human shape, in the towns and cities, woods and thickets. The exact number of his victims, men, women and children, as well as every conceivable species of animal, has never been ascertained. It is thought to be many hundreds, although he confessed to but sixteen. Eventually the inhabitants of Bedburg and neighboring towns feared to go out alone unless they were adequately equipped with a practical means of defense. Arms and

Woodcut from *The damnable life and death of one Stubbe Peeter* (1590), depicting the misdeeds, capture, torture, trial and execution of one of Germany's most notorious werewolves, Peter Stump. In the last frame, the decapitated Stump is flanked by his daughter Beell and his mistress Katherine, both of whom were accessory to several murders.

legs of dead men, women and children were daily found scattered up and down the fields. His luck eventually ran out and a search party, with a pack of dogs, went in pursuit of what they believed to be a real wolf. Stump, in his wolfish form, was presently cornered and made a hasty attempt to remove his Devil's girdle and change back into his human shape – but he was caught in the act. The game was up. He was swiftly frog-marched to the local magistrate, the captors amply convinced that he, Peter Stump, werewolf, was the demon responsible for the area's foul catalog of murders.

The pamphlet relates the trial and execution as follows:

After he had been imprisoned for some time, the magistrates found out through due examination that his (Stump's) daughter Beell and his mistress Katherine Trompin, were both accessory to divers murders committed, and with Peter Stump were condemned, and their several judgments pronounced the 28 of October 1589, in the manor. Peter Stump was judged to have his body laid on a wheel, and with red hot burning pincers in several places to have the flesh pulled off from the bones; after that, his legs and arms to be broken with a wooden ax or hatchet; afterwards to have his head struck from his body; then to have his carcase burned to ashes.

Also his daughter and his mistress were judged to be burned quickly to ashes, the same time and day with the carcase of the aforesaid Peter Stump. And on the 31 of

Another woodcut (the original, in the State and Town Library of Augsburg, West Germany, is colored) showing the life and death of Peter Stump, here being executed alongside his daughter and mistress. It was published in 1589, the year of Stump's death.

the same month they suffered death accordingly in the town of Bedburg in the presence of many peers and princes of Germany.

After the execution, there was by advice of the Magistrates of the town of Bedburg a high pole set up and strongly framed, which first went through the wheel whereon he was broken, whereunto also it was fastened. After that a little above the wheel the likeness of a wolf was framed in wood, to show unto all men the shape wherein he executed those cruelties. Over that, on the top of the stake, the sorcerer's head itself was set up; and round about the wheel there hung, as it were, sixteen pieces of wood about a yard in length, which represented the sixteen persons that was perfectly known to be murdered by him. And the same was ordained to stand there as a continual monument to all ensuing ages, what murders by Peter Stump was committed, with the order of his judgment, as this picture doth more plainly express.

I doubt if any witch, sorcerer or werewolf died in a more wretched manner; to be burned alive, albeit scarred by the hand of the torturer, but at least in one piece, was by comparison an almost humane end.

As for France's terrible Gandillon family in the Jura Mountains, and Jacques Rollet of Caude, their crimes of werewolfery were marked equally by the stench of blood. They were all brought to book in the same year, 1598, for committing the same type of offence, yet the attitude of the courts towards the individuals varied considerably: literally a difference in the sentences between life and death.

As we have seen, the young, insane Perrenette Gandillon, who slaughtered many a young (and often not-so-young) child, never ventured as far as a courtroom: she was caught by her neighbors and systematically butchered. She was described by witnesses, after killing a sixteen-year-old boy, as resembling a huge, tailless wolf. Not long after, the girl's older brother, Pierre Gandillon,

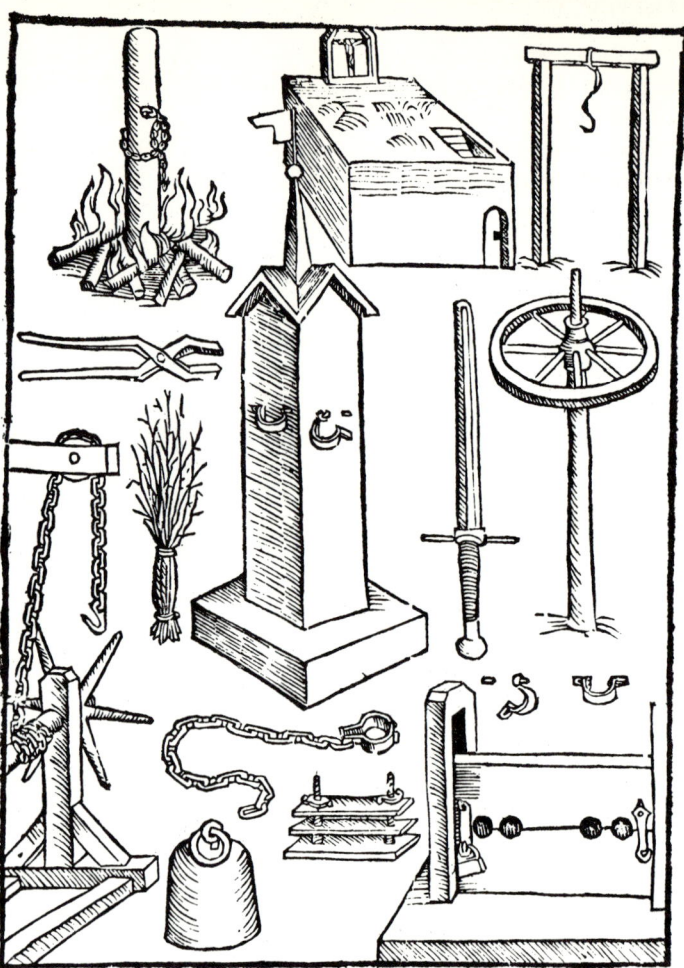

After suspected werewolves had been tortured and tried – always in that order – they were then quite often literally ripped to pieces to expose the wolf-hair that was said to be growing on the inside of their skins. Shown here are instruments of torture used on accused werewolves in the sixteenth and seventeenth centuries.

and his children, Georges and Antoinette, were accused of witchcraft and werewolfery. In court they were charged with leading children to the Devil's sabbath and of adoring the demon. It also came out that they received a salve from the Devil, with which they frequently anointed their bodies, and that they ran around the countryside in the form of the fiercest wolves. They admitted that, in their wolfish form, they had murdered and eaten many young children. A contemporary account describes Pierre and Georges as having "lost wellnigh any resemblance to humanity, loping on all fours rather than walking upright, creatures with foul horny nails, unpared and sharp as talons, keen white teeth, matted hair, and red gleaming eyes." Another observer found that "their faces, arms and legs were frightfully scarred with the wounds they had received from dogs when they had been on their raids."

All three, Pierre, Georges and Antoinette, were subjected to the obligatory sessions of torture prior to their appearances in court. All three were then taken to a place of execution, hanged, and finally burned. The presiding judge? Henry Boguet.

Rollet, for all his terrible deeds, fared rather better. Although he came from a parish in the vicinity of Nantes, he preferred to carry out his crimes in a desolate part of the country near Caude. Here an archer of the Provost's company and some villagers one day found the corpse of a fifteen-year-old boy, whose name was Cornier; his body was grievously mutilated and drenched with blood. As they approached the body three wolves bounded away into the undergrowth. They gave chase and suddenly stumbled across a half-naked man, his hands splattered with fresh blood, his long talons stuffed with red human flesh; his teeth were chattering with fear. The man was the accused, Jacques Rollet, who told the court at Angers, on August 8, 1598, that he had been prevented from eating the body only by the intervention of the men.

Under examination the thirty-five-year-old Rollet explained that he was a beggar who, with his brother Jean and a cousin, Julien, vagabonded from village to village. He further confessed to the judge, Pierre Hérault, the Lieutenant-Général et Criminel, that his parents had delivered him to the Devil and that by using the unguent they had given him he could at will take the form of a wolf with a bestial appetite. The other two wolves were his accomplices, Jean and Julien, who also knew the secret of animal-transformation. He confessed to the murder of countless children while in his wolfic guise. His guilt was confirmed by the fact that he could give precise details of locations and dates of former child atrocities.

"What are you accused of having done?" asked the judge.

"Of being a thief – of having offended God," replied Rollet. "My parents gave me an ointment; I do not know its composition."

"When rubbed with this ointment, do you become a wolf?"

"No; but for all that, I killed and ate the child Cornier: I was a wolf."

"Were you dressed as a wolf?"

"I was dressed as I am now. I had my hands and my face bloody, because I had been eating the flesh of the said child."

"Do your hands and feet become the paws of a wolf?"

"Yes, they do."

"Does your head become like that of a wolf – your head become larger?"

"I do not know how my head was at the time; I used my teeth; my head was as it is today. I have wounded and eaten many other little children; I have also been to the sabbath."

The judge then pronounced sentence. Rollet the werewolf would be burned at the stake. And then something rather odd happened. While the prisoner was locked in his cell awaiting the day of his appointed execution, the Parliament of Paris decided, for some inexplicable reason – and it was an act of compassion rare for that age – that Rollet should instead be confined for two years in the mental hospital of St. Germain-des-Prés, and there be instructed in the knowledge of God, "whom he had forgotten in his utter poverty." It was mercy indeed.

Four months later, on December 14, 1598, a tailor from Châlons was tried in Paris for crimes of werewolfery which probably surpassed, and certainly equaled, those committed in a later age by Jack the Ripper, the Boston Strangler, and the fictionalized "demon barber," Sweeney Todd. The werewolf of Châlons, like the murderers above, must be known by a pseudonym – the Demon Tailor – because the details of the case were so revolting that all documents pertaining to it were ordered by the court to be destroyed.

The court heard (and it is from contemporary accounts and not from that of the court itself that we have details of this case today) that the tailor would lure children of both sexes into his shop and, having abused them sexually in all manner of ways, would slit their throats and dress their flesh in much the same way as a butcher. This meat he would eat with great relish. At other times, when the sun was setting, he would head for the woods and, in the form of a wolf, leap at unsuspecting ramblers and tear out their throats. He told the court that on such occasions he fully believed he was a savage wolf, and it would certainly seem he behaved like one. The number of young people he attacked and consumed is not known, but when his house was raided by local officials, barrels of bleaching human bones were found hidden in the cellars, together with fragments of human legs and arms and other hideous things. Many lycanthropes, as this gaunt creature seems to have been, died repenting their sins; but the Demon Tailor, a hard, cold man, wanted nothing to do with God. As the flames at the stake licked around his body on December 15, 1598, the people of Paris, who had gathered to see the execution, heard him blaspheming everybody and everything in God's kingdom.

In the present century mass-mutilators like the Demon Tailor would almost certainly be certified by the court as victims of delusion, and tried as such; if proved insane they would be committed to a sentence of life imprisonment. In the sixteenth century things were quite different, and murderers of this nature were almost always charged with being servants of the Devil; under torture, that would quite often mean they were, quite simply, werewolves. "Dreams" and "visions," especially if they involved Satan, were considered valid forms of evidence of guilt.

"Dreams" and "visions" continually plagued John George Haigh, an inventor of South Kensington, London, who was executed on August 15, 1949 for the murder of nine people, all of whom he decoyed into a basement, shot or clubbed from behind, opened their jugular vein at the neck and drank a glassful of the hot blood. What, I wonder, would Boguet or Camus or Hérault have made of Haigh's recurrent dreams? "The dream was," said the psychiatrist who attended him, "that he went into a forest of crucifixes, and these turned gradually into trees with branches at right angles dripping with dew or rain. As he got near he saw it was blood dripping from the trees. One of the trees gradually assumed the shape of a man who held a bowl and collected blood from one of the trees. This tree got paler, and he himself felt that he was losing strength. Then the man, when the bowl was full, approached and invited him to drink it. At first he was unable to reach the man, who receded, and the dream ended." After experiencing this dream three or four more times, Haigh began his murders "and after one or two of them he dreamt again. Then the man did not recede from him and he was able to drink the blood." (*The Times*, July 20, 1949.)

Boguet, by aligning these dreams with the nature of the murders, and by eliciting other "confessions" under torture, would have found little difficulty in pronouncing Haigh a sorcerer and werewolf of the first order. And if many of the so-called werewolves were deluded and their confessions wrung from them by torture, is it therefore not likely that a great bulk of them were falsely accused? By this I mean they were victims of people whose motives, in court, for accusing them of practicing werewolfery, was one of revenge. This was certainly the case at the trials for sorcery and witchcraft in England. How easy it was to make false accusations of werewolfery, to trump up testimony and get the accused convicted. In the sixteenth century, particularly, witnesses were rarely subjected to a searching examination; the court was invariably presided over by a Boguet type, and was therefore blatantly biased; and if a confession of guilt was not forthcoming voluntarily, well, the accused could always be subjected to torture and in this way the necessary statement of guilt

THE WEREWOLF OF ANSBACH

RIGHT The history of an extraordinary werewolf case appeared in a document published in Germany in 1685, the year of several alleged werewolf attacks in the Bavarian hamlet of Brunnen, close to the town of Anspach (now Ansbach). The supposed incarnation of the town's dead burgomaster was said to be attacking and devouring women and children and animals – in the form of a wolf. The beast was eventually caught and slaughtered. Its carcase was dressed in a flesh-colored shroud and its head and face were adorned with a chestnut-colored wig, after the snout had been cut off and a mask resembling the burgomaster substituted.

BELOW The burgomaster and his wolfic incarnation are depicted in an engraving of the period by George Jacob Schneider.

ABOVE Another engraving by Schneider is a composite portrayal of the werewolf on its bloody expeditions, pursued by its subsequent captors, with the doomed creature finally strung up on a gibbet.

LEFT A painting unique in composition (oil on cardboard) of the hanged wolf, with a huge crowd standing around, is believed to be the work of the Ansbach court painter, Johann Michael Schwabeda (1737–1817).

LEFT The reputed home of the ill-fated burgomaster still exists.

obtained. One recognized "werewolf test" involved dipping one of the accused's fingers into boiling resin; if the finger was withdrawn unhurt, innocence was established. There can be no doubt that many were falsely accused. It is also relevant to note that there is no statement on record of an accused werewolf actually turning himself into a wolf in full view of the assembled court.

This much is true. Yet it is just as true to say that not all those unfortunate wretches who were subjected to the rack, and other types of torture, and confessed themselves werewolves, were necessarily confessing falsely. There is every reason to acknowledge the existence of a certain type of human-animal transformation, as will be investigated more fully later.

Not all accounts of accused werewolves can be traced to a malicious agency, or to that of a victim of torture. Many were genuinely deluded into believing that, at certain periods, they *were* wolves; they were the lycanthropes and many were guilty of barbarous crimes. Others swore that, with the help of the Devil and special potions and animal skins, they could transform their human shape completely into that of wolves; they were the werewolves.

In 1589 in France the judicial approach to werewolfery took a dramatic turn: fourteen people charged with sorcery and wolf transformations, and tried (but not by Boguet) on that charge, were acquitted. But although checked in one place, the crusades against werewolves went on elsewhere with undiminished ardor. Eventually, however, at the beginning of the seventeenth century, judges began to listen to the doctors, who were now convinced that a vast number of suspected werewolves – which, to the legal men, meant practitioners of witchcraft – were in fact patients suffering from various forms of mental delusion. The courts, having their suspicions awakened by the great number of self-accused werewolves placed before them, and fearful of wrongly sentencing so many otherwise respected people – civil officials for instance – acquitted most of them. These werewolves were, they said, the victims of delusion and hysteria. In many cases they were probably right.

But by acknowledging a more enlightened seventeenth century we cannot possibly wipe out a superstition of the preceding two thousand years; and if we disregard many accounts of werewolves, those from Ancient Rome and Greece on up to the present, as the reports of a gullible people easily swayed by the natural phenomena of events around them, then, for the same reason, we would also have to negate much of The Bible. The werewolf myth, like Christianity, is there – and it won't go away.

8 Man into Wolf – Wolf into Man

Make me a werewolf! make me a man-eater!
Make me a werewolf! make me a woman-eater!
Make me a werewolf! make me a child-eater!
I pine for blood! human blood!
Give it me! give it me tonight!
Great Wolf Spirit! give it me, and
Heart, body and soul, I am yours.

THIS, THE FINAL INCANTATION of a macabre black magic ritual practiced during the last century in the Urals, the Caucasus, the plains of East Russia and in various parts of Siberia, is quite explicit. The bewitched chanter-of-magic-words wishes to become a werewolf. In every country where the werewolf has waged its fearful campaign of bloodlust, whether in antiquity or in a time nearer our own, you will find evidence of incantations and initiation ceremonies conducted very much along these lines. We are told they actually worked. Should one doubt that such things are possible? Most people do, because most people are by nature skeptical of the bizarre powers of the supernatural. Let us suppose, anyway, that the initiates themselves at least *believed* that these ceremonies "worked." Afterwards we will examine the soundness of these claims.

A man, evil and debase, wishes to become a werewolf. Many have no choice: werewolfery, we have seen, afflicts some men in the form of a curse; some, the hereditary werewolves, are born to it, possessing as their birthright the power of metamorphosis. But our man is the most despicable of all Satan's servants, for he freely wishes to become a werewolf, and will consequently, for the most part, be a ravenous destroyer of all that falls in his way. There are as many ceremonies which dealers in the black

RIGHT Hemlock

FAR RIGHT Henbane

arts might embark upon to reach the desired end as there are magic potions, spells and materials to effect the crucial change.

In Siberia the usual initiating ceremony involved drawing a circle of seven to nine feet in radius on the ground; in the center a fire consisting of black poplar, pine or larch (but never ash) was kindled. Over this fire, in an iron pot, a special fumigation was heated. The ingredients comprised any four or five of the following substances:

Hemlock......*2 to 3 ounces*   *Opium*......*$\frac{1}{4}$ ounce*
Henbane......*1 to 1$\frac{1}{2}$ ounces*   *Asafoetida*...*2 ounces*
Saffron......*3 ounces*   *Solanum*.....*2 to 3 drachms*
Poppy seed...*Any amount*   *Parsley*......*Any amount*
Aloe........*3 drachms*

The selected substances were stirred thoroughly in the pot while heating, after which the would-be werewolf assumed a kneeling position inside the circle and recited a preliminary prayer of his own invention. He would then be called upon to deliver his first incantation:

> Hail, hail, hail, great Wolf Spirit, hail!
> A boon I ask thee, mighty shade,
> Within this circle I have made.
> Make me a werewolf strong and bold,
> The terror alike of young and old.
> Grant me a figure tall and spare;
> The speed of the elk, the claws of the bear;
> The poison of snakes, the wit of the fox;
> The stealth of the wolf, the strength of the ox;

FAR LEFT Poppy seed

LEFT Aloe

The jaws of the tiger, the teeth of the shark;
The eyes of a cat that sees in the dark.
Make me climb like a monkey, scent like a dog,
Swim like a fish, and eat like a hog.
Haste, haste, haste, lonely spirit, haste!
Here, wan and drear, magic spell making,
Findest thou me – shaking, quaking.
Softly fan me as I lie,
And they mystic touch apply –
Touch apply, and I swear that when I die,
When I die, I will serve thee evermore,
Evermore, in gray wolf land, cold and raw.

Now, in a distinctly agitated frame of mind, the initiate would first kiss the ground three times and then remove the pot from the fire and launch it whirling and smoking around his head, while chanting loudly the lines which opened this chapter: "Make me a werewolf! make me a man-eater! a woman-eater! a child-eater!" Witnesses tell us that at this point the trees would:

> begin to rustle, and the wind to moan, and out of the sudden darkness that envelops everything glowed the tall, cylindrical, pillar-like phantom of the Unknown, seven or eight feet in height. It sometimes developed further and assumed the form of a tall, thin monstrosity, half human and half animal, grey and nude, with very long legs and arms, and the feet and claws of a wolf. Its head was shaped like that of a wolf, but surrounded with the hair of a woman, that fell about its bare shoulders in yellow ringlets. It had wolf's ears and

a wolf's mouth. Its aquiline nose and pale eyes were fashioned like those of a human being, but animated with an expression too diabolically malignant to proceed from anything but the superphysical. It seldom if ever spoke, but either uttered some extraordinary noise – a prolonged howl that seemed to proceed from the bowels of the earth, a piercing, harrowing whine, or a low laugh full of hellish glee, any of which sounds may have been taken to express its assent to the favor asked. It only remained visible for a minute at the most, and then disappeared with startling abruptness.

The initiate was now a werewolf. Next evening, at sunset, he would experience the "thrill" of his first transformation into the form of a wolf; at dawn, he would resume his human shape. This cycle would continue daily until his death. At the point of death he would automatically effect his last metamorphosis: so if he was in human form at the final hour, he would change slowly into a wolf, and this was the form which his corpse would retain. Far-fetched, perhaps, even by the bizarre standard of most werewolf stories; but the Slavonic race, it seems, believed in it utterly.

The power of Russian wizards was said to be absolute. If one of them wished to turn into a werewolf, he would employ one of several verbal charms, including this *zagovór*:

Cinematic metamorphosis. David Rintoul plays the title role in the 1975 British film, *Legend of the Werewolf*.

In the ocean sea, on the island Buyán, in the open plain, shines the moon upon an aspen stump, into the green wood, into the spreading vale. Around the stump goes a shaggy wolf; under his teeth are all the horned cattle; but into the wood the wolf goes not, in the vale the wolf does not roam. Moon, moon! golden horns! Melt the bullet, blunt the knife, rot the cudgel, strike fear into man, beast and reptile, so that they may not seize the grey wolf, nor tear from him his warm hide. My word is firm, firmer than sleep or the strength of heroes.

Foliage of aspen stump.

The stump of the aspen is probably mentioned in this spell because a buried werewolf or vampire must be pierced with an aspen stake if the creature is to meet its eternal end.

The rites in which these spells are employed vary from country to country, from one region to another, but there is one consistent factor: for the rites to work, the initiates must believe wholeheartedly in mystical powers. "Believe and you shall *be*" seems to be the prime maxim. The choice of location is also important. Areas of human desolation, such as the wildest deserts, woods and mountain peaks, are the types of locale dictated by the powers of the paranormal whose favors are being solicited. And, because psychic influences vary according to the position of the planets, a bright new moon is an integral part of the ceremony; at this time the earth is literally "bathed" in sinister supernatural presences.

 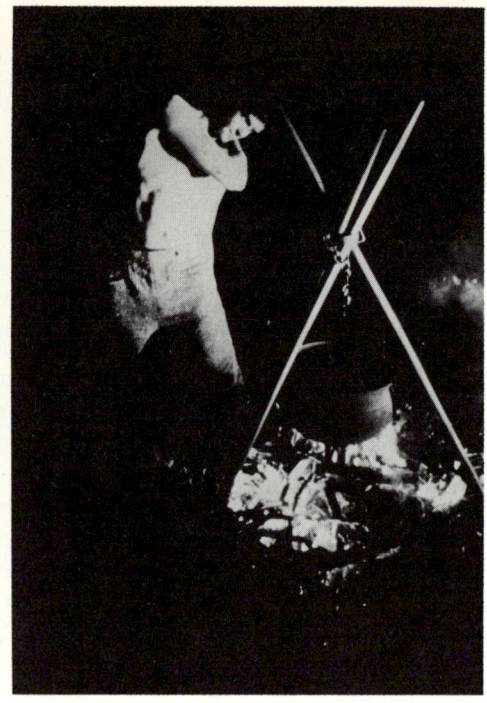

Metamorphosis by ritual sorcery. The initiate werewolf (ABOVE LEFT) prepares a boiling cauldron of specified herbs and drugs. He then (ABOVE RIGHT) strips naked to the waist (often he strips completely naked), smears his body with a previously prepared ointment, and (OPPOSITE LEFT) fastens a wolf-skin girdle around his waist – and then awaits some unknown demon, some supernatural power which the sorcerer hopes will transform him into a ravening beast. Having recited one or more of several magic incantations, the initiate begins to metamorphose (OPPOSITE RIGHT) into a werewolf . . . and soon his night of savage horror will begin (OPPOSITE BELOW).

A Slavic werewolf ceremony, with certain similarities to the black-magic rites of many countries, takes place on a level plot of land, where the werewolf candidate marks out, with string, chalk or pitch, a circle not less than seven feet in radius; another circle, this time three feet in radius, is then drawn inside it. A fire must be lit within the inner circle, an iron pot of water brought to the boil, and handfuls of three or four of the previously-mentioned substances thrown into the bubbling cauldron. As he is doing so, the initiate recites this incantation:

> Spirits from the deep
> Who never sleep;
> Spirits from the grave
> Without a soul to save;
> Spirits of the trees
> That grow upon the leas;
> Spirits of the air,
> Foul and black, not fair;
> Water spirits hateful,
> To ships and bathers fateful;
> Spirits of the earthbound dead
> That glide with noiseless tread;
> Spirits of heat and fire,
> Destructive in your ire;
> Spirits of cold and ice,
> Patrons of crime and vice –
>   Oh spirits, be kind to me!

> Wolves, vampires, satyrs, ghosts!
> Elect of all devilish hosts!
>   I pray you send hither,
>   Send hither, send hither,
>   The great grey shape that makes
>   men shiver!
>   Shiver, shiver, shiver!
>   Come! Come! Come!

Having taken off all his clothing and footwear – nudity being an important requisite in a number of obscure magical rites, including those of werewolfery – the initiate smears his body with a concoction (previously prepared for the purpose), consisting principally of the fat of a cat, or some other animal which has been recently killed, mixed with camphor, aniseed and opium. This done, he fastens a wolf-skin girdle securely around his waist and, kneeling inside the larger circle, awaits the arrival of the Unknown – some malevolent, supernatural, creative power which the initiate believes contributed to the creation of this and other planets. It is the summation of countless devils and, according to O'Donnell, an enthusiast in these matters, the spirit's advent is sometimes announced by a preliminary deep unnatural silence, sometimes by crashes and bangs, groanings and shriekings. If it arrives in its invisible state, then its presence is felt by a sensation of abnormal cold and the most acute terror. More frequently it can be seen in the external appearance of a huntsman;

at other times in the form of a monstrosity, partly man and partly beast; and there are occasions when it appears ill-defined and in a state of partial materialization. But, however the Unknown makes its presence felt, the omen is in the initiate's favor, for he has now achieved his wish to become a werewolf. The Unknown cannot be sought promiscuously; it comes only to those (usually loathsome characters with a demoniacal thirst for evil) who go to great pains to search it out. There are several other methods by which the sorcerer may acquire the property of werewolfery, as we shall see, but they lack the conviction of the full-scale initiating ceremony.

In the North, particularly Norway and Sweden, it used to be said that drinking from a lycanthropous stream at midnight, during the evening of a full moon, was the first stage towards becoming a werewolf. The next stage was to chant these words:

> 'Tis night! 'tis night! and the moon shines white
>   Over pine and snow-capped hill;
> The shadows stray through burn and brae
>   And dance in the sparkling rill.
>
> 'Tis night! 'tis night! and the Devil's light
>   Casts glimmering beams around.
> The maras dance, the nisses prance
>   On the flower-enamelled ground.
>
> 'Tis night! 'tis night! and the werewolf's might
>   Makes man and nature shiver.
> Yet its fierce grey head and stealthy tread
>   Are nought to thee, oh river!
>   River, river, river.
>
> Oh water strong, that swirls along,
>   I prithee a werewolf make me.
> Of all things dear, my soul, I swear,
>   In death shall not forsake thee.

The following formal declaration was then made:

> I (*here insert name*) offer to thee, Great Spirit of the Unknown, this night (*here insert date*), my body and soul, on condition that thou grantest me, from this night to the hour of my death, the power of metamorphosing, nocturnally, into a wolf. I beg, I pray, I implore thee – thee, unparalleled Phantom of Darkness – to make me a werewolf... *a werewolf*!

He then struck the river bank three times with his forehead. Finally, he submerged his head into the river, again three times, and on each occasion he swallowed a quantity of water. He was now a werewolf.

Lycanthropous water? O'Donnell again:

A strange, faint odour, comparable with nothing, distinguishes lycanthropous water; there is a lurid sparkle in it, strongly suggestive of some peculiar, individual life; the noise it makes, as it rushes along, so closely resembles the muttering and whispering of human voices as to be often mistaken for them; while at night it sometimes utters piercing screams, and howls, and groans, in such a manner as to terrify all who pass near it. Dogs and horses, in particular, are susceptible to its influence, and they exhibit the greatest signs of terror at the mere sound of it.

The girdle required for the ceremony of transformation usually consisted of a wolf's pelt (or that of the animal whose shape the man wished to adopt), which was worn around the waist. In other instances, a girdle of human skin was necessary, and it had to come from a murderer, or, failing this, from a criminal who had either died on the scaffold or been broken on the wheel for his offences. This derives from an old judicial usage, because the Northern nations at one time used to class the proscribed murderer and robber with the wolf, making that animal the symbol of his crime. The girth was three fingers wide, and the belt had to have a buckle which possessed seven tags or tongues; it was powerless when not affixed to the body. It should be remembered, incidentally, that a girdle was formerly a common, and often essential, item in a man's wardrobe; to wear such a belt, therefore, would not in itself be regarded as an act warranting suspicion. Peter Stump told the court that the demon had bestowed a girdle upon him and Jean Grenier told de Lancre that he was given a magic wolf-skin by the Lord of the Forest.

The ancient legends of Scandinavia and Germany provide many accounts of similar uses of animal skins and girdles. The ancient Norse legends in the *Volsunga Saga* tell how the heroes Sigmund and Sinfyotl came across two men fast asleep, wearing magic golden rings; suspended above them were two wolves' pelts, which they removed every fifth day, putting them on again by means of the said rings. The two Volsungs donned the wolves' pelts, became werewolves and killed numerous people until they succeeded in shedding the skins and burning them. Sometimes, in the *Saga*, a mere girdle of wolf's skin, wolf's hair or leather works the transformation.

Closely associated with both the North and the wearing of animal skins for purposes of transformation is the aforementioned berserker: the bear-man, or were-bear, a man who, historically at least, has acquired superhuman

OPPOSITE There is reason to believe that marauding raids of fur-clad barbarians like these plunderers from Scandinavia, who dressed in full bearskins, may have given rise to many of the early werewolf stories. These *berserkers* acquired, historically at least, superhuman strength by transformation.

strength by transformation. In battle berserkers were subject to fits of frenzy, when they howled like wild beasts, foamed at the mouth, and bit through the iron rim of their shields – thus the modern phrase "going berserk." Several ancient kings had a corps of berserkers attached to their battalions, and sometimes a corps of *ûlfhednar* (that is, "wolf-skin shirted"). The *Volsunga Saga* seems to imply that this epithet signifies that the ûlfhednars wore coats of wolf-skin over their armour; but this is not so, for the original conception was that of men who possessed *ulfahamir*, wolf-shirts, and were in fact werewolves. The derivation of berserker is more certain, being a warrior who has a bear-skin shirt (*berr*, bear; *serkr*, sark, shirt), and who possesses the strength of a bear through its transforming power.

To the berserker, remember, paradise was a place where people could hack each other to pieces through all eternity. In the ninth century, the chief business and amusement of these men of the North was to set sail for some pleasant country, like Spain or France, and make all the coasts and navigable rivers hideous with rapine and massacre. When at home, in the intervals between these expeditions, they were liable to become possessed by a strange homicidal madness – the celebrated "berserker rage" – during which they would array themselves in the skins of bears and go out by night to snap the backbones, smash the skulls, and sometimes to drink with fiendish glee the blood of unwary travelers or loiterers. Later they would suffer, as well they might, periods of utter exhaustion and nervous depression. To the trembling peasant, at home as well as abroad, the savage fury of these wolf- and-bear-skinned rovers became attached to local folklore and superstition: the berserker was gifted with the same supernatural powers as the Trollman and the werewolf. It was the donning of the animal skin which, to all intents and purposes, effected the transformation.

Boguet also encountered the transforming power of the animal skin:

> The confessions of Jacques Bocquet, Françoise Secretain, Clauda Jamguillaume, Clauda Jamprost, Thievenne Paget, Pierre Gandillon, and Georges Gandillon are very relevant to our argument; for they said that, in order to turn themselves into wolves, they first rubbed themselves with an ointment, and then Satan clothed them in a wolf's skin which completely covered them, and that they then went on all-fours and ran about the country chasing now a person and now an animal according to the guidance of their appetites.

LEFT A die used for preparing helmet plates from Torslunda, on the Baltic island of Öland. It dates from the sixth century and the wolf-headed figure on the right is thought to represent one of the *berserkers*, warriors said to assume animal form in time of battle.

But the most common accessory in the business of metamorphosis, after the use of the girdle (and sometimes in conjunction with it), was the magic unguent or salve. Most demonologists agree that the ointments used by werewolves were practically identical to those employed by witches to effect their journey to the sabbath, or when they wished to change into wolves. Jean Grenier, Pierre Bourgot, Michel Verdung, Jacques Rollet, as well as those mentioned above and countless other accused werewolves, all testified that a special unguent was instrumental in their transformations. By standing accused of werewolfery, of course, they were automatically regarded as practitioners of witchcraft.

Few people will deny today, as they once denied not so long ago, the very real effect which these old unguents and potions can have on those who employ them. From a purely scientific point of view, we know that they work – that is, that they induce on the patient a certain soporific and hallucinatory condition whereby almost anything will seem to be possible. They consequently produce marked aberrations of behavior. A modern parallel might be such psychopharmacological drugs as lysergic acid diethylamide (commonly known as LSD), mescaline, psilocybin, psilocin, bufotenine, harmine, and the synthetic compounds methyltryptamine (DMT) and dimethoxyphenylethylamine; cannabis could also be included.

Our knowledge of the effects of these potions is nothing new. The Italian physicist, Giambattista della Porta, in a book on magic and alchemy published in 1562, talks about "Medicines which cause sleep," and describes "How to make men mad with mandrake," and how "To make a man believe he was changed into a bird or beast." This was done by infusing mandrake, stramonium or solanum manicum, belladonna (deadly nightshade), and henbane into a cup of wine.

Johann Wier, the sixteenth-century Belgian physician who was one of the first to challenge, and ridicule as superstition, the then universal belief in witchcraft, has left us valuable details of the principal ingredients of several other unguents. One recipe is composed of the fat of young children "seethed in a brazen vessel until it becomes thick and slab, and then scummed." With this are mixed eleoselinum (hemlock), aconitum (aconite), frondes populeae (poplar leaves), and fuligo (soot). Another recipe for the magic liniment comprises sium (cowbane), acorum uulgare (sweet flag), pentaphyllon (cinquefoil), uespertilioris sanguis (bat's blood), solanum somniferum (deadly nightshade), and oleum (oil). All in all (with the exception of the fat of young children) these are potent

Aconite

Deadly nightshade.

substances, some of a deadly compound. One sixteenth-century scientist and physician, the Italian Geronomo Cardono, was even brave (or foolish) enough to try out a number of these unguents on himself, which he said induced hallucination, sleep and fantastical dreams.

It would be wrong as well as misleading to suggest that all or even most animal "transformations" were the mere consequence of wild hallucinations – for we have yet to consider the very important area of theosophy and spiritualism – yet there can be little doubt that in many instances lycanthropes and so-called werewolves were in fact the victims of often overtly excessive drug-taking. It is interesting to note that a large proportion of suspected werewolves were shepherds, often mentally sub-normal and frequently psychologically deranged – easy victims for black magic rituals and the attendant incantations, unguents and drugs. Shepherds, of course, were in daily contact with the dreaded wolf. In a period of history when wolves and other savage beasts roamed the land in vast numbers, these shepherds commonly bore nasty bodily scars as a result of protecting their flocks from marauding wolves (it is undoubtedly no coincidence that a notable characteristic of many captured werewolves and lycanthropes was the marked profusion of skin lesions on their bodies). It would be only natural that if they were to become involved in drug-taking rituals they would at some point imagine themselves to be metamorphosed into these wild beasts, which, in the victims' day to day occupations, brought such fear, depredation and personal injury into their lives.

Jean de Nynauld recognized this proposition as long ago as 1615 in his book *Lycanthropie*. The eighth chapter deals with "those natural things which have the quality of presenting to the imagination things which are not present in reality but only in effect." He mentions various drugs and potions, including those containing cannabis and strychnine, as well as the vapor of strong perfumes which "dazzle and cheat the senses." All shape-shifting, he concludes, is "mere hallucination." Dr H. J. Norman, writing in 1933, agrees in several respects with Nynauld, noting that some of the drugs used by werewolves

> were very potent, especially if taken internally; but there also seems to be no doubt that absorption would take place through the skin, for it was the custom to mix them with some fatty substance: for example, the fat of children. Even so it is unlikely that any considerable amount of the drug could be absorbed in this way, for it was not probable that it could be in any

degree of concentration. The chief effect was brought about as the result of the high degree of suggestibility of the individuals, who were undoubtedly in numerous instances psychopathic and mentally deranged.

Dr Norman then discusses the effect on the patient of several of the drugs used in the magic unguents and potions. Belladonna, or deadly nightshade, says the doctor,

> is a powerful poison, acting locally on the sensory nerve-endings and also on the central nervous system. According to Professor Dixon, "in man, after a large dose, there are general excitement, restlessness, vertigo, talkativeness, laughter, and disturbance of vision giving rise to illusions generally of a pleasing character." The well-known effect of dilation of the pupils of the eyes might assist in the production of the illusions of sight – the "seeing of visions." Henbane also contains potent alkaloids, or active substances; with it there is the tendency to the production of illusions of sight. Aconite root contains aconitine and other alkaloids; it acts on the sensory nerve-endings, producing tingling, numbness, and anaesthesia: and when absorbed has a definite effect on the heart and on respiration. Hemlock tends to produce loss of muscular power and eventually paralysis. The list of potent drugs employed might be easily extended, but it will be gathered from what has already been mentioned that the witches' armamentarium was by no means an ineffective one.

So, medically speaking, we know that the drugs employed by many early werewolves actually produced the desired effect: that is, the illusion that transformation into wolf-form had taken place. Legend, superstition and the diabolical imagination of man then took over.

Yet the use of hallucinatory unguents and potions is by no means the complete or final answer to the werewolf legend. A vast number of the stories never mention salves or drugs or girdles, nor the all-important initiating ceremonies. My own records of lycanthropic transformations, containing material collected from sources all over the world, verbally and from historical documentation, are bulging at the seams with the various methods used to effect metamorphosis: to drink water out of the footprint made by a savage wolf; to consume its brains; to drink from certain enchanted streams or pools; to pluck, wear or smell a lycanthropic flower; to haunt the lair of a werewolf, to eat his food or make any form of contact with him or his possessions ... it is pointless to continue. But these and many, many more were all means of voluntary or

The moment of werewolfic metamorphosis – as seen by American artist Joseph Krucher for the first issue in 1962 of a supernatural magazine.

involuntary transformation, and they might be permanent or merely transitory. Interesting as they are, and as "relevant" as we may wish to make them, they amount in sum to little more than the whims and fancy of folk-lore, and it would be futile and misleading to attach to them any undue significance.

The actual hour of metamorphosis seems to vary not only from district to district but from one individual to another, no doubt dictated by whether or not the person is a voluntary or involuntary werewolf. But sunset seems to be the time when transformation customarily takes place; the transmutation back to man generally happens at dawn. In most cases the werewolf's return to human shape is an automatic occurrence. At other times the werewolf needs a little help. Often the simple expedient of laying aside the wolfskin or girdle is enough to effect the change and remove the enchantment; sometimes burning it, or piercing it with a knife, does the trick; plunging into water or rolling over and over in dew is also said to be effective. Other methods include asking a trusted friend to recite a certain formula, rubbing the body with a particular ointment (Pierre Bourgot favored this method), being touched with a pitchfork or a flail (popular in the Ukraine), slipping through a hoop made of a shoot of a year-old birch, and being recognized by a relative.

A Swedish legend tells of a cottager who, on entering the forest one day without remembering to say the Lord's Prayer, got into the power of a Troll, who changed him into a wolf. For many years his wife mourned him as dead. But one Christmas Eve the old Troll, disguised as a beggar-woman, came to the house for alms; and being taken in and kindly treated, told the woman that her husband might very likely appear to her in wolf-shape. Going at night to the pantry to lay aside a joint of meat for the following day's dinner, she saw a wolf standing with its paws on the window-sill, looking wistfully in at her. "Ah, dearest," she said, "if I knew that you were really my husband, I would give you a bone." At this point the wolf-skin fell off, and her husband stood before her in the same old clothes which he had on the day that the Troll got hold of him.

Having examined the background to metamorphosis provided by the black arts, with their magical accessories, as well as the modern science of psychiatry, it is important to take up another vital element of this subject: spiritualism. Theosophists believe that during the Middle Ages, when one of the most popular forms of entertainment was public execution, many people sunk so low mentally that their astral bodies, those human spirits which we are said to use after death, actually linked with an animal. Among such theosophists are many distinguished scientists and men of medicine. They will affirm that it is just possible for a man to live a life so absolutely depraved, so utterly wicked and brutal, that the whole of his lower mind may become enmeshed in his desires, and finally separated from its spiritual source in the higher self.

"To attain the appalling pre-eminence in evil," says C. W. Leadbeater in *The Astral Plane* (1895), "a man must stifle every gleam of unselfishness or spirituality, and must have absolutely no redeeming point whatever; and when we remember how often, even in the worst of villains, there is to be found something not wholly bad, we shall realize that the abandoned personalities must always be a small minority. Still, comparatively few though they be, they *do* exist." And it is from their ranks that many of the famous werewolves were drawn.

We know that low spirit entities can possess an animal; we know that dogs, for instance, can be possessed. The Bible talks of the Devil entering into swine. Spiritualists and the Church are in agreement on this: that animals and human beings can be taken over by evil spirits. We speak of "evil people," but what we really mean is the *manifestation* of evil. A child is not born evil: that condition is acquired, usually involuntarily. The lower spirit entity is rarely evil, but there are forces that are neither human nor spiritual – unknown forces without a name – which can be manipulated and used by the minds of man: by witches, wizards and occultists generally; and they can be used either for good or for evil. These low forces, too, according to the theosophical credo, can be formed into, or given the shape of, animals; these thought-forms can be energized (by witch-doctors, say, or dabblers in black magic) and directed on to a mission of bloodshed. My discussions with exorcists suggests that there is much in these propositions which we would be foolish to ignore.

Rose Gladden, one of Britain's most respected exorcists, and a renowned clairvoyant-healer with clients all over the world, has, at her Hertfordshire clinic, treated literally dozens of men, women and children suffering from diabolical possession of evil spirits. She has had on her books, and indeed still has, several psychic vampires. From our numerous conversations together she has formulated a number of plausible and original theories on lycanthropy generally and, along the way, has made what I wish to acknowledge as a notable contribution towards

Rose Gladden, British exorcist and clairvoyant healer: "They've seen wolves and bears come jumping through their bedroom windows."

our greater understanding of the werewolf as a psychic phenomenon.

She explains that the will to commit werewolfic acts would not come to a person unless he was of low passion and limited desires. We come across fewer instances of reported werewolves today, she says, not because the wolf populations of the world are drastically reduced, but because man is now more spiritually enlightened. Rose Gladden insists that the wizards, magicians, witch-doctors, sorcerers, occultists – call them what you may – understood the power of thought. She observes:

> They wielded such a strong power over the minds of other people that I would put nothing past them whatsoever. I know – I have actually seen the results of their power from the many people, colored people especially, who come to me, frightened to death because of the dreadful things they've seen. They've seen wolves and bears come jumping through their bedroom windows. They come to me for help, quite often, because they are trying to get away from satanist groups, black magic groups, and they tell me that the groups refuse to let them go. I am absolutely convinced that many of these groups use a form of hypnosis without the person knowing it; the person imagines all sorts of things, and it is not inconceivable that he imagines himself to be a werewolf. If people in our more enlightened world are susceptible to auto-suggestion, hypnosis, persuasion and so on, just think how easy it must have been for occultist groups to sway the mind of an uneducated peasant in earlier times.

Rose Gladden believes, and I am inclined to agree, that the archetypal werewolf of the Middle Ages, and later, was a creature which existed on an astral level. The werewolf was an astral body. The following passage is from *The Occult and the Supernatural* (1975):

> This astral body is an exact copy of the flesh and blood body but is made of a finer material and has a shining and luminous appearance. It is supposed to be capable of separating itself from the physical body and travelling about, passing through walls, ceilings and other solid obstructions. It is also said to survive death, when it leaves the physical body. It exists in what is called the astral plane, which excludes the normal everyday world but extends beyond it.

> The astral body can manifest itself initially only during a man's physical life, and he would need to have some knowledge of the magical arts to project it. There is a

greater understanding of the technique today, due to the proliferation of books on astral projection. So, if a cruel and brutal person (whom we might define as a "low astral person") was to use the technique, his body could be seized upon by astral entities and materialized – that is, made solid – not into human form but into that of an animal, usually the wolf. In that condition it would certainly range the country, it would kill other animals, even human beings, and would need to satisfy its own craving for blood. The entities which drive on that astral body would also demand the replenishment of blood. If the astral body was in the form of a wolf, and it was subsequently wounded – its paw cut off, say, by a hunter – that wound would be duplicated on the wolf's human physical body; that is, one of the hands would be badly wounded or missing.

Rose Gladden explains the relationship of astral projection to werewolfery like this:

> If I was to sit here and close my eyes, and breathe deeply, I could quite easily project my astral body out of my physical body to the other end of the room. I could stand down there and look back and see myself sitting here. Now while I have retention of my full consciousness, and I know what I am doing, I am safe. But suppose I was a cruel person who enjoyed the horrible things of life – well, as I came out of my physical body and moved down to the other end of the room, all the surrounding evil could grasp me. And it would be the evil grasping my astral projection, or grasping my "double," which would transform me into an animal, into a wolf. The atmosphere is always full of evil forces, and these evil forces find it much easier to exist within mankind – within an evil man, say – than in a nebulous vacuum. People addicted to werewolfery were – indeed, still are – the most evil manifestations of humanity. I can well understand why there are so many instances on record of "wound-doubling." It would be impossible for it not to happen.

A werewolf's wound in animal form being later duplicated when he returns to human form was always, in an earlier period, regarded as an infallible test of a werewolf's guilt. No doubt there have been errors of identification and interpretation in some ancient werewolf accounts, but on the whole the theosophist explanation has much to commend it.

There are numerous examples of wound duplication. One involves a German farmer and his wife who were cutting hay together when suddenly the wife requested

This German wood engraving dated 1722 illustrates one of several werewolf stories "on a theme": the haymaker who, feeling he is about to metamorphose, instructs his son not to harm any wild beast which might approach him but simply to throw a hat at it. Seeing the wolf, though, the fear-struck boy strikes the animal with a sickle, piercing its heart. Transformation again takes place . . . and there lying on the ground is not the body of a wolf but the corpse of the boy's father.

her husband to throw his hat at any wild beast that might come his way. She then disappeared. Soon afterwards a wolf was seen to be swimming across a neighboring river in the direction of the party of haymakers. The farmer, remembering his wife's order, threw his hat at the wolf, which the ravenous beast seized upon and tore to pieces. One of the men, however, stabbed the wolf with a pitchfork. This dissolved the spell; the wolf-form disappeared – but the body of the wife lay bleeding from a pitchfork wound on the ground before the eyes of the astonished spectators.

From Baring-Gould's *Were-Wolves* we learn:

The wife of a nobleman in Livonia expressed her doubts to one of her slaves whether it were possible for man or woman to change shape. The servant at once volunteered to give her evidence of that possibility. He left the room, and in another moment a wolf was observed running over the country. The dogs followed him, and not withstanding his resistance, tore out one of his eyes. Next day the slave appeared before his mistress blind of an eye.

Bodin tells some werewolf stories on good authority. He says that the Royal Procurator-General Bourdin has assured him that he had shot a wolf, and that the arrow had stuck in the beast's thigh. A few hours after, the arrow was found in the thigh of a man in bed. In Vernon, about the year 1566, the witches and warlocks gathered in great multitudes, under the shape of cats. Four or five men were attacked in a lone place by a number of these beasts. The men stood their ground with the utmost heroism, succeeded in slaying one puss, and in wounding many others. Next day a number of wounded women were found in the town, and they gave the judge an accurate account of all the circumstances connected with their wounding.

Nynauld relates that in a village of Switzerland, near Lucerne, a peasant was attacked by a wolf, while he was hewing timber; he defended himself, and smote off a fore-leg of the beast. The moment that the blood began to flow the wolf's form changed, and he recognised a woman without her arm. She was burnt alive.

We have seen in earlier parts of the book how it is often necessary for the human werewolf to discard his clothes before he can achieve successful metamorphosis into wolf form. The Arcadian and German legends, especially, provide abundant evidence of this. Rose Gladden offers an observation on this subject which must be regarded as a real breakthrough in understanding the black science of werewolfery:

> Can't you see how this procedure of undressing has got slightly twisted in the re-telling. What most likely happened is that instead of coming out of their clothes they came out of their body. In one sense, therefore, they wouldn't be "in" their clothes, because the astral body doesn't need clothes. So what you would see lying on the ground is a pile of clothes, yes, but inside them would be the physical body, sound asleep. The astral form would take the shape of something which in those days was most feared, which was the wolf. The wolf was the most aggressive, most evil creature they could think of. They couldn't think of a lamb, for instance, because the astral form would want blood; that meant assuming the form of a wolf. And this is why the werewolf went into the countryside and killed people: to gratify the astral body.

This is a very probable explanation for the many werewolfic mutilations which were committed while the particular man was asleep, either in his bed at home or in a field somewhere. The sleeping werewolf, in his human physical form, projected his astral body elsewhere – perhaps many miles away – in the materialized, solid shape of a savage wolf.

Eliphas Levi, the nineteenth-century occultist, discusses this phenomenon in relation to "wound-doubling" in *The Mysteries of Magic* (where, incidentally, he says werewolfery is due to the "sidereal body, which is the mediator between the soul and the material organism"). He explains that while a man is in bed dreaming that he is a real wolf, his body, because it is subject to nervous and magnetic influences, will receive the blows and cuts dealt at the fantastical shape. C. W. Leadbeater, in *The Astral Plane*, corroborates this:

As so often with ordinary materialisation, any wound inflicted upon that animal form will be reproduced upon the human physical body by the extraordinary phenomenon of repercussion; though after the death of that physical body, the astral (which will probably continue to appear in the same form) will be less vulnerable. It will then, however, be also less dangerous, as unless it can find a suitable medium it will be unable to materialise fully.

Rose Gladden has treated, and exorcised, many human patients who have been able to project their foulest thoughts into animal form and "attack" not only their enemies but also, ironically, themselves. To conclude this chapter, I will quote one particular case in full, exactly as Mrs Gladden related it to me, because I feel it perfectly illustrates, and goes a long way to explain, the origin of many a macabre werewolf tale, particularly those where revenge has been the prime motive.

A boy of seventeen or eighteen came to me for help. He told me truthfully that he was surrounded by evil and that he himself was riddled with terrible demons. I tried to find out what influences were responsible for the evil attacks on him, and was amazed to find very little – but what I did discover was that he himself was producing the dark images that were afflicting him with such terrible harm and fear. So I asked him if he hated people. He told me a strange story. As a child, he said, he wore glasses; and he wasn't as pleasant-looking as some of his friends. He was often laughed at. So he was determined to avenge them somehow. Well, he discovered that just by concentrating on them very deeply and wishing them ill, within two days those boys who had tormented him were taken ill. Consequently, after every period of torment suffered because of their jeers, he would concentrate illness on them, and on each and every occasion when they were taken sick, he was absolutely delighted.

He exercised this power all through childhood and into early manhood. He told me, "It was my way of getting my own back." But then his thoughts got out of hand, and it got to the stage where he was not just wishing people ill but wishing the total collapse of their lives; eventually he was wishing them death. He himself was building the "salt forms", the evil thoughts, and sending them out; but the auric field (the field of energy which surrounds all living things) of the people he had been directing them against had been so strong that it couldn't accept his thoughts. Therefore they bounced

It is believed by some experts that the werewolf is the manifestation of a person's evil thoughts. The wolf, because it was formerly considered to be the most evil of all beasts, was the form usually assumed by these evil thoughts. This print of a werewolf ripping out a man's throat first appeared in Sabine Baring-Gould's classic *The Book of Were-Wolves* (1865).

back – this will happen – they bounced back and attacked him. It means he was being attacked by the manifestation of his own evil thoughts. These were in the form of animals, including wolves. And do remember that when his enemies were hurt by them, that what they caught sight of on each occasion was a savage animal – a savage animal coming at *them*. That animal, that wolf, would have been very real to them. It is more likely that they became ill through absolute shock; it could have been to the point of having them sent to a mental hospital.

I told him, "I will help you, my friend – but only if you will pray for those you have hurt." At first he said, "I can never pray for them." But I insisted, and eventually we sat down together and prayed; and we prayed together for God to forgive him for what he had done, and for health and strength to be given to his enemies, and for love and light within himself. We did this, and he left me a much happier person.

So, when people ask whether man *can* be transformed into a wolf or some other animal, it is never a simple matter of answering Yes or No. As Rose Gladden says, "The power of thought and auto-suggestion is tremendous. We can't begin to understand it. There are a few who do: the sorcerers of the mind. Among their number, unquestionably, is the werewolf."

9 "The Devil is Exceedingly Chastised": Cure and Exorcism

THE WEREWOLF MAY WELL DERIVE a certain perverted gratification from his loathsome life-style. Yet for every ten which, historically, revel in the gore and mangling mess of their own making, there are another ten which clearly do not. The lycanthrope certainly does not; he is a morbidly unhappy creature, suffering as much mentally from the excesses of his own bouts of melancholia and hypochondria as his victims suffer physically. But whereas, since the eighteenth century, the lycanthrope has so often been treated psychoanalytically, the werewolf will never subject himself – not willingly at least – to the couch. He is committed irrevocably to the Devil. There are, however, other methods of curing him.

Traditionally, there are three principal ways in which a werewolf can be scourged of his demons: he may be cured medicinally and surgically; he may be exorcised; and, the more drastic, he may be shot with a special bullet. The idea behind the first two procedures was to enable the wolf part of his nature to be destroyed; the latter method, on the other hand, took care quite nicely of both the human and the animal elements. Often a combination of the "cures" was used, and this was certainly the case during the lifetime of the seventh-century Greek surgeon Paulus Aegineta, or Paul of Aegina. In one of his books, *De Re Medica Libra Septem*, still extant, he suggests the following course of treatment:

> You may know that lycanthropia is a species of melancholy which you may cure at the time of the attack, by opening a vein and abstracting blood to fainting, and giving the patient a diet of wholesome food. Let him use baths of sweet water, and then milk-whey for three days, and, twice or thrice, purging with the hiera from colocynth [*a purgative drug obtained from the bitter pulp of the fruit of the wild gourd*]. After the purgings use the theriac [*ancient antidote for poison,*

composed of certain drugs mixed with honey] of vipers, and administer those things mentioned for the cure of melancholy: sprig of thyme, epithymus; aloes; wormwood after purging, pungent vinegar as a beverage; squills, poley, slender birthwort; phlebotomy and hot poultices. In chronic cases evacuation, by vomiting with hellebore [*a purgative drug prepared from the Christmas rose, or black hellebore*]. When the disease is already formed, use soporific embrocations, and rub the nostrils with opium when going to rest.

It is not too difficult to imagine what agonies many suspected werewolves were forced to endure in the cause of medicine and, if these lycanthropic "remedies" were well-known to them it is perhaps not surprising why so many of their kind preferred the way of Satan and black magic to the way of Hippocrates and medical science. So severe, so brutal, were the cures advocated by early medical practitioners that, not surprisingly, a great many werewolfic patients died by the hands of those who had promised them salvation. Conversely, death was perhaps the ultimate act of redemption – although, if their bodies were then not cremated, they stood a fair chance of joining the kingdom of the Undead. Salvation for these werewolves was short-lived, and not very sweet.

Among the more excessively bloody means of administering lycanthropic cures were those practiced in the eleventh century by Avicenna, the Middle East's most famous Islamic physician and philosopher. If the customary methods failed he would then cauterize the forehead with a red-hot branding iron; the good Arabian doctor does not say how many coronary cases he acquired as a result of this dramatic treatment. Copious bloodletting was also a remedy for lycanthropy greatly favored

A Greek surgeon collecting medicinal herbs. In ancient times, and even within living memory, a great variety of magic plants were used for their supposed protection from evil creatures, including werewolves and vampires. From a seventh-century Turin manuscript.

by the early Arab physicians, as well as treatment which required that blows and lashes be delivered to the skin with a thin wooden rod. (A close parallel to this treatment was the Roman custom of whipping all sufferers of nymphomania.) In chronic cases of lycanthropy, and as an alternative to cauterization, the Arabs advised excessive castigation. Where the European werewolf was tortured in order to elicit an appropriate confession, his Arabian counterpart first confessed and then received his due "cure": in any other language it would be called torture. (Admittedly, though, such "cures" often took place in Europe as well. During the Counter-Reformation of the sixteenth century, it was dangerous to fall into the diagnostic and therapeutic machinery of the Catholic Church, because exorcism, the treatment of werewolves and the possessed generally, could assume the form of torture; the purifying treatment of witches had this character to begin with.)

In nearby Sicily, where the werewolf tradition is long and colorful, the Arabian belief in the werewolf's forehead as a vulnerable spot, occultly, is reflected in several local remedies. A sharp blow to the forehead or the scalp with a knife, resulting in a flow of blood, is said to cure the werewolf forever of its black affliction. The spell can also be broken, according to peasant tradition, if the backs of his paws or hands are pierced. The blood in both cases, apparently, will be black and thick, and it will well in great clotted gouts, which the islanders refer to as "sangue pazzo." In the province of Messina, too, it used to be said that the *lupo manaro*, those loathsome witches dressed as wolves, could be cured by striking them with a key of a certain (unspecified) shape.

The Ancient Romans and Greeks were great believers in the overwhelming power of exhaustion as a suitable cure for lycanthropia, therioanthropia, and other forms of delusional insanity. The treatment was used when the daughters of King Proitos of Argos, by refusing to be initiated into the mysteries of Dionysus, were compelled to roam the country naked, during which time they believed themselves to be transformed into cows. The women of the island of Cos, seat of the first school of scientific medicine, were similarly transformed into cows as a penance for having exalted their own beauty above that of the goddess Aphrodite. The cure, advocated by the prophet and healer Melampus, was to have such women chased by young men, "roaring and dancing after them over the mountains and valleys, until they fell down exhausted and came to their senses, with the exception of the eldest among them who died from the effect of the cure."

The idea that exhaustion is an infallible healer of lycanthropic madness probably stems from a knowledge that, following a werewolf's period of morbid abnormality, he is left feeling tremendously weak and debilitated – with dry throat and tongue and feeble vision – and generally exhausted. The Romans and Greeks believed that exhaustion was the werewolf's Achilles' heel, and subjected him to periods of enforced physical activity in the hope that it would effectively purge him of the malady. As in the case of the women of Cos and Agros, the mortality rate must have been high following the inevitable heart-attacks.

We saw earlier how the French infantry officer Bertrand, and other victims of the disease, experienced these characteristic bouts of exhaustion; the condition can also be compared with the utter exhaustion which followed the excesses of the berserker rages of the Northmen. There is a plausible answer to this, as Rose Gladden, the exorcist and clairvoyant-healer, explains:

> I would be very surprised if, after returning to his normal self following a period of astral projection in animal form, a werewolf did not suffer extreme exhaustion. Astral projection occurs many times when the werewolf is asleep in his bed; the reason why we go to sleep in the first place is so that the etheric body, the vital force which gives the body life, can be energized. Our body is literally boosted, during sleep, like a car-battery on a charger. Now if a depraved, brutal person was to project his astral body in wolf form, and energized it in order to accomplish his evil deeds, this energy would have to come from the etheric matter normally used to vitalize the physical body. It means that when the werewolf "wakes up," or changes back from his animal form to that of his human shape, he will feel absolutely drained. He will be suffering, in fact, from classic "werewolf exhaustion."

Elsewhere, in later times, less extreme methods were often (though by no means always) favored. In the north German lowland of Schleswig-Holstein, for instance, it used to be said that if a werewolf was addressed three times by his Christian name, he resumed his human form; the cure was absolute. Dosing a patient with a magic narcotic also often did the trick. Some old books on black magic say that if the human being retains a material object acquired by his wolfic replica, it will effectively free him from his obsession; while severely scolding a werewolf, according to Danish folklore, will also work. Self-control, too, has long been popular as a cure for werewolfery, ranging from not eating meat for nine years to kneeling in one spot for one hundred years. It was also believed that if a priest first cursed a werewolf, and then drew its blood, the man could be considered cured.

If all these methods failed to cure a werewolf of his affliction, then the community would often try to find a means to protect itself from possible harm. The "safety" methods employed were often as fanciful as some of the prescribed cures. In many country areas, rye and mistletoe are still looked upon as effective safeguards against werewolves. So is a sprig of mountain ash; in fact, many country people in Belgium do not consider they are safe from evil influences unless a mountain ash is growing close to their house. Elsewhere, many people would build or buy a house near to running water in the belief that it would repulse werewolves.

Although shooting a werewolf with a bullet made from inherited silver, or stabbing him with a silver dagger, was said to be a sure method of finishing off a man's werewolfic spirit, along with his life, exorcism of some form or other was a more popular choice. The ceremonies themselves ranged from the incredibly simple to those which were as elaborate in routine as many of the actual werewolf initiating ceremonies. Into this latter category comes a ritual reported by Elliott O'Donnell as occurring near Orsk, in the Orenburg region of Russia, earlier this century. A wealthy landowner and his two servants, long suspected of being werewolves, were eventually brought before a high priest, who performed the following exorcising rite:

> A circle of seven feet radius was drawn on the ground in white chalk. At the centre of the circle were inscribed, in yellow chalk, certain magical figures representing Mercury, and about them was drawn, in white chalk, a triangle within a circle of three feet radius – the centre of the circle being the same as that of the outer circle. Within this inner circle were then placed the three captive werewolves. It would be well to explain here that in exorcism, as well as in the evocation of spirits, great attention must be paid to the position of the stars, as astrology exercises the greatest influence on the spirit world. The present occasion, the reverend Father pointed out, was specially favourable for the casting out of devils, since from 8.32 p.m. to 9.16 p.m. was under the dominion of the great angel Mercury – the most bitter opponent of all evil spirits; that is to say, Mercury was in $17° 11'$, on the cusp of Seventh House, slightly to south of due west:

☽ going to ☌ with ☿ in 14° ♊
☿ to ☌ ♅ ☿ 130° ♄

Round the outer circle the reverend Father now proceeded to place, at equal intervals, hand-lamps, burning olive oil. He then erected a rude altar of wood, about a foot to the south-east of the circumference of the inner circle. Exactly opposite this altar, and about one and a half feet to the far side of the circumference of the inner circle, he ordered the soldiers to build a fire, and to place over it a tripod and pot, the latter containing two pints of pure spring water.

He then prepared a mixture consisting of these ingredients:

- 2 drachms of sulphur
- $\frac{1}{2}$ oz. of castoreum
- 6 drachms of opium
- 3 drachms of asafoetida
- $\frac{1}{2}$ oz. of hypericum
- $\frac{3}{4}$ oz. of ammonia
- $\frac{1}{2}$ oz. of camphor

When this was thoroughly mixed he put it in the water in the pot, adding to it a portion of a mandrake root, a live snake, two live toads in linen bags, and a fungus. He then bound together, with red tape, a wand consisting of three sprigs taken, respectively, from an ash, birch and white poplar.

He next proceeded to pray, kneeling in front of the altar; and continued praying till the unearthly cries of the toads announced the fact that the water, in which they were immersed, was beginning to boil. Slowly getting up and crossing himself, he went to the fire and dipping a cup in the pot, solemnly approached the werewolves, and slashing them severely across the head with his wand, dashed in their faces the seething liquid, calling out as he did so: "In the name of Our Blessed Lady I command thee to depart. Black, evil devils from hell, begone! Begone! Again I say, Begone!" He repeated this three times to the vociferous yells of the smarting werewolves.

A similar, but less involved, form of werewolfic exorcism, was practiced in many European countries as late as the turn of the last century. When the accused werewolf was secured within the prescribed chalk circle of seven feet radius, three girls, with the aid of ash twigs, committed on the patient the most brutal acts of flagellation. As they were doing so, they called out:

The exorcism of people suffering from lycanthropic mania was much described and depicted in the Middle Ages and even later. This victim is being exorcised in the presence of nobles and the clergy in the castle of Cappeln, at Starnberg, Austria, in 1574.

> Greywolf ugly, greywolf old,
> Do at once as you are told.
> Leave this man and fly away,
> Where 'tis night and never day.

They maintained their barrage of chants and unmerciful whippings until the whole of the werewolf's body, including his face, was covered with blood. A person of senior rank, or the oldest person present, then gave the werewolf a severe blow with his or her foot, exclaiming:

> Go, fly, away to the sky;
> Devil of greywolf, thee we defy.
> Out, out, with a howl and yell,
> 'Twill carry thee faster and surer to Hell.

From a concoction of sulphur, tar, vinegar and castoreum (a pungent oily substance obtained from the beaver), which had been bubbling at boiling-point in a heated cauldron, every one present scooped out a mugful and, positioning themselves in a circle around the werewolf, dowsed him all over with it. As he was squirming from the painful effects of the boiling substance, they would all chant:

> Away, away, shoo, shoo, shoo!
> Do you think we care a jot for you?
> We'll whip thee again, with a crack, crack, crack!
> Scourge thee and beat thee till thou art black;
> Fool of a greywolf, we have thee at last,
> Back to thy hell home, out of him fast –
> Fast, fast, fast!
>
> Our patience won't last.
> We'll scratch thee, we'll prick thee,
> We'll prod thee, we'll scald thee.
> Fast, fast, out of him, fast!

All this continued, over and over again, until the cauldron was empty and the hour struck one o'clock. Everyone then departed, leaving the werewolf on the ground in a condition of severe physical depredation and, I suspect, shock. The werewolfic spirit was then said to leave the man. When he recovered from his wounds, his disposition would be sunny and bright – *if* he recovered from his wounds, of course, he had every right to feel joyful. There was an element of sadism about these rites which makes one skeptical of their principal function.

Saint Cyprian, the third-century Christian martyr and Bishop of Carthage, was one of the first scholars to note that "by the power of the exorcist, whose words are energized in the sovereignty of Almighty God, the Devil

A boiling cauldron of herbs and drugs is prepared for a ceremony of werewolfic exorcism. A sixteenth-century woodcut.

143

is exceedingly chastised, yea, and burned as with fire and sore tormented." So exorcism has always been associated with an element of pain. In a letter to Demetrianus, proconsul of Africa, Cyprian again writes: "If you could but hear and see how what time the possessed and demoniacs are exorcised and smitten, as it were, with spiritual blows; the demons screeching and howling, are compelled to abandon the bodies they have so foully invaded, and release the afflicted from their travail and pain."

Often a form of "deception" was adopted by Renaissance physicians to rid a werewolf of his demons. This is affirmed by the *World History of Psychiatry*, published in 1975, which explains: "On the advice of doctors, a manic patient was not treated by exorcism but by medicaments. Since he believed himself to be possessed, these were applied under the pretext of exorcising manipulations. The patient was cured, though he believed that not bodily medicine but exorcism had restored him." This is a fact of such overwhelming significance that it should always be taken into account when considering those early exorcising ceremonies where medication formed a principal function.

In Haiti, an island much plagued by a unique werewolf-vampire, exorcism is a serious and extreme business. Alfred Métraux, who (as author of *Voodoo in Haiti*, 1959) probably knows more about Haitian voodooist folklore and superstition than anybody else, provides details of the following "magic treatment" as a protection against werewolves:

> The peasants are not entirely helpless in face of their children's danger from werewolves. Since the numerous available talismans are not always effective, it is thought wise to immunise new-born babies by "spoiling their blood." This is done as soon as possible; during pregnancy, the mother must drink bitter coffee laced with *clairin* and flavoured with three drops of petrol. Then she bathes in water infused with garlic, chives, thyme, nutmeg, *bois-caca* leaves (*Capparis cynophallophora*), manioc mush, coffee and *clairin*. Some time after its birth the child is plunged into a similar bath. It is also given a tisane made of various herbs. For good measure of precaution *clairin* is burnt in a plate and the child passed through the resulting flames. The exorciser who is "drugging" it asks three times: "Who wants this little one?" The mother replies, "I do." In these words she affirms her determination to resist any werewolf who may take advantage of her sleep to come and demand her child. Then the calabash used in the

Exorcism in 1978. A sixteen-year-old schoolgirl, possessed by the spirit of a savage wolf, is "crucified" on a Brazilian hillside.

ablutions is buried open-side downwards. If a *loup-garou* turns up near the house and tries by deceitful utterances to obtain the mother's consent to her own loss, the calabash must answer it. In some families the children's blood is made bitter by feeding them with cockroaches – first trimmed of their legs and wings and fried in castor oil, syrup, nutmeg and garlic. Some children have blood that is naturally salty or bitter and these therefore have nothing to fear from werewolves. The werewolf who drinks "spoilt blood" is seized with violent vomiting.

A unique form of lycanthropic exorcism occurred at Rosário do Sul, in Southern Brazil, early in 1978. A sixteen-year-old schoolgirl, Eliana Barbosa, was secured to a makeshift cross and crucified in an attempt to exorcise her of her "evil visions and demons"; at times, it is said, she felt she was possessed of the spirit of a savage wolf. The Roman Catholic girl was roped to the cross after dragging it 450 feet up a hillside. For three days she hung there as racketeers, out to make a fast buck, set up makeshift food stalls to cash-in on all the ghoulish sightseers which the exorcism attracted – estimated at more than five thousand. Eliana was later taken down in a state of deep shock. But the exorcism failed. She was still plagued, it seems, by the werewolfic visions and demons.

Rose Gladden, whose work as an exorcist is widely known, pursues, as we might expect, a somewhat more humane and Christian attitude with her own patients. If she were approached by a person suffering from lycanthropia, and asked to help, she would

> ... look at the person very carefully, clairvoyantly, to determine first of all whether or not there were any influences within the auric field – which, as I mentioned earlier, is the field of energy which surrounds all living things. With man it varies in size from inches from the body to perhaps yards from the body, depending entirely on the spirituality of the person. Now if the lycanthrope's own auric field was narrowed because of any unhealthy desires, and remembering that there are other lower forces which will seize upon a person's depraved desires to give him greater depraved strength, I would try to find out who or what was doing the manipulating. If the lycanthrope was receiving images which had been projected into his mind by these lower evil forces, then I would help him fight them.
>
> But I know from experience that a person cannot be possessed by these lower forces unless he himself happens to be a low, evil type of person. Well, assuming he wants to be helped, I would try to uplift him spiritually. I would try to fight, on his behalf, whatever evil influences are troubling him. I would get him to try and understand God and the higher nature of man, because once you're uplifted and you understand that we are all a part of God, the way is clear for the road to salvation. The light exists within all men, no matter how "bad" they are; they still have this tiny light. In the case of the lycanthrope, it is true, it may be almost extinguished; but I would help him to brighten it. Once it has brightened again, once it is shining out, then the evil around him will dissolve and he will be ultimately cleansed. Exorcism, when it works, can be such a beautiful thing.

When it *works* – that is the crux of the whole damnable matter. There are many who believe, despite all the evidence to the contrary, that the pathway of the werewolf is irresolvable: once a werewolf, always a werewolf. Spiritual healers from the ancient Greeks to Rose Gladden, along with thousands of others through the ages, are fortunately not so fatalistic.

10 The Vampire Connection

YOU ARE WITNESS to a most bizarre apparition. It is the dead of night and the moon has cast hideous shadows from the tombstones in the country graveyard. The morbid silence is broken only by a gentle breeze and the squeaking of bats in the black sky. Underneath an old willow in one corner of the cemetery we stumble across the grave of a recently-buried corpse. There is life here, more life than we would dare to imagine.

Six feet below ground, inside the noxious coffin, the corpse has begun to quiver and to gnaw and tear at the cloth which covers its face. A demonic ferocity overtakes it and we hear horrible wails and shrieks and other blood-curdling noises issuing from the ground. The cemetery echoes with the sound of a mad beast. The coffin then bursts open, the earth which lay upon it is thrown into the air, and flames of Hell leap and soar from the grave. A pale-skinned specter, half-man, half-wolf, with blazing red eyes, clambers from its former prison and disappears into the darkness. An orgy of midnight murders is about to begin....

The scenario for a Gothic horror movie? Perhaps. But such a creature is still believed to exist in many rural areas of Germany and Poland and, until comparatively recently, in certain parts of northern France. It is quite distinct from the ordinary werewolf and nearer to the vampire, for it is not a transformed living man but a corpse that has risen from the grave in the form of a wolf. Such a fate, it used to be said, quite commonly befell the remains of a man or woman who died in mortal sin; an area harboring such a creature in its cemetery would invariably be overwhelmed by death and ominous onslaughts on the population.

At one time, when a neighborhood recognized the frequent deaths all around as the dastardly work of the wolfish vampire, the priest of the parish would be called in. He would arrange for the corpse to be dug up and, after cutting off its head with the sexton's spade – which must never have been used before – he would exorcise the remains. He would then carry the head to the nearest

A 1970s sketch of a vampiric-werewolf by Carey Miller.

BELOW A graveyard werewolf flees from its would-be captors. A nineteenth-century engraving.

stream and throw it in. It sank immediately. But, according to custom, this was not all it did: for, weighed down with its terrible sins, it would pierce the bottom of the river and would press slowly downward through the earth until it reached the place of everlasting torments.

The methods of exorcism meted out to these wolf-vampires was not dissimilar to those for vampires proper:

A werewolf, unless exorcised, will traditionally become a vampire, a belief which is strikingly illustrated in this double-page spread by Boris Dolgov for the American magazine *Weird Tales* (September 1942).

a stake was driven into the corpse, it would let out a frightful cry, half-human and half-animal, and then it would be decapitated, its trunk and head burned. Innumerable exorcisms of this nature were carried out in France during the reign of Louis XV, who even ordered a report to be prepared on the subject. This document, bearing the date June 7, 1732, is still in existence, and is signed and witnessed by three surgeons and several other people. Life after death, under such circumstances, was rightly feared.

In many East European countries, particularly Bulgaria, Serbia and Slovakia, the werewolf is also linked with vampires. The same is true in Greece today (although, of course, it was not always so). In all these countries, and a few others – save for Serbia – the werewolf collapses into a state of catalepsy, during which his soul departs from his body and enters that of a wolf, when it preys voraciously on blood. When his soul returns he aches with exhaustion. In Serbia, the vampire and the werewolf are known collectively as one creature, the *vulkodlak*, and these are most active during the bleakest winter months. At their annual gatherings they strip off their wolfskins and hang them on the nearby trees. If any of them succeeds in getting hold of another's skin and burning it, the *vulkodlak* whose skin it was will be freed forever from its fiendish enchantment. It is a touching story.

Unless a werewolf is exorcised, folkloric tradition tells us, it will become a vampire. A hundred years ago, for instance, the Ukrainians and Russians looked upon vampires as dead people who, in their lifetime, were wizards, witches, and werewolves. Until the end of the last century, too, the Greeks believed that these werewolf-transformed vampires haunted battlefields in the shape of wolves and hyenas, and that they sucked the last remaining lifeblood from dying soldiers and broke into houses to steal babies from their cots.

A very similar belief is still very much alive today in voodoo-ridden Haiti, where most of the population, from every level of society, trembles with fear at stories of witchcraft and vampires-cum-werewolves. While most Haitians have been educated to disregard, or at least react against, these evil influences, a small proportion of the population do succumb to them and secretly consult a voodoo priest. There are particular spirits known locally as *Jé-rouge*, or "red-eyes," which are without exception evil and cannibalistic and which have much in common with the wolf-vampires of Germany, Poland and northern France.

Two decades ago Alfred Métraux wrote in *Voodoo in Haiti* (1959) that the fear inspired by werewolves on the island was as sharply felt among Protestants and Catholics as it was among voodooists:

> At Marbial my friends gave me, in confidence, the names of all the werewolves in the district. These lists always agreed with each other, which suggests that there is more in this than superstition, a tale with which to frighten children. In 1948 several families lodged complaints with the *Chef de Section* against such and such a neighbour, accusing her of being the werewolf who had come to "drain" (*sécher*) their sick children. I have also seen an enraged mother, who had just lost her baby, insult the woman she suspected of having killed it. Only very rarely does a woman become a werewolf of

her own accord. She nearly always acts in obedience to an impulse of which, to begin with, she remains unconscious. The occult power which enables her to journey through the air and abandon herself to cannibalism with impunity is often the result of a hereditary taint which has passed from mother to daughter. It can also be a sort of contagious illness which can be transmitted to anyone who, without knowing, wears a garment or jewel which has belonged to a werewolf.

In the early stages of their career werewolves commit their crimes without knowing. Night excursions, cannibal meals are for beginners no more than nightmares which haunt their sleep. Then, gradually, the terrible truth dawns on them – but by now it is too late to stop: the taste for human flesh which these unfortunates have by then acquired, has become an uncontrollable vice.

Haitian werewolf-vampires, unlike normal werewolves but with certain similarities to normal vampires, are passionately impelled to increase their numbers. Métraux continues:

> They lay ambushes for women, surprising them at night in remote spots and obliging them to take part in their sabbath. Whoever has fraternised with werewolves can never again live a normal life. He is bound to them with a complicity which, however involuntary, still alienates him for ever from normal human feelings. Nevertheless a person does not become a werewolf overnight; a novice must learn the secrets of this wretched profession under the guidance of a veteran.

An Haitian werewolf will usually do no harm to children of its own kind, according to Métraux.

> But if no other prey is available, then it knows no scruple. Even less does it hesitate if it cherishes a secret grudge against the child's mother or father. One of the laws of the supernatural world requires that no werewolf may "eat" a baby unless its mother has expressly "given" it. Such a gift is obtained by the following trick: having gone up close to the house where the child they want to "eat" is sleeping they find out their chances of success by shuffling clover-leaves together like playing-cards. Success is certain if all the leaves fall shiny-side down but if only three fall thus it means there will be some snag and the attempt is usually abandoned. When the signs are favourable the werewolf first goes into the kitchen which, in the country, is a small shelter not far from the dwelling-place. From there she calls the child's mother. The latter, half-

asleep, hears her name and answers, "Yes." The werewolf then asks, "Will you give me your child?" If then, drowsy and only half-awake, she still replies, "Yes" – then that's that: the child is lost.

We are finally asked:

What motives drive *loups-garous* to feed on the blood of children? Peasants say that it starts as a perverted taste and grows into an insatiable yearning. When a werewolf has succeeded in killing a child he goes with his colleagues, digs it out of the cemetery and eats it, having first turned it into "cod, herring, goat's meat or pork." There are, however, cases when cannibalism is not the sole motive for these murders. A werewolf may avenge itself on a child for an insult suffered from its parents; others simply kill children out of jealousy.

It is clear that some of the symptomatic behavior patterns of Haitian werewolves – a love of preying on children, particularly babies; reddish eyes during spells of demoniacal frenzy; a lust for ravaging corpses newly buried – are also to be found elsewhere. As well as purely werewolfic symptoms we also encounter here well-defined traces of similar types of vampirism, cannibalism and monomaniacal insanity which are also evident in other parts of the world. It has been said that the French lycanthrope, Bertrand, whom we met earlier, was in fact a vampire; though there is little to suggest from his trial that he was suffering from vampirism, we could quite easily, and with some scientific justification, equate his mental symptoms with those of the Haitian werewolf-vampires of today.

Those loathsome fiends who burst with a flaming fury from their coffins in certain parts of Europe have far more in common with vampires than with demonically obsessed creatures like Bertrand. For a vampire is an element which, under certain conditions, inhabits a dead body and, in this way imprisoned, comes out of a grave at night to suck the blood of a living person. Unlike the normal werewolf, or even the more sinister werewolf-vampire of Haiti, the normal vampire has absolutely no interest in the dead. And whereas the werewolf customarily bites, savages and generally mutilates its victim, the vampire pierces the skin of its prey with extremely sharp incisor teeth and laps up blood with the tongue in such an imperceptible way that the sleeping victim probably knows nothing about it.

It is interesting to note that some demonologists believe that Bertrand was a ghoul, one of those evil spirits which supposedly haunts burial-places and feeds on the dead; and certainly in many respects ghoulism bears a

Ghouls, like the two in this 1941 print, devour corpses and possess a striking psychological affinity with werewolves and werewolf-vampires.

greater affinity with werewolfism or werewolf-vampirism than with vampirism proper. A ghoul digs up and devours corpses, and has a particular liking for brains, which it sucks in much the same way as a vampire sucks blood.

Earlier this century the Irish author Elliott O'Donnell explained:

> Ghouls either remain in spirit form or steal the bodies of living beings – living beings only – either human or animal. They can only do this when the spirit of the living person, during sleep (either natural or induced hypnotically), is separated from the material body; or, in other words, when the spirit is projected. The ghoul then pounces on the physical body, and, often refusing to restore it to its rightful owner, the latter is compelled to roam about as a phantasm for just so long a time as the ghoul chooses to inhabit the body it has stolen.

A werewolf-vampire watches a fellow sorcerer prepare a black-magic potion for purposes of future werewolf transformation. An eighteenth-century print.

O'Donnell, a prolific writer on the supernatural, was prone to allow his imagination to get the better of him, but I believe that if what he says about ghouls is right, many of the old stories of werewolves and vampires inhabiting graveyards may have a firm basis in ghoulism. It would certainly explain why a certain type of werewolf prefers the vicinity of burial grounds to almost any other environment; but this is also the territory of the vampire, of course, and so the werewolf and the vampire will forever be linked one with the other. Perhaps because of this apparent affinity, the Gothic horror movie has perpetuated much mythical nonsense about the werewolf and the vampire and, largely because of this, most people today cannot think of either one of these terrible creatures without regarding it in connection with the other.

Both in the cinema and in modern and ancient literature we meet a wild assortment of "variations on a theme": the vampire whose behavior resembles that of the werewolf, and the werewolf who after death becomes a vampire. The latter occultist species, at least, is based on historical documentation. But there is one area where the two species differ in a most significant way, and this applies wherever the belief in them was, or still is, to be found: quite simply, there are innumerable accounts of individuals becoming werewolves by their own choosing, but *never* do they voluntarily become vampires.

Werewolfism is not infectious, but vampirism most certainly is. Any individual who is sucked by a vampire becomes, on physical dissolution, a vampire, and remains afflicted in this way until his corpse is destroyed in the specific manner already illustrated. The werewolf's fate, according to a variety of legends, unless exorcised or killed (and sometimes both) in a certain prescribed way, is one of double damnation, for on death he will assuredly become a vampire.

This form of occultist aberration appears to have something in common with, but in fact is separate from, those creatures who rise after death as werewolves. There are many stories from which to choose. Paracelsus, the sixteenth-century Swiss alchemist and physician, believed that men of a particularly evil and bestial nature returned after death as ghostly werewolves; England's cruel King John is said to have done such a thing; and innumerable ghost-wolves were seen in Britain during the nineteenth century with human features and identified as werewolves. But they appear to be neither werewolves nor vampires as we customarily know them.

Many sex murderers and child rapists were accused at one time of being practitioners in lycanthropy, mainly, I would hazard, because of the awful mangled bodies which were frequently found. They were left in such a terrible state of mutilation that it was often assumed to be the work of wolves. There is, it is true, a certain sexual element associated with the werewolf, although it does not approach the sado-erotic subtlety of the vampire. The werewolf is a crude and aggressive rapist; the vampire is a Don Juan among Demons. The werewolf-turned-vampire is doubly sensuous, doubly amorous, doubly treacherous. He is the one to watch – and avoid.

11 Bloodlust

AN, BY NATURE a predatory animal, knows the feeling of intoxication when the knife enters into the flesh of the enemy and brings to the triumphant senses groans and the smell of blood. Many of the so-called "war heroes" were in fact men who derived a sense of overwhelming elation, a kind of mental "high," from each new killing. But cannibalism, which springs from this bloodlust, is a characteristic depravity of man. Juvenal, the Roman satirist, made a valid point when he said:

> What lion takes advantage of his strength
> To kill his kind? What bear will e'er succumb
> To boar with larger tusks?

There is much truth in the old saying that "dog does not eat dog," although there are one or two exceptions, such as when food becomes scarce on Polar expeditions and dogs have to be fed to other dogs. Yet the psychological effect on animals which, on occasion, consume each other, is said to be grave and damaging. On September 9, 1948, the *News Chronicle* in England brought our attention to the following peculiar situation:

> A lady member of the recent International Congress of Mental Health in London who keeps lions "had observed that they ate rabbits or anything like their normal prey without digestive anxiety." But when she fed them Great Danes, one of which they had "known socially," they showed signs of severe guilt.

As man eats man rather more frequently than dog eats dog, and has done so for thousands of years, it is perhaps not surprising that a similar "severe guilt" condition should weigh down just as heavily on the subconscious of man-eating man, to the extent that it colors his entire psyche. And as most lycanthropes and werewolves are traditionally manic-depressives, the significance of "severe guilt" following an attack is all the more striking. As with the dogs on the Polar expeditions, it was hunger which turned the original peaceful hominids of the woods into

Another werewolf victim. In both the cannibal and the werewolf, the passion for blood is clearly developed alongside an indifference to suffering. An illustration by John Giunta for Manly Banister's classic werewolf tale, "Loup-Garou" (*Weird Tales*, May 1947).

carnivorous and even cannibalistic beasts. Hunger, too, has made cannibals of shipwrecked sailors, the "lost" survivors of air disasters, and starved Japanese troops in the Second World War.

In 1846, in the village of Polomyia in Austrian Galicia, a starving beggar named Swiatek happened to pass a Jewish tavern soon after it had been burned down. Among the charred rafters of the house he came across the half-roasted corpse of the publican and, suffering from the pangs of extreme hunger, the sight and smell of the roasted flesh inspired the beggar to taste it. "He tore off a portion of the carcase and satiated his hunger upon it," explains a contemporary report (*Niedersächsiche Sagen und Märchen*, 1854), "and at the time he conceived such a liking for it that he could feel no rest till he had tasted it again." From that moment he was tormented by a craving for human flesh. So Swiatek became a cannibal primarily as a result of hunger, although it is possible that he always had leanings in that direction. Two centuries earlier he would have been more than likely tried and accused of werewolfery. "When taken before the Protokoll at Dabkow," says the same document, "he stated that he had already killed and – assisted by his family – eaten six persons. His children, however, asserted most positively that the number was much greater than he had represented, and their testimony is borne out by the fact that the remains of *fourteen* different caps and suits of clothes, male as well as female, were found in his house." He later hanged himself, in 1849, from the bars of the window in his prison cell.

The atavistic urge in man to attack and kill members of his fellow race is usually held in check by the employment of other less violent means, from the use of verbal weapons like "a good argument" to the more physical throwing-of-plates when words alone seem to be ineffective. Contact sports have also helped to serve this need. A very small percentage resort to a more extreme form of violence, including murder (these people have much in common with other flesh-eating mammals, including the most ferocious beasts-of-prey, in that they are activated by an impulse to kill and by a love of destroying life); while an even smaller percentage of this small percentage are overtaken by an irresistible urge to consume the victims of their attacks, the actual act being symbolic of one man's dominance over another, his enemy. Here the passion for blood is clearly developed alongside an indifference to suffering. Among these people, less so now than was previously the case, could be numbered the cannibals, the lycanthropes and the werewolves, and all others who attacked and consumed their own kind either out of necessity or out of diabolical choice. Throughout history modern man has shown himself to be the most formidable of all the beasts-of-prey and, indeed, the only one that preys systematically on its own species.

The actual line of demarcation which separates the cannibal from the werewolf is tenuous and often difficult to define. For instance, a man possessed with homicidal cravings for human flesh may hallucinate sufficiently to convince himself that he is a savage animal; he may in turn, under the delusion that he is this savage animal, go in search of human prey and, finding it, attack, mutilate, kill, and subsequently devour his victim. Now physically – to us at least – he seems to all intents and purposes a perfectly normal human being; but mentally and spiritually he is a wolf. So, from a purely scientific point of view, is he a lycanthrope or a cannibal? In the sixteenth and seventeenth centuries there is no question but that he would be accused of practicing werewolfery, especially if the animal he imagined himself to be was a wolf. Today, though, the word "cannibalism" might more graphically describe the nature of his crimes. In fact a close examination of the records of many of the werewolf trials, especi-

The actual line of demarcation which separates the cannibal from the werewolf is tenuous and often difficult to define. Boris Dolgov's illustration of a ghoulish cannibal in the company of a werewolf first appeared in *Weird Tales* (November 1942).

ally those concerning Pierre Bourgot, Michel Verdung, Jacques Rollet, and the Demon Tailor of Châlons, might quickly lead us to suppose that a primeval cannibalistic bloodlust motivated these men as much as, if not more than, a wholly satanic-werewolfic one.

On the other hand, if proof could be found retrospectively to confirm that Bourgot, Verdung, Rollet and other accused werewolves had in fact successfully directed their foulest thoughts into animal (wolf) form – by projecting their astral body out of their physical body in the manner

Some authorities on the supernatural support the theory that many accused werewolves directed their foulest thoughts into wolf-form via astral projection.

described earlier – then in the theosophical-spiritual sense at least it could be said that as they *were* animals at the time of their crimes, they should not therefore be accused of pursuing essentially cannabilistic desires. It was, at the time of astral projection, wolf against man, *not* man against man. Admittedly, even if the complexities of astral projection and the etheric double were psychic phenomena with which the judges of the great werewolf trials were familiar, the sentences they meted out would probably have remained the same; as far as the judges were concerned, transformation into wolf form (by whatever means you wish to name) *had* taken place and therefore the accused stood charged with the heinous crime of werewolfery. Witchcraft and the black arts alone were responsible, and so the sentence was death.

A good example of how cannibalism might easily be misconstrued as werewolfery occurred in Scotland during the reign of James I. At this time a certain man and his wife withdrew from society and set up "home" in a cave facing out over the wild, rugged sea coast of Galloway, many miles from the nearest village or human habitation of any kind. Here, in this hideous hiding-place, they lived undetected for twenty-five years, during which time they produced eight sons and six daughters, who in turn produced eighteen grandsons and fourteen granddaughters.

The common-denominator between the cannibal and the werewolf is an overriding passion for blood. A late-nineteenth-century print by L. Fillol.

Incest alone accounted for some abysmal mental aberrations. Their way of life was wholly cannibalistic, their food being the flesh of unsuspecting human beings, who were either ambushed or lured into the cannibal family's cave, murdered and torn apart, cooked and roasted. Some of the human joints were even pickled like dried beef. The surrounding communities, now increasingly suspicious of friends and relatives who were periodically disappearing, banded together to search the area for possible clues. When, eventually, they found the family of cave-dwellers, they were justly horrified at the sight which greeted their eyes: for there before them, strung up around the roof, was a cave full of salted and dried human meat.

The whole family were tried and sentenced by the court to burn at the stake for being witches and werewolves. In demon-bewitched France and Germany, there is every chance they would have been tried and condemned as "a wondrous family of damnable werewolves." They would certainly have been accorded an element of notoriety that was ultimately not theirs in down-to-earth, matter-of-fact Scotland. Yet only when cannibalism and a lust for blood are united with a particular kind of hallucinatory insanity can the condition correctly come under the definition of lycanthropy; and only when it is accompanied by the additional agency of black magic can the possibility of werewolfery be entertained.

So although the connection between the cannibal and the werewolf appears on the surface to be an obvious one, in reality the only common-denominator between the two happens to be an overriding passion for blood. The mental state of the two, the actual psyche which motivates the crimes they perpetrate on their fellow men, is quite different. It *is* worth noting, though, that the very same prejudices which led men to look upon an insane or epileptic person as a changeling, and which allowed them to explain away catalepsy as the temporary departure of a witch's soul from the body, would also enable them with very little difficulty to equate the behavior of the maniac or idiot with cannibal appetites with that of a wolf's savage nature. Having gone this far, too, the myth-forming process would not have stopped short of attaching to the poor cannibal wretch a definite lupine body . . . and it really is a sobering thought that *all* ancient mythology teems with precedents for similar "transformations". As mentioned right at the beginning, the werewolf and the cannibal may be poles apart, yet they share a common mythology – a mythology which wishes to marry them off to one another.

12 Rabies and the Werewolf: A Case of Mistaken Identity?

IN THE AUTUMN OF 1976, at the North Manchester General Hospital in England, a fifty-three-year-old chef spent his last hours enduring periods of diabolical horror. "He looked like a scared animal," said a doctor. The man, Mohammed Muslim, who died of rabies, was bitten earlier in the year by a dog while visiting his family in Bangladesh. In hospital he displayed the following symptoms: he foamed at the mouth, he screamed uncontrollably, and he bit a nurse; at one point it took five strong men to get him up off the floor, so immense was his rabid strength. The supervising physician explained how the patient's "uncontrollable screaming attacks" were unabated by the use of drugs which would have sedated an ordinary patient.

The symptoms experienced by Mohammed Muslim during his "attacks," symptoms shared by hundreds of other victims of rabies, today and in former times, point irrefutably to one unavoidable conclusion: that a certain proportion of the many early eye-witness accounts of werewolves did, in fact, pertain to human sufferers in various stages of *rabies canina*. Dryness of the tongue, inordinate thirst, an abhorrence of water, foaming at the mouth, super-human strength, violent tendencies – these are some of the symptoms common to both the werewolf and the victim of *rabies canina* in human beings, the latter being bitten by rabid dogs or wolves, and driven themselves to bite others.

Frothing at the mouth, which characterizes the human rabid patient, has been a distinguishing factor of the werewolf for thousands of years. The Roman poet Ovid, referring to Lycaon's transformation into a wolf, writes:

> In vain he attempted to speak; from that very instant
> His jaws were bespluttered with foam, and only he thirsted
> For blood, as he raged among flocks and panted for slaughter.

His vesture was changed into hair, his limbs became
  crooked;
A wolf – he retains yet large trace of his ancient
  expression,
Hoary he is as afore, his countenance rabid,
His eyes glitter savagely still, the picture of fury.

The foaming jaws, the animal rages, the crooked limbs, the savage eyes, the rabid countenance – these are the symptoms of one of the most terrifying and hideous diseases ever to afflict humanity, and their description here stems no doubt from a man who knew, or had been told about, its dreadful effects. Yet Ovid is talking about a werewolf. A rabid wolf, the head and jaws all splattered with foam, is a frightening enough sight; but the wild ferocity of its attack on man is chilling in the extreme. Being bitten by a werewolf, according to some traditions, will make the victim a werewolf. Being bitten by a rabid wolf will also surely make the victim rabid. To the rustic mind, a rabid wolf would more than likely be seen as a werewolf, especially if that person was attacked by the diseased animal and subsequently developed all the symptoms of rabies.

Rabies, which is the Latin word for madness, is usually spread to a victim in a violent tooth-and-claw manner, the virus itself being transmitted by acutely infectious saliva; having been deposited in the tissues of the victim, the virus can then start its cycle of infection and multiplication. But it can also be transmitted by the infected saliva coming into contact with cut or split skin or even undamaged mucous membrane, including the eyelids, mouth,

A rabid dog in quarantine at Denmark's State Veterinary Serum Laboratory in Copenhagen. A rabid wolf would display identical symptoms. Note the animal's savage aggressiveness, foaming jaws and markedly exposed teeth. A rabid wolf would obviously present a chilling sight to the unsuspecting, unsophisticated medieval mind. There would more than likely be a cry of "Werewolf!"

nose, anus, and external genital organs, as well as through eating infected food or drinking infected water. To drink water out of the footprint made by a werewolf, or to drink from a lycanthropous pool, was said to transmit the disease of werewolfery to the drinker. So could not the "lycanthropous pool" be little more than a water-hole frequented by rabid animals? And as wolves fastidiously lick their paws after eating a meal, could not the footprints be simply the saliva-infected impressions of rabid wolves? If such was the case, it would certainly help to explain the origin of one aspect of the werewolf legend.

Historical accounts also talk of lycanthropes who go about their morbid business only at night; or, if during the day, only in places which are heavily shaded, such as dense forests. Since in some cases of rabies the human patient experiences an extreme sensitivity to bright light, it could well be that at least a few of the past's reported lycanthropes were in fact people suffering, in varying degrees, from this disease. The rabies victim would certainly choose darkness as the most convenient period in the day for venturing out of doors.

There is then the question of the extraordinary strength and periods of violent spasms shared by the human and animal rabies victim. As we have seen in the case of the fifty-three-year-old chef, a human rabid patient (including a child) frequently has moments when an increase in strength is so marked that it requires five people to hold him down. Historical accounts of the werewolf often refer to its extraordinary strength, and to the fact that several people who have gone to a victim's rescue have been powerless to overcome the beast's brute savagery and physical toughness. In the Middle Ages a rabid wolf such as this, if it got away, would certainly pass into werewolfic legend – as would the victims if they contracted the disease and developed the symptoms of the werewolf/rabid patient. According to Geoffrey P. West in his *Rabies: In Animals and Man* (1972) these symptoms include:

> a feeling of apprehension; a burning or tingling sensation at the site of the bite; an excess of saliva in the mouth (so that the patient may be constantly spitting); intermittent mental derangement, which may be associated with periods of mania, when bedclothes may be torn to shreds; pain; and convulsions. The name "hydrophobia" (meaning fear of water, but used in past centuries as a synonym for the illness) derives from the horror which the mere sight of water can bring to the human patient, who may suffer agonising muscular spasms if he attempts to drink.

A subsidiary symptom of a hydrophobic patient's repulsion of water – or indeed *any* liquid – is an hysterical barking sound: very similar, by all accounts, to the terrible "barking" which many werewolves in their human shape were said to make. David A. Warrell, consultant physician and clinical lecturer in tropical medicine at the Radcliffe Infirmary, Oxford, describes in *Rabies: The Facts* (1977) the progression of symptoms which eventually climax with the characteristic barking:

In the Middle Ages a rabid wolf such as this would certainly pass into werewolfic legend. A dramatically disturbing illustration by the American artist Howard Pyle for *Harper's Monthly Magazine* (December 1909).

Patients show an extraordinary ambivalence about drinking. They avoid drinking for some time, fearing the effects, but finally become unbearably thirsty. Attempts to lift the cup to their lips are thwarted by violent trembling of the arm. They try desperately to snatch a sip of water before a last-minute terror makes them fling away the cup and dive under the bedclothes. During spasms the drink or saliva may be spat or coughed out in showers over bystanders. Patients may retch or vomit so violently that tears are made in the gullet near its junction with the stomach. Cries of alarm may be distorted by paralysis or swelling of the vocal cords which alter the voice so that the shouts sound more like barks.

At the peak of an attack the whole nervous system seems to be aroused. The patient is in a state of extreme agitation and has frightening hallucinations. His face is a mask of terror. His body is racked with tremors or spasms. He may struggle frantically to free himself and try to escape from the room.

As we saw earlier, many werewolves in the past were said to lock themselves in a room when they felt their ravening spasms approaching. I wonder, though, whether or not this has been twisted in the telling? It may well be that it was those nearest to the "werewolf," fearing for their own safety as a consequence of his impending mad rages, who locked him in the room. If the "werewolf" was in fact a victim of rabies or hydrophobia, they had every reason to fear him and to take all necessary precautions.

Historical documentation shows that the incidence of rabies rises and falls in cycles of roughly one hundred years, a century of epidemic being separated by a century of relative calm. We are now living at a time when the

Rabid wolves are known to display a certain preference for biting their human victims about the head. A sketch by Dudley Tennant for Alan Sullivan's short story "Loup-Garou" in the English periodical *The Windsor Magazine* (July 1905).

disease is rapidly building up to explosive proportions. A conservative estimate of worldwide deaths from rabies today is thirty thousand, of which India alone accounts for half this figure. Rabies was certainly raging in the Middle Ages, especially between 1500 and 1600 – and so, of course, was werewolfery; and although foxes, badgers, bears and other animals were also affected, people most feared rabid wolves (not that the country people necessarily *knew* they were rabid) because of the sheer savagery and unpredictable nature of their character. A great many of the reported werewolves were undoubtedly rabid wolves: sufficient in number (as indeed were their rabid human victims) to sow the seed for many a good werewolf story.

Rabid wolves are known to display a certain preference for biting their human victims about the head, a form of attack which all too easily deposits the rabies virus near the brain and thus increases the risk of fatal illness. As one of the earliest treatments consisted of cauterization of the bite wound, we can perhaps understand the reasoning behind a similar cauterization procedure adopted by Avicenna in the eleventh century as a remedy for lycanthropy – except that he may sometimes have been unknowingly treating victims of rabies and hydrophobia. Many other ancient treatments for rabid madness were as colorful as (and sometimes similar to) those for lycanthropy – including medical preparations containing such ingredients as asses' milk, child's urine, and the "stones" of a hedgehog, plus bleeding the patient, giving him cold baths (preferably salty water), and administering doses of liverwort with black pepper.

One further point of interest is that France has a history of periodic rabies going back at least a thousand years. A new cycle of the disease began in the north-eastern region of the country in 1968 and has been spreading west and south ever since. Significantly, the area so far covered by the spread of rabies in France is identical to those areas most afflicted with werewolfery in the sixteenth and seventeenth centuries. In the nearby Jura region, well-known for its werewolfic associations, an epidemic of animal rabies raged there between 1803 and 1835, subsequently spreading throughout Switzerland; it had already reached Germany by 1820. Rabid wolves were attacking the inhabitants of Crema, Italy, in 1804, from which many died; other rabid wolves in France in 1851, in Turkey in 1852, Russia in 1866, and elsewhere, attacked and subsequently caused the deaths of many people through rabies . . . in earlier times, I am certain, an accusatory finger would have been pointed at many a werewolf. It is also possible, of course, that genuine werewolves might be misdiagnosed as rabies victims, the symptoms being caused by the transformation rituals and the werewolf's psychological make-up The restriction of salivation and the drying-up of the tear-ducts, in the case of werewolves who have participated in black-magic transformation ceremonies, can be accounted for by the drugs they used. Henbane and stramonium, for instance, with which initiate werewolves drugged themselves in order to evoke soaring and flying dreams, produced a sensational dual-condition: first an abhorrence of water while the werewolf is in his animal form, and then an insatiable thirst when he returns to his normal human shape.

As far as a hatred of water is concerned, the sixteenth-century physician, Petrus Salius, laid particular stress on this when describing werewolves "aquam perhorrescunt." One possible explanation for this unnatural dread of clear water among werewolves and lycanthropes may be due to the fact that for thousands of years water was one of the principal ordeals to which sorcerers were subjected by the guardians of law and order. Nearly four thousand years ago, Hammurabi, the greatest of the first-dynasty Babylonian kings, used water as a test in all cases of sorcery; in England, Germany and the United States the water-ordeal also has an old association with witchcraft (the practice, for instance, of "swimming a witch"). Water also has a certain connection with "holiness" – running water for dissolving spells and evil charms, true and natural water in the "first sacrament," the "living water" of the old Hebrews.

King James I of England, writing in the sixteenth century of the witches receiving their just reward by "fleeting on the water," added that this ordeal was appointed by God "for a supernatural sign of the monstrous impiety of the witches, that the water shall refuse to receive them to her bosom, that have shaken off them the sacred Water of Baptism, and wilfully refused the benefit thereof." Having made a covenant with the Devil, a werewolf has therefore renounced his baptism, and one result of this may be an antipathy between him and water.

In any case it would be difficult to decide who is the most cursed, the practitioner of werewolfery or the unfortunate victim of rabies. Each has inspired dread for centuries. Each, during this time, has frequently been confused one with the other. But I have no doubt that, because of the shared symptoms, a vast proportion of history's dreaded "werewolves" were in fact either rabid wolves or their rabid human victims. The facts seem to speak for themselves.

13 A Bizarre Contradiction of Terms

A BENEVOLENT or protective werewolf sounds about as likely, and as frightening, as a well-meaning poltergeist. Yet there are stories – not many, admittedly – of werewolves who have gone out of their way to be kindly and helpful. So who are they and what is their business? Basically they are people who have been transformed into wolves against their will, either as a curse stemming from the spite, jealousy or revenge of a witch or wizard, or because they have incurred the wrath of the Devil.

The werewolf or *volkolak*, for instance, is a man in White Russia who, for some reason or other, has angered the Devil. His punishment is to be metamorphosed into a wolf and despatched to his relations who, recognizing him, provide him with all the food he needs. He shows his gratitude by licking the hands of his sympathetic benefactors. The nature of his particular curse, however, is that he is not permitted to "stay put" for any length of time, but is doomed to an irresistible passion for change of scene; and so he prowls from one household to another, from village to village, for the rest of his days. As a curse, it shows the Devil at his most malicious.

These gentle werewolves, and others like them, attempt by tears and deprecatory pawings to apologize for their brutal appearance. Unless driven beyond endurance by hunger, they never slay and eat, and when they must kill a sheep, they look for one belonging to some other neighborhood and not from the area in which they themselves once lived.

Perhaps the most well-known of all these protective creatures is the werewolf who appears in the twelfth-century romance *William of Palermo*. King Apulia's jealous brother has arranged the murder of the king's son, William, heir-apparent to the throne. But "while the boy William is at play a werewolf runs off with him, swims across the Straits of Messina, and carries him into a forest near Rome, where it takes care of him and provides him

"... while the boy William is at play a werewolf runs off with him...." Woodcut from the title page of a nineteenth-century edition of the legend *The Ancient English Romance of William and the Werewolf,* by Frederick Madden. This book was published in 1832 from a fourteenth-century manuscript (an English translation of the French original by Guillaume de Palerne) preserved in the library of King's College, Cambridge.

with food. The werewolf in reality is Alphonso, heir to the Spanish throne, who has been transformed by his stepmother, Queen Braunde, who desires her own son Braundinis to wear the crown of Spain." As true a guardian angel among werewolves as you are likely to encounter! These lines illustrate his characteristic gentleness:

> The werewolf embraces the king's son
> With his fore-feet,
> And so familiar with him
> Is the king's son, that all pleases him,
> Whatever the beast does for him.

Marie de France's werewolf, in her *Lay of the Bisclavaret*, could also be described as a benevolent creature, since he lacks all savage instincts except against those who have wronged him – in this case, his wife and her lover. He is one of Brittany's most gallant knights who, without explanation, leaves his wife for three days in every week. One day, exasperated at being denied knowledge of her husband's regular disappearances, his wife insists that he explains everything to her. He finally reveals all:

"Learn then that I become a werewolf during my absence. I go into the forest, hide in the thickets and seek my prey."

"But, my dear," says the wife, "tell me whether you take off your clothes or whether you keep them on?"

"I am naked when the transformation occurs, Madame."

"And where do you leave your clothes?"

"I must not tell you, because if I were seen when I take them off I should remain a werewolf for the rest of

The benevolent werewolf (in reality one of Brittany's most gallant knights) featured in Marie de France's late-twelfth-century *Lay of the Bisclavaret*. "Bisclavaret" is the Breton term for the Norman *Garulf*, werewolf. Decoration from the front binding of Frank Hamel's *Human Animals* (1915).

my life. I can only recover human form at the moment I put them on again. After that you will not be surprised if I say no more."

But, with her considerable feminine guile and charm, she obtains from him the information she desperately requires, tells the young man with whom she is in love, and persuades him to go and steal her husband's clothes. Her husband, the werewolf, unable to change back into human shape, is assumed by the king – whose favorite he is – to be dead. The wife is now free to marry her lover.

Some time later the king and his hunting party give chase to a werewolf in the forest and succeed in wounding him. Fearful for his life, the werewolf in desperation licks the king's boots. Greatly impressed by the gentleness and humility of a beast renowned only for terrible savagery, he orders that it should be taken back to the castle and cared for. And here, indeed, the wolf is pampered and given every comfort and he, in turn, is meek and gentle and harms no one. His behavior only changes to one of ferocity whenever his former wife and her new husband visit the king, or the king visits them. And so, the king's suspicion aroused by the wolf's change of character, orders an investigation into the matter. The lady then confesses her misdeeds and suggests that the werewolf must be her husband. The king orders the immediate return of the werewolf's clothes to a private place in the castle frequented only by the wolf, and it is soon revealed that the werewolf was none other than his former gallant knight, his dear friend. The lady and her false husband are banished from the kingdom, while the knight resumes his former life of valor and chivalry. A fine tale.

Another protective werewolf story, also from France, concerns one Abbot Gilbert of the Arc Monastery, on the banks of the Loire. Gilbert, returning one afternoon from a village fair – where he had consumed rather too much ale – was saved in a forest from the attack of some savage wildcats by a friendly werewolf. At the monastery the next day the werewolf assumed its natural shape – that of a stern dignitary of the Church – and immediately rebuked Gilbert for drinking too much vintage the previous day. As a punishment he was ordered to embark on a course of severe penance.

Protective werewolves, benevolent werewolves, and, in this case, a werewolf who moralizes! Whatever next? Listen to this account of the werewolf who preached goodness and light. During the reign of Louis XIV, André Bonivon commanded the schooner *Bonaventure*, which for some time had been engaged in usurping the Huguenots – French Protestants – who lived along the shores of the Gulf of Lions, on the Mediterranean coast of France. After one of these raids, the ship floundered in the wild waters of the Rhône estuary during a terrible night storm. There was panic, and Bonivon would certainly have drowned in a whirlpool if someone had not come gallantly to his rescue. On dry land he took his rescuer by the hand to thank him, but was horrified to find the "hand" he was shaking was in fact a huge hairy paw. The wolf then led the captain to a house close to a village, placed him in a darkened room, and departed. A moment or so later the rescuer returned with a lantern,

A kindly wolf-headed man, believed in ancient times to inhabit certain regions of India. Woodcut from Hartmann Schedel's *Liber Chrinicarum Mundi*, published in Nuremberg in 1493.

when, for the first time, Bonivon saw the man's face – the face of a werewolf. The captain's heart was filled with terror. His fear was multiplied many times over when later in the evening, alone, he discovered in one corner of the bolted-and-barred room the body of a woman, nude and terribly mutilated. With no means of escape, he awaited the dawn with a feeling of unspeakable horror. Would such a terrible fate soon be his? His heart very nearly exploded when, eventually, the door of his room slowly opened ... but there by the gaping door was not the form of a werewolf but that of a human being, and a Huguenot minister at that. Bonivon's relief was enormous. The Huguenot then asked him:

> Do you know now where you are? Do you recognize this room? No! Well, I will explain. You are in the house of Roland Bertin, and the body lying over yonder is that of my wife, whom your crew barbarously murdered yesterday when they sacked this village. They took me with them, and it was your intention to have me tortured and then drowned as soon as you got to sea. Do you know me now?

The captain, dumb with shock and surprise, nodded, and the minister continued:

> Well, I am a werewolf – I was bewitched some years ago by the woman Grenier [*that name again*], who lives in the forest at the back of our village. As soon as it was dark I metamorphosed; then the ship ran ashore, and everyone leaped overboard. I saw you drowning. I saved you ... you who had been instrumental in murdering my wife and ruining my home! Why? I do not know! Had I preferred for you a less pleasant death than drowning, I could have taken you ashore and killed you. Yet – I did not, because it is not in my nature to destroy anything. Assassin, I have spared you. Be not ungenerous. Spare others.

Romantic accounts of benign werewolves like the Huguenot minister, although rare, are not uncommon. The piety of many a man, impelled by an unwanted curse to range the countryside in the form of a wolf, has been so strong as to render the werewolf's natural instincts harmless. The difference between the involuntary and the voluntary werewolf is usually the difference between lightness and darkness. Perhaps, in the tales of the protective, benevolent werewolves we may find somewhere the basis for a Christian allegory which preaches that good will always triumph over evil. It is a nice thought, a Christian thought, but hardly a werewolfic thought. That is its supreme fascination.

14 "An Unsettling Display of Bare-Chested Lycanthropy": The Werewolf in Literature

IN HIS SHORT STORY "The Priest's Tale," the Greek author Demetrios Bikelas reflects: "Fear fills the heart of the ignorant with the passions of wild beasts." It was these same passions, of course, which fanned the flames of the earliest werewolf stories of folk-legend. But in this particular tale Bikelas, who died in 1908, is writing of the reaction of the fearful, almost demoniacal villagers towards an unfortunate peasant who, having been bitten by a ferocious she-wolf, is beginning to show all the symptoms of lycanthropia. Whatever the peasant's real complaint, whether it be rabies or dementia, fear and ignorance will assuredly have him branded a werewolf.

It seems an ideal subject for an author of fiction. But is it? Strangely enough, prior to nineteenth-century Romanticism, which recognized the claims of the supernatural and the power of passion, the werewolf makes but a few fleeting appearances in full-length fiction. And even among the Romantics you will look in vain for all but a few passing references to either lycanthropy or werewolfery, for it seems that more obviously "poetic" themes were occupying the minds of men like Goethe, Byron, Scott, Heine, Vigny, Wordsworth, Hugo, Schiller, Coleridge, Musset, Keats, Lamartine, and Shelley. In 1818, of course, Shelley's second wife, Mary, gave the world an archetypal monster in *Frankenstein*, but that's another story, as is the monster's subsequent filmic meeting with the wolfman a century and a quarter later.

So, because the werewolf legend is arguably less erotic than, say, the vampire legend, and therefore less stunningly poetic, evocative or beguiling, and because, historically, it lacks an element of visual, mental and spiritual beauty, the whole area has been largely overlooked by most of the sensitive literary giants. Yet understandable as this may be, it is nonetheless a crying shame that so monumentally complex a theme should so rarely have benefited from the same creative gifts which have elevated the ghost-story into the domain of a respected literary genre. Werewolfery, because it is less easily defined, less easily understood, and because it brims with more enigmas and doubts than vampirism, has undoubtedly frightened off many a good author of fiction.

But not entirely.

Bram Stoker's *Dracula*, published in 1897, quickly became recognized as a landmark in the area of Gothic horror fiction and sold over a million copies – deservedly so, for it is certainly one of the most blood-curdling horror stories in English literature, and nothing else in the genre, before or since, can quite match that peculiar impression of cold terror which runs throughout its pages. In the sequel, *Dracula's Guest*, published posthumously in 1914, Stoker has an unexpected surprise in store for us – he introduces into the story a chilling werewolf incident. The whole episode occupies seventeen turbulent pages, and is conveyed with the same evocative style which makes the original book such compulsive reading. It can only be lamented that Stoker never developed the werewolf theme into a full-scale novel. Imagine: *The Werewolf* by Bram Stoker. What wonderful shivers we have been denied! What nightmares!

And then, in 1933, the New York publishing house of Farrar & Rinehart published *The Werewolf of Paris*. Written by the then thirty-three-year-old Harry Relis, whose work was published under the pseudonym of Guy Endore, it quickly consolidated the New Yorker's existing reputation as a novelist and biographer (including brilliant studies of Casanova and Joan of Arc). Two years later Hollywood released *The Werewolf of Paris*, the first film to be based on Endore's macabre novel, followed in 1961 by the British-made *Curse of the Werewolf*. Endore's book is finely crafted, with an economy of style, a vividness of imagery, and an almost Germanic breadth of fantasy, an influence which can certainly be traced back to the author's early education in Vienna. It also possesses those passages of erotic passion that are so conspicuously absent from practically every other werewolf story. *The Werewolf of Paris* is a milestone in its genre. Endore had obviously done his homework; a great deal of pure, hard werewolfic fact is put into the mouths of the story's principal characters. Thus, when the werewolf of the story is a week or so old, his concerned guardians exclaim:

"Have you ever noticed his eyes?"

"Yes, of course; they are very fine eyes, I should say."

"Well, I don't mean his eyes so much as his eyebrows."

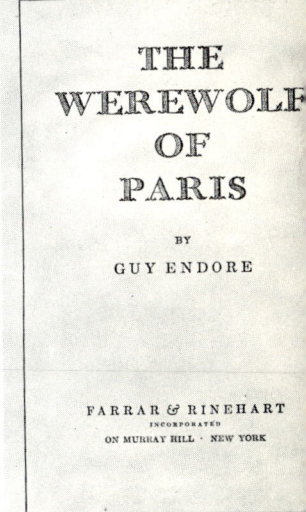

Title page of Guy Endore's novel *The Werewolf of Paris* (1933): a landmark in werewolfic fiction.

"What about them?"

"They are very full and join together across the nose."

"And what do you deduce from that?"

"In our part of the country that was a sign of a low nature."

What is more, the baby was born on Christmas eve, and he had hair on the palms of his hands. The boy was christened Bertrand. As a young man he joins the National Guard. If all this strikes a chord . . . well, that may be because it so easily recalls the real-life case of the French lycanthrope Bertrand, the junior officer in the 1st Infantry regiment whose atrocities shocked Paris between the autumn of 1848 and the summer of 1849. Endore's novel is depicted in approximately the same period and setting.

When Bertrand knew his attack was coming on,

> . . . he would arrange his window [*that is, leave it open*] and lock his door, and having taken his precautions, he would lie down. Frequently he would wake in the morning, in bed, with no recollection of what had happened at night. Only a wretched stiffness in his neck, a lassitude in his limbs, that could come from nothing but miles of running, scratches on his hands and feet, and an acrid taste in his mouth argued that he had spent the night elsewhere. On one such occasion, however, full conviction awaited him when he rose. Under his bed he caught a flash of white. It was a human forearm! A man's. The fingers were clutched tightly into a fist. Hair, as if torn from a fur coat, protruded from the interstices between the fingers.

Endore's shock-tactics are grave and severe, never crude or over-explicit. He leaves much to the imagination, and it pays handsome dividends. Bertrand in the novel "made few friends of his comrades"; Bertrand in grim fact was of retiring habits. The two Bertrands mutilated and devoured the recently-buried. Aymar Galliez, Bertrand's uncle in the novel, refers to the fact that when his nephew feels his change is about to overcome him, and he has accordingly removed his clothes, "he finds it imperatively necessary to urinate." The uncle then quotes "Petronius and other more obscure sources" to prove that urination "is a universal trait of werewolves before the metamorphosis." Endore had clearly referred to Petronius Arbiter's *Satyricon* for this "fact," but, as is suggested earlier, the old belief that a werewolf must strip prior to metamorphosis may now reasonably be said to be an error of interpretation.

Yet with all the novel's vivid detail, it is Endore's *questioning* of the whole subject of werewolfery that gives it its inner strength and impetus. It is such admirable skepticism, mixed with the horrible reality of historical fact, which contributes to the greatness of *The Werewolf of Paris*. It can stand proudly on the bookshelf alongside *Dracula*. But in the werewolf genre, as with Stoker's tale in the vampire genre, it has been condemned to stand alone. Werewolf short-stories, of varying quality, abound; the full-length werewolf novel does not.

Yet there is another, earlier example of the werewolf novel. In *Wagner: The Wehr-Wolf*, published in London in 1857, the prolific George W. M. Reynolds managed to sustain his bizarre theme over no less than seventy-seven chapters. The book originally appeared as a serial in *Reynold's Miscellany*, between November 7, 1856 and July 24, 1857; it was re-published the same year as twenty-four weekly "penny dreadfuls," in which form Reynolds and his colleague Thomas Preskett Prest, author of *Varney the Vampire*, were past masters. *Wagner: The Wehr-Wolf* hardly qualifies as *literature*, but its racy, breathless momentum, its rapidly-changing locale (from the Black Forest to Florence and the Island of Snakes off the African coast, to Syracuse and Tuscany), its melodramatic turn-of-phrase, its banal imagery, its sheer length – all this provided a certain section of the Victorian public with the sort of florid, harrowing adventure in which they could unashamedly lose themselves. The extracts which here accompany the two illustrations certainly say all that needs to be said about Reynolds' style.

Whereas Reynolds pulls out all the stops and deals with the theme of werewolfery in a colorfully implicit, high-

Two of the Henry Anelay's twenty-four illustrations for *Wagner: The Wehr-Wolf* (1857).

LEFT The author writes: "The solemn spectacle seemed to madden the Wehr-Wolf. His speed increased – he dashed through the funeral train – appalling cries of terror and alarm burst from the lips of the holy fathers and the solemn procession was thrown into confusion. The coffin-bearers dropped their burden – and the corpse rolled out upon the ground. . . ."

RIGHT The author continues: ". . . the Wehr-Wolf falls in writhing agonies upon the fresh dew, whence in a few moments rises Fernand Wagner – a man once more! But he starts back with mingled aversion and alarm: for there – with folded arms, eyes terrible to gaze upon, and a countenance expressing infernal triumph and bitter scorn – stood the Demon."

flown manner, most other authors of werewolf novels either treat the subject in a key which is essentially cool, half-hearted, even restrained (an approach quite unsuited to the theme) or they use the werewolf or lycanthrope character simply as a device by which to drum up sham atmosphere – the *dénouement* revealing that the man-beast is not all we have been led to believe him to be. Into the latter category fall three books in particular: Charles Swem's *Were Wolf* (London, 1929), about a seemingly bed-ridden old man who regularly attires himself in a wolf's skin and embarks on a lycanthropic orgy; Frederick Marryat's decidedly old-fashioned supernatural yarn, *The White Wolf of the Harz Mountains* (sometimes called *The Werewolf*), which originally formed part of the English author's three-volume romance, *The Phantom Ship* (London, 1839); and *The Wolf Demon* (London, 1907), credited as "by the Author of *Buffalo Bill*," with its terrible feuding villains confronting the demon of Wolf River Canyon.

The she-werewolf, known as White Fell, drawn by Laurence Housman for Clemence Housman's novelette *The Were-wolf* (1896). Here, White Fell surveys the body of the man Christian who was foolish enough to be beguiled by her fatal beauty.

In *Prince Godfrey*, a tale by Polish writer Halina Gorska, the hero frees mountain dwellers and shepherds from a savage werewolf. The werewolf is particularly voracious, consuming (among others) numerous goats, a ram, four sheep, various cows, a bull, two shepherds, numerous children, and a sharpshooter named John. In this illustration, from an English translation of the story published in New York in 1946, Godfrey is asking the werewolf about his hoofs. "They are not quite hoofs," says the werewolf, "but constant walking in the mountains has given me corns and bumps which make them look like hoofs."

Clemence Housman's *The Were-wolf* (Chicago, 1896; also London same year), a beautifully produced novelette with six romantic illustrations by Laurence Housman, sits naturally in the category of those volumes of fiction which treat the werewolf in an utterly cool, albeit *poetic* way. This is no *horror* story, but a dire romance about a she-werewolf – "the dreadful Thing" known as White Fell – who "cleared the ground at times by long bounds." At death her "great grim jaws had a savage grin, though dead-stiff." Another werewolf book is Gerald Bliss's *The Door of the Unreal* (*circa* 1905), described by one critic as "a lycanthropic novel of great power and tension."

So much for the full-scale treatment of the werewolf by the novelist. In several other works of novel-length fiction, the werewolf or the lycanthrope appears as an important subsidiary character of the main plot. There is the lycanthrope in Charles Maturin's last extended romance, *The Albigenses* (London, 1824, four volumes), whom we encounter crouching in a corner of its lair, gnawing at a skull snatched from the graveyard; later, in the dungeons of l'Aigle sur la Roche, it lets out horrible bestial yelps and growls, while snarling "I am a mad wolf.... The hairs grow inward – the wolfish coat is within – the wolfish heart is within – the wolfish fangs are within!" In Frank Norris's posthumous *Vandover and the Brute* (New York, 1914), the young lycanthrope experiences terrible paroxysms of insanity during which he is utterly convinced that his body is transformed into the beast that his soul symbolizes. He runs growling and snarling about his room, naked, four-footed, uttering raucous cries of "Wolf! Wolf!" His madness is diagnosed by the doctors as "lycanthropy-mathesis." Impressive-sounding, but bogus.

Samuel Rutherford Crockett, in his dramatic *The Black Douglas* (London, 1899), paints a dynamic, often harrowing portrait of the "woman-witch or werewolf," Astarte, who procures children for the Black Mass; while in *The Wolf's Bride* (London, 1930) the Finnish author, Aino Kallas, writes stirringly and poetically (shades of Clemence Housman) of the she-werewolf who, by day, is a loving wife, by night a blood-lusting wolf of field and forest. The she-werewolf theme appears frequently in novels and short-stories from the turn of the century, rarely prior to it. A parallel can be drawn, actually, between the emergence of the she-werewolf in literature and the worldwide movements of women's suffrage.

Cervantes makes clever use of werewolfic folklore in *Los trabajos de Persiles y Sigismunda* (Madrid, 1617), Alexandre Dumas conjures with it in *Le Meneur des Loups* (Paris, 1857, three volumes), and so does Maurice Barrès in *La Colline inspirée* (Paris, 1913). L'Abbé Laurent Bordelon, in his *History of the Ridiculous Extravagancies of Monsieur Oufle* (London, 1711; original French edition, 1710, two volumes), makes our hero – "the *Don Quixote* of occultism" – don a bear-skin one carnival night and imagine himself a wolf; he runs howling into the streets, and soon there are rumors that a *loup-garou* is abroad. The word "werewolf" in Edgar L. Cooper's novel *The Werewolf's Helmet* (London, 1931) is used jocularly, and to give color to the title. The helmet in question belonged to Hermann Karl Stendahl, alias Gröner, the Phantom Werewolf, "a Continental Jekyll and Hyde." And for a fictionalized account of the Society of Human Leopards, John Cameron Grant's *The Ethiopian* (Paris, 1900) makes a good read.

While the novel may lack a representative quota of

Monsieur Oufle frightens the carnival revelers, who fear they have seen a werewolf. An engraving from Laurent Bordelon's comical *History of the Ridiculous Extravagancies of Monsieur Oufle* (1710).

supremely chilling, full-blooded werewolf sagas, the short-story certainly does not. A multi-volume anthology could certainly be compiled with infinite ease and consummate pleasure. There are many fine examples to choose from, but among the Top Ten in this anthology I would have to include Eugene Field's masterly "The Werewolf" (1911), in which the St Louis-born author sees the wolf-man not as a supernatural wretch but as the victim of an atavistic throw-back and as the reincarnation of a wicked grandfather. Also included would be Saki's understated but brilliantly drawn picture of the malevolent werewolf-boy in "Gabriel-Ernest," published in 1910, and Algernon Blackwood's perceptive "Camp of the Dog" (1908), in which the unknowing werewolf's etheric double takes the form of a wolf in his sleep. Catharine Crowe's well-spun "A Story of a Weir-Wolf" (1846), set in a village of Auvergne in 1596; Sutherland Menzies' demoniacally powerful "Hugues, The Wer-Wolf" (1838), subtitled "A Kentish Legend of the Middle Ages"; Fred Whishaw's Russian-based "The Were-Wolf" (1902), about a man condemned to be a werewolf by the Liéshui, or spirits of the forest – each of these three longish short stories is notable for a narrative that is bold, descriptive, well-told, with a somber, compelling power, too, which invites repeated reading.

For lighter relief – for humor is as rare in lycanthropic fiction as it is generally unsuited – the reader will find much to enjoy in Dudley Costello's comical, accurately-researched "Lycanthropy in London; or, The Wehr-Wolf of Wilton Crescent" (1855). In "The Kill" (1931), Peter Fleming, brother of James Bond author Ian Fleming, graphically updates the ancient werewolf legend and sets his story in a drab railway waiting-room – a macabre mystery which has you guessing literally until the very last paragraph ("Very slowly he lifted one hand and removed his bowler hat. Of the fingers about its brim, the young man saw that the third was longer than the second.") Guy de Maupassant, that great master of the short story, chose the lycanthrope for the cruel protagonist in "Le Loup" (1884), a sinister yet often poignant story about men who are more savage than the beasts they hunt, and about, more particularly, a man who displays all the bestial instincts of the wolf yet never changes his form; one of the few classic tales of lycanthropy (as opposed to werewolfery).

To conclude the anthology in an atmosphere of lusty Grand Guignol, Sir Gilbert Campbell's "The White Wolf of Kostopchin" (1889), about a beautiful she-werewolf in Poland, could hardly be bettered. It has everything we require of an absorbing tale of the macabre. A continual thread of fear and terror pervades the writing, with an eye for bizarre detail, occultist charm, and an almost theatrical melodrama which propels the tale towards a finale of brute savageness and unashamed sentimentality.

Of the many other short-stories in the catalog of the werewolf literature, some admittedly of dubious quality and historical content, the following are at least worth mentioning: H. Beaugrand's "The Werewolves" (1898), Count Eric Stenbok's "The Other Side" (1893), Algernon Blackwood's "Strange Adventure" (1906) and (with

Wilfred Wilson) "The Empty Sleeve" (1921), the Hon. Mrs Greene's "Bound by a Spell" (1885), Rudyard Kipling's "The Mark of the Beast" (1891), Eden Phillpotts' "Loup-Garou!" (1899), E. F. Benson's "The Shootings of Achnaleish" (about were-hares) (1912), Hugh Walpole's "Tarnhelm; or, The Death of My Uncle Robert" (about a were-dog) (1933), Ambrose Bierce's "The Eyes of the Panther" (about a were-panther) (1893), Erckmann-Chatrian's "Hugues-le-Loup" (1869), Prosper Mérimée's "Lokis (about a were-bear) (1868), Robert Louis Stevenson's "Olalla" (1887), Allan

An 1850 French comic strip entitled "Le Loup-Garou." Drawn by d'Epinal.

"... the armed man lifted his pistol, aimed between the eyes of the great bull-like head before him, and fired...." Painting from Eden Phillpotts' short story, "Loup-Garou!" It originally appeared in a collection of the author's work, published in 1899.

OPPOSITE A daring cover illustration – daring for the period, that is – for Seabury Quinn's werewolf story, "The Thing in the Fog" (*Weird Tales*, March 1933). The yarn provides a resumé of the werewolf superstition via the quoted conversation of one Justin de Grandin, a mercurial French scientist, occult detective and ghost-breaker. Along the way it draws an interesting parallel between hydrophobia and lycanthropia.

BELOW Werewolf logo used in the South African magazine *Die Brandwag* (November 29, 1974) to illustrate J. A. Rio-Neuhof's short story, "Die Weerwolf."

BELOW "A man doomed to assume the shape of a savage wolf," reads the caption to this illustration. It tops the first page of "The Woman at Loon Point" by August W. Derleth and Mark Schorer (*Weird Tales*, December 1936).

ABOVE The she-werewolf depicted so chillingly in Manly Banister's "Eena" (*Weird Tales*, September 1947). Boris Dolgov is the artist.

LEFT Title illustration for H. Warner Munn's "Tales of the Werewolf Clan" (*Weird Tales*, January 1931), a lycanthropic story which revolves in and around seventeenth-century Germany.

Roderic's "Night of Horror" (1962), and J. A. Rio-Neuhof's "Die Weerwolf" (1974).

In the 1920s, 1930s and 1940s, an absolute glut of werewolf short-stories appeared in the American pulp magazine, *Weird Tales*. As might be expected, inspiration and quality varied considerably from author to author as well as from story to story, but from the cauldron of dross emerged several werewolf stories of considerable distinction. Among such lycanthropic *crème de la crème* can be included Seabury Quinn's "The Blood Flower" (1927), "The Wolf of St Bonnot" (1930), "The Thing in the Fog" (a gripping cover-story) (1933), "Fortune's Fools" (1938), "Uncanonized" (1939), and "The Gentle Werewolf" (1940); August W. Derleth's "The Werewolf of Tottenham" (1928) and (with Mark Schorer) "The Woman at Loon Point" (1936); H. Warner Munn's "The Werewolf of Ponkert" (a fine cover-story evocatively illustrated by A. Brosnatch) (1925), "The Return of the Master" (1927), "The Werewolf's Daughter" (1928), and "Tales of the Werewolf Clan" (1931); Manly Banister's "Eena" and "Loup-Garou" (both 1947); Fritz Leiber's "The Hound" (1942); Mary Elizabeth Counselman's "The Cat Woman" (1933); Robert Bloch's "The Black Kiss" (1937) and "Nursemaid to Nightmares" (1942); and – the most unlikely, not to say bizarre permutation of all – Manly Banister's cover-story (with splendid artwork by A. R. Tilburne), "A Werewolf Western" (1942). The werewolf

The lycanthrope Ferdinand, Duke of Aragon (portrayed here by Robert O'Mahoney) creating havoc with the jugular vein of actress Jane Lapotaire, who played the title role in the Bristol Old Vic's 1976 production of Webster's *The Duchess of Malfi*.

ABOVE LEFT Title page of Francis et Ourry's stage comedy, *Le Loup-Garou* (1807).

RIGHT Title page of Scribe and Mazères' comic opera, *Le Loup-Garou* (1827).

short-story-writer's imagination was certainly vivid, if occasionally crude; the reader never lacked entertainment.

As far as entertainment in the theater is concerned, the playwright who tackles the werewolf theme is confronted with a number of apparently insurmountable hurdles. Whereas the cinema and television can produce all kinds of disturbing supernatural effects, by an astute use of camera-work and imaginative editing and dubbing, the theater largely cannot. A determined effort to be eerie and chilling usually results, in my experience, in the absurd and often frankly comical. To produce a convincing scene of metamorphosis on stage is, of course, a non-starter. Nevertheless, despite such obstacles, dramatic authors have not been dissuaded from attempting the subject. The lycanthrope Ferdinand, in Webster's *The Duchess of Malfi* (1613; published 1623), immediately springs to mind; Robert O'Mahoney's Ferdinand, noted the *Financial Times* of the Bristol Old Vic's 1976 production, "teeters on the brink of fantastical madness from the very outset, finally growing in physical and vocal stature to an unsettling display of bare-chested lycanthropia." It is a meaty part.

A, by all accounts, insignificant one-act comedy by Francis et Ourry (pseudonym of E. T. Maurice and

Francis Ourry), *Le Loup-Garou*, was published and performed in Paris in 1807; while in 1827, also in the French capital, playwright Eugène Scribe collaborated with Mazères on the libretto of (again) *Le Loup-Garou*, an attractive comic-opera with music by Louise Bertin. A century and a half later, Brian Hayles (whose screenplays have distinguished many Hammer horror movies) conceived what was described on the posters as "the first-ever horror play written especially for children" – *The Hour of the Werewolf* (1975; published 1976), which was performed with great Gothic gusto by London's Unicorn Theatre for Young People ("the unimpeded action pleased the eight-plus children," said *The Stage*).

A recent adult attempt at the macabre theme, Ken Hill's *The Curse of the Werewolf* (premiered in 1977 by London's Theatre Workshop, Stratford East), is updated to the year 1922 and given a traditional East European setting – the unlikely-sounding Walpurgisdorf – where a spooky psychoanalyst is engaged in the even more un-

Vincent Brimble in the title role of Ken Hill's play for the theater, *The Curse of the Werewolf* (1977).

likely pursuit of trying to create a new species by mating a human with a werewolf. (This outlandish idea brings to mind Jaroslav Hašek, the Czech author of *The Good Soldier Svejk*, a noted confidence trickster who once ran a kennel of forged pedigrees where he advertised thoroughbred werewolf pups for sale.) Hill's stage play, said the critic of the *Financial Times*, provides "a lot of entertaining hokum, with bloodied hands, mad creatures in the wood, the strange appearance of a headless hunter and a vampiric interlude in which Dr Bancroft nearly loses his neck." The ingenious program was in the form of a cardboard cut-out mask of a werewolf's head – great for parties!

Victor Pemberton's radio play, *Night of the Wolf* (BBC Radio 4, 1975), set in Cambridge at the end of the last century, revolved around an arrogant, wild-eyed, red-haired family whose sons and lovers were doomed to turn into werewolves. It enjoyed the benefit of chilling sound-effects and two committed performances by Vincent Price and Coral Browne; the latter, "as lady of the manor and the grandmother of werewolves, had immense dignity" (*Daily Telegraph*). Also steeped in neo-Transylvanian atmosphere was Robert Muller's television play *The Werewolf Reunion* (BBC1, 1977); less successful, on the other hand, was Nigel Kneale's *What Big Eyes* (London Weekend Television, 1976), set in a laboratory at the back of a pet shop, where the proprietor (an unsettling performance by Patrick Magee) conducts experiments in so-called "lycanthropy": that is, he voluntarily transmutes his soul into that of a wolf secured in the yard.

The Devil, the witch, the ghost, the vampire – they have all figured prominently in poetry, whereas this can hardly be said of the werewolf (the banal rhyming lines of incantation used in the bizarre initiation ceremonies do not qualify as poetry). Marie de France's late twelfth-century lay, *Bisclavaret* (this is the Breton term for the Norman *varulf*, or werewolf) is familiar enough, yet it makes for difficult reading; while the old folkloric *Ballad of the Loup-Garou* (included in William J. Thoms' *Lays and Legends of Various Nations*, London, 1834), although scanning prettily on the page, is perhaps too coy for the modern reader. Stronger stuff is *Romanze vom Werwolf* (1883), by the German poet Emanuel Geibel. Yet we really strike gold with Graham R. Tomson's *Ballad of the Were-Wolf*, a grim, historically accurate tale about werewolfic "wound-doubling." The poem first appeared in the September 1890 issue of *Macmillan's Magazine*, and is written in Scottish dialect. The werewolf, at last, is accorded due poetic justice.

15 A Mere Twist of Fact: Wolfman and the Cinema

Even a man who is pure in heart,
And says his prayers by night,
May become a wolf when the wolfsbane blooms
And the autumn moon is bright.

HAT UTTER NONSENSE! Yet even those who do not know the difference between an historically authentic werewolf like Peter Stump and an absurdly made-up actor like Lon Chaney, Jr, will almost certainly be familiar with this Hollywood jingle. The lines, conceived by scriptwriter Curt Siodmak for Universal's 1941 production of *The Wolf Man*, symbolize all too clearly everything that is bad, silly and often downright inaccurate about the filmic werewolf. The first line alone is way off the mark. Benevolent or protective werewolves apart, a potential werewolf candidate – as we have already seen – must be devoid of all decent human qualities and be completely lacking in spiritual enlightenment. Such a man could never be "pure in heart," nor would he say his "prayers by night" – not *Christian* prayers, at least.

In horror films, a full moon is all-important to the werewolf, and the curse of metamorphosis is involuntary. Never do you see a character portrayed on the screen who actually *wants* to be a werewolf, never do the elements of black magic and witchcraft come into it, never a glimpse of the bizarre and horrible initiating ceremonies, the donning of wolf-girdles, the smearing of unguents, the drinking of potions. The terrible affliction of werewolfery in the cinema is simple and clear-cut: the werewolf of the film must himself first be bitten by another werewolf. That is all. What the screenwriter, the producer and the director do not take into account is the fact that the werewolf of folklore was not simply in business to go around biting people for the sheer hellish, fetishist fun of it. Being utterly depraved and of the lowest animal creation, he

Lon Chaney, Jr (the wolfman) and Evelyn Ankers in a tender moment from Universal's *The Wolf Man* (1941).

wanted blood, he wanted flesh, and to get it he ripped his victims to pieces. What remained was a sorry sight. Except for those few occasions when the werewolf was perhaps disturbed in his horrendous crimes, his victims were left in no fit state to become werewolves themselves.

The werewolf of the cinema, again, slowly transforms into a sort of hairy, long-toothed, foul-mouthed Mr Hyde figure. Yet the folkloric werewolf, in his animal form, is to all intents and purposes a *wolf*: his feet and hands change to paws, his arms to legs. The creature is a four-legged wolf, not a glorified caveman. Only the eyes retain the glint of humanity: being a mirror of the soul, they *cannot* change.

From the moment the filmic werewolf finds himself cursed by the power of metamorphosis, a distinctive five-pointed symbol – called a pentagram – appears on his body, usually in the palm of his hand, and it cannot be removed. In turn, Lawrence Talbot, the college-student werewolf portrayed in several Universal horror-pics by Lon Chaney, Jr, only pounces on his victims when he notices a facsimile of the mysterious pentagram in the palms of their hands. This is Hollywood's method of saying, in a simplistic cut-and-dried way, *why* their tame werewolf must stalk and attack people. The pentagram

LEFT "Even a man who is pure in heart...."
Poster for Universal's *The Wolf Man* (1941).

ABOVE Universal Pictures' famous pentagram medallion, one of three in existence. Two became the property of the directors of Pentagram Pictures, while the other is housed in the Universal City prop department. They are said to be made of pure, solid silver, although their effectiveness against evil influences cannot be vouched for.

(see illustration above right) is the *motivation* which lies behind the werewolf's crimes. It is, dramatically, a weak, pathetic device; historically, it is sheer hokum, an invention of Hollywood. Yet, in a comparatively short space of time, it was to become an integral part of the cinema's werewolfic mythology.

In the 1941 version of *The Wolf Man*, the first and best-crafted of the Lon Chaney, Jr, werewolf films, an old gypsy woman, Maleva (played by the superb Maria

Ouspenskaya, a former star of the Moscow Arts Theater), gives Talbot a pentagram medallion charm to wear over his heart as a form of protection against impending evil, the generous gesture being inspired by the fact that her werewolf son (played by Bela Lugosi in a brief guest appearance) attacked Talbot, thus transferring to him the curse of the werewolf. Talbot in turn presents the charm to his girlfriend, Gwen (played by Evelyn Ankers), daughter of the local antique-shop owner, so that she might be protected from his own werewolf rages. It was Gwen who first told Talbot about the area's local legends and recited him the old gypsy verse which prefaces this chapter: "*Even a man who is pure in heart . . .*" etc. Later, alas, he notices with nauseating numbness that the pentagram sign has now appeared in the palm of her hand. He recoils from the terrible knowledge that Gwen must be his next victim.

Siodmak was clearly inspired in his werewolf-pentagram creation by the "mark of the Devil" in werewolfic folklore; but the Devil's mark could not be obtained involuntarily, and certainly not as a result of being bitten by another werewolf. But this was hardly going to inhibit Hollywood. So the movie capital turned to the vampire legend for help. To be bitten by the folklore vampire, and more specifically by Bram Stoker's Count Dracula, was to become a vampire oneself. Why not, someone in the studio script department must have said, combine the marvellous legends of the vampire and the werewolf? This they did, and they did so several years *before* Curt Siodmak cut his teeth on the lycanthropic tale in *The Wolf Man*. The vampire-werewolf mix-up, in fact, first made the big screen in 1935, in *The Werewolf of London*, based on Guy Endore's novel *The Werewolf of Paris* – a novel which, twenty-six years later, was also to provide the inspiration for Hammer Films' masterly *Curse of the Werewolf*, with the up-and-coming twenty-three-year-old Oliver Reed as the beast.

By the time of the arrival of the wolfman in *The Werewolf of London*, in which Henry Hull portrays an English botanist bitten by a Japanese werewolf in Tibet, the vampire theme was already a well-established horror-movie favorite, from Max Schreck's spine-chilling portrayal of the Transylvanian vampire in Murnau's German silent film *Nosferatu* (1923) to Bela Lugosi's definitive *Dracula* (1931). Although the cinema *did* make an early shot at the werewolf theme, in Universal's two-reeler "short," *The Werewolf*, released in 1913, a period of twenty-two years was to elapse before, with Henry Hull's *Werewolf of London*, the subject was ever attempted again on the screen. But despite its title, the 1913 silent movie was not

Henry Hull as the devil's-peaked werewolf in Universal's *The Werewolf of London* (1935).

about a wolfman but a wolf *girl*, and was based on an old Navajo legend; it further had the Indian girl, Watuma, being reincarnated one hundred years after her death, and doing so in wolf-form. Since reincarnation and metempsychosis – the transmigration of a human soul at death into a new body of the same or different species – has nothing to do with either werewolfery or lycanthropy, the 1913 silent-reeler is not strictly speaking a werewolf film. Nor was *The Werewolf of London* a wholly successful interpretation of the werewolf story, because director Stuart Walker seemed to confuse the theme not only with the vampire legend but also with Robert Louis Stevenson's *Dr Jekyll and Mr Hyde*. With no werewolf precedent in the cinema at the time, someone must have thought, who is going to know the difference? Well, we know now.

For all its inaccuracies, *The Wolf Man*, by treating the werewolf as an individual theme – and by the use of magnificent, atmospheric studio sets, imaginative black-and-white camera work, and a polished cast – subsequently achieved an element of super-charged Gothic horror which was not to be surpassed until the appearance of Hammer's *Curse of the Werewolf*. But once Universal strove to cash-in on the success of the explosive Chaney/wolfman combina-

ABOVE American comedian Lou Costello meets the wolfman (as ever, Lon Chaney, Jr) in Universal's degenerate *Abbott and Costello Meet Frankenstein* (1948). "Abbott and Costello ruined the horror field," said Chaney. "They made buffoons out of the monsters."

RIGHT A twenty-three-year-old Oliver Reed, adorned with fur-lined vest and matching gloves, provides a stunning performance in the title role of *The Curse of the Werewolf* (1961).

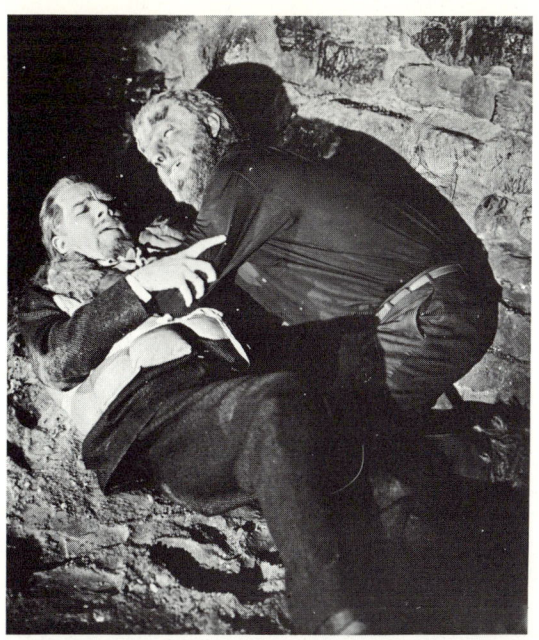
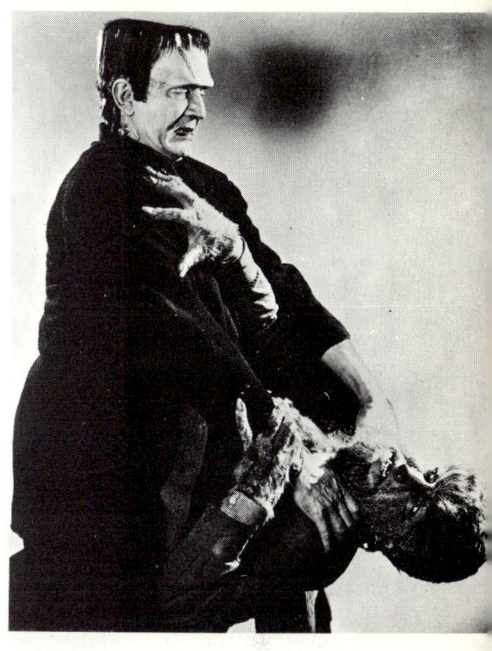

ABOVE LEFT Too many ghouls spoil the brew in Universal's *House of Dracula* (1946). Scientist Dr Edelmann (played by Onslow Stevens) treats Dracula, Frankenstein and Wolfman . . . although the wolfman (Lon Chaney, Jr) here seems to be treating the scientist.

ABOVE Lon Chaney, Jr.'s wolfman in the Frankenstein monster's deadly and not-too-friendly embrace – Bela Lugosi's first and last attempt at the role, incidentally – in *Frankenstein Meets the Wolf Man* (1943).

LEFT Sporting a fine crop of yak's hair and stranded kelp: Lon Chaney, Jr, as the supernatural beast of prey in Universal's *House of Frankenstein* (1945).

American supporting actress June Lockhart took the title role for Universal's low-grade thriller, *She-Wolf of London* (1946).

OPPOSITE TOP Columbia's *The Werewolf* (1956): juvenile treatment of the lycanthropic superstition under Fred F. Sears' direction.

OPPOSITE BELOW Royal's witless, plotless *Werewolf in a Girls' Dormitory* (1961). The film gave the world, for better or worse, a theme song single called *The Ghoul in School*.

tion by casting him alongside a variety of ill-assorted horror-character permutations, the werewolf as a serious screen subject became impossible as well as ludicrous. Following *The Wolf Man* of 1941, the studios had Talbot rising from the family crypt for *Frankenstein Meets the Wolf Man* (1943), thawed out from a block of ice for *House of Frankenstein* (1945), revived for *House of Dracula* (1946), and placed in ridiculous situations for *Abbott and Costello Meet Frankenstein* (1948). The level at which Universal Pictures were now treating the werewolf theme can be best gauged from the goings-on in *House of Frankenstein*, where Lon Chaney, Jr's Wolf Man has to compete with Boris Karloff's Mad Doctor, John Carradine's Dracula, J. Carrol Naish's Hunchback, and Glenn Strange's Monster. As a matter of interest, Glenn Strange, a B-western "heavy" on the Universal payroll, had himself earlier played a wolfman in *The Mad Monster* (1941), a film and a performance which seems to have sunk into oblivion.

Chaney himself lamented the decline of the werewolf genre in the cinema. In 1973, at sixty-seven and just before his death, he told one reporter:

> I used to enjoy horror films when there was thought and sympathy involved. Then they became comedies. Abbott and Costello ruined the horror field: they made buffoons out of the monsters. Then the cheap producers came along and made worse buffoons of them, because they killed for the sake of killing, there was blood for the sake of blood. There was no thought, no true expression of acting, no true expression of feeling. We used to make up our minds before we started that this is a little fantastic, but let's take it seriously. And they were sold seriously. But all this foolishness today, it isn't sold seriously. It's made as a joke, a laugh, for the kids to go in and have a ball.

By and large, Chaney was right. He himself even made a light-hearted appearance as the Wolf Man in one of television's *Route 66* stories. Some of the other werewolf films included Twentieth Century-Fox's *The Undying Monster* (1942), Columbia's *The Return of the Vampire* (1943) and *The Cry of the Werewolf* (1944), Universal's *She-Wolf of London* (1946), Columbia's *The Werewolf* (1956), American International's *I Was a Teenage Werewolf* (1957), Royal's *Werewolf in a Girls' Dormitory* (1961; a German film released in that country as *Lycanthropus*, in the United States as *Werewolf in a Girls' Dormitory*, and in Britain as *I Married a Werewolf*), Universal's *The Boy Who Cried Werewolf* (1973), Marron Films' *Werewolf of*

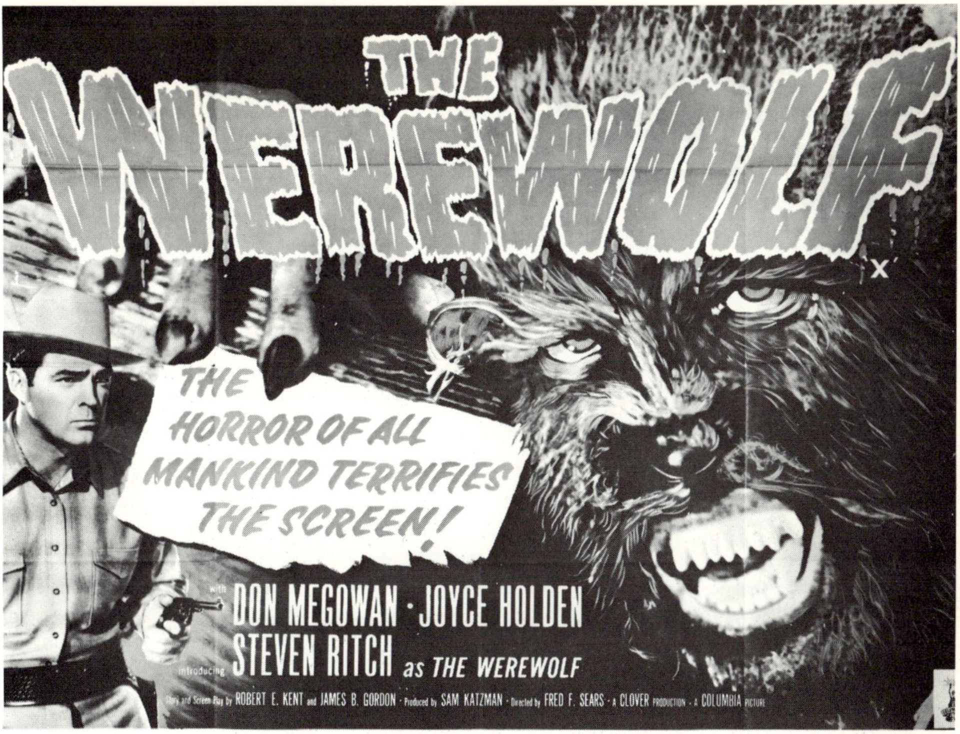
THE
WEREWOLF
THE HORROR OF ALL MANKIND TERRIFIES THE SCREEN!
with DON MEGOWAN · JOYCE HOLDEN
introducing STEVEN RITCH as THE WEREWOLF
Story and Screen Play by ROBERT E. KENT and JAMES B. GORDON · Produced by SAM KATZMAN · Directed by FRED F. SEARS · A CLOVER PRODUCTION · A COLUMBIA PICTURE

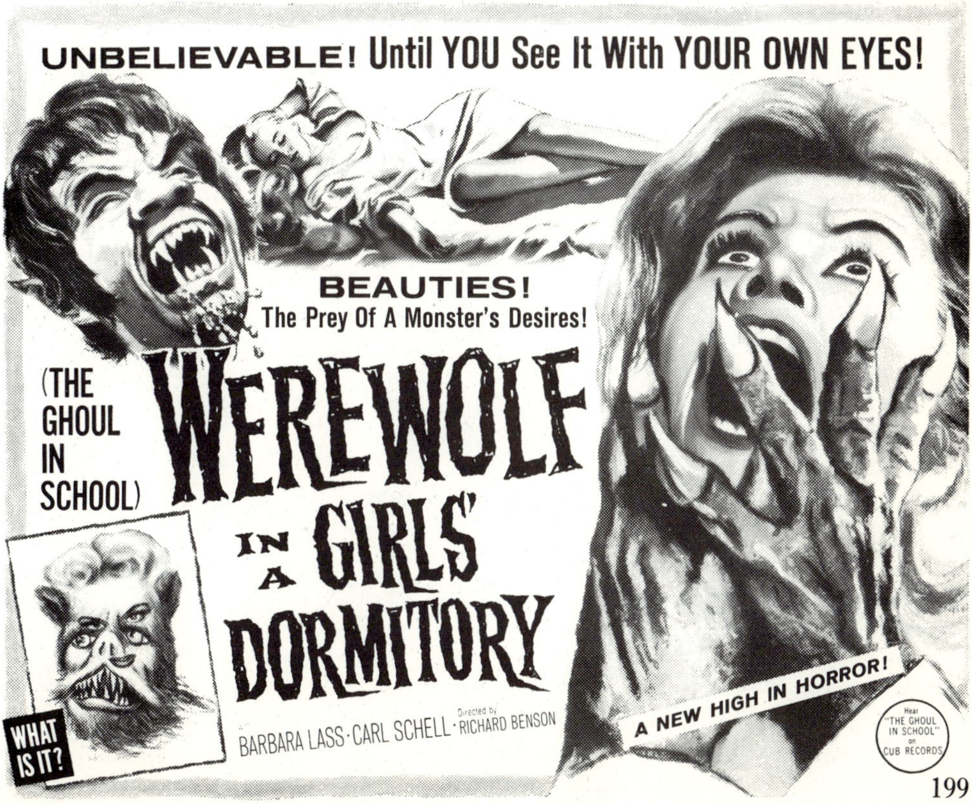
UNBELIEVABLE! Until YOU See It With YOUR OWN EYES!
BEAUTIES!
The Prey Of A Monster's Desires!
(THE GHOUL IN SCHOOL)
WEREWOLF IN A GIRLS' DORMITORY
WHAT IS IT?
BARBARA LASS · CARL SCHELL · Directed by RICHARD BENSON
A NEW HIGH IN HORROR!
Hear "THE GHOUL IN SCHOOL" on CUB RECORDS

Washington (1973), and British Lion's *The Beast Must Die* (1974). Most of these films have little to recommend from the point of view of historical credibility, although *Werewolf of Washington* achieves the dubious distinction of being the only politically satirical werewolf film, being a send-up of America's Watergate affair, with Michael Dunn as Dr Kiss and Dean Stockwell as a werewolfic Nixon aide; the posters proudly billed it as "A biting picture of America." The title-role in *I Was a Teenage Werewolf*, incidentally, was played by the then unknown twenty-year-old Michael Landon; he was yet to win fame – and the hearts of women the world over – as Little Jo in TV's *Bonanza* series. Two British films, the already-mentioned *Curse of the Werewolf* of 1961 and Tyburn Films' *Legend of the Werewolf* of 1975, the latter with David Rintoul as the werewolf, are arguably two of the most intelligent films of their kind, dealing with the legend as sanely as the demands of the commercial film business will allow . . . although the barrel-chested werewolf of Oliver Reed more resembles a were-bear than a werewolf.

Walt Lee's three-volumed *Reference Guide to Fantastic Films* lists an incredible *fifty-eight* werewolf films, although a number of them are amateur productions. The pro-

The werewolf of actor David Rintoul tries to escape capture in the sewers of Paris. A climactic moment from Tyburn Films' *Legend of the Werewolf* (1975).

A Tyburn Film Production photograph

fessional feature films range from the classic *Wolf Man* to such bewildering absurdities as *Nympho Werewolf* and *Munster, Go Home!* Most of these werewolf films fall down as soon as the camera gives us even a moderately close view of the beast's face, since the make-up in most cases is laughable and about as horrific as cherries atop a walnut cake. It was Jack Pierce, the make-up genius of Universal Studios and the man responsible for transforming Boris Karloff into the horrendous Frankenstein monster, who designed the werewolf features which millions all over the world must now regard as the definitive wolfman. His work in black and white has yet to be surpassed. Pierce first invented the werewolf make-up for Henry Hull in *Werewolf of London*, but it was his painstaking attention to detail on the Chaney wolfman films where his craftmanship really achieved distinction, even if the werewolf he finally evolved was pure fairy-tale fantasy.

Chaney, who was fitted with a moulded rubber nose, plastic fangs, hairy palms, padded paws (for those scenes where his feet came into frame), yak's hair and stranded kelp, had to endure a daily six-hour make-up session whenever he was involved in scenes depicting him in animal werewolf-form. In the episodes showing actual metamorphosis, those eerie "dissolves" from human to beast, and vice versa, Chaney apparently suffered as much physical agony as his screen victims. Chaney recalls the experience:

Michael Landon, yet to bite the dust as Little Jo in TV's *Bonanza* series, here shows utter werewolfic contempt for a pretty face. From American International's *I Was a Teenage Werewolf* (1957).

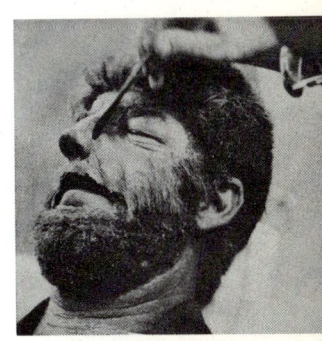

Lon Chaney, Jr, endures the long and tedious daily process of being made up as the wolfman.

> The day we did the transformations I came in at two a.m. When I hit that position they would take little nails and drive them through the skin at the edge of my fingers, on both hands, so that I couldn't move them any more. While I was in this position they would build a plaster-cast of the back of my head. Then they would take the drapes from behind me and starch them, and while they were drying them, they would take the camera and weigh it down with one ton, so that it wouldn't quiver when people walked. They had targets for my eyes up there. Then, while I was still in this position, they would shoot five or ten frames of film in the camera. They'd take that film out and send it to the lab. While it was there the make-up man would come and take the whole thing off my face, and put on a new one, only less. I was still immobile. When the film came back from the lab they'd put it back in the camera and then they'd check me. They'd say, "Your eyes have moved a little bit, move them to the right . . . now your shoulder is up. . . ." Then they'd roll it again and

Paul Naschy, Spain's answer to Lon Chaney, Jr, as the excitable werewolf in *Nacht der Vampire*.

shoot another ten frames. Well, we did twenty-one changes of make-up and it took twenty-two hours. I won't discuss about the bathroom!"

Most later werewolf films brilliantly solved the question of transformation: they did without it.

On the Continent – where, after all, the werewolf of history flourished – the werewolf film industry is thriving in, of all places, sunny Spain. In recent years, Paul Naschy has become Spain's answer to Karloff-Chaney-

Lugosi-Lee-Cushing, having played the full gamut of cinematic monsters; but, like Chaney, he has become principally associated with the werewolf roles, playing the Talbot-like Waldemar Daninsky, a Pole tormented by the affliction of werewolfery, in some ten werewolf films (including a couple of made-for-television films and the Mexican movie, *La Casa del Terror*), among them *La Marca del Hombre Lobo* (which appeared throughout Europe with such titles as *The Wolfman of Count Dracula, Hell's Creatures, The Vampires of Dr Dracula*, and, in the United States, as *Frankenstein's Bloody Terror)*, *Las Noches del Hombre Lobo (Night of the Wolf Man)*, *The Fury of the Wolfman* (obviously inspired by *The Werewolf of London)*, and *Los Monstruous del Terror* (English substitute title: *The Man Who Came from Ummo*). This last film, made in 1969, is a sort of Spanish version of Universal's *House of Frankenstein*, throwing into one movie practically every known monster, including alien invaders from the planet Ummo, Dracula, Frankenstein's Monster, the Mummy and, of course, the werewolf of Paul Naschy. Other werewolf films made by Naschy include the German-Spanish co-production of *La Noche de Walpurgis* (or *The Werewolf's Shadow*), made in 1970, and its 1973 sequel, *El Retorno de Walpurgis*.

As in the Lon Chaney, Jr films, silver objects, especially silver bullets, are positively fatal to the Spanish werewolf. But whereas Hollywood allowed Talbot to mysteriously come back to life again in each new production after being despatched in previous films with either a silver wolf-headed walking-stick or a silver bullet, the Spanish studios solved the problem by having the slugs removed from Daninsky at the beginning of later films. Perhaps the fact that wolves still thrive in Spain partially explains the success of these films.

Naschy's howl, in his werewolf scenes, is truly hair-raising. How he, or the studios, produce that nasty sound I cannot say; but I *can* reveal the secret of Henry Hull's yelpings for *The Werewolf of London*, from an explanation given by Ron Haydock in the magazine *Fantastic Monsters of the Movies* (Vol. 1, No. 5, 1963).

> The note sought for London's werewolf was one of ferocity, mixed with protest and near-human grief. What key should be selected for this howl? How long should each howl endure? What animals should be tested for the best sound? These were moot points thrashed out in hours of discussion between director Stuart Walker and Gil Kurland, Universal's sound supervisor. Hyena shrieks, wildcat yowls, and bear

growls were found unsatisfactory. Visits to the zoo by night and day failed to elicit a single adequate yelp from the big gray lobos or coyotes or even the jackals. While on location in Alaska for another Universal film, Kurland was able to record the bay of a wild timber wolf, full of menace and curdling with melancholy, and upon his return to Hollywood, he played the recording for Walker. Although Walker was satisfied with the genuine wolf howl, he decided the human element in the voice was still lacking. Using a sound mixer, Kurland blended the timber wolf's baying with Indian yells, crowd roars, every tragic cry in his sound library, but to no effect. Valerie Hobson, Lester Matthews, Warner Oland, and other members of the cast tried their luck at supplying the right whoop, but their sounds were too flat. Then Walker hit on the notion of seeing what Hull himself could do. As the record was played, Hull shouted with it, and reports filtered back from the mixer's booth that this attempt was more encouraging. However, only certain notes would blend effectively with the baying. At Walker's direction, Kurland edited out all of Hull's high notes, re-recorded the remains, and a realistically terrifying howl was finally throated by the London werewolf. Six years later the second werewolf film was produced, *The Wolf Man*, also from Universal – but the painstaking Walker-Kurland-Hull yelp was nowhere to be heard.

But it was heard by a number of children in San Diego in 1967. *Monsters Unleashed* magazine, in the issue dated February, 1974, provides a poignant obituary to a man whose private life was often far from happy:

> Lon Chaney, Jr, one of the most versatile horror movie stars of the 1940s, died at age sixty-seven in San Clemente, California, on July 12, 1973. There is some speculation that a contributing factor in Chaney's death *might* have been cancer of the esophagus, the disease that claimed his famous father in 1930. On Hallowe'en Night in 1967, at the request of a large group of trick-or-treaters gathered outside his large ranch in Warner Hot Springs in San Diego County, Chaney gave out with a blood-curdling "Wolf Man growl" that permanently damaged his voice, reducing his distinctive baritone to little more than a whispery croak.

How paradoxical that the man who came in like a lion, or rather like a wolf, should go out like a lamb. But his filmic werewolf lives – even though, like his less convincing successors, he should be depicted portraying so much werewolfic hokum.

16 The Commercial Werewolf

HE COMMERCIAL MARKET, using the werewolf as a money-spinning theme, has certainly not lacked ingenuity. The wonder is that the world has not yet been driven werewolf crazy by the sheer volume of wolfman products it has been made to endure. Werewolf home movies are at the top of the list for instant chills and thrills, with werewolf masks of all types to "petrify and amaze," packs of werewolf photographs "suitable for framing," and werewolf T-shirts and special iron-on werewolf transfers. The Smiths Food Group in Britain recently produced a special, werewolf bookmark made from colored plastic and included it in packets of potato chips (renamed Horror Bags for the occasion) as a free gift. A manufacturer of chewing gum also cashed-in on the werewolf mania by inserting werewolf joke-cards with their product. Then there are werewolf signet rings, werewolf fun stamps (with the legend "Lycanthropy Lives"), werewolf "bank notes" ("This note is illegal tender and must be honored under penalty of pain and death – yours"), glow-in-the-dark werewolf model kits, werewolf coloring books, and "easy-to-fly" werewolf kites. The American choreographer Raymond Johnson even based a modern ballet – *Wolfman* – on the werewolf theme. Werewolf comics (*Werewolf by Night*, etc.) and magazines have always proliferated. So the man in the street, not to say the man in the store, is stuck with the werewolf whether he likes it or not.

Werewolf fun stamps, issued in the United States by *The Monster Times* magazine.

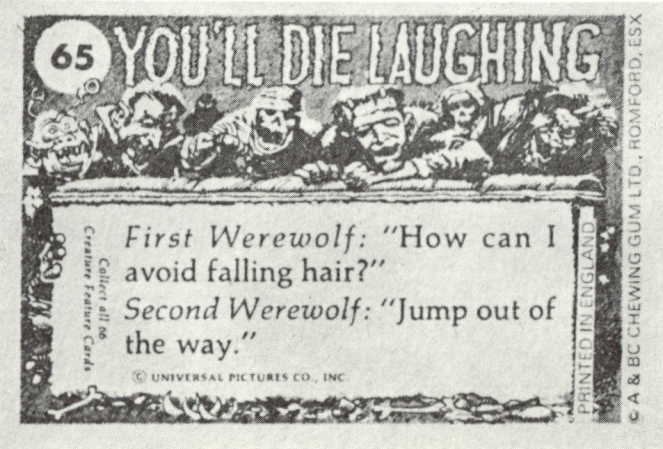

TOP Wolfman "bank note," again produced by *The Monster Times*.

ABOVE LEFT Front cover of the British glossy magazine *Legend Horror Classics: Werewolves* (No. 11, 1976).

ABOVE RIGHT Werewolf mask boasting the latest in streaked coiffure.

RIGHT "You'll Die Laughing" werewolf joke cards, courtesy of chewing gum.

ABOVE Free with Smiths' potato chips: a werewolf bookmark.

LEFT The proud owner of a werewolf T-shirt.

ABOVE Latin werewolf. A frame from the Italian comic *Lycantropus* (No. 6, 1977).

17 Were-Animals

HERE ARE FEW PLACES on earth which do not possess a local equivalent of the werewolf superstition – the were-tiger, were-eagle and were-serpent in Mexico, Peru and Central America generally; the were-vulture and were-calchona in Chile; the were-jaguar, were-tiger and other were-animals in South America; the were-bear in Europe and northern Asia; the were-hyena and were-leopard in Africa; the were-tiger in India, China, Japan and other parts of Asia; and, elsewhere, such varied were-creatures as were-crocodiles, were-foxes, were-lions, were-boars, were-cats, were-dogs, were-badgers, were-coyotes, were-buffaloes, were-horses . . in fact, literally hundreds of animals, birds and reptiles, because the wolf is far from being the only wild creature whose shape man may possess the power of assuming. Usually the particular were-animal of the particular area will be dictated by certain considerations: it will be commonly found in the region; it will be notorious for its attacks on humans and animals alike; and it will consequently be much feared by the local people. For the second and third reasons, therefore, the likelihood of encountering (from a folkloric point of view) a were-sheep or a were-wallaby would be extremely remote.

Fear, where human-animal transformation is concerned, is a key element; it is the same fear which a particular locality will have for the wild animal itself. This is why the werewolf, or rather the *dread* of the werewolf, is rare today; the wolf has become extinct in so many parts of the world. As Montague Summers explains in *The Werewolf*:

> For long centuries throughout all Europe there was no wilder brute, no more dreaded enemy of man than the savage wolf, whose ferocity was a quick and lively menace to the countryside such as perhaps we cannot in these later days by any stretch of imagination even faintly realise and comprehend. While yet large tracts of every country, steppes and moorland, sierra and wold, upland, fell and plain, were utterly deserted and only trodden by man with peril and mortal danger

to himself, the wolf proved a fearful foe. . . . What better guise, what better shape of fear and ferocity could the shape-shifting sorcerer in Europe assume?

By substituting, say, *tiger* or *leopard* for *wolf*, this could apply equally to the fear and superstitions of were-animals in Asia, Africa and elsewhere. There can be no doubt, though, that many stories of were-tigers and were-lions, for instance, are little more than the bizarre figment of the storytellers' imagination.

The medicine man or wizard, as we all know, can exert an extraordinary hold on the primitive mind. He tells his people that he is going to transform himself into a tiger or some similar ferocious beast and then mutilate and devour them; and hardly has he started to roar and snarl than the frightened natives, their minds easily swayed by the spell of suggestion, run for their lives. "Look," cry the women, who are so fear-struck as to let their eyes deceive them, "his body is covered with spots like a tiger! Horrible! His nails are turning into claws." The sorcerer meantime is hidden inside his hut, performing all manner of mysterious rites designed to work on the wild imagination of his people. Ask them to explain the terrible fear they experience and they will tell you it is because, being unable to see and kill the savage tiger-image, they feel vulnerable and threatened. But they will tell their neighbors, boastfully, that they have "seen" a were-tiger.

It should certainly come as no surprise to learn that the vast continent of Africa is abundantly rich in legends concerning the were-lion, the were-hyena and the were-leopard. Bornu, a region of the central Sudan and now a province of Northern Nigeria, has a local word for the were-hyena – *bultungin*, which means "I change myself into a hyena." It used to be said that one or two villages in the region, including Kabutiloa, were populated entirely by were-hyenas; while on the other side of Africa, in Ethiopia – formerly Abyssinia – every wizard was believed to be a were-hyena. A superstition very much alive

Title illustration by A. Brosnatch for Frank Belknap Long Jr's short story, "The Were-Snake" (*Weird Tales*, September 1925). The story concerns "the great mother-goddess Ishtar, the *magna mater* of the Babylonians, the Assyrians and darker, more sinister peoples whose civilizations were legends in the age of Homer."

in Ethiopia today is that every blacksmith, whose trade is hereditary, is a sorcerer who has the power to change himself into various kinds of animals. He is distinguished from other people by wearing gold ear-rings. And it was formerly believed – may *still* be believed, for all I know – that he robbed graves at midnight. He is accordingly viewed with suspicion by most of his countrymen, who refer to him as the *bouda*. Mansfield Parkyns writes in *Life in Abyssinia*, published just over a hundred years ago:

> I remember a story of some little girls, who, having been out in the forest to gather sticks, came running back breathless with fright; and on being asked what was the cause, they answered that a blacksmith of the neighbourhood had met them, and entering into conversation with him, they at length began to joke about whether, as had been asserted, he could turn himself into a hyena. The man, they declared, made no reply, but taking some ashes, which he had with him tied up in the corner of his cloth, sprinkled them over his shoulders, and to their horror and alarm they began almost immediately to perceive that the metamorphosis was actually taking place, and that the blacksmith's skin was assuming the hair and colour of the animal in question. When the change was complete he grinned and laughed at them, and then retired into the neighbouring thickets. They stood rooted to the spot from sheer fright; but the moment the hideous creature withdrew, they made the best of their way home.

Another case of the frightened onlookers seeing what they wanted to see, of coming under the magical influence of a man whose mystical reputation was well-known to them? More than probable. But to their friends, again, they would say they had "seen" a were-hyena.

The same belief in were-hyenas occurs from the Sudan to Tanzania, and as far afield as Morocco, where the fair-skinned, brown-eyed Berbers regard the *bouda* as a man who *nightly* turns into a hyena and resumes his human shape at dawn. There are other African were-hyena stories which differ intrinsically from European werewolf stories in that it is the hyena itself which is capable of changing into a man, rather than the other way around. The metamorphosis is very similar, in fact, to that of the strange were-fox and were-vixen encountered in Chinese and Japanese folk legends. In northern China especially the were-fox is said to inhabit the borderline between the earth and the underworld. When it changes into its human form it appears as a young and pretty girl; but in Chinese legend it betrays its real nature by the possession of a tail,

A Chinese were-fox, a creature said to inhabit the borderline between the earth and the underworld, and noted for its great sexuality and amorousness. A nineteenth-century painting.

in Japanese legend by its reflection in water, which is always that of a fox. As in China, the Japanese were-fox prefers the shape of a beautiful girl. In both countries, male were-foxes have sexual intercourse with women, were-vixens with men. In either case, notes Robert Eisler, a morbid state results, resembling that caused by the medieval *incubi* and *succubae*. Their animal shape becomes visible when they sleep or are under the influence of drink, of which they are as fond as the Maenads of Dionysus. In fact, adds Eisler, the Chinese and Japanese were-vixen is an exact counterpart to the Thracian "vixen" of Dionysus, the Roman *lupa*, and the English "bitch" – a "harlot". But whereas the Japanese *nogitsone*, or "wild fox," can assume any shape – human being, bird, reptile, or animal, the were-rat and were-badger being especially common – the Chinese were-fox or were-vixen is exclusively the wild fox assuming human shape. Here, legend has it, the fox lives to an age of eight hundred years, and sometimes more, but only when it reaches five hundred years does it acquire the mystical property of human metamorphosis.

The were-fox of China may lack the ferocity of its Western counterpart, the werewolf, but it makes up for this by its overt sexuality and amorousness. The greatest wrong they do is to seduce men and women and lead them on through passion to their doom. No human animal can be more seductive than the were-vixen. Japan's were-fox, on the other hand, is rather more mischievous than

A trio of Japanese were-rats, one of whom has already metamorphosed into the form of a rat. A late-eighteenth or early-nineteenth-century painting by Osaka.

amorous, and sometimes extremely dangerous. There *are*, incidentally, numerous accounts of Chinese werewolves, but the stories are so similar to those stemming from the West that it seems pointless to do other than acknowledge their existence.

Tales of were-cats and were-dogs have also existed for some two thousand years in China and Japan. Again, they are normal cats and dogs which assume human shape; the dogs in particular take human form in order to gratify their sexual lust through women. Were-dogs proper, men who can transform themselves into dogs, appear occasionally in the folk-tales of Germany, Romania, Russia, parts of Africa (especially Guyana) and South America

(especially Argentina, Brazil and Uruguay) and, not surprisingly, Japan. Perhaps the were-dog should be as familiar as the werewolf in folklore, certainly where the Eskimos are concerned, who believe that all Indians and all Europeans are descended from the dog.

Were-cats have likewise been part of European folklore. There is a German story of a carpenter at Bühl who, being bothered by a nightmare, saw an elf enter his room, through a hole, in the shape of a cat. He caught the animal and nailed one of its paws to the floor. In the morning he was surprised to find his feline prisoner transformed into a beautiful naked young woman. He later married her and they had three children. But she suddenly disappeared one day, in the form of a cat, through the hole by which she had entered – because her husband inadvertently removed the material with which he had blocked it up. Another story, originating in what was formerly eastern Prussia, now western Poland, concerns a girl who, without her knowledge, was transformed into a cat every evening and awoke each morning in a state of complete exhaustion. One night her lover caught a cat, which had regularly tormented and scratched him at night, and placed it securely in a sack. Next morning he found the cat transformed into his naked sweetheart. The story adds that she was cured by the parson of the parish.

To return to the larger members of the were-cat family, the jaguar is as feared today in the midland provinces of Argentina as was the European wolf in the Middle Ages. To the local population the jaguar, or *tigre capiango*, is not a jaguar but a man who, at will, can assume the jaguar's form. His purpose is usually to frighten friends in a spirit of rustic jesting, but highwaymen have also availed themselves of the guise. During the civil wars of the last century, General Facundo Quiroga was popularly supposed to have under his command an entire regiment of *capiangos*, evocatively recalling the corps of berserkers and ûlfhednars attached to the battalions of ancient Norse kings. In many parts of South America, especially among the Arawak groups, totemism was rife, and the natives had as their god a deity in the form of a jaguar, to whom they prayed for vengeance on their enemies and for the property of lycanthropy. In the remoter regions of Guyana the locals still believe that certain tigers are possessed by human spirits who, as men, devote themselves to cannibalism. Taking the shape of the jaguar, they approach the lonely sleeping-places or pounce on men in the forests. No were-animal superstition, even today, causes more terror. In some other African tribes, tailless leopards are believed to be transformed men, stemming no doubt from

The were-jaguar, South America's equivalent of the werewolf, is represented in this pottery figurine from Mexico.

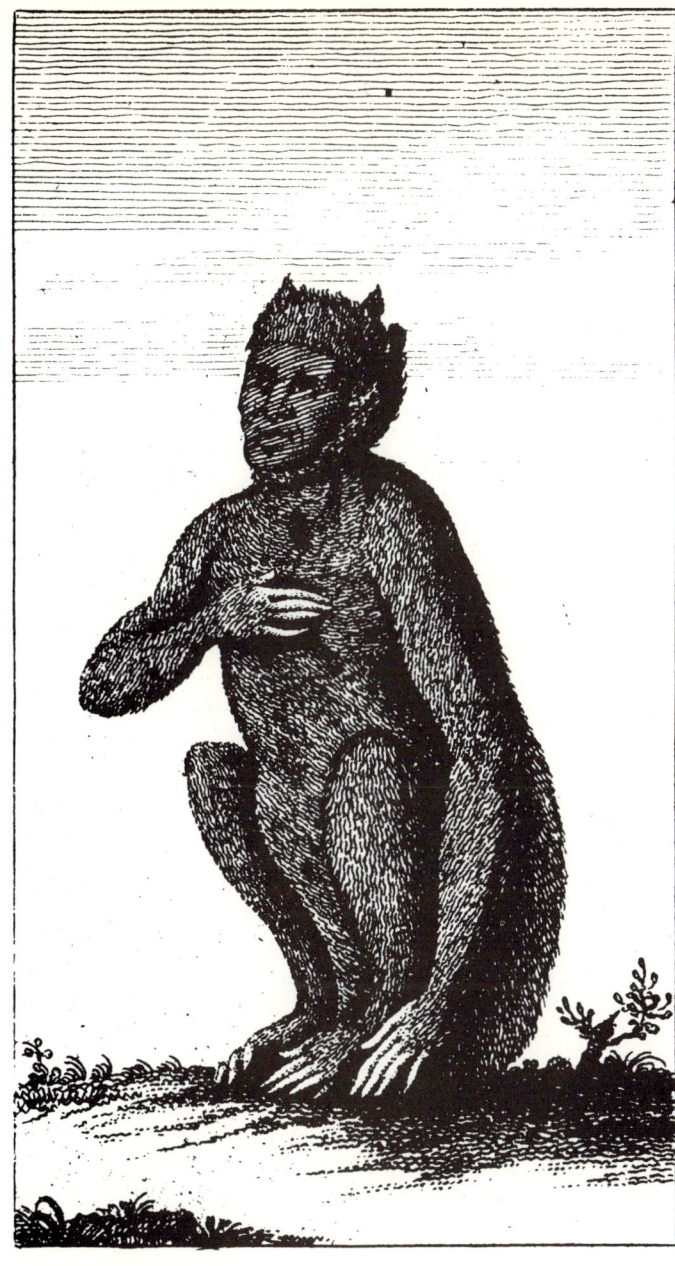

The were-tiger, depicted in this print dating from 1763, is held in great fear throughout India.

the belief that the were-animal usually has no tail.

As one might expect, the were-tiger is still held in great fear throughout India; in the constituent state of Orissa, the power of transforming into a tiger is said to be hereditary, and also to be acquired through the practice of magic. The lycanthropy of the were-tiger, says Elliott O'Donnell in *Werwolves*, differs from that of the werewolf

> ... inasmuch as there is a definite god or spirit, in the shape of a tiger, that is directly responsible for the

215

bestowal of the property. This tiger deity is looked upon and worshipped as a totem or national deity – that is to say, as a divine being that has the welfare of the Kandh nation especially at heart. It is communed with at home, but more particularly in the wild dreariness of the jungle, where, on the condition that the prayers of its devotees are sufficiently concentrated and in earnest, it confers – as an honour and privilege – the power of transmutation into its own shape.

Because the doctrine of metempsychosis, or reincarnation and the transmigration of souls, is prevalent throughout India, actual belief in transformation is understandably diffused, although traces of genuine lycanthropy can be found in all regions where Buddhism exists, including Sri Lanka.

The stories surrounding Africa's were-leopards and were-lions are usually rather more sinister than mystical, and refer more specifically to the murderous "leopard-men" and "lion-men". Paul B. Du Chaillu, writing just a hundred years ago about his journeys into equatorial Africa, recalls a curious illustration of the existence of a belief in men being sometimes transformed into lions and leopards:

> I cannot avoid relating a strange and horrid form of monomania which is sometimes displayed by these primitive negroes. It was related to me so circumstantially by Akondogo, and so well confirmed by others, that I cannot help fully believing in all the principal facts of the case. Poor Akondogo said that he had had plenty of trouble in his day, that a leopard had killed two of his men and that he had a great many palavers to settle on account of these deaths. Not knowing exactly what he meant, I said to him, "Why did you not make a trap to catch the leopard?" To my astonishment, he replied, "The leopard was not the kind you mean. It was a man who had changed himself into a leopard, and then became a man again." I said, "Akondogo, I will never believe your story. How can a man be turned into a leopard?" He again asserted that it was true, and gave me the following history: While he was in the woods with his people, gathering india-rubber, one of his men disappeared and, notwithstanding all their endeavors, nothing could be found of him but a quantity of blood. The next day another man disappeared, and in searching for him more blood was found. All the people got alarmed, and Akondogo sent for a great doctor to drink the mboundou, and solve the mystery of these two deaths. To the horror and astonishment of

the old chief, the doctor declared it was Akondogo's own child (his nephew and heir), Akosho, who had killed the two men. Akosho was sent for and, when asked by the chief, answered that it was truly he who had committed the murders; that he could not help it, for he had been turned into a leopard, and his heart longed for blood; and that after each deed he had turned into a man again. Akondogo loved his boy so much that he would not believe his own confession, until the boy took him to a place in the forest where lay two bodies, one with the head cut off, and the other with the belly torn open. Upon this, Akondogo gave orders to seize the lad. He was bound with ropes, taken to the village, and then tied in a horizontal position to a post, and burnt slowly to death, all the people standing by until he expired.

I must say the end of the story seemed to me too horrible to listen to. I shuddered, and was ready to curse the race that was capable of committing such acts. But on careful enquiry, I found it was a case of monomania with the boy Akosho, and that he really was the murderer of the two men. It is probable that the superstitious belief of these morbidly imaginative Africans in the transformation of men into leopards, being early instilled into the minds of their children, is the direct cause of murders being committed under the influence of it. The boy himself, as well as Akondogo and all the people, believed he had really turned into a leopard, and the cruel punishment was partly in vengeance for witchcraft, and partly to prevent the committal of more crimes by the boy in a similar way, for, say they, the man has a spirit of witchcraft.

I have quoted this story (from *Explorations and Adventures in Equatorial Africa,* 1861) at length because it clearly shows how a local primitive culture, taught in adolescence, can induce people to believe what they want to believe. The delusion is no less real for the African patient than is the delusion of werewolfery for the Western lycanthrope. The boy Akosho also recalls, in a different culture, the French boy Gilles Garnier. They both suffered from lycanthropia. Unlike the werewolf, though, the "wereleopard's" history has sustained its grip on popular imagination well into recent times. The London *Evening Standard,* dated January 10, 1948, reports from Dar-es-Salaam, Tanganyika (Tanzania): "Three women have been hanged in Tanganyika for the first time in the country's recorded history. They died, with four men, for their part in the lion-men murders in the Singida district last spring, when more than forty natives were slaughtered by people dressed in lion skins." Other examples in recent times include reports in *Wiener Tagblatt*, the issue of May 3, 1934 (execution of nine Negro members of the sect of "leopard-men"), and *Neue Freie Presse*, May 16, 1936 (execution of eight Anyotos in Stanleyville, Belgian Congo). On June 20, 1937, the *Neue Freie Presse* described the masks of the leopard-men as being made of brown tree-bark, painted with black and yellow spots, with a real leopard's tail attached to the back. The Anyotos in question dragged young people, chiefly women and girls, by night from their huts, lacerated them with knives shaped like leopards' claws, pierced the heart with a trident knife (probably representing forked-lightning) and devoured the bodies. On April 9, 1947, the *Daily Telegraph* reported: "Sixty-one native men and women have been arrested during inquiries into alleged

A murderous Leopard Man from the former Belgian Congo in central Africa contemplates his next victim.

murders by 'lion-men', or witch-doctors, in the Singida district of Tanganyika. The police said they expect to bring the total to seventy. Many of those arrested will be brought before the Tanganyika High Court for trial on murder charges."

For some inexplicable reason, most cases of sham lycanthropy seem to come from West Africa, where a secret brotherhood of Human Leopard Societies is formed from time to time by young natives. It is often difficult to bring the criminals to justice, because when questioned the victims (terrified of the consequent reprisals if they identify the men concerned) will simply declare that they have seen nothing. The leopard sprang from the bush, they will say, and it merely seemed as though a great wind had rushed by. Yet there are many ancient tribes who *are* convinced of the existence of the were-leopard, and other were-animals, as a very real phenomenon to be avoided at all costs.

Among these other were-animals, the were-bear has been a feared foe in Europe, Scandinavia and parts of Asia for two thousand years: the berserkers of the North, it will be recalled, by donning their bear-skins, were contriving as much to be were-bears as the West Africans, in their leopard skins, are still contriving to be were-leopards. Björn (this common Norse name means "bear"), in the ancient saga of *The History of Hrolf Kraka*, is transformed into a bear by his stepmother. He lives as a bear and kills many of his father's sheep, but by night he always becomes a man, until he is hunted and slain. The

A fine wood-engraving by Cornelius Matthäus Weindel, dated 1701, showing the transformation of a Polish nobleman into a were-pig. The original print in the Augsburg archives is in color.

story was later re-written by Sir Walter Scott. A Danish song makes a man's transformation into bear-form take place by tying an iron collar round his neck, and as late as the turn of the century it was believed in Norway that all Finns and Laplanders, who from time immemorial have been regarded as the world's most skilful wizards and witches, turn into bears.

Until the middle of the last century, if we are to believe Charles Hardwick and his *Traditions, Superstitions and Folklore* (1872), a common belief in Denmark, Iceland, Germany and the North of England was of the transformation of a man into a horse, by a woman throwing a magic halter over his head while he is lying in bed. The woman, who is a disguised witch, then mounts the horse and gallops to the trysting place, where her fellow-witches meet for their revels. If the were-horse can contrive to slip the magic bridle from his head, and throw it over that of the woman, she is suddenly transformed into a mare, and in turn is ridden almost to death by her previous victim. I admire the element of justice in this tale.

The Ethiopian sorcerers are still believed to possess the power to transform themselves into virtually any animal – not just the expected jaguar, leopard and lion, but such dissimilar creatures as the elephant, the crocodile, the alligator, and even fish, the shark especially, the sea's equivalent of the wolf. Modern Greece has its were-boar tradition, while the Wallachians of southern Romania fear the were-dog, or *priccoltish*. The wizards on Indonesia's mountainous island of Celebes are said to possess great powers of animal metamorphosis, ranging from transformation into cats, wild pigs and crocodiles to buffaloes, deer and apes. Were-animals will exist, if only in popular folklore, for as long as man fears, esteems or generally honors the wild creature or creatures nearest to his own local habitat.

A were-boar being tormented by another of Satan's demoniac disciples. An engraving by the sixteenth-century French artist, James Callot of Nancy.

18 A Chamber of Global Horrors

ITH ALL OUR apparent sophistication, the bizarre primeval myth of the werewolf, as emphasized elsewhere in this book, has remained very much alive. It still conspires to stir many a poor soul in France, Germany, Scandinavia, the Slavic lands, and elsewhere, even if these days an element of incredulity may be in many people's minds. France remains the nerve-center for all things werewolfic, with an unbroken lineage from the dawn of history to the present day. You would find little difficulty, believe me, should you question local people, in unearthing many a fine werewolf story in the region of France lying between the Saône, the Loire and the upper Seine, and around Finistère, Côtes-du-Nord, Morbihan, Ille-et-Vilaine and Loire-Atlantique. The memory of the French countryman is amazing, and stories passed down from one generation to another, through many centuries, are to be found everywhere.

On a motoring holiday in France one year I stayed the night at a small farm just outside Guingamp, in the foothills of the Monts de Bretagne, and here my host related a marvelous werewolf tale from the Auvergne Mountains in the south of the country. Here, at the end of the sixteenth century, a gentleman was looking out one evening from a window of his château when he saw a hunter friend of his passing by. He asked the man to bring something back on his return from the hunting expedition. The hunter was subsequently attacked by an enormous wolf, and after a bitter battle with the beast he managed to cut off one of its fore-paws with his hunting-knife. On his way back to the château, and putting his hand into his game-bag to show the gentleman the wolf's paw, he drew out a human hand with a gold ring on one finger, which the gentleman at once recognized as his wife's. He immediately went to look for her, and found her sitting in the kitchen with one arm concealed under her apron, and on uncovering it he saw that the hand was gone and that she was nursing a bloody stump. The lady was later brought to trial, confessed that she was a werewolf, and was burnt at Ryon.

This is the country which produced the tyrannical High Court judge, Henry Boguet, who drew up a code in 1601 in which he stated that, while sorcerers should be first strangled and then burned, werewolves should be burned alive. The belief in werewolfery in France, as well as the theological animus against it, often led to "werewolf epidemics"; the people in a district, such as Lombardy, would become terrorized by the idea that all around them were *loups-garous*. In Normandy during the Middle Ages it was believed that any man who was excommunicated by the Church would become a werewolf for a period of between three and seven years; in Brittany, too, as late as the eighteenth century, a person who had not been to confession for ten years, nor used Holy Water, stood a good chance of becoming a werewolf.

One of France's most notorious "werewolf epidemics" occurred between 1764 and 1766 when half the country was terrorized by a terrible monster – or, as it was popularly called, the Wild Beast of Gévaudan. Six districts lived in daily fear of a wolf-monster which killed and consumed more than a hundred men, women and children; and not just solitary individuals, for even armed stage-coaches came under attack. "A detachment of dragoons has been out six weeks after him," reported the *London Magazine* in December, 1764. "The province has offered a thousand crowns to any persons that will kill him."

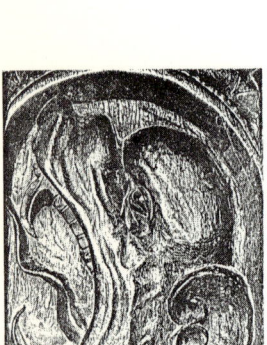

A werewolf's head carved into one of the pews in the ancient church of Cuiseaux, in the Saône-et-Loire, an area in east-central France with a grim werewolf tradition.

Its teeth were said to be formidable, its tail immense and lethal if it chose to strike a blow with it, and it could leap enormous heights and run "with supernatural speed." Its smell, we learn, was beyond description. Its fur was tinged with a reddish color. The people of Gévaudan were quite convinced that the beast was a sorcerer who had indulged in a wicked game of shape-shifting. An anonymous author of an eighteenth-century manuscript even gave the monster a scientific name, calling it *Lycopardus parthenophagus*. "Parthenophagy, or a peculiar delight in the flesh of girls," he writes, "is an enormity of the lycanthropes and not of wolves; from which we may infer in what light the people of the Gévaudan regarded that famous beast." Baron von Grimm, meantime, corresponding on April 1, 1765, informed a friend that "for several months now the *Gazette de France* has been chronicling exploits of a new kind, for it never misses to give us an extraordinary recital of this ferocious beast in the Gévaudan, and loudly praises the heroic and memorable feats of those who take the field against this monster."

The manner in which the beast attacked its victims – by tearing away the face with its razor-sharp teeth –

horrified the populace beyond belief and wherever it waged its bloody campaign its evil presence assumed that of the worst specter of the supernatural. After a unit of dragoons, under the command of Captain Jean Duhamel, had failed to track down the beast, the Church was called in. Public prayer for the safety of the community was led by the Bishop of Mende. Prayer did not help.

Yet its end, after dozens of terrible mutilations, was soon within view. During one of several hunts, on June 19, 1766, in the Forest of la Tenazière, where hundreds had assembled with guns, pitchforks and hatchets, the beast amazingly came within the gun-sights of a Monsieur Antoine. He could not believe his luck. The monster, catching sight of the man, lurched towards him in a demoniacal fury. M. Antoine took careful aim – and fired; the beast collapsed within a few feet of him, snorted and convulsed once or twice and then lay motionless. The beast, with the reddish tinge to its fur, was at an end. So, too, were the savage killings, which ceased from that happy day on. Whether or not the Beast of Gévaudan was a real wolf; whether or not more than one animal was involved in the war of terror . . . this is open to discussion. But to the local population, who were appalled by the creature's trail of depredation and superhuman savagery, it was quite simply a werewolf. Certainly no other wolf

Between 1764 and 1766 it was popularly believed that half of France was being terrorized by a grotesque werewolf monster – or the Wild Beast of Gévaudan – which was said to have killed and consumed more than a hundred men, women and children. But on June 19, 1766, it was eventually shot by a Monsieur Antoine, who can be seen on the left in the picture and on the right in the picture on page 224. One area of France slept peacefully that night.

Death of the Wild Beast of Gévaudan. This print, and the one on the previous page, dates from 1766.

story since then has so assuredly caught the imagination of the French man-in-the-street.

My investigations into the supernatural have, in the case of Germany, surprised me many times, for the Germans undoubtedly possess a very real affection – I might even say *a need* – for belief in the apparently incredulous. I have in front of me a letter from the distinguished director of the Lemgo town archives, Dr Hans Hoppe, in which he informs me: "I remember my father telling me that he was once told by a man that one evening he came across a friendly stray dog. The man stroked the dog for a few minutes when, quite suddenly, the dog started to grow bigger and bigger – and the man ran away in terror." Fantastic stories like this are frequently told in bier kellers and elsewhere throughout Germany. The werewolf is still high in the occult stakes, and the Germans still talk about the trial and execution of Peter Stump as if it was yesterday. One German told me an old tale of a farmer who was driving his wife through a wood in their cart when he suddenly stopped and got down, ordering his wife to drive on. He told her to throw her apron at any beast that might attack her. A few moments later she was savaged by a fierce wolf, which tore her apron to shreds, and then retreated into the woods. When her husband returned home she noticed some threads of her apron lodged between his teeth, and she instantly knew that all these years she had been married to a werewolf. This verbal story, like many another brought to my notice, must be read with the understanding that the gist of it is to be found in werewolf stories stemming from all over Germany and surrounding countries. Many are considerably embroidered.

North and East Germany provide the richest vein of werewolfic tales. It is said that in the village of Hindenburg (a part of Poland since 1945) there was a werewolf of such devastating strength that he could carry off a cow in his mouth. It seems he worried cattle and devoured human beings, but never harmed his wife because she could keep him at bay with magic words he had taught her for any eventuality of danger; then she used to unbuckle the belt he wore for purposes of transformation, and once again he was his old rational self.

Although accounts of female werewolves occur in many European countries, Germany has by far the most abundant crop. One of them concerns a farmer's wife in Hesse who used to serve fresh meat at every meal, although she would never tell her husband where she bought it. Eventually, unable to contain his curiosity any longer, he insisted that she should let him in on the secret. She agreed, but only on condition that, while she was doing so, he should not call her by her Christian name. So they went outside to find a field where sheep were feeding, and there the woman threw a ring over herself: instantly she was transformed into a wolf, and in no time at all she had a sheep in her mouth. The farmer was terrified; but when the shepherd and his dogs pursued the wolf, the danger in which the farmer saw his wife made him forget his promise, and he cried out, "Oh, Margaret!" With that word the wolf had vanished – and his wife stood naked in the field. (The reader will remember that calling out a werewolf's Christian name is one of several infallible ways of permitting the creature to resume its human form.)

Walter Kelly, a respected nineteenth-century folklorist, quotes three very different historical accounts in his *Curiosities of Indo-European Traditions and Folk-Lore* (1863) to illustrate the extent to which, during the second half of the nineteenth century, the werewolf superstition still sustained a firm grip on the German imagination:

> A sale was made, by order of the authorities, of a heap of old things that lay in a room in the Erichsburg. Among them were old implements of the chase which had been taken from poachers, and also some werewolf girdles (for purposes of transformation). The bailiff's assistant, having a mind to try the effect of the latter, buckled one of them on, was immediately turned into a wolf, and started off for Hunsrück. The bailiff rode after him and, cutting at his back with a sword, severed the girdle,

Germany's Harz Mountains, rich in spruce and firs, and situated between the Weser and Elbe rivers, once provided an attractive haven for werewolves. When they sought seclusion from their enemies – mostly the courts of law – they escaped to the Harz's series of terraced plateaus, rounded summits and narrow, deep valleys.

whereupon the man resumed his proper shape.

A man in the neighbourhood of Steina forgot to lock up his wolf-girdle, and it was later found by his little boy, who put it on and was transformed. He looked like a bundle of peastraw, and lumbered off with the clumsy gait of a bear. His father overtook him and unfastened the girdle before any mischief was done. The boy afterwards stated that the moment he put on the girdle he was seized with so ravenous a hunger that he could easily have devoured everything that came in his way.

Of all the German tales of werewolves, the most widely diffused is that of the mower, herdsman of horses, or charcoal-burner, who, believing that his two comrades are asleep in the meadow, fastens a strip of wolf-skin about him, becomes a wolf, and eats up a whole foal. All this has been observed by one of his comrades, and on the way home, when he complains of pain in his body, the man says "That is not to be wondered at, when a fellow has got a whole foal in his belly." "Had you said that to me yonder," replied the werewolf, "you would never have reached home again;" and with these words he vanished, never to return.

The Harz Mountains were formerly a favorite haunt of werewolves, where the monster was more dreaded than any other visitor from the Unknown. The Rhineland, too, with its dark woods and haunted castles and accompanying phantoms, has yielded many a savage werewolf. Fifty miles due west of the Rhine, in the forested Ardennes, the Belgian werewolf has also firmly made its bloody mark, while still further west, around the Sambre district, and along the beaches on the coast, werewolf stories come literally thick on the ground. The belief is still so strong in some rural districts that a great many country people in Belgium would not feel entirely safe from the werewolf's curse unless a mountain ash were growing only a matter of feet from their house.

According to German legends by the redoubtable Grimm Brothers, two sorcerers were executed at Liège in 1810 for having, in the form of werewolves, killed and eaten several children. In the neighboring Netherlands the werewolf has made much less impact, although there are one or two interesting facts to tell. Werewolves, for instance, according to the Dutch, are restricted almost entirely to the male sex; while in the north, in an area bounded by the Waddenzee and the Ijsselmeer, home of the famous Friesian breed of cattle, it is believed that when seven girls succeed each other in one family, that among them one will automatically be a werewolf. Consequently, young men of a superstitious frame of mind are wary of courting one of seven sisters.

Over a drink the Dutch still like to tell anyone who cares to listen about their most famous werewolf from the Hague, a certain burgomaster of Delft. A young man, Van Renner, was on his way to an archery contest when, in a thicket, he saw a large wolf spring from some bushes and bound towards a young girl sitting by the roadside. He wasted no time, and took aim and fired one of his arrows, which hit the beast on the right-hand side of its body, and it fled howling into the thicket. On his return home that evening a message was awaiting him: would he please visit his friend, the burgomaster. When he arrived at the household, he found his friend lying in bed at the point of death, suffering from a severe wound in his right side.

"I can't die without telling you," he whispered, clutching Van Renner by the hand. "God help me, I'm a werewolf! I've always been one. It's in my family – it's hereditary. It was your arrow that has wounded me fatally."

The burgomaster handed him the offending arrow. Van Renner felt utterly miserable with himself. He did not know what to say. "Don't say you hate me," cried the dying man. "There is little hope for me, if any, in the next world. In all probability I shall either go direct to Hell or remain earthbound; but, for God's sake, let me die in the knowledge that I leave behind me at least one friend!"

The burgomaster confessed that he, and his family before him, had devoured many little children. He died the following day. I have been told this story by several Dutch people, friends and drinking companions alike, and the details varied with each telling. In some versions it is not the burgomaster, but the burgomaster's servant who is the werewolf; in other tellings, Van Renner, to avoid being accused of murder, forces the dying man to confess that he was a werewolf. I have no doubt that *somewhere* here there is the germ of authenticity.

Across the English Channel, where the wolf was formerly man's most common enemy, werewolves certainly once existed, although for only a comparatively short time. When the Anglo-Saxon kings waged war on the wolf, drastically reducing its numbers to near-extinction, the people's principal terror ceased, and so very nearly did the werewolf superstition as it then existed. But the werewolf must have made some impact on the English, because the creature crops up in numerous old ballads and romances; such as—

> O was it *war-wolf* in the wood?
> Or was it mermaid in the sea?
> Or was it man, or vile woman,
>   My ain true love, that mis-shaped thee?

An English werewolf. From Boaistuau's *Histoires Prodieuses* (1597).

And Gervase of Tilbury, the thirteenth-century English churchman, who lived at a time when the final destruction of British wolves was not yet complete, explains that "We have frequently seen men in England transformed into wolves, for the space of a lunar month, and such people are called Gerulphs by the French, and werewolves by the English." England's King John, a contemporary of Gervase, was suspected of being a werewolf; such frightful noises were heard coming from his grave soon after his burial in Worcester Cathedral, before the high altar, that the pious monks dug up his body and (according to Gabriel de Moulin, writing in 1631) "flung the vile carcase, which had been embalmed by the Abbot of Croxton, out of the sanctuary and on to a tract of unconsecrated ground, where the king's blackened features were distorted in a hideous grin." After death he became a werewolf.

When wolves finally became extinct in England during the early sixteenth century, it became the fashion for sorcerers to change themselves into cats, weasels or harmless hares; in rural areas of Somerset and Devon, as late as the last century, witches were said to roam the moors in the shape of black dogs. Some medical experts, too, believe that the cases of cattle-maiming that still break out in England could be the result of attacks by mentally-deranged people who believe themselves to be wolves or some other fierce animal. Perhaps the lycanthrope still exists; perhaps a prolonged period of peace in the land merely stokes the dormant fires of the frustrated lycanthrope. But is it not strange that in a country once heavily populated by savage wolves that it should be so barren of convincing werewolf stories? Yet facts are facts, and from what few records are available it would seem that werewolfery was a branch of sorcery which simply wielded precious little fascination for Anglo-Saxon warlocks. Another possibility, as O'Donnell rightly observes, hinges on the temperament of the race itself: "The country folk in all parts of the British Isles are so sensitive to ridicule, and so suspicious of being 'got at,' that it is very difficult to extract any information from them with regard to the superphysical." The French and the German, on the other hand, *talk*!

The Welsh and the Irish do better in the way of werewolves than the English, and they also do rather better as talkers: of course, the Irish, like the French and the Italians, are great romantics, as any country which worships the leprechaun must be, and so their werewolf tradition is correspondingly strong and of immemorial antiquity. We saw earlier how certain inhabitants of sixth-century Ireland were transformed into wolves every seven years, and a Norse book (*Kongs Skuggsjo*) compiled in about 1250 explains that "when the holy Saint Patrick was preaching Christianity in Ireland, there was one great race more hostile to him than the other people . . . for it is said that all men who come from that race are always wolves at a certain time, and run into the woods and take food like wolves." Another thirteenth-century source, *The Wonders of Ireland*, reveals that "there are certain men of the Celtic race who have a marvellous power which comes to them from their forbears; for by an evil craft they can at will change themselves into the shape of wolves with sharp tearing teeth." But the seventeenth-century English historian, William Camden, writing of wolfmen in Tipperary, is little impressed by these tales and, in *Britannia* (1610), perceptively likens Irish werewolves to deluded lycanthropes: "that certain men in this tract are yearly turned into wolves I suppose to be a mere fable, unless they be possessed with the malady which engenders such fantasies that they *imagine* themselves to be transformed into wolves."

Irish werewolf stories flourished well into the nineteenth century, and this can be explained by the fact that the wolf survived in Ireland later than in any other part of the British Isles. In England it was extinct by about 1530, in Wales by 1576, and in Scotland sometime in the fourth decade of the eighteenth century; but in Ireland (according to *The Irish Penny Journal* for 1841) a wolf was killed in the Wicklow Mountains as late as 1770.

In Wales, my place of birth, I have visited many of the spots where, according to local tradition, werewolves once flourished, including those in my own county, Breconshire. Here, in Mynydd Eppynt (Epynt Hills) and the high plateau of the Black Mountains, the Brecon Beacons, the werewolf formerly reigned supreme. Here, too, St Patrick turned the Welsh king, Vereticus, into a wolf; while in nearby Radnor the werewolf daughter of a Welsh prince waged war against her father's enemies. Some people believe that werewolfery may still exist in the more desolate areas of Wales, although I can find no evidence to support the idea.

While Scotland is rich in stories of cannibalism, through many centuries, actual werewolfic transformations have been rare, although (according to *Chronicles of Scotland*, published in 1814) a certain late-eighteenth-century werewolf, named Saunderson, is said to have lived in a cave at the foot of Ben Macdhui – "a mon with evil, leerie eyes, and eyebrows that met in a point over his nose." His forefathers were also suspected of being werewolves; and on Saunderson's death, visitors to his cave found a quantity of "queer bones," some human and some belonging to wolves.

Those other ancient Celts, the Italians, especially those from the north, have given us some of the earliest and most colorful of all werewolf stories, and we have already heard the well-known werewolf episode from the *Satyricon*. In general, the transformation of men into wolves is treated by Roman literature purely as a work of magic; Virgil (in the Eighth Eclogue, the *Pharmaceutria*) is the first to mention it ("These herbs and these poisons, culled in Pontus, Moeris himself gave me – they grow plenteously in Pontus – and by their aid I have oft seen Moeris turn wolf and hide in the woods, oft call spirits from the depth of the grave, and charm sown corn away to other

fields . . ."), followed by Propertius, Petronius, and Apuleius. But belief in the superstition largely faded with the decline of the Roman Empire itself, and apart from a few accounts in the eleventh and twelfth centuries, and the solitary incident of the Paduan lycanthrope of 1541, the Italian werewolf is virtually dead – which is odd, to say the least, bearing in mind that the wolf maintains its supremacy as a feared predator along the isolated mountain ranges of central Italy.

Equally inexplicable is the fact that, despite the wolf's frequency of attacks on human life in Spain, the werewolf is little known there, and then confined (as you might expect) to the mountainous regions. I have been able to locate only one authenticated account of a Spanish werewolf, and that from the Pyrenees in 1853. He was a man by the name of Juan de Nurrez, whose wife Isabelle provided him with suitable victims by luring them to a lair in the mountains. In adjoining Portugal the werewolf has not been heard of since the fifteenth century, although its place is taken by the curious *lobis-homem*, a timid creature with a short yellow tail; it labors under the charm of the wolf, whose shape it assumes, although it differs from the werewolf in that it is shy and wishes to do no harm.

At the other end of the Mediterranean, in the Balkan countries bordering the Adriatic and Aegean Seas, the werewolf begins to come back into its own. Greece, earliest home of lycanthropy, remains strong in werewolfic superstition; nearby Turkey is weak in it, although in the year 1542 the streets and lanes of Istanbul (then Constantinople) were apparently so overrun with werewolves that Sultan Suleiman II the Magnificent led an attack against them, killing at least a hundred and fifty of these monsters. Nearly six hundred years earlier, Prince Bajanus, son of Simeon, Emperor of the Romans and Bulgars, was credited with magic power; with the aid of the Devil he could turn himself into a wolf – or, indeed, into any other beast – as often as he chose. And in Romania, legend has it, a man nightly transformed himself into the form of a dog and roamed the countryside, killing and devouring horses, cows, sheep, swine and goats, as a consequence of which he appeared to be in "continual rude health and vigor."

The Welsh priest-historian, Giraldus Cambrensis (1147–1220), tells in *Topographia Hibernica* of a Celtic priest who was met by a wolf in Meath and asked to give his dying she-wolf wife the sacrament. By turning down her skin a little, the husband then revealed that she was in reality an old woman. An eighteenth-century engraving of the tale.

Lily-of-the-valley.

Azalea

In the Transylvanian Alps, and the mountainous regions of Hungary, Austria, Czechoslovakia and the Balkan Peninsula, local folklore has it that if certain flowers are picked and worn, the wearer will be transformed into a werewolf. (Universal's 1935 movie, *The Werewolf of London*, adopted this superstition in reverse – the plant *cured* a werewolf of its curse – although the locale was transferred to the mountains of Tibet, where the plant in question, the so-called *Marifesa lupina*, bloomed only in the moonlight.) These flowers (according to O'Donnell) are variously white or yellow and the same shape and size as a snap-dragon; or red, similar to an ox-eyed daisy, and they all "have the same peculiar vividness of colour, the same thick, sticky sap, and the same sickly, faint odour." Hungarian and Romanian lilies-of-the-valley, marigolds and azaleas, as well as diamonds, are also supposed to attract werewolves, "thus proving a source of danger to those who wear them." These lovely flowers, alas, will now never be quite the same again

If werewolf stories are numerous in Hungary, they are positively commonplace in Poland; the Poles, like the Irish, assail you with their blarney, and my own experience shows that when it comes to a good werewolf yarn the Poles, of all the East European *bloc*, cannot be surpassed. Here there are traces of the old belief that werewolves were bound to assume that form twice a year, at Christmas and at midsummer; in later legends the *wilkolak*, or werewolf, is generally the victim of a spiteful sorceress's vengeance. A Pole recently told me of a peasant who, having been a wolf for seven years, was permitted by the witch who had transformed him to resume his natural shape. Although hungry and without clothes, he walked the whole day to reach his home where he had left his wife and children. He arrived at his hut late at night, and knocked on the door.

"Who is there?" demanded a voice from within; and the peasant at once recognized it as that of his wife.

"It is I – your husband. Open the door, quick!"

"Heaven help us!" cried the terrified woman. "Here, husband, get up!"

The wondering peasant soon saw before him his former servant, who, having married his wife, had come into all his property. The new husband rushed out of the hut armed with a pitchfork, determined to drive away its rightful owner. The unhappy man-wolf, exasperated at his wife's inconstancy, cried out in anguish –

"Oh, that I were again a wolf, so that I might punish my faithless wife, and never feel my misery!"

His wish was instantly granted, and once again he was

transformed into a wolf. Maddened with rage, he attacked his wife, who stood by holding a child of the second marriage in her arms. He pulled her down to the ground, devoured the child, and revenged himself upon its mother by mangling her body in a terrible manner.

At the cries of the wounded woman the neighbors ran to her assistance and set upon the furious animal. The wolf was unable to defend itself for long and soon fell beneath the repeated blows of his attackers. When the peasants, shouting with joy at their victory, began to examine the creature by the light of the burning pine splinters, they found to their surprise and horror that, instead of a wolf, they had killed their country-man who, seven years earlier, had been assumed lost and changed into a wolf. They tried to restore him, but it was too late. While they were lamenting his unhappy end, the faithless wife died of the wounds she had received.

In the Soviet Union, the Caucasus and Ural Mountains are to the Eastern werewolf what the Harz and Jura Mountains are to those in the West: a focal-point of weird psychic phenomena, where, writes Elliott O'Donnell

> ... all the primitive conditions favourable to such anomalies, still exist, and where they have undergone but little change in the last ten thousand years. Here, at night, werewolves wander over the rough, stony, arid ground, picking their way surreptitiously through the scant vegetation, and avoiding all frequented localities; pausing, every now and then, to slake their thirst in deep-sunk wells, or to listen for the sounds of quarry ... nothing is so heartily appreciated by werewolves as fat tender children and plump women.

There was once a Russian prince who, hearing that a shape-shifting warlock was in the area, ordered him to go through his feats of transformation. The enchanter disappeared into a small room, crouched down, muttered some incantations and presently assumed the form of a wolf, grinning with his open jaws, glaring with his eyes, and raging so fiercely that the guards had to restrain him. But the prince played a dirty trick and set two large hounds upon him, which tore the wretched man-wolf to pieces.

An interesting story of Armenian werewolfery is told by August von Haxthausen in his *Transcaucasia* (1854):

> A man once saw a wolf, which had carried off a child, dash past him. He pursued it hastily, but was unable to overtake it. At last he came upon the hands and feet of a child, and a little further on he found a cave, in which

lay a wolfskin. This he cast into a fire, and immediately a woman appeared, who howled and tried to rescue the skin from the flames. The man, however, resisted, and, as soon as the hide was consumed, the woman had vanished in the smoke.

Such tales are told frequently throughout the vast Soviet *bloc*, enough to fill a book. The Russians, as well as the Finns and Lapps, are also held by their Swedish neighbors to be very potent wizards, with the power to change people into wild beasts. In the last war between Sweden and Russia, when the province of Kalmar was overrun with wolves, it was generally believed that the Russians had turned the Swedish prisoners into wolves, and sent them home to ravage their own country. One such Swede, a soldier in the Kalmar regiment, having been transformed into a wolf, made his way back from Finland in order to see his wife and children again. But on the journey he was shot by a hunter, who brought the dead wolf into the village; and when it was flayed a shirt was found beneath the wolf's skin, which was later recognized by the soldier's wife as one she had made for her husband before he went to war.

Not surprisingly, Lapland and Finland – like the North in general – literally teem with stories of werewolves. The curse is said to be both hereditary and acquired through spells and black magic, and some streams are reputed to be lycanthropous. We have already covered at some length the werewolves of Scandinavia, the true home of lycanthropy. Tales of werewolves still exist in the remoter parts of these countries, although tourism and the opening up of once uninhabitable tracts of land seem to have put a halt to stories of modern werewolves. But in Sweden the influence of *vargamors* – old women who live in the forests, keeping complete control over all the wolves – is as strong as ever; and, because the *vargamors*' job is to keep the wolves well supplied with food, preferably human, they are closely associated with werewolves. Another werewolf variation exists in Norway, where it is believed there are people who can assume the form of a wolf, and then their own again, with the help of the Troll-men. Those possessing the property naturally are the true Trolls: they are said to be *eigi einhamir* ("not of one form"). Similar, and very special to Norway and the North, are the berserkers.

Across the Atlantic, the werewolf is most commonly met among the North American Indians, although in South America it is replaced by were-animals in general. There are also, among the North American Indians, secret societies of wolfmen. "The Nooktas relate that wolves once took away a chief's son," explains anthropologist Robert Eisler in *Man into Wolf*. "They became his friends and ordered him on his return home to initiate the other young men into the society, the rites of which they taught him. In the ceremony a pack of 'wolves', that is, men with wolf masks, appears and carries off the novice; next day they bring him back apparently dead (presumably drugged) and the society has to revive him." A similar recruiting system is practiced by the African leopard-men, as we have seen in the chapter on were-animals; and an account from *Traditions of the North American Indians*, published in 1830, illustrates a belief in animal transformation among the ethnic peoples which resembles in many respects a shape-shifting superstition we find the world over.

When the Vikings crossed the oceans and, antedating Columbus, reached North America, they naturally brought with them their belief in werewolves. Although the traditions, legends and superstitions of North America were then not properly formed, we can be certain that among the earliest notions to strike a common chord was a belief in, and a fear of, the wolf-demon. The wolf was common and pretty well evenly distributed throughout the North American continent, although it was known only in its natural shape and condition, for the inhabitants were not yet in the habit of supposing that, as in Europe and other countries, the fiercest wolves were men, transformed by magic into that shape for the purpose of devouring their fellows, or, at least, their flocks and herds. The marauding Vikings and, later, the European settlers, changed all that: first the Indian tribes were influenced by the proposition that a man could be transformed into the animal he feared most, the wolf; and then the white man, hearing about the strange stories of wolf-men among the Indians, and relating it to those he had heard from European superstition, slowly formulated his own werewolf "tradition". They were not as frequent, or as convincing, as those from across the ocean, mainly because they came late, at a time when people were more enlightened and less gullible than was the case with their European counterparts. Neighboring Canada was equally affected, although, because many French people settled there, the creature became known by the name *loup-garou*.

Late the werewolf may have been in making its fiendish impact in North America. Yet once the country had adopted the superstition, it could never again be accused of ignoring it: cinematically at least America put the werewolf firmly on the international map.

19 Fact or Fancy?

HETHER IT STEMS from black magic, cannibalism, insanity, low intellect, gullibility, sadism, curse, inebriation, susceptibility, fantasy, rabies, astral projection or sheer stupidity, the werewolf superstition has endured thousands of years. What is the power that has energized its survival well into the twentieth century? If it is so much nonsense, why should learned men of science and medicine in all ages have been interested in it? Can hokum, pure and unadulterated hokum, live on puerile fantasy alone? A friend of mine, a man of mathematics and therefore a man who requires a clean scientific solution to every problem, said to me when I was halfway through writing this book: "I appreciate everything you've just told me about the werewolf – but I'm sorry, I can't take it seriously." I could, and still do, understand that sentiment (although I hope after I have presented him with a copy of this book he may think differently).

The werewolf is so complex a creature, and it can be discussed on so many levels, that it defies simple definition. It invites protracted analysis. You cannot "convince" people in a few sentences of the possibility of the existence, past or present, of the werewolf. Give me an hour and perhaps, just perhaps, I might do so. The question I still hate being asked is, "*Are* there such things as werewolves?" I wish I could think of an easy answer, but there isn't one. Well, there is one – "Yes, I believe so" – but that will not satisfy the curious and certainly not the persistent. "How can you prove it?" I am then asked. And so I am back with the old problem, and therefore my reply must be: "Have you got a couple of hours to spare . . . ?" Not a very satisfactory response, I know. If ever a subject required serious, studied reflection on the printed page, it is the werewolf delusion.

You have now heard the story. One of the great enigmas of all time. Do you believe it, or disbelieve it? You now have most of the facts . . . and some of the fancy. Space and time for my own argument has run out. But this much I ask: keep an open mind.

The mystery is now *yours*. . . .

Appendix: What's in a Name?

A facsimile of the first seven lines of the fourteenth-century English translation (from the original twelfth-century French) of *The Romance of William and the Werewolf*. The manuscript, which is housed in the library of King's College, Cambridge, is arranged in single columns of 36 lines to a page, and the writing is in a remarkably distinct but rather thick and inelegant script – as can be seen here – with small blue and red initials.

TRYING TO UNRAVEL the mystery of the term "werewolf" is a task fraught with danger. Even the clever word-smiths, the etymologists, find immense difficulty in agreeing on anything connected with the word. They go as far as to question its most commonly held meaning – that is, that *werewolf* = *man-wolf*, *were* meaning "man." And the French equivalent – *loup-garou* – is debated with some relish. *Loup*, meaning "wolf," is clear enough; but since *garou* is a Gallic corruption of *wehrwolf*, it follows that *loup-garou* is a tautological expression.

The first authenticated use of the word werewolf appears in *Otia Imperialia*, by Gervase of Tilbury, in about 1212, although in the form *werewolf* = *man-wolf*. A little more than a century later, in the poem *William of Palermo* – now better known as *The Romance of William and the Werewolf*, after being translated from the French twelfth-century original at the command of Sir Humphrey de Bohum – we find the word *werewolf* referred to frequently throughout the text.

Richard Rowlands, in his *A Restitution of Decayed Intelligence*, published in 1605, tells us: "*Were* our ancestors vsed somtyme in steed of *Man* yet should it seeme that *were* was moste commonly taken for a maried man. But the name of *man* is now more knoun and more generally vsed in the whole Teutonic toung then the name of *Were*.

"*Were-wulf*. This name remaineth stil knoun in the Teutonic, & is as much to say as *man-wolf*, the greeks expressing the very lyke, in *Lycanthropos*.

"*Ortelius* [Abraham Ortell, the sixteenth-century Flemish scholar and geographer] not knowing what *were* signified, because in the *Netherlands* it is now clean out of vse, except thus composed with *wolf*, doth misinterpret it according to his fancie."

But Ortelius was not alone – and is still not alone – in misinterpreting the prefix *were* according to his fancy. In fact the prefix "were" in the word werewolf has caused mythologists before me many sleepless nights: *Wer*, or *wera*, a man, being the same as the Gothic *wair*, Teutonic *wer*, Francic *uuara*, Celtic *gur*, *gŵr* or *ur*, Irish *fair*, Latin *vir*, Icelandic *verr*, old Prussian *wirs*, Persian *vîra*, Balto-Slavonic *wîrs*, Sanskrit *vîra*, Bengali *bîr*, etc. Oskar Schrade, in his *Altdeutsches Wörterbuch* (1872–82), uses the prefix *wër*. But, most significant of all, is the West Frisian *waer*, as in *waerûl* and (in a modified form) *waerwulf*, the latter derived from the Middle Dutch (and Modern) *weerwolf*.

Waer is of special interest when applied to the term werewolf, because of its two quite distinct connotations. In Anglo-Saxon, it is true, the word *waer* (or *wær*) means "a man"; but, in the same tongue, *waer* also means "war": waer-boda, a herald or war-declarer; waered and werod, an army; werian, to destroy; werig, cruel, hostile. *Were*, as already noted by Rowlands, was most commonly used by the Saxons for "a married man" – that is, a man of an age to kill one man and procreate another in his place. *Weren*, defendere, is the parent verb of *wer*. It soon came to signify all acts of warlike violence, both defensive and offensive ("There must you draw your swerde of were"). By a second transition the word passes into all the bad consequences of hostility and violence. Waergian is to cure; waergad, accursed. *Were* is trouble, uneasiness, sorrow. *Wer* in German became a word of evil and deprecation – immensely suitable as a prefix to a man-turned-wolf whose deeds were foul and loathsome, but signifying "evil-wolf" rather than "man-wolf."

But, to confuse the issue, in other dialects the combination of *waer* (or *wehr*) and *wolf* can mean something other than "evil-wolf" and "man-wolf" (or "wolfman"). Glance at the pedigree below:

```
                          A 1 waeren, defend
                                 ↓
       B waer, defensive hostilities    2 waer, defender
                      ↓
           C waer, any hostility    3 waer, a man adult and able-bodied
                      ↓
D waer, any violence, injury or contention    4 waer, a man
                      ↓
   E waer, all evil of condition, whatsoever
```

This is based on the family of words already described and stems from the original terms, their compounds and derivatives. This procession of ideas may be authenticated out of the leading dialect of High Dutch or German. In this dialect, *wehren* is to defend, to oppose, to *ward* off or repulse; and *wehrung* is defense, resistance. So a *wehr-man* is someone who maintains, renders safe and sure, or *warrants*, anything. *Wehr* is rampart or barrier of defense. *Wehr-wolf*, then, would have a quite different meaning to that with which it is commonly associated.

This pedigree, therefore, illustrates that there are two *waers* – and it does not really help us to know that etymologists cannot make up their minds as to whether *werewolf/waer-wolf* is derived from letters C and D or from number 4. So we take our choice: *waer* (*wer*, *were*, *wër*, *wehr*) can mean either a man or an act of war or evil. My definition would be a marriage of the two meanings: "evil man."

So this is how I would arrive at the real and, I hope, most accurate meaning of werewolf –

Evil + Man + Wolf
↓
Evil Wolfman
↓
Werewolf

One etymologist, Ernest Weekley, having informed us that *were* died out in early Middle English, then offers an interesting clue in his *More Words Ancient and Modern* (1927). "The disappearance of the simple *were*," he writes, "led Middle English writers to explain the first syllable as *ware*, and, as late as 1576, Turberville tells us, 'Such wolves are called "warwolves," bicause a man had neede to be ware of them.'"

Another interesting *phonetic* derivation of werewolf is mentioned in the famous *Discourse of Witchcraft as it was acted in the Family of Mr Edward Fairfax* (1621). It occurs in the passage: "Above all [the transformation of] the Leucanthopoi is most miraculous . . . which Witches that people do call *weary wolves*."

After "werewolf," which is the spelling I have chosen as the most suitable for general use, the French *loup-garou* is the form most popularly used as an alternative. The seventeenth-century English lexicographer, Randle Cotgrave, defines *loup-garou* as "A mankind Wolfe; such a one as once being flesht on men, and children will rather starue than feed on any thing else; also, one that, possessed with an extreame and strange melancholie, beleuues he is turned Wolfe, and as a Wolfe behaues himselfe."

There seems to be almost as many variations of the word *loup-garou* as there is of werewolf. The ones I have

France's nineteenth-century wolf-charmer, the *Meneur des Loups*, who would sometimes take the form of a wolf. An 1858 painting by Maurice Sand.

most frequently come across, in differing dialects, are *loup-garoun, loup-carou, louparou, loup-paumè, loup-berou, loubérou, leberou* and *garuló*. In two old French provinces, Limousin and Dauphiné, a werewolf is *leberoun* and *lamiaro*, respectively. I have also seen a werewolf described as *brouch*, and sometimes as *borouch*, although this is normally used to denote a wizard or sorcerer.

In many parts of France during the last century there was a well-known figure, said to be a wizard, known as the *Meneur des Loups*, who, when the werewolves of the district had met and were sitting together in a hideous circle around a fire in the heart of some forest, would charm the howling pack and encourage them to do their foulest deeds. Sometimes he himself would assume the shape of a wolf, although he would speak with a human voice.

Writing in 1858, the French novelist George Sand explains: "I know several persons who, at the first faint rising of the new moon, have met near the carfax of the Croix-Blanche old Soupison, nicknamed *Démmonet*, walking swiftly along with great giant strides followed in silence by more than thirty wolves." Her son, Maurice Sand, painted such a scene (see above).

The *loup-garou* of the French is known in Italy as the *lupo manaro* or *versiero*. The *lupo manaro* of the Middle Ages was a witch dressed as a wolf; but the same term was also associated with a certain hobgoblin who was peculiar to the city of Blois and whose chief occupation seems to have been to inspire deadly fear in young children.

241

In every country where tales of the werewolf exist, there is an appropriate word to describe it. Sometimes, as in France and Italy and other nations, several regions within one country may each have their own individual names for the creature: the Norse *vargulfr* (literally "rogue wolf"), the Norwegian and Swedish *varulf* (which may be connected with an Old Norman *varulf*), the Danish *vaerulf*, the Icelandic *varg-úlfr* (literally a "worrying wolf"), the Sicilian *lupu-minaru* (one of at least ten dialects), the Portuguese *lobis-homem*, *lycanthropo* or *lobarraz*, the Spanish *lobombre*, the Greek λυκάνθρωπος or *vrykolakas*, the Bulgarian *vulkolak* (in ancient Bulgarian it is *vlukodlak*, meaning literally "wolf-haired" or "wolf-skinned"), the Polish *wilkolak*, the Serbian *vulkodlak* or *vlkoslak* (the Serbs connect the vampire and the werewolf together and call them by either of these two names; the Greek werewolf is also closely related to the vampire), the Czech and Slovak *vlkodlak* (a term they also call a drunkard, because he makes a beast of himself), the White Russian *volkolak*, the Russian *volkulaku* (prior to the 1860s it was *oborot*, meaning "one transformed"), the Romanian *vęlkolak* or *vęrkolak*, the Albanian *vurvolak*, the Lithuanian *vilkakis*, and the Latin *versipellis* (literally "changing one's skin"; hence "changing one's form"). A formidable list.

Further Reading

Three monographs in particular are an invaluable source of reference to the student of werewolfery:

Baring-Gould, Sabine: *The Book of Were-Wolves.* London, 1865.
O'Donnell, Elliott: *Werwolves.* London, 1912.
Summers, Montague: *The Werewolf.* London, 1933.

The werewolf-theme in literature is discussed at length elsewhere in these pages. A necessarily selected list of non-fiction works on the subject includes:

Beauvoys de Chauvincourt, Le Sieur de: *Discours de la Lycanthropie ou de la transformation des hommes en loups.* Paris, 1599.
Black, George F.: *A List of Works Relating to Lycanthropy.* New York, 1920.
Bodin, Jean: *De la Démonomanie des Sorciers.* Paris, 1580.
Boguet, Henry: *Discours des Sorciers.* Lyon, 1590. English translation: *An Examen of Witches.* London, 1929.
Burton, Robert: *The Anatomy of Melancholy.* London, 1621.
Eisler, Robert: *Man into Wolf.* London, 1951.
Fischer, Wilhelm: *Dämonische Mittelwersen Vampir und Werwolf in Geschichte und Sage.* Stuttgart, 1906.
Hamel, Frank: *Human Animals.* London, 1915.
Hertz, Wilhelm: *Der Werwolf.* Stuttgart, 1862.
Lancre, Pierre de: *L'incredulité et mescréance du sortilège plainement convaincue.* Paris, 1622.
Lauben, Theophilus: *Dialogi und Gespräche von der lycanthropia oder der Menschen in Wölff Verwandlung.* Frankfurt, 1686.
Leadbeater, C. W.: *The Astral Plane.* London, 1895; reprinted many times to the present day.
Leubuscher, Rudolph: *Über die Wehrwölfe und Thieverwandlungen im Mittelalter.* Berlin, 1850.
Levi, Eliphas: *Mysteries of Magic.* London, 1897.
Loyer, Pierre le: *Discours des Spectres, ou Visions et Apparitions d'Esprits, comme Anges, Demons, et Ames, se monstrans visibles aux hommes.* Paris, 1608.
McNeil, Elton B.: *The Psychoses.* New Jersey, 1970.
Malleus Maleficarum (English translation by Montague Summers). London, 1928.

Métraux, Alfred: *Voodoo in Haiti.* London, 1959.
Mei, Michael: *De Lycanthropia.* Witteburgae, 1654.
Müller, Jacobus Fridericus: *De transmutatione hominum in lupos.* Lipsiae, 1673.
Nynauld, Jean de: *De La Lycanthropie, Transformation, et Extase des Sorciers.* Paris, 1615.
Prieur, Claude: *Dialogue de la Lycanthropie.* Louvain, 1596.
Stewart, Caroline Taylor: *The Origin of the Werewolf Superstition.* Missouri, 1909.
Wantscherus, Christopherus: *De lupo et lycanthropia.* Witteburgae, 1666.
Wolfeshusius, Joannes Fridericus: *De Lycanthropis.* Lipsiae, 1591.

Title page of Claude Prieur's *Dialogue de la Lycanthropie* (1596). Prieur, a perceptive Franciscan of the Louvain house, quotes several doctors, philosophers and a saint or two to demonstrate that "there cannot be a corporeal transformation, whether wrought by an enchanted girdle or unguents or by any means whatsoever."

Picture Credits

The author and publishers wish to thank the following for permission to reproduce illustrations on the pages indicated:

A.&B.C. Chewing Gum Ltd., England. Photograph: Zenka Woodward Picture Library: 206 (bottom)
Acorn Photographics, England: 129
Aldus Books Ltd., England: 118, 119
Ampliaciones y Reproducciones Mas, Spain: 86
Antikvarisk-Topografiska Arkivet (ATA), Sweden: 123 (bottom)
Associated Newspapers Ltd., England: 61
Associated Press, England: 41
Alan Austin, Fantasy Unlimited, England: 66
The Bettmann Archive, Inc., USA: 196 (bottom)
Bibliothèque Nationale, France: 65
Bildarchiv Preussischer Kulturbesitz, West Germany: 111 (top)
Die Brandwag, South Africa: 22, 184 (bottom)
Bristol Old Vic, England. Photograph: Derek Balmer: 187
The British Library, England: 19, 59, 90, 92, 93, 97, 106, 170, 177, 178, 181, 184 (top), 185, 186 (center and bottom), 188, 209, 245
Trustees of the British Museum, England: 214
Charlton Publications, Inc., USA: 127, 159
Jean-Loup Charmet, France: 16, 71, 77, 78, 95, 183, 211, 212–213
Columbia Pictures, USA: 199 (top)
Daily Express, England: 35
Daily Mail, England: 23, 29
Walt Disney Productions, USA: 38
Mary Evans Picture Library, England: 54, 73, 82, 148 (bottom), 160, 215
Fantasy Fiction, USA: 67 (center)
Farrar & Rinehart, USA: 175
Harpdown Ltd., England: 206 (center left)
Harper's Monthly Magazine, USA: 165
John Hillelson Agency Ltd., England: 27
The Mansell Collection, England: 43, 76, 81, 84, 89, 110 (bottom), 154, 226, 231
Marvel Comics Group, USA: 207 (bottom)
The Monster Times, USA: 205, 206 (top)
Morning Star, England: 34
J. Müller, State Veterinary Serum Laboratory, Copenhagen, Denmark. Photograph by Bjørn Gierløff: 163
National Film Archive, England, and American International Pictures, Inc., USA: 201 (top)

247

National Museum of Wales: 33
Picture Collection, Newark Public Library, USA: 21, 228
La Palatine, France and Switzerland: 222
Pan Books Ltd., England, from Carey Miller's *A Dictionary of Monsters and Mysterious Beasts* (1974): 147
Plata Films, Spain: 202
Popperfoto, England: 145
Radio Times Hulton Picture Library, England: 18, 32, 70, 74, 83, 85, 123 (top), 137, 142, 153, 218
H. Roger-Viollet, France: 47, 53, 223, 224
Ann Ronan Picture Library, England: 172
Roy Publishers, Inc., USA: 179
Royal, Germany: 199 (bottom)
Smiths Food Group, England. Photograph: Zenka Woodward Picture Library: 207 (top right)
Staats- und Stadtbibliothek, Augsburg, West Germany: 104–105, 132, 219
Sunday Express, England: 28
Theatre Workshop at the Theatre Royal, England. Photograph: Malcolm Goy: 189
Charles C. Thomas, publisher, Springfield, Illinois, USA, from *Diseases of Porphyrin Metabolism* (1962) by A. Goldberg and C. Rimington: 50
Tyburn Film Productions Ltd., England: 116, 117 (bottom left and right), 200
Ullstein GmbH: Bilderdienst, West Germany: 88
Universal Pictures, USA: 67 (top), 192, 193, 195, 196 (top), 197, 198
Universitätsbibliothek, Erlangen-Nürnberg, West Germany: 110 (top), 111 (center and bottom)
Brent Walker Film Distributors Ltd., England: 26
Weird Tales, USA: 25, 148–149 (top), 157, 158, 186 (top)
The Windsor Magazine, England: 166
Zenka Woodward Picture Library, England: 15, 20, 31, 62, 91, 99, 103, 114, 115, 117 (top), 124, 135, 143, 171, 206 (center right), 207 (top left), 220, 232, 241

Acknowledgments

An author who elects to embark on so vast an investigative canvas as werewolfery must by necessity call on the specialist expertise of many people. In this respect, much invaluable groundwork has been provided by Montague Summers, Elliott O'Donnell and Sabine Baring-Gould in their respective books, *The Werewolf* (1933), *Werwolves* (1912) and *The Book of Were-Wolves* (1865); my debt to them cannot be over-emphasized. I have also called on the help of museums, galleries, libraries, universities, archives and collections of institutions and individuals all over the world; and although it would be impossible to name them all here, my gratitude to them is nonetheless immense. Yet I must single out the respective staffs of the New York Public Library and of the Reading Room of the British Library in London, where so much of this book was researched and written; the British Library, particularly, helped enormously in my search for pictorial documentation. For valuable assistance with historical and illustrative research I am also indebted to Walter Grantham, assistant chief, Social Sciences and History Division, the Chicago Public Library; J. A. Bateman, keeper of zoology, the National Museum of Wales; Margaret F. Sax, assistant curator, the Watkinson Library, Trinity College, Hartford, Connecticut; the Library of the Museum of Ethnology, Berlin; David Easson and the Social Sciences Department of the Metropolitan Toronto Library, Toronto; Dr György Pajkossy, head of the Department of Printed Books and Periodicals, the National Széchényi Library, Budapest; the Staatsliches Museum für Völkerkunde, Munich; the Biblioteca Nacional, Lisbon; the Carnavallet Museum, Paris; the Bibliothèque Nationale, Paris; the Nordiska Museet, Stockholm; the State Archives Museum, Bucharest; and William J. Dane, supervising librarian of the Art and Music Department of the Newark Public Library, New Jersey (the latter for two important discoveries – the illustration of the English werewolf on page 228 and the werewolf from the medieval bestiary on page 21). For assistance in helping to track down a number of obscure werewolf cases I am greatly obliged to Dr Bernhard Schemmel and Dr Wilhelm Schleicher of the Bamberg Staatsbibliothek; Prof Dr Wendehorst of Erlangen-Nürnberg University; and Dr Hans Hoppe, director of the State and Town Archives of Lemgo. In Denmark, J. Müller of the State Veterinary Serum Laboratory, Copenhagen, kindly placed at my disposal a series of photographic negatives produced in conjunction with research on rabid animals; one of these appears on page 163. My thanks must also be extended to the Royal Society of Medicine, London, for furnishing me with research material on congenital porphyria; to Atlas Translations for coping so admirably with the bulk of my foreign-language translations; to the Incorporated Society for Physical Research, London, for much help; and to Peter Haining, author of *Terror!* (1976), for providing the lead to a number of illustrations. For permission to quote copyright texts I wish to acknowledge: the Hamlyn Group (publisher of Robert Eisler's *Man into Wolf*, 1951); Routledge & Kegan Paul Ltd. (Montague Summers' *The Werewolf*, 1933); A. P. Watt Ltd. (Richard Cavendish's *The Powers of Evil*, published in 1975 by Routledge & Kegan Paul Ltd.); David & Charles Ltd. (Geoffrey P. West's *Rabies: In Animals and Man*, 1972); Octopus Books Ltd. (*The Occult and the Supernatural*, 1975); Curtis Brown Ltd. (Pierre van Paassen's *Days of Our Years*, published in 1939 by William Heinemann Ltd.); Associated Book Publishers Ltd. (Thomas Freeman's *Psychopathology of the Psychoses*, published in 1969 by Tavistock Publications Ltd.; and Elliott O'Donnell's *Werwolves*, published in 1912 by Methuen & Co. Ltd.); Oxford University Press (Colin Kaplan's *Rabies: The Facts*, © Oxford University Press, 1977, by permission of the Oxford University Press); André Deutsch Ltd. and Schocken Books, Inc. (Alfred Métraux's *Voodoo in Haiti*, 1959, reprinted by permission of the respective publishers, © 1959 by Alfred Métraux); Prentice-Hall, Inc. (Elton B. McNeil's *The Psychoses*, 1970); the American Folklore Society (Dr Nandor Fodor's "Lycanthropy as a Psychic Mechanism," from *The Journal of American Folklore*, Vol. 58, 1945); Brunner-Mazel, Inc. (John G. Howells' *World History of Psychiatry*, 1975); Farrar, Strauss & Giroux, Inc. (Guy Endore's *The Werewolf of Paris*, 1933). Every effort has been made to trace the owners of copyrights, but I take this opportunity of tendering apologies to any owners whose rights may have been unwittingly infringed. I also wish to thank: Rose Gladden for answering so many of my questions on exorcism and on more technical matters concerning materialization and astral projection; and Margaret Wilkinson for typing the manuscript with such skill and fortitude. Finally, and most important of all, my gratitude to all at Paddington Press for making the whole thing possible: to John and Janet Marqusee for their faith in the project, to Sandra Shafee for her superb-layouts and designs, and to Catherine Carpenter for her creative editorial assistance.

Index

Page numbers in *italic* refer to the illustrations and their captions

Abbott and Costello, 198
Abbott and Costello Meet Frankenstein, 198; *196*
Aesop, 39
Africa, 18, 31, 60–1, 84, 208, 209–10, 213, 214–15, 216–19, 235
Agrigento, 39
Argos, 138, 139
Akondogo, 216–17
Akosho, 217
Alaska, 35
Albertus Magnus, St, 91; *91*
Alsace, 27
Altomarus, 51
American International, 198
Anelay, Henry, *177*
Ange, Daniel d', 97–8
Anglo-Saxons, 40
Angurboda, 79
Ankers, Evelyn, 194; *192*
Annales Medicopsychologiques, 55
Ansbach, *110–11*
Anthos, 72
Antoine, Monsieur, 223; *223, 224*
Apuleius, 77, 231
Arabs, 137–8
Arawak tribes, 214
Arcadia, 70–3, 77, 133; *73*
Ardennes, 26, 227
Argentina, 214
Ati Hin Frode, 78–9
Armenia, 233–4
Aryans, 75
Asgard, 79
Asia, 208, 219
astral body, 12, 128, 130–1, 133–4, 139, 159–60
The Atlantic Monthly, 68
Augsburg, *88*
Augustine, St, 88–90; *89*

Austria, 33, 157–8, 232
Auvergne Mountains, 221–2
Aveyron, 31
Avicenna, 55, 137, 167

Babylon, 168
Bajanus, Prince, 231
Balkans, 45, 231–2
Bangladesh, 162
Banister, Manly, 187; *157, 186*
Barbosa, Eliana, 145–6
Baring-Gould, Sabine, 22, 31, 55–7, 76, 81–2, 132; *135*
Barnum, P. T., 52
Baronius, Caesar, 39
Barrès, Maurice, 180
BBC, 190
Bear Boys of Lithuania, 31
The Beast Must Die, 200
Beaugrand, H., 182
Bedburg, 102–4
Belgian Congo, *218*
Belgium, 26, 33, 140, 227
Ben Macdhui, 230
Benedict, 45
Benson, E. F., 183
Berbers, 210
berserkers, 79, 121–2, 139, 219, 234; *123*
Bertin, Louise, 189
Bertin, Roland, 173
Bertrand, 56–7, 139, 152, 176
Besançon, 14
Bible, 39–40, 85, 129
Bierce, Ambrose, 183
Bikelas, Demetrios, 174
Bjelasica Mountains, 36
black magic, 113–21
Blackwood, Algernon, 182–3
Bliss, Gerald, 179
Bloch, Robert, 187

Boaistuau, *228*
Bocquet, Jacques, 122
Bodin, Jean, 87–8, 90, 100, 132
Boguet, Henry, 45, 52, 96–7, 99–101, 107, 109, 112, 122, 222; *19, 97, 99*
Bohum, Sir Humphrey, 238
Boin, Jean, 14
Bonaventura, St, 94
Bonaventure, 172–3
Bonivon, André, 172–3
Bordeaux, 48
Bordelon, Laurent, 180; *181*
Bornu, 209
Bosnia, 37
Bourdin, 132
Bourg-la-Reine, 27–8
Bourgot, Pierre, 14–17, 124, 128, 159
The Boy Who Cried Werewolf, 198
Die Brandwag, 22, *184*
Brazil, 145–6, 214; *145*
Breber, Count von, 42
Breconshire, 230
Brimble, Vincent, *189*
Bristol Old Vic, 188; *187*
British College of Psychic Science, 60
British Lion, 200
Brittany, 170–1, 222
Brosnatch, A., 187; *209*
Browne, Coral, 190
Brunnen, *110–11*
Buddhism, 216
Bühl, 214
Bulgaria, 149
Burton, Robert, 21, 58, 59

Callot, James, 220; *62*
Camden, William, 229–30
Campbell, Sir Gilbert, 182
Camus, Henry, 96, 97–8

251

Canada, 35, 69, 235
cannibalism, 156–61; *158*
Canon Episcopi, 91–4
Cappeln, *142*
Cardono, Geronomo, 125
Carradine, John, 198
Carre, Isadore, *41*
Catholic Church, 138
Caucasus, 113, 233
Caude, 49–50, 107
Cavendish, Richard, 67
Celebes, 220
Celts, 69, 229
Central America, 208
Cervantes, 180
Challemaison, Matthieu de, 97
Châlons-sur-Marne, 31, 108
Chaney, Lon Jr, 44, 191–4, 195–8, 201–2, 203, 204; *67*, *192*, *196*, *197*, *201*
Chastel Charnon, 15
Chile, 208
China, 39, 208, 210–13
Chronicles of Scotland, 230
Chusnée, M. de, 16
cinema, 44, 175, 191–204
Coccagna, Peter, *67*
Cologne, 79
Columbia, 198
Columbus, 235
Comestor, 20
Cooper, Edgar L., 180
Cornier, 107
Cos, 138, 139
Costello, Dudley, 182
Costello, Lou, 198; *196*
Cotgrave, Randle, 240
Counselman, Mary Elizabeth, 187
Counter-Reformation, 138
Cranach, Lucas, *65*
Crema, 167
Crockett, Samuel Rutherford, 180
Crowe, Catharine, 182
The Cry of the Werewolf, 198
Cuiseaux, 222
Curry, Francis, 189
Curse of the Werewolf, 175, 194, 195, 200; *196*
Cyprian, St, 143–4
Czechoslovakia, 232

Dacians, 30
Daily Express, 35
Daily Mail, 23, 29
Daily Telegraph, 190, 218–19
Daily Worker, *34*
Dar-es-Salaam, 217–18
De Virtutibus Herbarum, 39
Della Porta, Giambattista, 124
Demaentus, 72
Demetrianus, 144
Demon Tailor of Châlons, 108–9, 159
Denmark, 72, 139, 220
De Nobilis, Dr Joseph, 69
d'Epinal, *183*
Derleth, August W., 187; *186*
Devil, 80–95; *et passim*
Devon, 229
Disney, Walt, *38*
Dolgov, Boris, *148–9*, *158*, *186*
drugs, 124–6
Du Chaillu, Paul B., 216–17
Dufthac, 78–9
Duhamel, Captain Jean, 223
Dumas, Alexandre, 180
Dunn, Michael, 200

Eccleshall, 23–4
Edmund the Martyr, St, 39
Eisler, Dr Robert, 30, 60, 77, 211, 235
Elisha, 84
Endore, Guy, 175–7, 194; *175*
Engel, Katherine, *27*
Erckmann-Chatrian, 183
Eskimos, 214
Ethiopia, 209–10, 220
Evening Standard, 217–18
Exmoor, 25
exorcism, 140–6, 147–9

Fantastic Monsters of the Movies, 203–4
Fantasy Fiction, 67
Farrar & Rinehart, 175
Fenris, 75–6, 79
Field, Eugene, 181
Fillol, L., *160*
Financial Times, 188, 190
Finland, 37, 78, 220, 234
Fiske, John, 68
Fleming, Peter, 182
Fodor, Dr Nandor, 61–6, 67; *61*
Formosa, 31
Fortune, Dion, 67
France, 11, 12, 14–17, 19, 27–8, 29, 33, 42–3, 48–50, 55–7, 80–2, 96–101, 105–8, 112, 147, 149, 167, 170–3, 221–4
Francis et Curry, 188–9; *188*
Frankenstein Meets the Wolf Man, 198; *67*, *197*
Freeman, Dr Thomas, 68

Gaillard, Clauda, 101
Galicia, 157–8
Galloway, 160–1
Gandillon family, 45, 105–7
Gandillon, Antoinette, 106–7
Gandillon, Georges, 106–7, 122
Gandillon, Perrenette, 45, 105–6
Gandillon, Pierre, 106–7, 122
Garnier, Gilles, 96, 97–8, 217
Gaul, 78
Gazette de France, 222
Geibel, Emanuel, 190
Geiler von Kaisersberg, Dr Johann, 82–5; *15*, *83*
Germanic tribes, 69
Germany, 11, 30, 34, 42, 55, 102–5, 121, 139, 147, 167, 168, 213, 214, 220, 224–7
Gervase of Tilbury, 228, 238

Gestosa, 35–6
Gévaudan, 222–4; *223, 224*
ghouls, 152–4; *153*
Gilbert, Abbot, 172
Giraldus Cambrensis, 231
Giunta, John, *157*
Gladden, Rose, 129–31, 133, 134–5, 139, 146; *129*
Goebbels, Joseph, 34
Golnier, 59
Gomesende, 36
Gornia Teslic, 37
Gorska, Halina, *179*
Goya, Francisco de, *86*
Grant, John Cameron, 180
Great Britain, 19, 23–5, 28–9, 40, 155, 168, 228–30
Greece, 30, 149, 150, 220, 231
Greece, ancient, 11, 69–74, 138–9
Greene, Mrs, 183
Grenier, Jean, 48–9, 53–4, 81, 121, 124
Grimm, Baron von, 222
Grimm Brothers, 227
Guazzo, Francesco Maria, 87, 94; *54*
Guillemin, 16
Guingamp, 221
Gulf of Lions, 172
Gustavus I, King of Sweden, 77
Guyana, 213, 214

Hack Tuke, Dr Daniel, 59
Hague, 227–8
Haigh, John, 109
Haiti, 144–5, 150–2
Hamadan, 35
Hamel, Frank, 87; *171*
Hammer Films, 194, 195
Hammurabi, 168
Hardwick, Charles, 220
Harold I, King of Norway, 79
Harper's Monthly Magazine, 165

Harz Mountains, 227; *226*
Hašek, Jaroslav, 190
Haxthausen, August von, 233–4
Haydock, Ron, 203–4
Hayles, Brian, 189
Hérault, Pierre, 107–8
Hermetic Order of the Golden Dawn, 66
Herodotus, 72
Hesse, 225
Hill, Ken, 189–90; *189*
Himmler, Heinrich, 34
Hindenburg, 225
Hindus, 76–7
Hirpini, 40
The History of Hrolf Kraka, 219–20
Hitler, Adolf, 34, 60
Hobson, Valerie, 204
Homo ferus, 31
Hoppe, Dr Hans, 224
House of Dracula, 198; *197*
House of Frankenstein, 198, 203; *197*
Housman, Clemence, 179, 180; *178*
Housman, Laurence, 179; *178*
Hubsch, Dr, 31
Huguenots, 172–3
Hull, Henry, 194, 201, 203–4; *195*
Human Leopard Societies, 219
Hungary, 33, 45, 232
hypertrichosis, 52; *53*
Hyrcanians, 30

I Was a Teenage Werewolf, 198, 200; *201*
Iceland, 72, 220
Illis, Dr Lee, 50–2
India, 18, 31, 35, 78, 167, 208, 215–16; *172*
Indians, North American, 234–5
Indonesia, 220
Inquisition, 91
International Congress of Mental Health, 156
Inverness-shire, 26
Ireland, 79, 229–30

The Irish Penny Journal, 230
Istanbul, 31, 231
Italy, 30, 35, 37, 40, 55, 167, 230–1

James I, King of England, 21–2, 65, 168
Jamguillaume, Clauda, 122
Jamprost, Clauda, 122
Japan, 157, 208, 210–13, 214
Jesus Christ, 40
John, King of England, 155, 228–9
Johnson, Raymond, 205
The Journal of American Folklore, 62
Journal of Mental Science, 59
Jung, C. G., 30
Jura Mountains, 45, 167
Juvenal, 156

Kabutiloa, 209
Kallas, Aino, 180
Kalmar, 234
Karloff, Boris, 198, 201
Kelly, Walter, 225–6
Kipling, Rudyard, 183
Kirkland, Dr Gerald, 60–1
Kneale, Nigel, 190
Kongs Skuggsjo, 229
Krucher, Joseph, *127*
Kurland, Gil, 203–4

Lancre, Pierre de, 48–9, 52, 54, 121
Landon, Michael, 200; *201*
Lapland, 220, 234
Lapotaire, Jane, *187*
Latvia, 87, 94–5
Laube, Theophilus, *92–3*
Leadbeater, C. W., 128, 133–4
Lee, Walt, 200
Legend Horror Classics: Werewolves, 206
Legend of the Werewolf, 200; *116–17, 200*
Leiber, Fritz, 187

Lenin, 60
Leningrad, 37–8
Lerugen, Pierre, 17
Levi, Eliphas, 133
Liège, 227
Linnaeus, 31
literature, 174–88, 190
Lithuania, 31
Little Red Riding Hood, 75–6; *75*
Lockhart, June, *198*
Loki, 79
Lombardy, 222
London, 29
London Magazine, 222
London Weekend Television, 190
Long, Frank Belknap Jr., 209
Louis XV, King of France, 149
Loup Garou, 69
Lucanians, 30
Lucian, 77
Lugosi, Bela, 194; *197*
Luvians, 30
lycanthropy, 12, 19–22, 46–9, 59–66, 96–101, 136–9; *47*; *et passim*
Lycantropus, 207
Lycaon, King of Arcadia, 70–2, 73–4, 77, 162–3; *71*
lycorexia, 47
Lyon, 80, 85–7

MacGregor, Mathers, 66
Macmillan's Magazine, 190
McNeil, Elton B., 58
The Mad Monster, 198
Madden, Frederick, *170*
Madden, Richard, 59, 94–5
Maeterlinck, Maurice, 13
Magdeburg, 42, 43–4
Magee, Patrick, 190
Marcellus Sidetes, 72
Maréville, 48
Marie de France, 170–1, 190; *171*
Marron Films, 198–200
Marryat, Frederick, 178
Maruts, 75

Matthews, Lester, 204
Maturin, Charles, 180
Maupassant, Guy de, 182
Maurice, E. T., 188–9
Mazères, 189; *188*
Medicina de Quadrupedibus, 38–9
medicine, 38–9
Meheux, F., *82*
Melampus, 138
Menzies, Sutherland, 182
Mérimée, Prosper, 183
Merionethshire, 24–5
Messina, 138
Métraux, Alfred, 144–5, 150–2
Mexico, 208
Michigan, 35
Midnapur, 31
Miller, Carey, *147*
Milo, 40
Minnesota, 35
Mongolia, 39
Monster, Go Home!, 201
The Monster Times, 205 206
Monsters Unleashed, 204
Montana, 35
Montefredane, 35
Montot, Philibert, 17
Morel, Dr, 46–8
Morocco, 210
Moulin, Gabriel de, 228–9
Moyset, 15–16
Muller, Robert, 190
Munn, H. Warner, 187; *186*
Murnau, F. W., 194
Musi, Agostino de', *71*
Muslim, Mohammed, 162

Nacht der Vampyr, 202
Naish, J. Carrol, 198
Nantes, 107
Naschy, Paul, 202–3; *202*
Natalis, St, 79
National Museum of Wales, *33*
Navajo Indians, 195
Nazis, 34
Nebuchadnezzer, King of Babylon, 77; *76*
Neocleus, Nick, *66*

Netherlands, 227–8
Neue Freie Presse, 218
Neurians, 72
News Chronicle, 156
Nigeria, 209
Nooktas, 235
Norbert, St, 39
Nordic myths, 31
Norman, Dr H. J., 125–6
Normandy, 82, 222
Norris, Frank, 180
Norsemen, 121–2, 139
North America, 234–5
North Manchester General Hospital, 162
Norway, 37, 72, 120, 220, 234
Nosferatu, 194
Nurrez, Isabelle de, 231
Nurrez, Juan de, 231
Nymph Werewolf, 201
Nynauld, Jean de, 90–1, 125, 133; *59, 90*

O'Donnell, Elliott, 119, 121, 140–1, 153–4, 215–16, 229, 232, 233
Öland, *123*
Oland, Warner, 204
Olaus Magnus, 40, 77–8, 91; *77*
O'Mahoney, Robert, 188; *187*
Orissa, 215–16
Orsk, 140–1
Ortell, Abraham, 239
Ouspenskaya, Maria, 193–4
Ovid, 18, 162–3; *18*

Paassen, Pierre van, 27–8
Padua, 231
Paget, Thievenne, 122
Palerne, Guillaume de, *170*
Paracelsus, 155
Paris, 29, 55–7; *29*
Parker, Dr N., 59
Parkyns, Mansfield, 210
Patrick, St, 229, 230
Paul, St, 40
Paul of Aegina, 136–7
Pauli, Johann, 82

Pausanias, 70–2
Pemberton, Victor, 190
Périgord, 81
Perrier, Peter, 101
Perrin, Jeanne, 101
Persia, 35, 36
Peru, 208
Petit, Léonce, 47
Petrof, Théodore, 52; *53*
Petronius Arbiter, 74, 176, 231; *74*
Peucer, Gaspar, 46
Phillpotts, Eden, 183; *184*
Pierce, Jack, 201
Plato, 70; *70*
Pliny, 73
Pluto, 40
Poland, 35, 147, 150, 232–3
Poligny, 17
Polomyia, 157–8
Ponce de Santa Cruz, Alfonso, 59
porphyria, 50–2; *50*
Portugal, 231
Price, Vincent, 190
Priest, Thomas Preskett, 177
Prieur, Claude, *245*
Proitos, King of Argos, 138
Propertius, 72, 231
Prussia, 214
Psychic Science, 60
Pyle, Howard, *165*
Pyrenees, 231

Quebec, 69
Quinn, Seabury, 187; *185*
Quiroga, General Facundo, 214

rabies, 38, 162–8; *163*
Reber, Keith, 27
Reed, Oliver, 44, 194, 200; *196*
Regino, Abbot, 91
Relis, Harry (Guy Endore), 175–7, 194
Remy, Nicolas, 87
The Return of the Vampire, 198
Reynolds, George W. M.,
177–8
Reynold's Miscellany, 177
Rhineland, 227
Rhône estuary, 172
Rintoul, David, 44, 200; *116–17, 200*
Rio-Neuhof, J. A., 187; *22, 184*
Roderic, Allan, 183–7
Rollet, Jacques, 49–50, 59, 105, 107–8, 124, 159
Rollet, Jean, 107
Roman Empire, 11, 31, 69–70, 72, 84, 138–9, 230–1
The Romance of William and the Werewolf, 238
Romania, 213, 220, 231–2
Rome, 28
Romulus and Remus, 31; *32*
Rosário do Sul, 145–6
Rowlands, Richard, 238, 239
Royal Society of Medicine, 50
Russia, 33, 37–8, 49, 60, 113–17, 140–1, 150, 167, 169, 213, 233–4

Sabzavar, 36
Saki, 181–2
Salius, Petrus, 168
San Cyprian, 37
Sand, George, 241; *78*
Sand, Maurice, 241; *16, 241*
Saunderson, 230
Scandinavia, 11, 77–9, 121–2, 219–20, 234
Schedel, Hartmann, *172*
Schenck von Grafenberg, Johannes, 21, 59
Schleswig-Holstein, 139
Schneider, George Jacob, *110, 111*
Schorer, Mark, 187; *186*
Schrade, Oskar, 239
Schreck, Max, 194
Schwabeda, Johann Michael, *111*
Scotland, 26, 160–1, 230
Scott, Sir Walter, 220

Scribe, Eugène, 189; *188*
Sears, Fred F., *199*
Secretain, Françoise, 122
Serbia, 149–50
Servius, 40
She-Wolf of London, 198; *198*
Shelley, Mary, 174
Sherkot, 35
Siberia, 113–16
Sicily, 39, 54–5, 138
Singapore, 28; *28*
Singh, Rev J. A., 31
Siodmak, Curt, 191, 194
Slavs, 118–19
Slovakia, 149
Smiths Food Group, 205; *207*
Somerset, 229
South America, 208, 213–14, 234
Southern Rhodesia, 60–1
Spain, 35–6, 37, 202–3, 231
Sprenger, Jacob, 91–4
The Squirm, 26
Sri Lanka, 216
Staffordshire, 23–4
The Stage, 189
Stanleyville, 218
Stenbok, Count Eric, 182
Stevens, Onslow, *197*
Stevenson, Robert Louis, 183, 195
Stockwell, Dean, 200
Stoker, Bram, 175, 177, 194
Storwolf o' Whale, 78–9
Strange, Glenn, 198
Strasbourg, 27, 82
Struys, John, 31
Stump, Beele, 102, 103–4; *103*
Stump, Peter, 79, 101–5, 121, 191, 224; *103, 104–5*
Sudan, 209, 210
Suleiman II the Magnificent, Sultan, 231
Sullivan, Alan, *166*
Summers, Montague, 24–5, 30–1, 54, 88, 94–5, 208–9

Sunday Express, 28
Sweden, 35, 77–8, 120, 128, 234
Swem, Charles, 178
Swiatek, 157–8
Switzerland, 133, 167
Syria, 35

Tanzania, 210, 217–19
television, 190
Tennant, Dudley, *166*
theater, 188–90
Theatre Workshop, 189–90
Theosophy, 128
Thirty Years' War, 34
Thoms, William J., 190
Tilburne, A. R., 187
The Times, 109
Tomson, Graham R., 190
Torslunda, *123*
Transylvania, 232
Trompin, Katherine, 102, 103–4; *103*
Turberville, 240
Turkey, 167, 231
Twentieth Century-Fox, 198
Tyburn Films, 200

Ukraine, 128, 150
Ulfhednar, 79
The Undying Monster, 198
Unicorn Theatre, 189
United States of America, 35, 37, 168
Universal Pictures, 191, 194, 195–8, 201; *27*, *193*

Ural Mountains, 113, 233
Uruguay, 214
Uttenheim, 27

Valerius Maximus, 84
vampires, 147–55; *147*, *154*
Van Renner, 227–8
Verdung, Michel, 14–17, 124, 159
Vereticus, King, 230
Vernon, 132
Vienne, 42–3, 44
Vikings, 235
Vincentius, 84
Virgil, 72, 230–1
Volsunga Saga, 121, 122

Wales, 24–5, 229, 230
Walker, Stuart, 195, 203–4
Wallachia, 220
Walpole, Hugh, 183
Warrell, David A., 165–6
Webster, John, 20, 188; *187*
Weekley, Ernest, 240
Weindel, Cornelius Matthäus, *219*
Weird Tales, 187; *148–9*, *157*, *158*, *185*, *186*, *209*
were-animals, 208–20
The Werewolf, 194, 198; *199*
Werewolf in a Girls' Dormitory, 198; *199*
The Werewolf of London, 194–5, 201, 203–4, 232; *195*

The Werewolf of Paris, 17;
Werewolf of Washington, 198–200
Werewolf Organization, 34; *34*, *35*
West, Geoffrey P., 164–5
Whishaw, Fred, 182
White Russia, 169
Wiener Tagblatt, 218
Wier, Johann, 59, 124
Wild Beast of Gévaudan, 222–4; *223*, *224*
Wild Boy of Aveyron, 31
Wild Peter, 31
William of Palermo, 169–70
William of Paris, 84
Wilson, Wilfred, 183
The Windsor Magazine, *166*
Wisconsin, 35
The Wolf Man, 191, 193–4, 195–8, 201, 204; *192*, *193*
Wolfeshusius, Joannes Fridericus, 91
Wolfman, 205
wolves, 32–41
The Wonders of Ireland, 229
World History of Psychiatry, 68, 144
World War II, 34, 157

Yugoslavia, 36

Zabadani, 35
Zender, *32*

LIZARD PEOPLE

NOVELS BY EVE OTTENBERG

Roman Summer

Hope Deferred

Bonkers

Troglodyte

Birdbrain

Wages

Further Adventures of Feckless Frank

Carbon

Sanctuary City

Hometown, U.S.A.

Tainted Water

Homegrown

Sunset at Dawn

The Race of Men

Zone of Illusion

Realm of Shadow

Sojourn at Dusk

Dark is the Night

The Walkout: A Tale in Three Parts

Reluctant Reaper

Suburbia

Dead in Iraq

The Unblemished Darlings

Glum and Mighty Pagans

The Widow's Opera

Short Story Collections

Anxiety, and Other Stories

What They Didn't Know, Stories and Essays

EVE OTTENBERG

LIZARD PEOPLE

THREE BLUEBIRDS PRESS

THREE BLUEBIRDS PRESS

This book is a work of fiction. Names, characters, places, and incidents are either the product of the author's imagination or are used fictitiously, and any resemblance to actual persons, living or dead, business establishments, events, or locales is entirely coincidental.

LIZARD PEOPLE

Copyright ©2023 Eve Ottenberg

All rights reserved.
No part of this book may be reproduced in any manner without the express written consent of the author, except in the case of brief excerpts in reviews and articles.

Cover art © SUNWARDS
Cover design & Interior layout by Vanessa Anderson
at NightOwlFreelance.com

Paperback ISBN-13: 9798399394572

1

AFTER HER EVENING shower, Philippa Philpot dried off vigorously with a towel – too vigorously, for she soon noticed on her left forearm that she had rubbed off a patch of skin, and where her tan should have been, she now saw bright green, glittering scales. She poked them tentatively with her index finger. They felt, she thought, like the skin of her friend Doobie Dimly's iguana. But then, she had only touched that iguana, named Monster Mouth, once, and very gingerly the year before, so she couldn't be sure. "I have scales under my skin," she murmured to herself. "How odd. Maybe I have superpowers! Maybe I'm invulnerable!" She kicked the toilet to see and hurt her big toe. No, she wasn't invulnerable to pain.

She decided not to wake her mother, Floozy Philpot, to impart this earth-shaking news. Instead, she pulled her phone out of her pants pocket and dialed Doobie Dimly. He answered on the first ring.

"I have green scales on my arm," Philippa said, combing her brown, purple-streaked hair with her free hand.

"Who is this?" The video game addict demanded. "Hey! I'm winning! I'm winning!"

"I'm afraid to dry off with a towel because when I rub, my skin might come off."

Doobie paused his game and peered nearsightedly at his phone. "The Illuminati don't exist," he said.

"Who're the Illuminati?"

"Who're you?"

"It's Philippa, you imbecile, who else?"

"Some psycho who thinks they have scales, that's who else." Doobie Dimly paused a moment, considered, picked his nose, wondering if he should tell his Dad, Delbert, that apparently Delbert had been correct to join Q-Anon. Instead, he said. "Hallie Gas tried to convince me that the Illuminati, aka the lizard people, rule the world."

"I rule the world," Philippa said dreamily.

"Fat chance."

"Then how come I got glittering scales?" She asked. "Like a fish."

Stumped, bored, and eager to resume his video game, the twenty-something told her to come over to prove it, thinking that with any luck this birdbrain would decline.

"But how do I dry off? If I rub myself with the towel, my skin will come off."

"Air dry. Or use your hair dryer," Doobie suggested, telling his dog, Pooper, "Some people are stupid."

Philippa, offended, ended the call. But she took Doobie's suggestion and dried herself with the hair dryer. Then she put on her underwear and pants, and continued blowing the hair dryer at her stomach, as she stepped out into the second-floor hall.

"Why are you blow-drying your stomach?" Floozy asked groggily, stepping out of her bedroom, her gray and black hair a mess, her pajama pants and top rumpled.

"So my skin won't come off."

"How odd."

"That's not the only thing that's odd. A mother who goes to bed at 7 p.m. – that's odd."

"I have sleep issues," Floozy sniffed offendedly. "Like massive insomnia. I think I'm addicted to Xanax."

"Go to the sleep lab in Bethesda. It's the best in the Washington, D. C. metro area. They'll cure you," Philippa suggested.

"You have green stuff on your arm."

"Scales, mother."

"Great. I gave birth to a frog."

"Not a frog," Philippa corrected. "A lizard."

"You know, I think you may have lost your mind."

"Whatever," her daughter sniffed. "While you're making condescending remarks, I'll be ruling the world."

Floozy rolled her eyes and went back to bed. It was 8:30 p.m. Her daughter, she concluded, had succumbed to delusions of grandeur. Maybe it was time for a shrink. Her acquaintance from her book group, a Mrs. Schmutz, raved about her therapist, Dr. Klutz. She called him "a political genius," though what that had to do with her therapy, Floozy had not been able to ascertain. She crawled into bed, dozed briefly to thoughts of her daughter discussing a Biden-Trump rematch election campaign with a politically savvy psychiatrist. She wondered if her health insurance would cover it. She wondered if her friends, the Sniffles, were still selling pot. She wondered if her deceased mother, lying in a coffin in the Schlimizzle funeral home would mind if she didn't get buried in a top-of-the-line casket. Her mind raced. Floozy Philpot couldn't sleep.

Sighing, she threw back the covers and marched downstairs to the kitchen of her townhome in downtown Silver Spring, Maryland. Philippa thrust her arm under her mother's nose. "See?" She demanded.

Floozy screwed up her eyes. "Yes, you have scales. I'll schedule a session with Dr. Klutz."

"Who dat?"

"Some doctor Mrs. Schmutz says is the cat's meow."

"I don't want the cat's meow, and Schmutz is a lunatic. She wears a 'Stop ISIS' T-shirt." Philippa sat at the dining table, staring at her laptop screen. She had googled "chat with a lizard person" and found exactly what she was looking for, something called the Lizard Collective.

"Mrs. Schmutz is a very astute judge of character. She knows a terrorist when she sees one."

"She gets her knowledge of the world from that supermarket tabloid. You know, the one that says all the men on earth will die from the Penis Plague."

"You mean Scuttlebutt? Or National Disgrace, or Gossip?"

"I wouldn't know," Philippa sniffed condescendingly. "I don't read that trash."

"You do too, and so do I. All three were very informative about the covid menace in the produce section and how infected individuals handling bananas could pass the virus on to you."

"So you decided to shop with surgical gloves," Philippa said sourly.

"And I only got covid once."

"Maybe it was covid that turned me into a lizard person," Philippa mused.

"You weren't careful. You caught it three times at that ridiculous dog-walking job of yours."

"Canines are a vector."

"It rotted your brain," Floozy told her daughter.

"Thanks, mother."

"At least at the pharmacy, everyone I work with wears a mask," Floozy continued.

"Well, I couldn't very well ask the Schnooks or Miss Squish to put masks on their dogs, could I?" Philippa huffed.

Silence descended on the tenebrous little kitchen and dining room, silence in which Floozy's thoughts took a maudlin turn. "I wish you'd get married," she sighed.

"I'm turning into a lizard, and my mother wants me to get married," Philippa groused, "so I can lay lizard eggs."

"Why not Doobie Dimly? He's not too particular."

"Thanks Mom. He's also high all the time."

"What I meant was, he wouldn't care if you have green scales."

Philippa rolled her eyes, thinking, "I'm turning into an iguana and my mother wants me to marry an unemployed video gamer, so she can have grandchildren, who'll probably also have green scales. I wonder if they'll have tails too? Well, while my idiot Mom is daydreaming about my marriage to a nincompoop, I'm gonna get this iguana business under control."

"What do you do if you start developing green scales?" Philippa tapped into her computer.

"You are one of us! One of the elect! We Illuminati will meet soon in

Langley Park, Maryland. It's a party, but there's also a discussion on the topic 'how to pass unnoticed when you look like an alligator.' Bring your own beverage."

"Do I look like an alligator?" Philippa asked her mother.

Floozy's eyebrows lifted in surprise. "No, but you have a raspy voice like an alligator."

"Gators have raspy voices?"

"Or maybe a snake."

"I don't hiss, mom."

"Just trying to be helpful. I'll call Dr. Klutz in the morning. Mrs. Schmutz says he's politically savvy."

"You do that," Philippa frowned. "But I warn you, if he mentions terrorists, I'll walk out."

"Why would he do that?"

"Mrs. Schmutz raves about him, she raves about terrorists, claims he talks about politics – ergo."

"Who's ergo?"

"Never mind, Mom. Get some sleep."

Worried about her daughter thinking she might resemble an alligator, Floozy rose and meandered through the shadows to the stairs. "I just want you to know," she called over her shoulder, "that if you start having the urge to eat live animals, grow a tail and your teeth turn sharp and pointy, I will stand by you."

"Good to know," Philippa muttered.

Her mother thudded up the steps.

Someone named Seymour Burp began g-chatting with her. He was, he said, a 40-year-old insurance adjuster, who wondered if she'd been in any car collisions recently.

"No," Philippa typed back. "I have not."

He also claimed to have a long, green, scaly tail. Did she?

"I'm not there yet," Philippa typed.

Disappointed non-responsiveness ensued. Finally, Seymour sent her another message. Would she like to get together for a late dinner and how old was she?

"No and none of your business," she replied.

"Well, I guess I'll see you at the upcoming Illuminati shindig," he wrote her.

"Yes, well, that's something to look forward to," she scowled, as she typed back. She had a burning burst of liquid in her mouth as she wrote this reply. "Great," Philippa huffed to the empty room. "Twenty-eight years old, and I got acid reflux, an appointment with some idiot named Dr. Klutz, an upcoming get-together with a group of psychotics, no job and I'm turning into an alligator. What's freakin' next?" Fortunately, the silence of the nocturnal dining room did not reply.

DR. KLUTZ WAS a tall, sleek, slightly portly, silver-haired psychiatrist given to ponderous pretentions and fond of expensive suits. He greeted Philippa with the question: "Are you a Democrat or a Republican?"

"Neither. You're not a dermatologist."

"Why should I be?" Dr. Klutz asked.

"Because of this." And Philippa pulled back her sleeve to reveal green glittering scales on her left forearm.

"Hmm. A bizarre psychosomatic reaction to your apolitical stance on the upcoming election campaign."

"Come again?" Thus Philippa.

"I prescribe Zyprexa, 20 milligrams. That should get this psychosis under control."

The patient tucked her brown, purple-streaked hair behind her ears, revealing multiple piercings.

"Make that 30 milligrams, considering all the earrings," Dr. Klutz said.

"What do my earrings have to do with anything?"

"I have observed a correlation between multiple piercings and paranoid schizophrenia. You're sure you don't prefer one of our two political parties?"

Philippa, seated now on the couch, cast a critical, sidelong glance at the psychiatrist. Bright April sunshine flooded the room from its large windows.

"Nice weather we're having," she commented.

"Patient tries to deflect painful consideration of Democrats and

Republicans onto the weather," Dr. Klutz spoke into a small recording device.

"What do I do about these green scales?" Philippa demanded.

"Take your anti-psychotic medication."

"What if I grow a long, green alligator tail?"

"Patient clearly delusional. Electro-shock therapy may be in order. Consult with expert, Dr. Schnook."

"Oh, is he related to the famous Al Schnook?" Philippa asked. "I know Al's sons, Herm and Hinchy."

"Patient hallucinates about Dr. Schnook," Dr. Klutz intoned.

Philippa sighed. "Whatever. You can't prescribe a cream or something?"

"Young lady, since when could a cream possibly cure your florid, psychotic and psycho-somatic symptoms?"

"I don't know. You tell me. You're the Democrat – oops, I mean the doctor."

"Patient is a Republican, but for some neurotic reason wishes to conceal this fact."

"Well, that's about enough of that. See you around, Dr. Klutz."

"That'll be $300."

"Bill my insurance, they'll pay," Philippa lied. "It's under my mother's name, Floozy Philpot."

"How odd."

"That ain't the only thing around here that's odd," Philippa said and left Dr. Klutz to his musings into his tape recorder. She took the elevator down to the lobby and thence walked to her 20-year-old Volkswagen compact. It sported a parking ticket on the windshield, as the meter reader who had just affixed it walked toward the next car.

"Hey," Philippa called. "I'm here."

"Good for you," the rather overweight, middle-aged woman said.

"Couldn't you, um, take back this ticket?"

The woman glared at her. "No."

"But it was an emergency."

"What emergency?"

"This!" And Philippa showed her the green scales on her forearm.

"A lizard person!" The woman screamed. "Don't eat me, eat my kids.

They're younger, tastier, and they give me a pain."

"Ew. I won't eat anybody," Philippa told her. "That is, if you take back my parking ticket."

The woman lumbered back to the Volkswagen and retrieved the ticket. "We good?"

"Never better," Philippa said.

"Since you're part of that pedophile cabal who rules the world, who will be our next president – Trump or Biden? I figure the lizard people want one of their own and that would be Biden."

"Gimme a raincheck on that," Philippa said, opening the driver's door.

"Okey doke."

"Some people," the young woman muttered to herself, as she turned the key in the ignition, "are crazy."

She drove to Kemp Mill, to the home of Hubert Poop, a residential mortgage specialist at a local bank, whose bulldog, Hubert Poop Junior, she was scheduled to walk. She parked in front of his modest split-level and strolled up to the front door. His scantily clad, live-in girlfriend, Lila Hanger, answered. Lila had been puffing away on weed, and clouds, literally cumulus clouds of marijuana smoke wafted out through the open front door. Peering past Lila in her skimpy, less than half-length bathrobe, Philippa noted that a blue gray layer of smoke enveloped the living room.

"Ya got the pooper scooper?" Lila asked, cracking gum.

"You're supposed to supply that, remember?"

"Oh yes. I knew that. Come in."

Philippa entered the vestibule and gagged on the smoke. "No thanks," she said. "I'll wait on the front walk." So she stood in the too warm April sun, twiddling her thumbs, wishing she'd worn shorts instead of her ripped jeans and long-sleeved pullover. Finally, Lila Hangar opened the door, handed her the leash and pooper scooper and gave the bulldog, Hubert Poop Junior, an affectionate kick.

"Whatever you do, don't let this mutt crap in Maynard Ploshinsky's potted begonias."

"Who's Maynard Ploshinsky?"

Lila Hangar pointed at a very peculiar individual, crouching on the lawn next door and filming them with his phone.

"Why would I let Hubert Poop Junior crap in that strange person's potted begonias?"

"Cause it's convenient," crack, on the gum.

"It might also cause trouble," Philippa said.

"You can say that again. Lotsa trouble, in the form of a restraining order from a lunatic judge who wears a hazmat suit on the bench, saying that if I ever let that bulldog crap in Maynard Ploshinsky's potted plants again, I'll have to pay a six-figure award in damages to that nut next door and maybe do prison time," crack on the gum. "That's how come we hired you."

"Well, this is only my second time out with your dog, but I'll be sure to avoid that," Philippa squinted at the crouching middle-aged neighbor in his rumpled tan summer suit and tie and his thick, dark-framed glasses, "that person."

"I'm surprised Hubert didn't give you the lowdown on Ploshinsky the last time you came."

"He seemed kinda...unfocussed and frazzled," Philippa thus referred as discreetly as possible to what she regarded as the weirdo with the pronounced lisp, who had hired her.

"That's cause of the wild and crazy life of a residential mortgage specialist," Lila told her, cracking again, on her gum.

"If you say so."

"Wanna come in and share a joint?"

"I think I have to walk Hubert Poop Junior. We wouldn't want him to defecate in the house," Philippa said, giving the leash a yank.

"Just so he doesn't defecate on Ploshinsky's property," Lila said. "'Cause I do not, repeat not, want to do time on account of some dog turds setting off a raving lunatic who floods people's phones with photos of a bulldog crapping in his begonias."

"How strange," Philippa murmured, edging away. "C'mon Hubert."

Maynard Ploshinsky rose out of his crouch, snapped a picture of Lila Hanger giving him the finger before she stepped back inside and slammed the front door, then approached his potted begonias.

"If that disgusting creature craps in my potted plants, I will take you, young lady, to court, where the one and only Judge Fibble DuCouk will make you wash your hands 10 times during every session and may spray you with Lysol, if you try to breathe on him." Maynard Ploshinsky told an astounded Philippa Philpot.

"You see this?" She asked after a moment, waving the pooper scooper and the plastic bag toward the irate homeowner. "That's so I can clean up after the dog."

"Humpf," thus Maynard Ploshinsky.

Hubert Poop Junior defecated on the sidewalk.

"Well, that's an improvement," Ploshinsky said, as Philippa Philpot bent to collect this mess in the plastic bag. "What did you say your name is?"

"Philippa Philpot."

"And why is there green glitter on your arm?"

"Cause I'm a lizard."

Maynard Ploshinsky gaped at her a moment, then snapped a photograph of her scaly arm and her hand holding the pooper scooper. He told her she was going to be famous.

"I don't want to be famous."

"How about famous and rich?" He asked.

"I could do that," she conceded, then, "rich enough to stop walking crazy people's dogs?"

"Don't stop. You're so much better than that Lila Hanger, who… desecrated my begonias for months on end."

"How will I be rich?" Philippa decided to cut to the chase.

"We'll sell your story to the supermarket tabloid, Scuttlebutt or to National Disgrace, whichever bids the most on it," and Maynard Ploshinsky nodded at her eagerly, as if to suggest that she agree. "Or we'll cheat and sell it to both."

"I could do that without you," Philippa said, the eager light of calculation and greed flickering in her blue eyes.

"But I know the editors-in-chief of both publications," Ploshinsky said.

"We split it 70-30. I get 70 percent," Philippa snapped.

"Sixty, 40. You get 60 percent."

"Deal," Philippa replied and reached out to shake the hand Maynard Ploshinsky extended to her. Unfortunately, as she did so, Hubert Poop Junior's turd fell out of the pooper scooper into a begonia pot.

"I'll get that right now!" She exclaimed.

"You do that, Miss Philpot, or I'll make it 50-50!"

Philippa scooped up the crap without further ado.

"You're so...normal," Maynard Ploshinsky marveled.

"Except for turning into a lizard, yes, that's me – normal."

AFTER WALKING HUBERT Poop Junior, Philippa returned the dog to its owner. "So we're on for tomorrow?" Lila Hanger cracked her gum.

"Sure. Same time," the young woman replied.

"I saw you talking to Maynard 'Off His Rocker' Ploshinsky. Don't believe a word he says about me. In fact, I may sue him for defamation, like poor Hubert did."

"How did Mr. Ploshinsky slander my employer?" Philippa asked.

"By announcing at a community meeting that Hubert was harassing him by leaving dog turds in his potted begonias. What did he say about me?"

"Nothing," Philippa lied, then left. She went next door and rang the bell. Maynard Ploshinsky answered at once. "What did she say about me?" He demanded.

"Who?"

"That Lila Hanger person, who never gets dressed."

"Nothing," Philippa lied.

"Humpf. Come in. I was about to call Bull Bruiser, editor-in-chief of Scuttlebutt."

They entered the Ploshinsky's living room, filled with overstuffed armchairs, ottomans and an overstuffed couch. The carpet was very thick.

"Don't you have to go to work, Maynard?" A scratchy voice shouted from the kitchen.

"I took the day off." Then Maynard Ploshinsky dialed and demanded to speak to "the one and only Bull Bruiser."

"He's busy," the receptionist lied, cracking her gum. She knew for a fact that the editor-in-chief was alternating between swatting flies and pursuing suburban matrons on social media.

"I have a hot tip for him," Ploshinsky said.

"How hot?"

"Lizard people."

"That's old news," crack on the gum. "We covered it repeatedly, just again last week, with a focus on lizard people taking over the pentagon." And the receptionist blew a huge pink bubble with her gum and popped it.

"That sounded like gunfire!" An alarmed Ploshinsky exclaimed.

"Who is this?" She demanded.

"Maynard Ploshinsky. Your publication covered the famous defamation case, *Poop v. Ploshinsky*. I countersued and won. Does the name Judge Fibble DuCouk ring a bell?"

"The insane jurist? Yes. Well, enough of that," and the receptionist prepared to end the call.

"I have an actual lizard person in my living room," Ploshinsky proclaimed.

"Sure you do."

"Here, lemme call you back on FaceTime, and I'll show you her scales." He did so. The blue-haired receptionist was impressed and so finally consented to put the call through. Soon they were connected via FaceTime, with bald, ugly, paunchy but muscular Bull Bruiser, whose angry, bored, little, dark eyes glinted at them with frank disbelief, as he removed the cigar that was usually a fixture in the corner of his mouth.

"Show me that arm again!" He snapped.

Philippa did so.

"How do I know it's not just green glitter?"

"Because it doesn't come off," Philippa said. "If I rub my skin with a towel, the skin flakes off and there are scales underneath."

"You work for the pentagon?"

"I work for Hubert Poop."

"And now you're conspiring with his mortal enemy Maynard 'the Crab Person from the Crab Nebula' Ploshinsky."

"That's slander!" Ploshinsky exclaimed. "And I'll sue!"

"Our impeccable source, Albert Pop, insists you're spreading microscopic crabs."

"The last time I saw scrawny, dirty, old Pop, he was in a straitjacket, tied to a chair in Judge Fibble DuCouk's courtroom," Ploshinsky snapped.

"He's certifiable. Bonkers!"

"Well, he's still in a straitjacket at an undisclosed location overseen by the CIA, but I can assure you, from my regular FaceTime interviews with him," here Bull Bruiser scowled very sourly, "he still insists, among other insanities, that you are a crab person from the Crab Nebula."

"He also claims to have a pink plastic brain and wires in his head. Don't you believe a word out of his mouth, Mr. Bruiser."

"You think I'm an idiot? You think I believe someone who tells me he's a robot from the Andromeda galaxy, here to suction all the salt out of my body by inserting hoses in my orifices? You think I'm stupid, Ploshinsky?"

"I think I have a bona fide lizard person in my living room and you should pay for her story," Ploshinsky said.

"Five hundred dollars," the bored editor replied. "That's my best offer."

"We want $50,000, and we're going to the competition to get it!" Ploshinsky huffed.

"Maynard!" The scratchy voice shouted. "Go to work."

"Knock yourself out," thus Bull Bruiser, who then swatted a fly on his desk and ended the call.

Long, lean, dour Maynard Ploshinsky grumbled something unintelligible, while his guest gazed out the front picture window at a gorgeous April day, thinking that she would rather be driving home with all the windows down, enjoying the fresh air, than sitting in the living room of this very strange person who, if she had heard correctly, hailed from the Crab Nebula and was spreading microscopic crabs.

"Futz Fraud, editor of National Disgrace, please," Maynard Ploshinsky said into his phone.

The image of a tall, obese, frizzy gray-haired woman in a tight, blue poncho, with foggy, cat's-eye glasses balanced crookedly on her nose, appeared on FaceTime. "Fraud's busy throwin' darts," she snapped, then peered closely at her phone. "Oh hi, Mr. Ploshinsky. How's the Crab Nebula been treatin' ya?"

"Stop it, Stella," Ploshinsky grumbled. "Still wearing your poncho, I see."

"That's cause Fraud still vomits on me, every chance he gets," Stella said.

"How peculiar," Philippa said.

"Who said that?" Stella demanded.

"A lizard person."

"Oh?" Stella perked up. "Put her on."

So Philippa took the phone and proved she was a lizard person by displaying her arms, because, by now, her right forearm had begun to display scales, too.

"We been gettin' our ass kicked on lizard people by Scuttlebutt," Stella explained, "with their blockbuster series on how the lizard people infiltrated the pentagon via the space force. Are you military?"

"I'm a dog walker," Philippa said.

"Military canines?" Stella asked hopefully.

"I'm open to any dogs."

"Fraud!" The secretary hollered. "Fraud! Get out here. I got a lizard person on the line."

Small, stringy, warty, nebbish, unimpressive Futz Fraud stepped out of his cramped, cluttered editorial suite, bent over his secretary and promptly vomited on her.

"Dammit Fraud!" Stella exclaimed, then left for the ladies' room to rinse her poncho.

"How long have you had those scales on your arms?" The editor asked Philippa.

"Since last night. After a shower I toweled off my arm, the skin flaked off, and there they were. I must've rubbed the other one today, because after the experience with my left arm, I didn't towel off the right one."

"If you towel off the rest of you and have green scales from head to toe, we're prepared to pay good money for the exclusive rights to your story and pictures of your person," Futz Fraud told her.

"We want $50,000, "Maynard Ploshinsky said.

"I'm not toweling off the rest of me," Philippa put her foot down.

"Why not? We'll pay $5000 for your story," Futz Fraud wheedled.

"I don't wanna look like a freak," Philippa complained.

"Twenty thousand dollars," thus Maynard Ploshinsky.

"You'll be a rich freak," Futz Fraud said.

Stella reappeared. Her boss opened his mouth, but she was too fast for him. She grabbed the super-soaker on her desk and blasted him in the face.

"Not the water gun, Stella!" Futz Fraud cried.

"Don't even think about puking on me again today!" She huffed. "Some people! I been sayin' it for months, Fraud, either you have your stomach removed or you raise my weekly pay one hundred bucks for every time you barf on me. Where's the lizard girl?"

Philippa waved.

"We'll pay you good money for your story," Stella told her.

"Even if my scales are only on my arms?" Philippa asked.

"Where else should they be?"

"Well, your boss wanted me to rub the skin off all my body, so I'd have green scales from head to toe," Philippa complained.

"Don't listen to that birdbrain. All he knows how to do is vomit on his long-suffering, inoffensive amanuensis. Come downtown to our D. C. office, and we'll take care of all the details," Stella advised.

"We want $20,000," Maynard Ploshinsky said.

"You can WANT it all you like, but you're only gettin' 15," Stella snapped.

"Fifteen thousand?" Ploshinsky asked hopefully.

"Yes, moron. Isn't that what I just said?"

"You got a deal!"

"Can we come now?" Philippa asked. "I have a busy dog-walking schedule for the rest of this week and then a lizard people shindig coming up in the not-too-distant future."

"Take photos," Stella promptly said.

"Photos of what?" Philippas asked.

"The lizard people at the lizard people party. And yes, come now. We might go back to our Miami headquarters next week, though you can be sure I won't be sittin' next to Futz Fraud on that plane trip. Let him puke on some unsuspecting passenger, not me."

"How strange," Philippa murmured.

Stella squinted at her. "You seem…normal."

"That's the second time today somebody said that to me."

"Even with your green scaly arms. How'd you get mixed up with kooks like Poop and Ploshinsky?" Stella demanded.

"I answered an ad for a dog walker."

"This ain't Poop's bulldog?" Stella asked.

"Yes, as a matter of fact, it is."

"I'll have you know we made that canine world famous for leaving turds in Ploshinsky's potted begonias," Stella informed her.

"How odd," Philippa repeated.

Stella chuckled wickedly. "You're gonna be sayin' that a lot in the coming months, 'cause you, Philippa Philpot, have stumbled your way into a nest of raving lunatics."

"Great," Philippa said sourly. "I want my money."

"Everything, especially money, comes with a price," Stella instructed her.

MAYNARD PLOSHINSKY PARKED his car on Eighteenth Street Northwest in the nation's capital, then he and Philippa strolled through the splendid April afternoon to the high-rise that housed the local offices of National Disgrace. Not a cloud marred the cerulean blue of the early spring sky, and fresh breezes washed their faces.

The receptionist on the twelfth floor was very busy blowing humongous pink bubbles with her gum, and they had to wait until she had popped three of them before receiving any attention from her. "Oh yes," she finally drawled, "lizard girl. Now I've heard everything."

"For a paper that covered Al Schnook's reincarnation as Frank Fart, who had two brains in his skull and was covered with a thick pelt of fur, I'd think this is small potatoes for you," Ploshinsky griped.

"Let's have a look see," the girl said.

Philippa rolled up her sleeves. The receptionist screamed.

"What?" Ploshinsky demanded. "You never seen a lizard person before?"

"Down the hall to the desk at the end," the receptionist hyperventilated. "Don't eat me!"

"Ew," Philippa said. "I'd much rather eat that unopened bag of Doritos on your desk."

The receptionist quickly handed it to her, then the two arrivals ambled down the newly, beige-carpeted corridor to the desk at the end, behind which, in her triple extra-large, ergonomic, swivel chair sat obese Stella, her blue poncho stretched taut over her vast midriff, her sharp eyes agleam, behind fogged, crooked glasses, with intelligence and malice. "Go away," she said. "We don't want any."

"It's me, Maynard Ploshinsky."

"I repeat," Stella said.

"And me, lizard girl." And Philippa stretched out her forearm with its green, glittering scales.

"Humpf," thus Stella. "That's the most impressive deformity I've seen since we published Pinky Pimple's dick pics with all his furry junk."

"Maybe you don't need my story," Philippa whined querulously. "I mean, if I have to hear about these freaks every time I turn around…"

"You know where you are, Philippa?" Stella asked, tucking a stray wisp of unattractive, frizzy, gray hair behind her ear. "You're in the offices of National Disgrace, the nation's leading supermarket tabloid that specializes in cannibalistic fetuses that eat their way out of their mothers' wombs then bite off the fingers from the obstetricians' hands, that publishes interviews with custodians in straitjackets, who are, naturally, off their rocker and believe they have wires in their heads and pink plastic brains that they regularly must plug into CIA computer servers, and," she raised a fat, didactic index finger "who insist that they are robots from the Andromeda galaxy come to earth to steal all our salt and conquer the planet and, in the meantime, contend with their enemies, the crab people from the Crab Nebula, an ancient race of midget poisoners who dispense toxins into our coffee creamer. We also publish screeds by high falutin' CIA frauds like Charlemagne Crackers on the Penis Plague, causing de-evolutionary degradation, so that its sufferers slide back down the evolutionary scale to become apes, then reptiles, then giant, homicidal amoebas, or tuna fish, I could never keep it straight. We also ran a ground-breaking series on the world-famous 40-year constipation of a local undertaker, Buddy Schlimizzle, and we cover the Russian plot to take over our all-Amurican insect populations with nuclear centipedes, the Liverwurst Plague, Bat-Brain Fever, as well as the depredations of the Arcturans – space invaders who abduct unsuspecting Republicans and sell them into sex slavery in interstellar bordellos. I could go on. But I'm sure you get the idea."

"You don't think my story measures up?" Philippa asked.

"Oh, it measures up, though it would be better if you were covered with green scales from head to toe. Fraud! Fraud!" She hollered. "Get out here!"

Scrawny, little, warty, gray-haired Futz Fraud was busy in his office throwing darts at the front page of his paper's chief rival, Scuttlebutt, with its tale of an evil granny with killer vision who could murder lovable tots just by looking at them. Fraud had pasted this best-seller onto the wall and spent the last 40 minutes pitching darts at it from across his office.

"Fraud!" Stella shouted again.

"What?" He snapped, stepping out of his office, then leaning over his secretary and vomiting on her.

"Dammit, Fraud. I wanna raise." Stella lumbered to her feet, then down the hall to the lavatory to clean up.

Futz Fraud burped. Philippa stepped away. "Don't barf on me," she pleaded.

"Who're you?" The editor demanded.

"This," Maynard Ploshinsky grandly announced with a theatrical sweep of the arm toward Philippa, which happened to swat her with his hand on her shoulder, "is lizard girl." And Ploshinsky pushed his thick, black-framed glasses up to the bridge of his prominent nose and peered eagerly, greedily at Futz Fraud.

"She doesn't look like a lizard," Fraud complained.

"Here," Philippa bared her forearms and held them out for inspection.

"Hmm…" The editor murmured, gingerly poking at the scales. "They look real," he muttered.

Stella reappeared, and slid back into her triple extra-large ergonomic chair.

"Five thousand dollars," he said to Philippa.

"No, Fraud. We're paying $15,000. I already arranged it."

"Who's in charge here?" And Futz Fraud puffed out his puny, bony chest.

"The long-suffering secretary who gets puked on twice a day," Stella snapped.

"Young lady," Futz Fraud addressed Philippa. "When those scales cover you top to bottom, then we'll pay $15,000."

"No then you'll pay me $150,000," Philippa snapped, surprising herself with her own boldness. "Come on Mr. Ploshinsky. Let's go to Scuttlebutt."

"Ploshinsky?" Fraud asked. "Of *Poop v. Ploshinsky*? The crab person from the Crab Nebula who defamed Hubert Poop at the community meeting?"

"Look who's talking about defamation!" Maynard Ploshinsky huffed. "I am not a crab! But Philippa Philpot IS a lizard, and if you won't pay the agreed-on price for exclusive rights to her story, that's your loss. C'mon, Philippa."

And the unlikely pair tramped away down the newly carpeted corridor.

"Good work, Fraud. You just lost us about 20 million additional readers," Stella snapped.

The editor stepped closer and opened his mouth, but Stella was faster. She grabbed her super-soaker and blasted him in the face.

"No need to drench me," he whined, retreating to his office doorway.

"Yes, there is a need. Apparently there is."

The editor began drifting toward her.

"Back Fraud, or I'll blast you again."

Waiting for the elevator, a fat, white-haired fellow in a rumpled suit joined them, looked at Ploshinsky closely, then tentatively said, "Maynard? Maynard Ploshinsky?"

"Who're you?" Ploshinsky asked.

"I'm Fevereau Slop, senior editor at National Disgrace. I remember you from Judge DuCouk's courtroom. Now there's a lunatic."

"Where?" Ploshinsky asked.

"The judge."

"Yes, he was a little off," Ploshinsky said.

"What brings you here?" Slop asked.

"None of your business."

The elevator door opened.

"Be that way," Slop said, and then, as Ploshinsky and Philippa stepped in, he sniffed: "I'll take the next one."

The elevator zoomed down. Then they walked through the gorgeous spring afternoon breezes to another high-rise, took the elevator up and found another bored receptionist with purple hair, cracking gum.

"Oh, if it isn't the crab person from the Crab Nebula," she said.

"Maynard Ploshinsky," he corrected her rather stiffly.

"Don't come any closer. I don't wanna catch your microscopic crabs."

"Is Bull Bruiser in?"

"He's in conference with our chief terrorism and alien abduction reporter, Jeremy Spit. They are interviewing a confidential source in a…er, straitjacket."

Maynard Ploshinsky grimaced. "Tell him I have the bona fide lizard person with me, who wants to sell her story to Scuttlebutt."

The receptionist picked up the phone, then waved them down the hall.

Again they traversed plush carpet, coming to a stop at a spacious corner suite, where a very unfocussed, slobbering individual stood in the doorway. This was Jeremy Spit, who, because of his habit of involuntarily spitting at whomever he spoke to, was regularly banished by his superior to the threshold.

"Where's the lizard girl?" A voice boomed.

"Here!" Spit spat, lobbing a gob of saliva onto one of the thick lenses of Maynard Ploshinsky's glasses. Ploshinsky pulled a Kleenex out of his pants' pocket and cleaned it off. Then he and Philippa slipped past this slobbering menace into the editor-in-chief's suite.

Bald, muscular, bored and annoyed, Bull Bruiser sat behind his desk, his shirt sleeves rolled up, his muscular elbows planted on the desk, twiddling his stubby thumbs and glaring at the scrawny, short man with cracker crumbs in his gray-streaked goatee, who wore a straitjacket and sat off to one side. This was Albert Pop, Scuttlebutt's famous, psychotic source.

"The crab person from the Crab Nebula," Pop said.

"Nice to see you too, Albert," thus Maynard Ploshinsky, rather sourly.

"I will eat your liver," Pop said.

Behind the back of her hand, Philippa whispered, "Did he just threaten to eat your liver?"

"So you came here after all. Good, I like someone who doesn't give up. And those scales did look genuine," Bull Bruiser said. "We'll start bargaining down from Ploshinsky's original demand. Come here, young lady."

"Philippa Philpot," she corrected.

"I don't care if you're Marilyn Monroe. Show me your arms."

Philippa rolled up her sleeves, past the elbows.

"A war of the worlds has begun," Albert Pop intoned, his eyes rolling wildly in his head. "The lizard people have formed an alliance with the crab people. Send all the coffee creamer out for testing. Alert the NSA and CIA. Remove this straitjacket."

"Never, Pop," thus Bull Bruiser.

"I will eat your spleen," Pop said.

"Good to know," the editor replied sourly.

"We Andromedans will ally with the Arcturans. We will sell all the Republicans into sex slavery in the bordellos orbiting Alpha Centauri."

"YOU'RE orbiting Alpha Centauri," Bull Bruiser snapped. "And if you don't shut up, Spit here will gag you."

Albert gargled something incomprehensible.

The editor reached out and touched Philippa's scales. "Haven't seen anything like this since Frank Fart grew fur."

"Don't forget Pinky Pimple's fur," Spit spat. A huge blob of saliva splattered on a framed supermarket chain circulation award, one of several framed awards on the wall, behind Bull Bruiser's head. "Shut up, Spit," the editor said.

"But Pinky's fur was limited to his junk," Spit spat again, this time zapping Albert Pop in the eye.

"I was afraid you'd mention that," Bull Bruiser grumbled. "I find it very disturbing."

"As we all know," Spit continued spluttering, spraying saliva in all directions as he drifted from the threshold into the room.

"Back Spit! At once! All the way to the door!" Bull Bruiser shouted.

"Because Pinky sent everyone dick pics."

"The threshold, Spit!" Bull Bruiser growled. "And no more yakking about that pervert's furry dick pics!"

"I wonder why he didn't send them to me?" Albert Pop mused.

"Am I surrounded by psychos or what?" Bull Bruiser asked.

HOLDING PHILIPPA'S SCALE-COVERED forearm, Bull Bruiser's little dark eyes flickered malevolently, as he gazed at her face. "So what did you do?" he demanded.

"Come again?" Philippa replied.

"How'd you get these scales? Did you drink Pinky Pimple's non-FDA-approved anti-baldness concoction, Bush? Or his equally non-FDA-approved anti-constipation elixir, Explosion? Or did you go to that freak proctologist, the one who perfumed Fred Fart's gas…"

"Dr. Butt," Spit clarified. "Whose assistant, Bunzi Schlimizzle was fixated on getting him the Nobel Prize."

"Oh right. I remember," Bull Bruiser said. "Did you get Butt's anti-constipation and flatulence perfuming device,"

"The pump," Spit spat helpfully.

"Yes, the pump? Did you get that inserted in your rectum?"

Philippa's eyes widened in horror.

"I take that as a no," the editor said sourly.

"I will sautee this lizard person's scales in butter sauce," Albert Pop informed the room.

"Good to know," Bull Bruiser said as sourly as before.

"It just happened, last night after my shower," Philippa explained. "I was rubbing myself dry with a towel, and the skin flaked off, revealing these…these…"

"Scales," Bull Bruiser said.

"Right. So I ditched the towel and finished drying myself with a hair dryer."

"Hmm. So conceivably, if you lose all your skin, you'll have green scales from head to toe," the editor mused. Then he rubbed the skin at the edge of Philippa's forearm. It flaked off, revealing more scales. "I'm a freakin' genius," he exclaimed.

"But I don't wanna be a freak! You stop that!" Philippa snapped, pulling her arm out of his grasp.

"If you don't wanna be a freak, why'd you come to Scuttlebutt?" The editor demanded, that bored, annoyed light flickering in his little dark eyes.

"To sell her story to you for $50,000," said Maynard Ploshinsky.

"Twenty-five thousand dollars seals the deal," Bull Bruiser snapped. "We'll get photos, it'll be a front-page spread. This is blockbuster stuff, Spit! The lizard people exist! We have photos of one of a real, true Illuminati!"

"I'm not an Illuminati," Philippa said.

"Oh yes you are. And if you towel off the rest of your skin, so you're covered with scales head to toe, we are prepared to pay you $100,000 for the exclusive rights to your story and pictures. And I mean exclusive – no hanky-panky with that twerp Futz Fraud over at National Disgrace." Bull Bruiser interlaced his stubby fingers and twiddled his thumbs.

"I will insert hoses in all your orifices," Albert Pop told the editor, "to suction out your salt, which I will store in my intestines until the mother ship arrives."

"No you won't," Bull Bruiser said evenly, between clenched teeth. "Because I'm never again making the mistake of removing your straitjacket."

"Yes you will," Pop asserted. "You will need me to protect you from the lizard queen, when she decides to eat your appendages."

"Not MY appendages," Bull Bruiser snapped.

"I resent that remark," Philippa huffed.

"My associate is no cannibal," Maynard Ploshinsky said.

"Is the Lizard Queen a Cannibal?" Bull Bruiser murmured. "It has headline potential."

"If you call me a cannibal, I'll sell my story to National Disgrace or Gossip," Philippa warned.

"Those cheapskates won't give you half of what I'm offering," Bull Bruiser snapped.

"We will have to confer," Maynard Ploshinsky intoned rather pompously.

"Well, here's my card," the editor handed one to Philippa. "We'd like to record a session between you and our outside consultant, the prestigious," here he looked like he was strangling over this word, "CIA biologist, Charlamagne Crackers."

"That's an extra $5000," Philippa snapped.

"The Lizard Queen is greedy," thus Albert Pop.

Bull Bruiser glared at Philippa.

"She catches on fast, boss," Spit spat, launching a gob of saliva that landed in Philippa's ear.

"Ew!" She cried, as the editor handed her a Kleenex. "Will that… person," she jerked her head in Spit's direction, "be interviewing me? Because if so, I deserve combat pay."

"Alright," Bull Bruiser snapped. "My final offer. Thirty thousand dollars for photos and interviews with Crackers or Spit – oh and the rights to any future developments in this ongoing story, like if you sprout an alligator tale."

Albert Pop's eyes rolled wildly in his head.

"How odd. My mother worried about that too," Philippa said.

"I'm not worried," Bull Bruiser clapped his hands together and rubbed them eagerly. "I look forward to it."

Philippa Philpot eyed him with scorn.

"I will eat the lizard queen's alligator tail," Albert Pop told them.

"OUR ENEMIES ARE the radical left-wing Marxist communist agitators," someone from the website Illuminati Central typed to her. Philippa had clicked on "chat with a lizard" and got a reply from Expert-Q Lizard, who told her that the Illuminati had infiltrated Q-Anon, because their goals were really in sync, namely expunging radical leftism from the world. It was 9 p.m., and the Philpot townhouse was shadowed and silent, as Floozy Philpot had gone visiting at her friend, Maybelline Schnook's house in East Silver Spring.

"Do you have scales?" Philippa typed.

"Of course I have scales, on my toes and my nose," Expert-Q Lizard replied. "I'm not like that phony, Seymour Burp, who attaches a fake iguana tale to his behind with a belt."

"Let me see your scales on FaceTime," Philippa suggested.

"No," came the definitive reply.

Philippa ended the chat. "I'm dealing with frauds," she said aloud into the semi-darkness, then fell into a fit of melancholy: she was a freak, a monstrosity, the only lizard person in the world. Her phone beeped. It was Seymour Burp texting her and asking her out for a drink and did she need homeowner's insurance? "No and no," she angrily replied.

"Well, I guess I'll see you at the shindig in Langley Park." He repeated what he had said the last time they communicated, and then: "Since you live in downtown Silver Spring, I could swing by from Takoma Park and pick you up. We call it the People's Republic of Takoma Park."

"Are you a radical Marxist leftist?"

"No, I'm in insurance. I hope you haven't been talking to that phony, Expert-Q Lizard."

"Just a little," Philippa replied.

"He glued green glitter to his nose and his toes."

"Good to know."

"Everybody wants to be an Illuminati," Seymour texted.

"Why?" She asked.

"To rule the world, why else?"

Her friend Mimi Schnook, nee Schlimizzle, texted her. "Your mom says you have scales."

"Tell her to stop gossiping about me," Philippa texted back, accidentally sending this note to Seymour Burp.

"Expert-Q Lizard is a he, not a she," Burp replied.

"And my mom says this lizard people conspiracy theory is for nuts," Mimi continued.

"You mean Q-Anon?" Philippa asked.

"Yes."

"Well rest assured," Philippa continued, "my research so far reveals that I'm the only real lizard person in the world. All the others are fakes."

"Not me," Seymour Burp texted back. "I have an alligator tale."

"Oh, shut up about your alligator tale," Philippa wrote.

"I don't have an alligator tale," Mimi texted back.

"Not you," Philippa attempted to correct the confusion.

"Yes me," Seymour Burp replied.

"I give up," Philippa texted.

"See a dermatologist," Mimi suggested helpfully. "Hinchy Schnook saw one for the purple spots on his leg."

"Maybe he's a lizard person," Philippa texted, and inadvertently managed to send it out on both threads.

"Who?" Seymour Burp asked.

"No, he just had spots and had to stop drinking vinegar."

"Who in their right mind drinks vinegar?" Philippa asked.

"What are we talking about?" Thus Seymour Burp.

"Hinchy Schnook, apparently," thus Mimi Schnook, nee Schlimizzle. "My husband Herm does it too."

"You married into a very peculiar family," Philippa texted.

"I'm not married," Seymour Burp texted back. "But I'm open to the idea of marriage."

"What are you talking about?" Philippa asked.

"About the Schnooks drinking vinegar. They started when their father, Al Schnook, came out of his nine-month coma and claimed he was animal trapper Frank Fart reincarnated. That's when the MRI showed he had two brains in his head, proving that he really was reincarnated."

"That didn't prove reincarnation," Philippa texted.

"What?" Seymour Burp asked. "What's going on?"

"It just proved he was a freak with two brains."

"I'm not a freak with two brains," Seymour Burp texted. "I'm a lizard person with an alligator tale who's open to the idea of marriage."

"I give up," Philippa texted.

"Don't give up," Mimi advised. "See Dr. Hiccup."

"Who's Hiccup?" Philippa asked.

"Come again?" Thus Seymour Burp.

"The dermatologist who cured Hinchy Schnook's spots. He," Mimi texted definitively, "is your guy."

THE NEXT MORNING, a bright, cool, early April day, Philippa drove her rattling old car over to the Schnooks' small, crowded house. Fifty-something Maybelline Schnook, pudgy and frazzled, her dark, gray-streaked, chin-length hair still fly-away, despite having been combed, answered the door, announcing that the toy poodle, Fart Schnook, a name which combined those of the previous householder, Al Schnook, later Frank Fart reincarnated, had already crapped in the hall. "But take him out anyway, maybe he'll go again," Maybelline said. "I'm late for work at Jumbo Mart, because I had to clean that mess up."

"I still don't see why Hinchy can't walk the damn dog," Mimi said, emerging from the basement staircase. The basement was very full – she and her husband Herm Schnook had a bedroom there, as did Hinchy. "It's not as if he has a job or even does anything all day."

"I look for work on Craigslist," the nearly 30-year-old Hinchy Schnook called from the kitchen.

"Oh bother," thus Maybelline. "He doesn't walk Fart Schnook because he refuses to clean up after him. And after Fart Schnook left a few small… turds on the neighbor's front yard a couple of times, we began to get threatening texts on our phones."

"I'm not cleaning up turds after that midget poodle that does nothing besides crap all day," Hinchy called.

"Good to know," thus his older brother Herm, in khaki pants and a white button-down shirt. "Should I wear a tie?" He asked his barista wife.

"Fresh Feet is a freakin' podiatry supply shop! No, you don't need a tie," Mimi huffed.

"But I'm in retail. I face the public," he whined.

"Wear a tie, knock yourself out," she said.

"Hey Philippa," Hinchy came out into the living room from the kitchen. "Lemme see your scales."

Philippa pulled up a sleeve. Everyone's eyebrows rose in shock.

"You didn't, by any chance," Maybelline haltingly began, "ingest any non-FDA approved elixirs, did you Philippa?"

The dog walker shook her head.

"I ask because my husband, Al Schnook,"

"Who thought he was Frank Fart," Mimi put in.

"Al got a lot of one of Pinky Pimple's men's health products, a non-FDA approved powder, on his skin, and he, um, grew fur over half his body. It looked very odd."

"Bush. The men's anti-baldness product is called Bush," Herm said. "Remind me never to use it."

"You're going a little bald at the temples," his 20-something wife said, casting a critical glance at his hairline.

"Better that than a full-body pelt of brown and silver fur," Herm huffed.

"Maybe just a few flakes of Bush," thus Mimi.

"We still have it in the medicine cabinet," Maybelline said.

"No," Herm replied.

"I don't think I used Bush," Philippa said.

"Well, not Bush, but maybe some other non-FDA approved elixir,"

Maybelline continued. "Because I don't see how else you got those scales. That," she said, pointing at Philippa's arm, "is not normal."

Everyone goggled at Philippa's green scales.

"So the lizard people exist after all," Hinchy finally said, crunching on a celery stalk. "And here I thought it was all fake news."

"Philippa's not a lizard person," Mimi defended her friend.

"Oh yes she is," Hinchy continued, then reached into a pile of Scuttlebutts, National Disgraces and Gossips on the coffee table and pulled out an issue of National Disgrace, whose front page announced in 50-point type: "Lizard People Rule the Earth! Illuminati Eat Children, Expert-Q Lizard Says."

"Hey, I was texting with Expert-Q Lizard last night," Philippa exclaimed.

"I'd avoid that freak, if I were you," Hinchy advised. "He's a cannibal."

"You're not a cannibal, are you, dear?" Maybelline asked.

"Eat the poodle, if you get hungry," Herm advised Philippa.

"No. I'm a vegetarian," Philippa said.

"A 28-year-old, unemployed vegetarian with scales," Mimi said. "Come work at Starbucks. I think we're gonna have an opening. Pedro says the smell of coffee makes him sick. He almost puked on a customer the other day, and yesterday he DID puke in an extra grande latte. When he offered to remake the latte, the woman said, 'no, never mind. The sight of you vomiting into my coffee took away my appetite.' Management was very unhappy with him."

Fart Schnook defecated on the parquet floor next to the beige carpet's edge.

"At least it's not on the rug," Mimi said, wrinkling her nose in disgust.

Maybelline handed the pooper scooper to Philippa. "I don't have time," she explained. "I'll be late for my shift at the supermarket bakery, if I clean that up."

"Why'd we have to get that damn dog anyway?" Herm wanted to know.

"In memory of your dear departed father," Maybelline Schnook sniffed, "and his untimely demise."

"He got dragged off a tour fishing boat near Miami, 'cause he wouldn't let go of his freakin' fishing rod when he'd clearly hooked a monster squid," Herm said. "I don't see what that has to do with an incontinent, midget poodle."

"It was a very moving ceremony," Maybelline continued. "Buddy Schlimizzle is the best undertaker on the east coast, even if he has been constipated for 40 years."

"As the whole world knows," Herm said sourly, "since those supermarket tabloids," and he pointed to the stack on the coffee table, "got into a circulation war on the subject."

"And you don't know Al hooked a squid," Maybelline continued. "It could've been a shark."

"A shark would have eaten him," Herm said. "And his corpse was intact."

"Buddy Schlimizzle did a wonderful embalming job," Maybelline enthused dreamily.

"It could've been a whale," thus Hinchy, who had returned to the kitchen and then come back out eating a bagel with cream cheese.

"And he gave us a discount," Maybelline continued.

"I should hope so. I was engaged to his daughter," Herm said.

"A BIG discount," Maybelline said.

"He opposed our engagement," Mimi recalled. "He told my mother that we would produce a brood of furry little Al Schnooks, who would send dick pics to their preschool playmates, for which the Schlimizzles, all of us, would probably be arrested and sued."

"Al never sent anybody any dick pics," Maybelline huffed.

"But he did use Bush, and it covered him with fur," Mimi said, "like Pinky Pimple, who DID send out dick pics, lots of them."

"To everybody and their grandmother," Herm said sourly.

"Pinky did it 'cause he had the Penis Plague," Mimi continued. "I read all the stories about it in National Disgrace and Scuttlebutt."

"Well, Al never had the Penis Plague," Maybelline huffed again.

"Scuttlebutt said otherwise," Mimi contradicted.

"That rag also said he would de-evolve into a homicidal giant amoeba," Maybelline continued huffing in great umbrage. "I don't know why Al didn't sue them and that idiot CIA biologist, Charlemagne Crackers."

"Because they paid Dad thousands of dollars for his story," Hinchy said, chewing his bagel. "And because Frank Fart was a freakin' publicity hound."

"You mean Al Schnook," Maybelline sniffed in offended tones. "Al Schnook, who was in INSURANCE."

"Well, when he came out of his coma, he insisted he was an animal trapper from Miami named Frank Fart," Herm contradicted his mother.

"Whose cousin Fred Fart stayed with us," Mimi frowned, "and nearly asphyxiated the entire family with his stinky flatulence."

"Enough," thus Maybelline.

"Good thing your Mom works for that proctologist, Dr. Butt," Herm mused. "He put that anti-constipation pump that can also deodorize flatulence into Fred Fart's colon, and then it was all roses and honeysuckle. No more swamp gas."

"That's not what his boss, the exterminator who owns Pest Patrol says," Mimi contradicted.

"You mean Lucas Flush," Herm said.

"Yes him."

"I know all about Lucas Flush," Philippa put in. "I read in Scuttlebutt how he was directing the commander of the Space Force, leading the attack against the enemy flying saucers with the Andromedans and the crab people."

"Yeah, and he lost the nation's nuclear codes, "Herm said.

"He stapled them to an invoice for cleaning out a spider infestation in a Miami townhome, owned by a spinster named Miss Pinch," Philippa said.

"Wow!" Thus Hinchy. "Some memory for detail!"

"Yeah, well, the whole country thought we were under attack and the world was about to end. And this pest control expert lost the freaking nuclear codes. And General Boom couldn't find them. The president couldn't find them," Philippa went on. "And for a while they thought that, uh, DARPA had miniaturized them and attached them to the, uh, pump, in that person's colon."

"You mean Fred Fart," Mimi scowled.

"He NEVER, NEVER sets foot in this house again," Herm told his mother.

"I said the same thing about my parents' house," Mimi said. "And my brother Marty explained that if Fred Fart ever came back, he and my father would sleep at the funeral home like they did before. The coffins are apparently very comfortable."

"But now Fred smells like perfume," Maybelline objected, heading toward the door.

"Yeah, but sometimes that perfume runs out," Herm said sourly. "I read about that in National Disgrace. There was a diagram on the front page and everything. The caption said: 'The pump in Fred Fart's rectum.' And the story told how the perfume ran out on a Baltimore to Miami flight and nearly asphyxiated the passengers and crew."

"I don't think I want to meet this person," Philippa said, scooping up Fart Schnook's leavings.

"Well, I'd say you never will," Herm replied. "But I don't wanna jinx it."

DR. HICCUP WAS so boney, it looked like his skeleton was trying to poke out of his skin. He sported an ugly, brown moustache, very short, sparse and bristly.

"Hmm, lizard scales," he said, examining Philippa's arms. "Young lady, you have lizard scales."

"I knew that," Philippa said.

"You may turn into an alligator."

"Great."

"Or a large iguana."

"Thanks, Dr. Hiccup. That's really helpful."

"If you have the urge to plunge into large bodies of water and catch fish with your teeth, then we'll know," the idiot doctor told her.

"Know what?"

"That you're becoming an aquatic reptile."

"Excuse me, Dr. Hiccup," an exasperated Philippa began, "but can you recommend a cream or ointment I could use to make these scales go away?"

"Yes. There's a non-FDA approved gel, Derma-Lube, marketed by the estate of the online men's body products mogul, Pinky Pimple. That should do the trick," and Dr. Hiccup rubbed his ugly, uncomfortable looking, little moustache and then some of the other many bristles that poked out on his face and hands.

"I already use Derma-Lube," Philippa said, and then a light went on in her brain. "In fact, it was a day after I started that I developed these scales! I'm gonna sue Derma-Lube!"

"Wouldn't it be better to find out from the estate's manager, the well-known widow and Lorena Bobbitt admirer, Prissy Pimple, if they market an 'Anti-Derma-Lube?'" With that, Dr. Hiccup began opening drawers in the examining room, shuffling things around, pulling them out and generally, noisily making a mess. A nurse opened the door and poked her head in. "Stop that, Dr. Hiccup," she snapped.

"I'm looking for Derma-Lube," he complained.

"That's not FDA-approved," She sniffed haughtily.

"The patient wants it."

"I want Anti-Derma-Lube," Philippa corrected.

"Hmm. I'll see what I can do." The nurse left, and Dr. Hiccup resumed making a mess. Philippa phoned Mimi Schnook.

"Doesn't your Mom know that insane widow, Prissy Pimple?" She asked.

"Who is this?" Mimi replied, shouting over the clatter of Starbucks.

"Me, Philippa. I want to meet her. I think her husband's Derma-Lube made me grow scales."

"Well, you're in luck," Mimi said. "My parents are having her over to dinner tonight, and Herm and I have to go. We're expected. We'll bring you along."

The nurse reappeared with a small sample tube of something called "Desert."

"This is for patients with oily skin," she said.

"I don't have oily skin," thus Philippa.

"I didn't say you did," Mimi said.

"It may make those scales," the nurse pointed at Philippa's arm, "drop off."

"Well, I do want the scales to drop off," Philippa replied. "What if Desert has the opposite effect?"

"What desert?" An exasperated Mimi asked. "Are you coming to dinner or not? It's at seven. I have no idea what's for dessert, but the main course will undoubtedly be flank steak or meatloaf – two of the four dishes my

Mom knows how to cook."

"Why are you telling me about your Mom's culinary skills?" Philippa asked.

"I'm not," the nurse said. "I'm telling you about Desert."

There came a loud crash, as a drawer, which Dr. Hiccup had opened too far, fell on the floor. He yowled, because it partially landed on his foot.

"I told you to stop that, Dr. Hiccup," the nurse said.

"Dr. Hiccup's cookies are cracked," Philippa said.

"I thought he was a very good dermatologist," Mimi sniffed. "That'll be eight dollars," she told a customer.

"It'll be a lot more'n eight dollars," Philippa said. "You can be sure of that."

AFTER THE LONG drive home, Philippa phoned her mother to tell her she was having dinner at the Schlimizzles with Prissy Pimple that evening.

"Aren't we moving up in the world," Floozy said. "The Kaopectate's in aisle seven," she told a pharmacy customer.

"I don't need Kaopectate. I need to get rid of these scales. That's why I'm going to dinner at the Schlimizzles," Philippa said.

"Consorting with the well-known undertaker and his world-famous constipation," Floozy marveled.

"I don't want constipation," the short, fat, elderly customer with a goatee told her. "I just want to get this diarrhea under control."

"You know that Dr. Butt that Bunzi Schlimizzle works for was nominated for the Nobel Prize by the American Proctological Society," Floozy continued.

"Good to know," the customer replied.

"He was nominated for his internationally renowned anti-constipation pump, that goes in the rectum. It also deodorizes flatulence," Floozy said.

"Too much information," the man told her.

"But Buddy Schlimizzle claims it causes the Penis Plague and can be fatal," Floozy went on.

"Fantastic," Philippa muttered sarcastically.

"I haven't heard about the Penis Plague since covid," the man said. "As

I recall, it causes its sufferers to grow two brains, a thick pelt of fur and to become sexually insatiable, before they degenerate down the evolutionary scale and become fully aquatic, either a giant homicidal tuna or amoeba. The stories were never too clear which. It was very alarming."

"You should wear a mask," Floozy told him.

"What are you talking about? I'm home alone, making myself a veggie burger," Philippa snapped.

"And don't get me started on Prissy Pimple," Floozy went on. "The last time I saw her at Maybelline Schnook's, she argued that all males who cheat on their wives should be castrated. Hard to believe she heads up a men's body products empire."

"That doesn't include Kaopectate, does it?" The customer asked nervously.

"Last I checked, Kaopectate wasn't a men's body product. It just stops you, man or woman, from going too much," Floozy said.

"What's all this about Kaopectate?" Philippa demanded. "Dr. Hiccup gave me Desert. I realized, no thanks to him and his three-figure fee, that Derma-Lube probably caused my scales."

"And here I thought my daughter was one of the Illuminati."

"This pharmacist is crazy," the customer murmured under his breath and wandered off.

Meanwhile, Mimi Schlimizzle had phoned her mother at work to alert her that Philippa would come to dinner.

"It'll be a party!" Bunzi enthused, clapping her hands.

"Just two guests," Mimi said.

"No, three. Fred Fart's coming up to see Dr. Butt."

"Oh no!" Mimi wailed. "I thought he had a proctologist in Miami who refills the perfume in his rectal pump."

"I'll get that latte later," a customer said and promptly left the premises.

"He does, Dr. Posterior. But Posterior's on a two-week vacation in Puerto Rico, and Fred Fart's back to, um…" Bunzi paused.

"Passing smelly gas?"

"Yes, you could put it that way. I had a very disjointed conversation with Fred and his boss, Lucas Flush, the famous pest exterminator who lost the nation's nuclear codes. Lucas Flush claimed that if Fred Fart didn't get a perfume refill, pronto, he, Lucas, was going to hang himself. Well, of course I didn't want to be responsible for a celebrity suicide," here, all the patients in the waiting room dropped their mouths open, as they gaped at her. "So I invited Fred up for the night. He sees Butt tomorrow. He's Butt's 9 a.m."

"Excuse me, Mrs. Schlimizzle," one patient said, approaching the desk, "but I think I'll cancel today's exam."

"Oh, Dr. Butt will be so disappointed."

"I don't wanna hang myself," the patient said.

"Oh, you won't hang yourself," Bunzi assured him.

"If I have to smell Fred Fart throughout dinner, yes, I may very well hang myself," Mimi Schlimizzle snapped.

EARLIER THAT DAY in north Miami, as the Pest Patrol pickup bounced along through a wealthy subdivision on its way to a domicile "crawling, literally crawling with silverfish," so the householder claimed, bushy gray-haired Lucas Flush, behind the steering wheel turned to dull-eyed, dull-witted, dull brown-haired Fred Fart in the passenger seat and told him to open the window, or else.

"Or else what?" Fred Fart looked alarmed, then, as no answer was forthcoming, went on: "It's a cool day," he whined. "And your window's already wide-open."

"Fred, I'm desperate here," and Lucas squinted at his employee.

Fred Fart looked alarmed. "What's goin' on, Lucas?"

"Your perfume ran out. We're gonna hafta take a detour to Biscayne Boulevard."

"Someone there has a worse silverfish infestation?"

"Nope. We're goin' to Posterior."

"Oh. But he's in Puerto Rico. When I saw him three weeks ago, he said he needed a vacation from all his patients who pass enough gas to asphyxiate an entire metropolis. Who do ya think he was talking about, Lucas?"

The proprietor of Pest Patrol ran his fingers through his thick gray hair, which stuck out in all directions, and squinted at his employee.

"Then ya gotta go up to Maryland, to see Butt. Because he's the only other proctologist in the country who knows how to refill that perfume cannister you got in that, um, unmentionable place."

"You mean up my ass?"

"I was trying to be polite, Fred."

"Oh, don't stand on ceremony with me, Lucas."

His boss gagged, waved a hand in front of his nose, then poked his head out the window. "Get a grip, Fred," he said.

"I got digestive issues," Fred Fart whined.

"As the whole world knows, from the in-depth coverage of the goings on in your colon by Scuttlebutt and National Disgrace. Hmm…" Lucas paused. "I got an idea. I'll call the head of the space force. General Boom may be able to recommend a local proctologist."

Lucas dialed, then said, "The rectal pump ran out of perfume and now the cab of my truck stinks to high heaven."

Space force commander General Boom concluded this was a crank call and hung up. He told the driver of his black SUV to take him to Heaven's Lobby cemetery, outside Miami, as he had some lilies "to put on mother's grave." His phone rang again.

"I'm dyin' here. I need a proctologist, pronto!" Lucas said.

General Boom hung up again.

"We got a bad connection," Lucas said on the third try. "But Fred Fart's in a lot of trouble."

General Boom's eyebrows rose in alarm. "He hasn't been abducted by the crab people, has he?"

"I wish. Hey, Fred," Lucas turned to his employee. "Think you could get yourself abducted by some sexually insatiable aliens?"

"Who is this?" General Boom demanded.

"Lucas Flush."

"Oh hello, commander Flush, how can I help you?"

"I need a proctologist."

"Is this to miniaturize the nation's nuclear codes and store them in a certain, um, person's, certain, um, place?"

"You mean Fred Fart's rectum," Lucas clarified. "And no. It's not about that. Does the space force have a proctologist in the greater Miami metropolitan area?"

General Boom pondered, and finally, after a long pause, delivered his weighty answer: "No." Then he said, "Rendez-vous at Heaven's Lobby in 30 minutes."

"No can do," Lucas replied. "I got a 9 a.m. silverfish infestation in North Miami."

Fred Fart, who had heard every word, because the volume on Lucas' phone was turned up high, shouted: "I'd appreciate it if you could pay my respects to my cousin Fatso's grave."

"Fatso?" Thus General Boom.

"Frank Fart."

"Python man? Who abducted the president after snacking on some Amtrak passengers in the dining car?" General Boom asked.

"And he ate some of the white house staff," Fred Fart added, at the top of his lungs.

"No," General Boom said. "I will not."

After this fruitless call, Lucas Flush phoned Bunzi Schlimizzle at Dr. Butt's reception desk.

"The canister in his rectum ran dry, and I'm gonna hang myself if it don't get a perfume refill," Lucas said.

An alarmed Bunzi promptly ended the call. She ran her beautifully manicured fingers through her blonde-highlighted hair. In her close-fitting designer ensemble, she looked much younger than her nearly 60 years, as she told Dr. Butt's 9:30 patient that a little constipation was nothing out of the ordinary. Her phone rang, she answered it, telling the patient, "In fact, my husband has been constipated for 40 years."

Lucas Flush hung up. "Must be a wrong number," he muttered and dialed again. "Fred Fart stinks to high heaven," he announced.

"Who is this? Is this the Nobel committee?" Bunzi asked.

"No. It's Lucas Flush. And if you don't schedule Fred Fart for a perfume refill tomorrow morning, I'm gonna hang myself." And he squinted over at his employee. "Stop it, Fred."

"But what about Posterior?" Bunzi asked.

"He fled to Puerto Rico."

"Okay, I scheduled him. I assume he'll want to stay with us," she said.

"Hotel prices bein' what they are," Fred shouted. "Yes."

Her phone beeped. She switched calls.

"I ran outta Explosion, and I think I'm gonna explode," Buddy Schlimizzle at the Schlimizzle Funeral Home told his wife.

Bunzi promptly ended the call. He called back. "Bring me a bottle of Explosion on your lunch break. I need a laxative." She accidentally switched calls, demanding, "Who is this?"

"Lucas Flush, I told you."

She inadvertently switched calls again. "Well, I can't say I'm too enthusiastic about Fred Fart stinking up my dining room tonight."

"Bunzi, I put my foot down! No Fred Fart!"

"Who is this?" She demanded.

Long, lean Buddy Schlimizzle in his black undertaker's suit frowned at his phone, then said, "It's Buddy, your husband, who else?"

"Well, we're having Fred Fart, Prissy Pimple and Philippa Philpot to dinner."

"No, no and no."

"You don't know Philippa Philpot," Bunzi said.

"I'm sure she's awful. If Fred Fart stays at our house, stinking like he does, I'll spend the night at the funeral parlor and sleep in a coffin." Buddy snapped.

Bunzi accidentally switched calls. "Don't you think sleeping in a coffin is a little…odd?"

Lucas held his phone out and stared at it, then said, "This conversation's a little odd."

The 9:30 patient's eyes rounded and his eyebrows lifted in shock. "I'm not gonna sleep in a coffin. It's just a little constipation. Maybe I'll go home and try Miralax again." And with that, he slipped out of the office.

Bunzi accidentally switched calls again.

"I got a 10:30 funeral," Buddy said.

And again, she unwittingly switched her call. "I don't care if you got a 10:30 funeral," Bunzi told Lucas Flush. "I can't leave. Buy your own Explosion."

"I think something's wrong with my phone," Lucas Flus said and squinted at it.

Bunzi switched calls again. Fat, white-haired, medium height Dr. Butt in his white jacket wandered out. "Where's my 9.30?" He asked.

"I think he went to sleep in a coffin or hang himself, I'm not sure which or in which order," Bunzi told him.

THAT EVENING, WHEN the doorbell rang at the Schlimizzle residence in leafy Kemp Mill, their 30-year-old son Marty, who lived in the basement, went to answer it, while his mother tended the meatloaf in the oven, and his father scowled and demanded to know why he couldn't get take-out sushi.

"Because that would be rude, Buddy," Bunzi said, wiping her hands on her white apron with the red flower print. "How do you think our guests would feel if I served them meatloaf, while you and Marty ate tekka maki? No self-respecting guest,"

"They're not self-respecting guest. Two – Fred Fart and that man-hating Prissy Pimple – are dimwits. One smells and the other talks about nothing besides castrating unfaithful husbands."

"Prissy does have a one-track mind," Bunzi conceded. "I'll grant you that."

"If you dignify what's in her skull as a mind," Buddy groused. "I guess you could put it that way."

Marty opened the front door.

"Surprise! We all came at once," Mimi told her brother, who froze in horror at the sight of Fred Fart and Prissy Pimple. He ran his fingers through his brown curly hair and moaned.

"It'll be over soon, Marty," Herm Schnook told him. "That is, if you survive your mother's meatloaf."

Long, lean, dark-haired, dark-suited, dyspeptic Buddy Schlimizzle poked his head into the vestibule, saw who was there, sniffed the air, frowned and said: "I'm goin' for sushi."

"Get some for me," thus Marty.

"And me," thus Herm.

"How rude," Mimi said.

"What's on the menu besides sushi?" Philippa asked politely.

Buddy Schlimizzle frowned sourly, "meat loaf, dry as dust."

"I resent that, Buddy Schlimizzle!" Bunzi called from the kitchen.

"Keep it up, and I'll stop cooking at all."

"There's hope for us yet," Marty breathed.

"Would it be okay if I got sushi too?" Philippa asked Mimi.

"No," Mimi replied.

"You seem normal," Buddy addressed her. "How'd you wind up in this crowd?"

"I used Pinky Pimple's patented Derma-Lube, and it had very, um, bad effects," Philippa began.

"That louse. I shoulda cut off all his junk years ago and tossed it out the car window," Prissy Pimple muttered, thus dispelling the previous, usual and correct impression of bovine stupidity that she made on all around her.

Fred Fart's eyebrows rose in alarm. "I remember you," he said and edged away from the widow, who, despite her husband having expired several years before, still wore black. "In mourning," as she explained to anyone who asked, "at having missed my opportunity to castrate that philanderer like he deserved, that louse who sent dick pics to half the housewives in this county."

Philippa also edged away from the widow. Buddy noticed this and nodded approvingly.

"I was hoping," Philippa said, "to find out how I can purchase Desert, so as maybe to, um, reverse the effect of Derma-Lube."

"On my website," Prissy said, "the Pinky Pimple, may he rot in hell, men's body products website. But I also brought a can of Desert, because Mimi phoned me." And as this crowd moved into the front room, Prissy extracted the spray can from her large purse, handed it to Philippa and said, "That'll be $20."

Philippa paid, then looked at the canister skeptically. As she held it up, the white silk sleeve of her blouse fell to the elbow, revealing her green glittering scales.

"Wow!" Marty exclaimed, very nasally, for he was holding his nose. "What's that?"

"That's what Derma-Lube did to me," Philippa explained.

"Sue," thus Buddy Schlimizzle. "I have a great lawyer, Morris Finkelstein in D.C. I'll get his card for you."

Prissy Pimple gaped from Buddy to Philippa.

"Philippa's a lizard person," Marty said.

"No," his father contradicted, "she's another victim of Pinky Pimple's phony body products with their horrible side effects."

"Look who's talking!" Bunzi stepped into the living room from the kitchen, her hands on her hips. "The man who's addicted, ADDICTED, to Pinky Pimple's ghastly laxative, Explosion."

"One of our best-selling products," Prissy simpered. "That and Bush."

"You'd think people would be more careful about Bush, after what happened to Pinky and Al Schnook," Buddy said sourly.

"Frank Fart," Herm corrected.

"Schnook, Fart. I never believed that reincarnation song and dance," Buddy said. Everyone except Bunzi sat in the armchairs or crowded onto the couch.

"Lotsa bald men don't care about possible dangers of Bush," Prissy said.

"Would you rather be bald or look like a gorilla?" Buddy demanded.

"*I* wouldn't be bald," Prissy rather obviously stated.

"Pinky didn't look like a gorilla," Herm corrected.

"He just spilled it on his junk and then sent disgusting photographs of his furry equipment to MY WIFE!" Buddy roared in anger.

"Careful Buddy!" Bunzi called from the kitchen. "Your blood pressure!"

"If I'd known, I would have severed that furry equipment from his body and tossed it out in the trash," Prissy Pimple averred.

Fred Fart's eyebrows lifted. He left his seat and began tiptoeing toward the stairs. Meanwhile Buddy Schlimizzle, Marty and Herm Schnook all paled. "I woulda used shears," Prissy elaborated.

Fred Fart bolted for the staircase and vanished up into the second floor.

"What is that smelly person doing upstairs, Bunzi?" A shaken Buddy Schlimizzle called into the kitchen. Bunzi came out, a large knife in hand. "What's wrong with you three? You look like you saw a ghost," she said.

"This discussion of castration gave me gas," Buddy complained and burped discreetly.

"Oh, what's a little castration?" Bunzi asked. "That's just Prissy. She talks about it all the time. Where's Fred Fart?"

"Up here. I don't want someone going after my junk with shears," the pest technician called from the top of the stairs.

"Stinking up our bedroom," Buddy grumbled. "Well, no matter, I'll be sleeping at the funeral home, in a deluxe coffin."

"Me too," Marty said.

"You get down here, Fred!" Bunzi snapped and walked over to the foot of the stairs.

"What's the knife for?" Dull-witted Fred Fart asked. "And where is that witch with the shears?"

"The knife's for meatloaf, and Prissy doesn't have shears. You're not allowed on the second floor," Bunzi said. "Get down here."

Fred Fart phoned Lucas Flush for a consult.

"That witch I've mentioned before, she's a very strange woman who wants to cut off my junk with shears," he said.

Lucas disconnected the call at once, climbed out of the cab of his Pest Patrol pickup and walked with his distinctive limp into a Dairy Queen for an ice cream cone. His phone rang again.

"She thinks I got fur on my privates and wants to turn me into a gorilla – maybe," a confused and terrified Fred babbled.

Lucas' bushy gray eyebrows rose in shock. "These crank calls are gettin' weirder and weirder," he told the pimply teenager behind the counter, after ending the call.

"Get down here, Fred," Bunzi snapped, waving the knife, "this instant."

Fred dialed again. "Butt's receptionist is threatening me with a knife," Fred babbled.

"You probably deserve it," Lucas snapped, "for harassin' random citizens with insane phone calls."

"I'm in danger, Lucas."

"Who is this?"

"Me, Fred Fart."

"Chocolate," Lucas told the teenager. "Extra-large."

"Chocolate what?" Fred asked. "What's chocolate got to do with these bloodthirsty women?"

"Fred, nobody's going to castrate you," Bunzi placated.

"Well, that's reassuring," Buddy said, then, "Ow, all this talk about mutilation has given me a monster case of gas. I don't think I can go get the sushi."

"For once, Buddy Schlimizzle, your gas is good for something," his wife unsympathetically said.

"Do you think if I spray Desert on my scales, they'll go away?" Philippa asked Prissy, who gaped at her idiotically.

"Dinner is served!" Bunzi announced, in the hopes of luring Fred Fart down the stairs.

"Act like a man," Lucas told his employee. "You can't let these women intimidate you."

Fred Fart tiptoed down a step or two and peered through the railing at the living room. Black-clad Prissy was gone. "I thing that castratin' female may have left," he told his boss.

"There you go," Lucas said, paying for his ice cream and returning to his pickup. "I ate at the Cuban place tonight and ran into your girlfriend. She was there with her receptionist, that freak Lolo Chandry, who's always threatening to chop people's heads off."

"Now you depressed me, Lucas," Fred said.

"Sorry. See you after you get your perfume refill. What'll the scent be this time?"

Fred Fart came downstairs and walked into the dining room. He sat at the table as far away from Prissy Pimple as possible. "What'll the scent be this time?" He asked Bunzi, who, with oven mitts on her hands was placing the platter with the meatloaf in front of her disgusted husband.

"Lakeside Laurel," she told him.

"Lakeside Laurel is sounding pretty good just about now," said Marty, holding his nose.

"Mom! Get the air freshener!" Thus Mimi.

"We tried that when he stayed with us a few years back," Herm Schnook said in a very nasal voice, holding his nose. "It didn't work."

Buddy began serving the meatloaf.

"Help yourselves to green beans and red roasted potatoes," Bunzi told her guests, then clapped her hands happily. "Oh, it's so nice to see everybody together at a dinner party! Just like old times! Old times before covid!"

"Yeah, when that raving lunatic in the straitjacket stayed with us and threatened to eat my liver," Buddy grumbled.

"Lakeside Laurel," Fred said into his phone. "I don't know what that smells like."

"Whatever it smells like," Lucas told him, "it's bound to be an improvement."

Philippa, seated next to Fred Fart, reached across his plate for the bowl of roasted red potatoes, revealing her green, glittering scales.

"I'm sitting next to a lizard girl," Fred Fart told his boss.

Lucas Flush's bushy, gray eyebrows rose in shock, as he squinted at his phone. "How do you know she's a lizard girl, Fred?"

"She's got scales."

"I read about these people in Scuttlebutt," Lucas said.

"They eat children," Fred Fart told him.

"Who eats children?" Buddy asked, chewing his meatloaf and scowling.

"The lizard people," Fred explained, his dull brown eyes riveted on Philippa's scales.

"Well, *I* don't eat children," Philippa huffed.

"Maybe this is a job for one of them patriotic veterinarians, "Lucas said. "The ones who helped us out with the crab people invasion, like your girlfriend, Ducky Finch."

Fred ended the call and phoned Ducky. "I'm eatin' dinner with a lizard person," he said, as all the other diners stared at him, chewing.

Ducky Finch decided this was a crank call and hung up.

Fred dialed again. "She has scales on her arms, and you bein' a patriotic veterinary dentist could help."

"Who is this?" Ducky demanded, trying not to watch Lolo make a mess of his chicken.

"Me Fred Fart. I'm eating dinner with a lizard person."

"Better that than with Lolo," she grumbled, tucking her pink hair behind her ears.

"Mom, the meatloaf's dry," Marty whined.

"You shoulda bought sushi," Herm Schnook mumbled to Buddy.

"I couldn't. That so-called conversation about castration upset my stomach," the undertaker said sourly and scowled at Prissy Pimple, cutting her slice of meatloaf into tiny pieces. "Bunzi," he called down the table, "where's the Maalox?"

"I don't see why you go out with that weirdo," Fred Fart complained.

"Because you went away, and I got lonely," Ducky said.

"You tell that stinky Fart, if he tries to come between us, I'll chop his freakin' head off," Lolo snapped. "And his fingers, too."

"I heard that, Lolo," Fred Fart shouted.

"Fred is my boyfriend, Lolo," Ducky told him.

"I don't know what you see in that smelly old exterminator," Lolo griped.

"He has a certain something," Ducky said.

"Yeah, clouds, I mean clouds of perfume that landed me in the hospital with hives all over my body," Lolo frowned.

"And nobody, not Lolo, not Pinky Pimple's widow, is chopping any… any," Fred Fart groped for le mot juste, "part offa my body."

"You tell 'em Fred," thus Herm Schnook.

"Calm down Fred," his girlfriend soothed. "Lolo has anger management issues."

"Could this veterinarian help me get rid of my scales?" Philippa asked.

Fred Fart repeated the question, and one thing led to another and soon Ducky had arranged to fly up sometime in the near future to spend a few days with Fred at the Schlimizzles'. Buddy Schlimizzle listened to these developments frozen in horror. Bunzi was delighted. "It'll be like old times, Buddy!" She enthused.

"We'll all be asphyxiated," he said.

"No, you forgot, tomorrow morning Fred Fart will start smelling like Lakeside Laurel, when Butt refills the canister in his rectum."

"In whose rectum?" Herm Schnook asked.

"This is not proper dinner table conversation," Prissy Pimple sniffed.

"Look who's talking," Buddy snapped at her, "the bloodthirsty witch who yammers on about cutting off male private parts with such gusto that it upset my stomach. Bunzi! The Maalox!"

Bunzi brought the requested medicine to her husband, and he guzzled from the bottle.

"I'll also be able to receive my award," Ducky told Fred. "From Senator Barnard Bustup. He's giving all us patriotic veterinarians plaques. We couldn't have the ceremony for two years because of covid, but now, I'll finally get it, you know, for helping save all those Republicans from sex slavery in interstellar bordellos."

"My girlfriend's getting' a plaque from Senator Barnard Bustup," Fred told the dinner table.

"That lunatic," Marty said.

"Aren't you excited for me, Fred?" Ducky asked. "There'll be a ceremony in his office and everything."

"Cash would be better than a plaque," Fred said.

"When can she examine my arm?" Philippa asked.

"The lizard girl wants to know," Fred began.

"My name's Philippa."

"Whatever," Fred said. "When can you look at her scales?"

"When I come up. How'd she get them?" Ducky asked.

Philippa explained that she believed Derma-Lube was to blame.

"I'll sue you for defamation," Prissy said, her insipid features dully contorted with anger.

"No one could defame you, no matter what they said," Buddy told her. "And if I were you, I'd slap a warning on that Derma-Lube, tout de suite."

"What kind of warning?" Prissy warily asked, but not so warily that it in any way ruffled her bovine placidity.

"Like that it causes users to grow scales," Buddy said.

"That could hurt sales," Prissy said.

"Bunzi, this discussion aggravated my gas."

"And I don't wanna hurt sales," Prissy ponderously continued. "Besides, who knows if Derma-Lube really causes scales?"

"Ow, ow, ow," said Buddy Schlimizzle.

2

THAT SAME EVENING, at a Burger Burg in nearby Takoma Park, Maryland, Seymour Burp sat at a table with Expert-Q Lizard, chowing down on the establishment's signature Gutbuster burgers. Seymour sat a little uncomfortably, however, and kept shifting from haunch to haunch, due to the long, large, green alligator tail he had strapped onto his behind, with an elastic waistband, and which he half concealed, by tucking it into one pants leg. Expert-Q Lizard of course, as always, sported green glitter on his nose and fingers, and Seymour Burp's blue eyes could not stop staring at the glitter-bedecked wart in the deep cleft of Expert-Q Lizard's chin. Burp was hefty, medium height, with thin, limp, brown hair, combed over his very visible pate. Expert-Q, stringy and tall, had close-cropped black hair, whose bristles stuck out all over his head like those of a brush. They were somehow not an appealing pair.

As they chewed, the conversation having stalled, in waltzed loutish, perennially unemployed Hinchy Schnook in jeans and a T-shirt that blared the unfriendly logo "Fuck Off." His frizzy black hair glistened at the temples with perspiration, as if the effort of walking from his unlovely, very old compact vehicle into the Burger Burg had strained him. He took one look at Seymour's tail and Expert-Q's glitter and snickered.

"You got a problem?" Expert-Q rather belligerently demanded.

"Lizard people wannabes are everywhere," Hinchy chuckled.

"I'm no wannabe," Seymour asserted, rising to throw out his trash.

"What's that tail of yours held on with?" Hinchy snickered again. "Duct tape?"

Seymour Burp did not dignify this comment with a response.

"I saw a real lizard girl with real scales today," Hinchy continued, walked to the counter and ordered a Gutbuster. "No duct tape, no glitter."

"We're gonna rule the world," Expert-Q Lizard loudly told him.

Hinchy Schnook snickered again.

"You laugh," Expert-Q continued. "But you won't be laughing when we cook your sorry ass for dinner."

"Not my sorry ass, you phony," Hinchy said. "All the trimmings," he told the woman behind the counter. He turned and said to Seymour behind him in line for a second Gutbuster: "This girl got her scales from Derma-Lube."

"Is that a lizard person?" Seymour asked.

"It's a men's body lotion. But women use it too. It turns your skin to scales – if you're into that sort of thing."

Expert-Q Lizard rose, left the fast-food restaurant, walked to a pharmacy and bought a tube of Derma-Lube. He returned, rubbing it on his arms and neck. He sat back down and handed it to Seymour. Uninvited, Hinchy joined them.

"It's non-FDA approved, bozo," Hinchy said.

"I don't give a crap," thus Expert-Q Lizard, rubbing his arms and neck.

"She said after her shower," Hinchy continued chattily, "when she toweled off, her skin flaked off, revealing the green scales."

Expert-Q walked to the counter and requested a cup of water, "extra-large." Then he returned to the table. He sprinkled the water on his arms and neck, then wiped it off with napkins. To his companions' astonishment, the skin peeled off, revealing very green, glittering scales.

"Holy cow!" Thus Seymour.

Expert-Q Lizard rolled up his jeans and massaged the Derma-Lube into his calves.

"I deserve a finder's fee," Hinchy said.

"I won't eat you," Expert-Q Lizard replied. "That's you finder's fee."

Hinchy chewed his Gutbuster thoughtfully. "You gonna go around in public like that?"

"Where do you think I am now, idiot?" The lizard person replied. "Want some, Seymour?"

"Nah, I got my tail," Seymour hiccupped in reply.

"Chicken."

"I don't think scales would go over at the office," Burp explained. "Insurance is not a lizard-friendly field."

"Fortunately, I'm rich and retired," the lizard person said.

"From what?" Hinchy asked.

"The drug trade."

"Good to know," thus Hinchy.

The lizard person squinted at the fine print on the tube of Derma-Lube. "It says 'ingest at your own risk.'" He told his companions.

"I wouldn't do that if I were you," Seymour warned.

"I knew the guy who ran the company that makes that stuff," Hinchy pointed at the Derma-Lube. "He died cause his anti-constipation rectal pump malfunctioned, causing the shit to back up to his heart and kill him."

Seymour Burp burped.

"Well, he was a genius," the lizard person said.

"Pinky Pimple. His company also makes Bush," here Hinchy glanced significantly at Seymour Burp. "The anti-baldness concoction."

"That covered people with fur, caused them to develop a second brain and de-evolve into a giant cannibalistic toad," Seymour said. "No thanks. I read they almost took it off the market."

The lizard person squeezed the Derma-Lube into his mouth.

"Our company was involved in the lawsuits," Burp continued. "It was an insurance claims adjuster's nightmare."

"That's the second time you've mentioned insurance," Hinchy observed.

The lizard person keeled over.

"I guess the Derma-Lube didn't agree with him," Hinchy said.

"What happened here?" The Burger Burg manager asked, coming over to their table.

"I think our companion just had a seizure," Hinchy replied, still chewing.

The manager dialed 911. EMTs arrived shortly thereafter and proclaimed Expert-Q Lizard quite thoroughly dead.

"I'm definitely not using that Derma-Lube," Seymour Burp told Hinchy.

"Wise move," said Hinchy Schnook.

THE NEXT MORNING, stringy, scrawny, warty, nebishy and generally unimpressive Futz Fraud sat behind the massive desk that dwarfed him to even greater insignificance, glaring at the front page of the competition with its 50-point headline: "Interview with a Lizard Girl." The front page also featured a color closeup photo of Philippa's arms.

"Stella!" Futz Fraud hollered. "Stella! Get in here!"

"Never, Fraud," she yelled back from her desk, stationed just outside his office. "You ain't vomitin' on me this morning."

"It's an emergency!"

"Go to the bathroom!" She shouted.

"I got my throw-up bag," the editor wheedled.

Stella poked her head, with her frizzy, unattractive, salt and pepper hair coming out of its ponytail, into the doorway and saw her boss waving the white bag of the sort distributed to passengers by some airlines. She rose, her blue poncho taut across her vast midriff, pushed her befogged, crooked, cat's-eye glasses up her nose and, glaring angrily, lumbered into the room. She was careful, however, to keep a good distance from her employer, whose habit of puking on her was the scandal of the office, had been going on for years and had thus thinned the ranks of supplicant editors and reporters flowing into his suite, as they all preferred to text Futz Fraud about their stories and thus not become a barf target.

"National Disgrace got scooped by Scuttlebutt," Futz Fraud told her, his face very long.

"Thanks to your stinginess, yes, we did," Stella snapped.

"Get Fevereau Slop in here."

"You get him."

"No. You tell him to use his spies in the Scuttlebutt newsroom to find out how much that rag paid Philippa Philpot. I am the editor-in-chief. I'm in charge here." And Futz Fraud thrust out his thin, scrawny chest and projectile vomited over the top of his desk.

Stella smiled nastily at not having been doused with this effusion and texted Slop. "Get in Fraud's office, on the double!"

"No," Slop texted back. "I don't want him to vomit on me."

"He won't. He just did all over the desk. We should be good for a couple of hours. And get the custodian."

Minutes later, the fat, white-haired, exhausted, medium-height editor in a rumpled gray suit, appeared in the doorway to the boss's decidedly small-time suite, with a reluctant janitor in tow.

"Mr. Fraud needs to see a doctor," the custodian grumbled. "I clean up his vomit every day."

"He needs to have his stomach removed," Stella snapped. "So he can stop being a menace to the public in general and his inoffensive, hard-working secretary in particular."

"We got scooped," Fraud told Slop.

"I saw. They paid her almost $26,000. Why didn't we offer her more?" Slop asked.

"'Cause Fraud is cheap," Stella said.

"I thought we were bargaining, and she'd come back," the editor-in-chief whined.

"Well, now you gotta pay her $30,000," Stella said.

"Twenty-seven thousand," Fraud snapped.

"No, 30," thus his secretary.

"And I want our prophet, Nostradamus on the case, "Fraud added.

"That lunatic?" Slop asked. "All he ever says is 'The end is nigh!'"

"Invasion of the Lizard People!" Futz Fraud crowed. "The End Is Nigh!" He paused and burped. "Great headline, if I do say so myself."

"I think we used something like it last week," Stella said.

"Genius," the warty little editor told her, "never grows old."

LONG, LEAN, CONSTIPATED, dyspeptic Buddy Schlimizzle stared in perplexity at the corpse he had just cleaned. It was covered with green, glittering scales. He read the text on his phone that had preceded it: "My son, Wilfrid Doofus, expired last night in the Takoma Park Burger Burg.

Please make him presentable for his funeral." He phoned Bunzi who was on a call with Fred Fart.

"I got a corpse covered with green scales. How am I supposed to make a dead lizard presentable?"

Bunzi accidentally shifted the call back to Fred. "You got a dead lizard?" She asked.

"I don't think so," Fred replied.

"Who is this?" Bunzi demanded.

"Fred Fart," he answered.

Bunzi inadvertently switched the call back to her husband. "Butt had to bump you to a later appointment, because his 8 a.m. colonoscopy was so massively constipated they couldn't see a thing. That patient's getting the pump."

"Butt's not bumping me anywhere," Buddy rather aggressively replied, "because I am never, I repeat NEVER, getting that pump up my ass."

"But you already have it," Bunzi said.

"Not unless you inserted it in my sleep I don't," Buddy snapped.

His wife again accidentally switched the call and huffed in very offended tones, "How dare you insinuate that I inserted anything into your rectum in your sleep."

"Something's wrong with my phone," Fred Fart told Marty, who sat across from him on the Schlimizzle's living room couch, holding his nose. "Things are gettin' very confused."

Bunzi unwittingly switched back to her husband.

"What do I do about this dead lizard?" He demanded.

Bunzi decided it was a crank call and disconnected it.

Dr. Butt waddled out into the waiting room, very professional in his white lab coat and asked, in a whine, why he had to see Fred Fart again. "I thought Posterior had that covered down in Miami," he concluded.

Buddy called his wife back.

"Posterior couldn't take it and fled to Puerto Rico," she told Dr. Butt, speaking into the phone.

"Whose posterior?" Buddy demanded. "What couldn't he take – the rectal pump? And what's this got to do with my dead lizard.?"

"What dead lizard?" Bunzi asked.

"Now there's a dead lizard involved?" Dr. Butt asked. "I hope that doesn't have anything to do with Fred Fart's pump, 'cause he's already got the pump, the perfume canister and, if I recall correctly, the nation's nuclear codes, miniaturized by DARPA onto a jump stick in his rectum. It's getting kinda crowded in there. I don't think there's room for a dead lizard."

Dr. Butt's 8:30 patient, who had followed this discussion closely and with alarm, quietly packed up his magazine in his briefcase and left.

"Now look what you did, whoever you are with your dead lizard!" Bunzi snapped into the phone. "You scared off Butt's 8:30."

"Butt's what?" Buddy asked.

"Who is this?" His wife demanded.

"Your husband, who else? And I got a very dead Wilfred Doofus covered with scales. I think his mother may sue," Buddy said.

Bunzi accidentally switched the call.

"Put on lots of make-up," she advised.

"Your Mom wants me to put on lots of make-up," dull-witted Fred Fart told Marty.

"Will it help with the smell?" Marty asked hopefully.

"Will it help with the smell?" Fred Fart asked.

Bunzi accidentally switched the call. "What smell?"

"I'm confused," Dr. Butt said.

"Doofus doesn't smell," Buddy said.

"Who said Doofus smells?" Bunzi asked.

"What doofus?" Dr. Butt wanted to know.

"Though he's a corpse," Bunzi mused, "so I guess it's logical he would smell."

"He doesn't freakin' smell," Buddy hollered. "He looks like a dead lizard!"

Bunzi again unknowingly switched the call.

"Well, some people look like lizards," she said.

"You think I look like a lizard?" Fred Fart asked.

"Who is this?" Bunzi demanded.

"Fred Fart."

"Come now. Butt can see you after all. His 8:30, um, fled," Bunzi said.

"Not if he looks like a lizard, he can't come," Dr. Butt warned. "Whoever he is."

"It's Fred Fart," Bunzi explained.

"Tell him to see Posterior," Butt said stubbornly.

"That shirker's in Puerto Rico," Bunzi repeated.

"Hello! Hello Bunzi?" Buddy shouted into his phone.

His wife came back on the line. "No need to shout."

"Yes, apparently there is a need. What do I do about this dead, man-sized iguana?"

"Like I said, put on lots of make-up."

"I'm not gay," Buddy huffed.

"On the corpse, stupid."

"And I'm not stupid, either," her husband snapped.

THAT EXHAUSTED HACK, medium-height, fat Fevereau Slop was in a funk. He sat in the National Disgrace lunchroom, his gray suit rumpled and ran the thick fingers of one hand through his white hair, in need of a trim. Futz Fraud had assigned him to interview Nostradamus in person about the invasion of the lizard people, something he was loath to do, as he considered the prophet an obese, dirty, potentially dangerous nutjob. But Slop had been unable to sluff this task off onto any other reporter. All had the impudence to insist to the senior editor that they were too busy. So Slop decided to phone Nostradamus and entice him to the newspaper's office, "because I am not, repeat not, interviewing that kook in his filthy RV in the Walmart parking lot," he said aloud.

"What kook?" Stella asked, lumbering into the lunchroom and pouring a cup of coffee.

"Nostradamus," Slop said.

"Don't you interview him anywheres near me, that's all I gotta say," she told him.

"Thanks Stella," Slop grumbled.

"Hey, it's everyman for himself around this madhouse," Stella said. "And I got my hands full, fending of Fraud's vomit attacks. You wouldn't have a recommendation for a good gastroenterologist?"

"Do I look like a nurse?" Slop rather ungraciously demanded.

"I want one for Fraud. I think he needs his stomach removed."

"So you've been saying for months," Fevereau Slop dialed Nostradamus' number.

"I got it!" Stella exclaimed. "I'll call that wife of the undertaker, whose 40-year constipation we covered in depth."

"I think she works for a proctologist, and you don't need a proctologist," Slop said.

"Who says I need a proctologist?" Nostradamus demanded, sitting at the little fold-out Formica table in his phenomenally cluttered RV with the shotgun over the door. Before him lay a half-eaten Domino's, extra-large, pepperoni pizza and an enormous cup of Mountain Dew. His pimply companion sitting across from him, gazed hungrily at the pizza.

"The end is nigh!" Tall, fat, disheveled Nostradamus boomed into his phone. It was his signature pronouncement, and everyone at National Disgrace was sick of it, except Futz Fraud, who found it "inspired," and "riveting."

"Just one piece," his companion begged.

"No, Pimples. Get your own pizza," the prophet replied, digging a fat index finger into the deep coal pit of his navel, exposed by his too-tight T-shirt with the "Wellesley College" logo in big black letters, a T-shirt which had ridden up over his vast, hairy belly. He fished out a fingerful of gray lint and wiped it on the table's edge.

"I did get my own pizza," Pimples whined. "I bought this one for you for breakfast at the crack of dawn, and you won't even give me one piece!" Pimples ran his fingers through his thick, greasy brown hair. "And you haven't paid me for it!" Nostradamus' guest concluded.

"Oh, all right, take one piece of pizza," the prophet conceded, as he had no intention of paying for this meal and hoped, by this generosity, to distract Pimples from that unpleasant expectation.

"What pizza?" Fevereau Slop demanded.

"Who is this?" Nostradamus demanded back, trying to wipe the tomato sauce out of his long, rather unclean gray beard.

"National Disgrace. I want to interview you on the invasion of the lizard people."

"Who are you?"

"Fevereau Slop, senior editor. Meet me in my office here in half an hour."

"No can do. You come here," Nostradamus said.

"No. Your RV is too crowded, and I'm allergic to cats."

"It's not crowded. Just me and Pimples," the prophet said.

"Tell him you'll pay him an extra $50 if he consents to be interviewed IN YOUR OFFICE," Stella said. "That means nowhere near me."

"I'll pay you an extra 50 bucks to come here," Slop wheedled.

"So…$850," Nostradamus said.

"No. $550."

"Five-hundred fifty bucks seal the deal. The end is nigh!" The prophet boomed again.

"Whatever," Fevereau Slop said.

"**I NEED A** ride to National Disgrace," Nostradamus told Pimples.

"We gotta stop by the hospital," the prophet's guest discreetly belched. Nostradamus scowled.

"I promised Albert Pop, I'd help him escape first thing this morning. The CIA is giving him mind-altering drugs," Pimples said.

The prophet's scowl deepened. "His mind's already altered," he grumbled. "Pop doesn't need drugs, not that raving lunatic." Nostradamus had concluded years earlier, when Albert Pop informed him that he had wires in his head, a pink plastic brain which he regularly connected to CIA computer servers at Langley where he worked as a custodian and that he was a robot from the Andromeda galaxy – from this Nostradamus had concluded that Albert Pop was insane. And if the supermarket tabloids' looney prophet concluded someone was crazy, there was no doubt that person was flat-out psychotic.

"Maybe I'll uber," Nostradamus said.

"He'll be in his straitjacket," Pimples assured him, to make the prospect more palatable.

"He better be," the prophet remarked, thinking that since his credit card was maxed out, he probably couldn't uber. "But Pop doesn't set foot in my

RV," Nostradamus warned.

"No, we'll stay at his place out in the Virginia sticks. The CIA won't catch on or think to look for him there," Pimples said. "The last time they searched it, they proclaimed it unfit for human habitation. They also worried they might catch a disease."

Nostradamus decided not to dignify what he considered revolting idiocy with a response.

"Question," Pimples continued, reaching for another slice of pizza, which caused his host to frown. "How come the CIA operates so freely in this country? I thought that wasn't legal."

"Since when are those psychopaths bothered by what's legal?" Nostradamus pointed his remote at the TV, and switched it off silent.

"Do you have irritable bowel syndrome?" An advertiser asked.

"They're not psychopaths," Pimples began.

"Then how come they think brainless Albert Pop, who's off his rocker, is an expert on China?" Nostradamus snapped.

"You got me there," Pimples said, and wolfed down his second slice of pizza, beneath the prophet's angry, offended glare.

SEATED IN HER ergonomic, triple extra-large swivel desk chair, Stella phoned Dr. Butt's office and said: "This is National Disgrace."

"Oh my God!" Bunzi squealed in delight. "Is this about Butt's Pulitzer?"

"Butt's Pulitzer," Stella said flatly, a little, annoyed light flickering in her dark, intelligent eyes.

"Yes, for his lead article in American Anus," Bunzi said.

A look of profound revulsion spread over Stella's usually imperturbable features. "Fraud!" She hollered into the open doorway to his office behind her desk. "Get out here. I think we got a story about the Pulitzer committee losin' its mind."

"Oh, I'm so excited!" Bunzi enthused.

Futz Fraud was busy throwing darts at the Scuttlebutt front page with its best-selling fabrications about lizard people. He had pasted it to the wall opposite his desk, but he stopped pitching darts and poked his head out the doorway. "Say what?" he asked.

"They gave a Pulitzer to American Anus," Stella said.

"What anus?" A horrified Futz Fraud asked.

"Butt's anus," Stella replied.

"What butt? What anus?" Fraud demanded.

"You know, I think this discussion's disgusting," Stella said.

Fraud returned to throwing darts. One missed and whizzed past Stella's desk.

"Stop throwin' darts or shut the door Fraud," she snapped.

"Butt's not a fraud," Bunzi huffed. "He's a brilliant, under-appreciated proctologist, who deserved that Nobel Prize."

"I need a recommendation for a gastroenterologist," Stella said.

"Butt's your guy," Bunzi told her.

"American Anus and all," Stella muttered. "I thought he was a proctologist."

"He, er, took some night school courses," Bunzi explained, "and now he's a certified gastroenterologist, too."

At that moment Fred Fart waltzed into the waiting room, and the other two patients looked up sharply, sniffing. Bunzi perceived this and astutely concluded it would be best to remove the new arrival to an examining room, pronto. Holding her nose, she buzzed the nurse, who stepped out into the lobby and told the receptionist that some large animal must have crapped in the waiting room.

"What large animal are you talking about?" Bunzi asked.

"I don't think I mentioned a large animal," Stella said.

"Maybe an elephant," the nurse said. "Or maybe someone died." She scrutinized the patients waiting in the room. "You don't look dead," she told a man reading an issue of Your Colon. He closed the magazine nervously and asked, "Is there something going around?"

"Sure smells like it," the nurse said. "Smells like a ripe corpse."

"That's just Fred Fart," Bunzi told her, pointing at the pest control technician.

"Don't tell me that smelly dimwit's at your office!" Stella exclaimed.

"Take him to an examining room," Bunzi told the nurse, "before we all expire."

"I swear it smells like a decomposing corpse," the nurse said.

"Well, I'm married to an undertaker, and I know from decomposing corpses!" Bunzi nearly shouted.

"What does that have to do with our appointment with Butt?" Stella demanded.

"It's a group appointment?" Bunzi asked.

"No. It's an appointment for an editor who won't stop vomitin' on people," Stella grumbled.

"Take Fred Fart away," thus Bunzi. The nurse did not do so.

"By all means," Stella said. "Take him away. And if you think we're setting foot in that office while that stinky old Fart is there, you've got another thing comin.'"

"Too bad. Our only opening today is in 30 minutes," Bunzi told her.

The patient who had been reading Your Colon approached the desk and whispered, "Did someone die?"

"No need to whisper," Bunzi admonished.

"I ain't whisperin,'" Stella said, then yelled into her boss's office. "Fraud! Get your vomit bag. We're going out to the suburbs."

"There are no corpses in this office," Bunzi assured the anxious patient.

"Good to know," Stella said. "But there is a smelly member of the Fart clan."

"By the time you get here, he'll smell like Lakeside Laurel, that is, provided the pump in his rectum is in working order," Bunzi said.

"You know, maybe I don't have to come on this little sojourn," Stella said.

"You don't go, I don't go," Fraud told her and pitched another dart at the Scuttlebutt front page.

"You just go back to reading Your Colon," Bunzi told the patient.

"Nobody's reading MY colon!" Stella snapped.

"You want the anti-constipation pump?" Bunzi asked. "It's Butt's patented device, and it works like a charm."

"No," Stella said and ended the call. "Well," she told Futz Fraud, "that was an experience."

LOUTISH, UNEMPLOYED, 20-SOMETHING Hinchy Schnook lounged in his mother's basement, where he lived, bored to tears. It was still early morning and he had just sent out five resumes over Craigslist, but he was not optimistic about snagging a job. This pessimism stemmed from years of such attempts, all of which ended in abject failure. As he stewed over this, his sister-in-law, rising, stumbled out of her bedroom in her robe and made for the bathroom.

"Hey," Hinchy had an idea. "Give me your friend Philippa's number." Moments later she picked up the phone.

"Don't ingest Derma-Lube," he told her.

"Who is this?" Philippa demanded.

"Hinchy Schnook."

"How'd you get my number?" She asked in annoyance, as she walked Hubert Poop Junior past Maynard Ploshinsky's potted geraniums. From his front picture window, Ploshinsky waved a copy of Scuttlebutt at her. She stopped, then traipsed up the walk, through brilliant April sunshine to the front door.

As she did, the bulldog crapped on the walk, and she got another incoming call, this one from her mother. Maynard Ploshinsky opened the door.

"The dog just crapped on the walk," she said.

"Sorry, I must've misdialed," Floozy Philpot apologized, hung up and dialed again.

"I hope you intend to clean that mess up," Maynard Ploshinsky said.

"Of course I will," Philippa said. "You think I leave dog turds in people's yards?"

"Who is this?" Floozy asked. "You sound familiar."

"Mom?" Thus Philippa.

"I'm not your Mom, and I have to go to work," long, gangly Maynard Ploshinsky told her, peering at her through thick, black-framed glasses.

"You're famous!" Floozy exclaimed.

"You're famous!" Ploshinsky said, pointing to the front page of Scuttlebutt.

"I'm famous?" Philippa asked, accidentally switching the call.

"Who says you're famous?" Hinchy demanded.

"The front page of Scuttlebutt, about lizard people," she told him, scrutinizing the color photo of her scaly arms.

"Well, Expert-Q Lizard ate Derma-Lube and it killed him," Hinchy reported. "I was there in the Burger Burg when it happened."

"Sounds like somebody has a first-person story for Scuttlebutt," Philippa said.

Hinchy sat up straight. "You know? You're right! If my Dad could make thousands of dollars from that rag, selling it the story of his reincarnation as Frank Fart, I sure can get a fee for having seen Expert-Q Lizard turn into a lizard and croak."

Soon Hinchy Schnook had the editor of Scuttlebutt on the line. Bull Bruiser sat at his desk, his muscular elbows planted on it, as he twiddled his thumbs, with this tipster on speaker.

"I want $5000 for my first-person account of how I witnessed Expert-Q Lizard grow a neck full of scales and then croak in a Takoma Park Burger Burg," Hinchy told the editor.

"Sounds like we got a dead lizard person," chief terrorism and alien abduction reporter Jeremy Spit spat from the threshold of his boss's office. He had been warned not to approach any closer, and Bull Bruiser observed with smug satisfaction that the spray his reporter constantly emitted did not, from that distance, even reach his desk.

"You think I'm an idiot, Spit?" Ugly, bald, blunt-nosed Bull Bruiser snapped. "There are no lizard people."

"Well, this guy was covered with scales," Hinchy said over the speaker phone.

"What'd you say your name is?" Bull Bruiser demanded.

"Hinchy Schnook."

"That rings a bell," the editor grumbled.

"Al Schnook? Reincarnated as Frank Fart?"

"How could I forget? Five thousand dollars is a lot of money. We'll need pictures."

"Well, I got pictures," Hinchy said, "and the corpse is at the Schlimizzle funeral home in Silver Spring. Call Buddy Schlimizzle there."

"Oh yes, the famously constipated undertaker," Bull Bruiser scowled, then muttered, "Is my life a goddamn freak show or what?"

"I'm related to him," Hinchy continued.

"Good to know. You got scales too?"

"No – related to the undertaker, that is," Hinchy clarified. "And remember: I can give you an eye-witness account of how this scaly weirdo kicked the bucket. It was awesome."

So Bull Bruiser phoned Buddy Schlimizzle. "I understand you have a man-sized lizard corpse on the premises."

"Who is this?" Buddy demanded.

"Bull Bruiser, editor-in-chief of Scuttlebutt."

"The sleazos who paid that pervert Pinky Pimple to send dick pics to my wife!" Buddy hollered.

"Calm down, Mr. Schlimizzle. That was years ago. And now there's money involved."

That got Buddy Schlimizzle's attention. "If you want pictures, that's a thousand bucks, and I gotta clear it with Doofus' mother. She may want a cut."

"What Doofus?" Bull Bruiser demanded.

"Wilfred Doofus. This dead person who looks like a giant iguana, except without the tail," Buddy clarified.

"On the case, boss," Spit spat.

"Just so long as you're not in my office," Bull Bruiser said.

"IT'S FOR REAL!" Jeremy Spit hollered into his phone, spraying a disgusted Buddy Schlimizzle with saliva, as the two stood beside Wilfred Doofus' remarkable, scaly corpse.

"That's a thousand for me and another thousand for Mrs. Doofus," Buddy Schlimizzle said sourly, stepping away from the reporter, whose spit range, he recalled from past experience, was quite extensive.

Seated at his desk, Bull Bruiser began scrolling through the photos his star terrorism reporter had just sent him. Astonishment spread over his ugly, blunt, bulbous features. "Put Schlimizzle on the line," he commanded.

"No," Buddy said. "I refuse to touch that…person's wet phone."

Buddy Schlimizzle called Bull Bruiser on his own phone. "So we have a deal?" He asked.

"This is amazing!" Bull Bruiser marveled.

"After all the astounding tales your publication has paraded on its front page, from aliens abducting Republican senators, to nuclear centipedes, to Al Schnook de-evolving into a sex-crazed giant carnivorous toad, I would think," Buddy said, "you'd be a little more blasé. And don't think for a minute, Mr. Bruiser, that I've forgotten you put that pervert, Pinky Pimple, up to sending his dick pics to my wife to improve your story. If my wife receives any dick pics from anyone associated with this story – you, Mr. Spit, Hinchy Schnook or one of Mr. Doofus' relatives – I'll sue. And I have a gun."

"Schnook! I need Hinchy Schnook!" Bull Bruiser yelled.

"That loser who's almost 30 and still lives in his mother's basement?" Buddy asked. "He doesn't even wash under his armpits, according to my daughter."

Bull Bruiser held his phone out and scowled at it. "I didn't need to know that," he said.

STILL EARLY THAT morning, Nostradamus packed his impressive girth into the cramped space of Pimples' car's front passenger seat, amid many complaints about lack of room, clutter and the generally unlovely aspect of this vehicle, to which he referred as a "piece of junk." Pimples defended his Honda compact hatchback as a 1980s "vintage" machine. The prophet riposted that it was falling apart and covered with rust. Thus bickering, this unlovely pair exited the Walmart parking lot and thence Virginia, under a bright sky, marred, however, by huge gray cumulus clouds rumbling in from Washington, D.C.

Once in the city, Pimples became briefly flummoxed and lost his way.

"You shoulda turned left there, dimwit," the prophet rather ungraciously informed him.

The driver corrected his mistake and soon pulled into the District Medical Center drop-off point, where, lurking in a corner, stood short, scrawny Albert Pop in his straitjacket, pajama pants and socks, his gray-streaked hair a wild mess, his salt and pepper goatee sporting cracker crumbs. Spotting the hideous Honda, he darted out, as Pimples exited the vehicle and opened the back door for him.

"Remove this straitjacket," Albert commanded.

"No," Nostradamus snapped to Pimples through his rolled-down window. "Don't even think about it."

Pimples said nothing, but gently shoved the lunatic into the back seat.

They soon zipped back onto a wide boulevard and before long were in downtown D.C., looking for parking.

"After our invasion, there will be no more parking," Albert informed them. "We Andromedans will abolish it."

"Good to know," Nostradamus said.

"We will declaw our ancient and devious enemies, the crab people from the Crab Nebula," Pop continued.

"No," Pimples said. "No crab people today. Today you tell this editor about the lizard people, so we can collect our honorariums."

"Lizard people," Pop muttered. "They have taken over the Agriculture Department."

Nostradamus's bushy brown and gray eyebrows lifted in surprise. "The Ag department?" He asked. "Now I've heard everything."

"Lizards plot to release cows and pigs," Pop continued.

"Apparently you ain't heard everything," Pimples told the prophet.

"Soon farm animals will overrun the cities," Pop proclaimed. "Starbucks will be selling cowpies."

Pimples and Nostradamus looked at each other.

"You think National Disgrace will buy this crap?" The prophet asked.

"Cowpies, not crap. It's very alarming news," Pimples averred.

"To a moron, yes, I guess it is," the prophet said.

It started to rain.

"Lizard people love rain," Albert Pop rambled.

"The end is nigh!" Nostradamus said.

"Save it for Fevereau Slop," Pimples said. "So he can quote you."

"That's the plan," the prophet told him.

WHEN STELLA AND her boss entered Dr. Butt's waiting room, they saw Fred Fart seated along with two other patients and Bunzi Schlimizzle behind the reception desk, frantically rummaging through drawers in search of air freshener. All the examining rooms were, apparently, occupied. Another nurse stepped into the room and sniffed.

"Mrs. Schlimizzle, I believe there is a large, dead animal in the waiting room. Maybe a buffalo." The nurse said. "Call custodial to remove it."

The two patients beside Fred Fart looked around nervously, as they held their noses. One rose and approached the reception desk.

"Is Dr. Butt in the habit of keeping large dead animals in his office?" The man asked anxiously.

"Go back to Your Colon, Mr. Fink," Bunzi said. "Everything is under control."

"It doesn't smell like it's under control," Mr. Fink said. "And I fail to see what my colon has to do with it. I hope you're not implying some connection between my colon and this...this stench."

"Phew," Sttella said, waving a fat hand before her nose. "Put Fred Fart in an examining room, pronto, before we all expire!"

Bunzi buzzed yet another nurse and spoke into the phone. "Butt's morning rectal pump is here. Put him in a room and shut the door."

"Rectal pump?" A voice squawked back. "There's no rectal pump on the schedule."

"It's an emergency," Bunzi said, "involving deodorizing flatulence. The canister in the patient's colon needs a refill. Lakeside Laurel."

The nurse returned. "Did you call custodial?" She asked.

"No, but I found the air freshener," Bunzi said.

"Well, that's a start," Stella grumbled.

"You're next Fred," Bunzi told him. "We moved you to the front of the line. Now skedaddle."

"I don't see a line," thus Fred.

"You're ahead of Fink and Snit," Bunzi told him.

"What snit?" Dull-eyed, dull-witted Fred Fart asked.

"Is he stupid?" The nurse whispered to Bunzi.

"Just put him in an examining room now," Bunzi said, exasperated.

"Then you'll deal with the dead buffalo?" The nurse asked.

"He's not the only one who's stupid," Stella muttered, sitting as far away from Futz Fraud as possible.

The editor had opened a back issue of Your Colon. After a moment, he surreptitiously slipped it in his briefcase.

"I saw you stealin' that colon, Fraud," Stella said.

Mr. Fink and Mrs. Snit looked up, confused.

"What colon?" The editor innocently asked.

"The one in your briefcase," Stella snapped.

"It's a good resource for our newspaper," Futz Fraud said.

"Now folks are stealin' each other's colons," Fred Fart remarked, as the nurse led him out of the reception area. "What if someone tries to steal mine?"

"You should look into that, Fred," Stella told him.

NOT FAR AWAY, at the Schlimizzle funeral home, chief terrorism and alien abduction reporter Jeremy Spit was in a veritable frenzy of excitement over the bizarre and scaly appearance of Wilfred Doofus's corpse. This hysteria caused his usual unpleasant habit of spitting, for which many shunned him, not that he could care less, to intensify, much to Buddy Schlimizzle's revulsion. As Spit snapped pictures of the corpse, he talked; as he talked, he spat; his spit more than once moisturized the undertaker's face.

"Have you thought about seeing a doctor?" Buddy asked. "About your condition. Maybe an oral surgeon, someone who could give you a procedure, maybe to sew your mouth shut."

"Then how would I talk or eat?" Spit spat a huge gob of saliva that landed in Buddy's eye. The disgusted undertaker wiped it away with a Kleenex.

"We all have to make sacrifices," Buddy said.

But Jeremy Spit's thoughts had meandered back to the corpse. "Remove the towel from the groin area," he said.

"So you can snap more perverted dick pics of Doofus's scaly pecker? No. You got enough."

The reporter ignored him, removed the towel and snapped more photos. Then he demanded Hinchy Schnook's phone number, only to learn that Buddy's wife had it. Spit dialed, but as he did a call from Bull Bruiser came in.

"I got great photos of Doofus's scaly dick," Spit said, mistakenly thinking he was talking to his boss.

Bunzi promptly ended the call. "Pervert," she snapped.

Spit inadvertently switched calls. "The question is, how do lizard people have sex, with these deformed peckers?"

Bull Bruiser decided he had an insane Scuttlebutt reader on the line and hung up.

"Crank call?" Futz Fraud asked, lounging now at the reception desk.

Her phone rang again.

"I need Hinchy Schnook's phone number."

"Who is this?" Bunzi demanded.

"Scuttlebutt's chief terrorism and alien abduction reporter, Jeremy Spit."

Bunzi put a hand over her phone and said to Futz Fraud: "Scuttlebutt's on the line. Maybe they heard about Butt's lead article in American Anus."

"Oh, ho!" Thus the National Disgrace editor. "Put him on speaker."

Bunzi did so. "Why should I give you Hinchy Schnook's number?"

"Because he witnessed the death of a lizard person honcho, Wilfred Doofus at the Takoma Park Burger Burg," Spit told her. "I'm here in your husband's funeral parlor, looking at his green, scaly corpse."

Stella joined her boss at the desk. "Ask him how much Scuttlebutt is payin' for this blockbuster," she whispered to Bunzi, who complied.

"One thousand for Buddy, 5000 for Hinchy, who witnessed this freak eat a Gutbuster and croak." Spit said. "Maybe lizard people can't eat burgers."

"We'll pay your husband $10,000!" Futz Fraud proclaimed.

"Who's that?" Spit spat.

"Futz Fraud," Bunzi answered.

Alarmed, Spit ended the call.

Bunzi phoned her husband and told him the Schlimizzles were in a bidding war between two leading newspapers, and he should hold out for more money.

"So National Disgrace will pay me many times more than what Scuttlebutt offered," the undertaker told the reporter. "What do you say to that?"

Spit snapped a few more pictures, then headed to the exit.

"Well?" Buddy demanded.

"I'll get back to you," Jeremy spit said, then mendaciously added, in the hopes of preventing the competition from photographing Doofus: "But you should hurry up and bury that corpse. It smells."

"Bury this goldmine?" Buddy chortled. "Not till I get my money."

UGLY, VERY BALD Bull Bruiser sat at his desk, his muscular elbows planted on it, as he twiddled his stubby thumbs. An annoyed, bored, malevolent gleam lit his little dark eyes, as he listened to his reporter, Ruffles Johnson – who loathed Jeremy Spit and was engaged in a years-long feud with that slobbering reporter – pitch him a story about celebrity sexual abuse of their pets. Johnson sat, donut in hand, facing the editor.

"Been there, done that," the editor muttered, but then jerked his bald head up as he espied the signature slouch and shower of dandruff from his chief terrorism and alien abduction reporter, Jeremy Spit, in the doorway. So consumed was Bull Bruiser with sudden fury, that he forgot his habitual admonition for Spit not to dare cross the threshold. As a result, the reporter drifted into his office, and snarkily greeting Rubbles, managed to spray that disgusted journalist with saliva, also thus drenching his chocolate donut.

"What's this I hear about you alerting National Disgrace to our scoop about the lizard corpse?" Bull Bruiser demanded, turning a dangerous shade of purple and leaping to his feet.

"Well, er," Spit stuttered, sending a gob of saliva shooting past the ear of the editor, who was so enraged, he hardly noticed.

"Fire him, boss," thus Ruffles Johnson, wiping his wet face with a tissue and dropping the now slimy donut in the trash.

"And now," Bull Bruiser hollered, approaching Jeremy Spit, "you got us into a bidding war with that revolting nonentity, Futz Fraud!"

"There was a mix-up at the Schlimizzle funeral home," Spit slobbered.

"There was a mix-up in your brain, Spit!" Bull Bruiser yelled and pounced on the reporter, throttling him with his stubby fingers. The pair crashed to the floor.

"Give it to him, boss!" Thus Ruffles Johnson.

"Now I gotta pay that idiot Schnook $20,000 instead of five!" The editor grunted, grappling with Jeremy Spit. "That's comin' outta your paycheck, moron!"

"Make him pay for my donuts, too," Johnson put in. "He freakin' contaminated a whole box, spraying his spit on them, yesterday afternoon."

Jeremy Spit, being strangled, began to turn purple. Who knows where this would have ended, had not the copy chief, a very tall, broad-shouldered fellow and the production manager, equally big and fit, not passed the editor's open doorway and decided to halt a murder in progress by pulling their boss off his delinquent underling. Bull Bruiser did not want to let go.

"I heard Spit tested positive for covid," the copy chief lied. That did it – Bull Bruiser allowed himself to be separated from his prey.

"You're demoted to the celebrity pet beat, Spit!" The editor hollered, "and any complaints will get you fired!"

"What about my donuts?" Ruffles Johnson wanted to know.

"Forget those donuts. You're on the dead lizard person beat," Bull Bruiser snapped.

Ruffles Johnson snickered at a wretched Jeremy Spit, who was straightening his tie, then added, "Spit spoiled the whole box."

"You know what?" Bull Bruiser snarled, his bulbous nose and bald head pink with fury. "*I'll* interview that imbecile Schnook. If you want something done right, you gotta do it yourself."

"Ain't it the truth, boss," Jeremy Spit ventured.

"You," Bull Bruiser pointed a stubby index finger at him, "better keep quiet!"

"I SMELL FLOWERS," Mr. Fink exclaimed, looking up from the issue of Your Colon that he had been reading, as Fred Fart waltzed back into Dr.

Butt's reception room, reeking of perfume.

Mrs. Snit sniffed. "Lakeside Laurel," she added definitively.

"Much better, Fred," thus Stella, who sat in her blue poncho very far away from her boss, who had now filched three issues of Your Colon. "You're now fit for something other than skunk society."

Fred Fart's dull, usually impassive features expressed alarm. "What skunk society?" he asked.

"The one you belonged to," Stella said.

Futz Fraud threw up in his vomit bag.

"Mr. Fraud!" Bunzi Schlimizzle exclaimed, leaping to her feet, her hazel eyes, her blond-tinted hair, her arresting form in her white and gold designer ensemble, all somehow exuding anxiety. "Are you alright?"

Noting that this explosion had not landed on her, Stella snickered rather unkindly. "Missed me that time, Fraud," she said.

"He does this often?" Bunzi asked.

"Multiple times a day, and it almost always lands on me. That's why I'm in this poncho, and that's why we're here," Stella explained.

Hefty, white-haired Dr. Butt in his white lab coat ambled into the reception room.

"Dr. Butt, your 10 a.m. just threw up," Bunzi told him.

Dr. Butt turned to Mr. Fink. "I'll have to inspect your rectal pump," he told him.

"Not MY rectal pump," Mr. Fink exclaimed. "His," and he pointed at Futz Fraud.

"Fraud doesn't have a rectal pump," Stella clarified. "But if it would stop him puking on his innocent, inoffensive secretary, when she's doin' nothing besides mindin' her own business, by all means, put one in."

"What secretary?" Butt asked.

"I don't need a rectal pump," Futz Fraud whined. "Stella, help! Come over here."

"Not on your life," she snapped.

"I still feel sick."

"Hmm. Mr. Fink, Mrs. Snit," Dr. Butt said, "I believe I need to bump you behind Mr. Fraud here. This appears serious."

"Finally," Stella breathed, "we're getting some action on this." Then she said to her boss. "You heard the doctor, Fraud. Time for your exam."

"I don't feel good," Fraud whined.

"He needs the pump," Bunzi put in.

"Hear that, Fraud?" Stella asked. "You're gettin' off easy." And she pushed her crooked, befogged glasses up to the bridge of her nose. "I woulda thought you needed your stomach removed."

Fred Fart looked alarmed.

"My, that Lakeside Laurel is everywhere," thus Mr. Fink.

"Don't remove my stomach," Fred Fart babbled nervously to Dr. Butt.

"Don't worry, Mr. Fart," the doctor soothed. "That's not the part of you that's the problem."

"So you won't be removin' it?"

"No, nitwit," Stella snapped. "That's Fraud's department."

"From here on out," Dr. Butt said with great satisfaction, "or as soon as he returns from Puerto Rico, Posterior will look after your, um, digestive difficulties."

"What department?" Fred asked. "What difficulties?"

Stella rolled her eyes.

"Someone help me up," Futz Fraud said plaintively.

"Not me," thus Stella rather brutally.

Bunzi and Dr. Butt approached and got the editor to his feet, then walked him to an examining room. Bunzi soon returned to her desk. Moments later, a nurse stepped out into the reception area.

"I need your help, Mrs. Schlimizzle," the nurse said. "A patient just threw up on Dr. Butt."

Stella chuckled evilly.

"Oh my goodness!" Bunzi exclaimed. "It must be Mr. Fraud."

"Yes, him," the nurse said.

Bunzi turned to Stella. "I hope this won't affect your coverage of Butt's Pulitzer for his lead article in American Anus."

Stella decided to ignore what she considered a bizarre remark and instead asked the nurse: "What's Butt's recommendation? Stomach removal?"

"The rectal pump, of course," the nurse said.

"It works like a charm," Bunzi added. "It's the best thing since sliced bread, for regularity, that is. You can quote me on that, in your article."

A cloud of Lakeside Laurel filled the room.

"Will it stop him vomitin' on people?" Stella demanded, then said: "Get a grip, Fred."

"All this talk about stomach removal makes me nervous," Fred Fart whined. "And when I get nervous…"

"I get the picture," Stella interrupted him.

"I've had the pump for years," Mr. Fink confided in Stella. "And I never threw up on anybody."

"SO ALBERT," NOSTRADAMUS addressed the passenger in the back seat of the "vintage" Honda, without turning to look at him. "Why'd the CIA take you back into custody?"

"They caught me backing up my pink plastic brain on one of their servers at Langley. I got wires in my head, you know," the lunatic replied.

"Of course I know. The whole world knows, thanks to Scuttlebutt and National Disgrace," Nostradamus said. "I suppose the CIA allowed you to return to your janitorial job, after they seized you, back before covid."

"They need janitors," Albert said. "They got lots of dirt."

"So they found you poking around a computer server," Pimples said. "I guess they concluded you were a spy."

"More likely they concluded they had a psychotic on the payroll," Nostradamus said. "And that's why he's back in the hospital in a straitjacket."

"Remove this straitjacket," Albert Pop commanded.

"No," Nostradamus said.

"Fevereau Slop was real clear," Pimples said. "No straitjacket, no interview about the lizard people. And no interview," the driver scratched a zit on his chin definitively, "no moolah."

They parked in downtown Washington, D. C. and walked under gray skies to the building that housed National Disgrace's offices. Up they zoomed in the elevator and then approached a bored, blue-haired receptionist, blowing big pink bubbles with her gum.

"I will eat your bubble gum," Albert Pop told her.

"No you won't," she retorted.

"And your esophagus," the madman continued.

"Ew," thus the receptionist.

"Pop, don't you know it's rude to threaten to eat random strangers' body parts?" Nostradamus asked, combing pizza crust crumbs out of his messy, long gray beard with his fingers. They drifted down toward the floor, but were intercepted by his enormous belly, over which the Wellesley College T-shirt had ridden up, to reveal his coal pit of a navel.

Albert Pop's eyes rolled wildly in his head.

"Look's like whoever's 'pop' he is," the receptionist made quote marks with her fingers, "doesn't know his...behind from his elbow."

"Albert has ocular problems," Pimples explained helpfully.

"I am an Andromedan robot," Pop told her. "I have wires in my head."

"Okey doke," the receptionist cracked her gum.

"We're here to see Fevereau Slop," Pimples continued. "Pop here is a source."

"So now Mr. Slop's sources are people in straitjackets," the young woman mused.

"I will put hoses in your orifices," Pop continued, hopping now from one foot to another.

"Is that before you eat my esophagus or after?" The receptionist asked.

"We will crush this puny planet," Albert Pop continued.

"That's enough of that," Nostradamus said, pushing the lunatic aside. "Just tell Mr. Slop we're here. The end is nigh."

"Oh, you must be Nostradamus," the receptionist said chattily. "I read all your predictions."

"The end is nigh," the prophet repeated.

"Especially that one."

"It always kinda comes down to that," Pimples said. "Don't it?"

Paunchy, tired Fevereau Slop did not look happy to see them. In his rumpled gray suit, with pouches under his eyes, the editor was clearly the worse for wear.

"If you tie me to a chair again, I won't talk," Pop told him.

"Is that a promise?" The senior editor asked, leading them along the beige-carpeted corridor.

"I never forget a person who ties me to a chair."

"That was years ago, Albert," Slop said. "Get over it."

"Like that crab person who masqueraded as a judge," Pop continued. "He had me tied to my seat."

"Oh, judge Fibble DuCouk?" Slop asked. "He's off his rocker, but still on the bench, I see, from the multitudes of freakish reports from his courtroom that it is my," here he nearly strangled in disgust over the word, "PRIVILEGE to edit."

The editor ushered his three visitors into his office. They sat and faced him, as he slipped into his chair at his computer and picked up a pen and notepad. "So Albert, tell me about these lizard people," Slop began.

"What lizard people? It's our ancient and devious enemy, the crab people from the Crab Nebula that I worry about. You may be one."

"No, I may not," Slop glanced in annoyance at Pimples. "Your so-called client won't deliver the goods."

"The end is nigh!" Nostradamus boomed.

Medium-height, frizzy-haired Hinchy Schnook slouched in the doorway. "You the editor on the death of Expert-Q Lizard story?" He asked.

"Yeah," Slop sighed. "What of it?"

"I witnessed his death at a Takoma Park Burger Burg, after he ate a Gutbuster," Hinchy said.

"So now burgers are killin' people," Pimple mused sagely, straightening his thick, greasy brown hair with his fingers.

"People who look like giant lizards, yes," Hinchy said. "I want my money."

"I want my pictures," Slop snapped.

Hinchy Schnook pulled his phone out of his jeans pocket, approached the editor and showed him the photos.

Fevereau Slop's gray eyebrows lifted in shock, as Albert Pop, somewhat constrained by his straitjacket, leaned over and peered at the phone.

"That's a lizard person," he announced. "From the lizard planet."

"No," Hinchy carefully corrected. "He was from Takoma Park."

"The lizard people are retards," Pop continued.

"Look who's talking," Slop muttered.

"No surprise there," Hinchy replied. "I saw this nitwit eat the entire contents of a tube of Derma-Lube."

"Was that before or after he kicked the bucket?" Fevereau Slop asked.

"Before, of course. He couldn't eat after dying," Hinchy clarified. "That's not possible."

"I will eat your liver, dead or alive," Albert Pop somewhat confusedly told him.

Hinchy stepped away from Albert Pop.

"So I think we can put the 'burger killed him' narrative to rest," Slop said. "What's Derma-Lube? Oh, here, I googled it. A non-FDA approved skin-care product marketed by the estate of Pinky Pimple. I should have known. The pervert who sent dick pics to half the housewives in suburban Maryland, which our competitor, Scuttlebutt, paid him to do. They will stoop to anything. Then we had to follow them down the primrose path and pay that perverted exhibitionist to send out more dick pics."

"Perverts who eat Derma-Lube?" Pimples asked in some confusion.

Fevereau Slop frowned at him.

"Lizard people have lizard brains," Albert Pop said. "Very small lizard brains. That's why we Andromedan robots are so successful at putting wires in their heads."

"That's enough of that," thus Slop.

A startled Hinchy Schnook stared at Albert Pop in astonishment.

"I have wires in my head," the lunatic continued, "Connected to my pink plastic brain. That's why I'm constipated."

"Good to know," Hinchy Schnook said and edged further away from Albert.

"He's harmless," Slop reassured him.

"I will eat your kidneys," Pop told Hinchy Schnook

"He doesn't sound harmless," Schnook said.

"At least as long as he stays in his straitjacket, he is," Slop clarified.

"Remove this straitjacket, I'm hungry," Albert Pop said.

"So you can eat our internal organs?" Slop demanded. "I think not."

"I want pizza," Albert Pop said, eyeing a slice on the editor's desk.

"Go ahead, one of you. Give him the pizza," Slop sighed. "But don't ask me to feed him."

"Me neither," Nostradamus said.

"I just met the guy," Hinchy remarked. "And frankly I don't think I want anything to do with feeding him."

Pimples fed Albert Pop the slice of pizza. But he did so rather absentmindedly, while explaining to Fevereau Slop that as Pop's "agent," he got a 30 percent cut of whatever they paid for the lizard people story. As a result, he often held the pizza slice out of Pop's range, so the hungry, crazy CIA custodian had to lean far forward and snap at the food. As a result, he fell to the floor.

"You're fired," he told Pimples.

"You can't fire me," Pimples said, looking down at Pop sprawled on the carpet. "I'm your agent for life."

"You got pizza in my nose."

"Get that insane person off my office carpet," Fevereau Slop said.

"This is not the way I imagined a newspaper interview," Hinchy Schnook said.

Fevereau Slop pushed a chair toward him, and Hinchy sat.

"So you were in Burger Burg with this lizard person," Slop began, pen poised to take notes.

"Yes. Wilfred Doofus."

"What kind of a name is that?" Nostradamus demanded.

"The name of a very stupid, odd someone," Hinchy said, "who was also a conspiracist."

"What conspiracies?" The editor asked.

"The crab people," Albert Pop said.

"Crab?" Hinchy Schnook asked. "No. He talked about lizard people, the Illuminati. He and Seymour Burp seemed convinced the lizard people rule the earth."

"Lizard people are morons," thus Albert Pop.

"Look who's talking," Nostradamus said sourly.

"So this Burp has the inside track," Pimples said.

"Inside track to the loony bin," thus Slop.

"What Burp?" Albert Pop reasonably asked.

A frustrated Fevereau Slop phoned Futz Fraud. "This is a three-ring circus. How can you expect me to conduct an interview with four weirdos, one in a straitjacket, none of whom can stay on topic for more than five seconds? I've got lizard people, crab people, Andromedan robots, and the end is nigh."

Futz Fraud decided he was listening to a lunatic and hung up. "So how much for today's procedure?" He asked Bunzi Schlimizzle.

"Uusually $10,000. But we gave you a discount on your rectal pump, seeing as you're covering Butt's American Anus Pulitzer."

Futz Fraud gaped at her.

"Don't even go there, Fraud," Stella warned, then asked what guarantee she had that the device in Fraud's colon would prevent him from vomiting on her.

"It's FDA approved," Bunzi sniffed touchily, as if Stella's evident doubts offended her.

The editor-in-chief's phone rang again.

"And I got a Schnook who claims you owe him tens of thousands of dollars," Slop said.

Alarmed, Futz Fraud hung up. His phone dinged again.

"The Schnook who witnessed the lizard person croaking," Slop said.

"So lizard people croak," Futz Fraud said.

"Yes of course!" A very exasperated Fevereau Slop cried. "That's what we're doing our story on!"

"Who is this?" Futz Fraud demanded.

"Fevereau Slop."

"Lizard people croak like bull frogs?" Futz Fraud stated flatly, in disbelief.

"Now that's a new angle," Stella said, "and one I'm sure our illustrious publication will cover in depth."

"Mr. Schnook – did Mr. Doofus croak like a bull frog?" Slop asked his source.

"Um, I'm not sure," Hinchy Schnook replied. "When do I get paid?"

"Schnook wants to know when he gets paid," Slop said.

Futz Fraud repeated this to Stella.

"When we get the goods," she snapped.

The editor-in-chief repeated this to Fevereau Slop.

"The corpse is at my in-law's funeral home," Hinchy said.

"How'd your in-laws get involved?" Slop asked.

"I didn't know they were involved," Hinchy Schnook said.

"This is very confusing," Slop griped into his phone.

Futz Fraud relayed this message to his secretary, who snatched the phone away and told Slop if he couldn't handle a simple interview then to wait 30 minutes until they returned. "Fraud will interview this Schnook," she snapped.

Futz Fraud vomited on her.

"We want our money back," Stella told Bunzi Schlimizzle. "The rectal pump doesn't work."

"You don't know that," Bunzi protested.

"Yes," Stella growled, looking at the puke on her blue plastic poncho. "I do."

AS NOW COMPLETELY purple-haired Philippa walked Hubert Poop Junior through warm, fresh, spring breezes, Seymour Burp phoned her.

"That Derma-Lube is powerful stuff," he said. "It turned Expert-Q Lizard into a giant iguana, and he croaked."

Alarmed at what she took to be aggressive harassment based on coverage of her scales in Scuttlebutt, Philippa ended the call.

Burp phoned back. "The idiot ATE the Derma-Lube."

Philippa ended that call, too.

Burp phoned again. "Philippa, I think we have a bad connection."

"Who is this?" She demanded. "If you think you can harass me based on that story, think again. I'll call the cops!"

"It's me – Seymour Burp."

"Why didn't you say so?"

"Where are you?" He asked.

"The Kemp Mill shopping center."

"I'm on my lunch break in the neighborhood," he fibbed. "Meet me outside the Motor Vehicles Administration office in 10 minutes." He hung up before she could say no.

Standing at the MVA entrance, gentle spring breezes caressing his snout, Herbert Poop Jr. decided to leave a turd for officialdom right in front of the glass door. Philippa, on the lookout for Seymour Burp – "I look like your typical claims adjuster, nothing fancy" – did not notice what the dog had done.

"Uh, Miss," an annoyed MVA employee stuck his head out the doorway. "You'll have to clean that up."

"What? Oh sorry, I'm waiting for someone," Philippa said.

"You got MVA business? I ask, 'cause I don't want that canine crapping in our office."

Philippa cleaned up the mess with the pooper scooper.

Medium-height, stocky, scanty light-brown-haired Seymour Burp in a rumpled navy-blue suit accosted her.

"I hope you didn't use that Derma-Lube on your whole body," he said, "'cause that'll turn you into a lizard."

"I did not and I ain't no lizard," the MVA staffer said with obvious annoyance. Seymour Burp ignored him.

"Whatever you do, don't eat it," Seymour warned.

"You think we eat lizards at the MVA?" The employee demanded.

"Not you," Seymour said. "Her."

"*I* certainly don't eat lizards," Philippa huffed.

"Not lizards, Derma-Lube."

"That's the second time you've mentioned an automotive lubricant with which I am not familiar," the man said.

"Why would I eat Derma-Lube?" Philippa asked.

"Just sayin.' Expert-Q Lizard did, and he turned into a man-sized iguana and croaked." Seymour told her.

"Now I've heard everything," the MVA staffer said.

"He was covered with scales," Seymour continued.

"The question is, will he leave lizard poop on MVA premises?" The man asked.

"I told you, he's dead," Seymour said. "He can't poop anymore."

"I guess we here at the MVA lucked out."

"I gotta take this creature home," Philippa said.

"I'm not a creature, and I'm not going to your home," the man told her.

"Things got confused," Seymour said.

"I'll say," the man snapped and went back into the MVA office.

Philippa tossed the plastic bag with the dog's mess into a garbage can, and they ambled out of the shopping center, then along somnolent suburban streets, past tidy bungalows and split-levels, until they came to

Hubert Poop's abode. Lila Hanger, in her signature bathrobe, flip-flops flapping, came out onto the front walk and took the leash. Hubert Poop Jr. peed in the daffodils.

"So you're a famous lizard person," Lila addressed Philippa.

"You allow that mutt to pee on your flowers?" Seymour asked.

Maynard Ploshinsky, in a brown suit and tie, stepped out into the front yard next-door and snapped a photo with his phone of Hubert Poop Jr.

"Don't you ever go to work?" Lila drawled.

"I could ask you the same question," Ploshinsky said.

"Whatever. Leave me alone. I'm talking to lizard girl here," Lila said.

Philippa frowned.

Just so long as that canine stays away from my begonias," Ploshinsky snapped. "If he comes any closer, you'll be in violation of Judge DuCouk's restraining order."

"He's busy peeing on these daffodils," Seymour said.

"Judge DuCouk doesn't pee on my daffodils," Lila Hangar said.

"Judge DuCouk's off his rocker," Ploshinsky put in. "But he had enough sense to rule in my favor."

"How did you turn into a lizard person?" Lila Hanger asked.

"Read the story in Scuttlebutt," Philippa said sourly.

"I tried, but I got distracted by an article about a resurgence of the Penis Plague. It had statistics about men sending dick pics to housewives in the D.C. metro area. I didn't get any," and Lila sounded disappointed.

"You're not a housewife. You're a lazy, live-in girlfriend, who encourages her bulldog to crap in my potted plants," Ploshinsky said.

"Scuttlebutt once wrote about me," she said sadly, like a star whose fame has faded, "about my wandering breasts. They had wandered to someone with a very odd name."

"I read that," Seymour said. "They wandered to Bunzi Schlimizzle, whose husband worried about the location of his wife's breasts and the legal ramifications of intimacy with yours. That was quite a story," and he goggled at Lila Hanger as if she were a celebrity.

"So," Lila cracked her gum and pointed at Seymour Burp. "He's your new boyfriend?"

"We're just acquaintances," Philippa replied, annoyed at her employer's nosiness.

"And fellow lizard people," Seymour Burp put in.

"I don't believe you. I've seen her scales," Lila said. "But not yours."

Seymour lifted his pants leg to reveal a broad strip of green, glittering scales on his calf.

"You used Derma-Lube!" Philippa cried.

"Just on my leg. Did you use it on your whole body?" Seymour asked again.

"No. Or I'd be suing that moron, Prissy Pimple," Philippa said.

Seymour's even features contorted slightly in confusion. "The famous Prissy Pimple's a moron?"

"Her company makes and markets Derma-Lube," Philippa explained.

"And Bush," Lila put in. "I been tryin' to get Hubert to use it, but he says he doesn't want to become furry, like you know, that famous person Frank Fart, who used it and grew fur all over his body, and that equally famous pervert, who sent out all the dick pics."

"Sounds like Prissy Pimple could use more insurance," Seymour said. "Her company's a customer of ours."

"She could use a brain," Philippa muttered unkindly.

"What about you, Miss Hanger?" Seymour continued. "You wanna insure against future lawsuits for damages caused by that canine?"

"I thought you were in claims," Philippa said.

"I pitch in in other departments, too," Seymour said.

"Well, this is all very interesting," Maynard Ploshinsky grumbled, "but when will that dog be removed from proximity to my lawn, that is, into the house?"

"When I freakin' feel like it," Lila snapped.

"If I sell a policy, in addition to claims adjusting, I get a bonus," Seymour said.

"I'm not leaving till that four-legged menace does," Ploshinsky threatened.

"Suit yourself," thus Lila Hanger.

Philippa's phone beeped, as Hinchy Schnook texted her. "Sell your story to National Disgrace. You could get in the high five figures."

"What's that?" Seymour asked, watching her read her phone.

"A sales pitch, apparently," Philippa sighed, "Who knew celebrity could be so tiresome?"

"I didn't find it tiresome," Lila Hanger sighed too.

Philippa's phone rang.

"I could put in a word with the big Fraud for you," Hinchy said. On the other line, a call from Floozy Philpot came in. Her daughter accidentally switched calls saying, "And I could sue you for harassment."

Alarmed, Floozy Philpot ended the call.

"Whaddya say?" Hinchy continued.

"Who is this?" Philippa demanded.

"Hinchy Schnook. National Disgrace pays big bucks."

"I'm tired of fame," Philippa complained.

"But I'm not," Seymour Burp said loudly in the direction of his friend's phone.

"Who said that?" Schnook demanded.

"Just Burp."

"Didn't sound like a burp. It sounded like someone who wants to get his name in the papers," Schnook said, in some irritation at finding the, to him, alluring Philippa in the company of another man.

"That's Burp," Philippa said.

"I didn't burp," a befuddled Hinchy told her.

"This conversation is tiring me out," Philippa whined.

"Well, if you didn't keep repeating nonsense about burps, because I am NOT burping," Schnook said, "maybe it wouldn't."

"Burp's a lizard person," she tried to explain.

"Come again?" Thus Hinchy.

"Here," Seymour offered. "Let me talk to him. What's his name?"

Philippa handed him her phone, saying, "Schnook."

"Listen Schnook," Seymour began.

"What happened to my call with Philippa. Who're you? How did you get my number?" Hinchy demanded.

"I'm Philippa's lizard person friend," Seymour said.

"A likely story," thus Hinchy.

"And I'll sell my story to any supermarket tabloid that wants it."

"Fine. Manage your own sales, put Philippa back on," Schnook said.

"Do you need insurance?" Seymour suavely asked.

Hinchy Schnook held his phone out and stared at it in disbelief for a moment, and then put it back to his ear, "uh…what's going on?" he asked.

"Been in any accidents lately?" Seymour Burp continued.

Hinchy, alarmed now, ended the call.

HINCHY SCHNOOK HAD been happy to leave what he had dubbed "those three losers" – Albert Pop. Nostradamus and Pimples – in Fevereau Slop's small, overcrowded office, when he received a summons from Futz Fraud. Those "losers" would only earn in the three figures for their lizard people fabrications, while he, Hinchy Schnook, unemployed nearly full time since dropping out of college, living in his mother's basement and now approaching age 30, would be rich! Tens of thousands of dollars from Scuttlebutt and tens of thousands from National Disgrace. It was so much money, it dizzied him. What would he do with it? Why, buy a new car, of course, hopefully to impress blue-haired, or was it purple? He couldn't remember – foxy Philippa Philpot. Walking on air, he waltzed through the editorial offices to Stella's desk.

"You can tell Mr. Fraud, his primo, first-rate, unbeatable lizard people source is here," he announced to her. "I can describe a lizard person in detail."

Immense, annoyed Stella sat back in her triple extra-large, ergonomic, desk chair, her vast blue poncho stretched taut across her even vaster, obese midriff, her befogged, crooked, cat's eyes glasses having slid down her nose, and eyed him warily. "Someone's got a swelled head," she muttered.

"Lizard people don't have swelled heads," Hinchy corrected.

A little flicker of irritation glimmered in her dark eyes. "Not exactly the ace when it comes to conversational synapses," she said. "Are you?"

"You lost me," Hinchy Schnook told her.

"If only," she sighed, then turned and yelled into the open doorway into the boss's office. "Fraud! Get out here!"

A dart whizzed by her desk.

"You throwin' darts, Fraud?" she shouted.

The stringy, warty, little editor appeared on the threshold, darts in hand. "So what if I am?" He approached her, but Stella, with amazing speed and agility for one of her enormous girth, reached across her desk, grabbed her super-soaker and drenched him.

"Not the super-soaker!" Futz Fraud wailed.

"You're not vomitin' on me!" She snapped.

"Vomiting? Who's vomiting?" Hinchy asked.

"I know the signs, and you're read to puke. Throw up on your lizard person source, Fraud, not your secretary!" Stella snapped.

Hinchy Schnook's eyes narrowed. "Someone's gonna barf on me? I came here for my money, not throw-up."

"Well, too bad for you, Schnook," Stella said. "Fraud'll interview you, cause I ain't. I hope you brought a change of clothes."

Futz Fraud turned green.

Stella rolled her chair as far away from him as possible. "I say we sue Schlimizzle and Butt. That pump up your ass made things worse!" She snapped.

"I certainly don't have a pump up my ass," thus Hinchy.

"Work on your conversational synapses," Stella snapped.

"I don't understand," Schnook began.

"Well, that's obvious," the secretary snapped again.

"Stella, take me back to Butt. I want this pump removed," Futz Fraud whined.

Stella phoned the proctologist's office. "Fraud's vomitin' worse than ever!" She angrily announced.

"Who is this?" Bunzi Schlimizzle demanded.

"National Disgrace," Stella barked. "And it's not about any Pulitzer for an American Anus article."

Hinchy's face contorted in disgust. "I don't think I need to hear this."

"That pump in Fraud's rectum has done nothing about him puking on his secretary. Give me Dr. Butt!" Stella commanded, then repeated her assertion to the doctor.

"But is he regular?" The proctologist asked.

"You regular?" Stella asked her boss.

"Regular what?" Fraud demanded.

"Your bowel movements, that's what."

The editor averred that he was.

"Then the pump is working," Dr. Butt informed her complacently.

"But he still vomits," Stella objected.

"Tell him to sit on the toilet." This was the proctologist's cure for everything.

"Go sit on the toilet," she said.

"Who, me?" Thus Hinchy.

In a spectacular display of projectile vomiting, Futz Fraud threw up on his secretary.

"Dammit, Fraud!"

At that moment Fevereau Slop lumbered by, complaining that he had three psychos in his office and didn't know how to get rid of them.

"Fraud!" Stella snapped, heading off to the ladies' room to wash up. "Go vomit on the lunatics in Slop's office."

"No," Futz Fraud said. "I feel better.

"Maybe *you* could?" Slop asked Hinchy hopefully.

"Could what?" Hinchy Schnook responded in a rather surly manner.

"Vomit on them," Slop suggested.

"I didn't come here to vomit, have a bowel movement, hear about an American Anus or about pumps in people's rectums. I came here for my money!" Schnook said.

"Who are you?" Futz Fraud demanded. "What money?"

"My $25,000," Hinchy Schnook said.

"That's too much," Fraud peremptorily replied.

"Maybe he could get rid of the raving lunatics in my office," Slop repeated. "For $25,000, he should make himself useful."

"I witnessed a giant lizard person croak in a Burger Burg." A frustrated Hinchy Schnook explained.

"Remind me not to eat there," Futz Fraud told a returning Stella, whose poncho, just rinsed, gleamed wetly.

"You better not eat anything ever again," Stella snapped, slid into her chair and dialed Dr. Butt's office. "Now he's projectile vomitin'," she snapped. "He barfed all over me from across the room!"

Alarmed at what she took to be harassment, Bunzi Schlimizzle ended the call.

"It's amazing how that scent of Lakeside Laurel lingers," mused Mrs. Snit wonderingly, still waiting for her exam from the illustrious proctologist.

"Fred Fart's odors always…linger," Bunzi said, into her phone, as she answered it.

"Don't you send that smelly Fart my way!" Stella hissed, glaring for no particular reason at Hinchy Schnook.

"I didn't fart," Schnook said.

"Who is this?" Bunzi demanded.

"National Disgrace. The pump backfired!"

"Oh my God!" Bunzi cried, then shouted, "Dr. Butt, Dr. Butt! Get on this call."

Dr. Butt waddled out into the waiting room.

"One of your pumps backfired," his receptionist told him.

"I only have one pump," he clarified. "And it's in good, working order."

"I mean in a patient," Bunzi explained. "I think that strange little man from National Disgrace."

"Oh yes, who threw up on me," Dr. Butt frowned.

"We need to get it removed, pronto," Stella said into her phone.

"I'm not going back to that proctologist," Futz Fraud announced his decision, then turned to Hinchy. "Now what's this about Burger Burg?"

"The lizard man kicked the bucket there," Hinchy said.

"Ate too many Gutbusters? 'Cause that's been known to result in a number of celebrity deaths," Futz Fraud said.

"Ate too much Derma-Lube. I want my money for my eye-witness account," Hinchy Schnook said.

"Who's Derma-Lube, and why do lizard people want to eat her?" Futz Fraud asked.

"Could she come eat the nutjobs who won't leave my office?" Fevereau Slop pleaded.

"This interview isn't going the way I envisioned it," Hinchy Schnook said.

BUDDY SCHLIMIZZLE DECIDED to demand more money from both supermarket tabloids. "Especially from Scuttlebutt," he thought sourly, recalling that that rag had been the first involved in the dick pics that Pinky Pimple had sent to his wife's phone. In fact, his contact with Jeremy Spit and phone call with Bull Bruiser had put him on high alert: There were lizard people out and about; who knew how their perverted minds worked; wouldn't one likely succumb to Scuttlebutt's blandishments to start sending obscene phones of his scaly junk to unsuspecting women? And wouldn't Bunzi Schlimizzle be at the top of that list?

Already fuming with fury, he phoned his wife at work. "Did you receive any dick pics?" He demanded.

"Well, I never!" Bunzi huffed, and ended the call, as Mr. Fink, a very satisfied customer approached the reception desk to pay.

"Never what?" Fink asked.

"Got such an obscene phone call," she said absently, "that's $400."

"For the phone call?" A confused Mr. Fink asked.

"It was you? It couldn't have been you. I saw you right here in front of me, not talking on the phone."

Buddy called his wife back. "These lizard people are perverts!" He hollered. "If one of 'em sends you dick pics, save the text, so I can sue!"

"I'll be suing you, whoever you are," Bunzi snapped. "If you don't stop harassing me."

"I'm not harassing you," Mr. Fink said.

"Not you," she soothed. "This bozo on the phone."

"What bozo?" Buddy Schlimizzle demanded. The long, lean undertaker in his black suit, though distracted, heard the funeral home's doorbell ring. It chimed an appropriately muted version of the tune, "I will survive." Buddy liked to hear this melody, whenever someone arrived at his establishment, because it reminded him that while most everyone around him was dead, he still was not. "Oh," he said, "another corpse."

"Necrophiliac perverts got my number," Bunzi said.

"Call the cops," thus Mr. Fink and Buddy at the same time.

Four peculiar men clad in green, sporting green glitter on their faces, most notably on their noses, stepped into Buddy's reception area.

"It's not St. Patrick's Day," he said.

His wife looked at her phone oddly, then ended the call.

"We're from the L.C.," one announced. "The Lizard Collective."

Buddy's jaw dropped.

"Here to gather up the corpse of our brother, Expert-Q Lizard," the man continued.

"Oh no you don't," Buddy snapped, "Mrs. Doofus didn't give me any instructions about a so-called Lizard Collective."

The men opened the door to Buddy's corpse prep room.

"You can't go in there!" He snapped again. "Doofus isn't done."

"What doofus?" One man asked. "You calling me a doofus?"

"The man-sized iguana," Buddy elucidated.

"He's no doofus. He's a god," the man told the astonished undertaker. "And we have a taxidermist, who's going to stuff, preserve and mount him at the L.C. headquarters, so he can preside there, in perpetuity."

"A taxidermist," Buddy repeated, stepping into the room with the four, green-clad arrivals. Wilfred Doofus lay naked and scaly on a long narrow table, while the visitors mumbled something in what he accurately pegged as pig-Latin, over the corpse.

"Why are you talking in pig-Latin?" Buddy asked.

"It's not pig-Latin. It's the royal reptile tongue," one man sniffed in offense at Buddy's gauche question. "Think he'll fit in the back of the station-wagon?" He asked.

"Who?" Buddy demanded. "'Cause my corpse isn't going anywhere."

"He'll hafta," another replied, then mumbled more pig-Latin. The four "weirdos," as Buddy Schlimizzle had mentally dubbed them, continued their mumbling for another minute, then all laid hands on scaly, dead Doofus.

"Hey, you can't touch the corpse!" Buddy yelled.

"Think again, bozo," one said, as all four picked up Wilfred Doofus, two at the shoulders, two at the knees, and carried him to the exit.

"That's the second time today somebody called me a bozo," Buddy complained, then, loudly, "I'm gonna call the cops!" He followed them out into the parking lot, where a blue station-wagon with the back open stood waiting in the bright April sunshine.

"We may have to eat this undertaker," one man said, as they slid the green, scaly corpse into the back of the car. They shut the door. The back window was down, and Doofus's dead feet stuck out.

"Not this undertaker," Buddy said.

"Lizards eat any undertaker they want," the man told Buddy, "especially ones that call the cops." With that, all four climbed into the car, and away it zipped.

Buddy Schlimizzle was fit to be tied. Standing on the asphalt, amid fresh spring zephyrs, he dialed 911 and was put on hold. By the time a bored operator picked up, several minutes had passed. "Please state the nature of the emergency," she said.

"They stole my corpse!" He shouted.

The operator hung up. Buddy dialed again, again was put on hold and finally, when a woman answered, he had collected himself enough to say, "Four freaks just stole a corpse outta my funeral home."

The operator was taken aback, but had the presence of mind to question Buddy and to learn that no, he had not noted the license plate number. Soon Buddy Schlimizzle, fuming furiously, had a Detective Dump on the phone.

"Four weirdos just walked into my funeral home and absconded with the corpse of a man-sized lizard," Buddy began.

"The ALA struck again," Detective Dump rather ponderously announced.

"The American Library Association?" Buddy demanded, "'cause these guys didn't look like librarians."

"The Animal Liberation Army. How long have you been keeping dead lizards on the premises?"

"Since last night," Buddy said.

"That's what attracted these fanatical, radical Marxist vegans," Detective Dump informed him.

"They said they belonged to the Lizard Collective," Buddy elaborated.

"Collective is the giveaway," Dump pontificated. "We're dealing with a Marxist-Leninist soviet right here in Maryland."

"Great. How do I get my corpse back from these communists?"

"You really want that dead lizard back?" Detective Dump sounded surprised.

"I don't. But Mrs. Doofus will."

"Hmm…there's a doofus in the picture."

"The mother," Buddy clarified.

"The mother lizard?"

"Yes, well, I guess you could put it that way," Buddy said. "These nutcases said some kinda prayer over the corpse in pig-Latin, then announced they were gonna have a taxidermist preserve it and stuff it."

"Where is this mother lizard located at this time?" Dump asked.

"In East Silver Spring."

"She would be the next target," Dump informed him.

"You mean these loons will kidnap Mrs. Doofus?" Buddy asked.

"If they haven't done so already. Check your terrariums."

"What terrariums?" Buddy snapped.

"Well, you don't let these lizards roam free, do you?"

"I imagine Mrs. Doofus has the run of her house," Buddy said.

"Now we got lizards owning property in this county," Detective Dump mused. "The ALA is definitely involved. Hmm. Didn't know they speak pig-Latin, though. That explains a lot."

"Like what, Detective Dump?" Buddy Schlimizzle asked in some exasperation.

"Like why we can never understand ALA messages that we intercept."

"Have you intercepted any about the Lizard Collective and where it might be located?" Buddy asked. "'Cause I want my corpse back."

"Now we got undertakers buryin' dead lizards."

"It's a living," Buddy snapped.

BALD, UGLY, MUSCULAR yet paunchy, a cigar planted firmly in the corner of his mouth, Bull Bruiser sat behind his desk, a light of bored annoyance flickering in his little dark eyes. He had been pursuing a flirtation on twitter and was irritated to have been interrupted by tall, ordinary Ruffles Johnson and the loutish 20-something he had in tow.

"This is your eye witness, boss." Johnson said, as he and Hinchy Schnook sat in the two chairs facing the editor-in-chief's desk. "And by the way, Spit slobbered all over my box of donuts. I should be reimbursed by that cheapskate who can't keep his oral fluids offa my food."

"Any other earth-shaking news?" Bull Bruiser grumbled.

"I witnessed Doofus turn into a lizard and croak," Schnook said.

"Now you bring me raving psychotics, Johnson? I thought that was Spit's specialty," the editor snapped.

"In the Takoma Park Burger Burg," Hinchy clarified.

"Oh yes," Bull Bruiser said. "This sounds familiar. And you sound familiar."

"The moron ate a tube of Derma-Lube, turned green, sprouted scales and croaked," Hinchy Schnook pitched his tale.

"You can't make this shit up," Bull Bruiser chortled.

"Front-page material, boss," thus Ruffles Johnson.

"I want my money," Hinchy Schnook said.

"Everybody wants their money," a bored, annoyed Bull Bruiser said, "including that famously constipated undertaker."

"I sent you photos," Hinchy continued.

"Yes, those were…disturbing," Bull Bruiser said. "But they'll undoubtedly rivet the rubes' eyes to the tune of a 10 million circulation boost. So yes, you'll get your money." Hinchy Schnook smirked smugly.

Meanwhile Buddy Schlimizzle, still enraged over his stolen corpse, decided to demand a bigger compensation for his role in the Lizard Man Croaks in Burger Burg story. He phoned Bull Bruiser.

"Four weirdos, dressed in green, stole my corpse. They're gonna stuff and mount it," he said.

Bull Bruiser, alarmed that an apparent psychotic had his number, ended the call.

The undertaker called back. "They stole the dead lizard man," he shouted.

"Who is this?" Bull Bruiser demanded.

"The undertaker, Buddy Schlimizzle, and if you want my first-person account of how the Lizard Collective stole dead Doofus, you're gonna hafta pay me more money!"

"How much?" the editor asked warily.

"Ten thousand dollars."

"What's this Lizard Collective? It sounds like communists are involved," Bull Bruiser said.

"Maybe they're Marxist lizards, who knows? When do I get my money?"

"Marxist Lizards Steal Man-Sized Iguana Corpse," Bull Bruiser mused. "This has front-page headline potential."

Ruffles Johnson's mouth fell open. "Somebody stole our corpse?!" He exclaimed.

"That's what I just said in English," his boss snapped in exasperation. "Good thing we got Schnook's photos." Then into his phone, he barked. "I want photos of this man-sized lizard stuffed and mounted."

"Doofus?" Buddy asked.

"What doofus?" Bull Bruiser replied.

"My corpse," the undertaker said.

"Now you're dead? You trying to say I'm talking to a corpse?" Bull Bruiser nearly shouted. "Am I surrounded by nutcases or what?"

"I don't know where lizard man's corpse is," Buddy explained. "They kidnapped it, this, this collective or soviet or whatever it is."

"Necrophiliac Lizard Soviet on the Loose!" Bull Bruiser exclaimed. "Write that headline down, Ruffles."

"Ruffles?" Buddy Schlimizzle was confused. "They didn't wear ruffles. They wore green."

3

IN SHABBY, RUN-DOWN Langley Park, Maryland, behind a forlorn little strip mall, whose liveliest feature was a pawnshop, stood a small rec center, long closed. The county-paid groundskeeper had, however, given a key to the Lizard Collective, for a fee, of course, and allowed them to maintain the small, unimposing building as their headquarters. It was here, after the taxidermist had done his work, that the four corpse-thieves decamped and with the taxidermist's help mounted the now stuffed and very scaly Wilfred Doofus in the Lizard Collective's main meeting room. There he stood, clad only and quite bizarrely in a green thong, casting a dead, doleful, green-lidded eye over the preparations for that evening's meeting of the collective's central committee and general assembly. It was also the much-ballyhooed lizard shindig, and these commissars had resolved attendees were allowed to bring dates. And so, Seymour Burp arrived at the Philpot townhouse in the warm twilight, to escort the, to him, dazzling Philippa to this one-of-a-kind event. Little did he know, however, that he was followed by that intrepid fabricator, plagiarist and so-called reporter, Jeremy Spit, whom Bull Bruiser had seen fit to reassign to the story, having lost faith in Ruffles Johnson, when that journalist made the error of responding to Hinchy Schnook's demand for an extra $30,000 with a "sure, Schnook, whatever you want, Bull Bruiser will be happy to oblige."

Shocked and offended, the editor hollered for Jeremy Spit, who quickly appeared, to learn he was back on the big story. Ruffles Johnson's jaw fell open, as he gaped from Spit to Bruiser, a most unfortunate development, for when the chief terrorism and alien abduction reporter, Jeremy Spit, said "I'm on it, boss," the "t" in the word "it" was pronounced with such percussive effect that it launched a huge gob of saliva into the air, across the room and into Ruffles Johnson's open, gaping mouth.

Even Bull Bruiser, given usually to snickering nastily when Spit's oral effusions decorated someone else's face instead of Bruiser's, was horrified at this wet bullseye and for a full 30 seconds everyone in the editor's office froze in revulsion, especially Ruffles Johnson, who finally had the presence of mind to spit into a trash can, before leaping to his feet and pouncing on Jeremy Spit.

"Does this happen often?" Hinchy Schnook had asked, as the two reporters rolled on the carpet, grunting and grappling with each other.

"Multiple times a day," the now bored editor told him.

"Shouldn't you, um, stop it?" Schnook asked.

"Hopefully one of them will kill the other," Bull Bruiser said, puffing on his cigar. "Then we'll have one less moron in the newsroom and a page three story as well: 'Reporter Spits in Colleague's Mouth, Is Strangled to Death in Editor's Office.'" Then Bull Bruiser leaned over to the side, the better to see this writhing mass of furiously fighting journalists and shouted: "Give it to him, Johnson! The jerk spat right into your mouth!"

So Spit was back on his beat and happy as a clam, as he sat in his Toyota compact in the gloaming down the block from the Philpot residence and watched medium-height, chunky, brown-haired Seymour Burp, who had changed out of his usual suit into khaki pants and a pull-over shirt that sported the logo, "Insurance Adjusters Are Sexy" – yes, Spit watched and chortled wetly, as Seymour Burp trundled up the walk to Philippa's door. Something odd, however, long and green, waved from Burp's behind. Spit squinted through the dimness at this appendage, but could not imagine for the life of him what it could be. It was Seymour's detachable tail, of course, but Spit, never having seen anyone sporting a tail before, didn't know that and concluded that some piece of furniture or part of a pillow or clothing had somehow become attached to Burp's behind.

Frazzled Floozy Philpot answered the door. "Philippa!" She yelled over her shoulder, "there's somebody here for you," she peered through the dusk at the green tail, which waved from side to side whenever Seymour moved. "Somebody with…a tail!"

"Tell her it's the treasurer of the Lizard Collective," Seymour Burp put in modestly.

Floozy repeated this, then added: "He thinks insurance adjusters are sexy."

"Been in any car accidents recently?" Seymour asked her.

Floozy was tempted to shut the door in this very strange person's face, but her daughter hollered from the kitchen, "Oh, that's Burp."

"Are you…" Floozy peered at him again, this time somewhat apprehensively, "Burp?"

"That's me," Seymour replied.

"I see, well, come in, I guess, you and your tail," Floozy said.

Seymour Burp followed the lady of the house into the living room.

"Wall-to-wall carpeting," he decided to make conversation. "Nice."

Floozy eyed him warily. "Glad you like it," she finally said, and then, "What's the Lizard Collective?"

"Group of lizard people like me and Philippa, who rule the world," Seymour Burp explained.

"Not my Philippa," Floozy said.

"You don't think she rules the world, Mrs. Philpot?" Seymour began.

"I think she's a part-time dog walker," Floozy said. "Last I checked dog walkers don't rule the world, and neither," she stared at the logo on his T-shirt, "do insurance adjusters."

"I'm not a lizard person," Philippa said, stepping out of the kitchen and standing beside her mother. They were exactly the same, average height, had the same compact figures, though Floozy had grown a little pudgy around the midriff with age; both had chin-length, fly-away dark hair, though the mother's was streaked with gray, and in their jeans and matching "Stop Big Pharma" T-shirts, they looked almost like twins.

"What's big pharma?" Seymour asked, and then, "I thought you were a pharmacist, Mrs. Philpot."

"She's a rebellious pharmacist," Philippa said, then, "why the tail, Seymour?"

"I thought you said he was Burp," Floozy interrupted.

"When you could just use Derma-Lube," Philippa continued, "and cover yourself with scales?"

"A little on my leg's enough. I don't wanna croak, like Doofus."

"Doofus?" Thus Floozy.

"The man-sized lizard," Philippa reminded her, "who kicked the bucket in the Takoma Park Burger Burg."

"Oh yes. I read about that in National Disgrace on my lunch break today," Floozy said. "Very disturbing."

"The moron only died 'cause he *ingested* it," Philippa clarified. "I used it on my arms, and I'm fine."

"Except for the scales," her mother said.

"I'm suing the Pinky Pimple men's body products company," Philippa said. "But the owner claims she got a brand-new product in the works to undo the Derma-Lube damage, seeing as Desert was a dud."

Seymour Burp gaped: "You mean to bring Doofus back to life?!"

"There's a thought," Philippa said dryly.

"But his body was kidnapped," Floozy said. "And if I read the story correctly, the kidnappers intended to employ a taxidermist to stuff and mount his corpse. I don't see how Prissy Pimple can expect to come out with a product to reverse that!"

"To de-scale me, mother," Philippa elaborated.

"So I guess," Seymour Burp said pensively, as he had clearly been pondering this news in all its implications, "if we applied it to Doofus, his, uh, corpse would return to normal."

"I think all the stuffing would come out," Floozy Philpot informed him.

BUDDY SCHLIMIZZLE WAS working late. Wilfred Doofus' mother, Carmelita Doofus had demanded to see him but not till after twilight, "'cause I'm a night owl," she had explained, "like my son was a lizard, a drug-dealing, degenerate lizard, may he rest in peace." The undertaker took great satisfaction in missing a meal with smelly Fred Fart, still at his home –

he had lengthened his stay so Dr. Butt could "keep an eye on his rectum," a turn of phrase from Bunzi which her husband found very unpleasant – and also in eating sushi takeout instead of spaghetti and meatballs, one of the four dishes his wife could cook, or rather over-cook. So he sat at his desk in his shadowed office, savoring his California roll and delighted that he was not eating mushy pasta, while overpowered by the scent of Lakeside Laurel. The front door jingled the tune of "I will survive."

Carmelita Doofus was short and skinny, with sharp, darting, dark eyes, gray hair and, oddly, Buddy thought, given her age, clad in yoga pants and a T-shirt with the bizarre logo, "EZ-Pass."

"You, uh, work for the Motor Vehicles Administration?" Buddy asked.

"What kind of question is that?" She demanded, sitting in the chair beside his desk. "You think the MVA could find my freakish son's corpse?"

"Don't mind me, I'm finishing dinner," Buddy said and resumed eating his sushi.

"Go ahead. I already ate my peanut-butter and jelly sandwich. You couldn't pay me to eat sushi," she commented.

Buddy Schlimizzle decided to let this remark pass without probing and so, chewed his food thoughtfully.

"Did you get a good look at the kidnappers?" Carmelita asked.

"They were very ordinary," Buddy belched discreetly. "Except they all wore green."

"That's the Lizard Collective," his customer said grimly.

Buddy's phone rang. He excused himself to answer it.

"This perfume is enough to asphyxiate a person," his son Marty said, "though I guess it's better than the usual putrid odors that this person emits."

Buddy hung up. "Crank call," he told Carmelita Doofus.

His phone rang again. "Get back here, so you can drive Fred Fart to the airport!" Bunzi snapped. "Butt's done with him, and he smells."

"He always smells," Buddy grumbled.

"I think Butt put too much perfume in the canister. I'm dyin' here," Bunzi complained.

"Why do I have to drive that smelly Fart to the airport?" Buddy demanded, then, "Ow, Bunzi, mention of Fred Fart and his odors gave me gas."

Carmelita Doofus, who had followed this conversation closely, looked startled.

"Get the pump, Buddy," his wife said. "It will solve all your problems."

"Never!" Buddy Schlimizzle snapped. "I'm never getting that lethal device that killed that pervert Pinky Pimple, up my ass. You tell Butt to forget it."

"Whose Butt?" Carmelita Doofus, both eyebrows raised in astonishment, asked.

"Then find your own Maalox," his wife said.

"I'm the one dyin' here, and all you can do is yammer on about pumps and Fred Fart."

"Well, if you kick the bucket," Carmelita said, "you're already in a funeral home. So that's a consolation."

Buddy scowled at her.

"Provided, of course, four weirdos in green don't steal your corpse," she added.

"Not MY corpse," Buddy informed her.

"What corpse?" Bunzi asked. "There you go, exaggerating again."

"No Lizard Collective's getting their hands on ME, dead or alive," Buddy said.

"Don't be too sure," Carmelita told him.

"I think your father has lost his mind," Bunzi told Marty.

"Just so he doesn't lose his way home, because this perfume is too much," Marty snapped. "I can't breathe."

"Marty can't breathe," Bunzi said.

"Tell him to eat dinner on the back deck, away from that retarded Fart," Buddy said rather unsympathetically.

"What retarded fart?" Carmelita Doofus wanted to know.

"The one stinking up the room," Buddy explained.

"I don't smell anything," Carmelita said.

"Doofus' mother doesn't smell anything," Buddy said.

"Are you calling me a doofus, Buddy Schlimizzle? Because if you are," Bunzi began.

"No, I'm not," Buddy belched less discreetly. "I think all this talk about Fred Fart and smells and that rectal pump made me lose my appetite."

"It made me lose mine, and I wasn't even eating," Carmelita Doofus said.

Buddy ended the call.

"Well, that was rude," Buddy said.

"You can say that again," his visitor grumped.

"So why are you here?" The undertaker asked.

"My idiot son's corpse is stolen out of your funeral home and you ask why I'm here?" Carmelita said.

"The cops are looking into it," Buddy said. "They'll find out where it leads."

"Those cops couldn't find their way out of a paper bag, if their lives depended on it," Carmelita snapped. "I talked to Detective Dump. All he did was babble about some Animal Liberation Army."

Buddy pushed his plate of mostly finished sushi away. "Well, I got more money for us from the papers," he said.

"How much?" She asked, a flash of greed in her dark, darting eyes.

"I bargained 'em up to $25,000 apiece."

"From each paper or for each of us?" She asked.

"Both."

"I'm confused," Carmelita whined.

"We each get $25,000 apiece from Scuttlebutt and $25,000 apiece from National Disgrace, but we have to consent to be interviewed by a reporter who spits and an editor who vomits," Buddy explained.

Carmelita Doofus gaped at him. After a moment, she began: "When you say spits…"

"As in he'll coat your face with saliva if you get too close to him," Buddy scowled. "At least the editor seems to prefer to vomit on his secretary, but you never know, so I'd keep my distance from him, too."

"You should have asked for more money," she snapped.

"I did," Buddy said gloomily, "but both newspapers said they were already paying a fortune to a 20-something Schnook, to whom I happen to have the misfortune of being related, and so their budgets were tight."

"Who is this Schnook?" She demanded. "And what's so special about him?"

"He's managed to spend the last 10 years in his mother's basement without doing a lick of work."

"He won't help around the house?"

"No. And he's unemployed."

"Sounds like Wilfred," Carmelita frowned sourly. "Except he sold drugs."

"I wish Hinchy Schnook sold drugs, something, anything, other than mooching offa his relations and expecting me to pay for his sushi whenever he comes to dinner," Buddy frowned.

"Did you try Gossip?" Carmelita asked.

"Yes, they hung up on me."

"Well, Scuttlebutt and National Disgrace it is, spit and vomit. I've seen worse. Working in a plumbing supply office, you wouldn't believe the shit you see. Oh, excuse me, no offense."

"None taken," Buddy belched even less discreetly.

"It's just that around plumbers, you get kinda…casual about the, um, stuff they gotta work with," she explained.

"I can see that," Buddy said. "Do your plumbers need an extra hand in the office?"

"I thought you were busy running a funeral home, and with kidnappers who make off with your corpses," she said.

"Not for me, for my son, Marty."

"As a matter of fact, we need someone to take charge of inventory," Carmelita explained.

"Marty Schlimizzle's your guy, though he's been unemployed for a while," his father said.

"How long?"

"Forever," Buddy frowned.

JEREMY SPIT FOLLOWED Seymour Burp and Philippa Philpot from downtown Silver Spring east into the run-down precincts of Langley Park. He watched them park in the crowded little lot outside the rec center, and, joined by a couple, both also sporting green tails, enter the building.

He dialed his boss, Bull Bruiser, who was relaxing in his tony Bethesda townhome, drinking a Margarita and pursuing several flirtations on twitter.

"I flushed 'em out," Spit said. "Green tails and all."

"Who is this?" Bull Bruiser demanded.

"Your chief terrorism and alien abduction reporter."

"Oh, hello Spit," the editor decided to make his move on an attractive Rockville housewife – at least her photo on her twitter page was attractive, but, he thought sourly, you could never be too sure. More than once he had found out to his profound disappointment that those photos were decades old. "How about we meet for a drink," he mumbled as he typed.

"I thought you wanted me to infiltrate the Lizard Collective," Spit said.

"Not you," Bruiser snapped.

"Oh. So I'm off the story? You gave it back to Johnson?"

Bull Bruiser sighed, removed the cigar from the corner of his mouth and asked: "So where's this collective?"

"Langley Park."

"Sounds like a dump."

"I haven't even described it," Spit said.

"You think I'm an idiot, Spit? I know you haven't freakin' described it. But Langley Park and everything in it is a goddamned dump."

"Sooo…I should make it sound swanker to impress our readers?"

"Our readers are sub-moronic imbeciles without IQs," Bull Bruiser snapped, noting a new female on his twitter time-line. He clicked on her name – Bunzi – and saw the photo of an attractive woman with blonde-tinted hair, who described herself as the assistant to an award-winning proctologist.

"What awards?" He typed his question to her.

"The Pulitzer," she typed back.

Bull Bruiser's eyebrows lifted in surprise. "I'm in the journalism field myself. I didn't hear anything about a Pulitzer to a proctologist. What for?"

"His lead article in American Anus."

Bull Bruiser gagged.

"You alright, boss?" Thus Spit.

"Something's goin' on in the Pulitzer committee," he said. "Deep, profound perversion. That's your next assignment, Spit – 'The Pulitzer Dives in the Tank for American Anus.' That's our headline."

"Ew," Spit spat, spraying his already damp windshield.

"My reaction exactly. But this would rivet the rubes' eyeballs." Then Bruiser texted Bunzi: "What exactly in American Anus?"

"Oh, it's too technical for me to explain, but it had something to do with the efficacy of vinegar enemas," Bunzi elaborated.

Bull Bruiser gaped at his phone. "You can't make this shit up!" He exclaimed.

"What shit?" Spit demanded. "Should I infiltrate this confab or no?"

But his editor did not answer. He was busy texting Bunzi about getting together for drinks.

"I couldn't, because I'm not available," Bunzi replied. "My husband, a very hot-headed undertaker, would object. Also, he has a gun."

"Forget that loser," Bull Bruiser typed.

"I couldn't," she replied. "He relies on me for everything, all his medicines."

"Oh, he's an invalid?" Bull asked hopefully.

"No. He's constipated."

"Maybe I don't wanna date this woman," Bull Bruiser muttered. Instead, he asked: "What medicines?"

"Explosion."

"That sounds dangerous," Bull Bruiser wrote.

"You should hear him howling from the toilet," Bunzi replied.

"I'll pass," the editor wrote.

"Boss…" Jeremy Spit began.

"Quiet Spit. I'm texting a very hot lady about constipation."

"I'm goin' in," the reporter announced.

"You do that," Bull Bruiser replied, then texted: "How about a bite, if you're not up for drinks, maybe sushi?"

"My husband loves sushi," Bunzi typed.

"Forget that constipated mortician."

Jeremy Spit exited his car and crossed the twilit parking lot. He joined a small crowd of what he considered very odd people, sporting green tails and green glitter on their faces, entering the rec center. Inside, he saw Wilfrid Doofus, magnificently stuffed and mounted, covered with scales, wearing only a green thong and glaring down at the gathering collective. Recognizing Philippa, he drifted her way.

"Oh," she said, "you're that reporter who spits."

"Shh." He told her. "I'm undercover."

"Whatever."

Seymour Burp eyed Jeremy Spit jealously.

"Oh Burp," she said, "meet Spit. The only thing you two have in common is your names."

"I fail to see," Seymour began.

"Spit spits but you, thank goodness, don't burp."

"Not unless I've had a big meal," Seymour explained.

"Keep it to yourself," Philippa told him.

"These lizard people are phonies," Spit spat. "But I won't put that in my story."

"We rule the world," a short, obese fellow in green with green glitter on the end of his nose informed him.

"Mind if I take notes? I'm writing a novel," Spit prevaricated.

The fat man preened. "About the Lizard Collective?"

"Yes: How long have you been a follower of Karl Marx?"

The man looked confused. "I'm a lizard, from outer space," he explained.

"Oh? What star system?" Jeremy Spit scribbled on his notepad.

"One in Orion's Belt."

"And why are you here?"

"To eat novelists," The man told him.

"So you're cannibals," Spit spat, zapping the man in the eye with a glob of saliva.

"No need to spit," the man complained. "And while we may look like cannibals, we're not."

Philippa rolled her eyes.

"We're another species," the man rather ponderously explained, "so when we eat people it's not cannibalism."

"Well, that settles that," Philippa Philpot told Jeremy Spit.

SEATED IN THE Schlimizzle's living room, Fred Fart phoned his boss. "My gas smells like laurel," he said.

Lucas Flush ended that call, taking it to be harassment. Fred Fart phoned back.

"Lakeside Laurel, to be exact."

"Listen here, whoever you are," Lucas Flush began, seated in his Pest Patrol pickup and squinting, as was his wont, through the windshield at an aggressive pack of possums on the front lawn of a desperate North Miami householder's yard.

"See?! See?!" The very rotund fellow in a gray bathrobe and flip flops shouted to Lucas from his front threshold. "They've taken over the yard!"

"Yes, I see those possums," Lucas said, climbed out of his truck and advanced up the walk, limping and squinting, as always.

"What possums?" Fred Fart asked. "Do they have gas?"

"They better not," Lucas said and then, "look here, you. I'm a busy exterminator and my chief trapper's out of town."

"You mean me, Lucas?"

"Who is this?"

"Fred Fart," Lucas' employee said.

"That explains the opener about gas."

"Can you get rid of them?" The homeowner called.

"I'm talking to my trapper right now," Lucas shouted back.

"What trapper?" Thus Fred Fart.

"You," Lucas said. "I'm glad you got yourself deodorized, Fred, I really am. But you need to hightail it back to Miami. We got a situation."

"What kinda situation?" Fred Fart asked warily.

"Pack of very bold possums," Lucas explained.

"I don't wanna get abducted," Fred Fart whined.

"That's been your excuse ever since you heard aliens was posin' as racoons and abducting unsuspecting pest experts to their spaceships in geosynchronous orbit," Lucas said.

"And sellin' 'em into sex slavery in the Alpha Centauri system," Fred Fart added. "All the best newspapers covered it."

"Well, these possums are just possums," Lucas said.

"Don't be too sure. Aliens could look like possums," Fred said.

Seated across from him on the couch, Marty muttered "This is unbelievable," and rolled his eyes. "Mom," he called into the kitchen. "Dad got me a job."

"Ooo!" Bunzi exclaimed, stepping out into the living room in her gold designer ensemble covered by her white apron with the red floral design.

"With the mother of a man-sized lizard," Marty continued, staring at his phone.

"Well, you can't be too choosy," Bunzi said.

"I don't know about this," her son equivocated.

"Marty! You're 30. You haven't worked since you dropped out of college. Seize the day! This is your chance, your opportunity, your future! Who cares if you work for a lizard?"

"One of my hosts works for a lizard, "Fred Fart told his boss.

"From what galaxy?" Lucas Flush asked.

"What galaxy is this lizard's mother from?" Fred Fart asked Marty, who frowned.

"Don't discourage him, Fred," Bunzi admonished.

"Doofus," Marty said.

"I'm not a doofus," thus Fred.

"The lizard's mother is," Marty said absentmindedly, as he texted with Buddy. "I'm not sure about this, Dad," he wrote.

"Tell your father I'm finally on twitter," Bunzi said. "And the first thing that happened is some journalist, who never heard of the American Anus, asked me out."

Marty texted this news to his father.

"He says he's gonna kill this asshole," Marty told his mother.

"He's mixed up. It's American Anus, not Asshole," Bunzi elaborated.

Fred Fart, following this exchange closely, looked alarmed.

"Someone's gonna kill an asshole," he told Lucas.

"I'm not innarested in that asshole, whoever he is. I got a pack of possums to deal with."

"What galaxy is this asshole from?" Fred Fart asked Marty.

IN YOGA PANTS and a ripped T-shirt, Philippa walked up to the counter at Starbucks and thanked her friend, Mimi Schlimizzle, who worked there, for the free cappuccino.

"Keep your voice down," Mimi whispered. "You'll upset the other customers. Is Prissy coming?"

"I told her either she pays me a LOT of money or that lawyer your Dad recommended will sue her for millions. She claims to have a new product, 'Scale-off' that will cure me. We'll see," Philippa harrumphed and moved off to a table to wait.

Soon Pinky Pimple's ferocious and ferociously stupid widow, all in black, entered, waving an aerosol can. She sat across from Philippa and said, "my chemist says this'll cure you." She sprayed Philippa's arm. The green scales glittered wetly. But they didn't do anything else.

"Your chemist is a dud," Philippa said. "Is he the one who came up with the Derma-Lube formula?"

"And Explosion and Bush. They all are super-effective," Prissy said.

"Well, if I gotta live with these disfigured arms, I'm suing," Philippa snapped.

Prissy Pimple gaped.

In walked a couple, both older, spherical and very unappealing. They wore red MAGA hats and they addressed Mimi like gangsters. "The usual. Make it snappy, and enough syrup or else."

"Hi Mrs. Schlumpf," Mimi said. "Hi Mr. Schlumpf."

They grunted their hellos.

"Make me an offer!" Philippa snapped again.

"Uh, $30,000," Prissy Pimple said.

"I'll take a check."

As the bloodthirsty but otherwise bovinely placid Mrs. Pimple wrote out a check and Philippa pocketed it, the Schlumpfs turned around. Mrs. Schlumpf saw Philippa's scales and screamed.

"An Illuminati!" She shrieked. "A lizard person!"

"Where, sweetiekins?" Her husband asked. "Where?"

Mrs. Schlumpf pointed. Both Schlumpfs stared in horror.

"It's okay," Philippa tried to appease them, rising and approaching. "I'm not a lizard person. It was the Derma-Lube."

"Don't you touch my sugarpie!" Mr. Schlumpf warned.

"What sugarpie?" Philippa asked, unwisely stepping closer. Both Schlumpfs tackled her. All three crashed to the ground, overturning a table.

The other customers screamed. Mimi Schlimizzle called the cops. She was put on hold. The Schlumpfs and Philippa rolled from one end of the coffee shop to another.

"Nine one one. What is the nature of your emergency?"

"We got an assault at Starbucks!" Mimi shouted.

Mrs. Schlumpf detached herself from the mass of furious, writhing limbs to inform Mimi that she was just doing her duty as a patriotic American, member of Q-Anon and Trump supporter to kill any Illuminati pedophiles wherever she found them. She picked her MAGA hat up off the floor and put it back on.

"Make that attempted murder," Mimi spoke into the phone.

Philippa sat on the spherical Mr. Schlumpf's chest. "I think I had an aneurism," he muttered.

"Then you shouldn't assault strangers in coffee shops," Mimi snapped.

"Free the January 6th protesters!" Mrs. Schlumpf bellowed to the few remaining customers.

"We've got two dangerous ignoramuses here," Mimi said into her phone. "Hurry."

Two policemen entered. "What's this?" One asked.

"An attempted murder," Mimi said.

"I knew we shoulda skipped the cappuccinos," the other officer complained.

"I just called 911," Mimi elaborated. "These people, the Schlumpfs, assaulted a customer, Philippa Philpot."

Philippa, still sitting on Mr. Schlumpf, waved.

"She's a lizard person!" Mrs. Schlumpf huffed. "Look at her arms."

The policemen approached Philippa.

"Green scales," said one.

"Trump mentioned this," said the other.

"I got them from using Derma-Lube," Philippa explained.

The first officer frowned in consternation. "I just bought some for my dry skin."

"Don't use it," Philippa advised.

"It's in the squad car," he continued rather ponderously. "You think I could get a refund if I return it? I don't wanna grow green scales."

"Are you going to arrest the Schlumpfs or what?" Mimi demanded.

"Who are the Schlumpfs?" One officer asked.

"The two fat people who assaulted the customer intending to kill her," Mimi explained.

"Where are our café mochas?" Mrs. Schlumpf asked.

"You're under arrest," the first officer said. "You and your café mocha." Philippa got off Mr. Schlumpf.

"What about lizard girl?" Mrs. Schlumpf demanded.

"I don't feel good," Mr. Schlumpf groaned, still lying on the floor.

"Then maybe you shouldn't attack random strangers," Philippa said again, "quietly minding their own business in coffee shops after receiving a $30,000 settlement."

Both officers looked impressed.

"For the scales," she told them.

"Maybe I'll use that Derma-Lube after all," one said. "I could use $30,000."

Prissy Pimple gaped at him.

"I want $30,000," said one customer.

"Me too," thus Mrs. Schlumpf.

"So you concede I'm not a lizard person," Philippa snapped.

Two more police cars parked out front. More officers entered. "What's going on here? Where's the attempted murderer?" One new arrival asked.

"There!" Mimi pointed at Mrs. Schlumpf.

"No murder. It was an attack of the lizard people," Mrs. Schlumpf said. "An Illuminati."

"A what-who?" The officer asked, attempting to snap handcuffs on her. "Her wrists are too fat. Get the extra-large cuffs from the car, Hank."

Meanwhile the policeman who had bought the Derma-Lube went to his car, got it and returned. He approached Philippa. "Now what do I do?"

"Rub some on your arm. Don't eat it. Then rinse it off with water," Philippa advised.

He did so. Moments later green scales appeared.

"You violated our non-disclosure agreement," Prissy Pimple told Philippa. "You infringed on my rights as the owner of the Derma-Lube patent."

The officer looked at her. "I want $30,000."

Prissy stared at him, then Philippa. "I want my money back," she said.

"Quiet, or I'll demand more," Philippa replied.

DR. ELBERT POSTERIOR strolled into his Biscayne Boulevard, Miami office, tall, paunchy, his thin, limp brown curls neatly combed, and greeted his receptionist, dyspeptic Sylvia. "It's good to be back from Puerto Rico," he said, "especially with no Fred Fart expected in the office for another month."

"Except he came by twice while you were gone," she said sourly. "The stink was enough to knock you out."

"Please Sylvia," Dr. Posterior said. "Show some consideration."

"I've shown lots of consideration. Fred Fart passes too much gas. He uses up the perfume in the canister every three weeks, so we should schedule refills accordingly, not on the monthly or even two months basis, by which time the smell is toxic," Sylvia said.

"But then I have to see him every three weeks," Posterior complained.

"But *I* won't have to smell him," Sylvia snapped. "It's either that or I get a raise for hazard pay."

"Let me think about this," Posterior said and then: "I must call Butt and thank him. Could you get his office on the line?"

"That bedlam? Maybe we should rethink this."

"I'm going to suggest that Butt develop a more…capacious canister."

"As in bigger?" Sylvia asked. "'Cause last I heard, Fred Fart's got a lot of stuff in his colon – a rectal pump, the nation's nuclear codes on a jump drive, and a perfume canister. I don't think a bigger one will fit."

"You're behindhand, Sylvia. We never did actually insert the nation's nuclear codes, because DARPA refused to miniaturize them when they found out what the purpose was," Posterior explained.

"You mean putting 'em in Fred Fart's behind."

"Um, ah yes. Call Butt, please," Posterior said and walked back to his office.

"It's your funeral," Sylvia said then dialed.

"Oh, I'm so excited about Butt's Pulitzer for his lead article in American

Anus. That must be what this call's about," Bunzi enthused to a patient, Mr. Fink, as she answered the phone.

"No. I didn't know the Pulitzer was giving awards to proctologists," Sylvia said.

"Who is this?" Bunzi demanded. "Another award-giving body?"

"No awards from this body."

"Because Dr. Butt's an under-appreciated, proctological genius, no matter what the Pinky Pimple men's body products corporation claims. The rectal pump does not kill people by backing their shit up to their hearts and causing heart attacks. It's okay Mr. Fink," she turned back to him. "The pump in your rectum has not malfunctioned."

"I don't want to die," he said.

"You won't. Your pump just needs adjustment," Bunzi said. "That's why you're not having regular bowel movements."

Sylvia rolled her eyes.

"Posterior wants to thank Butt," she finally said.

"Oh?" Bunzi asked. "For what?"

"For refilling Fred Fart's perfume canister."

"He can thank me. I'm the one who had to put up with that person in my house for a few nights so he could make his morning appointment and then stay on while his rectum was under observation," Bunzi sniffed in offended tones.

Sylvia's features contorted in distaste at Bunzi's last turn of phrase, and then, as the whole message sank in, looked aghast. "You let Fred Fart stay in your house?"

"He was Butt's first patient to receive the device that deodorizes flatulence. We put him up at the Schlimizzle home to help advance science."

"How does your husband feel about this?" Sylvia couldn't help asking.

"He sleeps in a coffin," Bunzi replied.

Sylvia's eyebrows lifted in shock. "Come again?"

"He's an undertaker. So when Fred Fart walks in the door, Buddy walks out, goes to his funeral home and spends the night in a coffin," Bunzi said.

"Vampires," thus Mr. Fink.

"How unusual," Sylvia commented.

"He says the smell may kill him," Bunzi went on.

"I agree with him there," Sylvia said and transferred the call to Posterior.

"So he sleeps in the coffin in case Fred Fart's fumes have a delayed reaction. That way his corpse will be ready to be interred," Bunzi concluded.

"Who is this?" Dr. Posterior demanded.

"I could ask you the same question. Where's Sylvia? The lines must've crossed." And Bunzi ended the call.

"Sylvia," Dr. Posterior came out to the reception area, looking worried. "I think I just got a harassment call."

"Could be."

"Someone who sleeps in a coffin to be prepared for death due to Fred Fart's fumes," he continued.

"That wasn't harassment. That was Dr. Butt's receptionist, Bunzi Schlimizzle, whose husband Buddy, if I got his name right, sleeps in a coffin at his funeral home whenever Fred Fart comes to town," Sylvia explained.

"Doesn't that seem, um," Dr. Posterior lowered his voice. "Rather extreme to you?"

"No. If Fred Fart slept in my house, I wouldn't just sleep in a coffin, I'd ask to be buried," Sylvia said.

"Maybe we could cut a deal with an airline for him to fly up to Washington every three weeks," Dr. Posterior said hopefully. "Get a discount."

"There's a thought," Sylvia said sourly.

FRED FART WALTZED into Woof Woof's Teeth, the offices of his girlfriend, veterinary dentist Ducky Finch in South Beach.

"Outta here, Fart!" Snapped the receptionist, Lolo Chandry, waving the shorter of his arms at the pest expert – shorter because it had been bitten off by an insufficiently sedated patient, a crocodile, and then surgically reattached. "Your perfume gives me hives."

"I don't see any hives."

"You will if you stay, moron," Lolo snapped again.

"Where's Ducky?"

"None of your business. She's my girlfriend now, Fart – got that? 'Cause if you don't, I'll cut your fucking head off!"

"Lolo has been skipping his anger management classes," Ducky said, stepping out into the reception room. Then she sniffed. "I like that Lakeside Laurel."

"I'm gonna have hives all over my body," Lolo snarled at Fred. "Like the last time and the time before that. You think I like spending the night in the hospital, you dimwit?"

"Stop it, Lolo!" Ducky snapped, then, straightening her white lab coat, turned to Fred Fart. "I can't talk long. I'm treating a mouse that ate too much cheese and got constipated."

"That doesn't sound like a dental problem," Fred Fart said slowly and dully.

"We're very versatile here at Woof Woof's Teeth, Fred," and Ducky tucked her pink hair behind her ears with the multiple piercings. "You know that."

"The imbecile forgot," Lolo muttered.

"I forgot," Fred Fart said.

Ducky returned to the examining room.

"Get out," Lolo told him. "Ducky and I have a dinner date tonight."

"No you don't," Fred Fart smirked.

"You contradictin' me?" Lolo leapt to his feet and in a flash had rounded the reception desk and tackled the Pest Patrol employee. They rolled on the floor, grappling, as the doorbell chimed and an elderly woman stepped in. "I must have come to the wrong place," she said, turning to leave.

But Ducky, who'd heard the doorbell, popped out and stopped her with a "How can I help you?"

"By telling the wrestlers to stop," the customer said. "They make me nervous."

Indeed, Fred Fart and Lolo rolled wildly from one end of the room to the other, grunting, sweating and grappling ferociously.

"Ignore them," Ducky said.

"Kinda hard," the dowdily attired senior citizen said.

"Oh, I do it all the time," Ducky continued. "What seems to be the problem?"

"Well," the woman stepped further in, as Ducky approached her. "I used this product, a skin cream called Derma-Lube."

"This is a veterinary practice, ma'am," Ducky explained.

"And this is a veterinary problem," the gray-haired grandmother said, then pushed up her sleeves, revealing green, glittering scales from her wrists to her elbows.

Fred Fart, seated now on Lolo's chest, looked at the old woman's arms and said, "another lizard person."

"I am NOT a lizard person," the woman snapped.

"Shut up, Fred," thus Ducky.

"Any idea how I…de-scale?" The woman asked.

"I have a product I use for reptiles when their scales need to be… thinned." Ducky said.

"What's it called?"

"De-Scale."

"Let's give it a go!"

So with Fred Fart still seated on Lolo, Ducky fetched a tube of the medicine and rubbed it on the old woman's arm. Several scales fell off.

"Well, that's disappointing," Ducky said.

"What's that perfume you're wearing?" The woman asked.

"Ignore that," the veterinary dentist said.

"Okey doke."

"I'm sorry De-Scale didn't work better, Ms….Ms…"

"Miss Pit. But it's better than nothing. I'll take it," the old woman said.

"You should sue Derma-Lube," Fred Fart said. "That's what this lizard girl I met in Maryland did. And according to an award-winning proctologist's receptionist, she got $30,000."

"What award?" Miss Pit asked.

"An American Anus award," dull-eyed Fred explained.

"I shouldn't have asked," she muttered.

"That's enough of that, Fred!" Ducky snapped.

"Well, she asked," Fred Fart whined.

"Ow, get offa me!" Lolo howled. "The perfume," he gasped. "It's overpowering. It's making me itch."

"You should wear less perfume," Miss Pit advised Ducky. "For the sake of whoever that person is, lying on the floor." Miss Pit paid for the De-Scale, then turned to Fred Fart. "Who do I sue?"

"Prissy Pimple. Don't mention me," Fred said.

"Why not," the old woman inquired.

"I wanna keep all my private parts," he replied.

"Logical enough, for a lunatic," Miss Pit said. "How do I find this Prissy Pimple?"

"Uh, the Derma-Lube website, I think." Fred Fart said. "Just don't mention me."

"I won't, whatever your name is. I intend to forget you forever, as soon as I walk out that door."

"My name is Fart, Fred Fart."

"That's a joke, right?" Miss Pit asked Ducky.

"What's a joke?" Fred asked.

"He's a little slow?" Thus Miss Pit.

"We all have our failings," Ducky simpered.

"Well, thanks to this stupid Fart's so-called failings, I now got hives, all over my body," Lolo snapped. Indeed, big, raised, red splotches covered all of Lolo's visible skin.

"I better call an ambulance," Ducky said.

"I think I'll leave," Miss Pit said.

"What's your hurry?" Fred Fart rather chattily asked.

"I don't wanna get hives," she said. "The scales are enough."

PHILIPPA PHILPOT HAD dyed her hair green to match her green yoga pants, green top and the green scales on her arms. This verdant spectacle presented herself very early for work at the crowded Schnook abode, just off University Avenue in East Silver Spring, so early that Maybelline Schnook, who rose with the sun to arrive at the supermarket, Jumbo Mart, where she managed the bakery, was still in her bathrobe. When Philippa stepped into the living room, zaftig Maybelline took one look at the scales on her arm and screamed. This geschrei did nothing to dislodge her loutish sons from their basement beds, but her daughter-in-law, Mimi Schlimizzle, came running, thumping noisily up the stairs.

"Where's the burglar?" She panted, belting her blue satin robe around her skimpy pajamas, which consisted, in fact, of little more than a gold thong.

"Philippa's turning into a lizard," Maybelline gasped.

"Old news, Maybelline. And besides," Mimi snapped grouchily, "you already knew that. You saw her scales before."

"It's still a shock. To see it suddenly, unexpectedly in the…the flesh," Maybelline stammered. "Or rather the scales."

"Why are you here at this ungodly hour?" Mimi asked her friend.

"To walk Fart Schnook," Philippa explained.

"He's asleep on Hinchy's bed. Don't disturb him. He may bite."

"He never bit me," Philippa said.

"That dog wakes up on the wrong side of the bed," Mimi explained. "Regularly."

"I shouldn't have screamed," Maybelline apologized to the visitor. "After all, at one point Al was covered with a complete coat of fur."

"That was bizarre," thus Mimi.

"Lots of things were," her mother-in-law continued. "Like him coming out of a nine-month coma with two brains in his head."

"I think I read about this in detail, years ago," Philippa said.

"Yes, in Scuttlebutt," Maybelline continued. "They did ground-breaking coverage on how Fatso was de-evolving and would end up a gigantic, fanged amoeba."

"Fatso?" Philippa asked.

"When Al came out of his coma, he insisted he'd been reincarnated as Frank Fart, an animal trapper whose nickname was Fatso," Maybelline explained.

"How odd," Philippa murmured.

"That wasn't the only thing that was odd. Living with a fur-covered, lecherous…creature, who sold the story of his every bowel movement to supermarket tabloids for thousands of dollars – now that was odd."

A yell could be heard in the basement, followed by the shout: "He bit me! Fart Schnook bit me!"

"You woke up the whole house," Mimi said sourly. "Why aren't you at home, recovering from being assaulted by the Schlumpfs?"

"My Mom has insomnia."

Mimi was fazed by this non-sequitur and said so.

"Very noisy, demanding insomnia," Philippa explained.

"She should try E-Z-Sleep," Maybelline said. "Prissy Pimple's new product."

"I don't think I want Floozy sleeping for one hundred years," Philippa objected.

"What makes you say that?" Maybelline asked, leading them into the sun-filled kitchen, where she began to make coffee.

"Or turning into a three-toed sloth," Philippa continued.

"Oh, the Pimple body products aren't that bad," Maybelline pooh-poohed these concerns. "Al, I mean Frank Fart, used their signature product, the laxative Explosion, all the time."

"Can we not talk about Explosion?" Mimi snapped. "I'm the one with the father whose 40-year constipation made headlines and was explicated in depth in supermarket tabloids, remember? My Dad drinks Explosion all the time. Then we hear him howling in the bathroom. It's kinda a sore subject."

They sat in the sun-filled kitchen, at the butcher-block table and drank their coffee, their slurps in syncopation to Hinchy's loud curses.

"I don't know about Fart Schnook, Maybelline," Mimi said. "Maybe we should donate him to the Humane Society."

"Excellent idea!" Hinchy snapped, poking his frizzy, black-haired head into the room. "Oh, hi Philippa. Why don't I come with you this morning, when you walk the dog?"

"'Cause you're still in your pajamas."

"I'll put on a jacket," Hinchy Schnook said, then joined them at the table. "I hope Fart Schnook has completed his rabies vaccines."

"Of course he has," Maybelline said, dusting a speck off the front of her bathrobe. "I keep all furry creatures up to date on their vaccines."

"You're thinking of Al Schnook?" Mimi asked.

"I am," Maybelline sighed sadly at the thought of her departed husband. "When he grew that thick pelt of fur, I insisted he get every vaccine Dr. Snot had, including rabies."

"Dr. Snot's been in National Disgrace," Hinchy Schnook said sourly. "Something about his patient, that psychotic Albert Pop who's always pictured in a straitjacket. Yes, Albert Pop and the lizard people."

"There are no lizard people," Mimi said.

"I beg to differ," Philippa put in. "I went to a meeting of the Lizard

Collective with Seymour Burp just the other night. There were dozens of maniacs in lizard suits."

"Seymour Burp, that loser," Hinchy grumbled. "I bet HE didn't figure out how to get tens of thousands of dollars from supermarket tabloids," and young Schnook preened proudly.

"I guess he didn't think it was decent to splash the story of Wilfred Doofus' untimely demise in a Takoma Park Burger Burg all over the headlines," Philippa sniffed.

"Like I said," Hinchy smirked, "a loser."

Herm thumped up the stairs, dragging the poodle on a leash. "This dog was a bad idea," he grumbled.

"I wanted something to remember your father by," Maybelline sniffled.

"How about a photograph?" Herm snapped, "instead of an incontinent poodle who bites?"

"I guess I should take him out before he has an accident on the living room carpet," Philippa said.

Hinchy Schnook eyed her lustfully. "I'm coming too. Think Philippa, we're both rich!"

Somehow the prospect of spending the morning gloating over her new-found wealth with Hinchy Schnook did not delight her.

CURLY BROWN-HAIRED Marty Schlimizzle went to Pipes Unplugged: Plumbing and Custodial Inventory in dreary Northeast Washington, D.C. and got hired on the spot.

"You're just what we need," the manager told him.

"What's that?" An astounded Marty asked.

"A warm body," was the reply.

"You're that constipated undertaker's kid," short, stringy Carmelita Doofus said, walking unevenly, as she always did, into the manager's office.

"What constipated undertaker?" The manager asked.

"He talked my ear off about his attempts to have a bowel movement over the course of many decades," she directed this grouchy complaint to Marty, "when I visited him to discuss the kidnapping of my no-good, drug-dealing lizard son's corpse."

"What drug-dealing lizard?" The manager asked.

"That's my Dad," Marty said sourly.

"He's a drug-dealing lizard?" The manager's eyebrows lifted in surprise.

"Evidently he sits on the toilet for hours," Carmelita continued. "I hope it doesn't run in the family, 'cause I need help in inventory, not somebody who spends the day in the bathroom."

"I'm not constipated," Marty said.

"I didn't say you were," the manager told him, then scrutinized him closely. "You don't look like a drug-dealing lizard."

"Apparently, his epic constipation made headlines for weeks on end in supermarket tabloids," Esmerelda continued. "Were you a party to that?"

"No," Marty said firmly but with evident irritation.

"A party to what? The undertaker's constipation?" The manager asked.

"Good," Carmelita continued, "'cause I can't abide publicity hounds. My worthless son was one, and styled himself some kinda unique lizard person. I wouldn't be surprised to learn he arranged that kidnapping after he died."

"So…lizard people can conduct business from beyond the grave?" The manager asked.

"I'm not a publicity hound," Marty said. "I just wanna work at Pipes Unplugged."

"Well, that's a peculiar aspiration," the manager said. "But knock yourself out."

A FEW HOURS later, as Marty stood behind the counter, looking out the front window at April showers, in walked short, scrawny, goateed Albert Pop in a straitjacket, blue jeans and work-boots, escorted by a greasy brown-haired Pimples also in jeans but wearing a yellow T-shirt that sported the logo "National Disgrace" in big black letters.

"Hi Albert," Marty said.

"You know him?" Pimples asked.

"Sure. He stayed at our house for a week, a couple of years ago, based on the promise of laxatives from another solar system, laxatives that never, uh, materialized."

"They're still in transit," Albert Pop informed him.

"Good to know," thus Marty.

"We need hoses," Pimples said. "Or, Albert does."

"To insert in your orifices," the lunatic clarified.

"Not MY orifices," Marty said.

"Everybody's orifices," Albert Pop explained.

"Which orifices?" Marty asked.

"Whichever are handy. That's how we Andromedan robots will conquer this puny planet. With our hoses, we'll suction all the salt out of your bodies. We'll steal all the salt in the oceans, all the salt in the ground,"

"I get the idea," Marty grumbled. "How many hoses?"

"Two for starters," Pimple said. "Albert plans to take them to the offices of Scuttlebutt."

"And you're abetting this psychotic?" Marty asked.

Albert Pop's eyes rolled wildly in his head. Outside the rain poured down.

"When in Rome," Pimples simpered.

"We're in D.C., not Rome," Marty said flatly. "And if I recall correctly this madman you're encouraging is a cannibal."

"I will eat your liver, and the liver of that constipated Andromedan, who betrayed us to the crab people," Albert informed him.

"You mean my father? Buddy Schlimizzle?"

Albert grunted assent.

"Look what our hospitality gets us," Marty grumbled.

"Then you know how it is," Pimples said. "Albert here lives with me."

Marty stared at him, aghast.

"He can't go back home, 'cause the CIA will kidnap him again," Pimples elaborated. "It's very trying. He goes on about hoses morning, noon and night. So I finally gave in. We want two."

"What?" Marty asked.

"Hoses." Pimples said.

"We need seven billion," Albert Pop clarified.

"I don't think we have that in inventory," Marty said, "or even on back order."

Albert Pop writhed in his straitjacket.

The manager stepped out. "Oh good," he said. "Customers." Then he looked at them more closely. "Is that man in a straitjacket?"

"What of it?" Albert Pop demanded.

The manager gaped.

"We Andromedans will crush this puny planet. We will suction the salt out of your bodies with hoses, store the salt in our intestines, then take it to the mother ship," Albert Pop told him.

"Okey doke," the manager said.

"Two hoses, coming right up," Marty said.

"Um, Schlimizzle," the manager said to his employee behind the back of his hand. "I'm not sure we should sell this person those hoses. He sounds dangerous."

"I will eat your liver," Albert Pop told the manager, whose jaw dropped.

"Don't worry," Pimples said. "He's in a straitjacket."

"Remove this straitjacket," Albert Pop commanded. "So I can defeat this lizard person."

"What lizard person?" The manager asked. "The corpse who got kidnapped?"

"Albert here read about the Lizard Collective in Scuttlebutt," Pimples explained. "He's got lizards on the brain."

"Lizards on the brain and an appetite for my liver," the manager said. "It doesn't sound good. It sounds like Mr. Albert here is a cannibal."

"He don't think so," Pimples said. "He thinks he's a robot."

"A hungry robot," Albert added.

"Maybe get him those hoses, after all," the manager, now eager to see these customers leave, told Marty.

"It won't do to humor no good, publicity-hound lizards," said Carmelita Doofus, who had been following this exchange from the desk and computer in a corner.

"Lizards or robots?" The manager asked.

"Either one," she snapped.

THE SCHLUMPFS' HOUSE in seedy Wheaton, Maryland, was an ordinary, red-brick, colonial affair, with a sign by the front hedge: "If your dog pees on our lawn, we will hunt you down." Onto these rather uninviting premises, one warm April evening at dusk, crowded a steady stream of visitors, for Mrs. Schlumpf had, post-arrest, convened a council of the Q-cell to which she and her spouse belonged. Many visitors wore red MAGA hats, as did the spherical Schlumpfs. Some wore "Trump" T-shirts. One, Delbert Dimly, sported a shirt with the logo "Stop the Illuminati." He escorted a friend of his son, Hallie Gas, who apparently wished to arrive incognito, as she wore sun-glasses and a ski mask.

In tromped this assortment of weirdos, all greeted in a rather surly manner by the Schlumpfs.

"We got trouble," Mr. Schlumpf announced, when they were all assembled, about 15 members of Q-Anon, in the living room. He held up an issue of Scuttlebutt with its banner headline: "Lizard Collective Worships Corpse of Iguana-Man, Stuffed, Mounted in Langley Park HQ!!!"

"I say we break in, steal that stuffed corpse and burn it!" Delbert Dimly shouted. All eyes fixed on the medium-height, paunchy, ordinary fellow with scanty brown hair, who stood in a corner.

"Good idea, Dimly," thus Mr. Schlumpf.

"That's me, full of good ideas," Delbert said. "That's why I'm in customer service."

Several members of the crowd nodded sagely.

"What're we gonna do about these lizard people?" Mr. Schlumpf asked. "Crawlin' around, drinkin' the blood of children."

"And rulin' the world!" One person put in.

"It's an atrocity," Mrs. Schlumpf huffed. "We need Trump."

"The real president," Hallie Gas said loudly.

"If Trump were in the white house," Mrs. Schlumpf said, "you can bet these lizard people wouldn't be so bold, parading around in respectable newspapers. I say we need drastic measures!" With that, she rubbed the bruise on her arm, sustained during her assault on Philippa Philpot in the local Starbucks.

The crowd murmured assent. "What does Q say?" One very adipose fellow asked.

"Armageddon's coming," Mrs. Schlumpf replied.

"He's said that before," the man complained.

"You questionin' Q?" Both Schlumpfs asked in unison, squinting at this fellow.

"I just want details," the man said.

"What details? It's the end of the world," Mr. Schlumpf said. "What that means should be obvious."

"Yeah, lizard people everywhere," said Dimly. "I say we need our guns."

"We take our AR-15s and storm that rec center," said another man, attired in red with a red T-shirt sporting the simple black logo, "Q."

"Hear, hear," went up in the crowd.

"Now don't get swept away in the tide of the moment," Mr. Schlumpf warned, "'cause that's what these lizard people are counting on."

"Meaning they know we'll be coming?" Delbert Dimly asked.

Both Schlumpfs nodded knowingly.

"My guess is, they'll have that rec center rigged to blow, the minute we enter," Mr. Schlumpf averred.

"They'll also probably alert the police that an armed Q cell is attacking," Mrs. Schlumpf said, then added sourly: "You can't trust the police. They innerferred with our recent, uh, action in Starbucks."

"So we don't go armed," the hefty man in red conceded. "We kill those lizard people with our bare hands."

Mrs. Schlumpf gazed skeptically at the crowd of mostly older, overweight Q members. "Bats," she finally said. "We take baseball bats."

A murmur of assent rippled through the crowd.

"But don't touch the lizard people with your bare hands," Delbert said. "You could catch the lizard virus."

Alarm spread over the features on every face in the room.

"Like…a covid virus?" Mrs. Schlumpf asked.

"A variant. It's highly transmissible. Gives you scales," Delbert said.

"Honeybunch, that lizard girl's scales," Mrs. Schlumpf babbled to her husband. "I touched them."

"Me too, sweetiekins," he replied somberly. People began to edge away from the Schlumpfs.

"But that was days ago, and still no scales," Mr. Schlumpf said bravely. "See?" And he held up his meaty arms for inspection.

The crowd grumbled.

"I say we beat those man-sized iguanas to a bloody pulp!" Delbert Dimly shouted.

"Till they're nothing but green goo!" Somebody else yelled.

"And hostages!" Mr. Schlumpf added. "Don't forget we gotta take lizard people hostages."

"Why's that?" Delbert asked, perplexed at anything other than the simplicity of his plan.

"Stands to reason the lizard queen will only relinquish her control of the U.S. capitol and white house, if we take hostages," Mr. Schlumpf said.

"I hadn't thought of that," Delbert Dimly confessed.

BUDDY SCHLIMIZZLE, IN his huge, gleaming black Escalade, whisked through evening traffic on the way home. After nearly 40 years of marriage and the same four dishes for dinner, rotating throughout the week, Bunzi had finally consented to cook something different. He didn't know why for sure, but he suspected that her enthusiastic, "I'll cook lamb chops to celebrate Butt's American Anus Pulitzer," had something to do with it, something whose details he did not want to know. So, salivating at the prospect of lamb chops, Bok choy – Bok choy! – and wild rice, three items that had never before made it onto his wife's menu, the undertaker hurried home.

He was not delighted to espy the frizzy black hair and loutishly bored face of his son-in-law, Herm Schnook, doodling on his iphone in the living room. His daughter's voice could be heard from the kitchen and someone else's. Buddy entered, saw green-haired Philippa Philpot and sniffed.

"Something's burning, Bunzi," he said.

"Nonsense. You don't want undercooked lamb chops, do you, Buddy?" His wife asked.

"I don't want burnt lamb chops," he sourly replied, then returned to the living room. Both Marty and Herm were busy on their phones. His son sported earplugs, so Buddy bellowed his momentous news – he had had a monster gas attack that day.

"Keep it to yourself, Dad," thus Marty, who turned up the volume on his phone in the hopes that louder noise would block out details of his father's digestive ailments.

The doorbell rang. Herm took it upon himself to answer it, and when he did, Pimples and Albert Pop, still in his straitjacket, promptly stepped in. Buddy Schlimizzle looked horrified.

"More guests! How delightful!" Bunzi said, coming out of the kitchen in her mauve designer wear and white and red apron.

"After seeing Marty today at Pipes Unplugged, we thought we'd drop in," Pimples explained.

Buddy Schlimizzle scowled.

"And I thought, since my place is so full of hoses there's nowhere to sit, maybe Albert here," Pimples continued, "could spend a few nights with you."

Buddy's scowl deepened.

"Only if he gets my husband those intergalactic laxatives," Bunzi said. "Otherwise, you're welcome to join the festivities."

"What festivities?" Her husband asked sourly.

"For Butt's American Anus Pulitzer Prize," his wife explained.

Albert Pop's eyes rolled in his head.

"Whose butt? Whose prize-winning anus?" Pimples asked.

"Ow, my stomach," Buddy groaned.

"I will eat your stomach," Albert Pop told him.

"Look what you've done, Bunzi!" Buddy complained. "Your talk about somebody's anus has lured two lunatics to our house."

"Our guests aren't lunatics," Bunzi said.

"Then how come one's in a straitjacket?" Her husband demanded.

"So he don't try to stick hoses in your orifices," Pimples explained.

"Mom, I think the lamb chops are overcooked," Mimi called from the kitchen.

Buddy Schlimizzle scowled again.

"Where do you keep your hoses?" Albert Pop asked the man of the house.

"In the garden," Buddy said sourly.

Herm Schnook, who had followed these exchanges, closely, spoke up. "Is that the famous Albert Pop who has wires in his head?" He asked. "And no brain?"

"I will eat your brain," Pop informed him.

"Great, a zombie," Marty muttered.

"And for your information," Pop continued, "I have a pink plastic brain full of all the latest data downloaded from CIA computer servers."

Herm Schnook gawked at him.

"Bunzi, that psychotic cannot stay here," Buddy snapped, stepping into the kitchen. "I put my foot down."

"He can stay at my house," Philippa said. "If you pay me."

Buddy and Bunzi looked at each other, then asked, "How much?" in unison.

"Four hundred dollars," Philippa said.

"Three fifty," thus Bunzi, as her husband frowned.

"Four hundred," Philippa offered stubbornly again.

"Let me write you a check," Bunzi said.

The smell of burnt meat pervaded the house.

"Are we having lamb chops or lamb charcoal for dinner?" Marty called.

"If I wanted burnt meat," Herm Schnook grumbled, "I coulda stayed home."

"Then go!" Buddy snapped. "I was against my daughter marrying a Schnook, and I still am."

"We have news," Mimi said, stepping into the living room.

"Uh-oh," thus Buddy.

"I'm pregnant!"

"Look what you've done Bunzi!" Buddy hollered.

"Well, I didn't get her pregnant," Bunzi called. "I think the culprit is lounging in the living room."

"You encouraged this unholy union with a Schnook, and now we'll have a whole pack of little Schnooks," Buddy shouted, "infected with the Penis Plague, sending dick pics to their preschool classmates and getting us entangled in law suits. Ow, this terrible news has given me gas."

"It's not terrible news!" Mimi huffed.

"I don't have the Penis Plague," Herm said. "That was my father, Frank Fart, originally Al Schnook."

"Mimi, get me the Maalox," Buddy said.

"Get it yourself," his daughter snapped.

Bunzi stepped out into the living room, wiping her hands on her apron. "The lamb and the Bok choy are a little overdone, but better safe than sorry."

"Sorry for what? That we'll be eating charcoal for dinner?" Buddy huffed. "Bunzi get me my ant-acid."

His wife handed him the bottle, from which he guzzled.

"And I, for one," Bunzi continued, "am thrilled that Mimi and Herm are having a baby. A grandchild! How wonderful!"

Her husband grumbled something unpleasant about little Schnooks infected with unmentionable diseases.

"I will take this baby back to the Andromeda galaxy," Albert Pop informed them.

"No," Herm said. "You won't."

Bunzi returned to the kitchen.

"He will be raised by Andromedan robot royalty," the lunatic continued.

"Soup's on!" Thus Bunzi.

As they all gravitated to the dining room, Herm said to Bunzi, "Your guest appears to have *Star Wars* on the brain."

"Our guest doesn't have a brain, but," she added cheerfully, delightedly, "he's not sleeping here tonight. So I don't have to listen to my husband's one thousand and one complaints."

"Bunzi, the lamb-chops are black," Buddy complained. "And so is the Bok choy."

"Eat the wild rice," she told him unsympathetically. "Albert," she sat next to this guest. "Since you're in that straitjacket, I will feed you."

"Kinda overcooked," Marty said, chewing.

Bunzi had raised a lamb chop to Albert Pop's face, but turned away to tell her son that if he didn't like the food, he could cook it himself.

Albert Pop snapped futilely at the lamb chop, waving just out of reach of his mouth. At last his teeth clamped down on Bunzi's hand. She screamed.

"He bit me!" She yelled. "This insane robot bit me!"

"Well, if you put the lamb chop, and not your hand, in front of his mouth," Marty said, "maybe that wouldn't happen."

"You're not missing anything, Mr. Pop," Buddy said, spitting out a mouthful of dry, black meat into his napkin. "This lamb chop is charcoal.

I'm calling for takeout sushi."

"Well I never," his wife huffed.

"I'll take tekka maki," Albert Pop told Buddy. "We robots are partial to tuna."

"SO LOONY ALBERT Pop filled your Springfield apartment with so many hoses you had to kick him out," Nostradamus said to Pimples. They sat at the prophet's little Formica kitchen table in his RV, stationed in a Walmart parking lot. Nostradamus was on his third Domino's pizza, extra-large. As always, Pimples hungrily eyed each slice from the box to the prophet's mouth. Some tomato sauce decorated Nostradamus's T-shirt with the logo "Wellesley College," which, per usual, being too small, had ridden up over his vast, hairy belly, revealing a deep, dark, lint-filled navel. "Who's the moron you palmed him off on?"

"Some girl who lives in downtown Silver Spring. She got the Schlimizzles to pay her $400 to take Pop off their hands," Pimples replied.

"Hmm. I could use $400," the prophet mused.

"Well, Albert Pop's already taken."

"I wasn't thinking of that nutcase, moron," Nostradamus delicately rebuked his guest. "Besides, where would a raving lunatic in a straitjacket fit here in my…home?"

"I don't know as Albert's a raving lunatic," Pimples began.

The prophet eyed him with scorn, then took a big bite of pizza.

"Sure could use a slice of that," Pimples said, gazing longingly at the sausage and pepperoni pizza.

"Two bucks," the prophet said.

"What? Now you're chargin' me?"

"Your freeloading is a big expense," Nostradamus said. "You're eatin' me outta house and home."

Grumbling, his guest fished in a jeans pocket, then handed him two very crumpled dollars. They ate in silence.

"Well, this is convivial," the prophet said.

"I'm concentrating on my pizza," Pimples said.

"How 'bout you drive me in that wreck of a car you own,"

"It's a vintage hatchback, I'll have you know," Pimples said.

Nostradamus rolled his eyes. "When we're done here, take me to National Disgrace."

"I will," Pimples said, "for two bucks."

The prophet glared at him, then snapped at his pizza.

"You ate two extra-large pizzas," Pimples marveled. "Just like that."

"Three. I had one before you got here," and Nostradamus pointed at the boxes on the floor. One of his two large, aggressive cats lay curled up on top of it. "Ugh. I don't feel so good."

"Whatcha gonna sell National Disgrace?"

"Lizard people," Nostradamus burped. "The end is nigh!"

"How much you gonna charge them?"

"Eight-hundred bucks."

"That's 10 dollars for the ride," the prophet's guest said.

"Pimples?" Nostradamus glared at him, shaking pizza crust crumbs out of his long, gray beard. "Don't push your luck."

"OH, HELLO PROPHET," the purple-haired National Disgrace receptionist greeted him, then popped a huge pink bubble of gum. "I see you still got your sidekick."

"The end is nigh!" The prophet told her.

"Down the corridor to Stella's desk," crack on the gum. "You're expected."

Nostradamus lumbered down the carpeted hall, Pimples trotting beside him, saying behind the back of his hand:" Don't you think eight hundred is kinda a lot?"

"Pimples, leave the negotiations to the people with brains," and Nostradamus belched loudly, as they stopped at Stella's desk.

The tall, frizzy gray-haired secretary sat there, fuming in her wet, blue poncho, taut over her enormously obese self. "Burpin's rude, prophet," she snapped at him.

"Well, somebody got up on the wrong side of the bed today," Nostradamus said.

"Somebody got vomited on by her very peculiar boss, not 30 minutes ago."

"Where is Futz Fraud?" Pimples asked.

"In his office, eatin' more ice cream sandwiches, which he no doubt plans to puke on me," Stella spoke with suppressed fury.

"I have a prophecy about the lizard people," the prophet informed her. "For 800 bucks, you can get a front-page story to rival all this hooey in Scuttlebutt about the Lizard Collective."

"Fraud!" Stella called out, leaning over and opening the door to his office.

"I'm busy with my ice cream sandwich," Futz Fraud called back. "I don't feel good."

"Well, get out here. Nostradamus has a prophecy about the lizard people, about 800 bucks."

"We don't need a prophecy about 800 bucks," little, scrawny, warty Futz Fraud said, stepping into the doorway. "We need a prophecy about the lizard people and the end of the world."

"The end is nigh!" Nostradamus boomed.

"That's the ticket," Futz Fraud said.

"Now pay me 800 bucks."

"No." The editor said.

"Don't be chintzy, Fraud," Stella warned him.

"For 800 bucks, we deserve more detail," Futz Fraud told the prophet.

Whereupon Nostradamus began circling his fat arms, as if he were a propeller plane ready for take-off. His eyes rolled up into his head, his vast, exposed belly shook like a bowl of hairy, beige jello, and he intoned: "The lizard people rule the earth!"

"That's the stuff," Futz Fraud belched. So did the prophet.

"They have taken over the pentagon," Nostradamus continued.

"Makes sense," thus Pimples.

"The army, they're in the navy, the air force, the marines!" The prophet hollered.

"I guess you got your money's worth, Fraud," Stella said. But Nostradamus wasn't done.

"Lizard people crawl through the space force!" Nostradamus hollered.

"The head of the space force, General Boom," here the prophet began foaming at the mouth, "is a lizard person! King Lizard Boom!" With that, the prophet's eyes rolled, sweat poured off him, and he croaked, "The end is nigh!" before collapsing, unconscious on Stella's desk.

"Well, this is a fine to-do," she snapped. "Look what your greed got us, Fraud."

He did not come to. So Stella dialed 911. The EMTs came and proclaimed that Nostradamus had had a seizure, followed by a coma. It took four, muscle-bound men to load him onto a stretcher, to take him to the hospital. When they finished getting him on the stretcher, Futz Fraud leaned over and vomited on his secretary.

"Take him too," she said to the EMTs, pointing at her boss. "Maybe you could put him into a coma till he stops vomitin' on people."

"I DON'T KNOW about this house-guest," Floozy complained to her daughter. "He seems a little peculiar."

"Is that because of the straitjacket?" Philippa asked. "'Cause lots of people belong in them."

"Yes, that and…telling me that his species will put wires in my head," Floozy complained again.

"Oh, ignore that. That's just Albert Pop."

"Kinda hard to ignore. I don't want wires in my head. I don't want to fall asleep knowing that some weirdo house-guest may try to…put wires in my skull while I'm sleeping," Floozy explained.

"He can't. He's in a straitjacket," Philippa said.

"What if he lures other members of his so-called species here, and they try to put wires in my head?"

"You mean what if he lures other raving lunatics to our house?" Philippa asked. "He can't phone them."

"Well, if he's another species," Floozy began.

"He's not. He's just quietly off his rocker."

"Not so quietly that he refrains from telling me he'll eat my kidneys," Floozy snapped.

"Mom – ignore Albert Pop. Here's $400 from the Schlimizzles for us keeping Pop out of their hair for the next two days, till he, uh, finds a new home."

"Well, for $400, I guess he can stay. Where's his new home?" Floozy asked.

"TBD," Philippa replied.

"I was afraid of that," Floozy said. They stood in the galley kitchen, where Philippa had been washing dishes. In wandered stringy, little Albert Pop in his straitjacket, jeans and work-boots, cracker crumbs dotting his salt and pepper goatee. "Great hotel you got here," he said. "I'll be sure to recommend it to all the other Andromedan robots."

"Really," Floozy said faintly, "you don't need to."

"When we invade this planet, we'll need comfortable accommodations, though nothing you have here can compare to the mother ship."

"I don't think I want to hear any more," Floozy murmured.

"On the mother ship," Albert Pop began.

"Well, it sounds like you're gonna," Philippa said.

"We sleep suspended in a gel that increases the conductivity of the wires in our heads," Albert Pop pontificated.

"Oh really? How nice," Floozy said.

"Our dreams are out of this world," Albert continued.

"So's this conversation," Philippa muttered.

"Well, if those accommodations are so great," Floozy said, "maybe you should return to your mothership."

"I can't. I need loafers," Albert said.

"Come again?" Thus Floozy.

"I'll never be allowed back on the mothership in these work-boots."

"Philippa, take Mr. Pop shopping for loafers right now," her mother said, "or would sneakers do?"

"Has to be loafers," Albert was implacable.

"Do I have to?" Philippa whined.

"You brought Mr. Pop here, you're responsible for his…exit." Floozy said.

"Remove this straitjacket," Albert Pop told Philippa, "so I can suction the salt out of your body, lizard queen."

Philippa and Floozy looked at each other.

"I don't think so, Mr. Pop," Floozy said. "Your friend Pimples was quite clear on that point – the straitjacket stays on."

"I will have to consult with him. Get him on the phone," Albert Pop said.

So Philippa dialed Pimples' number. "The straitjacket stays on, right?" She asked.

"Stupid crank callers," Pimples muttered and hung up.

Philippa called back. "Albert Pop's straitjacket."

"What about it?" Pimples asked.

"I'm not supposed to remove it, am I? 'Cause he's quite insistent about having it taken off," Philippa said.

"Remove it at your own risk. Who am I talking to?" Pimples asked.

"Philippa Philpot."

"Oh yes, lizard girl."

"Come get Albert Pop," Philippa snapped.

"No can do. I'm in the hospital."

"He's in the hospital," Philippa told her mother and Albert Pop.

"Just our luck," Floozy said, wringing her hands.

"The CIA runs that hospital," Albert Pop informed them.

"What's your problem?" Philippa asked Pimples.

"Problem? Me? What are you talking about? It's Nostradamus who's in a coma."

"Somebody named Nostradamus is in a coma," Philippa said.

"He has a lot of salt in his body," Albert told them.

"Maybe that's why he's in a coma," Floozy said, studying her houseguest closely. "You know what, Philippa? Take him out for loafers."

"Now we're getting somewhere," Albert Pop said.

"We are? Where?" Philippa asked.

"Outer space, if I heard Mr. Pop correctly," Floozy said.

Philippa and Albert Pop went to the shoe store. The short, rotund shoe salesman appeared perturbed about having a customer in a straitjacket.

"He's harmless," Philippa assured the salesman, "but he needs loafers."

"To return to my home planet," Albert Pop elaborated.

"Anything you say," the man replied. "The customer is always right."

"Not this customer," Philippa said.

Albert Pop tried on several loafers. It turned out he had corns on his toes, so it was difficult to get a good fit. They finally did.

"Now they'll let me back on the spaceship," he told the salesman.

"What spaceship?" The salesman asked.

"The one where you have to wear loafers," Philippa snapped.

"Send all your friends from outer space to my store for their loafers," the salesman told Albert.

"That's a lot of loafers," Albert said.

"And a lot of straitjackets," thus Philippa.

"Do all aliens wear straitjackets?" The chatty shoe salesman wanted to know.

"I should hope so," Philippa answered, paid and led Albert Pop out of the store.

She parked in front of her mother's townhouse, in the clear but shadowy early evening. The maple beside the car was coming into leaf early. Floozy, having espied her daughter's car through the front window, came out onto the doorstep.

"Is he going?" She called, as Philippa assisted Albert Pop out of the car.

"Is he going to outer space?" She called again.

"He's already IN outer space, mother," Philippa called back. She did not notice the minivan parked two cars away, with at least three people sitting inside in the semi-dark. But as she and Albert Pop started up the walk to the front door, three figures wearing ski-masks, one quite spherical, exited the van and hurried toward them.

"Come with us," a medium-height man said, poking something hard into Philippa's ribs, "and nobody gets blown away."

"Blown away?" Philippa asked in evident confusion.

"Be careful," the spherical bandit said. "They could be getting' reinforcements from outer space any minute."

"You look familiar," Philippa said to him and then, as she and Albert resumed walking toward   the house and were grabbed and pulled back toward the parked car: "I think I've been assaulted by you before."

"Come peaceably," the first man said, "and nobody gets hurt."

"Crab people," Albert Pop said. "Our ancient enemies, a race of midget poisoners."

"He doesn't look like a midget," Philippa said.

Albert Pop jerked his chin at the short spherical kidnapper. "Crab people are abducting us."

"Help!" Philippa wailed, as she was pulled toward the minivan. "We're being kidnapped. We're being abducted by," she squinted at the logo "Q" on the medium-height man's T-shirt, "by Q-Anon!"

Floozy called the police, but by the time they arrived, the van was long gone, having whisked its captives who knew where.

JEREMY SPIT HURRIED to his boss's office, forgot the rule that he was NEVER to cross the threshold, charged right up to ugly, muscular but paunchy Bull Bruiser's desk and spat: "The lizard queen's been abducted by Q-Anon!" Unfortunately, he emphasized the "t" in abducted with such percussive force, that he ejected a large blob of saliva, which shot through the air and landed smack in his thoroughly revolted editor's eye.

"Back to the doorway, Spit!" Bull Bruiser hollered, while wiping his eye with a Kleenex.

"I got a tip from a suburban police department," Spit continued, his oral fluids sailing toward Bull Bruiser's desk but falling, the editor noted with great satisfaction, short. He leaned over and looked at the damp spot on the rug.

"Gonna hafta get that carpet cleaned," he muttered. "Spit! Get me custodial."

"But what about the lizard queen?"

"Oh right. Remind me, who is she?"

"Philippa Philpot. We did front-page stories on her scaly arms. You know, the girl with multiple piercings." Spit spat – futilely, his editor noted, snickering.

"Girl's a goddamned lizard, and you yammer on about her piercings," Bull Bruiser snapped. "Am I surrounded by idiots or what?"

"Her mother, Floozy Philpot," Spit drifted into the room. This time his saliva smacked the back of Bull Bruiser's laptop.

"Back to the door!" Bull Bruiser roared. "Or you're offa this story. If you spit on me again, Jeremy, it'll be Ruffles Johnson interviewing this

Floozy Philpot."

Jeremy Spit retreated, as a disgusted Bull Bruiser wiped the back of his laptop with another tissue.

"We paid a lotta money to lizard girl," Bruiser said, when finished wiping the computer. He planted his muscular elbows on his desk and twiddled his stubby thumbs, a light of bored annoyance in his little, dark, porcine eyes. "Now she goes and gets herself kidnapped – by Q-Anon, you say?"

"Yup. But that's all we know. I'll have to dig in the dirt," Spit spat.

"You do that, Spit, but just not anywhere near me. What does the Lizard Collective say about this?"

"They're in an uproar."

"Well, they freakin' should be," the editor muttered.

"They're arming themselves, even the mini-Godzillas."

"What mini-Godzillas?" Bull Bruiser snapped.

"Some lizard people have become mini-Godzillas."

"You think I'm a moron, Spit? You think I believe this hokum about people with alligator tails and scales under their skin?" Bull Bruiser demanded.

"Well, Philippa sure had scales," Spit protested.

"That was a freak of nature, not proof that lizard people rule the world, though don't tell that to our sub-moronic readers, 95 percent of whom are still searching for their IQs," the editor snapped again.

"Q-Anon on Rampage. Abducts Lizard Queen," Spit spat. "How's that for a headline?"

"It lacks zing."

"How about adding, 'Mini-Godzillas Arm Up After Q-Anon Kidnaps Lizard Queen, Prepares to Storm the Capitol.'"

"I like it," Bull Bruiser said.

A GRIM, HAGGARD Seymour Burp, Doobie Dimly and several other members of the Lizard Collective stood around the unimposing entrance to the rec center in Langley Park, reading the note tacked to the door:

"Lizard people! We have abducted your lizard queen! If you ever want to see Philippa Philpot alive again, disarm and disband!"

Signed,

Q-Anon High Council

"This is the worst thing to happen in our long lizard history!" Doobie exclaimed.

"You just joined yesterday," a pudgy fellow whose cheeks sported green glitter said.

"But I got the feel of the Lizard Collective," Doobie said, brushing back his longish brown hair. Tall and blue-jeaned, he towered over the hefty lizard person who told him his name was Afflatus.

"You're kidding, right?" Doobie asked.

"Doobie Dimly's nothing to go preening about," Afflatus said.

Seymour Burp phoned Jeremy Spit. "We lizard people have to disarm and disband, if we ever want to see our lizard queen again," he said.

Spit, seated at his desk, across from an enraged Ruffles Johnson, whose open box of donuts Spit had just sprayed with saliva, snapped, "if you don't want my fluids on your donuts, close the box. I have orales effluvias!"

"I don't have any donuts," Seymour Burp said, and then, "what fluids? Something they're injecting into the captive lizard queen?"

Jeremy Spit decided he was talking to a deranged fan and ended the call.

Seymour Burp phoned him again.

"I'm gonna wring your neck, you slobbering freak," Ruffles Johnson shouted.

"I'll wring your neck first!" Spit spat.

"Sorry, wrong number," Seymour Burp said and ended the call. He dialed again. "The Q high council kidnapped Philippa Philpot," he said.

"The what who?" Spit spat, zapping Ruffles Johnson in the eye.

"That does it!" Johnson hollered, charging around the desk and tackling Jeremy Spit.

Bald, ugly, paunchy yet muscular Bull Bruiser was passing by, eating a donut. "You give it to him, Johnson!" He said. The two reporters rolled on the floor, grappling.

Seymour Burp phoned Bull Bruiser. "The lizard queen has been kidnapped!" He panted.

"Yeah, and so was your mother," Bull Bruiser snapped.

"My mother's fine," Seymour Burp said. "I tried to reach Jeremy Spit but couldn't seem to make contact."

"He's otherwise engaged at this moment," the editor said, as the two reporters wrestled ferociously on the floor. "Who is this?"

"Seymour Burp."

"You're joking."

"I'm serious."

"Okay Burp," Bull Bruiser said. "What's this about?"

"Philippa Philpot."

"Name rings a bell," the editor mused absentmindedly. "Watch out for that fist, Johnson!"

"You did a front-page story on her scaly arms," Burp burped.

"Oh yes. That boosted circulation. What about her? Has she sprouted more scales – or better yet, a green tail?"

"Our tails aren't real, Mr. Bruiser."

"You think I'm an idiot, Burp?" Bull Bruiser demanded. "I invent crap about lizard tails and homicidal fetuses 24-7. I don't frikkin' believe it."

"Well, Philipp's been kidnapped by the Q-Anon high council, and they say we'll never see her again unless we, the Lizard Collective, disarm and disband." Burp explained heatedly.

"'Civil War! Lizards Versus Q!' I like the headline possibilities," Bull Bruiser said, then shouted: "Spit! Spit! Get up off the floor and back to work! The Lizard Collective is calling!"

4

IN THE VAN, their kidnappers put hoods over their heads.

"The CIA got me," Albert Pop said. "Again."

"Not the CIA, pal," said Mr. Schlumpf, for it was he who adjusted their hoods. "Q."

"Just don't kill us," Philippa said.

"We won't, if the Lizard Collective cooperates," said Mr. Schlumpf.

Medium-height, scantily haired Delbert Dimly, at the wheel, complained that his dinner had not agreed with him.

"Great, one of our kidnappers has an upset stomach," Philippa grumbled.

"Gastritis, actually," Dimly explained.

"When did the crab people infiltrate Q?" Albert Pop asked.

"Crab people?" Dimly asked. "I thought it was lizard people."

"They didn't infiltrate us," Mr. Schlumpf said. "We took preemptive action, this kidnapping. Cut off the head of the snake."

"What galaxy is this snake from?" Albert wanted to know.

"You tell me," thus Schlumpf.

"I read the lizards came from a different solar system," Dimly belched discreetly, "not galaxy. Maybe the Crab Nebula."

Albert Pop gargled incoherently, then started yelling.

"I think you disturbed our captive," Mr. Schlumpf said.

"Best not to mention the Crab Nebula," Philippa advised.

"Is he wearing a straitjacket?" Dimly asked, scrutinizing Albert Pop in the rearview mirror.

"What of it, you loathsome, treacherous crab?" Albert Pop hissed.

"*I'm* no crab," Dimly said.

"We Andromedan robots will vaporize your nebula and slaughter your entire race of midget poisoners. Don't even think about making me drink coffee creamer," Albert snarled.

"I'm five-feet ten," Dimly huffed. "I'm no midget. Now Schlumpf here is another story."

"I knew it!" Philippa exclaimed. "I knew it was the Schlumpfs. Oh, am I gonna sue you!"

"Dimly! You weren't supposed to address me by name," Schlumpf huffed.

"Dimly? You don't sound like Doobie Dimly," Philippa said.

"That's because he's Doobie's father," the slow-witted third kidnapper explained.

"We're inducting Doobie," his father said. "Though so far he seems rather unenthusiastic about Q."

Philippa decided not to mention Doobie's keen interest in joining the Lizard Collective. "So what exactly do you want with us?" She asked.

"The end of the reign of the lizard people," Schlumpf said. "Nothing less. Trump will address that in his next letter to the Q high council."

"And you think by kidnapping a mostly unemployed dog-walker and a raving lunatic who believes he has wires in his head and a pink plastic brain that you can end this lizard rule – if the lizard people even exist," Philippa added, "which I doubt."

Mr. Schlumpf gaped at her. "You're the lizard queen," he began.

"I wish," She snapped.

"You runnin' for that office?" The third man asked.

"Whose office?" Albert Pop demanded. "The CIA's?"

"This conversation is confusing," thus Philippa.

"Don't try to muddle our brains," Schlumpf warned her.

"Any more than they already are?" She snapped. "I doubt I could."

A while later the van parked in seedy, suburban Wheaton, Maryland, and the two captives were led into a house, then down to a basement, where they were tied to chairs. Mrs. Schlumpf removed their hoods. "We have chicken noodle soup for dinner," she said.

"Homemade or out of a can?" Philippa asked.

"Robots don't eat soup," Albert Pop informed her. "Especially soup made by giant crabs."

"Did he say crabs?" Mrs. Schlumpf asked, startled.

"Welcome to my world," Philippa said.

SYLVIA PUT DOWN the phone at Dr. Posterior's reception desk and walked to his office in back.

"It's Fred Fart on the line. He wants to set up his appointment for a rectal perfume refill next month. He requests lily of the valley," she said sourly.

"Tell him I'll be in Puerto Rico," an alarmed Dr. Posterior replied.

"But that's not true."

"Lie. Say I'm moving my practice to San Juan," paunchy, ponderous Dr. Posterior looked very perturbed, as he ran a hand over his scanty, neatly combed brown curls. "I cannot face the prospect of that…person's smell again."

"Then maybe we should make the appointment before the perfume runs out."

"Sylvia, you're a genius," Dr. Posterior said. "But still lie about the upcoming appointment. Maybe I'll see him in two months."

Grumbling under her breath that a genius deserved a raise, Sylvia returned to the reception desk. "Dr. Posterior will be in San Juan next month."

"The whole month?" Fred Fart asked. He sat in the cab of the Pest Patrol pickup with his boss, squinty-eyed, bushy gray-haired Lucas Flush at the wheel. They were parked outside a Dairy Queen, where they intended to purchase chocolate ice cream cones.

Lucas Flush looked alarmed. "Posterior can't deodorize your flatulence, Fred?"

"Not next month," dull-eyed, dull-witted Fred Fart said.

"How about a June appointment," Sylvia suggested.

"They're givin' me a June appointment," Fred Fart explained.

"But what am I supposed to do for the month of May? You need that perfume, Fred," Lucas squinted at him.

"Lily of the valley."

"I don't care if it's Landfill Lily, you need another…fragrance," Lucas told him. "You gotta go back to Butt."

"I gotta go back to Butt," Fred Fart repeated.

"Excuse me?" Thus an offended Sylvia.

"Maybe I should come in today," Fred Fart said.

"Good idea," Lucas encouraged him.

"Posterior's booked solid till his flight to PR," Sylvia snapped.

"Buddy Schlimizzle ain't gonna like this," Fred Fart warned.

"Dr. Posterior can't be held responsible for the feelings of whoever that…oddly named person is," Sylvia said.

"He's an illustrious undertaker, world-famous for his 40-year constipation," Fred Fart said.

"I think I read about this. It was very disturbing. Please don't tell me any more," Sylvia said.

"She doesn't wanna hear any more," Fred Fart told his boss.

"Maybe you should clarify that maybe it was only 30 years of constipation," Lucas suggested, squinting at his employee.

"It was only 30 years," Fred Fart said.

Dr. Posterior approached the reception desk. "Did you get rid of that…person?" He whispered.

"On it, boss," Sylvia said. "He's telling me about some undertaker's 40-year constipation."

"Just so he doesn't refer him to me. I want no referrals from Fred Fart," Dr. Posterior said.

"We can't schedule the undertaker," Sylvia said. "Posterior isn't taking any new referrals."

"Buddy Schlimizzle can't get in to see Posterior," Fred Fart informed

Lucas Flush.

"Well, maybe he can see Butt," that worthy pest exterminator said.

"Maybe he'll see Butt," Fred Fart repeated.

"That's Mr. Fart's second rude reference to my butt," Sylvia told her boss.

"After all, he has an in with his wife," Fred continued.

"I don't even want to repeat what he just suggested," Sylvia snapped to Dr. Posterior.

"Don't. Repeat instead that I'm packing for Puerto Rico," Dr. Posterior said.

"Posterior's packing for Puerto Rico. He may move his practice to San Juan," Sylvia said.

"Ya hear that, Lucas?" Fred Fart asked.

Lucas Flush nodded, as the volume on his employee's phone was on high. "Maybe you could schedule an appointment in San Juan."

"Maybe I could see Posterior in San Juan," Fred Fart said.

Sylvia relayed this message to her horrified boss.

"He's booked," she said. "Packed solid."

"Like Buddy Schlimizzl,e" Fred mused.

"No," Sylvia snapped, "not like that constipated undertaker."

"He's comparing me to a constipated undertaker?" Posterior asked. "How constipated?"

"Forty years," Sylvia said dourly. "I already told you that."

"Tell him to get my colleague's rectal pump," Posterior said.

"He's already got it."

"Who – the constipated undertaker?" Posterior asked.

"I'm confused," Sylvia said.

"She's confused," Fred Fart told his boss.

"No surprise there, with a proctologist gallivanting off to San Juan every month, I should think she'd be confused," Lucas Flush said. "Stands to reason."

"Hunh?" Thus dull-witted Fred Fart.

"Never mind, Fred," Lucas sighed.

PHILIPPA PHILPOT AND Albert Pop sat tied to chairs in the Schlumpfs' damp, gloomy, unpleasant, unfinished basement. They had had Campbell's chicken noodle soup for dinner and again for breakfast. Apparently, it was the specialite de la maison. A noodle and a piece of chicken decorated Albert's salt and pepper goatee.

"The least you could do," Philippa whined, when spherical Mrs. Schlumpf came down to check on them, "is clean his beard."

"I don't wanna touch that psycho's beard," Mrs. Schlumpf informed her. "What he has may be catching."

"Paranoid schizophrenia?" Philippa asked.

"Yeah that."

"How long do we have to stay here?" Philippa asked.

"Till the Lizard Collective disbands or Trump answers our email," Mrs. Schlumpf told her.

"What email?"

"The one that says we captured the lizard queen, now what do we do with her? It also mentions that bye the bye we also kidnapped a weirdo in a straitjacket who eats like a slob," Mrs. Schlumpf concluded.

"I will eat your liver," Albert Pop told her.

"Not my liver, pal."

"And the livers of all the other crab people. Don't even think about putting creamer in my coffee," Albert Pop continued.

"Okay, so you take your coffee black," Mrs. Schlumpf said.

"You midget poisoner crab people have been lacing coffee creamer with arsenic for millennia."

Mrs. Schlumpf had nothing to say to that, so she turned and thumped back up the wooden stairs.

An hour passed. The house became quiet.

"Looks like they abandoned us," Philippa said.

"Good. That crab person was annoying," Albert Pop said. "She needs to go on a diet."

At that moment they heard the front door slam, then multiple footsteps from the entrance into the living room.

"Hey!" Philippa yelled. "Let us out! We're in the basement."

The footsteps moved to the kitchen.

"Down here!" Philippa hollered. "Help!"

Two men came down the stairs.

"I'm from the electric company," said the first, "here about possible flickering lights. I didn't get no message about people bein' tied to chairs."

Philippa craned her neck to see the other person.

"Philippa?" A voice asked in astonishment.

"Doobie? Doobie Dimly? What are you doing here?" She asked.

"They wanna induct me into Q. They don't know I'm already an Illuminati," Doobie told her. "Who's the psycho?"

"I'll just check the breakers," the electric company man said, eyeing Albert Pop with alarm.

"What psycho?" Albert Pop asked.

"The, uh, psycho in the straitjacket," Doobie said.

"Where?" Albert asked.

"Give it up, Doobie. Untie us," Philippa said.

Tall, bushy brown-haired Doobie Dimly set to work. "They really made a mess with these knots," he said.

"You untyin' that lunatic in the straitjacket?" The electrician asked. "'Cause I don't think that's a good idea."

"Maybe we could leave him?" Doobie asked.

"No. He has a friend living in an RV in a Virginia Walmart parking lot. We'll take him there," Philippa said. "Right, Albert?"

"Pimples and the prophet," he loudly replied.

"What prophet?" Doobie asked, struggling with a knot. "What pimples? How does a prophet having pimples figure into this, uh…er, situation?"

"The crab people abducted us," Albert Pop informed him

The electrician's eyebrows lifted in shock. "Okey doke, I'm about finished here. You tell the homeowner he's got some faulty wiring."

"I will eat that homeowner," Albert Pop said.

"Apparently Mr. Schlumpf isn't the only one with faulty wiring," Doobie commented.

"Did he say he'll EAT the homeowner?" The electrician asked.

"You heard him," Philippa said.

"Well, I'll be leaving now," the man told her and hurried to the staircase. "I can let myself out."

"What's your rush?" Asked oblivious Doobie.

"I don't wanna be eaten by what I take to be a cannibal tied to a chair," the man replied and thumped up the stairs.

"When are the Schlumpfs coming back?" Philippa asked nervously.

"Not for two hours. They're at a Weight Watchers meeting. They told me to heat up a can of chicken noodle soup and give it to the lizards in the basement for lunch," Doobie said.

"Speaking of which, would you mind removing the noddle and the chicken from Albert's goatee?" Philippa asked. "they've been bothering me."

"I don't want this…cannibal to eat my fingers," Doobie complained.

Philippa sighed. "Okay, skip it. Just get us out of here."

And Doobie did.

NOSTRADAMUS LAY IN his hospital bed, snoring loudly, his enormous belly rising and falling peacefully, rhythmically, like something very large, maybe the ocean. The nurses enjoyed checking his IV and vitals, because he made no fuss and no demands, was in fact the ideal patient, except, however, for those moments when his eyes flew open and he bellowed, "Lizard people! Lizard people everywhere! They will inherit the earth!" Then belched and subsided into his coma again.

"He's very concerned about these lizard people," a nurse told short, blond, pert-nosed Dr. Snot. "He wakes up yelling about them."

"Hmm. Increase the anti-psychotic medication by 10 milligrams," Dr. Snot prescribed, reaching for the prophet's fat wrist to take his pulse. "This is quite the situation. A patient who comes out of a coma shrieking, then falls back into it. There are only two such instances of it recorded in the medical literature and I," Dr. Snot pompously intoned, "was involved in both." He paused, as if awaiting applause.

"How remarkable," the nurse said.

"Yes. I *was* remarkable. One case involved the Liverwurst Plague. In that, the patient – obese like Mr. Nostradamus – came out of his coma periodically demanding liverwurst, would slobber over a whole roll of it, eat it all, then fall back into a coma. Has Mr. Nostradamus mentioned liverwurst?"

"All he's mentioned are lizard people," the nurse replied.

"Hmm," Dr. Snot stroked his chin authoritatively. "I think we can rule out the Liverwurst Plague."

The nurse nodded in agreement, suppressing a remark about her skepticism that that plague had ever existed anywhere other than the pages of supermarket tabloids.

"The other case," Dr. Snot droned on "involved a cuckold, the sight of whose wife in flagrante caused an aneurism. He was NOT obese, he was scrawny, though he had a very peculiar name, Bucky Buckeye. The police referred to him as a well-known burglar."

"Good memory," the nurse flattered Dr. Snot.

"We physicians must keep track of lots of details. Mr. Buckeye would wake from his coma shrieking, "That asshole! I'm gonna tear that asshole limb from limb.""

"Oh my," the nurse said.

"Yes. He was apparently actually referring to the behind of his wife's lover, which belonged to the editor of a leading newspaper, Scuttlebutt. Mr. Buckeye eventually recovered from his coma – the Liverwurst Plague victim expired – but is to this day apparently given to outbursts that he's quote seen enough of that asshole to last a lifetime unquote and he intends to quote tear that asshole limb from limb unquote," Dr. Snot concluded.

"How unsettling for his wife," the nurse remarked.

"And for the medical profession. We were never actually able to explain these two phenomena, and now, here we have a third."

Into the room stepped ponderous, white-haired, CIA-affiliated Dr. Schnook, distantly related to the Schnook family in East Silver Spring.

"Hello doctor," he said.

"Hello doctor," Dr. Snot pompously replied. "I read the report on Mr. Nostradamus. I believe these oddities are symptoms of his long latent Bat-Brain fever."

This disease was another complete fabrication of National Disgrace and Scuttlebutt, some years back, however mentions of it, discussions and hypotheses as to its origins and symptoms continued to percolate in some medical circles.

The nurse discreetly rolled her eyes.

"But Mr. Nostradamus recovered from Bat-Brain fever years ago," Dr. Snot protested.

"The virus lingers in the cerebral cortex, as several autopsies have indicated," Dr. Schnook said, approaching the prophet, lifting one eyelid and then another.

"Lizards!" Nostradamus shouted, his eyes flying open. "Lizard people rule the earth."

The sleek, eminent psychiatrist Dr. Klutz stepped into the room, pointed at the patient and announced. "This man's brain has decayed. I suggest an MRI at once."

Nostradamus opened one eye. "No," he said.

"Mr. Nostradamus!" The nurse exclaimed, "You're conscious!"

"I'm also claustrophobic," the prophet said. "No MRI for me. I need a mint."

"You need that MRI," Dr. Klutz insisted, "to determine how badly your brain has rotted."

"No," Nostradamus glared at the psychiatrist.

"Have you eaten any Chinese takeout, bat-brain soup recently," Dr. Schnook inquired.

"What kinda freak question is that?" The prophet demanded, taking the mint the nurse handed him and popping it into his mouth.

"We think the CCP has designs on you," Dr. Schnook continued.

"The what, who?" Nostradamus asked. "And who's this so-called we?"

"The CIA, of course."

"I was afraid of that," the prophet said.

TALL, BROWN-HAIRED, brown-eyed Doobie Dimly drove Philippa and Albert Pop to Virginia.

"What solar system is this spaceship going to?" Albert asked from the back seat.

"Uh, the Walmart parking lot solar system," Doobie replied, then: "You can sure pick 'em, Philippa."

"Hey, I got 400 bucks for putting him up for a night, so he wouldn't, um, eat the liver of a very constipated undertaker."

"Okey doke," thus Doobie. "Do we get 400 bucks for taking him to the Walmart parking lot?"

"No, we get peace of mind," Philippa snapped.

"What peace of mind?" Doobie asked. "'Cause I'd rather have 400 bucks."

"The peace of mind that comes from knowing a very strange somebody in a straitjacket is not going to attempt to dine on your internal organs," Philippa snapped again. "That peace of mind."

"I will eat the lizard queen," Albert Pop said. "And those fat crab people who tried to poison me with chicken noodle soup."

"Who's the lizard queen?" Doobie asked.

Philippa pushed up her sleeves and held up her arms for his inspection.

"Wow! How'd you get those?" The driver asked.

"A non-FDA approved skin hydrating lotion called Derma-Lube. Thank God, I only rubbed it on my arms," Philippa said.

"You should sue," was Doobie's considered advice.

"I threatened to," Philippa smirked, "and I got a $30,000 pay off."

Doobie's jaw dropped open. "So you're, like, rich! Could you help me launch my youtube channel?"

"No," Philippa said.

They continued in traffic in silence for a few minutes. It was a glorious spring day. The sun beamed down beautifully, and here and there cherry trees were in bloom, their blossoms hovering like pink clouds over the sidewalks.

"So, if the members of the Lizard Collective," Doobie began slowly, clearly working through a complex series of reasonings with difficulty, "if they all used Derma-Lube, they'd be, like, uh, real lizard people."

"Don't tell them. They're too stupid," Philippa said. "They'll probably try to eat it, grow scales all over their insides and out and kick the bucket, like that idiot they stuffed and mounted, Expert-Q Lizard."

Doobie gaped at her. "You follow that, Doobie?" she demanded.

"Uh, I don't think so. I had a lot of cannabis this morning." After a moment he added, "but I think I got the gist – don't eat the Derma-Lube."

Philippa sighed, as they drove into the parking lot. They spotted Nostradamus' RV in the far corner, under a maple tree. They parked near it, then stood in strong sunlight, knocking on the door.

"No one's here," came a voice.

"Well, someone appears to be," Philippa shouted.

"The prophet had a stroke, he's in the hospital," the voice called back.

"Are you Pimples? Albert Pop says you're his agent," she shouted again.

The door opened, and there stood an almost tall, very pimply fellow with thick, greasy brown hair, wearing jeans, work-boots and a white T-shirt that sported the black logo "Lizard Person."

"You agreed to house Albert," Pimples said.

"Not in perpetuity," Philippa snapped.

Pimples glanced nervously to the left and right. "Come in," he said, "before the CIA sees us."

They stepped into a cluttered RV, most of whose surfaces were covered with cat fur. The two felines lay curled up on the bed, and the smell of marijuana smoke was overpowering. A shotgun hung over the door, and cans and boxes of food crammed every available cranny. Pimples sat at the small Formica kitchen table, where Philippa joined him. Doobie and Albert sat on the bed, causing both cats to hiss.

"We got kidnapped by Q-Anon," Philippa said. "We just escaped. But they could come after us again, so we gotta separate. Albert Pop stays here at your place, with you."

"This isn't my place. It's the prophet's," Pimples clarified. "He's in the hospital."

"Why aren't you at your apartment?" Philippa wanted to know.

"'Cause somebody," he jerked his chin at Albert Pop, "insisted I fill it with hoses, and now there's no room for anything else, including people."

"We Andromedan robots must prepare for the invasion from our home world," Albert Pop informed them. "We must have large supplies of hoses, seven or eight billion, to suction all the salt out of human bodies."

"Come again?" Thus Doobie, edging away from him.

"We will insert the hoses in your orifices," Albert said.

"Uh, which orifices?" Doobie asked.

"Whichever are handy. I will suction out all your salt."

"Uh, Philippa, I don't know what arrangements you're making," Doobie said, "but this Albert Pop can't stay with me, even if someone pays me 400 bucks to put him up. No Albert Pop at the Dimly residence."

DUCKY FINCH HAD delayed her visit to the nation's capital, because the award ceremony for the patriotic veterinarians who helped thwart the invasion of the crab people had been postponed. But finally, it was rescheduled, and she and Fred Fart booked a flight to Washington.

"I have a surprise for you!" Bunzi Schlimizzle announced to her husband Buddy, as he crossed the threshold, coming home from work that evening.

Buddy stopped in the doorway and scowled. "I hate surprises," he said.

"This one smells good," she told him.

Buddy Schlimizzle's scowl deepened.

"It usually smells bad," she elaborated.

He sniffed. "I smell perfume," he said. "You got a new perfume?"

Fred Fart and Ducky Finch stepped into the living room from the den, where they were staying.

"You got two house-guests, Dad," Marty, seated on the couch, told him. "Now all we need is Albert Pop and that reporter who spits."

Buddy Schlimizzle turned red with anger and sputtered: "If that lunatic in a straitjacket shows up, Bunzi, I'll get my gun. I promise you that."

"Calm down, Buddy. Albert Pop is busy battling lizard people with an army of soldiers who have wires in their heads, at least according to National Disgrace," his wife told him.

"Ow, Bunzi, you gave me gas. Get the Maalox. I think it was that bit about an army of soldiers with wires in their heads," Buddy groaned.

"I hope they're not coming to dinner," Ducky Finch said.

"Don't worry," Bunzi told her, reaching into a kitchen cabinet for the Maalox, "Albert Pop, like his intergalactic laxatives, is always a no-show."

"You invited him?!" Buddy and Marty exclaimed in horror and in unison.

"I don't know how I feel about dining with someone with wires in his head," Ducky continued.

"Hunh?" Thus her dull-witted boyfriend.

"I received a call from Albert Pop's talent agent," Bunzi said.

"That psychotic has a talent agent?" Buddy asked, taking the Maalox from his wife and guzzling from the bottle, as Marty gaped at his mother.

"Yes. You remember Pimples," Bunzi said.

"He was dirty," Buddy scowled again, "had black under his fingernails. We paid another one of your guests, lizard girl, good money to take that insane person off our hands."

"Well, apparently Pimples' apartment in Springfield is filled with so many hoses, there's no place to sleep," Bunzi said.

"That's what comes of indulging someone who's bonkers," Buddy Schlimizzle frowned. "Which yours truly has no intention of doing. Bunzi, I put my foot down. If Albert Pop darkens my door, I will get my gun and run him off the premises – an army of soldiers with wires in their heads or no."

"You won't have to," Bunzi placated her spouse. "He can sleep on the floor of someone called Nostradamus' RV."

Everyone gaped at Bunzi.

"Well, he can't very well sleep in the bed with Pimples," she said. "And the RV apparently only has one bed."

"Where will this Nostradamus person sleep?" Buddy asked warily. "'Cause if he's coming here…"

"He's in the hospital. He just came out of a coma, caused, if I heard Mr. Pimples correctly," Bunzi said, "by a very vivid vision of lizard people overtaking the planet."

"Great, another nut," Marty breathed.

"But at least this one's in the hospital," Buddy belched. "And there's always the hope that he may fall back into a coma before he gets any ideas about spending the night in the upstairs guest-room."

"We're in the downstairs den," Fred Fart informed him.

"Fan-tas-tic," Buddy snapped. "For how long, Bunzi? How long will my house be filled with these perfumed farts?"

"Lakeside Laurel," Bunzi sniffed. "I rather like it."

"How long?" The man of the house demanded.

"One night," his wife replied.

"Ow, my chest! My gas!" Buddy groaned. "And I've been very backed up."

"Well, don't tell us about it," his wife said. "Because your constipation isn't polite dinner table conversation."

"Since when have we ever had polite dinner table conversation?" Marty asked, running his fingers through his curly brown hair. "As long as I can remember, going back to elementary school, our meals have been punctuated by the question, 'Do you know how long it's been since I was able to go?'"

"Well," Buddy Schlimizzle scowled. "Do you?"

SENATOR BARNARD BUSTUP was a cyclone of disorganization. Tall, paunchy, bald except for a gray fringe that garlanded his pate from ear to ear, sticking out in all directions, he gyrated around his office, picking up folders, putting them down, then complaining to his assistant, Fetch, that they were lost, but mostly reveling in the sacks of cash from SMOG (Society for More Oil and Gas) that arrived on his desk every couple of days, now that he was no longer prevented, by Justice Department order, from accepting such donations.

The original injunction, several years back, came while Bustup wore an ankle monitor to senate hearings and votes, being the first senator in the history of the republic to do so. This was because he had been convicted of embezzlement, corruption and fraud after many colorful escapades, which featured him going on the lam with the eco-socialist soviet of South Florida, called Carbon, when the FBI sought to detain him. Luckily for Bustup, the judge in his case, Hieronymus Squat, was so senile that the senator received no jail time, just a mandatory series of visits to a proctologist for daring to demand, "What's all this talk about my asshole?" at a particularly confused juncture in the proceedings.

When Ducky and Fred arrived the next morning, Bustup stood in the $60,000 plexiglass, bullet-proof, tax-payer-funded phonebooth in the middle of his office, talking on the phone, while gluttonously devouring the first of two enormous Gutbuster burgers. Other patriotic veterinarians sat around his office in chairs, most of them armed.

"Maybe we shoulda brought Buddy Schlimizzle's gun," Ducky said behind the back of her hand.

Fred Fart's eyebrows lifted in alarm. "You think we're in danger?"

"I think we lack the required accessories."

"Accessories?" Fred asked loudly. "I don't wear jewelry."

"I should hope not," one patriotic veterinarian said. "Manly men don't wear jewelry."

"Jewelry could get in the way when fighting off the crab people," another put in, cradling his AR-15. "While you're fiddlin' with your earrings, a crab invader could use his claw to snap your head off."

"Ducky, I think you should take off your earrings," her dull-witted beau warned her.

"The Amurican people won't stand for it!" Bustup told them, leaning out of the phonebooth. "They expect their patriotic veterinarians to be wearing semi-automatic weapons, not bracelets. The sacred right to bear arms, enshrined in the Ten Commandments, says nothing about rings or necklaces."

Ducky Finch raised a hand to her eyebrow ring.

"But you're okay, young lady," the senator intoned. "The Amurican people expect their lady veterinarians to be attractive." Then he moved back fully inside his secure booth, shut the door and hollered into the phone to his colleague, who many referred to as "bat-shit crazy" Republican senator Harley Hokum: "Martial law, Hokum. I say the Amurican people deserve no less. You introduce it in committee, and I'll back you up. We have a serious threat of invasion here. Lizard people. I saw the photographs in the papers. The Illuminati are getting ready to make their move. I have convened the patriotic veterinarians, and they'll, uh, take down, yes, take down any man-sized lizard threatening to eat red-blooded Amuricans, yes, take him down with one shot to the head. TV? Oh, the crew should be here any minute."

In a flash, with amazing speed for one so stout, Republican senator Harley Hokum arrived in Bustup's office, his facial tic twitching. Moments later, two TV crews followed, and for quite a while, it was pandemonium.

That is, until senator Barnard Bustup drew himself up and glowered into the camera.

"What's this about patriotic veterinarians wearing jewelry?" One breathless reporter asked. "What sort? Like an evil eye?"

"I say unto you, Steve, no patriotic veterinarian will…uh…sport anything besides the latest in military weaponry," Bustup intoned. "Not on my watch! Not in my 'murica! Because it's a sad day in Amurica when an ordinary citizen goes to order a burger and is confronted with the spectacle of a lizard man eating Gutbusters at the next table!"

"I read that lizard man croaked."

"He may have croaked, buzzed or hollered, I don't know, but he has no business eating the burgers that are the rightful inheritance of every red-blooded Amurican. The radical Marxist leftist lizard Illuminati want to steal this right away from us, purloin our burgers, our guns, our gasoline-powered cars and turn us into homosexual eunuchs, but I, senator Barnard Bustup, won't stand for it…"

Ducky dozed, Fred Fart gaped, several other patriotic veterinarians snored. Republican senator Barnard Bustup droned on.

BUDDY SCHLIMIZZLE HAD put his simmering rage over Bull Bruiser making a pass at his wife on the back burner. But once he deposited his check from Scuttlebutt, he phoned the editor.

"If you ever ask my wife out again, I'll blow your fucking head off," he said.

Ugly, paunchy yet muscular, bald Bull Bruiser hung up. He did not know which irate husband this was, but knew that it could have one of a dozen.

Buddy called back. "You leave Bunzi Schlimizzle alone," he hollered into the phone.

"Calm down, Mr. Schlimizzle," Bull Bruiser said. "You wouldn't wanna aggravate your constipation."

A call from Carmelita Doofus came in to Buddy's phone; unaware, he switched calls.

"And I don't need your false sympathy about my constipation," Buddy hollered.

Carmelita Doofus regarded her phone in shock, then put it back to her ear. "What constipation?" She asked.

"What constipation? I spent the entire morning on the toilet, I'll have you know, thanks to your philandering tweets!" Buddy shouted.

"I didn't tweet. I sent you a text about my no-good, dead lizard son," she said.

"Your no-good, dead lizard son?" Buddy asked, accidentally switching calls.

"MY no-good, dead lizard son?" Bull Bruiser asked, his eyebrows lifting toward his extinct hairline in shock. Jeremy Spit appeared on the threshold to his suite. "Back Spit. Don't come a step closer or you're on the celebrity pet beat."

"What's this about Spit?" Buddy sputtered furiously. "And my no-good, dead lizard son?"

"I'm dealin' with a case of conjugal jealously that has caused homicidal insanity," Bull Bruiser told his reporter.

"I'll blow your fucking head off!" Buddy hollered, but he had switched the call back to Carmelita Doofus. Alarmed, she hung up and called the police.

"I think a very violent someone is holding an acquaintance of mine hostage," she told Detective Dump.

"Could be the ALA," Dump said.

"It didn't sound like a librarian," she told him. "But I believe the life of Buddy Schlimizzle, the famous constipated undertaker, whose corpses get kidnapped – I believe his life is in danger."

Shortly thereafter, six squad cars swarmed the Schlimizzle funeral home parking lot.

"Come out with your hands up!" An obese police officer addressed the funeral home through a bull horn, as the other five cops surrounded the entrance, guns drawn. "And don't harm Schlimizzle!"

Buddy appeared on the threshold, hands raised, his phone still pasted to his ear, as he held it in place with his shoulder.

"I AM Buddy Schlimizzle," he said.

"I know that," Bull Bruiser said. "Are you done verbally abusing me, Mr. Schlimizzle? Have you calmed down?"

"It looks like I'm under arrest."

"Finally," Bull Bruiser told Jeremy Spit. "Law enforcement gets something right."

"Where's the gang that took you hostage?" The policeman asked through the bull horn.

"You can put that thing down. I'm right here," Buddy complained.

"No you're not," Bull Bruiser said. "Thank God. You and your gun are elsewhere."

"Let's see some ID," one officer said.

Buddy Schlimizzle presented his driver's license.

"Now I'll get back to twitter," Bull Bruiser said.

"You leave my wife alone, or you know what!" Buddy Schlimizzle hollered into his phone.

"The criminal's got his wife," one officer said.

"Where's Mrs. Schlimizzle?" Another asked Buddy.

"At Dr. Butt's office in Bethesda," and Buddy Schlimizzle gave them the address. The six officers, walked, some waddled, back to their squad cars, got in and tore off.

Carmelita Doofus called back. Buddy accidentally switched the call to her.

"I don't want your bald, ugly head to darken my wife's door ever again," he hollered.

Carmelita Doofus hung up.

FRED FART AND Lucas Flush sat in the cab of the Pest Patrol pickup, staring grimly at the pack of possums brazenly cavorting on their customer's front yard. For some reason best known to him, Fred Fart decided at that moment to phone Dr. Butt's office.

"Posterior can't deal with the rectal pump from San Juan, and the stink is outta control after three weeks," Fred Fart said, then addressing his boss, "those are some really aggressive possums. Are they mating?"

Bunzi Schlimizzle ended the call, pronto.

"See? They're worse today than ever!" The homeowner's fat wife called from the front step. She wore a purple bathrobe, flip flops, and her hair was in pink curlers. "And I think they've multiplied just in the past two days."

Fred Fart phoned Bunzi back.

"Posterior can't refill the canister in my rectum, and my boss says he'll hang himself if the perfume runs out," Fred Fart said.

"Who is this?" Bunzi demanded.

"Me, Fred Fart."

At that moment, five police officers, led by overweight Detective Dump swarmed into the proctologist's waiting room, guns drawn.

"Where are the terrorists?" Dump asked.

"There are terrorists?" Thus Bunzi.

"There are terrorists," Fred Fart informed Lucas Flush.

"Yeah, terrorist possums," his boss squinted through the windshield at the animals, reluctant to leave the safety of his truck.

"Terrorist possums?" Fred Fart asked.

"Terrorist possums?" Bunzi repeated.

"I knew the ALA was involved," Dump told an officer.

"I'm a librarian," one patient in the waiting room volunteered. "Maybe I can help you."

"We believe those man-sized possums kidnapped Bunzi Schlimizzle," Dump rather ponderously explained. "Or rather, that's what her husband Buddy Schlimizzle led us to believe."

At that moment a call from Buddy came into Bunzi's phone. She answered it, fuming, "You told the cops a gang of terrorist possums kidnapped me? You've finally lost your mind.!"

Buddy Schlimizzle concluded he had reached a lunatic by mistake, ended the call and phoned back. But by now Bunzi had, unbeknownst to her, switched back to Fred Fart.

"The nerve! Telling the police those terrorist possums took me hostage! Now I got a whole SWAT team in Butt's waiting room," She snapped.

"A SWAT team's involved," dull-eyed, dull-witted Fred Fart informed his boss.

"I don't see any SWAT team," Lucas Flush squinted at his employee, "though we sure could use one, just about now."

"So you gonna trap 'em or what?" The very hefty woman called from the front step.

"We're gonna trap 'em," Fred Fart shouted.

"You're an undertaker, not a trapper!" Bunzi snapped.

"Speak for yourself," Lucas told his employee.

"Apparently I'm an undertaker," Fred Fart informed his boss, whose eyebrows lifted in surprise.

"Ask that Bunzi Schlimizzle when you can get your anti-flatulence perfume refilled," Lucas said sensibly.

Fred did so.

"Who is this?" Bunzi demanded.

"Where is Bunzi Schlimizzle?" Thus Detective Dump.

"Fred Fart. I, uh, think I already told you."

Bunzi accidentally switched calls to her husband. "Why can't Posterior deal with all the devices in your rectum?"

"You think I got devices in my rectum?" Buddy demanded. "You think that's why I'm constipated?"

Fat, white-haired Dr. Butt in his white lab coat waddled up to the reception desk.

"Fred Fart's constipated," Bunzi told him. "His rectal pump may need adjusting." Then she told her husband to "Fly up to Washington tomorrow."

Buddy Schlimizzle held out his phone and gaped at it.

"Why can't Posterior handle it?" Dr. Butt whined. "And why are there policemen in my waiting room?"

"Hostage situation," Dump barked. "And who are you?"

"Dr. Butt, the proctologist who, just, um," he paused a moment.

"Got nominated for a Pulitzer for his ground-breaking work in the American Anus," Bunzi said.

Detective Dump stared.

"On second thought, I don't think this is something a librarian can help out with," the patient seated in the waiting room said.

"What hostage?" Dr. Butt asked.

"One Bunzi Schlimizzle, kidnapped by a man-sized possum, if I got my story right," Detective Dump said.

"You didn't," Bunzi told him.

"BOSS! BOSS!" JEREMY Spit spat, hurrying into Bull Bruiser's suite around the time the police left the funeral parlor.

"Back, back you slobbering menace! Don't you dare cross the threshold into my quarters!" the editor shouted.

"Quarters?" Spit asked, retreating.

"What else would they be?" Bull Bruiser demanded.

"Like hind quarters?"

A little light of dislike and bored annoyance glimmered in Bull Bruiser's small, dark, porcine eyes. "Shut up, Spit," he said.

"I got a tip. A hostage situation at a proctologist's office in Bethesda," Spit spat. But his oral emissions fell short of his editor's desk, causing said editor to snicker in nasty triumph that he had once again frustrated the chief terrorism and alien abduction reporter's attempts to moisturize his person with saliva.

"It's the same proctologist the Pulitzer nominated for his article in American Anus," Spit continued.

"American Anus Besieged," Bull Bruiser mused. "There are headline possibilities."

"American Anus Prize-Winner Kidnapped, Will Abductors Amputate Proctologist's Toes?" Spit elaborated.

"Not his toes, stupid, his butt," Bruiser said.

"How would they cut off his butt?" Spit spat.

"Use your imagination, and hoof it over to Bethesda."

When Jeremy Spit arrived in Dr. Butt's waiting room, everyone was talking at once, while over this hubbub could be heard Bunzi Schlimizzle's voice nearly shouting into the phone: "Well this is a fine to-do, you and your possum terrorists! Now I got a whole SWAT team here and some idiot babbling about the Animal Liberation Army."

"The Animal Liberation Army's involved too," Fred Fart sagely informed his boss, who squinted and nodded as if that was exactly what he would have predicted.

"I hope this army isn't involved in refilling my rectal perfume," Fred Fart said.

Bunzi accidentally switched calls. "Who is this?" She demanded.

"Your very confused husband," Buddy snapped. "Why would I want to fly up to Washington, D.C., when I'm here in Silver Spring."

"You have some nerve," Bunzi snapped, unwittingly switching the calls again. "I mean it, you have some nerve, sending the whole freakin' bomb squad to a proctologist's office."

"Will this army be planting a bomb in my you know what?" Fred Fart asked in alarm.

"Your what?" Bunzi demanded.

"My rectum."

"Why would the Animal Liberation Army plant a bomb in your rectum?" Bunzi confusedly snapped. The loud murmur in the waiting room came to an abrupt halt, as all eyes focused on the receptionist, most eagerly the filmy ones of Scuttlebutt's reporter, Jeremy Spit.

Bunzi again accidentally switched lines. "You think these terrorists want to put a bomb up an undertaker's ass? I thought you told the SWAT team they took your wife hostage?"

"What undertaker?" Buddy snapped. "Not the proprietor of the Schlimizzle funeral home."

Bunzi inadvertently switched calls. "Well, it certainly would cure your nearly 40-year constipation," she told Fred Fart, who relayed this earth-shaking news to Lucas Flush.

"Mrs. Schlimizzle, Mrs. Schlimizzle," Jeremy Spit panted with excitement. "Allow me to speak to your husband."

Bored and disgusted, Bunzi Schlimizzle gave her phone to the reporter.

"This is Scuttlebutt," Spit spat, zapping Detective Dump in the eye with a blob of saliva. "How does it feel to have a bomb up your ass, planted there by radical Marxist terrorists?"

Detective Dump wiped his eye with a tissue and glared at Jeremy Spit. "I think we've found our terrorist," he said.

DETECTIVE DUMP ARRESTED Jeremy Spit for "planting bombs in unmentionable places" and spitting on a police officer. This occasioned much protest from the reporter and thus, to the detriment of his case, much more spitting. He was handcuffed, placed in a squad car, then driven to the station, where he was charged with taking Bunzi Schlimizzle hostage and threatening one Fred Fart, over the phone with "a bomb up his ass."

Spit was instructed to call Fred Fart.

"I been arrested for asking you about the goings on in your behind," Spit said into his phone.

Fred Fart's eyebrows rose, as he turned to his boss in shock and relayed this astounding message.

"What goings on?" Lucas Flush asked, squinting at his employee.

Detective Dump seized the phone from Spit and warned Fred Fart above all to avoid a bowel movement, "until I call the bomb squad. What's your location?"

Truly alarmed now, Fred Fart explained that he was in the cab of the Pest Patrol pickup, in a North Miami subdivision. "What'll happen if I have a bowel movement?" He asked, trembling.

Lucas Flush was visibly startled. "Who ya talkin' to, Fred?" He asked.

"Who am I talking to?" Fred Fart asked.

"Detective Dump of the Montgomery County, Maryland police force."

"A detective," Fred told Lucas.

"Ask him what he detected," Lucas said.

"What did you detect?" Fred asked Dump.

"That if you have a bowel movement, you're gonna blow."

Fred Fart turned pale. "If I have a bowel movement, I'm gonna blow," he told his boss, who edged away from him.

"That sounds serious," Lucas Flush said.

"We got the perp at the station," Dump continued. "He spits."

"The perp spits," Fred said.

"Ask how this…perp wired you up," Lucas said. Fred did.

"That's what we're tryin' to get to the bottom of," Dump said.

"Call Scuttlebutt," Spit spat, zapping Detective Dump with a blob of saliva on the end of his nose. "They'll tell you I'm a reporter, not a terrorist."

"Stand by," Detective Dump told Fred. "I'll call you back."

The detective phoned Scuttlebutt and got put through to the editor-in-chief. "I got Jeremy Spit here," he said.

"Good. You can keep him," Bull Bruiser snarled and hung up, annoyed at being distracted from his multiple flirtations on twitter.

Detective Dump called back. "You know him?"

"Who?"

"Jeremy Spit," Dump said.

"I have that misfortune, yes. Who am I talking to?"

"Detective Dump. We believe Spit is a terrorist who tried to take Bunzi Schlimizzle hostage."

"Schlimizzle…Bunzi…" sounds familiar. Bull Bruiser paused to focus. "Oh yes, the hot lady and the Pulitzer for the article in American Anus."

"Would that American Anus belong to one Fred Fart?" Dump asked.

"Is this perverted or what?" Bull Bruiser asked.

"We believe Fart is a target of Spit's nefarious designs," Dump elaborated. "Spit claims he's a reporter."

"He's been claiming that for years," Bull Bruiser said.

"He's not?"

"Oh, he is, if you call his constant fabrications and plagiarisms reporting," Bruiser said.

"So I can call back this very concerned citizen, Fred Fart and assure him that Spit didn't, uh, wire him up to explode?" Dump asked.

A little annoyed light of intense dislike flickered in the editor's small, dark, porcine eyes. "You can tell that moron Fred Fart whatever you want. As for my reporter, you can keep him."

"Well, Mr. Spit, you're very lucky," Dump said. "You're not the terrorist."

"I told you," Spit spat, zapping Dump in the eyes with a blob of saliva. Dump pushed his chair as far away from his prisoner as possible.

"Just don't tell me any more," the detective said.

PHILIPPA PHILPOT HAD both Bull Bruiser's and Futz Fraud's cell numbers. So bright that cool April afternoon, she phoned the Scuttlebutt editor. "I was kidnapped by Q-Anon," she said.

"Sure you were," Bull Bruiser snapped, hung up and returned to eating his chocolate donut, which Ruffles Johnson had advised him to take, "before Spit gets back and slobbers over the whole box."

Philippa called back. "The Q freaks tied me and a lunatic in a straitjacket to chairs in a Wheaton, Maryland basement."

Bull Bruiser at once ended the call. Mention of Wheaton, Maryland reminded him of his dalliance with Matilda Mooch, whose common-law husband Bucky Buckeye had a seizure when he caught them in flagrante, thus ending the romance. Horny old Bull decided to give Matilda a call.

"Oh hi, Bull," she said.

"Better not be that asshole. I got a bird's eye view of that asshole. Seen enough of that asshole for the rest of my life," a voice shouted in the background. "I'm gonna tear that asshole limb from limb!"

"I see nothing's changed at your place," Bull grumbled.

Matilda tittered idiotically.

The editor inadvertently switched to Philippa's incoming call. "How about we meet at my place for drinks?"

"I'd prefer to discuss my kidnapping in your office," she said.

Bull Bruiser scowled at his phone and switched the call back to Matilda. "Drinks at my place?"

"Oh, I couldn't Bull," she tittered again.

In the background, short, scrawny, criminally inclined Bucky could be heard hollering: "I'm gonna tear that asshole limb from limb!"

Bull Bruiser ended the call, picking up Philippa's.

"Hello? Hello?" She was saying. "Did you hear me? I, the lizard queen, was kidnapped by Q."

"What fruitcake do I have the honor of talking to?" The editor demanded.

"Philippa Philpot."

"Oh yes. I remember you. Lizard girl."

"They kidnapped me and Albert Pop," she said.

"I hope they kept him," the editor grumbled.

"We both escaped," she said.

"Johnson!" Bull Bruiser yelled. "Call security. A lunatic in a straitjacket is headed our way."

"He might not be," Philippa said.

"He assaulted me and threatened to insert hoses in my orifices. I take no chances with Albert Pot," Bull Bruiser snapped.

"We were kidnapped by hard-core Q maniacs," Philippa continued. "They put hoods over our heads, but I recognized three of them anyway."

"Spit!" Bull Bruiser hollered, then muttered, "Oh right, he was arrested."

But Jeremy Spit had just returned. Since his boss usually did not summon him with such enthusiasm, he took this loud shout as an auspicious sign and hurried into the office, up to the desk and panted, "What is it, boss?" thus drenching a revolted Bull Bruiser's hand and cell phone.

"Back to the doorway!" The editor yelled, and as Spit drifted thither, he wiped his hand and phone with tissues.

"I see the police released you," the editor said sourly.

"The police didn't release me," thus Philippa.

"A case of mistaken identity," Spit spat, though his oral fluids fell short of Bull Bruiser's desk, much to the editor's satisfaction. "They mistook me for the terrorist who planted a bomb in Fred Fart's rectum."

Bull Bruiser glared at his reporter. "I'm sick of Fred Fart's rectum," he snapped. "I've edited enough articles on that stinky rectum to last me the rest of my life."

"Why are we talking about some oddly named person's rectum?" Philippa asked.

"It sells papers," Spit spat. "And I've got the exclusive. Here's the headline: 'One Bowel Movement Detonates Terrorist Bomb.' How's about it?"

Bull Bruiser glared at him in disgust. "Now you got a bomb in the rectum? Could this get any more disgusting if you tried?" He muttered.

"Hello? Hello?" Thus Philippa.

"I'm here," Bull Bruiser grumbled.

"I know you're here. How do you like my headline?" Spit spat.

"I got another story," the editor said. "Lizard girl and that…person, Albert Pop, got kidnapped by Q-Anon. They escaped."

"Ho, ho!" Spit chortled. "Where are they? I'll interview both, in person."

"If you bring Albert Pop into my suite, you will be demoted," Bull Bruiser told him.

"Pop's not so bad," Spit said, drifting toward his boss's desk.

"He's worse," the editor snapped.

"I expect to be paid," Philippa said.

"A thousand bucks," Bull Bruiser snapped. "That's my final offer."

"Five thousand," she barked.

"No."

"My story's worth more than a thousand bucks," Philippa whined.

"Young lady, your story is in stiff, front-page competition with a blockbuster about a pest exterminator walking around with a bomb in his rectum," Bull Bruiser snapped, the look of dislike in his small, dark eyes quite pronounced.

"A what, who?" Philippa goggled in amazement.

"You heard me," Bull Bruiser said, just as another call, this one from Fred Fart himself, came in on the other line. The editor inadvertently switched to it. "So don't expect big money for Q-Anon kidnapping a lizard and a lunatic."

"Q-Anon kidnapped a lizard and a lunatic," Fred Fart told his boss. They sat in the cab of the Pest Patrol pickup, watching in consternation as the wily possums figured out how to remove the lettuce and peanut butter treats from the traps they had set. The fat wife of the homeowner, still in a bathrobe, flip flops and curlers, frowned. "Your traps ain't working," she called.

"Well, how could we know these possums had such high IQs?" Fred Fart called back.

"What possums?" Bull Bruiser asked. "You were kidnapped by possums or Q-Anon?"

"We're in danger of being kidnapped by these possums," Fred Fart informed Lucas Flush.

"That wouldn't surprise me," the doughty pest expert squinted at his employee. "You talking to General Boom?"

"You're not General Boom, are you?" Fred Fart asked.

Bull Bruiser scowled at his phone and switched the call back to Philippa.

"Personally, I prefer Fred Fart's rectum to Q-Anon kidnappers," Spit spat, and an enormous blob of saliva whizzed past Bull Bruiser's ugly bald head and landed, zap, on a framed award from a supermarket association that hung on the wall behind his desk.

"That was too close for comfort," the editor muttered and then yelled at his reporter to retreat to the doorway, "or else!"

"I guess a thousand will do," Philippa complained.

"It better!" Bull Bruiser snapped.

PHILIPPA AND FRED Fart had the same idea to call Futz Fraud about their stories. They phoned within 30 seconds of each other.

"I was kidnapped by Q-Anon," Philippa said.

"Been there, done that," scrawny little warty Futz Fraud said, ended the call and resumed throwing darts at Scuttlebutt's front page, pasted on the wall opposite his desk.

She called back. "They took me and a raving lunatic in a straitjacket into a basement and tied us to chairs," Philippa continued.

Tall, obese Stella in her blue poncho opened the door and loomed on the threshold. "I got Albert Pop on the other line, or rather his so-called agent, Pimples, wantin' to sell us a story 'bout bein' kidnapped by Q-Anon."

"This sounds familiar," Futz Fraud said.

"I have only five words for you, Fraud: I will not interview Pop!" Stella glared at her boss through her foggy, cat's-eye glasses. "The last time, he bit me."

"Well of course," Fraud said, having switched calls to Fred Fart. "He's a cannibal."

"Who's a cannibal?" Fred Fart asked.

"Probably those possums," Lucas Flush told him.

"Who am I talking to?" Futz Fraud demanded.

"Me, Fred Fart, and I have a bomb in my rectum."

"Fred Fart has a bomb in his rectum," Futz Fraud told Stella.

"Wonderful," she snapped. "Tell him not to visit me."

Futz Fraud accidentally switched calls.

"Who put this bomb in your rectum?" He asked Philippa.

"You're the second person in 10 minutes to ask me that very rude question," Philippa snapped.

"We'll pay you $5000 for your highly unusual intestinal story," Futz Fraud offered.

"What do I tell Albert Pop?" Stella demanded.

"Not to eat me," Futz Fraud whined.

"Well, that would take care of you vomitin' on me," Stella said. "Now wouldn't it?"

BY SOME VERY confused judicial process, the case of Philippa Philpot's and Albert Pop's kidnapping wound up in the courtroom of the very senile judge Hieronymus Squat, who, perceiving Pop's straitjacket, immediately asked their attorney, the very dignified, well-dressed and well-groomed Morris Finkelstein, his short, dark curls with the occasional silver strand neatly trimmed, what institution Pop had escaped from and who he had kidnapped?

"Mr. Pop WAS kidnapped," Morris Finkelstein explained.

"Mr. Pop," Judge Squat sternly addressed Mr. Schlumpf, "who kidnapped you?"

"The lizard people!" Schlumpf snapped.

"Uh, your honor," thus began the Schlumpfs' lawyer, Howard Swindle.

"I have wires in my head," Albert Pop told the judge.

"This is some case," Judge Squat marveled, then forgot what it was about and mixed it up with a defamation case he had presided over earlier that day, in which a paranoid, suburban Maryland homeowner, Mr. Prick, wanted damages from his neighbor, an FBI agent, for spreading rumors about his pet ferret.

"How long have you been in the FBI?" Judge Squat asked Philippa.

"Excuse me, your honor," Morris Finkelstein began an attempt to correct the bench.

"Silence counsel. I intend to get to the bottom of this defamation. Mr. Prick," he turned to Mr. Schlumpf. "Explain what happened."

"While we were out at Weight Watchers, the lizard queen and her insane consort escaped," Mr. Schlumpf said.

Judge Squat's bushy gray eyebrows lifted in shock. "Who is this lizard queen? I think I know who the insane consort is, though," and he glowered at Albert Pop.

"They tried to poison me with chicken noodle soup," Albert Pop informed the judge.

"Still defaming Mr. Prick, are you? Even in court," Judge Squat said, then muttered something to himself about Weight Watchers.

"Your honor," Morris Finkelstein pointed at Mr. and Mrs. Schlumpf, "those are the defendants."

"I think I know who the defendants are in my courtroom, counsel. And I find it very offensive, yes, the court is most offended by the slanderous attacks of a government official on an innocuous homeowner because of his weight, which he attempts to control by joining Weight Watchers."

"He kidnapped my clients," a desperate Morris Finkelstein explained.

"So the defamation knocked you off the deep end – eh, Mr. Prick?" Judge Squat asked Mr. Schlumpf.

"The wires in my head are connected to my pink plastic brain," Albert Pop told the judge.

Judge Squat peered at Albert Pop, as Howard Swindle explained this was a case involving a lizard and a lunatic.

"What lizard?" Squat asked, then repeated: "Because I think I can tell who the lunatic is."

"I'm not a lizard!" Philippa snapped. "I'm being defamed!"

"Another defamation case!" Judge Squat marveled.

"Your honor," Swindle continued. "Look at her arms and you will see how my clients, the Schlumpfs, came to the conclusion that she was a lizard person."

Philippa duly exposed her scaly arms to the judge, who said, "Oh my," and then promptly gave his verdict: Philippa was to see a dermatologist. He also sentenced the Schlumpfs to 10 sessions with Weight Watchers.

"And you, you treacherous lunatic are to see an electrician at once, about all those wires in your head," he addressed Albert Pop.

PHILIPPA AND ALBERT Pop presented themselves at the office of Morris Finkelstein's law firm.

"You're saying Mr. Finkelstein has a client in a straitjacket?" The incredulous receptionist asked.

"Yes, and we're here about our case before the lunatic judge, Hieronymus Squat," Philippa said.

"Lunatic judge? People who live in glass houses," the receptionist muttered, "shouldn't throw stones."

Shortly Morris Finkelstein, tall, attired in a mutedly serious dark suit with a thin white pinstripe, his short dark curls combed and orderly, appeared in order to usher them back to his office.

"That…person," the receptionist pointed at Albert Pop, "claims to be your client."

"I will eat your liver," Albert Pop told her.

The receptionist's eyebrows rose in alarm.

"Don't worry, Selma," Morris Finkelstein said. "He's harmless."

"He doesn't sound harmless. He just threatened to eat my liver," she said.

"Well, he can't in that straitjacket, can he?" The attorney asked.

"Tell me if that straitjacket comes off," Selma said, "so I can arrange to be elsewhere."

"I think it's safe to say that straitjacket is never coming off," Morris Finkelstein told her.

"So says the shyster," Albert Pop snapped. "I'm hungry."

The receptionist regarded him with increasing alarm.

"Well, this is a law firm," Finkelstein said. "Not a restaurant."

"When I get hungry, the wires in my head tingle," Albert Pop informed them.

Selma gave the attorney a level stare. "Did he just say he has wires in his head?"

Finkelstein nodded.

"I presume that's from some previous procedure to try to induce, uh, normalcy," she continued.

"No, it's not," Finkelstein told her. "It's because Mr. Pop is bonkers. Just ignore anything he says."

"Your liver!" Pop hissed at her.

"That's kinda hard," Selma complained, and then, "how many other clients in straitjackets can I expect to come calling for you, Mr. Finkelstein, and when? I ask so I can get leave for those days."

"Mr. Pop is the one and only," the attorney said.

"I'll say," Selma breathed.

The trio moved down the carpeted corridor toward Finkelstein's office. His paralegal approached with some paperwork.

"Is that man wearing a straitjacket?" the paralegal asked in astonishment.

"Yes, Mr. Katz, he is," the lawyer replied.

"What of it?" Albert Pop demanded belligerently.

"You just don't, um, see that often around here," Katz said.

"I come from a long line of Andromedan robots," Pop told him.

"A long line of Andromedan lunatics," Philippa muttered.

"And we Andromedans will crush this puny planet!" Albert proclaimed.

"That's enough of that," Finkelstein said. "We heard all about it in Judge Squat's courtroom."

"Was he, uh, in restraints in the courtroom?" Katz asked in a low voice.

"Most certainly," Finkelstein replied.

Once seated facing the attorney across his desk, Philippa frowned and told Finkelstein how unhappy she was with Squat's ruling.

"I tried to get a different judge," the attorney sighed. "But my efforts were fruitless."

"I'll say. Squat didn't even issue a restraining order on the Schlumpfs. What's to stop them from kidnapping us again?" Philippa asked.

"We will bring a civil case," Finkelstein told her.

"Oh? Like for damages?"

"The Schlumpfs have no assets other than their home, so the main purpose would be a restraining order," Finkelstein said.

"Don't you think Albert's straitjacket will count against us?" She asked.

"Not with the judge I have in mind. Fibble DuCouk. Mr. Pop here has appeared before him previously," Finkelstein explained.

Albert Pop, who had followed this exchange with uncharacteristic attention, said: "That judge was eaten and replaced by a crab person from the Crab Nebula."

"So you have maintained," Finkelstein said, "with great obstinacy."

"He was very odd," Albert Pop observed.

"Look who's talking. But he did war a hazmat suit on the bench, and yes, that was peculiar," Finkelstein said.

"A hazmat suit?" Philippa's voice rose in shock.

"He is a germaphobe, who is also bonkers," Finkelstein said. "But he likes me, because for some reason, he has decided I don't spread any, um, contagious bacteria."

JUDGE FIBBLE DUCOUK had never caught covid, due to the fact that once he became aware of the virus, he switched from his decades-long attire of a surgical mask, hairnet and disposable gloves to his hazmat suit full-time, attire which had hung in his closet for years, waiting for just this moment of pandemic hysteria.

His clothing, however, appeared to disturb spherical Mr. Schlumpf, who, in a series of injudicious outbursts informed the judge that covid was a hoax perpetrated by the Illuminati.

"Counsel," Judge DuCouk thundered, his voice vastly amplified by the microphone, on which neither he nor his long-suffering assistant, Harris, could figure out how to lower the volume. "You will restrain your client and his bizarre ravings about the deadly covid virus or I will have him gagged."

That shut Mr. Schlumpf up.

"As I was saying, your honor," Morris Finkelstein continued, "Mr. and Mrs. Schlumpf,"

"Two crab people," Albert Pop interjected in a shout, "spreading microscopic crabs."

"Harris, Harris," Fibble DuCouk dithered. "The microscopic crabs!"

"There are no microscopic crabs, judge," Harris sighed. "That plaintiff is insane."

"How can you be sure?" DuCouk asked.

"Because he's wearing a straitjacket."

"What institution did you escape from?" DuCouk asked Albert Pop. "And what was the hygiene regime there?"

Albert Pop's eyes rolled wildly.

"That man is infected," Judge DuCouk boomed.

"With what?" The Schlumpfs' attorney, Howard Swindle asked.

"With anything that's going around. Court is adjourned for 10 minutes. Everyone is to go to the restroom and wash their hands with soap for 20 seconds. When you return, Harris here will inspect your fingernails for dirt. Bacteria colonize the dirt under the nails. Billions upon billions of bacteria. But if they're there, Harris will see the dirt," Judge DuCouk said.

"Lucky Harris," Philippa muttered, as everyone rose and shuffled out.

"Harris, where's my anti-bacterial decoction?" DuCouk asked.

"Right here, judge," Harris replied, handing him a small bottle from which the insane jurist guzzled.

After everyone returned and Harris had checked their fingernails, the judge summoned Morris Finkelstein to the bench.

"Counsel, I believe your client is harassing me," the judge said.

"Which one?"

"The one in the straitjacket," DuCouk murmured, but, due to the microphone, his voice boomed through the courtroom.

"How is he harassing you judge?"

"By continually reappearing in my courtroom," DuCouk said.

"I will eat the fingers of that judicial imposter, clean fingernails and all," Albert Pop announced.

"See?" DuCouk whispered – but everyone heard. "Last time he was here, he claimed I was a crab person from the Crab Nebula who had poisoned his coffee creamer and that he would roast and eat me for dinner. That insane person is a menace."

And indeed, at that moment, Albert Pop leapt out of his seat and charged at the bench. But DuCouk was faster. He grabbed his extra-large can of Lysol and sprayed it on the lunatic's straitjacket.

"No Andromedan bacteria will contaminate this judge," DuCouk snapped. "Officers, tie that plaintiff to his seat!"

After court officers had roped Albert Pop to his chair, the judge demanded to know why the Schlumpfs weren't in jail, for kidnapping Finkelstein's clients.

"Because Judge Hieronymus Squat oversaw those proceedings," Finkelstein said.

"Some people are senile," DuCouk averred. "And Squat is one of them. He doesn't know whether he's coming or going. We have some very odd jurists on the bench."

Harris rolled his eyes.

"All we want, your honor, is a restraining order against these dangerous, malevolent, kidnappers," Finkelstein said, and couldn't help adding, "who believe Covid-19 is a hoax."

Judge DuCouk ruled that neither Schlumpf was to come within 500 feet of Philippa or Albert Pop and that both had to wear surgical masks, in perpetuity, so as to stop spreading the Q-Anon virus.

"HOW DOES IT feel to be back in CIA captivity?" Spit spat at a prone Nostradamus in his hospital bed, zapping his left ear with a blob of saliva. The prophet reached for a Kleenex to dry his ear, all the while regarding the Scuttlebutt reporter with hostility and revulsion.

"None of your beeswax until I get my 500 bucks," Nostradamus snapped.

Spit phoned his boss. "The obese soothsayer demands five hundred bucks," he spat, this time spraying Nostradamus' forehead.

Bull Bruiser promptly hung up. At that moment, Bunzi Schlimizzle called.

"When will you run the story about Butt's Pulitzer for the American Anus article?" She asked.

"Do I get more crank calls than anyone else on the planet or what?" Bald, ugly, muscular Bull Bruiser snapped, ending that conversation also.

Jeremy Spit phoned back. "I need 500 bucks," he spat. This time his oral fluids reached Nostradamus' pillow.

"You and everybody else," the editor snapped again. "Bug off."

"But I won't get any prophecies from the CIA captive without it," Spit whined.

"To what nutcase do I have the privilege of speaking?" Bull Bruiser demanded.

"No nutcase, boss. It's me, Jeremy Spit."

"I shoulda known," the editor grumbled. "What's this about 500 bucks?" He accidentally switched calls to Bunzi Schlimizzle's incoming.

"You're gonna get scooped," she told him. "Butt won an award for best, most-read American Anus article of the year. National Disgrace is covering it. In fact, they're doing a profile of Butt and a feature on American Anus."

"And this Anus wants 500 bucks?" Bruiser demanded.

"They'll do it for free," Bunzi told him.

Bull Bruiser accidentally switched calls again. "So who wants 500 bucks?" he yelled.

"No need to yell, boss," Spit said. "Nostradamus."

"What's he got to do with the American Anus?" Bull Bruiser demanded.

"What do you have to do with the American Anus?" Spit asked the prophet, who glared at him.

"What anus?" Nostradamus snapped, throwing back the bed-covers to reveal his enormous hairy belly, exposed by his too-small T-shirt with the "Wellesley College" logo.

"The American one," Spit said.

"Unless I'm mistaken," the prophet snapped. "There are lotsa American anuses, a primo example of which I'm talking to right now."

"Nostradamus just called me an asshole," Spit told his boss.

"Well, he got that right. But you don't need a crystal ball for that. And it certainly ain't worth five hundred bucks," Bull Bruiser said sourly.

"It's a tell-all story about being back in CIA captivity," Spit spat.

"Soon to be not," the prophet said, swinging his massive legs over the side of the bed, reaching for his jeans on a chair and pulling them on. Then he hunted around for his sneakers and socks, put those on, checked his pockets for his wallet and phone, then tiptoed to the doorway, poked his head out, saw no medical staff and skedaddled to the elevator, his frothy companion at his heels.

"And about a daring escape from the CIA," Spit hyperventilated to his boss.

"I'll pay him $350," Bull Bruiser snapped.

"Four-fifty," Nostradamus demanded, as they exited the elevator and hurried to the taxi stand.

Bull Bruiser accidentally switched calls. "Okay, I'll pay you 450 bucks for the story. That's my final offer."

Bunzi Schlimizzle was thrilled. She hurried to the proctological genius' office. "Dr. Butt! Dr. Butt!"

"Calm down, Mrs. Schlimizzle, you're panting. You don't want to have an aneurysm," the great man advised.

"I got us a $450 honorarium from Scuttlebutt, for the privilege of doing an article on your American Anus award!" she announced.

Pink with pleasure, hefty, white-haired Dr. Butt turned from his computer to face his receptionist. "Well, well," he murmured. "And this is Scuttlebutt, you say?"

Bunzi nodded, her blond-tinted, beautifully coiffed hair gleaming in the sunshine from the window. "Maybe I should tell National Disgrace, you know, to nudge them to pay us for their article on you."

"We don't want to scare them off," Butt demurred.

"Oh, nothing could scare them off. Futz Fraud told me that this scoop on the American Anus was front-page stuff."

"Well, well," Dr. Butt murmured again.

ARRIVING IN HIS RV, stationed in the far corner of a Walmart parking lot under a maple tree, Nostradamus was not pleased to find Pimples and Albert Pop seated at his kitchenette table and demanding that they be permitted to stay and sleep on the floor.

"No," the prophet was categorical.

"But we can't go back to my place, there are too many hoses," Pimples whined. "And if we stay at Albert's dump out in the sticks, the CIA will catch him. They want his intel on China."

"What the CIA plans to do with so-called intel from a raving lunatic has always mystified me," Nostradamus said. "Outta my seat, Pimples."

Pimples rose and stood beside Jeremy Spit at the door, but this close proximity was noxious, as the reporter, breathing with his mouth open, had soon flooded the landscaper's face with saliva. Spit also scratched the veritable mountains of dandruff on his head, causing them to snow down onto Pimples' shirt.

Pimples wiped his face with a towel that had lain on the bed. "The CIA regards Albert as an expert on the…peculiar," Pimples said.

"On the outta this world," Nostradamus grumbled, "like his brain."

"They've consulted him for years," Pimples continued.

"No wonder the country's going to the dogs," the prophet grumbled again.

"Mr. Pop, Mr. Pop, what do you plan to tell your CIA handlers?" Spit asked breathlessly, filling the confined space with a mist of saliva, much to the disgust of the RV's owner.

"I play to eat my CIA handlers," Albert Pop informed him.

"Well, bon appetite," thus Nostradamus. "Now get out."

"Not me," Pimples said.

"Yes you, all of you."

"But my scoop – 'Soothsayer Escapes CIA Captivity.'" Spit whined.

"I'm over that," Nostradamus told him.

"Albert's got a story for you," Pimples said. "But as his agent, I insist that we will only discuss it with the editor. You know, the man who okays our fee."

Soon Nostradamus was happily rid of his unwanted visitors, who crowded in Pimples' "vintage" and rust-covered Honda hatchback.

"Make sure Albert keeps his straitjacket on," the prophet called from the doorway. "'Cause if he assaults Bull Bruiser again and attempts to put hoses in his orifices, that editor's likely to get a restraining order."

"No problem. Besides, Albert's the one with a restraining order," Pimples called back. "Against Q-Anon."

Nostradamus scowled at this further evidence of generally rampant lunacy. "The end is nigh!" He said, then "Ta, ta," and stepped back into his RV, shut and locked the door, and ordered a pizza for delivery.

Pimples' unlovely vehicle zipped through traffic and soon reached downtown D.C. He parked, conned the reporter into paying the meter with the app on his phone, and then this unlikely trio strolled into the high-rise that housed the headquarters of the illustrious supermarket tabloid.

"Out!" Bull Bruiser shouted when this threesome appeared on his threshold. He prowled menacingly to the center of his suite.

"As Albert Pop's agent, I have a story about his adventures in the courtrooms of not one, but two lunatic judges," Pimples said. "Right, Albert?"

Albert Pop's eyes rolled wildly. Then he answered, "Right! Judge DuCouk is off his rocker."

"Look who's talking," Bull Bruiser snarled.

"But that's because his flesh has been devoured and reconstituted by microscopic crabs who invaded form the Crab Nebula," Albert Pop said. The other three gaped at him.

"Take notes, Spit," Bruiser ordered his reporter.

"The microscopic judicial flesh-eating crabs are on a mission to take over the court system and replace all judges with raving lunatic crab people!" Albert Pop's voice, steadily rising as he spoke, had now reached a shout. "Then they will be in a position to poison all the coffee creamer on the planet. Only robots from the Andromeda galaxy can stop them, because we know about this plot by the race of midget poisoners. We have battled them for millennia. They plan to hijack the courts, issue subpoenas, injunctions and decisions that will enable the crab people to close their claws over human society and drive everyone bonkers. Did I tell you I have wires in my head?"

His three listeners goggled at him.

"But first we must conquer this planet. We Andromedans will steal all your salt. I, Albert Pop, will steal all your salt. I will insert hoses in your orifices!"

"Not my orifices," Bull Bruiser warned.

"Yes, yes!" The psychotic hissed, raced forward, straitjacket and all, and body-slammed the editor. Both toppled.

"Spit!" Bull Bruiser hollered. "Call the cops!"

ARRIVING AT WORK, Bunzi found a note from Dr. Butt: "Call that Fart person."

"Why am I supposed to call you?" She asked, having dialed Fred Fart.

This question genuinely stumped dull-eyed, dull-witted Fred Fart, who glanced out the window of the Pest Patrol pickup at his boss, chasing an iguana across a suburban Miami front lawn. "Why is someone supposed to call me?" He asked.

Bushy gray-haired Lucas Flush gave up his chase and limped over to the truck's passenger window.

"Someone's supposed to call me?" Fred Fart asked ponderously.

"Who?"

"That's what I can't figure out."

"Is it about a roach infestation?" Lucas Flush asked.

"Is this about a roach infestation?" Fred Fart asked.

"Unless you got roaches in your rectum, no," Bunzi replied.

Fred Fart's eyes widened in alarm. "I may have roaches in my rectum," he said.

"Well, I never sprayed nobody's roaches in their rectum before, so if that's your problem, don't ask me to do it, Fred," Lucas Flush told him.

"How, um, do you propose removin' these roaches from my rectum?" Fred Fart asked Bunzi.

"I propose Serene Snapdragon for your rectum," Bunzi said.

"Sounds like this somebody wants to plant flowers in my rectum," Fred Fart told his boss.

Lucas Flush squinted at him. "Ain't it getting' kinda crowded in there?"

"I don't think there's room," Fred Fart told Bunzi.

"Of course there's room. The canister's already in place," she said. "Now Butt's very busy with his American Anus award."

"What butt?" Fred Fart asked. "What American Anus?"

"I don't believe this," Lucas Flush said.

"You know what Butt," Bunzi said.

"She says I know what butt," Fred Fart spoke slowly, but still with alarm in his voice.

"Who ya talkin' to, Fred?" Lucas Flush demanded.

"Who am I taking to?" Fred Fart asked.

"Bunzi Schlimizzle," came the reply. "Butt's receptionist."

"Butt's receptionist," Fred Fart said.

"Well, that's a relief," Lucas Flush ran his stubby fingers through his thick gray hair that stuck out in all directions. "You wouldn't want some stranger callin' about plantin' flowers in your rectum."

Buddy Schlimizzle dialed his wife, who unwittingly switched the call to him. "Now when do you want Serene Snapdragon installed in the device in your rectum?" She asked.

"Never!" Buddy snapped and ended the call.

"Never?" Bunzi asked.

"Never what?" Fred Fart asked.

"You said it, not me," Bunzi said.

"What did I say?" Fred Fart asked.

Dr. Butt ambled out to the reception room, wearing his white lab coat.

"This half-wit can't even keep track of his conversation," Bunzi told him.

"What half-wit?" Fred Fart asked.

"What half-wit?" Butt echoed.

"That Fart," Bunzi explained. Dr. Butt's eyebrows rose, as he decided that would be a good moment to leave and return to his office.

"Whose fart?" Fred asked.

Buddy called back. His wife inadvertently switched calls. "Now you ask whose fart? What's wrong with your brain?" She asked.

"What's wrong with my phone," Buddy Schlimizzle grumbled, ending the call.

"Hello? Hello?" Bunzi said.

"I'm here, though I'm a little confused," Fred Fart said.

"That's the understatement of the year," Lucas Flush muttered, squinting at his employee.

In desperation, Buddy dialed his wife again.

"I want to schedule your perfume refill," she told Fred, "for mid-May. How's that?"

"If I can stay at your house, it's fine," Fred Fart said. "Hotels in the nation's capital are too expensive."

Bunzi unwittingly switched calls.

"So Fred Fart will stay with the Schlimizzles in mid-May, before the stink becomes intolerable," she called to Dr. Butt.

"What is this?" Buddy demanded. "The nightmare on the telephone?"

"What nightmare? What telephone?" His wife replied.

EJECTED FROM THE editorial offices of Scuttlebutt, Pimples and Albert Pop decided to try their luck at National Disgrace.

"Straight down the corridor," said the bored receptionist who recognized them, then blowing a big pink bubble with her gum.

"I will eat your bubble gum," Albert Pop hissed.

"Not my bubble gum, nutcase," she snapped.

"How rude," thus Pimples.

"He's the one threatening to eat me and my gum," she retorted. "Besides, he's in a straitjacket."

"Lotsa people are in straitjackets," Pimple defended his "client."

"Yeah, in insane asylums. Not too many in newspaper offices," she replied, "though I can think of a few who maybe should be."

They traipsed down the carpeted hall, to find tall, obese, unattractive, angry, frizzy gray-haired and poncho-clad Stella at the end, leaning back in her triple extra-large, ergonomic, swivel desk chair.

"Fraud's eatin' ice cream sandwiches," she said sourly. "Approach him at your own risk."

"We have two stories for Mr. Fraud," Pimples said. "First about Albert's adventures in two insane judges' courtrooms. Second about how the CIA wanted Albert Pop's intel on China so bad they abducted him."

Stella gave Pimples a level stare. "I refuse to believe the CIA turns to raving lunatics for its intel."

"They been doin' it for years," Pimples asserted. "Albert Pop is a long-time CIA intelligence asset, who deserves a medal for his service to our country."

"I woulda though he deserved a room in an appropriate institution for the mentally ill, but silly me. There's only one ground rule here, Pimples: the straitjacket stays on." Stella said, even more sourly than before.

Hefty, white-haired, exhausted Fevereau Slop in a rumpled tan suit passed by at that moment. "He still bites," the editor told Stella.

"I know," she said, yet more sourly. "Last time I saw Albert, he bit my arm, broke the skin. Pimples better be right about him bein' up to date on his rabies vaccine."

Scrawny, little, unimpressive Futz Fraud, with a wart on the end of his nose, opened the door to his office, belching. "I heard voices," he said.

"Then maybe you should join Albert Pop in the loony bin," Stella said.

"Very funny, Stella, you're a card," Fraud said.

"That's me, a card," she grumbled, eyeing her boss with dislike and annoyance.

"The CIA wants to kidnap Albert Pop," Pimples said.

"By all means, let them," Stella snapped.

"They already did, and he escaped," Pimples continued.

"Just like he escaped from the institution to which he should return at once," she snapped again.

"Now Stella, Mr. Pop could have a story for us," Futz Fraud said. "Come into my office, all of you."

"No way, Fraud. I ain't getting' vomited on again today," his secretary said.

"And I'm busy," Fevereau Slop said.

"You don't look busy," his boss commented.

"Looks are deceiving. Big edit. I have a big edit to attend to. Senator Barnard Bustup sent out a press release calling for martial law and allowing the CIA to establish concentration camps for lizard people." Slop said. "Liberal congressmen are in an uproar."

"Chaos in Congress. Will the CIA Uncover the Lizard People Conspiracy?" Futz Fraud said. "That's your headline."

"Uh, Mr. Fraud, I thought I'd highlight how an insane senator came up with the bat-shit crazy idea of detaining over 100 million Americans in concentration camps," Slop said.

"One hundred million crab people," Albert Pop put in.

"There's an angle for you," Futz Fraud said.

Fevereau Slop scowled. "I fail to see how the crab people are involved."

"The crab people are everywhere. They come from the Crab Nebula," Albert Pop enlightened him.

"This is a story about lizard people," Slop said sourly.

"Your story sucks," Albert Pop said. "Without the crab people, it is irrelevant."

"Shut up, Albert, Or I'll tie you to a chair again," Slop threatened.

"Look at yourself, Slop. Arguin' with a lunatic," Stella tsked.

"I do it every day, in this office," Slop grumbled.

ONE WARM, LATE April evening at dusk, the spherical Schlumpfs gathered a group of fellow Q-Anon members in their living room, to give them a pep rally.

"We gotta attack the Lizard Collective," Mrs. Schlumpf urged. "They're havin' a big meetin' tonight. I say we finally take our basket-ball bats and crack some green heads."

"You mean baseball bats, sweetiekins," her husband put in.

"Don't correct me in public, Schlumpf."

Chastened, her spouse clasped his hands over the giant beachball of his midriff and twiddled his thumbs. After much back and forth, the group gathered up the baseball bats and walked out into the tepid twilight to their cars.

"Rendez-vous in the rec center parking lot!" Mrs. Schlumpf called. Q was on the move.

Meanwhile, inside the rec center, things were popping. Many Lizard Collective members wore full-body Godzilla costumes, while others, who had smeared Derma-Lube on their cheeks and arms, glittered with green scales. Escorted by Seymour Burp in a Godzilla costume, Philippa wore a short-sleeved blouse, so her scaly arms were fully visible. A rock band consisting of three musicians dressed up as iguanas, blared music, so Philippa and Seymour stood far away from it, while she recounted the bizarre events in Judge Squat's and later Judge DuCouk's courtrooms.

Suddenly, the front door flew open, and in rushed a dozen Q-Anon fanatics, wielding baseball bats, but the sight of all the mini-Godzillas stopped them.

"You're in violation of DuCouk's restraining order!" Philippa shouted at the Schlumpfs.

Seymour Burp approached them. "I will call DuCouk myself!"

"Help!" Mrs. Schlumpf cried, dropping her bat. "The Godzillas control the courts!" She turned and fled. The rest of chicken-hearted Q followed suit.

"Well, that was surprising," one of the band members said, watching the last invader flee through the door. "Maybe they didn't like the music."

Printed in Great Britain
by Amazon